LEGISLATIVE
PRINCIPLES

Da Capo Press Reprints in

AMERICAN CONSTITUTIONAL AND LEGAL HISTORY

GENERAL EDITOR: LEONARD W. LEVY

Claremont Graduate School

LEGISLATIVE
PRINCIPLES

THE HISTORY AND THEORY OF LAWMAKING
BY REPRESENTATIVE GOVERNMENT

BY ROBERT LUCE

DA CAPO PRESS • NEW YORK • 1971

A Da Capo Press Reprint Edition

This Da Capo Press edition of *Legislative Principles* is an
unabridged republication of the first edition published in
Boston and New York in 1930. It is reprinted by permission
from a copy of the original edition in the collection of the
Law Library, University of Virginia.

Library of Congress Catalog Card Number 77-148083
SBN 306-70144-8

Published by Da Capo Press
A Division of Plenum Publishing Corporation
227 West 17th Street, New York, N.Y. 10011

Manufactured in the United States of America

LEGISLATIVE PRINCIPLES

THE SCIENCE OF LEGISLATION

LEGISLATIVE
PRINCIPLES

THE HISTORY AND THEORY OF LAWMAKING
BY REPRESENTATIVE GOVERNMENT

BY

ROBERT LUCE, A.M., LL.D.

*A Member of the General Court of Massachusetts for nine years; of the
Governor's Council, as Lieutenant-Governor; of a Constitutional
Convention; and of the Congress of the United States*

BOSTON AND NEW YORK
HOUGHTON MIFFLIN COMPANY
The Riverside Press Cambridge
1930

The Riverside Press
CAMBRIDGE · MASSACHUSETTS
PRINTED IN THE U.S.A.

CONTENTS

LEGISLATIVE PRINCIPLES

LEGISLATIVE PRINCIPLES

. .

CHAPTER I

WHAT IS LAW?

Law is that which systematically impels conduct.

It takes no feeble courage thus to hazard still another definition after the scores that have been given since Demosthenes
and Xenophon began the search. I am not unmindful of what
Sir Frederick Pollock says: " The greater a lawyer's opportunities
of knowledge have been, and the more time he has given to the
study of legal principles, the greater will be his hesitation in face
of the apparently simple question, What is Law?"

Nevertheless my definition is ventured, for some definition of
the basic fact seems desirable when engaging in a study of the
making of law, and this one may not be worse than any other.
At any rate it excels in brevity. It has the advantage of not
saying too much, for every explanatory term and modifying
limitation invites confusing controversy when law is the theme.
Indeed its chief value may be in its omissions.

Observe that it embodies but two affirmations — the force
must be exerted with some degree of system and it must tend to
coerce. Even these are wanting, or at any rate subordinate and
inferential, in such a definition as that of Emanuel Kant: " The
sum total of the conditions under which the personal wishes of
one man can be reconciled with the personal wishes of another
man, in accordance with a general law of freedom." [1] Does this
not describe the object toward which law strives, rather than
law itself? Savigny came nearer satisfying when he defined law
as " the rule whereby the invisible border line is fixed within which
the being and the activity of each individual obtains a secure and
free space." [2] This suggests both system and coercion, but the
emphasis here too is on one purpose. That makes each definition
inadequate, for there have been countless laws meant for quite

---

[1] *Rechtslehre, Werke*, VII, 27. [2] *Systema des Rechts*, I, 332.

another purpose, that of the common welfare regardless of individual rights or freedom.

Any attempt in definition to justify the rules that constitute law stirs up difficulties. When Cicero says, "*Lex est recta ratio imperandi atque prohibendi*," [1] or Hooker in English to like effect, "That which reason in such sort defines to be good that it must be done," [2] we are at once led to remonstrate that in many laws the element of reason does not enter at all. They are conventional, artificial, arbitrary, based on motives of convenience. They are standards of conduct meant to save time, labor, friction. This is notably true of customs, whether unwritten, as, for example, those of the table, or formulated, as in the case of certain laws of the road. Whether such rules are reasonable or not has no bearing on their existence. Indeed the complete absence of the element of reason is shown by the fact that hardly a rule of this class can be found which is not reversed in some other part of the world. Manifestly Cicero confused us when he implied that the reasoning must be correct. Hooker likewise led us astray when he intimated that reason is to vouch for inherent goodness. Mad tyrants have issued edicts that were none the less laws because unreasonable. Assemblies have enacted many laws not commending themselves to the common reason, laws generally denounced as bad and often quickly repealed, but none the less laws while in force. Not a few of the unwritten laws that meet with universal observance, notably those of fashion in dress, are admitted by everybody to be unreasonable — worse than that, not salutary, even distinctly harmful.

Uncertainty also comes when anything about the form of law is brought into the definition. Note that of Xenophon: "Whatever the ruling part of the State, after deliberating as to what ought to be done, shall enact, is called a law." Hobbes restricted it to a matter of "speech." Blackstone thought it "a rule prescribed." Bentham made it "a portion of discourse"; Lieber, an "expression of the will of human society"; Mulford, "the formal affirmation of the will of the people." All these phrases shut out that great mass of law which is unenacted — the law of custom. It is the law taught to the child from the dawn of his intelligence until he leaves the home — when the parent says, "You must always do this," or, "You must never do that." Some parts of it we call "manners." Some we call "morals." Its higher forms,

[1] *De Legibus*, i, 15.   [2] *Ecclesiastical Polity*, i, 3, 8.

dignified by the courts when applying the common law to specific cases, we call "precedents." These, to be sure, are affirmations, expressions, speech, or discourse, but they are not enactments. Yet they systematically impel the greater part of the social conduct of mankind, and they have all the necessary attributes of law, provided that by "systematically" we here mean normalcy, generality, some degree of continuity, and do not demand formulation.

Observe that customs and precedents "impel" rather than "compel." Around the difference between these two force-forms has gathered much controversy. They differ in that compulsion is usually effected with the help of a definite penalty, such as fine or imprisonment, whereas the penalties of impulsion may be indefinite, such as the loss of good-will or social standing. John Austin's declaration in his exceedingly abstruse but wonderfully logical lectures on Jurisprudence,[1] makes one view plain: "There can be no law without a judicial sanction, and until custom has been adopted as law by courts of justice, it is always uncertain whether it will be sustained by that sanction or not." [2]

Upon this with allied principles Austin, following Jeremy Bentham, and his immediate successors founded what is known as the English analytical school of jurisprudence. In harmony with their views various writers who seem to think that in definition something should be said about immediate sources, would require some form of recognized authority. Thus Lieber would have law "the public will of a part of human society constituted into a State." Mulford wants it "a rule of action made obligatory by the State." Woodrow Wilson thinks it is to be "backed and sanctioned by the force and authority of the regularly constituted government of the body politic." T. E. Holland calls for "a determinate authority."

Note that all these neglect the law of custom unless it has received some formal recognition. Yet this, the common law, which indeed may at some time be enforced by a State, may also exist regardless of expression by definite authority. Pressing this consideration, another school of thinkers developed, with Sir Henry Maine their leading champion in England and Savigny the best

---

[1] Vol. II, 564.

[2] It may be helpful to warn the reader unaccustomed to legal terminology or the technical language of the schools, that "sanction" is often used in such discussion where most men would say "penalty."

known to us on the Continent. The writers of this, the historical
school, argue that even if there is no live law without a penalty,
enforceable by somebody, it does not necessarily follow that a
law must have been adopted as such by courts of justice, or that
the penalty must be enforced by an organized government.

Put into the language of the philosophers, the arguments in
this matter suggest only the dreariest realms of abstract speculation, but in their concrete application to the affairs of men they
have led to wars, revolutions, epochs of history, and the problem
is to-day as much as ever it was, pregnant with tremendous possibilities. For practical purposes, however, it concerns the seat of
law rather than the source of law, and may be postponed for examination by itself, that we may first consider the ultimate
source from which law springs.

RELIGION AND LAW

Do the fundamental principles of law spring ultimately from
the human intellect, or are they divine in their origin?

There is reason to think that in prehistoric times all law was
believed to have a superhuman source. Law and religion were
one. In the illuminating pages of "The Ancient City," Fustel de
Coulanges tells us how it came about. An ancient belief commanded a man to honor his ancestor; the worship of the ancestor
grouped a family around an altar. Thus arose the first religion,
the first prayers, the first ideas of duty, and of morals. Thus,
too, was the right of property established, and the order of succession fixed. Thus, in fine, arose all private law, and all the rules
of domestic organization. When men began to perceive that there
were common divinities for them, they united in larger groups.
The same rules, invented and established for the family, were
applied successively to the phratry, the tribe, and the city. The
religious idea was the inspiring breath and organizer of society.

The traditions of the Hindus, of the Greeks, and of the Etruscans relate that the gods revealed social laws to men. The Cre-
tans attributed their laws, not to Minos, but to Jupiter. The
Lacedæmonians believed that their legislator was not Lycurgus,
but Apollo. The Romans believed that Numa wrote under the
dictation of one of the most powerful divinities of ancient Italy
— the goddess Egeria. The Etruscans had received their laws
from the god Tages. Solon, Lycurgus, Minos, Numa, might have
reduced the laws of their cities to writing, but could not have

made them. The veritable legislator among the ancients was not a man, but the religious belief which men entertained. Social laws were the work of the gods; but those gods, so powerful and beneficent, were nothing else than the beliefs of men.

During long generations the laws were not written; they were transmitted from father to son, with the creed and the formula of prayer. They were a sacred tradition, which was perpetuated around the hearth of family or city. On the day when men began to commit the laws to writing, they were consigned to the sacred books, to the rituals, among prayers and ceremonies. The laws concerning property and succession were scattered about among rules for sacrifices, for burial, and for the worship of the dead. Varro cites an ancient law of the city of Tusculum, and adds that he read it in the sacred books of that city. Dionysius of Halicarnassus, who had consulted the original documents, says that before the time of the Decemvirs all the written laws at Rome were to be found in the books of the priests. Later the laws were removed from the rituals, and were written separately, by themselves; but the custom of depositing them in a temple continued, and priests had the care of them.

Even when Greece was at the height of her culture, it was still the belief that the authority of law was religious. "This is Law," said Demosthenes, "to which all men should yield obedience for many reasons, and especially because every law is a discovery and gift of God, and at the same time a decision of wise men." In the terminology of the Roman jurisprudence, Bishop Stubbs [1] found proof of the special sanctity of the term "law." He suggests that the variety of expression by means of which men avoided giving the title of law to their various enactments may be thus explained. The Assizes of Jerusalem, Sicily, and Romania, the Establishments of Saint Lewis, the Recesses of the German diets, and many other like expressions, illustrate this reluctance.

Commingling of law and religion persists to this day in the case of that considerable part of mankind which adheres to the Mahommedan faith. Gibbon found from the Atlantic to the Ganges the Koran acknowledged as the fundamental code, not only of theology, but of civil and criminal jurisprudence; the laws regulating the actions and property of mankind are guarded by the infallible and immutable sanction of the will of God.

[1] *Constitutional History*, i, 574.

"The inspiration of the Hebrew prophets, of the apostles and evangelists of Christ," says Gibbon, "might not be incompatible with the exercise of their reason and memory; and the diversity of their genius is strongly marked in the style and composition of the books of the Old and New Testament. But Mahomet was content with a character, more humble, yet more sublime, of a simple editor; the substance of the Koran, according to himself or his disciples, is uncreated and eternal; subsisting in the essence of the Deity, and inscribed with a pen of light on the table of his everlasting decrees. A paper copy, in a volume of silk and gems, was brought down to the lowest Heaven by the angel Gabriel, who, under the Jewish economy, had indeed been despatched on the most important errands; and this trusty messenger successively revealed the chapters and verses to the Arabian prophet." [1]

In more recent times another great body of opinion about law has developed, ascribing to it human origin. Of course there have been overlappings of theory. Some say Moses was the medium through which God spoke. Others say he was inspired by God. Still others say he was the wisest man of his time, and like all other men owed his gifts to the Creator, differing from his fellows only in that his debt was the greater. And still others say all he did was to formulate the customs most followed by his people, thus so approving himself to them that they accredited him with miraculous sagacity, which they believed must have been more than human in its origin and exercise, though in fact it was merely the display of common sense, that is, a sense of what is common to all, which is the great requisite for leadership. The arguments shade into each other like the colors of the rainbow. Nevertheless it is possible to discriminate two broad bands of contrasting thought, even though their limits blur.

Modern discussion of the difference between these may be said to date from the famous book of Bishop Richard Hooker, "Ecclesiastical Polity," published 1594–1600, an argument for the Church as established by Elizabeth, against those who objected to a Church Polity having laws and usages of human institution. He sought to prove that laws are the products of man's reason; that they are maintained by the majority as long as they attain their end; and by the same action of human reason are readjusted for the more certain attainment of the ends desired. [2]

---

[1] *Milman's Gibbon*, chap. 50.

[2] Henry Morley, Int. to Locke's *Two Treatises of Civil Government*.

Hooker's purpose was to show that the Puritans were wrong when they looked wholly to the Bible for the foundations of church arrangements. Those Puritans who came to New England went beyond this and sought also in the Bible the foundations for civil arrangements, at any rate those not prescribed in their charters. The opening paragraph of the Body of Liberties, adopted by the General Court of Massachusetts Bay in 1641, declared that no man's life should be taken away, no man's honor or good name be stained, no man's person arrested, unless by virtue of some express law, or, in the lack of a law in any particular case, by virtue of the word of God. Three years later, the Elders, making formal answer to the General Court much after the fashion of Supreme Court Justices in later days, sustained the constitutionality of this, so to speak.

A more definite identification of human and divine command appears in the quotation borne by the title page of the Laws as first published, in 1648: "Whosoever therefore resisteth the Power, resisteth the Ordinance of God, and they that resist, receive to themselves damnation. Romanes 13." The same quotation appeared on the title page of the revisions of 1660 and 1672.

Another quotation to like purpose concluded the preface to the revision of 1660. After saying that the light of Nature taught the heathen to account both laws and lawmakers sacrosancto, inviolable, the revisers went on to declare: "Religion and civil Order should make as deep Impressions upon Christians, especially where Benefit and Damage are constant attendants. By this Hedge their All is secured against the Injuries of men, and whosoever breaketh this hedge, *a Serpent shall bite him:* They that rage against it, will find the *thorns will prick them:* They that fly to it for shelter, may find the *leaves to shade them:* To such as you we need no other inducements but the authority of the Apostle, 1 Pet. 2. 13. and 17. *Submit your selves to every Ordinance of man for the Lord's sake: Fear God; Honor the King.*"

Connecticut began still more definitely with God as its lawgiver. When the Reverend John Davenport and his company founded the settlement at Quinnipiack that was to become New Haven, they entered soon after their arrival (1638), at the close of a day of fasting and prayer, into what they termed a plantation covenant. In this they solemnly bound themselves, "That as in matters, that concern the gathering and ordering of a church, so also in all public offices which concern civil order; as choice of magistrates and officers, making and repealing laws, dividing allotments of inheritance, and all things of like nature, they would all of them be ordered by the rules, which the scripture held forth for them." In the following year on the 4th of June all the freemen assembled in a large barn and proceeded to lay the foundations of their civil and religious polity. They resolved that the scriptures held forth a perfect rule for the direction and government of all men in duties which they are to perform to God and men, as well in families and commonwealth, as in matters of the church; and went on to repeat the words of their first covenant.

CUSTOM AS A SOURCE OF LAW

Professor W. G. Sumner of Yale was not satisfied with the word "customs" for the title of an exhaustive treatise on human institutions. To his wonderfully instructive and illuminating book he gave the name "Folkways," in want of a better, unfamiliar though it is. Throughout his pages, however, he had constant recourse to the Latin word "mores," for which we have no precise English equivalent. It covers customs, habits, manners, fashions, traditions, institutions — what we sometimes call the unwritten laws of conduct. Here once more language is inadequate, or at least inaccurate, for the "mores" of a modern community are at least set forth in writing by a myriad Lord Chesterfields, or editors of periodicals for "ladies," or preachers of sermons, or expounders of ethics in portly volumes. Nevertheless the phrase "unwritten law" has had a conventional significance equal to the purpose ever since Thucydides in his famous "Funeral Oration of Pericles" spoke of the regard of the Athenians "for those unwritten laws which bring upon the transgressor of them the reprobation of the general sentiment."

"Custom" may serve as well as "folkways" or "mores" if we but agree so to understand it.

"Custom," then, in the wider sense, preceding religion, was undoubtedly the original source of law. Nobody to-day contends for the view made famous by Rousseau, that society began with a compact. It began with custom, which at the outset was hardly more than habit. Centuries slowly formed the idea that what had been done should be done. With it grew the belief that the reason for compliance with custom was supernatural, for primitive man early came to think that gods and demigods and all

sorts of spirits were the cause of all sorts of happenings, that they
bestowed all rewards and punishments, and that a violation of
custom would bring down their wrath. The first conception of
law, therefore, was that of a custom, and the first conception of
justice concerned the violation of custom. It is certain that in
the infancy of mankind no sort of legislation, not even a distinct
author of law, was contemplated or conceived. From some indefinite source at first, later from divinities or spirits localized
and personified, came the commands to be obeyed. Inevitably
the relations between men, as they began to be social, required
interpretation and application of these commands. Elders or
wise men, chiefs or kings or priests, gave judgments. As Sir
H. S. Maine says in his classic work on "Ancient Law," the only
authoritative statement of right and wrong was a judicial sentence after the facts, not one presupposing a law that had been
violated, but one breathed for the first time by a higher power
into the judge's mind at the moment of adjudication.

Next comes the epoch of Customary Law. Customs or Ob-
servances now exist as a substantive aggregate, and are assumed
to be precisely known to the aristocratic order or caste. Our authorities leave us no doubt that the trust lodged with the oligarchy was sometimes abused, but it certainly ought not to be regarded as a mere usurpation or engine of tyranny. Before the
invention of writing, and during the infancy of the art, an aristocracy invested with judicial privileges formed the only expedient by which accurate preservation of the customs of the
race or tribe could be at all approximated. Their genuineness
was, as far as possible, insured by confiding them to the recollection of a limited portion of the community.[1]

In the course of time declarers of law appeared in many guises
— rulers of all sorts, chiefs, princes, kings, every variety of
monarchs; men distinctively known as lawgivers, such as Moses,
Solon, Lycurgus; in aristocracies, small groups of the stronger
men; in democracies, the people themselves, as perhaps in all
the Germanic tribes; of late the people by their representatives,
in parliaments, congresses, and other forms of legislatures; and
through all periods, the judges.

With the invention of writing it was natural that the declaration of customs should be recorded. Hence came what are called
codes. The oldest of these yet known to us was the work of

[1] Sir H. S. Maine, *Ancient Law*, 4th Am. ed., 11.

Hammurabi, who reigned in Babylon about 2250 B.C. His full code, the most elaborate monument of early civilization so far discovered, he engraved on great stone stelæ, set up in the principal cities of his realm, where they could be read by all his subjects. There were about two hundred and eighty separate decisions or edicts, covering with great minuteness the rights of property, inheritance, marriage, divorce, injuries to life or person, wages for different kinds of service, rents of houses, boats, and other things, all showing a high state of civilization at the time of the patriarch Abraham; for Hammurabi is the Amraphel of Genesis xiv, who made a raid, with other kings, into Palestine, and captured Sodom. To a lawyer, familiar, as all lawyers must be, with the history of the modern Statute of Frauds, it is most interesting to find that more than four thousand years ago Hammurabi ordained that everything must be of record, written on tablets, or there was no obligation in case of loss. If stolen property was found on a man, and he could not show the bill of sale, he was regarded as a thief and punished with death. If a man had forgotten to take a receipt for money consigned to an agent for trade, he could exact no returns. It is no wonder that the soil of Babylon is full of these contract-tables.[1]

The civilization of Babylonia rested on this legislation, which probably remained in effect until the period of the Greek conquest under Alexander. Doubtless these laws were carried to all parts of the empire, even to Palestine, and very likely were there enforced, as far as conditions allowed, for centuries before Moses entered the Holy Land.

We speak of these as the laws of Hammurabi. So, if they were not perfectly familiar, we might go on to describe the laws of Moses, and follow with the laws of Solon, and the other great lawgivers of antiquity, as they are called, but detail is needless. The only important thing for us here is to realize what was common to all these codes in origin and development.

Codification, properly speaking, is not legislation. It is the writing of old law, not the making of new law. Codes have, indeed, sometimes contained new law, but that has been foreign to their real purpose, which is to put in convenient form rules of conduct already known. The earliest codes were formal declarations of venerable customs that had not before been authoritatively set forth in writing. Sometimes they crystallized custom,

[1] Dr. William Hayes Ward, "Who Was Hammurabi?" *Century*, July, 1903.

stopped its change, and were to that extent bad, for it is not well that custom should not have the chance to change. To illustrate, take the criminal law. Even those who doubt whether on the whole mankind has perceptibly improved since history began, admit that in respect both of mercy and of the giving of pain, we have made great advance. When codes attached to penalties a permanence they otherwise would not have received, the codes were unfortunate. On the other hand, in a deteriorating society such as that of Rome under the Emperors, old ethical standards embodied in law doubtless delayed disaster. Furthermore codes have played a useful part in helping to unify nations formed of heterogeneous elements. By reconciling diverse customs, or by selecting between those in conflict, they have given unity and solidarity, as in Rome, France, and Germany.

INNOVATION

Niebuhr was accurate in saying that no one in the ancient world took it into his head to make a new system of laws, but it does not follow that there were no new laws. Change was no longer spontaneous, from within; it had now to be artificial, from without. To alter old law embodied in a code was sometimes well-nigh impossible, always difficult. Only such a virile people as that of Rome, strong enough to grow and intelligent enough to bend the bars, could escape the prison of custom. The Roman jurisprudence, through a history longer than that of any other set of human institutions, shows a steady modification for the better, or, as Maine says, what the authors of the modifications conceived to be for the better.

In the gloom of the Middle Ages human aspiration toward better things disappeared. It was to come to the surface again in England. There as everywhere else ancient law was custom. The idea of "making" law did not exist. The Anglo-Saxon King never legislated. The Witenagemot, the Great Council of the realm, never made what we should call new laws. When it tried men for breach of the law, it might have to declare whether old law, that is, old custom, had been changed, and to tell what the old custom had become; but to devise out of its own wisdom what the custom ought instead to be, and to command its observance, was never contemplated. It is not probable there was anything we should call legislation before the Norman Conquest. Many writers say that English lawmaking began with Magna

Charta. J. R. Green, in his "History of the English People" (I, 245), observes that the Great Charter marks the transition from the age of traditional rights, preserved in the nation's memory and officially declared by the Primate, to the age of written legislation, of Parliaments and Statutes, which was to come. Pollock and Maitland speak of it as " the first chapter of the enacted law." Yet Magna Charta was a rehearsing and reviving of old liberties, and such were its various confirmations.

Originally all general statutes were intended to restate customs that had been violated or abused by King or Lords. As late as the seventeenth century, the Petition of Right and the Bill of Rights were of the same class, and indeed that may be said of our own Declaration of Independence. Burke gave the idea in his "Reflections on the Revolution in France": "You will observe that from Magna Charta down to the Declaration of Right, it has been the uniform policy of our constitution to claim and assert our liberties, as an *entailed inheritance* derived to us from our forefathers, and to be transmitted to our posterity."

Blackstone, writing just before America and France asserted the right of each generation to think for itself, had declared: "And it hath been an ancient observation in the laws of England, that whenever a standing rule of law, of which the reason perhaps could not be remembered or discerned, hath been wantonly broken in upon by statutes or new resolutions, the wisdom of the rule hath in the end appeared from the inconveniences that have followed the innovation." [1] In the essay just quoted, Burke also said: "A spirit of innovation is generally the result of a selfish temper and confined views." It is hard for us to realize that but a little more than a hundred years ago a leading English statesman and philosopher could pronounce such a belief. Since his time, however, we have traveled more miles on the road of innovation than the lawmakers of the world had traveled in all the centuries before. To-day we have almost come to look on change as the normal rather than the unnatural thing.

Nevertheless, it is not yet agreed that there can be or ought to be makers of law. The controversy over this is modern because the idea is modern. If that controversy did not begin with Rousseau, yet his powerful influence in contributing to the French Revolution, that brought out the strictures of Burke, will warrant the quoting of an eloquent passage in which Rousseau's

[1] *Commentaries*, I, 70.

belief in the artificial character of legislation clearly appears. "The Legislator," he said, "puts into the mouths of the immortals that sublime reason which soars beyond the reach of common men, in order that he may win over by divine authority those whom human prudence could not move. But it does not belong to every man to make the gods his oracles, nor to be believed when he proclaims himself their interpreter. The great soul of the legislator is the real miracle which must give proof of his mission. Any man can engrave tablets of stone, or bribe an oracle or pretend secret intercourse with some divinity, or train a bird to speak in his ear, or find some other clumsy means to impose on the people. He who is acquainted with such means only, will perchance be able to assemble a crowd of foolish persons; but he will never found an empire, and his extravagant work will speedily perish with him. Empty deceptions form but a transient bond; it is only wisdom that makes it lasting. The Jewish law, which still endures, and that of the child of Ishmael, which for ten centuries has ruled half the world, still bear witness to-day to the great men who dictated them; and while proud philosophy or blind party spirit sees in them nothing but fortunate impostors, the true statesman admires in their systems the great and powerful genius which directs durable institutions." [1]

Two score of years after Rousseau thus wrote, Napoleon Bonaparte, the greatest of modern lawmakers, was presiding as First Consul over the Council of State that passed upon the most noteworthy of constructive codes. Napoleon believed that law is a science, based on eternal principles of justice, to be set down by jurists rather than framed by a legislative body. His work it was that gave the great impetus to code-making.

In Germany, rather than in France, the discussion of the principles involved in the issue first became clear-cut. There in 1814 Thibaut, a Heidelberg professor, proposed the making of a code of laws that should be common to all the German States and so help toward unifying Germany. It was in reply to this that Karl Fried v. Savigny, professor at Berlin, won fame by an essay "On the Vocation of our Age for Legislation." Savigny's purpose was to show that laws may not be evolved from the reason of man, but grow out of the life of a people. He believed that they were the fruit of habit, and that the province of legislation was at

[1] *Social Compact*, book 2, chap. vii.

most to explain, to supplement, to modify, at most to improve, and not to create. To be sure, he admitted that as in the life of individual men no moment of complete stillness is experienced, but there is a constant organic development, such also is the case in the life of nations, and of every individual element in which this collective life consists. This he likened to the constant formation and development to be found in the life of a language, and he thought it no more feasible to command the habits of a people than to command their speech.

While Thibaut's theory has been marvelously vindicated by its practical application in the unification of Germany and in its legislation, that of Savigny has carried off the honors in the acceptance it has won from the writers on political science — a singular instance of the way in which rude statesmen sometimes ignore the logic of the closet philosophers. Yet although Germany, following Thibaut, has confuted a host of learned authorities by achieving what they in effect declared impossible, it will not do to omit a fair presentation of their arguments.

First note the view of an English contemporary of Savigny, Jeremy Bentham, who said, iconoclast and innovator though he was, that however odd or pernicious a religion, a law, a custom may be, is of no consequence, so long as the people are attached to it. The strength of their prejudice is the measure of the indulgence that should be granted. To take away a chimerical enjoyment or hope, is to do the same injury as if we took away a real hope, a real enjoyment. In such a case the pain of a single individual becomes, by sympathy, the pain of all. Thence results a crowd of evils: antipathy against a law that wounds the general prejudice; antipathy against the whole code of which that law is a part; antipathy against the government that carries the law into execution.[1]

According to Francis Lieber, all that in a code which is not conformable to the spirit of society must fall to the ground. Men like Solon and Lycurgus did not make Constitutions, like Condorcet, but rather collected them. This does not contradict the vast power of a great mind exercised over his community. That the community acquiesce in or support what he proposes or does, belongs likewise to the sense and sentiment of the community; and they will not, cannot acquiesce, except where that great mind acts out, completes, developes, and elevates, without mak-

[1] *Theory of Legislation*, trans. by R. Hildreth, 76.

ing the rash attempt to establish something absolutely foreign and heterogeneous.[1]

Of more recent writers, C. G. Tiedeman may be taken for illustration. The average common-sense of propriety, which is uniformly obeyed by the vast majority of the people, he believes to constitute in the main the standard after which rules of law are modeled. The morality commonly and uniformly practiced by the masses lends its character to the rule of law when it is first enunciated. And even when the rule is first promulgated, its ethical character is much lower than the standard of morality set up by ethical teachers; for only that code of morality can be enforced against delinquents which the people generally obey. If it were attempted to enforce a higher standard, for example, to compel every one to do unto others as he would have them do unto him, the sanction would be wanting, for no penalty is effective unless it is backed by the *posse comitatus*.[2]

In this matter of penalty Leslie Stephen has observed that although a legal sanction may of course be added to any custom whatever, and thus it may seem that a State can make its own Constitution and define its own organic laws, in reality, however, the power of making a Constitution presupposes a readiness to act together and accept certain rules as binding, and this again implies a whole set of established customs, such as are necessary to the constitution and authority of a representative body.[3]

While he was yet a Professor, Woodrow Wilson asserted that it is the function of the authorities of the State to direct, to lead, rather than to command. They originate forms but they do not discover principles. In a very profound sense law proceeds from the community. It is the result of its undeliberate as well as its deliberate developments, of its struggles, class against class, interest against interest, and of its compromises and adjustments of opinion. It follows, slowly, its ethical judgments, more promptly its material necessities. But law issues from the community only in vague and inchoate form. It must be taken out of the sphere of voluntary and uncertain action and made precise and invariable. It becomes positive law by receiving definition and being backed by an active and recognized power within the state. The sovereign organ of a State is, therefore, very properly said to be its law*making* organ. It transmutes selected tendencies

---

[1] *Manual of Political Ethics*, 2nd ed., I, 231.
[2] *The Unwritten Constitution of the U.S.*, 5.   [3] *The Science of Ethics*, 143.

into stiff and urgent rules. It exercises a sovereign choice in so doing. It determines which tendencies shall be accepted, which checked and denied efficiency. It forms the purposes of the State, avoiding revolution if it form them wisely and with a true insight. This is sovereignty — to sit at the helm and steer, marking out such free courses as wind and weather will permit. This is the only sort of sovereignty that can be exercised in human affairs. But the pilot is sovereign, and not the weather.[1]

Professor Sumner, having in his preface defined *mores* as "popular usages and traditions, when they include a judgment that they are conducive to societal welfare, and when they exert a coercion on the individual to conform to them," proceeded in the body of his book to show how acts of legislation come out of the mores. In low civilization all societal regulations are customs and taboos, the origin of which is unknown. Positive laws are impossible until the stage of verification, reflection, and criticism is reached. Enactment is not possible until reverence for ancestors has been so much weakened that it is no longer thought wrong to interfere with traditional customs by positive enactment. Even then there is reluctance to make enactments, and there is a stage of transition during which traditional customs are extended by interpretation to cover new cases and to prevent evils. Legislation, however, has to seek standing ground on the existing mores, and it soon becomes apparent that legislation, to be strong, must be consistent with the mores. Things which have been in the mores are put under police regulation and later under positive law. It is sometimes said that public opinion must ratify and approve police regulations, but this statement rests on an imperfect analysis. The regulations must conform to the mores, so that the public will not think them too lax or too strict.[2]

W. W. Willoughby, speaking of the Savigny doctrine, concludes that in the development of law, custom is the conservative element, legislative enactment the radical. The task of the true statesman is to give to both of these elements their due importance. It was the great merit of the work of Savigny that he showed the task of the legislator should be largely limited to the statutory confirmation of principles that common usage has already established, rather than the invention of laws according to individual caprice or judgment. As Count Portalis expressed it, "the legislature should not invent law, but only write it."[3]

[1] *An Old Master and Other Essays*, 94–96.   [2] *Folkways*, 55.
[3] *The Nature of the State*, 156.

Emerson put it still more succinctly: "The law is only a memorandum." [1]

Warrant for quoting at such length is to be found in the great practical importance of the issue. Every legislator is frequently told, "You can't make men good by law." Constant is the argument of the conservative that the people are not ready for reform, that they will not support a measure, that laws without public opinion behind them are worse than useless. Plutarch tells us that when Solon was asked if he had left the Athenians the best laws that could be given, he replied, "The best they could receive." Grote puts it: "He is said to have described them, not as the best laws which he himself could have imagined, but as the best which he could have induced the people to accept." From that day to this, legislators have been told they must give the people what the people want. Yet Sir H. S. Maine declares it to be indisputable that much the greatest part of mankind has never shown a particle of desire that its civil institutions should be improved since the moment when external completeness was first given to them by their embodiment in some permanent record.[2]

How are these things to be reconciled? If, as common observation teaches, most men do not want customs changed, and if no law unsupported by custom will avail, how can there be advance?

It may be that the view of law by the writers who have been quoted has been incomplete. Surely it does not take into account certain definite facts in legislation. In our time many countries have enacted many laws that have upset custom, that have not been based on any expression of popular will, did not spring from the people, were not wanted by the people. Yet probably in far the greater number of cases these laws have accomplished useful results and have in the end won approval. When the housewives of Berlin were forbidden to shake rugs out of their front windows and were promptly arrested if they continued their custom, and when Berlin accepted back yards as the proper place to shake rugs, it shattered the Savigny theory that law ought to be a formulation of custom, ought to grow out of the life of the people. When railroad rebates were made criminal in this country, it left little of Woodrow Wilson's theory that the function of the authorities of the state is to direct, to lead, rather than to command. A score of railroad practices to which a few thoughtful men ob-

[1] *Essay on Politics.*   [2] *Ancient Law*, 21.

jected were actually defended by the railroads on the ground that they were universal custom. Mr. Wilson himself, when he became Governor of New Jersey, was said to have struck stoutly and successfully and usefully at various things which at least wore the guise of customs and against which there was no really widespread revolt until he led revolt. Whether or not that statement could be substantiated with particulars, it is at any rate in accord with common experience, for reforms never spring into being full-fledged. They are always at the start and often at the end, the work of a minority, sometimes a very small minority; and frequently they are forced upon a reluctant or hostile constituency. Again to turn to antiquity for illustration, recall what was told by Plutarch, after rehearsing the long list of the laws of Solon:

"Now when these laws were enacted, and some came to Solon every day, to commend or dispraise them, and to advise, if possible to leave out or put in something, and many criticized, and desired him to explain, and tell the meaning of such and such a passage, he, knowing that to do so was useless, and not to do it would get him ill-will, and desirous to bring himself out of all straits, and to escape all displeasures and exceptions, it being a hard thing, as he himself says,

'In great affairs to satisfy all sides,'

as an excuse for traveling, bought a trading vessel, and, having leave for ten years' absence, departed, hoping that by that time his laws would have become familiar."

He quitted his native city in the full confidence that his laws would remain unrepealed until his return; for, says Herodotus, "the Athenians *could not* repeal them, since they were bound by solemn oaths to observe them for ten years."

The course of Lycurgus was even more compelling than that of Solon. Plutarch says of the Spartan lawgiver that he told the people to agree to observe his laws till he came back, and then going off killed himself by fasting, whereupon Lacedæmon "continued the chief city of Greece for five hundred years, in strict observance of Lycurgus's laws; in all which time there was no manner of alteration made, during the reign of fourteen Kings."

Human nature has not changed since the days of Solon and Lycurgus. The wise few must still cajole or coerce the stolid many. That small fraction of every community which takes an earnest, serious, and intelligent interest in public affairs must still make the decisions, and these will endure if in due time they win the approval of the majority. To argue the contrary is to put the cart before the horse.

Of course it is true that a law avowedly or even tacitly desired by the greater part of the people will be effective and efficient. This much of the argument of the Savigny school of writers is incontestable. When they go on to say that such a desire is an essential prerequisite, they err. Everyday experience disproves it. Fortified by this experience, legislators may well continue to study how to make such wisdom as they can command, of constructive benefit to their constituents. Let them not consent to be denied the right to create.

Bluntschli was wiser than Savigny. "While it may be true," said Bluntschli, "that the present rests upon the past and cannot be entirely separated from it, yet it is none the less true that the forms of different ages are variable, and out of the depths of Man's nature, and brought forth by the mutations in the spirit of the age, new forms are created. The critical examination of the past is necessary in order to discover the grounds upon which we rest, but the consideration of the future is none the less necessary in order to determine whither we are going.... The present is a union of the past and future. It alone is real. There is something that is not often sufficiently recognized by the historical school."[1]

Even if the future should be left to take care of itself, our duty to the present calls for us to free it from so much of the past as is dead. The forester helps a tree to new life by lopping off the dead and decaying branches. So the legislator should lop off rules due to customs once vital, but now abandoned. To formulate, to create, and to destroy, all are proper functions of the lawmakers of to-day.

CUSTOM AND THE COURTS

Let us pursue the problem farther by following it into the field of that most important group of law-declarers — the judges. The controversy reaches the heart of their function, and hence as to them has far more than academic significance. Underlying the question of "judge-made law," it affects the future of the judicial department of government. It brings in issue the very nature, purpose, and scope of justice.

As usual, definition makes much of the trouble. Men talk

[1] *Geschichte der neuren Staatswissenschaft*, 625.

about "custom" without meaning the same thing. "The common law" is used now in a popular, now in a technical, significance. Judges are said to "make" law, regardless of whether in fact they declare or apply or create.

Coke said that the laws of England are "divided into common law, statute law and customs." Without further discrimination, this would not meet technical demands, for though it be granted that custom is the source of law, custom is not necessarily law of itself, in the technical sense. General customs, as contrasted with particular or local customs, form the common law, but not all general customs, for only those are now avowedly applied as rules of the common law where judicial precedent can be found. The controversy comes over customs that have not received judicial recognition, or, more often, over inferences and analogies from customs whether hitherto recognized or unrecognized. In brief, may the judges in fact though not confessedly expand the common law beyond the artificial limits of precedent?

Many heated denunciations of the American judiciary in recent years have had no other excuse than the charge that the judges in thus expanding the common law, or in "making" law, as it is usually described, have usurped authority. Yet that has been the process and the practice from time immemorial. Back in the days of the Stuarts we find Sir Robert Filmer speaking of it as a natural thing. His "Patriarcha," published in 1680, had been written a generation before, for he died in 1653. In his third chapter he said: "Where precedents have failed, the judges have resorted to the general law of reason, and accordingly given judgment without any common law to direct them. Nay, many times where there have been precedents to direct, they, upon better reason only, have changed the law both in causes criminal and civil, and have not insisted so much upon the examples of former judges, as examined and corrected their reasons; thence it is that some laws are now obsolete and out of use, and the practice quite contrary to what it was in former times, as the Lord Chancellor Egerton proves by several instances."

Filmer gave more latitude to reason, independent and self-contained, than is necessary. If in his day judges commonly went that far, those of our time can here find proof that the judiciary has become more circumspect. It is not to be denied that judges sometimes make law, to the extent of applying to a fresh problem some principle not hitherto formulated — in other words, without precedent. But if the judge is true to his duty and equal to his task, he draws that principle from the common mind, the common sense, of the community in which he dwells, as it has been shown by the whole body of practice and experience. The bitter criticism of John Marshall by Thomas Jefferson and his followers did not delude that straight thinker Francis Lieber, who gave the fact when he said: "There is hardly such a thing as judge-made law, but only judge-spoken law. The doctrine pronounced to-day from a bench may, indeed, not be found in any law-book; but the judge has ascertained and declared the sense of the community, as already evinced in its usages and habits of business." [1]

If it be replied that since Lieber's time our courts have usurped more of power, take the judgment of a present day authority, F. J. Stimson, whose treatise attests his familiarity with the whole field of lawmaking — constitutional, legislative, judicial. Stimson reaches the belief that the phrase "judge-made law" is a misnomer in ninety-nine cases out of a hundred, and that a judge is a very bad judge who does not decide a point of law apparently new or doubtful according to the entire body of English-American precedent, experience, rather than by his own way of looking at things.[2]

On the other hand it is fair to recognize that a contrary view has been advanced by no less an authority on the common law than Oliver Wendell Holmes, Jr., whose book on the subject made reputation for him long before he reached the Supreme Bench. Holmes held that in substance the growth of the law is legislative, and this in a deeper sense than that what the courts declare to have always been the law, is in fact new. It is legislative in its grounds. "The very considerations which judges most rarely mention, and always with an apology, are the secret root from which the law draws all the juices of life. I mean, of course, considerations of what is expedient for the community concerned. Every important principle which is developed by litigation is in fact and at bottom the result of more or less definitely understood views of public policy; most generally, to be sure, under our practice and traditions, the unconscious result of instinctive preferences and inarticulate convictions, but none the less traceable to views of public policy in the last analysis." [3]

[1] *Manual of Political Ethics*, 2nd ed., I, 231.
[2] *Popular Lawmaking*, 122.   [3] *The Common Law*, 35, 36.

The vigorous independence with which Justice Holmes has applied his own views of public policy to the problems that have confronted him in the course of his long service, attests his faith in his theory of the judicial function, but is not the fact that such independence is so conspicuous by its rarity, proof that the contrary view is in practice well-nigh universal on the bench?

Two of the foremost American lawyers have taken opposite sides on the matter, in volumes of exceptional ability — one, "Law: Its Origin, Growth, and Function," by James C. Carter, a leader of the New York Bar, being a posthumous publication of lectures that were to have been delivered at the Harvard Law School; the other, "Nature and Sources of the Law," by John C. Gray, a leader of the Boston Bar and a Professor at the Harvard Law School. Mr. Carter found the origin of law in custom, the imperishable record of the wisdom of the illimitable past reaching back to the infancy of the race, revised, corrected, enlarged, open to all alike, and read and understood by all. "How poor the conclusions of the wisest of lawyers gathered from their own original reflections when compared with those garnered up in the actual customs of life!" Judges never make law, but it is always made by custom. "I know of no reason," he says, "why men were in the first instance compelled to perform their contracts except that such performance was in accordance with custom. It has often been said by the most approved writers that custom is *one* of the sources of the law, and indeed Blackstone views the body of our unwritten law as being custom, or founded upon custom; but the sort of custom thus intended is *ancient* custom, reaching so far back that its beginning is not known. Such a limitation of custom in the making of law seems to me to be without foundation." He goes on to cite a case where "there was no precedent, which is authenticated custom, nor any evidence of actual custom," and some would say it was clear the judges had *made* the law out of their own heads, upon a simple consideration of right or wrong. That the decision was based upon the consideration whether that action was right or wrong is, in a sense, true; but whose notion of right or wrong was it? It did not come from on High. It was not sought for in the Scriptures, or in any book on ethics. The judges in considering whether the act was right or wrong applied to it the method universally adopted by all men; they judged it by its *consequences*. Custom decided the case, for to determine whether it was right

or wrong by the *customary modes* of determining right and wrong
is to determine it according to custom.

To this Professor Gray replies: "The theory of his book seems
to be that Law is created by custom; that when the judges declare the Law, they are declaring that to be Law which already
existed; and that the declaration is only evidence, though a high
kind of evidence, of the Law. If this be his matured opinion, and
I think it is, I must say, with all diffidence, I cannot agree with
him, *Amicus Plato, sed magis amica veritas.*"

Professor Gray goes on to cite the famous case of Pells *v.*
Brown, decided by the court of King's Bench, in 1620, which
established that future contingent interests can be validly
created by will. He proceeds (p. 224): "Mr. Carter, I understand,
would say that the validity of this doctrine of future interests
was created by custom, and was Law before the case of Pells *v.*
Brown. Now what is custom? Custom is what is generally
practiced in a community and believed by the community generally to be a common practice. Now, is it conceivable that in
England, at the beginning of the seventeenth century, a belief
was prevalent in the community that an executory devise could
not be destroyed by a common recovery with single voucher?
Why, there was not one man in England out of ten thousand,
not one out of fifty thousand, who had any belief upon the question, or who would have even understood what it meant. To say
that there was a custom that future contingent interests were
indestructible is a baseless dream, invented only to avoid the
necessity of saying that judges make law.... And this is only one
case out of thousands where the Law stands as it does to-day
upon the opinions of individuals in judicial position on matters
as to which there was no general practice, no custom, no belief,
no expectation in the community."

To this it might be answered that the difficulty lies in the
definition of "custom." No doubt Professor Gray gives the usual
definition, but it is also possible that Mr. Carter meant something more. "I, the writer," says the author of the "Ottimo
Commento," "heard Dante say that never a rhyme had left him
to say other than he would, but that many a time and oft he
made words say in his rhymes what they were not wont to express for other poets."

Possibly Mr. Carter may have meant to cover by "custom"
the beliefs of mankind on which they have commonly acted. It
would not be far amiss to say that the generality of English-

speaking people have from time immemorial been accustomed to act on the belief that they may while living direct the disposition of their property after death; and if pressed, they would have added, "within reasonable limits." If that is the case, the task of the judge has been to define the "reasonable limits," and therein the word "reasonable" would restrict him to standards in harmony with the beliefs and practices of the mass of his countrymen. Supposing he could find no exact counterpart, would he be refused power to conclude from analogies?

Unless the common law is to be discarded and our reliance placed on code law, judges must continue to exercise functions of this sort. The body of the law they deduce from custom must change and grow because the body of custom changes and grows. The history of the common law is the history of social change and growth. The normal process is for new and extraordinary rules laid down in equity to become in course of time old rules, transformed into common law. The equitable decisions of one age become the strict legal rules of the next.

Modification and amplification have been enormously accelerated in the last century by the unprecedented advance in what is commonly spoken of as civilization, due not alone to inventions in the fields of industry and commerce — "business" — but also to inventions, new ideas, covering the whole range of human relations — "sociology." The effect has been shown by the staggering increase in the number of adjudications by those higher courts whose decisions make up the law reports. Where a century ago a volume of the reports of the Supreme Court of the United States covered a period of fourteen months, a single volume of the reports of that court covers the single day of June 16, 1913, in which decisions were rendered in about two dozen groups of causes. At the end of the eighteenth century the total number of printed volumes of reported cases in England, Ireland, the English colonies, and the United States of America was 260. At the end of the year 1865 they had increased more than twelvefold, to more than 3000, not including the Indian reports, and at the end of the nineteenth century the published reports of decisions in the United States alone required about 6000 volumes. Of course a great many of these decisions relate to constitutional, statute, municipal, or administrative law, and there is endless repetition, yet the determinations and applications of the common law are still plenty enough to show that it continues a vital and ever growing factor in the impelling of conduct.

CHAPTER II

MONARCHS AND SOVEREIGNTY

PRIESTS and judges would commonly be thought of as "law-declarers." The word "legislator" ordinarily conveys the idea of one chosen by his fellows, usually by vote, to enact laws. Whether law-declaring or law-making, the function during some part of the world's history and in many countries has also been performed by individuals known as kings, or emperors, or by rulers with corresponding title. Perhaps "monarch" is the best designation for our purpose, since "monarchy" means literally the rule of one. If Sir H. S. Maine and Fustel de Coulange are right in their theories, then monarchy is a comparatively recent development in respect of the legislating power. It would be interesting to see if this is borne out by the history of Egypt, Persia, China, Japan, Mexico, Peru, but that would take us too far afield. Our institutions are either Teutonic or Roman and it is enough for present purposes to recognize that they have had law-declaring or law-making monarchs as a feature only in that period of time commonly known as the Christian era, that is, for something less than two thousand years.

With the change of Rome into an empire, the Roman lawyers had to justify the assumption of power by a single Roman. Ulpian did it by saying: "That which is decided by the prince has the force of law, because the people delegates its authority to him by the *lex regia* which raises him to the empire." Most of the Roman lawyers of the Middle Ages interpreted Ulpian in the sense that, though the people were to be considered the original source of authority of the prince, they surrendered their authority once for all. This was the theory later on developed by the Jesuits.

The Norman Conquest brought into England the Roman theory, and the Norman Kings presently began lawmaking, which the Saxon Kings had never tried. The early history of the procedure is full of uncertainty. There is, however, reason to believe that it started with a custom permitting the King to issue proclamations for the enforcement of law. The custom grew until at last the King began to issue proclamations, not for the enforcement, but for the creation, of law. As a rule, this power was exercised only when Parliament was not in session, and when some urgent necessity called for immediate legislation. It was exercised by what came to be known as "ordinances." The distinction between ordinances and statutes is very obscure, and perhaps rests on no precise and uniform principle, but it seems to have been the case that whatever provisions altered the common law or any former statute, and were entered upon the statute-roll, transmitted to the sheriffs, and promulgated to the people as general obligatory enactments, were held to require the positive assent of both Houses of Parliament, duly and formally summoned.[1]

Whitelocke does not add much to our knowledge. "If," he says, "there be any difference between an ordinance and a statute, as some have collected, it is but only this, that an ordinance is but temporary until confirmed and made perpetual, but a statute is perpetual at first, and so have some ordinances also been." [2]

Ordinances that, if it were not for their restricted or temporary operation, could not well be distinguished from laws, were often established in Great Councils. These assemblies, frequently held in the reign of Edward III, were except in name hardly distinguishable from Parliaments, being constituted not only of those who were regularly summoned to the House of Lords, but also of deputies from counties, cities, and boroughs. Later on, more than once the King himself inquired of the Commons whether certain grants should be carried out by way of "statute" or "ordinance," to which they replied that the latter method was preferable, because requisite alterations could then be more easily made. Hence in parliamentary phraseology a distinction arose between two classes of statutory acts: (1) *ordinances* and *proclamations*, that is, decrees issued by the King in the old manner on his own authority — as a rule with the advice of the Council, and sometimes also with that of the Great Council; (2) *statutes*, which having been agreed upon in the new manner with the Estates, were, as being permanent enactments of the realm, entered upon the statute-roll and published.[3]

Furthermore, the King gradually came to legislate negatively, so to speak, by the exercise of suspending and dispensing powers.

---

[1] Hallam, *Middle Ages*, chap. VIII, part III.   [2] *On Parliamentary Writ*, II, 297.

[3] Rudolf Gneist, *Constitutional History of England*, II, 24.

Taswell-Langmead calls our attention to the fact that these two terms are frequently used indiscriminately; but there is an appreciable difference in their strict signification. (1) The *dispensing* power consisted in the exemption of particular persons, under special circumstances, from the operation of penal laws; being, in fact, an anticipatory exercise of the undoubted right of the King to pardon individual offenders. (2) The *suspending* power was employed in nullifying the entire operation of any statute or any number of statutes; and was in its nature incompatible with the existence of constitutional government. This encroachment on the liberty of the subject appears to have been derived from the practice of the Papacy, whose example in issuing Bulls "*non obstante*, any law to the contrary," was soon followed by Kings of England in their proclamations, grants, and writs. Henry III was perhaps the first to make use of the *non obstante* clause, and his successors throughout the Plantagenet period frequently exerted both the dispensing and suspending power. It was usually, however, asserted only in matters of small moment, and even then it was not allowed to pass without remonstrance and attempts at restraint.[1]

Hallam gives as an instance of the dispensing power an episode in the time of Richard II, when a petition that all statutes might be confirmed was granted, with an exception as to one passed in the preceding Parliament, forbidding the judges to take fees or give counsel in cases where the King was a party; which, "because it was too severe and needs declaration, the King would have of no effect until it be declared in Parliament." This, according to the Taswell-Langmead theory of differentiation, would seem to be rather an instance of the suspending power. It suggests the modern veto. Hallam, however, says the dispensing power, as exercised in favor of individuals, was of a different character from the general suspension of statutes, and but indirectly weakened the sovereignty of the legislature. The dispensing power was exerted, and even recognized, throughout all the reigns of the Plantagenets. In the 1st of Henry V the Commons prayed that the statute for driving aliens out of the kingdom be executed. The King assented, saving his prerogative and the right of dispensing with the statute when he pleased. To which the Commons replied that their intention was never otherwise, nor, by God's help, ever should be.[2]

[1] T. P. Taswell-Langmead, *English Constitutional History*, 289.
[2] Hallam, *Middle Ages*, chap. VIII, part III.

Nevertheless the Commons were not wholly subservient. Hallam further tells us that the apprehension of the dispensing prerogative and the sense of its illegality are manifested by the wary terms wherein the Commons, in one of Richard's Parliaments, "assent that the King make such sufferance respecting the statute of provisors as shall seem reasonable to him, so that the said statute be not repealed; and, moreover, that the Commons may disagree thereto at the next Parliament, and resort to the statute"; with a protestation that this assent, which is a novelty and never done before, shall not be drawn into precedent; praying the King that this protestation may be entered on the roll of Parliament.

Henry VIII having issued certain royal proclamations, the judges held that those who disobeyed them could not be punished by the Council. The King then appealed to Parliament to give his proclamations the force of statutes. This request was complied with, but not without "many large words."

Meantime on the Continent also the feudal system had helped develop the absolute authority of monarchs. They did not seize power; it was thrust upon them. It was not so much that the people wanted one-man rule as that they wished to get rid of few-men rule. They revolted against oligarchy. They tired of the injustice and the oppression worked by assemblies and diets and parliaments dominated by the nobles. They turned to monarchs for protection and relief. For instance, in an address to the King of France in 1412, profiteers were denounced, the King was blamed for inaction, and a blunt demand was made that he should grasp and use absolute power. Two centuries later the parlement of Paris, with the support of the third estate, probably representing the people as far as it then could be represented, declared it to be a fundamental law that the throne was absolutely independent, though the King himself demurred to a principle that ignored the privileges of the nobles. When absolute power was conferred upon the King of Denmark in 1660, he at first refused to accept it, but the burghers, closing the gates of the city so that the nobles could not leave it in order to collect their forces, carried their point by sheer intimidation.[1]

With the Revival of Learning men began to ponder these things; they began to seek causes and reasons, to justify or condemn. Slowly they formulated principles. In France they

[1] H. J. Ford, *Representative Government*, 299.

coined the word "sovereignty," and French scholars worked out its idea — the most important idea in political science. Bodin, who gained his reputation by "De La Republique," published in 1576, made sovereignty the basic principle of public or constitutional law. From that time men discussed with growing intelligence the great question of the source and location of authority. By what right does one command another? Who gave monarchs their power? In the last analysis who dominates and why? These and like questions became the fundamental inquiries of politics. The extremes were reached in France, first with the "*L'état, c'est moi*" of Louis XIV, and then with the opposite swing of the pendulum in the French Revolution. England never went so far in either direction, but handled the problem with Anglo-Saxon caution. On this side of the water, it played a great part in winning our independence. It came to the front again in the controversies over State Rights that led up to the War of Secession. The great mass of argument over it seems to this generation dry and dreary, uselessly abstruse, technical, and artificial. Yet it has been at the bottom of the most important political crises of the last three hundred years, and at least knowledge of its existence must be part of the equipment of whoever would understand how present processes of lawmaking came to be.

To hazard a conjectural definition: Sovereignty is the ultimate power that controls or might control in respect to the particular thing in question.

Where lies the ultimate power?

Absolute monarchs have believed that it was in themselves, put there by God. They have believed they ruled "by Divine right." James 1 was a passionate believer in this. Buchanan, his tutor, dedicated to him the "*De Jure Regni apud Scotus*," the gospel, as it were, of democratic government and popular liberty. In 1598 James replied to it with "*The True Law of Free Monarchies*," which is nothing more nor less than a treatise on absolute power. What he meant by a free monarchy was a government in which the monarch was free. The monarch is responsible to God alone, whose representative he is in the kingdom; he possesses power to make laws, and to suspend those which have been made, without having an account to give to any human authority. And when the law is passed, he is subject to it only as long as he chooses.

When James became King of England, he proceeded to live up to his beliefs by a more obnoxious use of royal proclamations than had before been known — the making of law by his personal edict. To this the Parliament vigorously demurred. "There is a general fear conceived and spread amongst your majesty's people, that proclamations will, by degrees, grow up and increase to the strength and nature of laws;... and this their fear is the more increased by occasion of certain books lately published, which ascribe a greater power to proclamations than heretofore had been conceived to belong unto them; as also of the care taken to reduce all the proclamations made since your majesty's reign into one volume, and to print them in such form as acts of Parliament formerly have been, and still are used to be, which seemeth to imply a purpose to give them more reputation and more establishment than heretofore they have had." [1]

In 1610 Lord Coke, as Hallam truly says, performed a great service to his country. Called to attend some members of the Council and advise, he declared the King could not change any part of the common law, "nor create any offense by his proclamation which was not an offense before, without Parliament." Asking time for consultation with his brothers, he secured the appointment of three judges to consider the matter with himself. They reached the same conclusion.

Thus was pronounced the modern doctrine that royal proclamations have in no sense the force of law; they serve to call the attention of the public to the law, but they cannot of themselves impose upon any man any legal obligation or duty not imposed by common law or by Act of Parliament. But this doctrine was not to be finally established until after a century and a half of contest. Under Charles I proclamations became more frequent than ever. It was his fate to be confronted by a new social force, religious in its inspiration, embodied in the people known as Puritans. From the outset they questioned the sovereignty of the monarch. For example: Robert Brown, whose ideas gave rise to the sect known as Brownists (the settlers of Plymouth), who had declared for local independent congregations in the time of Elizabeth, and who is looked upon as the founder of Congregationalism, averred: "Civil Magistrates are persons authorized of God, and received by the consent and choice of the people, whether officers or subjects."

[1] *Somers Tracts*, ii, 162.

Yet the Puritans were not democrats. John Winthrop did not believe he was helping to found a democracy in Massachusetts Bay. He thought it a "mixt Aristocratie," and in the last of his tracts on the negative voice (1643) he said: "A Democratie is, among most Civill nations, accounted the meanest and worst of all formes of Government: and therefore in writers, it is branded with Reproachfull Epithits as *Bellua muturū capitū*, a monster, etc.: and Historyes doe records, that it hath been allwayes of least continuance and fullest of troubles." [1]

Cromwell averred that "in England the whole struggle against regal power had been carried on by a minority." But in this struggle what appeared to Cromwell as the one thing necessary above all others, was that the whole burden of government in the interest of the nation must be entrusted to a minority composed of the godly or honest people of all the nation, in the hope that the broad views and beneficent actions of this minority would in time convert it into a majority. S. R. Gardiner, who speaks with authority, says that to the end of Cromwell's life he strove to maintain the ascendency of the Puritan oligarchy. If Gardiner is right, it must have been from policy or necessity that when Independency had developed into Democracy, Cromwell made the famous declaration that was repeated in the meetings, throughout the camps — "Every man is judge of just and right, as to the good and ill of a Kingdom." Government by one, government by the few — both ideas had gone by the board. When the Presbyterian minister Edwards, in 1646, published several tracts denouncing the errors of sectarians, under the significant title "*Gangraena*," he pointed to 1645 as the year in which the monstrous notion became prevalent, that the people, as sovereign, had the right to demand an account not only of the King and the Lords, but also of the Commons, as representatives receiving not full powers, but only a limited mandate. [2]

Turbulent John Lilburne was a prime instigator. He passed years of his life in prison as a result of conflict with this or that of the authorities. While in Newgate he wrote several pamphlets, in which he maintained the sovereignty of the people over the House of Commons. "Now," he declared in 1645, "for any man to imagine that the shadow or representative is more worthy than the substance or that the House of Commons is more valu-

[1] R. C. Winthrop, *Life and Letters of John Winthrop*, II, 430.
[2] Borgeaud, *Rise of Modern Democracy*, 50.

able and considerable than the Body for whom they serve, is all
one as if they should affirm that an Agent or Ambassador from a
Prince hath the same or more authority than the Prince himself."

In the same year John Cotton, whose influence on the course
of Puritan affairs was almost as great in England as in Massachusetts Bay, published in London "The Way of the Churches
of Christ in New England." In it he said: "It is evident by the
light of nature, that all civil Relations are founded in Covenant.
For to pass by natural Relations between Parents and Children,
and violent Relations between Conquerors and Captives, there
is no other way given whereby a people (*sui Juris*) free from
natural and compulsory engagements, can be united or combined
together into one visible body, to stand by mutual Relation,
fellow-members of the same body, but only by mutual Covenant;
as appeareth between husband and wife in the family, Magistrates and subjects in the Commonwealth, fellow Citizens in the
same cities."

The covenant idea appealed to both sides of the controversies
then dividing Englishmen into armed camps. Immediately after
the execution of Charles I, we find it used as a buttress of argument by Milton on the one hand and Hobbes on the other. "No
man, who knows aught," declared Milton, "can be so stupid as
to deny, that all men naturally were born free, being the image
and resemblance of God himself, and were, by privilege above all
the creatures, born to command, and not to obey: and that they
lived on, till from the root of Adam's transgression, falling among
themselves to do wrong and violence, and foreseeing that such
courses must tend to the destruction of them all, they agreed by
common league to bind each other from mutual injury, and
jointly defend themselves against any that gave disturbance and
opposition to such agreement. Hence came cities, towns, and
commonwealths." [1] Hobbes argued that the primitive state of
man was one of an unrestricted struggle for existence, a state of
war; and that men executed a contract with each other by which
they entered into commonwealths or politics.

Jean Jacques Rousseau developed the contract theory in his
famous "Social Compact," published in 1762, which played a
powerful part in the American and French crises of the generation
that followed. He held that government and the State are the result of a social compact, a common agreement between individuals

[1] *The Prose Works of John Milton*, ii, 176.

who voluntarily yield themselves to be subject to the common will; but he reached quite different conclusions from those of Hobbes by holding that such body politic is composed of equal members possessed of absolute authority; that sovereignty residing in the people can neither be delegated to representatives nor modified by contract with a King; and that the will of the majority, as expressed by universal suffrage, determines the form the government should take, and can at any time change the government if it desires.

Rousseau gave the contract theory a world-wide popularity, but he was not its author. Cotton and the Puritans did not invent it, though they were the first to give it practical application of importance. Its real source is the Bible. The publicists of the Reformation, and before them certain theologians of the Middle Ages, had drawn from sacred history, from the example of a treaty of alliance between Jehovah and his people, the idea of a contract that had taken place at the beginning between the sovereign and his subjects.[1]

The contract theory now finds few supporters. Its flame and heat have gone. Yet sparks smoulder under the ashes. As late as the Massachusetts Constitutional Convention of 1917 it was seriously urged that because of an original compact the accustomed form of representative government ought not to be changed by the adoption of the Initiative and Referendum. The same idea reappeared in some of the contentions advanced in 1919 and 1920 against the validity of the Prohibitory Amendment to the Federal Constitution. This was more like the notion of Hobbes than that of Rousseau. The unhappy Frenchman would have seen still more of misfortune in the prospect that his pet theory might be called upon to prevent change.

DELEGATED AUTHORITY

Along with the covenant idea came another, of equal consequence in the history of political science, of greater consequence to-day, for while few now urge the idea of a social contract, the idea that authority is delegated shapes the destinies of the civilized world. Once concluding that the authority of rulers had been delegated to them by the people, inevitably the leading Puritans began to ask whether that delegation was perpetual or temporary, whether it was with or without conditions or control.

[1] Borgeaud, *Rise of Modern Democracy*, 78.

For instance, when John Winthrop, in 1643, was arguing in Massachusetts Bay the question of the negative voice, he found it necessary to meet the contention that "the greatest power is in the people, therefore it should be in their Deputies." Winthrop, a trained lawyer and clear thinker, replied: "Answ: originally and virtually it is: but when they have chosen them Judges, etc.: their Judiciary power is actually in those to whom they have committed it and those are their magistrates in such order as before is declared." [1]

The figure first standing out in the controversy destined to become epoch-making was that of Thomas Hobbes. In 1651 Hobbes published "Leviathan, or the Matter, Forme and Power of a Common-wealth, ecclesiasticall and civill." He had fled to Paris to escape the dangers threatened by the views he had published in England, and it is commonly alleged that his greatest work, The Leviathan, was written in defense of the absolutism of the Stuarts and against the pretensions of Parliament. This may have been his immediate purpose, but Hobbes's doctrine was rather a vindication of the absolute rights of whatever government happened to be in power. The all-important thing was the clearness and force with which he expounded the absolute character of these rights, as he viewed them. Said he:

"The only way to erect such a Common Power, as may be able to defend them from the invasion of Forraigners, and the injuries of one another, and thereby to secure them in such sort, as that by their owne industrie, and by the fruites of the Earth, they may nourish themselves and live contentedly; is, to conferre all their power and strength upon one Man, or upon one Assembly of men, that may reduce all their Wills, by plurality of voices, unto one Will: which is as much as to say, to appoint one Man, or Assembly of men, to beare their Person; and every one to owne, and acknowledge himselfe to be Author of whatsoever he that so beareth their Person, shall Act, or cause to be Acted, in those things which concerne the Common Peace and Safetie; and therein to submit their Wills, every one to his Will, and their Judgements, to his Judgment. This is more than Consent, or Concord; it is reall Unitie of them all, in one and the same Person, made by Covenant of every man with every man, in such manner as if every man should say to every man, *I Authorise and give up my Right of Governing my selfe, to this Man, or to this Assembly of*

[1] R. C. Winthrop, *Life and Letters of John Winthrop*, II, 437.

men, on this condition, that thou give up thy Right to him, and Authorise all his Actions in like manner. This done, the Multitude so united in one Person, is called a *Common-wealth,* in latine *Civitas.* This is the Generation of that great *Leviathan,* or rather (to speak more reverently) of that *Mortall God,* to which wee owe under the *Immortall God,* our peace and defence. For by this Authoritie, given him by every particular man in the Common-Wealth, he hath the use of so much Power and Strength conferred on him, that by terror thereof, he is inabled to forme the wills of them all, to Peace at home and mutuall ayd against their enemies abroad. And in him consisteth the Essence of the Commonwealth; which (to define it), is *One Person, of whose Acts a great Multitude, by mutuall Convenants one with another, have made themselves every one the Author, to the end he may use the strength and means of them all, as he shall think expedient, for their Peace and Common Defence."* [1]

Yet Hobbes recognized clearly that sovereignty might take different forms. Indeed some have thought his most valuable contribution to political science is to be found in his explanation of this:

"The difference of Common-wealths, consisteth in the difference of the Soveraign, or the Person representative of all and every one of the Multitude. And because the Soveraignty is either in one Man, or in an Assembly of more than one; and into that Assembly either Every man hath right to enter, or not every one, but Certain men distinguished from the rest; it is manifest, there can be but Three kinds of Common-wealth. For the Representative must needs be One man, or More; and if more, then it is the Assembly of All, or but a Part. When the Representative is One man, then is the Common-wealth a MONARCHY; when an Assembly of All that will come together, then it is a DEMOCRACY, or Popular Commonwealth; when an Assembly of a Part onely, then it is called an ARISTOCRACY. Other kind of Common-wealth there can be none; for either One, or More, or All, must have the Soveraign Power (which I have shown to be indivisible) entire." [2]

Inasmuch as the Multitude had beforehand authorized the acts of him to whom they had delegated authority, they could not complain of the way in which this authority might be exercised. It could not be revoked. To change the form of govern-

[1] *The Leviathan,* chap. XVII.   [2] *Ibid.,* chap. XIX.

ment would be a breach of the original covenant, both so far as it related to the sovereign and so far as it related to the multitude who had made it between each other. It was permanent as well as absolute.

Spinoza, Pufendorf, and other writers on the Continent supported Hobbes. In England his ideas were to prevail through the course of two reigns after the Restoration, and then because no longer endurable were to aid powerfully in bringing about the Revolution that put an end to the theory and practice of absolute right in England. Charles II came to the throne with the impression that the divine right of Kings had been vindicated. When he issued his Declaration of Indulgence, he said therein: "We think ourselves obliged to make use of that supreme power in ecclesiastical matters which is not only inherent in us, but has been declared and recognized to be so by several statutes and acts of Parliament." And not long afterward: "We do declare our will and pleasure to be, that the execution of all and all manner of penal laws in matters ecclesiastical, against whatever sort of non-conformists or recusants, be immediately suspended, and they are hereby suspended." As we have seen, it was generally understood to be an ancient prerogative of the Crown to dispense with penal statutes in favor of particular persons, and under certain restrictions — a power akin to that of pardon. But, as Hallam says, a pretension in explicit terms, to suspend a body of statutes, a command to magistrates not to put them in execution, arrogated a sort of absolute power which no benefits of the indulgence itself (had they even been less insidiously offered) could induce a lover of constitutional privileges to endure. So the House voted that the King's prerogative in matters ecclesiastical did not extend to repeal of acts of Parliament. The King replied and received a fresh rebuke, the Commons, in a second address, positively denying the King's right to suspend any law.

Under James II the royal pretension was carried to its limit by a subservient court. A collusive action was brought against Sir Edward Hales, and this gave the Chief Justice a chance to lay down the proposition that the Kings of England were sovereign princes; that the laws of England were the King's laws; that it was consequently an inseparable prerogative of the crown to dispense with penal laws in particular cases, for reasons of which it was the sole judge. As a result, when William of Orange was put on the throne, one of the earliest doings of the Parliament of 1689 was to enact what became famous as the Bill of Rights. The very first complaint in the preamble read:

"Whereas, the late King James II, by the assistance of divers evil counsellors, judges, and ministers employed by him, did endeavor to subvert and extirpate the Protestant religion, and the laws and liberties of this kingdom;

"1. By assuming and exercising a power of dispensing with and suspending of laws, and the execution of laws, without consent of Parliament."

And the first declaration was:

"1. That the pretended power of suspending of laws, or the execution of laws, by regal authority, without consent of Parliament, is illegal."

Nevertheless the question was not settled for good and all until in the time of George III an act of Parliament definitely determined that proclamations creating law were illegal. It was in 1766 that Lord Chatham tried to prohibit by force of proclamation the exportation of wheat, and the Act of Indemnity (7 George III, c. 7), passed in consequence of the attempt, may be considered the final legislative disposal of the question. Ten years later the revolting Americans summoned the newly established doctrine to their help. A proclamation by the Great and General Court of Massachusetts January 23, 1776, declared: "It is a maxim, that in every Government there must exist, somewhere, a supreme, sovereign, absolute, and uncontrollable power; but this power resides, always, in the body of the people; and it never was, or can be delegated to one man or a few; the great Creator having never given to men a right to vest others with authority over them, unlimited, either in duration or degree." [1]

A dozen years afterward, in 1788, a celebrated speech of Pitt to the House of Commons showed that the dispute which agitated England for centuries had become history. "To assert the inherent right of the Prince of Wales to assume the government," he is averred to have said, "is virtually to revive those exploded ideas of the Divine and indefeasible authority of princes which have so justly sunk into contempt and almost oblivion. Kings and princes derive their power from the people; and to the people alone through the organ of their representatives does it appertain

[1] Force's *American Archives*, Fourth Series, vol. LV, 834.

to decide in cases for which the Constitution has made no specific or positive provision." [1]

Here was triumph for the doctrine of John Locke, who almost exactly a century before had come forward to demolish the theory of Hobbes that sovereignty was absolutely and permanently delegated to the monarch. More than any other writer of his age, Locke was destined to affect the development of the modern state. In the second of the "Two Treatises of Government" (1690) he held (chap. 7) that when men unite into one society, each man "authorizes the society, or which is all one, the legislature thereof, to make laws for him as the public good of the society shall require"; that (chap. 13) "there can be but one supreme power, which is the legislative, to which all the rest are and must be subordinate"; and that "the executive power placed anywhere but in a person that has also a share in the legislative is visibly subordinate and accountable to it." Furthermore, "the legislative being only a fiduciary power to act for certain ends, there remains still in the people a supreme power to remove or alter the legislative, when they find the legislative act contrary to the trust reposed in them."

In the latter part of the eighteenth century Locke's idea was so developed and expanded by Rousseau and other thinkers that it reached the point of declaring the supremacy of the people not only over princes and parliaments, but also over every other kind of authority. The National Assembly of France in its Declaration of War, April 20, 1792, officially proclaimed Rousseau's theory: "The French nation has undoubtedly declared that sovereignty belongs only to the people, who, limited in the exercise of its highest will by the rights of succeeding generations, cannot confer any irrevocable power; the nation frankly acknowledges, that no tradition, no legal decree, no declaration, no contract, can subject the society of men to any authority in such a manner that the nation should no longer have the right of revoking such power. Every people has alone the power to give itself its laws, and the inalienable right of changing its laws."

The failure to make any specific recognition of this principle was one of the defects charged against our Federal Constitution. It will be remembered that the ratification of this document was

---

[1] These precise words are not in the collection of Pitt's "Speeches" before me, but are in harmony with the tenor of his addresses on the occasion of the King's illness.

secured in various States only by a promise on the part of its
friends to consent to amendments virtually amounting to a Bill
of Rights. The tenth of these reads: "The powers not delegated
to the United States by the Constitution, nor prohibited by it
to the States, are reserved to the States respectively, or to the
people." Taken together with the provision for amendment of
the Constitution in the original instrument, this can leave no
doubt as to the limited nature of the delegated powers.

Note its last clause. Clearly a discrimination between "the
States" and "the people" is intended, but of themselves the
words used create perplexity. How do "the States" differ from
"the people"? Story, referring to this provision in his work on
the Constitution, says (Sec. 638): "A State, and the Legislature
of a State, are quite different political beings." He makes it
plain that in his belief the Legislature is not the equivalent of the
people, for he says that if a State in its political capacity has a
certain power, the possession thereof by the Legislature would not
follow. That must depend upon the powers confided to the
State Legislature by its own Constitution.

It is not easy to reconcile Story with the Tenth Amendment
unless we conclude that what he meant by the State was not
what the amendment meant, Story thinking of it as the people,
and the amendment having in mind the organ of the people.
However, the important thing is the fact of discrimination.
There can be no question that in the American view, as the
Massachusetts Supreme Court put it in Holden *v.* James (11
Mass. 396–1814), "the sovereign and absolute power resides in
the people; and the Legislature can only exercise what is delegated to them according to the Constitution." Herein, as the
Court pointed out, the principles of our government are widely
different from the theory of the English Constitution, whereby
"that absolute despotic power, which must in all governments
reside somewhere," is entrusted to the Parliament.

LIMITATION OF POWER

The general acceptance to-day of the principle that a people
has a right to control or change its government, makes further
discussion of absolutism largely academic, but political science
calls for its continuance in the search for truth. So it is to be
noted that when Austin came to deliver his Lectures on Jurisprudence he said: "It follows from the essential difference of a

positive law, and from the nature of sovereignty and independent political society, that the power of a monarch properly so called, or the power of a sovereign number in its collegiate capacity, is incapable of *legal* limitation. For a monarch or sovereign bound by a legal duty would be subject to a higher or superior sovereign." W. W. Willoughby has recently said much the same: "If, then, the only rules that possess legal validity are such as have received the sanction of the State, it follows as a logical deduction, that since no one can be bound by one's own will, the sovereign political power must necessarily be incapable of legal limitation." [1]

This can be reconciled with the declaration of Parliament and the assertion of American Constitutions by remembering that the King of England is no longer a monarch and that in this country there is no sovereign number acting in a collegiate capacity, that is, no legislative assembly beyond the reach of the people. The importance of each statement lies in its conclusion that the sovereign political power is incapable of *legal* limitation. Of course this turns on the meaning of the word "legal," and brings up again the question of whether the common law, customary law, is legal. If it is not a legal limitation, and if Hobbes and Willoughby are right, then the sovereign power could abolish customary law, the common law.

It has been alleged that this would transcend human experience, that as a practical matter no sovereign could by fiat overthrow a habit of a people, one of its customs, institutions, mores. This brings us again to the question, vital to present-day legislators, of whether even though they speak the voice of the majority of the people, they can in fact rightfully compel the minority to conform to their views in such matters, for instance, as the use of alcoholic liquors or habit-forming drugs, or such as gambling, schooling, vaccination, unorthodox methods of healing; and many others that perplex the legislatures of our times. Of course corollary is the question of whether the minority may rightfully refuse to obey.

Hobbes, as we have seen, held that as all power is turned over by the people of a State to their sovereign, who therefore becomes supreme, in consequence his will is to be implicitly obeyed, under all circumstances. Blackstone thought law the rule prescribed "by the supreme power in a State." Austin averred that

[1] *The Nature of the State*, 181.

"every positive law simply and strictly so called, is set by a sovereign person or sovereign body of persons." Holland wanted the authority "paramount in a political society."

Notice that these requirements do not agree in localizing sovereignty, nor do they all demand the apparent authority to be rightfully supreme. If, however, its nominal organ is commonly accepted, then inasmuch as sovereignty implies the duty of submission, the mere statement of law by the sovereign generally recognized as such should preclude dispute of its validity and compelling power. The practical importance of the point is illustrated by the story of the Missouri Compromise, the Dred Scott decision, the Legal Tender decision, and many another episode in our political and judicial history, indeed by the Civil War itself, and now by the contention of sundry citizens that the laws to enforce the Eighteenth Amendment, often spoken of as the Prohibition Amendment, need not be obeyed.

In support of such a contention it is argued that sovereignty does not in fact lie in the artificial thing we call our government, but is to be found in the minds of the people at large, in the shape of what we call public opinion. Some go to the extreme of holding that each human being embodies an independent element of sovereignty and may do that which is right in his own eyes.

Perhaps we will be aided toward a solution of the problem by putting together two views of sovereignty. First, that of Guizot: "When we speak now of a public power, of what we call the rights of sovereignty — that is, the right of making laws, of imposing taxes, of inflicting punishment, we know, we bear in mind, that these rights belong to nobody; that no one has, on his own account, the right to punish others, or to impose any burden or law upon them. These are rights which belong only to the great body of society, which are exercised only in its name; they are emanations from the people, and held in trust for their benefit." [1]

Next, that of D. G. Ritchie: "The ultimate political sovereign is not the determinate number of persons now existing in the nation, but the opinions and feelings of these persons, and of those opinions and feelings the tradition of the past, the needs of the present, the hopes of the future, all form a part." [2]

Sovereignty, then, is nothing definite, precise, palpable. It is

[1] *Civilization in Modern Europe*, Lecture IV.

[2] "On the Conception of Sovereignty," *Annals of the American Academy of Political and Social Science*, June, 1891.

an emanation. It cannot be localized. To try to isolate it is like trying to isolate the incidence of taxation, which one may pursue in a circle until he satisfies himself that everybody shifts the burden to somebody else, and nobody pays anything.

It would follow that as there is no infallible test for the location of sovereignty, so there is no way of knowing in advance whether one or another of its organs will function effectively on any particular occasion. This makes all legislation necessarily more or less empirical, experimental. This prevents lawmaking from being one of the exact sciences.

How about the ethical phase of it? Can the nominal sovereign do wrong? Is the individual believing the sovereign has done wrong, within his right in refusing to obey?

If there is such a thing as Natural Right, then the minority may have rights the majority is bound to respect, then one with God may be a majority. This cannot be admitted unless we deny that the purpose of the State is to achieve its own highest welfare. To admit it we should be compelled to say that there are particulars in which the wishes, feelings, or beliefs of the individual are of more consequence than the welfare of the community to which he belongs. That would be to deny sovereignty altogether.

The opposite view has to-day the more acceptance. Most men would agree with W. W. Willoughby when he says the State is supreme, not only as giving the ultimate validity to all law, but as itself determining the validity of its own powers, and itself deciding what interests shall be subject to its regulation.[1]

To be sure, this is utilitarianism, pragmatism, but are we not all now utilitarians, pragmatists, at any rate in practice? And after all is it impossible to reconcile the useful with the ethical? Guizot well put the two together: "The essence of government then by no means resides in compulsion, in the exercise of brute force; it consists more especially of a system of means and powers, conceived for the purpose of discovering upon all occasions what is best to be done, for the purpose of discovering the truth which by right ought to govern society, for the purpose of persuading all men to acknowledge this truth, to adopt and respect it willingly and freely." [2]

There is here no discord unless we hold that the best thing and

---

[1] *The Nature of the State*, 193.
[2] *Civilization in Modern Europe*, Lecture v.

the right thing can be different, and that is neither a utilitarian nor an ethical premise.

WHICH FORM IS BEST?

Modern political thought tends toward holding that sovereignty is a group rather than a unit; that government is but one of many forms in which dominating power shows itself. The argument is that in various aspects of our lives we are controlled by bodies of thought, organized or unorganized, religious, social, industrial, commercial, financial, or what not, each sovereign within its own sphere. The theory is interesting, but here we are concerned only with that sovereignty, whether it is the only sovereignty or not, which takes some form of what we usually mean by "government."

Of the forms of government it is commonly accepted that there are three which may be classed as primary — monarchy, oligarchy, and democracy. It is not well to assume that the experience of mankind has shown absolute perfection and therefore invariable superiority to lie in any one of these, or that it lies in any of the secondary forms therefrom developed. Somewhere and at some time each has secured peace, protection, and prosperity to a people. A comparative study of whether the making of law has been most wisely entrusted to one man, to a few men, or to many men, would be full of profit, but it would require illumination from the whole history of the world, and even an attempt at adequate treatment of the subject here is out of the question. All that will be ventured are a few phases of the problem chiefly as glimpsed through the eyes of men who at various epochs have thought deep and long on these things.

As to the attributes necessary for an acceptable monarch, ponder the words of Rousseau: "In order to discover the rules of association that are most suitable to nations, a superior intelligence would be necessary who could see all the passions of men without experiencing any of them; who would have no affinity with our nature and yet know it thoroughly; whose happiness would not depend on us, and who would nevertheless be quite willing to interest himself in ours; and, lastly, one who, storing up for himself with the progress of time a far-off glory in the future, could labor in one age and enjoy in another. Gods would be necessary to give laws to men." [1]

[1] *Social Compact*, book 2, chap. VII.

With the conclusions of the Genevan student, couple the judgment of a prince trained alike in the arts of war and administration, in philosophy and letters, Frederick II of Prussia, best known as Frederick the Great, who declared, according to Bancroft: "Kingdoms are subjected to the caprice of a single man, whose successors will have no common character. A good-for-nothing prince succeeds an ambitious one; then follows a devotee; then a warrior; then a scholar; then it may be, a voluptuary; and the genius of the nation, diverted by the variety of objects, assumes no fixed character. But republics fulfill more promptly the design of their institution, and hold out better; for good Kings die, but wise laws are immortal. There is unity in the end which republics propose, and in the means which they employ; and they therefore almost never miss their aim."

Lest this confidence in republics be implicitly accepted, recall what took place in Athens. Of this no more graphic account has ever been written than that by Lord Acton. For its eloquence as well as its scientific value, let it be quoted from at length. "Two men's lives," he says, "span the interval from the first admission of popular influence, under Solon, to the downfall of the State. Their history furnishes the classic example of the peril of Democracy under conditions singularly favorable. For the Athenians were not only brave and patriotic and capable of generous sacrifice, but they were the most religious of the Greeks. They venerated the Constitution which had given them prosperity, and equality, and freedom, and never questioned the fundamental laws which regulated the enormous power of the Assembly. They tolerated considerable variety of opinion and great license of speech; and their humanity toward their slaves roused the indignation even of the most intelligent partisan of aristocracy. Thus they became the only people of antiquity that grew great by democratic institutions. But the possession of unlimited power, which corrodes the conscience, hardens the heart, and confounds the understanding of monarchs, exercised its demoralizing influence on the illustrious democracy of Athens. It is bad to be oppressed by a minority, but it is worse to be oppressed by a majority. For there is a reserve of latent power in the masses which, if it is called into play, the minority can seldom resist. But from the absolute will of an entire people there is no appeal, no redemption, no refuge but treason. The humblest and most numerous class of the Athenians united the legislative, the judicial, and, in part, the executive power.

"The philosophy that was then in the ascendant taught them that there is no law superior to that of the State — the lawgiver is above the law.

"It followed that the sovereign people had a right to do whatever was within its power, and was bound by no rule of right or wrong but its own judgment of expediency. On a memorable occasion the assembled Athenians declared it monstrous that they should be prevented from doing whatever they chose. No force that existed could restrain them; and they resolved that no duty should restrain them, and that they would be bound by no laws that were not of their own making. In this way the emancipated people of Athens became a tyrant; and their Government, the pioneer of European freedom, stands condemned with a terrible unanimity by all the wisest of the ancients. They ruined their city by attempting to conduct war by debate in the market place. Like the French Republic, they put their unsuccessful commanders to death. They treated their dependencies with such injustice that they lost their maritime Empire. They plundered the rich until the rich conspired with the public enemy, and they crowned their guilt by the martyrdom of Socrates.

"When the absolute sway of numbers had endured for near a quarter of a century, nothing but bare existence was left for the State to lose; and the Athenians, wearied and despondent, confessed the true cause of the ruin. They understood that for liberty, justice, and equal laws, it is as necessary that Democracy should restrain itself as it had been that it should restrain the Oligarchy. They resolved to take their stand once more upon the ancient ways, and to restore the order of things which had subsisted when the monopoly of power had been taken from the rich and had not been acquired by the poor....

"The hostile parties were reconciled, and proclaimed an amnesty, the first in history. They resolved to govern by concurrence. The laws, which had the sanction of tradition, were reduced to a code; and no act of the sovereign assembly was valid with which they might be found to disagree. Between the sacred lines of the Constitution which were to remain inviolate, and the decrees which met from time to time the needs and notions of the day, a broad distinction was drawn; and the fabric of a law which had been the work of generations was made independent of momentary variations in the popular will.

"The repentance of the Athenians came too late to save the Republic. But the lesson of their experience endures for all times, for it teaches that government by the whole people, being the government of the most numerous and most powerful class, is an evil of the same nature as unmixed monarchy, and requires, for nearly the same reasons, institutions that shall protect it against itself, and shall uphold the permanent reign of law against arbitrary revolutions of opinion." [1]

Aristotle, most famous of Athenian students of government, saw this clearly, declaring: "He who bids the law rule, may be deemed to bid God and Reason alone rule, but he who bids man rule, adds an element of the beast; for desire is a wild beast, and passion perverts the minds of rulers, even when they are the best of men. The law is reason unaffected by desire."

We think we have met the danger by minimizing the human factor. As Charles Sumner put it, the object of free institutions is to withdraw all concerns of state, so far as practicable, from human discretion, and place them under the shield of determined principles, to the end, according to the words of the Massachusetts Constitution, that there may be a government of laws, and not of men. [2] More recently David Jayne Hill has said to kindred purpose: "What constitutional government intended to do, was to end forever the idea that there is any rightful depository of unlimited power; in brief, to destroy the error that *any one's will is law*, and to establish the principle that law is not a product of will, but a system of rules for the regulation of will derived from the authority of reason." [3]

Yet since the seat of reason is the mind, it can hardly be denied that the ultimate source of law is human, whether it be will alone or will controlled by reason, or reason alone. Therefore we have still to choose between one source, or a few sources, or many sources, all human. Those of us who prefer many sources nevertheless must admit that in spite of the confidence in democracy doubtless felt by most dwellers in democratic countries to-day, it would be rash to assume that the democratic principle is established beyond dispute. The Supreme Court of the United States said in 1874, by Justice Miller, in the great case of Loan Association *v.* Topeka (20 Wall. 655): "It may well be doubted if a

---

[1] Lord Acton, *The History of Freedom*, 11–13.

[2] *Debates in Mass. Convention of 1853*, ii, 593.

[3] "Taking Soundings," *North American Review*, May, 1914.

man is to hold all that he is accustomed to call his own, all in which he has placed his happiness, and the security of which is essential to that happiness, under the unlimited dominion of others, whether it is not wiser that this power should be exercised by one man than by many."

Since that was pronounced, we have gone far toward establishing the condition therein set forth, toward holding that an individual has no rights or possessions the community may not compel him to sacrifice for the common welfare. With the condition established, the doubt of the court gathers force. It is to be noted that writers on the science of government have from the earliest times assumed that if power were given to the many, they would use it to take property from the few. For example, Aristotle, in "The Politics" — "If justice is the will of the majority, they will unjustly confiscate the property of the wealthy minority." That apprehension is as prevalent now as ever it was, and not without ground, if we are to attach any significance to the brutal course of affairs in Russia after the World War or to the more refined processes resulting in certain classes of American statutes.

Because of these things there are those who look with equanimity, and even with approbation, on the reaction toward one-man government, whether as exemplified by the selection of an English monarch in the person of a Prime Minister, or the election of an American monarch, in the person of a dominating President. Pointing to the errors of democracy, they ask us to imagine how much better off we might have been had men not tried to govern themselves. Yet few pursuits are more idle than to conjecture what might have happened if on this or that occasion a different course had been pursued. Men will always say that the Civil War might have been avoided if some other way of meeting the slavery problem had been devised. President McKinley believed that war with Spain might have been escaped. The palpable fact is that as a consequence of the war with Spain, millions of human beings came to have a happier existence and the prosperity of mankind was advanced. The people of this country, through the pressure brought to bear upon their representatives, compelled that war. Had Congress not been in session at the time of the destruction of the Maine, the war might not have been fought. Congress was not in session when the Lusitania was torpedoed. When the horrors of that massacre revolted humanity, the country was told by the Washington correspondents the reason President Wilson did not call together his cabinet was that he did not wish his vision clouded by conflicting views. Who shall say that Lincoln and McKinley would have accomplished more beneficent results if they had been for the moment the sole lawmakers of the land, sagacious despots; that Wilson chose the best course because he followed one man's judgment, his own?

As a matter of fact, there is no such thing as an absolute despot, following his own fancy, enacting his own whim. Even when the power of a monarch is nominally, legally unlimited, its continuance depends on the skill with which the monarch gives voice to the will of others, be they few or many. If he disregards that will, then comes disaster. "The Soldan of Egypt, or the Emperor of Rome," Hume well observed, "might drive his harmless subjects, like brute beasts, against their sentiments and inclination; but he must, at least, have led his mamalukes, or prætorian bands, like men, by their opinions." [1]

Lord Bryce modified the thought by excluding even the Many from a real share in government. "In reality," said he in his presidential address to the American Political Science Association, "there is only one form of government. That form is the Rule of the Few. The monarch is always obliged to rule by the counsel and through the agency of others, and only a small part of what is done in his name emanates from his mind and will. The multitude has neither the knowledge nor the time nor the unflagging interest that are needed to enable it to rule. Its opinions are formed, its passions are roused, its acts are guided by a few persons — few compared with the total of the voters — and nothing would surprise it more than to learn by how few." [2]

Granted that this be the case, yet it is fair to say of modern government that it has somewhat expanded the share in political activity, has in some measure aroused a general will and organized its expression, has to a degree regulated the exercise of sovereignty. This has been accomplished by the development of what are known as representative institutions. They lie for the most part between oligarchy and democracy, bridging the two. Their study is the chief purpose of the volumes of which this is one.

[1] *Essays*, Green and Grose ed., i, 110.
[2] *American Political Science Review*, February, 1909.

CHAPTER III

LAWMAKING BY ASSEMBLIES

IN matter of public affairs the word "representation" may reach any political action by one man or some men in behalf of others, whether with or without declared authority. Common usage does not carry the phrase "representative government" that far, but restricts it to a system under which at least some part of those represented have in an avowed choice of a representative for the making of laws a share direct enough to disclose an organized source of authority.

Failure to discriminate in this regard has led to confusion in the search for the origins of representative government. Some writers have emphasized the factor of conscious choice; others have dwelt on the purpose or result of choice; others have made the method of choice the touchstone. Of course all the elements should be taken into account. If this be done, it will be found that representative government, as we now think of it, is of recent birth.

For this reason it is often said that representative government is a purely modern device, without any prototype among the Greeks or Romans or any of the older civilizations of which we have knowledge. The statement misleads. Though born in modern times, representative government had ancestors, and inherited from them some of its most striking features. For instance, action by a Body is nothing new. Tribes must have begun assembling as soon as there were tribes. When they clustered into small city communities as in Greece, history first tells us something of how their assemblages gradually organized political management. Originally, in the Grecian States, the assembly of free citizens was merely convened and consulted by the kings at their pleasure, and did not exercise any legal power; but in process of time its decisions acquired the force of law. Passing from kingship through oligarchy, Athens arrived at democracy with Kleisthenes, who, as Herodotus tells it, "being vanquished in the party contest with his rival, took the people into partnership."

The custom is to regard Athens as having achieved pure democracy, but this is not to be confounded with representative government, to which it was only a stepping stone. Some eminent scholars have thought that Greece never took the next step. Freeman, for instance, in writing of the Amphictyonic Council, the Achaian League, and the Lycian League, in which the cities had a certain proportion of votes in accordance with their size, declares that "the ancient world trampled on the very verge of representative government without actually crossing the boundary." Broadly speaking, that is no doubt true, at least to the extent that when the people of one State were admitted to the right of citizenship in another, they could exercise that right only by coming in a body to vote and deliberate with the people of that other State; or when two or more States confederated, they acted by ambassadors. Yet it is not wholly accurate to say that in no ancient State was any body of men ever constituted by the people to represent them in their internal affairs. The dikasteries, or jury courts, provided for Athens by Pericles and Ephialtes, had in legislation a share that was at least quasi-representative. Under this institution the judicial power of the magistrates and the Senate of the Areopagus was transferred to numerous dikasts, or panels of jurors, six thousand of whom were annually drawn by lot and sworn. Part of them, sometimes five hundred, sometimes one thousand, always a considerable number, were appointed and paid to pass upon laws, and were called *nomothetae*. The ecclesia, or public assembly, even with the sanction of the Senate of Five Hundred, became incompetent either to pass a new law or to repeal a law already in existence; it could enact only a decree applicable to a particular case. If it condemned any law, or if any citizen had a new law to propose, the nomothetae might be determined according to the number of measures to be submitted. Public advocates were named to undertake the formal defense of all the laws attacked, and the citizen who proposed to repeal them had to make out his case against this defense, to the satisfaction of the assembled nomothetae. The effect was to place the making or repealing of laws under the same solemnities and guarantees as the trying of causes or accusations in judicature.

Rome, also, though without representative institutions as we know them, certainly was not unfamiliar with delegated power. The Institutes affirm that "a law is an enactment established by the Roman people upon the rogation [proposal] of a senatorial magistrate or a consul." This would indicate that although the laws were enacted by the *comitia curiata* and the *comitia centu-riata*, popular assemblies, initiative by a higher authority was needed. This higher authority exercised delegated power, was an elected authority, for the consuls were elected and the road to the Senate was through the magistracies to which the people elected. Furthermore, measures to be submitted for the ratifi-cation of the comitia were first discussed in the Senate. With the transition into an empire, Augustus required that every measure should receive the assent of the Senate before it could be made law by the centuries. Not often after Tiberius were the people actually summoned to ratify a law at all.

In this development can there not be found a nearer approach to the representation idea than in the episode occasionally cited as the only instance of even quasi-representation in ancient times? That was the plan Augustus formed of giving to the Senates (decuriones) of the twenty-eight colonies he founded in Italy, the right of voting for the magistrates at Rome, their votes being sent under seal. The same device was adopted in the Massachusetts Bay Colony sixteen centuries later, but though interesting as a step in the development of our republic, nobody would think of it as a determining feature of representative in-stitutions.

Hearn has advanced a theory in explanation of the feeling of the ancients that political rights must be exercised in person, and in the General Assembly of the Citizens. He says that all the rights any Athenian or Roman enjoyed were his, not from any personal claim but because he was a citizen of Athens or Rome. It was therefore at once the highest privilege and the most urgent duty of each citizen to serve the State in his own person, whether at home or in the field. He was bound to accept any office that the State might place in his hands. He was bound to assist his fellow-citizens in enacting the laws by which the city should be governed, and in selecting the officers by whom her peace should be preserved and her honor defended. No delegation was admis-sible; and in no other place and under no other conditions than in the ecclesia or the comitia duly convened in the customary meeting-place of the city could these duties be performed.[1]

This accounts for the situation in Athens, and in Rome during the greater part of the time that it was a republic. They were city States, as were all the States of antiquity. Nations as we

[1] W. E. Hearn, *The Government of England*, 438.

know them had not come into being. Assemblies in the nature
of town-meetings could meet the needs of the time. The mystery
is that so intelligent a people as the Romans did not hit upon the
simple expedient of representation when after the Social War the
extension of the franchise to the Italians had brought the electorate of Rome up to nearly a million voters. The lack of some
orderly way for determining the popular will was one of the
potent causes for the downfall of the republic. While the inhabitants of so much of the Campagna as made up the territory
of early Rome could meet in the market-place and deliberate
without confusion, intelligent decisions were possible, and the
changes wrought by the growth of population were for a time
met by the practice of voting in centuries or tribes, but the
system was wholly inadequate when thousands of residents of
distant cities were made voters. Few of them could take the
long journey to the capital several times a year, unless paid by
the wealthy demagogues brought to the surface of public life by
the spoils from the conquered nations of the East. This contributed in no small degree to the corruption and debasement of
politics described so graphically by Ferrero in the first volume
of his "Greatness and Decline of Rome." Of all the privileges
that Roman citizenship brought, the right to vote at elections
was that by which most men set least store. The element of uncertainty given to the voting by the indifference of the newly en-
franchised was intensified by the nature of the electorate in Rome
itself, where the proletariat showed characteristics and developed
evils not unfamiliar in present-day cities of the same size. Few
of the mob would scruple to sell their votes. Skillful wire-pullers
organized the dregs into clubs or "colleges," and they were mar-
shaled to the polls at the will of the highest bidder, under contracts with complicated precautions to ensure the faithful execution of promises. Helpless and worthless, the assemblies of
the people became the prey of men strong and unscrupulous
enough to seize the reins of power. So Republic became Empire.

We may, then, give to neither Greece nor Rome as such any
credit for the discovery of representative government, but something can be said for the contribution of certain Roman citizens
or subjects. In the second century of Christianity its adherents
began to confer in synods, which were assemblies of the bishops
of the independent churches of a province, held to discuss doctrine and discipline. Out of them grew the great councils, which

might fairly be called religious parliaments. That of Nicæa ordered the provincial synods to be held twice a year (changed in 692 to annually). Though election of constituents does not yet appear, these were in a way representative bodies and must have spread surely even though slowly the idea of representation. Very likely this may have given to the prefect Pretonius early in the fifth century the notion of assembling once a year delegates from the seven southern provinces of Gaul for the transaction of public business. The troubles of the times interrupting the practice, we find the emperor Honorius in 418 ordering the prefect of Gaul to resume these assemblies at Arles, the metropolis. "Responsible persons or special deputies," said the mandate, "should be sent, not only by each province but also by each city, to your Magnificence, not only to render up accounts, but also to treat of such matters as concern the interests of landed proprietors." [1] The summons was to be sent to "all persons honored with public functions, or proprietors of domains, and all judges of provinces." There was to be a fine for non-attendance. The more distant provinces could send deputies for the judges, but if these deputies were to be appointed rather than elected, as probably was the case, what might be called positive representation was not yet accomplished, even if in fact these assemblies ever amounted to anything.

Meanwhile, farther northward and quite independently, the barbaric tribes known generically as Teutons, those whom we who speak English call our ancestors, were laying the foundations for kindred development of the arts of government. Because only after peoples of Teutonic origin had become masters of nearly all Europe, did representation begin to take its modern form, the historians have generally called it a Teutonic device. This of itself is not wholly without truth, but when the enthusiasts go so far as to ascribe that device to some peculiar aptitude of Teutonic peoples for politics, some exceptional genius for government, the claim may be fairly disputed.

Representative government was not discovered, and it was not an invention. It grew. And the reasons for its growth were the necessities of the case, working under the novel conditions of an intelligent and virile barbarism brought into touch with the remnants of Roman civilization. Our Teutonic ancestors were a group of nomadic tribes. When these tribes developed into peo-

[1] Guizot, *History of Civilization*, Lecture II.

ples — Huns, Vandals, Visigoths, Angles, Saxons, and all the
rest — their growth in numbers and their dispersion over a large
territory made conference by delegates natural and necessary.
Conference was nothing new; it began before History. And conference by delegates must have come when tribes first found
they had common interests.

Tacitus, in his "Treatise on the Situation, Manners, and
Inhabitants of Germany," written in A.D. 98, tells us something
of the political methods of the tribes: "On affairs of smaller
moment, the chiefs consult; on those of greater importance, the
whole community; yet with this circumstance, that what is referred to the decision of the people is first maturely discussed by
the chiefs.... When they all think fit, they sit down armed. Silence is proclaimed by the priests, who have on this occasion a
coercive power. Then the King, or chief, and such others as are
conspicuous for age, birth, or military renown, or eloquence, are
heard; and gain attention rather from their ability to persuade,
than their authority to command. If a proposal displease, the
assembly reject it by an inarticulate murmur; if it prove agreeable, they clash their javelins; for the most honorable expression
of assent among them is the sound of arms."

In the course of the next half-dozen centuries, these tribes, by
some process of which we have little or no knowledge, formed
themselves into confederacies or kingdoms. They swept across
the Alps, the Rhine, and the seas, pushed the Celts almost into
the Atlantic Ocean, crushed the once mighty Roman empire,
absorbed most of the Romans, destroyed some and adopted other
of their institutions. The general assembly of all the people became impossible, made so by geography, bad roads, numbers,
and expense. Gneist says the representation of the collective
people by the *boni homines*, who, under various national appel-
lations, had formed not the whole, but yet the leading element
of the popular assembly, now was limited to a narrower circle of
meliores seu optimates terrae, who included the most eminent
members of the army, the law courts, and the church. Just how
it came about, he makes no attempt to describe.[1]

Hucbald, the biographer of S. Lebuin, writing in the middle of
the tenth century about the Saxons of the eighth, particularized
thus:

"The race was, as it still is, divided into three orders; there are

[1] Rudolf Gneist, *History of the English Constitution*, I, 98.

those who are called in their tongue Edlingi; there are Frilingi; and there are what are called Lassi; words that are in Latin *nobiles, ingenui,* and *serviles.* Over each of their local divisions or *pagi,* at their own pleasure and on a plan which in their eyes is a prudent one, a single *princeps* or chieftain presides. Once every year, at a fixed season, out of each of these local divisions, and out of each of the three orders severally, twelve men were elected, who having assembled together in Mid-Saxony, near the Weser, at a place called Marklo, held a common council, deliberating, enacting, and publishing measures of common interest according to the tenor of a law adopted by themselves. And, moreover, whether there were an alarm of war or a prospect of steady peace, they consulted together as to what must be done in order to meet the case."

Stubbs thinks it may reasonably be doubted whether such a complete and symmetrical system can have existed, and points out that we have no distinct information about it from any other source.[1] Waitz allows that the passage is suspicious and Schaumann rejects it. Yet it could hardly have been altogether a figment of imagination. The fair inference rather is that the representative idea had by that time come to exist in some degree among the Saxons in their German home.

At a later period, in the little territory of Dithmarschen, in the immediate neighborhood of Saxony proper, we find the State governed by its own landrath, made up of forty-eight consules, twelve elected by each of the four marks, so that Hucbald may not have been dreaming.

Hincmar, Archbishop of Rheims in the time of Charles the Bald, has preserved, on the authority of a writer contemporary with Charlemagne, a sketch of the Frankish government under that great prince. Two assemblies (*placita*) were annually held. In the first, all regulations of importance to the public weal for the ensuing year were enacted; and to this, he says, the whole body of clergy and laity repaired; the greater, to deliberate upon what was fitting to be done; and the less, to confirm by their voluntary assent, or sometimes even to discuss, the resolutions of their superiors. In the second annual assembly the chief men and officers of state were alone admitted, to consult upon the most urgent affairs of government. Hallam thinks that in one of the assemblies of Louis the Debonair, who ruled from 814 to 840,

[1] *Constitutional History,* I, 44.

we can even trace the first germ of representative legislation.
Every Count is directed to bring with him to the general assembly twelve Scabini, if there should be so many in his country;
or, if not, he is to fill up the number out of the most respectable
persons resident. These Scabini were judicial assessors.[1]

We observe, then, that before the tenth century of the Christian era men had become familiar with assemblies gathered from
distant places for the transaction of public business. The spread
of the Christian religion and the structural growth of the church
had made the idea of representation familiar. Ecclesiastical
councils had revealed the possibilities of coördinating the thought
and action of widely separated groups. Men saw how the abbot
stood in the place of his monks. At the same time the feudal
system was beginning to teach the same lesson. Theoretically,
indeed, the feudal system was in its origin as pure an instance of
definitely delegated authority as history affords. It was a social
contract, by which the vassal agreed to serve his lord, delegating
to him authority over his person and property. So the ground
was preparing for representative government.

Genuine Representation Appears

It was on the outskirts of Teutonic influence that governmental development first reached what we may call a genuine
representative system. Possibly the priority should be accredited
to Iceland with its Althing, the thousandth anniversary of which
is about to be celebrated, and the Isle of Man with its Tynwald,
established about the tenth century and made up of elected delegates who prepared laws that were promulgated as the law of
the land. These, however, were rude and simple bodies compared
with that which came into existence in northeastern Spain, just
across the Pyrenees from France, in the region known as Aragon,
received in partition in 1035 by Ramiro I, son of Sancho III
of Navarre, who raised it from a county to a kingdom. The
fueros (constitutional charter) of the Aragonese embodied principles of self-government and popular rights not surpassed by
the liberal constitutions of our own time. Robertson tells us [2]
that, though the form of government was monarchical, the genius
and maxims of it were purely republican. The Kings, who were
long elective, retained only the shadow of power; the real exer-

[1] Hallam, *Middle Ages*, i, 212–13.
[2] *Charles the Fifth*, i, 159.

cise of it was in the Cortes, or Parliament of the kingdom. This supreme assembly was composed of four different arms or members: the nobility of the first rank; the equestrian order, or nobility of the second class; the representatives of the cities and towns, whose right to a place in the Cortes, if we may give credit to the historians of Aragon, was coeval with the Constitution; the ecclesiastical order, composed of the dignitaries of the church, together with the representatives of the inferior clergy. No law could pass in this assembly without the assent of every single member who had a right to vote. Without the permission of the Cortes no tax could be imposed, no war could be declared, no peace could be concluded, no money could be coined, nor could any alteration be made in the current specie. The power of reviewing the proceedings of all inferior courts, the privilege of inspecting every department of administration, and the right of redressing all grievances belonged to the Cortes. This sovereign court was held every year during several centuries; but, in consequence of a regulation introduced about the beginning of the fourteenth century, it was convoked from that period only once in two years. After it was assembled, the King had no right to prorogue or dissolve it without its own consent; and the session continued forty days.

In Castile the executive part of the government was committed to the King, but with a prerogative extremely limited. The legislative authority resided in the Cortes, which was composed of the nobility, the dignified ecclesiastics, and the representatives of the cities. The assembly of the Cortes in Castile was very ancient. The members of the three different orders who had a right of suffrage met in one place and deliberated as one collective body, the decisions of which were regulated by the sentiments of the majority. The right of imposing taxes, of enacting laws, and of redressing grievances belonged to the assembly; and, in order to secure the assent of the King to such statutes and regulations as were deemed salutary or beneficial to the kingdom, it was usual in the Cortes to take no step toward granting money until all business relative to the public welfare was concluded. The representatives of cities seem to have obtained a seat very early in the Cortes of Castile, and soon acquired influence and credit very uncommon at a period when the splendor and preëminence of the nobility had eclipsed or depressed all other orders of men. The number of members from cities bore such a proportion to that of the whole collective body as to render them extremely respectable in the Cortes.

Representative government of such a sort lasted in Spain about five hundred years, vanishing with the Emperor Charles V (1500–1558), who, though he allowed the name of the Cortes to remain, and the formality of holding it to be continued, reduced its authority and jurisdiction almost to nothing, and modeled it in such a manner that it became rather a junto of the servants of the crown than an assembly of the representatives of the people.

In France no such development is found as in Spain. "From the ninth to the sixteenth century," says Sir James Stephen, "the King was the real as well as the nominal lawgiver." [1] To be sure, there was an assembly, the States General, the name of which first appears in the fourteenth century, but it was an ineffectual body, the shadow of a Parliament. The three "Estates" — clergy, nobles, and commons — met at irregular intervals, whenever the King "condescended" to call them together. After a formal meeting to hear a speech from the King, the three groups sat, debated, and voted in separate chambers, and were quite independent of each other. Their functions were limited to expressions of opinion on points laid before them by the King, or on *gravamina* brought up by them from the country. They formulated their *cahiers* (or "quires") of grievances, which they laid solemnly before the King for his consideration, leaving all amendment entirely in his hands, for they had no power of redress. In a few instances they sanctioned taxation, and even voted subsidies; but this most important function was exercised rarely and uncertainly. Once only (in 1560) do they seem to have attempted actual legislation. With that exception they never got beyond advising. Voltaire tells us that Louis XIV "went from Vincennes in a hunting dress, attended by his whole court, and entering the parliament chamber in jack boots, whip in hand, made use of these very words: 'The mischiefs your assemblies produce are well known. I command you to break up those you have begun upon my edicts. Mr. President, I forbid you to permit these assemblies, and any of you to demand them.'" [2]

Guizot sums up their history: "No great measure which has truly had any influence upon society in France, no important

---

[1] *Lectures on the History of France*, ii, 345.

[2] *Age of Louis XIV*, ii, 8 (ed. Glasgow, 1763).

reform either in the general legislation or administration, ever emanated from the States General. It must not, however, be supposed that they have been altogether useless, or without effect; they had a moral effect, of which in general we take too little account; they served from time to time as a protestation against political servitude, a forcible proclamation of certain guardian principles — such, for example, as that a nation has a right to vote its own taxes, to take part in public affairs, to impose a responsibility upon the agents of power. That these maxims have never perished in France is mainly owing to the States General; and it is no slight service rendered to a country to maintain among its virtues, to keep alive in its thoughts, the remembrance and claims of liberty. The States General has done us this service, but it never became a means of government; it never entered upon political organization; it never attained the object for which it was formed, that is to say, the fusion into one body of the various societies which divided the country." [1]

Thierry thinks the failure to develop representative government in France may be ascribed to two causes — one, the instability of the Celtic race, who were loyal to persons rather than principles; the other, the effect of Roman domination in extinguishing the capacity for self-government. The difference of race kept the nobility and people asunder, and prevented that sincere coöperation of the various orders which had a marked and beneficent influence on the growth of English freedom.[2]

First or last in the course of the Middle Ages nearly every other country on the continent of Europe developed some sort of an assembly. One alone need have our attention, and that only because it was particularly familiar to the Puritans who founded Plymouth Colony and of course to the Dutch who founded New Amsterdam, with the result that at least one writer has traced to it the origin of many American governmental institutions. Although his theory has not carried conviction, yet the frequent reference to the history of the Dutch Republic by the American statesmen who devised our early Constitutions, State and Federal, show they were not unfamiliar with its lessons, and call for a word about them here. Motley's description will suffice. Writing of the Netherlands of the sixteenth century,[3] he says that the assemblies of the Estates were

[1] *Civilization in Modern Europe*, Lecture x.
[2] *History of the Tiers Etat*, chap. VII, 224, 243.
[3] *Rise of the Dutch Republic*, Historical Introduction.

rather diplomatic than representative. They consisted, generally, of the nobles and of the deputations from the cities. In Holland, the clergy had neither influence nor seats in the parliamentary body. Measures were proposed by the stadholder, who represented the sovereign. A request, for example, of pecuniary accommodation, was made by that functionary or by the Count himself in person. The nobles then voted upon the demand, generally as one body, but sometimes by heads. The measure was then laid before the burghers. If they had been specially commissioned to act upon the matter they voted, each city as a city, not each deputy individually. If they had received no instructions, they took back the proposition to lay before the councils of their respective cities, in order to return a decision at an adjourned session, or at a subsequent diet. It will be seen, therefore, that the principle of national, popular representation was but imperfectly developed. The municipal deputies acted only under instructions. Each city was a little independent State, suspicious not only of the sovereign and nobles, but of its sister cities.

The chief city of the Netherlands, the commercial capital of the world, was Antwerp, Motley further tells us. No city except Paris surpassed it in population, none approached it in commercial splendor. Its government was very free. The sovereign, as Marquis of Antwerp, was solemnly sworn to govern according to the ancient charter and laws. The stadholder, as his representative, shared his authority with the four Estates of the city. The Senate of eighteen members was appointed by the stadholder out of a quadruple number nominated by the Senate itself and by the fourth body, called the Borgery. Half the board was thus renewed annually. It exercised executive and appellate judicial functions, appointed two burgomasters, and two pensionaries or legal councilors, and also selected the lesser magistrates and officials of the city. The board of Ancients or ex-Senators, held their seats *ex officio*. The twenty-six ward masters, appointed, two from each ward, by the Senate, formed the third Estate. Their especial business was to enroll the militia, and to attend to its mustering and training. The deans of the guilds, fifty-four in number, two from each guild, selected by the Senate, from a triple list of candidates presented by the guilds, composed the fourth Estate. This influential body was always assembled in the broad-council of the city. Its duty was likewise to conduct the examination of candidates claiming admittance to any guild and offering specimens of art or handiwork, to superintend the general affairs of the guilds, and to regulate disputes. These four branches, with their functionaries and dependents, composed the commonwealth of Antwerp. Assembled together in council, they constituted the great and general court. No tax could be imposed by the sovereign, except with consent of the four branches, all voting separately.

On the Continent, representative institutions rapidly waned after the fifteenth century. By the last quarter of the eighteenth, when we were achieving our independence and establishing the first great republic of modern times, nothing but absolute monarchy was to be found between the North Sea and the Mediterranean. Then with the French Revolution began an era of revival or creation of Parliaments. One by one the nations copied the English model until at last even Russia was driven to yield, and that, too, in part as a result of defeat in war by an Oriental nation that had become one of the world-powers after adopting representative institutions. But great as was the marvel of Japan, greater still was that of China, when it astonished the world with the news that it had become a republic. This has all come about at any rate in sequence to what took place in the little island of Britain, if not as a result thereof. Let us see what that was.

DEVELOPED IN ENGLAND

When the Teutonic tribes overflowed from Germany into Britain, they brought with them the folkmoot, or popular assembly, in which each man had a right to share. As the group of invaders began to coalesce, to make larger groups each headed by a King, another kind of assembly was superimposed upon the folkmoots. This has come to be referred to by nearly all writers as the Witenagemot, the assembly of the wise men, although in the records it is styled simply "gemote," like all the Saxon Law Court Assemblies. Often the longer title is shortened into "Witan." It was a council, not a popular assembly, in fact, though perhaps in theory every man had a right to attend; nor was it a representative assembly in the sense that its members were sent by their fellows. Bishop Stubbs thought that the shiremoot, the popular assembly of the shire, which the folkmoot became after the kingdoms were formed, was a representative body to a certain extent. He believed it was attended by the representatives of the hundred and townships, and had a representative body of witnesses to give validity to its acts.[1] Taswell-Langmead thought he found still more proofs that the ideas of election and representation, both separately and in combination, had been familiar to the nation, in its legal and fiscal system, long before they were applied to the constitution of the national Parliament.[2]

Nevertheless, it is now denied that there was any such thing as formal representation in Saxon times, at any rate in the shire-moots. It is denied that there is a single authentic document to support the theory. However that may be, certainly the superior assembly, the Witenagemot, was made up of persons of rank because they were such, and not because they were delegates — for they were the great officers of the royal court, the magistrates, the bishops and high ecclesiastics — in brief, the aristocracy.

Kemble says that of the manner of the deliberations or the forms of business we know little, but it is not unlikely that they were very complicated. We may conclude that the general outline of the proceedings was something of the following order. On common occasions the King summoned his Witan to attend him at some royal vill, at Christmas, or at Easter, for festive and ceremonial as well as business purposes. On extraordinary occasions he issued summonses, according to the nature of the exigency, appointing the time and place of meeting. When assembled, the Witan began the session by attending divine service and formally professing adherence to the Catholic faith. The King then brought his propositions before them, in the Frankish manner, and after due deliberation these were accepted, modified, or rejected. Stubbs thinks it may be presumed that in the early stages and under the weaker sovereigns, the determination was elicited by *bona fide* voting.[3] Under the stronger and later Kings, it was decided by the sovereign himself, as he chose to follow or thwart the policy of his leading advisers. It is not until the reign of Henry II that we find any historical data as to deliberations in which the King does not get his own way. Yet, "it may be safely affirmed that no business of any importance could be transacted by the King in which they had not, in theory at least, a consultative voice."[4] The earlier records mention

---

[1] *Constitutional History*, I, 119. [2] *English Constitutional History*, 213, 214.
[3] *Constitutional History*, I, 126. [4] *Ibid.*, I, 133.

"counsel," "consent," and the like, making it clear that then the King was far from absolute or even dominant.

Bede gives an account of the Northumbrian council that received Christianity, and represents the King as consulting his princes and counselors one by one; each declares his mind; and the King decides accordingly. He also tells how Ethelbert made, "with the advice of his Witan, decrees and judgments." Edmund began his laws by declaring them to have been established with the counsel of his Witan, ecclesiastical and lay. Stubbs says the ancient theory that the laws were made by the King and Witan coördinately, if it be an ancient theory, has within historic times been modified by the doctrine that the King enacted the laws with the counsel and consent of the Witan. This is the most ancient form existing in enactments, and is common to the early laws of all the Teutonic races: it has of course always been still more modified in usage by the varying power of the King and his counselors, and by the share that each was strong enough to vindicate in the process. Until the reign of John the varieties of practice may be traced chiefly in the form taken by the law on its enactment. The ancient laws are either drawn up as codes, like Alfred's, or as amendments of customs; often we have only the bare abstract of them, the substance that was orally transmitted from one generation of Witan to another; where we have them in integrity the counsel and consent of the Witan are specified. The laws of the Norman Kings are put in the form of charters; the King in his sovereign capacity grants and confirms liberties and free customs to his people, but with the counsel and consent of his barons and faithful. From the reign of Edward I the forms are those of statutes and ordinances.[1]

There was no separation of powers in Saxon times. The Witenagemot was both legislative and judicial, a court and a conference combined. In fact, its primary purpose was judicial, to try men for the breach of law, to settle disputes between powerful thanes and prelates, to hear complaints of the denial of justice in the shire courts. Declaring what had been common law they made it statutory law. The law of Wihtraed reads: "There the great men decreed, with the suffrages of all, these dooms, and added them to the lawful customs of the men of Kent." "Ini, by the grace of God, King of the West Saxons," tells in the prologue of his laws how with the advice and by the teaching of Cenred his

[1] Stubbs, *Select Charters*, 46.

father, and of Hedde his bishop, and Ercenwold his bishop, with all his ealdormen and the most eminent Witan of his people, and with a great assembly of God's servants, he had been considering "concerning our soul's heal and the stability of our realm, so that right law and right royal judgments might be settled and confirmed among our people," etc.

After a Witenagemot the reeves, and perhaps on occasion officers specially designated for that service, carried the chapters down into the several counties, and there took a *wed*, or pledge, from the freemen that they would abide by what had been enacted. Possibly in very early times the local assemblies were required to give assent to the legal changes made by a central authority. Perhaps a publication of a new law in the shiremoot was regarded as denoting the acceptance of it by the people in general. Canute and the Conqueror heard the people accept and swear to the laws of Edgar and Edward. The Great Charter and the Provisions of Oxford were promulgated in the county courts, as if without acceptance they lacked somewhat of legal force. Yet this was a right of the nation to accept laws, not to frame them.[1]

Upon the conquest by the Normans, the people at large during the reign of William and that of his immediate successors, were without whatever little share they had before enjoyed in the matter of laws. The Witenagemot survived, the name Witan being used at least as long as the Chronicle continued, but another name more to the taste in language of the new masters, gradually came into use and at last supplanted the old one. It was the Latin translation, *Magnum Concilium*, for the Saxon *Mycel Gemot*. In nature the change was greater than in name, for although the Kings were supposed to act by the advice and consent of this Council, such was the authority they arrogated to themselves that the power of the Council was little more than a shadow. Its members now were the Barons — a name given to all who had the right to attend, whether earls, knights, bishops, abbots, or whatever their rank, episcopal or lay. In theory it included all the tenants-in-chief of the crown. Except in the anomalous period of Stephen's reign, there are no records of any such discussions as might lead to divisions. In private perhaps the sovereign listened to advice, but, as far as history goes, the counselors who took part in formal deliberations must have been unanimous or subservient.

[1] Stubbs, *Constitutional History*, ii, 245.

BEGINNINGS OF PARLIAMENT

Colloquium was the Latin word often used to describe a session of the Council. As early as 1175 Jordan Fantosme used the name "Parliament," and it may then have been in common use, but it is not found in the Latin chronicles for some years afterward. Its oldest Latin spelling is *parlamentum.* The interpolation of the letter "i" was doubtless the result of popular pronunciation at the time, but now the dictionary-makers would have us pronounce the word "parliament" in three syllables, slurring the second, which makes it correspond to its original form. In France where it appeared in the twelfth century, and where, by the way, it was never applied to legislative bodies, but to courts, the spelling is *parlement,* pronounced in two syllables. Both *colloquium* and *parlamentum* meant "a talk." Monastic statutes of the thirteenth century used *parlamentum* in speaking of the after-dinner talk of the monks in their cloisters, which was condemned as unedifying. Later it was used to describe solemn conferences such as the one held in 1245 between Louis IX of France and Pope Innocent IV. From all this it may be gathered that originally it signified in England simply the talk, the conference, the parley, between the King and his Council. Milton wanted it abolished as the name for the English legislature because it originally signified "the parley of our Lords and Commons with the Norman Kings when he pleased to call them." Note, however, that the word came into use long before the King called the Commons to his Council, and it was not restricted to the legislative assembly for a century or more after that time.

Woodrow Wilson, writing while a Professor, penned a passage on this subject that was more brilliant than accurate. Said he:

"We speak now always of 'legislatures,' of 'law*making*' assemblies, and are very impatient of prolonged debates, and sneer at parliamentary bodies which cannot get their 'business' done. We join with laughing zest in Mr. Carlyle's bitter gibe at 'talking shops,' at parliaments which spend their days in endless discussion rather than in diligent prosecution of what they came together to 'do.' And yet to hold such an attitude toward representative assemblies is utterly to forget their history and their first and capital purpose. They were meant to be talking shops. The name 'parliament' is no accidental indication of their function. They were meant to be grand parleys with those who were conducting the nation's business; parleys concerning laws, con-

cerning administrative acts, concerning policies and plans at
home and abroad, in order that nothing which contravened the
common understanding should be let pass without comment or
stricture, in order that measures should be insisted on which the
nation needed, and measures resisted which the nation did not
need or might take harm from. Their purpose was watchful
criticism, talk that should bring to light the whole intention of
the government and apprise those who conducted it of the real
feeling and desire of the nation; and how well they performed
that function many an uneasy monarch has testified, alike by
word and act." [1]

The trouble with this is in its implications. They do not harmonize with the fact that for many years the name described a
meeting of the King with his courtiers and other magnates, for
purposes having nothing like the scope that Professor Wilson
sketched. At the start the name did not imply an assembly
where the members were to talk with each other, a talking shop,
but an assembly to parley with the King. And many other years
were to pass before "watchful criticism" was to be a normal
function.

It is now believed that the first and capital function of Parliaments was to dispense justice or equity in particular cases. To
this end it was necessary to determine what might be the perti-
nent customs of the country. By the declaration of these customs in applying them to individual grievances, preëxisting laws
may have received some measure of form, but there was then no
novel lawmaking.

This aspect of the Parliaments that slowly developed into representative government was first brought forcibly to attention
by F. W. Maitland's introduction to the Records of the Parliament of 1305, which he edited under the title of *Memoranda de
Parliamento*, and which were published in 1893 as part of the
"Rolls Series," i.e. the official series of reprints of the rolls or
records of Parliament. The thesis of the Maitland essay has been
elaborated in two scholarly volumes, one published in 1910 by
an American, Professor C. H. McIlwain, on "The High Court of
Parliament," and the other in 1920 by an Englishman, Professor
A. F. Pollard, on "The Evolution of Parliament." These three
writers have completely demolished the theory that representative assemblies had a democratic origin, that they sprang from an

[1] *Constitutional Government in the U.S.*, 11.

intent to express the popular will, and that they were conceived for the purpose of making laws.

At first Parliaments were courts, and little else. In France they remained such. In England up to modern times the customary phrase was, "The High Court of Parliament." Massachusetts still has her "General Court," now the State Legislature.

The early Norman Kings found it convenient or advisable from time to time to hear petitioners for justice or relief while sitting with the Council. This was called "holding court in council." The petitions were not addressed to Parliament, nor to the magnates assembled, but to the King or to the King and his Council. Parliament had not then been conceived as a body that could be petitioned. A Parliament was rather an act than a body of persons. As Pollard says, one cannot present a petition to a colloquy, a debate. The prayer was generally for something the King could grant without transcending his powers, sometimes for relief the King was in common honesty bound to give, or sometimes for pure grace or favor. The response seldom gave all that was asked. Usually a record was entered to the effect that the petitioner had made out what we should call a *prima facie* case and the petitioner was referred to the proper court of the standing variety. The reason he could not go there in the first place was that then the jurisdiction and powers of the courts were greatly restricted.

Some of the petitions came from individuals, some from counties, cities, or boroughs, i.e. communities. Note that word, for out of it came the title, "Commons." It is believed that, before there was any formal recognition of the practice, counties had often sent to Westminster knights of the shire, and boroughs had sent burgesses, to prefer their requests, perhaps plead for them, much as a substantial citizen or an attorney might be sent to-day by an American city. The supposition is that presently this suggested the utility of making the practice regular, formal, and official, by the use of writs of summons. It was still the theory, however, that the men sent were the agents of the communities as such, and not of the separate individuals composing those communities.

Representation in matters judicial had long been familiar. McIlwain holds that jurors were from the very beginning "representatives." The verdict to which they swore was not their individual opinion; it was the common belief of the countryside.

This communal or representative element was no adventitious thing; it was an essential part of the institution itself. Quite naturally it came to be adopted as a means for furnishing to the King the general belief of a district on any topic as to which he wished to be informed. According to Hallam its first use for this purpose came four years after the Conquest, when William, if we may rely on Hoveden, caused twelve persons skilled in the customs of England to be chosen from each county, who were sworn to inform him rightly of their laws; and these, so ascertained, were ratified by the Great Council. Sir Matthew Hale asserts this to have been "as sufficient and effectual a Parliament as was ever held in England." There is, however, no appearance that these twelve deputies of each county were invested with any higher authority than that of declaring their ancient usages.[1]

In the next century came the practice of choosing assessors to fix the value of real and personal property for purposes of taxation. Thus, Henry II's Saladin tithe of 1188 — the first national imposition upon incomes and movable property — was assessed, at least in part, by juries of neighbors elected by the taxpayers of the various parishes, and in a way representative of them.

Stubbs tells us the first occasion on which we find any historical proof that representatives were summoned to a national council was the general assembly at St. Albans, August 4, 1213, called by the justiciar and archbishop, which was attended not only by the bishops and barons, but also by a body of representatives from the townships on the royal demesne, each of which sent its reeve and four legal men. They were probably called upon to give evidence as to the value of the royal lands; but the fact that so much besides was discussed at the time, and that some important measures touching the people at large flowed directly from the action of the council, gives to their appearance there a great significance. To this first English representative assembly on record was submitted the first draught of the reforms afterward embodied in Magna Charta. The action of this council was the first hesitating and tentative step toward that great act, in which church, baronage, and people made their constitutional compact with the King, and reached their first sensible realization of their corporate unity and the unity of their rights and interests.[2]

[1] Hallam, *Middle Ages*, part III, chap. VIII.
[2] *Constitutional History*, I, 527.

On the 15th of June, 1215, at Runnymede, John reluctantly and peevishly yielded to the barons the Great Charter, foremost of the landmarks in English constitutional history. Its chief interest here attaches to those articles that admitted the right of the nation to ordain taxation, and defined how consent should be given. Except the three customary feudal aids (payments on certain recognized occasions), no aid nor scutage (another form of levy under the feudal system) was henceforth to be imposed but by the common counsel of the nation. This was to be taken in an assembly duly summoned; the archbishops, bishops, abbots, earls, and greater barons were to be called up by royal writ addressed to each severally; and all who held of the King in chief, below the rank of the greater barons, were to be summoned by a general writ addressed to the sheriff of their shire; the summons was to express the cause for which the assembly was called together; forty days' notice was to be given; and when the day had arrived the action of those members who obeyed the summons was to be taken as the action of the whole.

Here, it will be seen, appears a new field for parliamentary activity. To the function of Parliament as primarily a high court of justice is now to be added the taxing and representative functions. Presently to provide money to the King on terms becomes the most important purpose of a national assemblage. Legislation and all other present-day parliamentary activities grow slowly out of this.

To the usefulness of representation for judicial purposes is now added that of representation for fiscal purposes. To handle money through an agent was customary in private affairs. It was a short and easy step to apply the same principle to public affairs concerning payments of money.

In another aspect the development was also purely natural, for it was the normal growth of the idea that a vassal of the Crown might by proxy, by an agent, perform his duty of attending meetings of the Great Council. It was inconvenient and expensive to try to assemble all the vassals, or separate agents for each. So it was well-nigh inevitable that there should come recourse to a few agents for many vassals — not representatives in the modern sense, but agents to share in transacting public business. So it was quite in accord with the feudal system that after the Charter instances of electing knights of the shire for this purpose by the county courts should become numerous.

Next came the matter of the cities and towns. They, too, must contribute to the needs of the royal purse. Here it was even clearer than in the case of the county gentlemen that the easy way was to deal with agents. Simon de Montfort was the first statesman to recognize this and systemize what was already practiced irregularly. To the Parliament summoned in Henry's name after the battle of Lewes, to meet in January of 1265, it was ordered that two burgesses should be sent from every borough in each county. Then for the first time were assembled the representatives of the towns together with those of the counties, for national purposes. That summer Simon de Montfort fell at Evesham and his party soon disappeared, but the victorious royalists saw the prudence of his policy in recognizing the towns.

In 1295 Parliament passed a milestone. To change the metaphor, it became of age. The assembly of that year is generally credited with having been the first real Parliament according to modern notions, although as a matter of fact it advanced but a little beyond its predecessors, and had yet before it much of change. To this Parliament King Edward summoned separately the two archbishops, all the bishops, the greater abbots, seven earls, and forty-one barons. The archbishops and bishops were directed to bring the heads of their cathedral chapters, their archdeacons, one proctor for the clergy of each cathedral, and two proctors for the clergy of each diocese. Every sheriff was directed to cause two knights of each shire, two citizens of each city, and two burgesses of each borough, to be elected.

→ The form of the summons addressed to the prelates began with a quotation from the Code of Justinian which was developed by Edward from a mere legal maxim into a great political and constitutional principle: "As the most righteous law, established by the provident circumspection of the sacred princes, exhorts and ordains that that which touches all shall be approved by all, it is very evident that common dangers must be met by measures concerted in common."

Although this prophesies the purpose of the representative system, there is not the slightest suggestion by any contemporary writer that anybody conceived the novelty of the political principles thus established or dreamt of what would be its momentous consequences. It was with this, Hearn points out,[1] as it

[1] *Government of England*, 457.

had been with almost every other great improvement in human affairs; and he aptly quotes Sir Walter Scott, who observed, writing of Lord Orford's "History of His Own Times," and Sir George Mackenzie's "Memoirs": "They show how little those who lived in public business and of course in constant agitation and intrigue knew about the real and deep progress of opinions and events. They put me somewhat in mind of a miller, who is so busy with the clatter of his own grindstones, and machinery, and so much employed in regulating his own artificial milldam, that he is incapable of noticing the gradual swell of the river from which he derives his little stream, until it comes down with such force as to carry his whole manufactory away before it." [1]

THE THREE ESTATES

It will have been noticed that the membership of the Parliament of 1295 was one of representatives of classes. The technical name for classes under the feudal system was "Estates," a term now most commonly used in property affairs, but originally describing status, whence confusion if the meanings are not discriminated. What in mediæval times it signified in the matter of tenure and service need not concern us here, beyond recognition of the probability that in the issuing of summonses to attend a Parliament the feudal relationships were more important than geographical, political, or social considerations. Inasmuch as these feudal relationships disappeared after having played no great part in the development of parliamentary institutions, the really interesting thing for us to observe is that whether intentionally or accidentally the classes summoned to the Parliament of 1295 did correspond, at least roughly, to social groupings with which we are to-day familiar, groupings based on condition in life or on occupation.

In all times the priesthood has generally been a class set apart. Other men have in common thought been divided into two groups — patricians and plebeians, or nobles and common people, or warriors and traders, or landowners and craftsmen, or rich and poor, according to the habit of the time and place. With some accuracy this grouping is reflected in the proper political use of the term, "the Three Estates," as referring to the clergy, the nobility, and the people at large, which is an inadequate way of describing the representation in the House of Commons.

[1] Lockhart, *Life of Scott*, VII, 12.

Improperly, and often, the term is used to designate King, Lords, and Commons, under an impression, probably, that it was conceived to describe the three factors of political power. The King cannot be an Estate, because he is not a class. It would be right to speak of the King and the Three Estates of the Realm.

Recognition of more than three "Estates" finds in theory no obstacle, and in fact has not been unknown. For example, Sweden made the number four until half a century ago. In England it was long uncertain what form of grouping would prevail. At times it looked as if the merchants or the lawyers or both might become Estates of the Realm. Early in the fourteenth century a singular Parliament was held at York, consisting solely of merchants and burgesses from the towns, who duly met and voted supplies, but it had no like successor. In 1381 the Commons petitioned the Crown to summon five separate assemblies — one each for the magnates, prelates, knights, judges, and commonalty, but this complicated gathering never took place.[1] Stubbs thinks that the failure of the lawyers to become an Estate is perhaps rather to be ascribed to the fact that the majority of the lawyers were still clerks by profession; that the Chancery, which was increasing in respect and wholesome influence, was administered wholly by churchmen; and that the English universities did not furnish for the common law of England any such great school of instruction as Paris and Bologna provided for the canonist or the civilian. Had the scientifio lawyers ever obtained full sway in English courts, the Roman law must ultimately have prevailed, notwithstanding the strong antipathy felt against it, and if it had prevailed it might have changed the course of English history. The summons of the justices and other legal counselors to Parliament, by a writ scarcely distinguishable from that of the barons themselves, shows how nearly this result was reached.[2]

Although there was no formal grouping into Three Estates in the Parliament of 1295, and indeed never has been in the Parliament of England, that classification may be accepted for convenience in discussion. First it may be said of the church that the notion of a complete clerical representation has never been realized. The archbishops, bishops, and greater abbots continued to attend in Parliament, as they had attended the Great

[1] Adrian Wontner, *The Lords*, 12, 13.
[2] *Constitutional History*, ii, 190, 191.

Councils of previous Kings, but they did it rather as great feudal lords and as great holders of lands than as churchmen. The clause by which they were directed to bring with them representatives of their clergy, which remains to this day in the writ by which they are summoned, has from the first been persistently ignored. In early days the lesser clergy pleaded all sorts of excuse for non-attendance — sickness, fatness, gout, incapacity to ride on horseback or in a litter, bodily infirmity, age, and domestic affairs. As a body they preferred to stand aloof, to meet in their own clerical assemblies or convocations, and to settle there what contribution they should make to the royal treasury. After the restoration of Charles II, in 1664, by a mere verbal agreement between Archbishop Sheldon and Lord Chancellor Clarendon, an arrangement was made under which the clergy waived their right to tax themselves, and agreed to be assessed by the laity in Parliament, gaining thereby the new right of voting at the election of the members of the House of Commons by virtue of their ecclesiastical benefices. At present two Archbishops and twenty-four Bishops sit in the House of Lords.

There was no essential change from the character of the representation of the nobility in the Parliament of 1295, and in principle it remains to-day what it was then, although greatly enlarged as the peerage has been extended. Freeman, indeed, thought there had been no change in principle from Saxon days. "Of one House of Parliament we may say," he observed, "not that it grew out of the ancient Assembly, but that it absolutely is the same by personal identity. The House of Lords not only springs out of, it actually is, the ancient Witenagemot. I can see no break between the two.... In the constitution of the House of Lords I can see nothing mysterious or wonderful. Its hereditary character came in, like other things, step by step, by accident rather than by design. And it should not be forgotten that, as long as the bishops keep their seats in the House, the hereditary character of the House does not extend to all its members. To me it seems simply that two classes of men, the two highest classes, the Earls and the Bishops, never lost or disused that right of attending in the National Assembly which was at first common to them with all other freemen.... The House of Lords, then, I do not hesitate to say, represents, or rather is, the ancient Witenagemot.... But the special function of the body into which the old national assembly has changed, the function of 'another House,' an Upper House, the House of Lords, as opposed to a House of Commons, could not show itself till a second House of a more popular constitution had arisen by its side." [1]

The third Estate, the Commons, began as virtually two Estates. More than a century was to pass after (1) knights of the shire and (2) citizens and burgesses were elected, before they coalesced. At the outset the knights of the shire were, as we have seen, in effect the agents of the landed gentry; the citizens and burgesses, the agents of the mercantile class. At home, there was a conspicuous difference in the social standing of these two groups, but at Westminster it disappeared in contrast with the difference between the two of them and the nobles of the court. They were called into being for the same purpose and had many interests in common. So it was natural that in the course of time they should be amalgamated. It is not found that they deliberated together before 1332, although they had before joined in petitions to the King. Historians differ as to when they were first united as one elected body, in contradistinction to another individually summoned as peers and barons; but it was undoubtedly about this period, sometime in the first half of the reign of Edward III. Toward the end of that long reign came the appointment of a permanent Speaker, marking the complete consolidation of the two groups into the House of Commons. At the same time (51 Ed. III) the imposition of a poll tax upon every adult person in the kingdom except mere beggars marked the fusion of the separate tax-paying classes into a united nation. [2]

The name "Commons" is inappropriate and misleading. It has no relation to "common people." It appears to have been an abbreviation of the Latin word "communitates," conveying the idea expressed in English by "communities." The House of Commons was simply the House of the Communities, originally groups of persons combined in a particular way for particular purposes, enjoying certain rights in common, and subject to common duties. The word "common" as applied to persons of a certain political standing does not seem originally to have had any flavor of odium or disparagement; nor did the man of democratic proclivities have any ground for using it with pride. The same was originally true of "commoner," although the modern usage that makes of some tribune of the people "a great

[1] *Growth of the English Constitution*, 60, 63.

[2] W. E. Hearn, *Government of England*, 402.

commoner," has given the word a significance it is not likely to
lose, in spite of the purists. "Commonalty," too, at first had a
technical meaning it would not now imply. Thus it was used in
that notable statute of 1322, in the reign of Edward II, which
provided: "The matters which are to be established for the estate
of our lord the King and of his heirs, and for the estate of the
realm of the people, shall be treated, accorded, and established
in parliaments, by our lord the King, and by the assent of the
prelates, earls, and barons, and the commonalty of the realm;
according as it hath been before accustomed." Notice that in
this there are but two parties — (1) the King and his heirs;
(2) the Estate of the realm of the people; and that the second
party is to give assent by four agencies. If it is to be assumed
that this was phrased with precision, the "commonalty" was
but one of the parts of the "people."

Of more consequence is it to observe that this statute recognizes
the assent of the commonalty is to be given to legislation, and
they are in this regard on a level with the others. That was
formally recognized in the last year of Edward I, and several
times under Edward II. It shows the Commons were beginning
to take part in the making of laws. From the time of the Conquest down to the period of Magna Charta lawmaking was in
practice a function of the King; if in theory his Council was to
approve, the royal power was such that the consent of the
Council was a nominal matter. In John's time the Great Council
won formal recognition of the right to advise and consent. Also,
it got some slight share in legislation by petitioning for amendments of the laws. During the minority and the troubled years
of Henry III, it fully vindicated and practically enlarged these
rights. In legislation it not only took the initiative by petitions,
such as those which led to the Provisions of Oxford, and by
articles of complaint, but, as in the famous act of the Council of
Merton touching the legitimizing of bastards by the subsequent
marriage of their parents, refused consent to a change in the law,
by words that were accepted by the jurists as the statement of a
constitutional fact. Under Edward I the laws again were issued
with counsel and consent of the Parliament, but legal enactments
might, as before, in the shape of assizes or ordinances, be issued
without any such assistance; and the theory of the enacting power
of the King, as supreme legislator, grew rather than diminished
during the period, probably in consequence of the legislative

activity of Frederick II, Louis IX, and Alfonso the Wise. The
legislation of the reign of Henry III, and most of that of Edward
I, was the work of assemblies to which the Commons were not
summoned. The statute *quia emptores* (1290) was not improba-
bly the last instance in which the assent of the Commons was
taken for granted in legislation.[1]

As in the case of the Great Council a century before, the path
of the Commons to a share in lawmaking was by way of petitions.
The King was asked to remedy grievances. If he consented and
a new law was necessary to accomplish the purpose, its promul-
gation implied the approval of the Commons, because they had
asked for it. From this the next step was to thinking that their
approval was worth having, and then to thinking it necessary.
Manifestly these steps did not follow as a matter of course, for if
that were the case all petitioners should have become lawmakers
everywhere since government began, which has rarely happened.
In England, in the early part of the fourteenth century it did
happen, because of the royal need of money. The usual purpose
of summoning agents of the commonalty of the realm to Parliament, to a parley with the King, was to tax the counties, cities,
and towns. These agents, finding they could bargain with the
King, gradually became bolder in their demands. At first it was,
"Your humble poor Commons beg and pray, for God's sake, as
an act of charity." By the time of Richard II the "humbles
pauvres communes" had become, in the royal eyes, "the right
wise, right honourable, worthy and discreet Commons."

The turning point in this situation is the long and financially
embarrassed reign of Edward III, in which there was, from year
to year, the continual necessity to summon complete Parliaments, in all not less than seventy times. The Commons, who,
until then, had been only occasionally mentioned in connection
with parliamentary statutes, are from this time seldom omitted
— nay, their assistance becomes more and more frequently
mentioned in the preamble to the statutes. The usual style now
distinguishes motion and consent; the King issues decrees on
motion of the Commons with the sanction of the lords and prelates.[2] Such at least was the general form, though for many years
there was no invariable regularity in this respect. The Commons,
who till this reign were rarely mentioned, were now rarely

[1] Stubbs, *Constitutional History*, II, 246.
[2] Rudolf Gneist, *History of the English Constitution*, II, 19.

omitted in the enacting clause. In fact, it is evident from the rolls of Parliament that statutes were almost always founded upon their petition.[1]

Pollard lays much stress on the part in the change played by petitions.[2] The importance of the Commons as a deliberative assembly grew with the gradual realization of the fact that individual petitions, arising spontaneously from different localities, dealt with grievances common to all and might well be fused into common petitions. The common petition required common deliberation, common action, and perhaps even a common clerk; the common action became a habit, the habit an institution, and the institution a House. Parliament became a political arena rather than a court of law; for, while individual grievances are matters of law, national grievances are matters of politics. Furthermore, common action was the cause as well as the result of community of feeling. By this process the locally minded representatives of heterogeneous communities were welded into a House of Commons, and in that House, more than anywhere else, the "Estates" were made into the State.

Along with this change, and as its result, went the organization of procedure. Hitherto single decisions, temporary administrative measures, and permanent ordinances had all been confused together. Frequently petitions that had been granted lay inoperative for years before the enactments giving them effect were put in force or published. As a rule, at the close of the parliamentary sittings, the Council sorted the jumbled mass of resolutions, and provided for their being duly carried out. It was especially the business of the justices to select such enactments as, being of a permanent nature, should be entered upon the "roll of the statutes" for the cognizance of the courts. But after the right of the Estates to take part in the framing of enactments had become established, they further demanded to take part in this selection. In the Parliament of 14 Edward III, a number of prelates, barons, and counselors were appointed, together with twelve knights and six burgesses, to formulate such petitions and decrees, and to direct the drafting of such as were suitable for permanent statutes.[3]

With the acknowledgment of the right of the Commons to

---

[1] Hallam, *Middle Ages*, part III, chap. VIII.
[2] *The Evolution of Parliament*, 60, 120, 127.
[3] Rudolf Gniest, *History of the English Constitution*, II, 23.

assent to laws, the belief grew that there was something more weighty and compelling and enduring in that to which they had assented than there was in a royal decree to which their assent had not been asked. Hitherto the more important enactments of King and Council had been distinguished from the simpler royal decrees, by the name of "assize." With the first year of Edward III began the *statuta nova*, and henceforward the distinction between statutes (parliamentary enactments), and ordinances (royal decrees), became clear.

Along with the right to assent came the conception that when a bargain had been made between the King and the Estates, the law thus enacted, like any other bargain, could not be changed without the consent of all parties to it; and this was expanded to cover all existing law, whether customary or statutory. Under Richard II we find the Commons petitioning, in 1390, that the Chancellor and Council might not, after the close of Parliament, make any ordinance "contrary to the common law or ancient customs of the land, and the statutes aforetime ordained, or to be ordained in the present Parliament." But the King replied that "what had hitherto been done, should be done still, saving the prerogative of the Crown." It was one of the charges brought against Richard that he had maintained the laws were "in the mouth and breast of the King," and he by himself could frame the laws of the kingdom. Yet the contrary principle gradually established itself.

Petitions of the Commons to the King naturally suggested that the petitions of private individuals might carry more weight if they went to the throne with the approval of the Commons. Under Henry IV the practice began. Under Henry VI the roundabout way of working through petitions led to the simpler process of bringing in the motions directly in the form of bills. Under Henry VII came another step forward taking the form of expressing the right of the Commons to assent to statutes in precisely the same manner as that of the Lords.

From this time on for more than a century parliamentary government made no important gain. On the contrary, it suffered distinct loss. With the Tudors reaction almost reached absolutism. Parliament became an almost negligible factor. Under Henry VIII there were two periods of more than seven years each when it did not meet at all. While that monarch was on the throne, the gain of struggle covering more than three hundred years, the struggle against the exercising of the law-making power by the King, was thrown away. In 1539 it was enacted that the proclamations of the King, with the advice of the Council, were to be obeyed and kept as acts of Parliament. To be sure, this was to apply only to the reigning monarch, but in effect it prevailed through the reigns of Edward VI, Mary, and Elizabeth, whose ordinances approached the efficacy of statutes. Elizabeth, who ruled for forty-five years, called her Parliament together only thirteen times, and in the course of her whole reign it sat not much if any more than eighteen months.

Upon the accession of James I in 1603 began a contest for the restoration of the rights of the Commons. James was a stubborn fighter for what he believed the royal prerogative, and the democratizing forces of Puritanism were not yet strongly organized. So Parliament did not achieve great progress in the vindication of its rights during the score and more years of his reign, though some things were accomplished, particularly in the way of parliamentary privileges. With Charles I the contest was renewed, the champions of popular liberty gaining strength until at last they got rid of absolutism by beheading the monarch. It is to be noted that the Petition of Right he so reluctantly accepted in 1628 asked nothing new, but simply a restoration of ancient rights, such as that taxes should not be levied without consent of Parliament. The reforms accomplished by the Long Parliament in its early days were rather returns than reforms — returns to old liberties.

CHAPTER IV

IN THE AMERICAN COLONIES

TURN now from the situation representative government had reached in England, to the lawmaking assemblies of her colonies beyond the sea, beginning to lay the foundations of another and a different representative system. While England was looking backward to old methods, America was looking forward to new methods. Before taking up the American story in detail, it may be well to forecast some of the contrasts. We have seen that in England representation was a matter of classes, Estates. In America it was to become one of persons, in some colonies from the start, in others gradually. Never in America was there to be anything corresponding precisely to the House of Lords, never a peerage, never an hereditary lawmaker (with the possible exception for a time in the case of certain New York manors). We find the clergy will still have here influence for a while, but never separate representation; on the contrary, the time will come when in many States they will be forbidden to sit in the Legislature at all. Although at the beginning the colonists will pay almost as little attention to numbers in the apportionment of representatives as was paid in England up to the time of men yet living, quickly the idea of an allotment by population will become general. From the very outset each colonial assembly will assert the right to make laws, and give scant sufferance to any imitation of lawmaking by ordinance if tried by any Governor. The requirements of colonial life will at once accustom representatives to think the making of laws a more important part of their work than the levying of taxes; and the budget, to this day the great feature of a Parliament, will be found here a minor consideration, in the Legislatures if not in Congress. With this will come a quite different conception of the nature, function, and purposes of representative government, and of the best way to achieve its ends.

America began by thinking of a legislature as a means to advance the safety, comfort, and happiness of the people. England first secured a representation of the people through the desire of its King to get more revenue; the general design of the system was to assemble representatives from the constituencies best able to contribute aids and subsidies for the service of the Crown. It might almost be averred that England has always placed the more stress on the raising of money, America on the spending of money. Our prime legislative purpose being the common welfare, not a financial transaction, we have developed a representative system meant to reflect and apply the common will, the will of all the people. If I mistake not, we shall find that England has developed the system best for government as a business; America, the best for government as a blessing.

De Lolme concludes with this sentence the remarkable book on "The Constitution of England" that he first published in 1771: "The philosopher, when he considers the constant fate of civil societies among men, and observes the numerous and powerful causes which seem, as it were, unavoidably to conduct them all to a state of political slavery, will take comfort in seeing that Liberty has at length disclosed her nature and genuine principles, and secured to herself an asylum, against despotism on one hand, and popular licentiousness on the other." In other words, Liberty had secured an asylum midway between absolutism and democracy. Under a government of classes, he thought he found the absence of political slavery. He wrote before the work of another Genevese, Rousseau, had ripened in the French Revolution. De Lolme's first edition was published five years prior to our Declaration of Independence, but the one before me (1784) revised though it was, betrays no doubt on his part that aristocracy — for such was the government of England — is the wisest of all forms of government. Yet already the Constitutions framed by American States had created not alone another asylum for Liberty, more secure than that of England, but also a workshop for Liberty, where it might create institutions for the prosperity and welfare of all the people.

It was singular that when England began her colonial system, in the sixteenth century, her monarchs, more nearly absolute than their predecessors for many generations, jealous of the royal prerogative, scornful of Parliament, should have either authorized or permitted colonies to make laws. The explanation is to be found in the necessities of the case. The early chartered companies were corporations for gain, not primarily public enterprises with philanthropic motive, whatever the pretext about spreading the Christian faith, converting Indians, or otherwise doing good. Manifestly they could not establish trading posts in barbarous lands without the right to exercise governmental authority there. The distance from home, the slowness and uncertainty of communication, compelled the granting of the power to meet local conditions on the spot. Furthermore, local self-government had been familiar to Englishmen from Saxon times. Our word "by-law," indeed, comes from "bye," the Saxon word for "town," — a by-law being the law of the town. Some measure of lawmaking, too, had been permitted to the older corporations as well as to the Guilds of the Middle Ages, voluntary associations for benevolence or to advance common trade interests, which organized themselves and made for their own government rules recognized to be binding if not repugnant to the common law. It was in the line of precedent, therefore, to put definite warrant to this effect in the colonial charters. Perhaps also there was some thought of adding thereby to the inducements that might attract colonists, for it was no easy matter to get men to leave home and take their families across the trackless ocean to an almost unknown wilderness peopled by savages.

VIRGINIA

Whatever the motive, powers such as those given to the Virginia Companies were common. They did not appear in the Virginia letters patent of April 10, 1606, but in the "Articles, Instructions, and Orders" of the November following, issued "according to the effect and true meaning of the same letters patents," which read as follows:

"The said President and Council of each of the said Colonies, and the more part of them, respectively, shall and may lawfully, from time to time, constitute, make, and ordain such Constitutions, Ordinances, and officers, for the better order, government and Peace of the people of their several Colonies, so always as the same Ordinances and Constitutions, do not touch any party in life or member; which Constitutions and Ordinances shall stand and continue in full force, until the same shall be otherwise altered or made void by us, our heirs, or successors, or our, or their Councel of Virginia, so always as the same alterations be such as may stand with and be in substance consonant unto the laws of England, or the equity thereof."

These were the letters patent and instructions given to two

groups of "knights, gentlemen, merchants, and other adventurers," who were to found colonies on the North American seaboard. One group, made up chiefly of Londoners, became known as the South Virginia, or London Company, the other as the North Virginia, or Plymouth Company. Their government was to be under the control of "the King's Councel of Virginia," with fifteen members specified by name or office. Each Company was besides to have its own "Councel" (virtually a Board of Directors), with thirteen members, named at the start by the "King's Councel," and afterward itself filling its vacancies. In 1609 the London Company secured a new charter. This put its government in the hands of a Council of fifty-two named members, with the important change that vacancies should be filled "out of the company of the said adventurers, by the voice of the greater part of the said company and adventurers, in their assembly for that purpose."

It has been declared that "this was the real beginning of American representative government," that the roots of the American House of Representatives started in this provision that members of the Council were to be elected by members of the corporation.[1] Yet surely it was nothing new at the beginning of the seventeenth century for English associations and corporations to elect their own officers. This Council was by specific charter provision to be resident in London. The colonists themselves were to have no share in the election unless they were members of the Company, what we should call stockholders; and after they had crossed the sea it was of course impracticable for them to attend stockholders' meetings. The provision is interesting and in its way important, but the roots of the American House of Representatives are to be found centuries behind it, and the actual beginning of American representative government was to take place when Americans first elected representatives.

The Council was empowered by the charter of 1609, "to make, ordain, and establish all manner of orders, laws, directions, instructions, forms, and ceremonies of government and magistracy, fit and necessary, for and concerning the government of the said Colony and Plantation; and the same at all times hereafter, to abrogate, revoke, or change, not only within the precincts of the said Colony, but also upon the seas in going and coming to and from the said Colony, as they, in their good discretion, shall think

[1] S. G. Fisher, *Evolution of the Constitution of the U.S.*, 118.

to be fittest for the good of the adventurers and inhabitants there."

It will be seen that the provision went into no detail as to how laws should be made. Later on, colonial charters or instructions to royal Governors would authorize lawmaking by assemblies. At first, the merchant adventurers had to work out a plan themselves. So we find that when Lord Delaware crossed the Atlantic in 1610 to take charge of the colony of Virginia, he took with him a code, compiled from the martial laws in force in the Low Countries. Sir Thomas Dale, appointed High Marshal of Virginia and arriving in 1611, confirmed this code and supplemented it with certain additions supposed to be specially applicable to the wants of a new country. It consisted of two parts, one military, the other civil. The extreme and pedantic minuteness of the first must have made it a dead letter in a rude and unsettled country. The civil code deserves more minute attention.[1] It is interesting both as an illustration of the legislative ideas of the day, and also as showing what manner of settlement some of the most energetic founders of America sought to establish.

It is scarcely too much to say, that in the hands of an unscrupulous or wrong-headed governor it would have given rise to a system of tyranny little more merciful than that which had goaded the Netherlands into revolt. For conformity to the Church of England to be required was in that day but natural, and in a newly settled community where none need go save of their own free choice it could not be regarded as a hardship. But even good churchmen might demur to a system which enforced attendance at daily worship by a penalty of six months in the galleys, and at Sunday service by a penalty of death. To blaspheme the name of God, to "speak against the known articles of the Christian Faith," or "to speak any word or do any act which may tend to the derision or despite of God's holy word," were all capital crimes. It was treason, punishable with death, not only to speak against the King's majesty, but even to calumniate the Virginia Company or any book published by its authority. A clause, perhaps more atrocious from its vagueness and even more opposed to all rational ideas of legislation, enacted that "no man shall give disgraceful words or commit any act to the disgrace of any person in this colony or any part thereof, upon pain of being tied head and feet together upon the ground

[1] J. A. Doyle, *English Colonies in America*, I, 135.

every night for the space of one month." Probably these laws applied only to the Company's servants and not to those independent planters who had settled at their own expense, or to the hired servants on their estates. Thus we may believe that this outrageous code had no operation over those who economically and socially formed the most important part of the colony, and to whom a large share of self-government was soon to be entrusted.

Glowing descriptions of the Bermudas incited the adventurers to seek still another charter, to include those islands within the scope of exploration, and such a charter was issued March 12, 1611–12. Far more important than the inclusion of the Bermudas turned out to be another change in the system of administration. It was now provided that once a week or oftener the "Treasurer and Company of adventurers and planters" should "hold and keep a Court and Assembly, for the better order and government of the said plantation, and such things as shall concern the same"; a quorum at such meetings to be five members of the Council (including the Treasurer or his deputy) and fifteen other members of the Company. Also there was to be held four times a year "one great, general, and solemn assembly, which our assemblies shall be stiled and called THE FOUR GREAT AND GENERAL COURTS OF THE COUNCIL AND COMPANY OF ADVENTURERS FOR VIRGENIA." These General Courts were to elect not only the members of the Council, but also the other officers of the Company; and were to "ordaine and make such laws and ordinances, for the good and welfare of the said plantation, as to them, from time to time, shall be thought requisite and meet: *so always as the same be not contrary to the laws and statutes of this our realm of England.*"

Sir Thomas Dale returned to England in 1616, leaving Sir George Yeardley in charge as Deputy Governor. A year later Yeardley too went home. Samuel Argall, a sea-captain and a masterful man, was put in charge and promptly got into trouble by domineering ways. The colonists complained and Yeardley was sent back to straighten out things. It is to be surmised that his previous experience stood the colony in good stead in the matter of pregnant instructions from the London Company, for when in 1619 he landed, on the 19th of April — fateful day for Americans, now celebrated in Massachusetts as Patriots' Day, though for other reasons — he brought with him the authority

for the first legislative assembly in the new world, after this
form:

"That the planters might have a hande in the governing of
themselves, it was graunted that a generall assemblie shoulde be
helde yearly once, whereat were to be present the governor and
counsell with two burgesses from each plantation, freely to be
elected by the inhabitants thereof, this assemblie to have power
to make and ordaine whatsoever lawes and orders should by
them be thought good and profitable for their subsistence."

From the official report by John Twine, clerk, it appears that
the first session "convented at James city in Virginia, July 30,
1619, consisting of the Governour, the Counsell of Estate and two
Burgesses elected out of eache Incorporation and Plantation, and
being dissolved the 4th of August next ensuing."

The church in what is now more commonly known as Jamestown was the place of assemblage. It is said that Governor
Yeardley had caused the building to be "kept passing sweet and
trimmed up with divers flowers." Twine's report reads: "The
most convenient place we could finde to sitt in was the Quire of
the Churche Where Sir George Yeardley, the Governour, being
sett down in his accustomed place, those of the Counsel of Estate
sate nexte him on both handes, excepte only the Secretary then
appointed Speaker, who sate right before him, John Twine,
clerke of the General assembly, being placed nexte to the
Speaker, and Thomas Pierse, the Sergeant, standing at the barre,
to be ready for any Service the Assembly should command him.
But forasmuche as men's affaires doe little prosper where God's
service is neglected, all the Burgesses tooke their places in the
Quire till a prayer was said by Mr. Bucke, the Minister, that it
would please God to guide and sanctifie all our proceedings to his
owne glory and the good of this Plantation."

The work of the session was classified with intelligent system.
The Speaker propounded "fower severall objects for the Assembly to consider on," viz. the charter; the instructions given by the
council in England to the Governors, to see what should be enacted into laws; "Thirdly, what lawes might issue out of the
private conceipte of any of the Burgesses, or any other of the
Colony"; and lastly, what petitions should be sent home to
England. These were taken up in order, and in due course the
records show a series of "lawes, suche as may issue out of every
man's private conceipte." For instance, there was one to require

returns of christenings, burials, and marriages; one about attendance at divine worship on the Sabbath; one about consent for the marriage of a maid or woman servant. No complete code was attempted, but apparently only such modification of common law as the peculiar needs of the colony suggested. Doyle thinks that "the new laws, though more lenient and moderate than the old code, showed the same tendency to regulate private life and to limit individual enterprise." [1] The suggestion implies the sort of criticism so commonly visited on the early legislation of the Puritan colonies at the north. Yet there was nothing novel to Englishmen in the scope of it or in what some would call its pettiness. Many instances of sumptuary legislation and interference with private affairs may be found in the records of the English Parliament before this time. Would it be expected that a score or more of representatives of a few hundreds of colonists should have occasion to concern themselves with great problems of statecraft? No, the business was small, the session was short, and altogether the episode has significance only because it was a beginning.

Two years later (July 24, 1621) the parent Company put the Virginia Assembly on a more definite footing, by an Ordinance, which, after setting forth the composition and duties of the "Councel of State," went on: "The other councel, more generally to be called by the governor, once yearly, and no oftener, but for very extraordinary and important occasions; shall consist, for the present, of the said Councel of State, and of two burgesses out of every town, hundred, or other particular plantation, to be respectively chosen by the inhabitants; Which councel shall be called THE GENERAL ASSEMBLY, wherein (as also in the Councel of State) all matters shall be decided, determined, and ordered, by the greater part of the voices then present; reserving to the Governor always a negative voice. And this General Assembly shall have free power to treat, consult, and conclude, as well of all emergent occasions concerning the public weal of the said colony, and every part thereof; as also to make, ordain and enact such general laws and orders, for the behoof of the said colony, and the good government thereof, as shall, from time to time, appear necessary or requisite." The commission to Sir Francis Wyatt, the first Governor under the new ordinance, greatly lessened the value of the legislative privilege by saying —

[1] J. A. Doyle, *English Colonies in America*, I, 160.

"No law to continue or be in force till ratified by a Quarter Court to be held in England, and returned under seal." It took experience to show the inconvenience of such provisions for the colonies, and to bring about the later practice of giving laws force until vetoed by the home authorities. The disregard of the instruction in Virginia was one of the reasons why the King in 1624 revoked the charter of the Company. This, however, does not appear to have interrupted the regularity of the meetings of the Assembly.

The most striking thing about the further legislative history of Virginia was the development of a high sense of the nature and value of representative institutions in spite of the fact that the colony was essentially and thoroughly aristocratic. It was a colony where the offices, the professions, and all occupations of dignity were kept in the control of a comparatively few families. Even the holders of small estates rarely achieved political preferment. The temper of the community is excellently shown by one of the objections embodied by the Assembly in its remonstrance to the King against restoring the charter to the London Company, in 1642. "We shall degenerate," it said, "from the condition of our birth, being naturalized under a *monarchial* government, and not a *popular and tumultuary* government, depending upon the greatest number of votes of persons of several humors and dispositions, as this of a company must be granted to be; from whose general quarter courts all laws binding the planters here, did and would issue."

Nevertheless, Virginia was not outranked by any other colony in early and emphatic and unmistakable declaration of the representative character of its Assembly. This came about in the session of 1658–59. Royalist to the core, the colonists had at first refused to accept Cromwell, had by act of Assembly denounced the traitorous proceedings against Charles I, had declared any person who justified his execution should be proceeded against as an accessory after the fact. Then, coerced by the commissioners of Parliament, sent over with a fleet, they had perforce yielded submission to the Roundheads. Thrown on their own resources to provide a new form of government, they decided to have the Assembly elect the Governor and other officers previously appointed by the Crown. In 1658 the first act of the Assembly was to choose Samuel Matthews for another term as Governor: and their second act empowered him to convene the

Assembly in the following January. The Governor and Council rashly assumed that the power to convene implied the power to dissolve, and on the 1st of April they withdrew from the Assembly (all sitting together in those days), and sent the Burgesses a formal notice of dissolution. The Burgesses promptly sent back word that this was not "presidentall, neither legal according to laws now in force, therefore we humbly desire a revocation of the said declaration." They voted unanimously that "if any member depart, he shall be censured as a person betraying the trust reposed in him by his country." The Governor and Council stood firm. Then the Burgesses asked that "the house remains undismissed, that a speedy period may be put to the public affairs." The Governor and Council seized at this offer of haste, called it a "promise of the speedy and happy conclusion," yielded the point for the time, and said they would "refer the dispute of the power of dissolving and the legality thereof to his highnesse the Lord Protector."

This, however, did not content the Burgesses. To vindicate their authority they appointed a committee to draw up a report, which presently was adopted. This report referred to the Burgesses as "the representatives of the people," and the Declaration the House thereupon drew up repeated this description twice. Upon this they based their claim to be dissolvable by no power yet extant in Virginia save their own. And, apparently to demonstrate their rights, they proceeded to declare all previous elections of officials null and void. Whereupon they gravely reelected "Coll. Samuel Matthews, Esq." as Governor!

Virginia has a double right to credit and honor for first establishing representative institutions in America if we may associate with her Bermuda, by reason of the charter of 1611–12. According to the History of the Bermudas attributed to Captain John Smith, as printed for the Hakluyt Society, the fifth Governor of the islands, Captain Nathaniel Butler, who arrived there October 20, 1619, brought with him instructions that in this particular are of especial interest because of the political doctrine set forth. "We require you," they said, "that as soon as you may after your arrival in the Islands, you do assemble your council and as many of the ablest and best understanding men in the Islands, both of the clergy and laity, as you and your council shall think fit, wherein we wish you to take too many rather than too few, both because every man will more willingly obey laws to

which he has yielded his consent; as likewise because you shall
better discover such things as have need of redress by many than
by few; and that in this assembly you deliberately consult and
advise of such laws and constitutions as shall be thought fit to be
made for the good of the plantation, and for maintenance of religion, justice, order, peace, and unity among them," etc.

The Governor opened the first meeting, August 1, 1620, with
an excellent speech, beginning: "Thanks be to God, that we are
thus met, to so good an end as the making and enacting of good
and wholesome laws; and I hope the blessed effect will manifest
that this course was inspired from Heaven into the hearts of the
undertakers in England, to propound and offer it unto us, for the
singular good and welfare of this plantation." Surely one man
had the prophetic vision to give him at least a glimpse of what
representative institutions would come to mean for those Englishmen who crossed the seas and for the generations to follow.

The Assembly was made up of the Governor, his Council, the
"baylies of the tribes," and two burgesses out of every tribe,
chosen by plurality vote. It had a Secretary to read the bills
proposed, and a Clerk to record those passed. Draw what inference you may from the fact that the Secretary was sworn to
secrecy, pledging himself to disclose nothing of the transactions
while the session lasted. By the speech of the Governor, reading
of the bills on each of three days was required. The Secretary
seems to have presided; at any rate all speeches were addressed
to him, and he put the question. On the last day the fifteen Acts
that had been passed were read in the Assembly (later in the
churches), and proclaimed to stand in force till England should
be heard from, for all laws were to be sent home to be approved.

PLYMOUTH

The North Virginia or Plymouth Company did nothing with
the privileges acquired by the letters patent of 1606. So in 1620
James turned the opportunity over to another body of specula-
tors, styled in their patent "The Grand Council of Plymouth for
Planting and Governing New England." Although their charter
was more liberal than that of 1606, they too made a failure of it,
from the business point of view. But from the religious, the
political, and the social point of view no corporation ever did
things more momentous, insignificant as they may have seemed
at the time. First, they permitted a small group of Brownists

(afterward to be known as Congregationalists) to settle at the place on Massachusetts Bay that was to become famous under the name of Plymouth. Next, they permitted another small group, under Captain John Endicott, to settle at what is now Salem. Thirdly, they consented that still another group, much larger, wealthier, and stronger, should apply directly to the Crown for a patent letting them settle also in Massachusetts Bay, with broader powers than the Company could convey under the charter of 1620. This third group got its patent and was incorporated March 4, 1629, as "The Governor and Company of the Massachusetts Bay in New England." It at once made an important settlement, soon centered at what became Boston. It swallowed the second group at the start and in 1691 was combined with the first group and other less numerous bodies of colonists, in the royal "Province of Massachusetts Bay in New England."

No attention need be given here to the 1620 charter, for it had no influence on our governmental institutions. No copy exists of the patent issued under it to the settlers at Plymouth and they seem not to have had that concern about charter provisions which was to be a feature of the history of their brethren in Boston. Before they began their settlement, they made a charter for themselves, the famous Pilgrim Compact, worth copying entire:

"In ye name of God, Amen. We whose names are underwritten, the loyall subjects of our dread soveraigne Lord, King James, by ye grace of God, of Great Britaine, France, and Ireland king, defender of ye faith, etc., haveing undertaken, for ye glorie of God, and advancement of ye Christian faith, and honour of our king and countrie, a voyage to plant ye first colonie in ye Northerne parts of Virginia, doe by these presents solemnly and mutually in ye presence of God, and one of another, covenant and combine ourselves togeather into a civill body politik, for our better ordering and preservation and furtherance of ye ends aforesaid; and by vertue hearof to enacte, constitute, and frame such just and equall lawes, ordinances, acts, constitutions, and offices, from time to time, as shall be thought most meete and convenient for ye generall good of ye Colonie, unto which we promise all due submission and obedience. In witnes whereof we have hereunder subscribed our names at Cap-Codd ye 11. of November, in ye year of ye raigne of our soveraigne lord, King

James, of England, France, and Ireland ye eighteenth, and of Scotland ye fiftie fourth. Ano: Dom. 1620."

This was not only the first self-constituted compact for government of which we have record: also it came nearer to pure democracy than anything that had gone before. For this reason, although the Plymouth Colony was small at the start and grew but little, although it lived only a trifle beyond the span of three-score and ten years, it shall be ever memorable for what it was. Still more memorable shall it be for the wondrous effect of its institutions on the life of the New World.

Governor Bradford follows the insertion of the Pilgrim Covenant in his history with this paragraph (p. 110):

"After this they chose, or rather confirmed, Mr. John Carver (a man godly and well approved amongst them) their Governour for that year. And after they had provided a place for their goods, or comone store (which were long in unlading for want of boats, foulnes of winter weather, and sicknes of diverce), and begune some small cottages for their habitation, as time would admitte, they mette and consulted of lawes and orders, both for their civill and military Governmente, as ye necessitie of their condition did require, still adding thereunto as urgent occasion in severall times, and as cases did require."

In other words, they gradually developed their frame of government as experience brought the need. That seems to us so natural a process as to make the statement of it a commonplace. It is the lesson of all political history. Yet among us there are still those who think frames of government and codes of law and systems of politics have been created *de novo*, or who dream that by the fiat of some reformer the course of our affairs could be changed, vastly for the better, in the twinkling of an eye. Instead let History show how

> "Step by step since time began
> We see the steady gain of man."

Plymouth took the next significant step in democracy with subdivision of the work of government in 1624. Bradford begins the story of that year with this paragraph (changed to modern spelling): "The time of new election of their officers for this year being come, and the number of their people increased, and their troubles and occasions therewith, the Governor desired them to change the persons, as well as renew the election; and also to add more Assistants to the Governor for help and counsel, and the better carrying on of affairs. Showing that it was necessary it should be so. If it was any honor or benefit, it was fit others should be made partakers of it; if it was a burden (as doubtless it was), it was but equal others should help to bear it; and that this was the end of annual elections. The issue was, that as before there was but one Assistant, they now chose five, giving the Governor a double voice; and afterwards they increased them to seven, which course hath continued to this day."

The word "Assistant," not now used as the substantive title of any political office, was common in the sixteenth century. Its early history shows the commercial origin of our forms of government, for at first it designated what we should call a "Director," although possibly of the class we speak of ironically as Directors who do not direct. It is probable, indeed, that in those days the Governors of trading corporations were the superiors, and their Assistants or Councilors were subordinates — a relation now reversed in most business corporations. With transition into political usage, the Governor remained and has continued to be the chief executive. Bradford's first Assistant undoubtedly did what his title would nowadays imply, that is, he assisted. When five and then seven Assistants were provided, they probably performed the office of what we should call a Council. By the record of a meeting of the Massachusetts Bay Company in London, April 30, 1629, it appears that thirteen persons were to be chosen to have "the sole managing and ordering of the government," and were to be entitled "The Governour and Councel," etc. At a meeting on the 20th of the following October a Governor and Deputy Governor were elected, and eighteen others "were chosen to be Assistants." The number was enlarged, but the nature of the service probably was expected to be the same as when the word "Councel" was used. There was in the early days of the colonies no separation of powers, and the judicial function fell for the most part to the Councilors or Assistants, according as they chanced to be designated in this or that colony. The result was that often they were referred to as "the Magistrates," and sometimes as "the Bench."

As far as we know, the Plymouth Colony was for some years not in law a body politic, and unless the missing patent of 1620 specified, its exercise of judicial and legislative powers was without authority save that of common consent. In 1629 it got a more satisfactory status by securing from the Grand Council of Plymouth a charter or patent. What the instrument should be called is of no great consequence, but lest it be thought that the words are being used inexactly, it may be well to point out that the original documents do not justify a common theory that a charter came from the Crown and a patent from a corporation. No precise differentiation of the terms appears.

Whatever the right name of the instrument, one clause in it read: "Also it shall be lawful and free for the said William Bradford and his associates his heirs and assigns at all times hereafter to incorporate by some usual or fit name and title, him or themselves of the people there inhabiting under him or them with liberty to them and their successors from time to time to frame, and make orders, ordinances and constitutions as well for the better government of their affairs here and the receiving or admitting any to his or their society as also for the better government of his or their people and affairs in New England or of his and their people at sea in going thither, or returning from thence, and the same to put in execution or cause to be put in execution by such officers and ministers as he and they shall authorize and depute: Provided that the said laws and orders be not repugnant to the laws of England, or the frame of government by the said president and councel hereafter to be established."

It is not known that before this the colonists at Plymouth had put in writing anything we should call laws.

MASSACHUSETTS BAY

In that same year, 1629, what was destined to be the larger and more important colony of Massachusetts Bay took shape. Its charter provided: "There shall or may be held and kept by the governor or deputy governor of the said Company, and seven or more of the said Assistants for the time being, upon every last Wednesday in Hilary, Easter, Trinity, and Michas terms respectively for ever, one great general and solemn assembly, which four general assemblies shall be styled and called the four great and general courts of the said company." At these "the Governor, or in his absence the Deputy Governor of the said Company for the time being, and such of the Assistants and Freemen of the said Company as shall be present, or the greater part of them so assembled, whereof the Governor or Deputy Governor and six of the Assistants at the least to be seven, shall have Full power and authority... to make Laws and Ordinances," etc.

In other words, there were to be held each year four of what we should call stockholders' meetings, with the Governor or his Deputy and at least six of the Directors present for a quorum. The language brings out clearly the fact that a "great and general court" was at the beginning nothing but a "general assembly." Indeed, "court" was then synonymous with "assembly." "Court" has since come in America to be connected most frequently in common thought with judicial proceedings only. Because of this the inference would be natural that the General Court got its name from its early function of being the court of last resort as well as the lawmaking body. Such an inference would be wholly wrong. By accident some colonies used the word "Court" for their legislatures, others used "Assembly," which in the end won far more general approval. Massachusetts, however, still calls her legislature the General Court, and when orators wish to be either particularly solemn or particularly ironical they preface its title with "great and," just as it was in the charter of 1629.

The charter was brought over here, or as we should say in the language of to-day, the headquarters or business office of the Company was transferred from London, first to Salem, then to Charlestown, and lastly to Boston. Governor John Winthrop, in the Arbella, reached Salem June 12, 1630. About July 1 the newcomers settled at Charlestown. Winthrop's diary has this brief entry relating to August 22: "Monday we kept a court." This appears to have been a Court of Assistants, that is, a directors' meeting, and it was followed by others of the same sort at frequent intervals, in 1632 ordered to be once a month. Although by the charter the General Courts were to make the laws, not much regard was paid to that, the Assistants mixing legislative with executive and judicial functions. For this there was excuse enough. Only seven or eight of the Assistants were on this side of the water, so that the peculiar provision about voting in a General Court required all or nearly all of them to be present and in accord, whereas seven made a quorum of a Court of Assistants and its decisions were by majority vote, with the result that it was much easier to handle everything possible in the Court of Assistants.

The first stockholders' meeting or General Court on this side of the water was held October 18 at Boston, the colonists on finding Charlestown unhealthy, as they thought, having crossed the Charles River to the three hills on which Boston grew. This meeting decided to put the government in the hands of the Governor and Assistants. The record says: "For the establishing of the government. It was propounded if it were not the best course that the freemen should have the power of choosing Assistants when there are to be chosen, and the Assistants from amongst themselves to choose a Governor and Deputy Governor, who with the Assistants should have the power of making laws and choosing officers to execute the same. This was fully assented unto by the general vote of the people, and erection of hands."

The colonists having shorn themselves thus of most of the occasion for frequent general assemblies, they proceeded to disregard the injunction of the charter that four mass meetings should be held each year. The next May they voted that "once in every year, at least, a General Court shall be holden," and in fact only once a year did they come together for some time. There is no reason to suppose there was anything contumacious in this disregard of the charter. They were engrossed with the huge labor of building homes, clearing farms, conquering the wilderness. It was easy and natural for them to turn the work of governing over to a few leading men chosen for that particular task.

Before long, however, they began to set bounds on the power they had delegated and then to take it back. Their declaration for a General Court at least once a year, made it clear that they had meant to have frequent chance to elect the Assistants. It begins, "For explanation of an order made at the last General Court": and says that at least once in every year "it shall be lawful for the commons to propound any person or persons whom they shall desire to be chosen Assistants, and if it be doubtful whether it be the greater part of the commons or not, it shall be put to the poll."

Governor Winthrop gave to this a far-reaching significance in connection with an important happening of the following winter. The occasion was the need of fortifying Newtown (now Cambridge) against the Indians, the intention being to make it the capital. The Court of Assistants assessed eight pounds on Watertown as its part of the cost, whereupon "the pastor and elder, etc. assembled the people, and delivered their opinions, that it was not safe to pay moneys after that sort, for fear of bringing themselves and posterity into bondage. Being come before the governor and council, after much debate, they acknowledged their fault, confessing freely, that they were in error, and made a retractation and submission under their hands, and were enjoined to read it in the assembly the next Lord's day. The ground of their error was, for that they took this government to be no other but as of a mayor and aldermen, who have not power to make laws or raise taxations without the people; but understanding that this government was rather in the nature of a parliament, and that no assistant could be chosen but by the freemen, who had power likewise to remove the assistants and put in others, and therefore at every general Court (which was to be held once every year) they had free liberty to consider and propound anything concerning the same, and to declare their grievances, without being subject to question, or, etc., they were fully satisfied; and so their submission was accepted, and their offence pardoned." [1]

Here was a rational, well-considered conception of the nature of delegated powers years ahead of their discussion by Hobbes and Locke. It explained government by elected representatives.

That the charter gave warrant for such government has been questioned by various writers. For example, James Savage in his note to the foregoing passage says: "In the objection of these gentlemen of Watertown, there was much force, for no power was by the charter granted to the governor and assistant to raise money by levy, assessment or taxation. Indeed, the same may be said of the right of making general orders or laws; for the directors of the company, or court of assistants, could only be executive." It is, indeed, true that the weight of judicial decisions within the last hundred years favors the doctrine that when a Constitution entrusts the lawmaking power to a given body, such as a State Legislature, the power cannot be delegated, or transferred by that body, as, for example, to the people. But is it not finical to apply this doctrine to the conditions of a new colony, operating under a commercial charter? That document said the general courts were "to make laws and ordinances for the good and welfare of the said company, and for the government and ordering of the said lands and plantations, and the people inhabiting and to inhabit the same, as to them from time

[1] John Winthrop, *Journal*, February 17, 1632.

to time shall be thought meet, so as such laws and ordinances be not contrary to or repugnant to the laws and statutes of this our realm of England." Were not Winthrop and his associates justified in assuming that this plenary power authorized them to impose such functions on the Assistants as they saw fit, provided they were not repugnant to English laws and statutes?

Winthrop's statement that "this government was rather in the nature of a parliament" than of a mayor and aldermen led H. L. Osgood, in his admirable work on "The American Colonies in the Seventeenth Century" to say (i, 156): "This is the earliest authoritative statement from a leader in the enterprise of a change which it was believed had been wrought by the transfer of government to Massachusetts. Expressed in modern scientific terms, it meant that by the change in the qualification of freemen the corporation had been raised from the domain of private law into that of public law. It was regarded as no longer in the proper sense of the word a corporation, but a commonwealth."

I submit this as the deduction of a competent scholar, and yet cannot myself read into the Watertown episode any such bearing. The increase in the membership of the corporation had, indeed, certain natural results in the way of governmental changes, but I find nothing to indicate that one of them was the early delegation of lawmaking to the Assistants. That can be sufficiently accounted for by motives of convenience, without supposing any change in the political nature of the colony had been then recognized. The transfer of the headquarters of the corporation from London to Boston did not in fact alter the terms of the charter one whit, and those who then drew or now draw any implication of essential change as a result of that transfer seem needlessly speculative.

At the General Court in the May after the Watertown affair, two steps were taken toward a more democratic form of government. "It was generally agreed upon, by erection of hands, that the Governor, Deputy Governor, and Assistants should be chosen by the whole Court of Governor, Deputy Governor, Assistants, and Freemen, and that the Governor shall always be chosen out of the Assistants." Evidently the indirect plan of electing the Governor, such as was to be used in the choice of United States Senators for a century and a quarter, proved itself unsatisfactory in the Massachusetts Bay Colony within two years.

More importance attaches to the other step. Winthrop's Journal has this entry for May 8, 1632: "A general court at Boston. Every town chose two men to be at the next court, to advise with the governor and assistants about the raising of a public stock, so as what they should agree upon should bind all, etc." It may fairly be presumed that this was the result of the protest of the Watertown men. To be sure, they had acknowledged their fault and made a "retractation and submission," but evidently the leaders of the colony thought it prudent, in matter of taxation at any rate, to make some concession. They were to be driven much farther. There is edification for us in the entry of Winthrop's Journal for April 1, 1634:

"Notice being sent out of the general court to be held the 14th day of the third month, called May, the freemen deputed two of each town to meet and consider of such matters as they were to take order in at the same general court; who, having met, desired a sight of the patent, and, conceiving thereby that all their laws should be made at the general court, repaired to the governor to advise with him about it, and about the abrogating of some orders formerly made, as for killing of swine in corn, etc. He told them, that, when the patent was granted, the number of freemen was supposed to be (as in like corporations) so few, as they might well join in making laws; but now they were grown to so great a body, as it was not possible for them to make or execute laws, but they must choose others for that purpose; and that howsoever it would be necessary hereafter to have a select company to intend that work, yet for the present they were not furnished with a sufficient number of men qualified for such a business, neither could the commonwealth bear the loss of time of so many as must intend it. Yet this they might do at present, viz., they might, at the general court, make an order, that, once in the year, a certain number should be appointed (upon summons from the governor) to revise all laws etc., and to reform what they found amiss therein; but not to make any new laws, but prefer their grievances to the court of assistants; and that no assessment should be laid upon the country without the consent of such a committee, nor any lands disposed of."

Savage's note to this reads: "No country on earth can afford the perfect history of any event more interesting to its own inhabitants than that which is here related. Winthrop seems to have spoken like an absolute sovereign, designing to grant a favor to his subjects, by admitting them to a representation at court. Such was the origin of most of the assemblies, in other nations, of delegates of the people, by whom some influence of the majority is imparted to the government.... The very humble powers, he proposed that the representative should receive from his constituent, it is hardly necessary to add, were immediately transcended: and the assembly, as it ought, was ever afterwards by itself thought competent to the enaction of any regulation for the public welfare."

This was what the General Court thereupon did: "It was further ordered, that it shall be lawful for the freemen of every plantation to choose two or three of each town, before every general court, to confer of and prepare such public business as by them shall be thought fit to consider of at the next general court; and that such persons as shall be hereafter so deputed by the freemen of [the] several plantations, to deal in their behalf in the public affairs of the commonwealth, shall have the full power and voice of the said freemen derived to them for the making and establishing of laws, granting of lands, etc., and to deal in all other affairs of the commonwealth, wherein the freemen have to do, the matter of election of magistrates and other officers only excepted, wherein every freeman is to give his own voice." [1]

Osgood says of this: "The merging of the corporation in the colony, taken in connection with the early dispersion of settlements and increase of the number of freemen, necessitated the development of the deputies, the element representing the localities in the general court. This was a change not contemplated in the charter, and it resulted in the creation of a colonial legislature by a process quite different from that followed in Virginia and the later proprietary provinces. It was created in Massachusetts not under authority of an instruction from the company or proprietor in England, but by the expansion of the general court of an open corporation when removed into the colony itself." [2]

This emphasis of the physical conditions, the dispersion of settlements and increase of the number of freemen, seems to me more justifiable than the theoretical argument referred to above, about a possible change in the very nature of the community produced by bringing over the charter. The vote of Plymouth to

---

[1] *Records of the Colony of the Mass. Bay in N.E.*, i, 118.
[2] *The American Colonies in the Seventeenth Century*, i, 155.

a like end, March 5, 1638, brings this out more clearly, showing
that convenience was the motive and excuse: "Whereas complaint was made that the freemen were put to many inconveniences and great expenses by their continual attendance at the
Courts It is therefore enacted by the Court for the ease of the
several Colonies and Towns within the Government That every
Town shall make choice of two of their freemen and the Town of
Plymouth for four to be Committees or Deputies to join with
the Bench to enact and make all such laws and ordinances as
shall be judged to be good and wholesome for the whole."

Neither Plymouth nor the Bay Colony at once abandoned
wholly the general assembly of all the freemen, each maintaining
it for the annual election. In 1636, through fear of Indian attacks, it was ordered in Massachusetts Bay that six outlying
towns, now known as Ipswich, Newbury, Salem, Saugus, Wey-
mouth, and Hingham, might for the next elections court appoint
any of their freemen to stay at home, for the safety of the town,
and that these might send their voices by proxy. An exciting
episode followed. Town and country were at odds. Governor
Vane and the Hutchinsonians were warmly supported by
Boston. Deputy-Governor John Winthrop, favored by the other
party, had to look for votes to the country towns, though himself a Boston man. The Court of Elections of May 17, 1637,
held at Newtown (now Cambridge) was a lively affair. Vane
wanted to read a petition preferred by the Boston men, but
Winthrop insisted the election should come off first. The controversy waxed warm and threatened to last all day. "Mr.
Wilson, the Minister, in his zeal gat up on the bough of a tree (it
was hot weather, and the election like that of Parliament men
for the Counties in England was carried on in the field) and there
made a Speech, advising the people to look to their Charter, and
to consider the present work of the day, which was designed for
the choosing of the Governor, Deputy Governor, and the rest of
the Assistants for the Governor of the Commonwealth. His
Speech was well received by the people, who presently called out
'election, election,' which turned the scale." [1]

Winthrop in his Journal tells us what then took place. Vane
and his friends would not proceed with the election, whereupon
Winthrop declared he and his followers would go on with it.
Vane yielded. Winthrop was chosen Governor, his supporters

[1] Hutchinson, *History of Massachusetts*, I, 62 note.

won the other places, and the other faction, Winthrop says with a touch of warrantable satisfaction, "were left quite out." A bit of human nature follows in the victor's description of the course followed by the vanquished.

"There was great danger of a tumult that day," he says, "for those of that side grew into fierce speeches, and some laid hands on others; but seeing themselves too weak, they grew quiet. They expected a great advantage that day, because the remote towns were allowed to come in by proxy; but it fell out, that there were enough beside. But if it had been otherwise, they must have put in their deputies, as other towns had done, for all matters beside elections. Boston, having deferred to choose deputies till the election was passed, went home that night, and the next morning they sent Mr. Vane, the late governour, and Mr. Coddington, and Mr. Hoffe, for their deputies; but the court, being grieved at it, found a means to send them home again, for that two of the freemen of Boston had not notice of the election. So they went all home, and the next morning they returned the same gentlemen again upon a new choice; and the court not finding how they could reject them, they were admitted."

On the 10th of October, 1638, it was proposed that each town might for every ten freemen choose one who should attend the Court of Election as a deputy with ten votes. This was to be considered at the next General Court, but no action appears to have been then taken.[1] It was in 1647, November 11, apparently, that provision for election by ballots cast in the place of residence, was first made; the Assistants were to be chosen by the use of white and black beans, the others by the use of papers, the votes to be taken by the deputies to the Court of Election.[2]

Plymouth, with fewer numbers and more compact territory, did not feel the need of voting by proxy for more than thirty years after its settlement. It was not till June 29, 1652, that it was "Ordered by the court That whereas in regard of age, disabillity of body, urgent occasions and other inconveniences that do accrue sundry of the freeman of this corporation shall have liberty to send his vote by proxy for the choice of Governor, Assistants, Commissioners, and Treasurer." [3]

The only break in the history of elected representatives in

[1] *Records of the Colony of the Mass. Bay in N.E.*, i, 33.   [2] *Ibid.*, ii, 220.
[3] *Plymouth Colony Records*, xi, 59.

Massachusetts came in what may be called the interregnum, between the years as a Company and those as a Province. In 1686 the Rose frigate arrived from England with a commission to Mr. Dudley, as President, and divers others, gentlemen of the Council, who took upon themselves the administration of government, the elected House being laid aside, but Hutchinson tells us, "the people, the time being short, felt little or no effect from the change." When Dudley's commission was laid before the General Court, the Court in its answer complained, "That the subjects are abridged of their liberty, as Englishmen, both in the matters of legislation and in laying of taxes; and indeed the whole unquestioned privilege of the subject transferred upon yourselves, there not being the least mention of an assembly in the commission, and therefore we think it highly concerns you to consider whether such a commission be safe for you or us." [1] Nothing came of the complaint, and when the provincial charter was granted, sittings of the Court went on as before.

At the time of the Revolution, the procedure in Massachusetts was typical of what took place in all the colonies. The Continental Congress, sitting in Philadelphia, by a resolve June 9, 1775, advised the Provincial Congress of Massachusetts (the continuation of the General Court), to summon an assembly, which should choose a Council, the two bodies to govern "until a governor of his Majesty's appointment will consent to govern the colony according to its charter" — a condition destined never to be met. In accordance with this advice, the "freeholders and other inhabitants" of each town, having an estate of freehold within the province of 40 s. per annum, or other estate to the value of £40 sterling (the previous qualification) were directed to send representatives to a great and general court. The third Provincial Congress was dissolved July 19, 1775, and forthwith the first House of Representatives of the State of Massachusetts Bay in New England began to function. Promptly it chose 28 Councilors from among its 203 Members, who represented 189 out of 268 towns. The Council and the House, "in General Court assembled," confirmed and established the proceedings of the three Provincial Congresses as lawful and valid. The charter was reënacted in slightly amended form, and served as a Constitution until 1780. During this period the Councilors, usually termed "The Honorable Board," combined executive and judicial functions with a share in lawmaking.

[1] Hutchinson, *History of Massachusetts*, 3rd ed., I, 397.

CHAPTER V

VARIED DEVELOPMENT

THE emigrants from Massachusetts Bay who settled in the towns of Windsor, Hartford, and Wethersfield, and in 1638 joined in a compact creating Connecticut, naturally began their lawmaking procedure at the point it had reached in Massachusetts when they took "the tedious and difficult journey" to their new homes. By their compact it was "ordered, sentenced, and decreed" that there should be held yearly "two general assemblies or courts." Notice the alternative in the name; "assembly" was beginning to have friends, even under the shadow of Massachusetts. As in the parent colony, one was to be the court of election, but as in the case of all election courts, the usual legislative work could be taken up when the election was out of the way. These two regular sessions were far from meeting the needs of even so little a colony. Many extra sessions were held. For instance, in 1645, there were seven in all. The compact provided that if the Governor and a majority of the magistrates neglected to issue a call for the regular sessions, or for a special session asked by a majority of the freemen, then the freemen petitioning could order the constables of the several towns to issue it, and might meet, organize, and proceed like any other General Court.

It is to be observed that these Fundamental Orders of Connecticut went into the matter of the Legislature with detail which astonishes when you reflect that its authors had the experience of less than ten years of general courts to guide them. In fact this, the first homemade frame of government in America, concerns itself almost wholly with this topic alone. The inference must be that in Massachusetts the problems of apportionment, nomination, election, summons, organization, and the like had already compelled consideration and probably aroused controversy, even though very little record thereof survives. At this early day we find conclusions that became guiding precedents with influence and effect reaching down to our own times.

In the same year New Haven likewise adopted a plan of government on much the same order, with a General Court consisting of the Governor, Deputy Governor, twelve Assistants, and two delegates from each town.

The Rhode Island towns came together under the patent in 1647. At a General Assembly in Portsmouth some towns were represented by delegates, and also the greater part of the freemen were present. Early in the meeting, provision was made against the withdrawal of so great a number as to defeat the object of the meeting by putting a stop to legislation. It was agreed that, the others departing, forty should be required to remain "and act as if the whole were present, and be of as full authority." Arnold sees in this compulsory quorum the germ of the representative system in Rhode Island. In the next year provision was made for a General Court of six men from each town. They soon came to be in fact the General Assembly, although if any others chose to remain, those whose help was desired were allowed so to do. In case any town refused to elect members, the Court, by this amendment, was required to choose for them. The General Court, as now constituted, was often called the Court of Commissioners, or the "Committee" — a name still preserved in styling the two branches of the Assembly, when united for the choice of officers, "the Grand Committee." [1]

If in electing representatives to the General Court, the New Englanders had adopted a device not warranted by any formal authorization from the home government, doubt as to the validity of the practice was removed by the charters of the last half of the century. First came that of Connecticut in 1662, saying that the "freemen of the said Company, or such of them.... who shall be from Time to Time thereunto elected or deputed, shall have a General meeting," etc. In the following year this language was followed in the Rhode Island charter, which read: "Such of the freemen.... who shall be, from time to time, thereunto elected or deputed, shall have a general meeting, or Assembly," etc. The Massachusetts charter of 1691 was more specific: "Each of the said Towns and Places being hereby empowered to Elect and Depute Two Persons and no more to serve for and represent them respectively in the said Great and General Court or Assembly."

Maryland, like Rhode Island, began with a composite lawmaking body, but took much longer to escape its inconven-

[1] S. G. Arnold, *History of Rhode Island*, I, 202, 219.

iences and evils. Maryland was one of what are styled the proprietary provinces, those founded under charters to proprietors,
rather than to corporations. The proprietary charters were
more explicit than those of the corporations in directing the assent of the colonists in the making of laws. The General Court,
the stockholders' meeting of a corporation, could be assumed to
protect the rights of all. Were unrestrained power to be given to
a proprietor, it might be grossly abused. Hence the difference in
the charters. In Maryland Lord Baltimore did not quickly
clarify the situation, probably because he was jealous of what he
thought his right to initiate legislation. In 1635, a year after the
settlement, all the freemen appear to have gathered in general
assembly for lawmaking. The Proprietor promptly annulled all
their proceedings. Three years later the colonists tried it again,
with the difference that this time those who could not come were
allowed to send proxies, a system that made trouble for a score
of years. The ground for it was the theory that the freemen were
supposed to sit in their own right, like Peers in the English House
of Lords, who could be represented by proxy.

At first the theory was carried to an extreme. In or about
1639, two burgesses being chosen for St. Mary's hundred, two
freemen presented themselves before the Assembly, and claimed
and were allowed seats on the ground that they had not voted
for the burgesses, and were therefore not represented. "By this
extraordinary application of the principle of minority representation, the votes of this minority of two would have counter-
balanced those of the whole body of electors, and had they been
there would have outnumbered them. It is probable that the ir-
rationality of the thing was at once seen, as the two do not appear in the records as voting on any question." [1] Another ridiculous conclusion drawn from the theory was that freemen represented by proxy were exempt from arrest for a reasonable time
after the dissolution of the Assembly as if they had occupied their
seats themselves. An evil early conspicuous was that proxies
could get into a few hands. When, in 1638, the set of laws sent
out by the Proprietor was rejected by a vote of 37 to 18, it appeared that a dozen of the minority votes were by proxies in the
possession of two men — the Governor and a Councilor. At
times the Governor and the Secretary, both of them appointed
by Lord Baltimore, held enough proxies to outvote all those

[1] W. H. Browne, *Maryland*, 46.

present. On the other hand in 1641 Giles Brent, with 75 proxies, formed a standing majority of the Assembly.[1]

In the attempt to avoid such difficulties the first step was an act providing for an Assembly to consist of the Governor and Secretary, those named by special writ, lords of manors, one or two burgesses from every hundred, and all freemen who had not consented to the foregoing election.

In the next Assembly the right of personal appearance was in at least one instance claimed and refused. Nevertheless, in 1642 the Governor reverted to the earlier system, and required the freemen of the colony to appear either by themselves or their deputies. Out of 106 persons who obeyed this summons, 72 availed themselves of the right to send. One of the first proceedings of the Assembly was to define the constitution of the legislature by limiting the popular representation to the elected deputies. Doyle says that with this reform the last trace of the earlier system disappears.[2] Osgood, however, finds that in the proclamation by which the assembly of April, 1650, was summoned, it was left to the option of the freemen to choose delegates or to attend personally or by proxy; all the hundreds showed their preference for the representative system by electing burgesses. Bishop says the proxy custom disappeared about 1658.[3]

If representative government begins when representatives are first elected, then C. Z. Lincoln is right in saying [4] that August 28, 1641, marks the beginning of representative government in what became New York. He tells us the masters and heads of families met that day at Fort Amsterdam, in response to a summons from Director Kieft, to consider what action ought to be taken toward the Indians in consequence of the murder of Claes Smits by one of their number. The Director wished severe measures for the punishment of the Indians, but evidently was unwilling to take the entire responsibility of any movement for this purpose. The population of Manhattan then was about 400. The assembly elected Twelve Select Men as their representatives to consider the matters submitted by the Director. These Twelve Men constituted the first representative body chosen in the colony. They used the opportunity presented by their elec-

---

[1] Edward Channing, *History of the U.S.*, I, 266–67.
[2] *English Colonies in America*, I, 290.
[3] *History of Election in the American Colonies*, 34.
[4] *Constitutional History of New York*, I, 414.

tion to try to reform some abuses that had become apparent in the administration of the colony, and to secure for the people some share in the government. The Director admitted the justice of some of the complaints presented and promised to reform the council, but he took occasion to say that the Twelve Men had in their memorial exceeded their authority, because they were chosen to consider only the question submitted relative to the course to be pursued toward the Indians.

It was an episode interesting enough in its way, but hardly to be called a beginning of representative government, for the quite sufficient reason that it produced no government. The Dutch rule of New Amsterdam was autocratic. In part this may account for a continuance of the same spirit after Charles II granted the place to his brother the Duke of York. The main reasons, however, were probably the autocratic powers given to James in his two charters, and the intolerant habit of James himself. With English control, naturally the colonists began to think of getting privileges such as other English subjects enjoyed. In 1669 eight of the towns petitioned Governor Lovelace for the fulfilment of a promise of such privileges, and foremost among them that of the annual election of deputies to join with the Governor and Council in the making of laws. The promise was denied. The next year inhabitants of various towns protested against a levy as illegal because it called for a grant without their consent. The protests were declared scandalous, seditious; and were ordered to be publicly burned. When Andros came, after the Dutch reoccupation had ended, he was at once met by a demand for an Assembly. Although for the moment he discouraged the movement, he seems to have written to James not unfavorably about it several times. James replied, April 6, 1675: "Touching General Assemblies which the people there seems desirous of in imitation of their neighbor Colonies, I think you have done well to discourage any motion of that kind," as not consistent with the form of government, nor necessary, since redress of grievances might be as easily obtained at the General Assizes, where the same persons were usually present as would be the Representatives if another Constitution were allowed.[1] In a letter without date, probably written later in the same year, James further said: "Unless you had offered what qualifications are usual and proper to such Assemblies, I cannot but suspect they

[1] *N.Y. Colonial Documents*, iii, 230.

would be of dangerous consequence, nothing being more known than the aptness of such bodies to assume to themselves many privileges which prove destructive to, or very oft disturb, the peace of the government wherein they are allowed." [1]

After Andros had been recalled, certain New York merchants, in 1681, began to refuse the payment of customs on an incoming cargo. Demands for an assembly gained fresh strength. Disorderly meetings followed, and disturbances were reported. The outcome was the yielding of the Duke, and a new Governor, Thomas Dongan, brought with him instructions to issue writs for the election of a General Assembly and to state in such writs that the Duke "had thought fit that there shall be a general assembly of the freeholders by the persons who they shall choose to represent them in order to consult with themselves and the said council what laws are fit and necessary to be made and established for the good weal and government of the said colony and its dependencies and of all the inhabitants thereof." Dongan reached New York in August, 1683, and called an assembly to meet October 17. Its most important act was the Charter of Liberties and Privileges, declaring that the "Supreme legislative authority under his Majesty and Royal Highnesse, James Duke of York, Albany, etc., shall forever be and reside in a Governor, Council and the people met a general assembly." James took umbrage at the high tone used and disallowed the Act. The royal commission of 1686 again vested full powers of legislation and taxation in the Governor and Council; and in 1688 New York was annexed to New England, in which the same despotic system was already in force, under Dudley, as we have seen. [2] With the accession of William and Mary a more liberal policy was adopted, and though New York continued without charter as a royal province, in 1689 Governor Sloughter was instructed to hold assemblies, "according to the usages of our other Plantations." Thenceforward there were regular sessions.

New Jersey and Elsewhere

"The Lords Proprietors of the Province of New Cæsarea, or New Jersey" made in 1664 a concession to and agreement with "all and every adventurers and all such as shall settle or plant there" that they should choose twelve "deputies or representa-

[1] *N.Y. Colonial Documents*, iii, 235.
[2] E. B. Greene, *The Provincial Governor*, 38.

tives" to join with the Governor and with the Council of from six to twelve members that he might appoint, in the making of laws, all together to be the General Assembly. In 1681 Samuel Jennings, Deputy Governor of West New Jersey, set forth an agreement with it that it should have a representative assembly, that he and his Council would make no laws without its consent, and—going far beyond most colonial authorities of the time— that the Governor of the Province should not suspend nor defer the signing of such laws as it might make — thus apparently disowning the right of veto. The Proprietors of East New Jersey, by the Fundamental Constitutions of 1683, likewise guaranteed representation to the people. The Great Council was to consist of the four and twenty proprietors or their proxies, and 72 (in time to become 144) to be chosen by the freemen. A two-thirds vote was necessary for the making of a law, and twelve of the proprietors (or proxies) must assent. For some time the government must have been precarious. We read that in 1698 one of Captain William Kidd's crew was arraigned for trial before the Supreme Court of the Colony at Monmouth. The accused admitted that he "had sailed" with Captain Kidd, but when the court proposed to punish him, the populace hastily assembled and locked up the Supreme Court, the Governor, and his Council, and kept them imprisoned for three days, by way of showing their contempt for the pretended authority of the East Jersey government.[1]

The eight proprietors of the province of Carolina entrusted the preparation of a frame of government for their dominions to one of their number, Ashley Cooper, afterward Earl of Shaftesbury, and he in turn had the help of John Locke, to whom the authorship is mainly credited. The "Fundamental Constitutions of Carolina," archaic, aristocratic, cumbersome, topheavy, were grotesquely unsuited to the primitive conditions of a feeble colony, never went into effect in full, and were abrogated by the proprietors in 1693. Before their existence was known in what became North Carolina, representatives of the people began making laws, and likewise the inhabitants of South Carolina worked out their own salvation through chosen delegates. So indistinct are the legislative doings of both these colonies in their early years that there is no important occasion to look to them for origins.

[1] *Annual Report of the American Historical Association for 1879*, i, 422.

The four towns that were the nucleus of New Hampshire long sent deputies to the General Court of Massachusetts. When it was decided that neither Massachusetts nor Robert Mason had the right to rule them, and instead New Hampshire was made a royal province, the commission to John Cutt (1679) made him President of a Council, six members of which were designated by name, who were to appoint three more. The President and Council were to summon a General Assembly of Deputies, and this Assembly was to make the laws, subject to the approval of the President and Council, and to the usual veto of the home government.

The charter to William Penn (1681), under which Pennsylvania was founded, gave him, his heirs, and successors, the power to make laws, "by and with the advice, consent, and approbation of the Freemen of the said county, or the greater part of them, or of their Delegates or Deputies." Penn at once provided for representative government by directing in his Charter of Liberties (1682) for the election by the freemen of a Provincial Council of seventy-two persons, who, among other things, were to agree "upon Bills to be passed into Laws." These bills were then to be presented to a General Assembly of not exceeding two hundred elected Representatives, which should give "their Affirmative or Negative." Doubtless by reason of the exigencies of the moment, that programme was not followed. The first Assembly was to consist of all the freemen, but they would not come together. They were too busy. So the counties chose only twelve men each — thirty-six from Pennsylvania and thirty-six from Delaware, asking Penn to accept this as a competent legislature.[1] Not all of them came, for only about forty persons met at Chester in December, 1682. These proceeded to act as a one-chambered legislature, adopting sixty-one bills before they adjourned.[2] In the following February Penn directed the freemen to choose seventy-two persons to serve as a Provincial Council and ordered that the freemen should assemble in a body with this Council to give assent to such laws as might be proposed, but before the Council came together he either suggested or accepted another arrangement, by which of the twelve persons chosen by each of the six counties, three should serve as Councilors and nine as members of the Assembly. After 1701 it was decided to constitute the Assembly of four members from each county.

[1] Isaac Sharpless, *A Quaker Experiment in Government*, 62, 72.
[2] Edward Channing, *History of the U.S.*, ii, 120.

In 1696 Markham's Frame of Government in effect recognized the right of initiative by the Assembly, by stipulating what was virtually an unqualified veto power for the Governor.

Delaware was an offshoot from Pennsylvania. Its three counties, known as "the territories," had been granted to Penn, and at first he tried to govern province and territories as one. The Delaware people, however, preferred to be by themselves and only on two occasions favored sending representatives to the legislature sitting at Philadelphia. In 1699 the county of New Castle would not elect assemblymen, in spite of the writ sent out by the Governor. In the next year the territories held an Assembly of their own. Penn, pacifist by nature and in principle, decided to let them have their own way and in 1701 gave a new charter in which it was permitted to the territories to legislate by themselves. From 1703 there were two Assemblies, one at Philadelphia, and one at New Castle, both under the proprietorship of Penn and with the same Governor.

The charter that George II issued for Georgia in 1732 was a corporation charter pure and simple. By this time England was chary of breeding any more of representative assemblies and nothing appears in the document intimating any measure of self-government for the indigent persons whom Oglethorpe might induce to settle beyond the Savannah. In 1750 matters were going so badly that the trustees proposed an annual assembly to which each town, village, or district of ten families or more should send one deputy, or two deputies if it had thirty families. Such an assembly was merely to present and debate grievances. It met once and once only. On the surrender of the charter, in 1752, a provincial government, with Governor and Council, came into being.

It will be seen that much the greater part of the American colonists had been experimenting in the development of representative institutions for a hundred years or thereabouts before they came to frame State Constitutions, and that the experience of Virginia and New England went back half a century farther. Taken by and large, only half the American acquaintance with representative government, measured in terms of time, has been acquired since the Revolutionary War. He sadly errs who presumes that our institutions were the work of Adams and Franklin, Hamilton and Madison and Jay. For the greater part they took that which they found, that which they inherited, that which they knew, and reshaped it to meet changed conditions.

Their writings might lead the reader to suppose that their intention was to profit abundantly by the experience of lands ancient and remote. The authors of "The Federalist" and their contemporaries showed remarkable unanimity in resorting chiefly to classic sources for illustrations and arguments. Somehow their homely surroundings seemed too commonplace for study, and they saw fit to argue instead from what happened in Greece or Rome two thousand years or so before. As a matter of fact all the vital features of our earlier Constitutions were but outgrowths of colonial experience. Yet in the discussions of the Revolutionary period next to nothing is to be found that throws useful light on the workings of representative government during the preceding century. "Publius" and all the rest ignored them. The authors of the Federalist drew somewhat from the experience of ten or a dozen years with State government. Sir H. S. Maine[1] has pointed out the remarkable scarcity of reference to England and explains that an appeal to British experience would have provoked only prejudice and repulsion. He argues that nevertheless "the Constitution of the United States is coloured throughout by ideas of British origin, and that it is in reality a version of the British Constitution, as it might have presented itself to an observer." With this I cannot agree. In some particulars it was a remote product of the British Constitution as transmitted through a century and a half of colonial modification. In other particulars, no less important and perhaps more numerous, it was an independent growth that responded to American needs.

Power of Assemblies Unlimited

From the first the belief was general among the American colonists that their assemblies were unlimited in lawmaking power, save in respect of matters covered by the laws of England. The reiterated declarations of this ripened in the conflict that led to independence. It would be superfluous to recite all of them. A few will show the temper of the people and the tenacity with which they held to this belief.

On the 16th of May, 1636, Plymouth ordered the following declaration, which has been called the first Declaration of Rights:

[1] *Popular Government*, 205 ff.

"We, the associates of New Plymouth, coming hither as free-born subjects of the State of England, and endowed with all and singular the privileges belonging to such, being assembled, do ordain that no act, imposition, law, or ordinance be made or imposed upon us at the present or to come, but such as shall be made and imposed by consent of the body of the associates, or their representatives legally assembled, which is according to the liberties of the state of England."

In 1640 a motion was made to Governor Winthrop and his Council of Massachusetts Bay, to send some person to England, to solicit favors and privileges of Parliament. They declined, observing that "if they should put themselves under the protection of Parliament, they should be subject to all such laws as might be imposed on them; in which, though their good might be intended, great injury might really be done them."

In June, 1661, the General Court of Massachusetts Bay adopted resolutions beginning: "We conceive the patent, under God, to be the first and main foundation of our civil polity, by a Governor and Company. The Governor, Deputy Governor, Assistants, and Representatives, have full power and authority, both legislative and executive, for the government of the people here, concerning both ecclesiastics and in civils, without appeals, excepting laws repugnant to the laws of England."

As to the force of acts of Parliament under the first charter of Massachusetts Bay, the House of Representatives in its "Answer" to Governor Hutchinson's speech to them of January 6, 1773, sought to confound him out of his own "History" of the colony:

"The first act of Parliament, made expressly to refer to the colonies, was after the restoration. In the reign of King Charles the II several such acts passed. And the same history informs us, there was a difficulty in conforming to them; and the reason of this difficulty is explained in a letter of the General Assembly to their agent, quoted in the following words; 'they apprehended them to be an invasion of the rights, liberties, and properties of the subjects of his Majesty, in the colony, they not being represented in Parliament, and according to the usual sayings of the learned in the law, the laws of England were bounded within the four seas, and did not reach America: However, as his Majesty had signified his pleasure, that those acts should be observed in the Massachusetts, they had made provision, by a law of the colony, that they should be strictly attended.' Which provision, by a law of their own, would have been superfluous, if they had admitted the supreme authority of Parliament. In short, by the same history it appears, that those acts of Parliament, as such, were disregarded; and the following reason is given for it: 'It seems to have been a general opinion, that acts of Parliament had no other force, than what they derived from acts made by the General Court, to establish and confirm them.'" [1]

The document gave instances in support of the contention that in the seventeenth century the Crown had viewed the colonies as outside the realm of England.

When in 1680 New Hampshire gained separate existence, as a royal province, the first of the code of laws framed by the assembly was that no act, imposition, law, or ordinance should be made or imposed upon them, but such as should be made by the assembly and approved by the President and Council. [2]

Of the attitude of Massachusetts when it became a Province, its House of Representatives told in the Answer to the Speech of Governor Hutchinson of January 6, 1773. "It appears by Mr. Neal's History of New England," they said, "that the agents, who had been employed by the colony to transact its affairs in England, at the time when the present charter was granted, among other reasons, gave the following for their acceptance of it, viz. 'The General Court has, with the King's approbation, as much power in New England as the King and Parliament have in England; they have all English privileges, and can be touched by no law, and by no tax but of their own making.' This is the earliest testimony that can be given of the sense our predecessors had of the supreme authority of Parliament, under the present charter. And it plainly shows, that they, who having been freely conversant with those who framed the charter, must have well understood the design and meaning of it, supposed that the terms in our charter, 'full power and authority,' intended and were considered as a sole and exclusive power, and that there was no 'reserve in the charter, to the authority of Parliament, to bind the colony' by any acts whatever." [3]

In 1692, it was declared by the General Court of Massachusetts, "that no aid, tax, assessment, loan or imposition whatever,

[1] *Massachusetts State Papers*, 360.

[2] Jeremy Belknap, *History of New Hampshire*, I, 146.

[3] *Massachusetts State Papers*, 361.

shall be laid, assessed, imposed or levied on any of his Majesty's subjects on any color or pretence whatever, but by the act and consent of the Governor, Council, and House of Representatives assembled; and that no freeman shall be taken, imprisoned or deprived of his freehold or liberty; nor be judged and condemned, but by the lawful judgment of his peers, or the law of his province." [1]

The famous Virginia Stamp Act resolutions, offered by Patrick Henry, May 29, 1765, declared that the colonists were entitled to all the franchises, privileges, and immunities of the people of Great Britain, and that among these was the right to be taxed only by themselves or persons chosen to represent them; and that they were "not bound to yield obedience to any law or ordinance whatever, designed to impose any taxation whatsoever upon them, other than the laws or ordinances of the general assembly."

To study the character of colonial lawmaking would take us too far afield. A sketch of the development of its processes would, however, be incomplete if it did not point out that from the beginning American Legislatures have been makers of law, not ratifiers, approvers, of law made by somebody else. This becomes of consequence because an eminent writer on political science, Woodrow Wilson, afterward President of the United States, held the contrary view. In his writings, as in his subsequent practice, Mr. Wilson continually emphasized the belief that the chief executive of a nation should be its chief lawmaker, the proper function of the legislature being to permit or deny, not to originate. Obsessed with this theory, he is open to the fair charge of having viewed the facts of history through colored spectacles. For instance, he said: "Parliament is still in all its larger aspects the grand assize of the nation, assembled not to originate business, but to apprise the government of what the nation wishes. Our own Legislatures were of the same character and origin. Their liberties and functions grew by similar processes, upon similar understandings, out of the precedents and practices of colonial laws and charters and the circumstances of the age and place." [2]

True as this may be of the English Parliament, it is not true of American Legislatures. I can find no scintilla of evidence that

[1] Bradford, *History of Massachusetts*, I, 269.
[2] *Constitutional Government in the U.S.*, 13.

they ever, from their first days, assembled not to originate business, but to apprise the Governors. The printed records of the colonial assemblies would furnish as many proofs to the contrary as they have pages, entries, lines. Where the Governors attempted to control initiation, they were met by stubborn resistance and in the end failed.

In the same book Mr. Wilson said: "It was as far as possible from the original purpose of representative assemblies that they should *conduct* government. Government was of course to be conducted by the immemorial executive agencies to which Englishmen had grown accustomed, and parliaments were to support those agencies and supply them with money, and to assent to such laws as might be necessary to strengthen the government or regulate the affairs of the country, public or private. Their function was common counsel; their standard of action the ancient understandings of a constitutional system — a system based on understandings, written or implicit in the experiences and principles of English life. They were expected to give their assent where those understandings were served, and to withhold it where they were disregarded. They were to voice the conscience of the nation in the presence of government and the exercise of authority. To recall the history is to recall the fundamental conception of the whole process, and to understand our own institutions as they cannot be understood in any other way." [1]

Again this is true of England, but the implication of the last sentence, that our legislative institutions were a continuance of English practice, may be squarely denied. Far nearer to accuracy is the statement of the case by Professor Osgood, made with especial reference to the proprietary provinces, but in substance equally true of the colonies: "The existence of a Parliament in England did not legally necessitate the existence of Assemblies in her colonies, though it greatly increased the difficulty of governing them without Assemblies. Moreover, their origin is not to be found in the natural or preëxistent rights of Englishmen. Like all their other organs of government the Legislatures of the provinces developed as the result of social and political causes operating upon the proprietors and in the provinces themselves." [2]

To understand our lawmaking institutions, it is not wise to

[1] *Constitutional Government in the U.S.*, 11, 12.
[2] H. L. Osgood, *The American Colonies in the Seventeenth Century*, ii, 74.

draw comparisons between them and those of the mother country, but it is wise to make contrasts. Our Legislatures were not assembled to grant money to the executive, except for his salary, and repeatedly great ingenuity was shown in depriving him even of his just dues in this regard. The Governors had their advisory Councils, but these were rarely law-approving bodies like the Great Council of the King in Norman times. As the upper branch of the Assembly or General Court, they were genuine lawmakers. Lord Baltimore's attempt to keep to himself the power of initiation in Maryland had to be abandoned. Penn gave his Assembly a free hand from the start. The General Courts of New England yielded deference to nobody save the clergy, and did their own conceiving, planning, thinking, deciding. In every essential particular the American lawmaking system always has been what it is to-day — the reverse of the English system. One has always worked from the bottom up, the other from the top down. England has been and is in essence aristocratic. America has been and is in tendency democratic, and for the most part in practice democratic.

Of late the power of the State Legislature and indeed its very nature have been brought in issue as a result of constitutional provisions exposing legislative acts to the Referendum. The Supreme Court of Ohio, supporting the constitutionality of the new system, held that "under the reserved power committed to the people of the States by the Federal Constitution, the people, by their State organic law, may create any agency as its lawmaking body." The Court declared it could not be maintained that the term "Legislature" necessarily implies a bicameral body, and quoted the definition of the New International Dictionary — "The body of persons in a state, or politically organized body of people, invested with power to make, alter, and repeal laws"; and that of the Century — "Any body of persons authorized to make laws or rules for the community represented by them." (The argument is that inasmuch as the electorate represents the community, the electorate can come under the Century definition.) [1] The decision in this case was sustained by the Supreme Court of the United States, [2] and this encouraged the Ohio court four years later, when the ratification of the Prohibition Amendment came up, to apply the principle thereto,

[1] State, ex rel. Davis, etc., *v.* Hildebrant, 94 Ohio St. 154 (1916).
[2] State of Ohio *v.* Hildebrant, 241 U.S. 565 (1916).

laying down the doctrine set forth in the syllabus of the former case, that "the term 'legislature' in Section 4, Article 1 of the United States Constitution comprehends the entire legislative power of the State." [1] The Federal Justices, however, drew a distinction, holding that though the referendum provision of the State Constitution when applied to a law redistricting the State with a view to representation in Congress was not unconstitutional, such legislative action is entirely different from the requirement as to a proposed amendment to the Constitution, no legislative action being authorized or required as to the expression of assent or dissent. The only question really for determination is: What did the framers of the Constitution mean in requiring ratification by "Legislatures"? The Court answered itself by saying that the term had no uncertain meaning when incorporated into the Constitution. "A Legislature was then the representative body which made the laws of the land." Citations of the use of the term in various parts of the Constitution showed that the framers clearly understood and carefully used it; and although the Court did not specify in so many words, the implication is that the term meant and still means what it was generally understood to mean when the early Constitutions were framed. So the decision of the Ohio court was reversed.[2]

The upshot of these and other cases on the subject seems to be that though a State may exercise its legislative power either through what is commonly understood to be a "Legislature" or by direct vote of the electorate, yet for certain purposes of the Federal Constitution the original significance of the term controls.

In English-speaking regions outside England and yet under her control, the power of legislating assemblies may be more restricted than with us. The curious may find a whole volume — "Are Legislatures Parliaments?" — devoted to answering the question of the title. The author, Fennings Taylor, writing with only Canadian conditions in mind, in 1879, argued the negative of the proposition. His logic may be summed up by a quotation from pages 15 and 16: "As a 'Legislature' is a body distinguished from and not identical with a 'Parliament,' so must it be ruled by the conditions of its creation, and not by the conditions under which the body from which it was distinguished was created. A 'Parliament' possesses hereditary as well as inherent rights . A

[1] Hawke v. Smith, 100 Ohio St. 385 (1919).   [2] Ibid., 253 U.S. 221.

Legislature possesses only charter rights; for it has no other or higher powers than those contained in the act under which it was established, and therefore its authority, like the authority of a municipality, is absolutely limited by the law." His conclusion is that the Canadian Legislatures do not inherently enjoy the "privileges, immunities, and powers" which from time immemorial have been held, exercised, and enjoyed by the Parliament of England.

CHAPTER VI

CONSTITUTIONS

"CONSTITUTION" is defined by Bouvier, in his Law Dictionary, as "the fundamental law of a State, directing the principles upon which the government is founded, and regulating the exercise of the sovereign powers, directing to what bodies or persons those powers shall be confided and the manner of their exercise."

This was not the original meaning of the word either in English or in its Latin form, "constitutio." In ancient Rome it meant a collection of laws or ordinances made by the Emperor. Brought to England with the Normans, it was at first applied only to important decrees or statutes, as, for example, the "Constitutions of Clarendon." Gradually it came to describe the fundamental law. For England it now denotes the mass of common law, statutes, decisions, and customs generally accepted as of fundamental importance, but that have never been brought together in one instrument. Common usage in the United States has restricted it to a document containing a body of organic laws, sometimes of late with the inclusion of provisions that are in essence statutes, but a document primarily devoted to the assertion of rights and to the frame of government.

Our Constitutions are developments of the charters under which colonies were established in America by trading companies, and those charters were developments from the charters of merchant guilds and other ancient corporations with origins that can be traced back to imperial Rome. The peculiar characteristic of American Constitutions is that they are charters not granted by external authority, but by the persons whom they control. Much enthusiasm has been used in contesting the honor due for the first exercise of that new idea. Because, after the first Assembly of Virginia, at Jamestown, in 1619, had begun lawmaking, the London Company two years later sent over Ordinances prescribing a structure of government, some would give the credit to Virginia. Others wax eloquent over the Pilgrim Compact, signed in the cabin of the Mayflower in 1620 by the forty-one men of the Plymouth colony, but inasmuch as this was an agreement to "frame such just and equal laws, ordinances,

acts, constitutions, and offices, from time to time, as shall be
thought most convenient for the general good of the colony," it
seems an exaggeration to call the instrument itself a Constitution.
Notice, too, that the word comes in between "acts" and "offices,"
with by no means the emphatic position that would have been
given to a designation of fundamental law. The agreement may
deserve the fame of the first self-created instrument of government, but even this would be contested, for Campbell has averred
that the "union of Utrecht," in 1579, was formed under a written Constitution pure and simple.[1] Motley, on the contrary, says
it was founded on a compact, not a Constitution.[2] It had but a
single object, defense against a foreign oppressor, and it secured
a confederation of sovereignties, not a representative republic.

The sons of Connecticut have shown more zeal than those of
any other State in demanding the honor for their ancestors, basing their argument on the instrument signed in 1639 by which
the towns of Windsor, Wethersfield, and Hartford became associated as a body politic. That instrument, however, though
entitled the "Fundamental Orders," lacked the characteristic
of superior authority, controlling the lawmaking body, that we
now deem essential to a Constitution, for it could be and was
changed like any other statute, by the General Court.[3] That the
right to frame it could be questioned was tacitly admitted by the
subsequent act of the colony in asking and getting a charter; and
examination of the instrument itself discloses nothing of genuine
importance not already embodied in either the charter or the
legislation of Massachusetts Bay. The men of Connecticut,
through the lack of a charter at the outset, won the credit of being the first by independent act to formulate on paper a democratic plan of government, but they adopted or adapted rather
than invented. The truth is that on the foundation of charters
to trading companies or provincial proprietors each of the colonies built frames of government which with their accompani-
ment of slowly developed customs were presently transformed
into State Constitutions. Besides grants of power these charters
embodied comprehensive regulations, often in some detail, meant
to anticipate as far as possible the governmental needs of colonies
several thousand miles away, which could get fresh instructions

[1] *Puritan in Holland, England, and America*, II, 417.
[2] *Rise of the Dutch Republic*, part 6, chap. 1.
[3] H. L. Osgood, *The American Colonies in the Seventeenth Century*, I, 311.

only after the lapse of months. That by themselves they were quite adequate as a basis for independent Constitutions would seem to be attested enough by the fact that one of the colonies, Connecticut, did not see fit to replace its charter with a Constitution for forty-two years after the Declaration of Independence, and another, Rhode Island, had as a State no organic law save its charter for sixty-six years.

Some writers would give a share, even the chief share, in the origin of Constitutions to church covenants — the agreements used in founding churches. These became familiar in Puritan times. In England their principle was transferred to the field of politics in the compacts formed to support Parliament in its struggle against the Crown. In America the same principle appeared conspicuously in the Puritan colonies, and the word "constitution" was used as at least akin to "covenant." For instance, Governor Winthrop of the Massachusetts Bay in his Journal (II, 239) spoke of "the covenant between God and man, in the moral law, and the politic covenants and constitutions, amongst men themselves." Farther on (II, 416), he said: "It is of the nature of every Society to be knit together by some Covenant, either express or implied." Traces of the same theory of relationship appear in some of the other colonies, but clearly it had no great influence, if any at all, in Virginia, Maryland, New Jersey, or New York. Taking the colonies as a whole, it could have had nothing like the effect of the factor common to them all — the charters. The most that can be said of church covenants is that they contributed to the belief in the need of formulating fundamental law and brought attention to the desirability of getting for it some sort of general acceptance either directly or indirectly expressed.

Other writers lay stress on the influence of the English precedents found in such famous documents as Magna Charta, the Provisions of Oxford, the Petition of Right, the Habeas Corpus Act, the Bill of Rights, the Act of Settlement. To be sure, these exemplified the value of quasi-constitutional documents in time of crisis, but they were largely reassertions of old rights that had been invaded, and in some part of rights springing from the Law of Nature. Doubtless they were the precedents for much of what is to be found in the Bills of Rights of our Constitutions, but no small part of this would have been enforced by the common law anyhow and the wise men who framed the Federal Constitution did not feel the inclusion of any of it to be necessary. In the matter of the Frames of Government, which have proved to be the far more important part of our constitution-making, these English precedents furnished practically nothing.

Whatever the influences, whether they were those of charters, of church covenants, or of English precedents, the colonists early began the codifying practice that was to end in general embodiment of the fundamental law in one comprehensive, systematic document, as contrasted with the fragmentary, disconnected, atomistic nature of the English Constitution. The first step in this direction appears to have been taken in Massachusetts. Winthrop entered in his Journal May 6, 1635: "The deputies having conceived great danger to our state, in regard that our magistrates, for want of positive laws, in many cases, might proceed according to their discretions, it was agreed that some men should be appointed to frame a body of grounds of laws, in resemblance to a Magna Charta, which, being allowed by some of the ministers, and the general court, should be received for fundamental laws." The work was delegated to the Governor, the Deputy Governor, Winthrop, and Dudley, but they did nothing. A year later another committee was appointed, this time with eight members, who were "entreated to make a draught of laws agreeable to the word of God, which may be the Fundamentals of this Commonwealth." One of this committee was the Reverend John Cotton. He made a code that somehow got into print, in London, at first anonymously. This long enjoyed undeserved credit as a genuine version of the early laws of Massachusetts. The real codification was the work of the Reverend Nathaniel Ward of Ipswich, who was named on still another committee, in March, 1637–38. According to Winthrop, the drafts made by Cotton and Ward were presented to the General Court in November of 1639, and turned over to yet another committee, which was to "peruse all those models which have been or shall be further presented to this Court," and draw them up into one body.

Winthrop explains the reasons for all this delay. One was the belief that the fittest laws would be those that grew out of the occasions, as the customs of England had grown. A greater reason was that the charter forbade laws repugnant to those of England. To get round this, it was shrewdly reasoned that customs having the force of laws might be gradually developed

without the risk òf running counter to the home government.
So for half a dozen years the anxieties of the people were skillfully evaded. At last the popular pressure became too strong and
the leaders yielded. In 1641 Ward's draft, with alterations by
the General Court, was adopted. It established one hundred
laws and was called the Body of Liberties.

This did not meet our modern idea of an enacted Constitution,
for it contained no frame of government. It was a code. Yet as
the provisions were deemed of fundamental importance, it was
what in England would be deemed constitutional. One American writer has been so laudatory as to declare it "a code of
fundamental principles which, taken as a whole, for wisdom,
equity, adaptation to the wants of their community, and a liberality of sentiment superior to the age in which it was written,
may fearlessly challenge comparison with any similar production,
from Magna Charta itself, to the latest Bill of Rights that has
been put forth in Europe or America." [1]

Connecticut established a code by vote in May, 1650. Many of
its sections are exactly the same as in the Massachusetts Body of
Liberties. New Haven published her code in 1656. It stated
that in preparing these Laws, Liberties, and Orders, "they have
made use of the Laws published by the Honourable Colony of
Massachusetts." Literal transcripts were made from the Body
of Liberties.

It may be that the news of what the Puritans of New England
were doing in the way of shaping their own destinies set the
Puritans of Old England to thinking. Certain it is that the happenings on this side of the water had no small influence on the
thought of the men left behind. There was constant correspondence, interchange of ideas, going and coming, printing of
pamphlets and books. Winthrop wrote in 1643: "It is well
proved and concluded by a late Judicious writer, in a book newly
come over, intituled an Answ: to Dr. Ferne, that though all
Laws, that are superstructive, may be altered by the representative body of the Commonwealth, yet they have not power to
alter any thing which is fundamental." [2] This notion of a fundamental law beyond the reach of the ordinary legislating body
accorded with the Puritan impulse to look to the Scriptures for
basic principles. So it fell on fertile ground and grew.

[1] Francis Calley Gray, *Massachusetts Historical Collections*, VIII, 3rd Series, 191.
[2] *Life and Letters of John Winthrop*, II, 438.

Radical change of government was not at first a part of the revolutionary program. Led by a moderate party, Parliament sought only religious reformation and some political guarantees. As the war progressed, an extreme faction, the Independents, with the support of Cromwell's soldiers, gained the upper hand, forced the execution of the King, and established a republic. A written Constitution was a natural consequence. Under the name of "Agreement of the People" there were three drafts: first, the original sketch proposed by John Lilburne and part of the army in 1647; secondly, a more detailed scheme drawn up by the leaders of the army and presented by them to Parliament in January, 1649; and thirdly, one by Lilburne and the Levelers put forward in the spring of 1649 as the manifesto of those extremists for whom the second scheme was too moderate. The principles propounded have now in large part been accepted and established in republican forms of government. Among them were: the sovereignty of the people; supreme power vested in a single representative assembly; the executive entrusted by the assembly to a council of state, elected for the term of one legislature; biennial parliaments; equitable and proportionate distribution of seats; extension of the right of voting and election to all citizens of full age, dwelling in the electoral districts, and neither hired servants nor in receipt of relief; toleration of all forms of Christianity; suppression of State interference in church government; limitation of the powers of the representative assembly, by fundamental laws embodied in the Constitution, especially with regard to the civil liberties guaranteed to citizens.

No attempt was made to put into execution any one of the three drafts of the Agreement of the People, but the discussion they aroused made familiar the idea of a written Constitution. The need for it was further and emphatically developed in 1653 by the fatuous conduct of the body that met July 4 upon the call of Cromwell, the body that became famous under the name given to it by reason of the presence in its membership of Praise-God Barebones. Although composed of men "faithful, fearing God, and hating covetousness," whose names were selected by the Council of the Army from lists furnished by the Congregational churches, they were so contentious and unreasonable that the question of controlling the Executive was replaced in importance by that of checking the despotism of a single House.

In December a majority of the members of the Barebones Parliament resigned in disgust, whereupon Lambert produced an "Instrument of Government" that the Army Council had worked out as a paper Constitution. Cromwell promptly accepted it and took oath to give it support. He seems to have been convinced of its need and for a time gave it what appears to have been sincere approval. "In every Government," he said, speaking in September of 1654, "there must be somewhat Fundamental, Somewhat like a Magna Charta, which should be standing, be unalterable.... That Parliaments should not make themselves perpetual is a Fundamental. Of what assurance is a Law to prevent so great an evil, if it lie in the same Legislature to unlaw it again? Is such a law likely to be lasting? It will be a rope of sand; it will give no security; for the same men may unbuild what they have built." [1]

Even while he was speaking, the trouble over what such a law should be was kindling anew. The first Parliament under the new Constitution had assembled a few days before. At once it began to consider the Instrument of Government with an eye to radical change or replacement by something else. Over this it fought for five months and then Cromwell dissolved the House in deepest anger. With the Instrument still in force, at least nominally, another Parliament was elected in accordance with it in September of 1656. That body drew, and in March of 1657 presented to Cromwell, what was in effect another Constitution, although it was called the "Humble Petition and Advice." It would have made Cromwell the King, but he refused the title and that was changed to Protector, whereupon he accepted the instrument. The chief change it made was the creation of a second House. A Parliament chosen under it met January 20, 1658, only to make itself obnoxious even quicker than its predecessors, with the result that it was wrathfully dissolved a fortnight later.

After Cromwell's death in the following September, his son Richard, succeeding him as Protector, carried on the government ostensibly along the lines of the Humble Petition and Advice, though when he called a Parliament to meet in January of 1659, he reverted to the old electoral system. In this Parliament the form of government and other constitutional questions were still to the fore. With its dissolution April 22 Richard dropped out

[1] Carlyle, *Letters and Speeches of Oliver Cromwell*, part VII; speech III.

and the Constitution disappeared. Anarchy and the sword prevailed till the Restoration.[1]

Our forefathers on this side the water, some of whom strongly sympathized with the English sectarians and others of whom were deeply concerned about their doings, must have been well informed about these pioneer attempts to frame Constitutions.

The States Organize

Governmental changes wrought by the Puritan Revolution did not survive in form, but the turmoils of the period brought to the basic questions of government the study of deep thinkers who illuminated them in writings that instructed all the English-speaking world. Furthermore, on this side of the water men became accustomed to definite, compact formulation of fundamental law in the shape of royal charters and proprietary patents, "Frames of Government" such as those devised by William Penn for his colony, "Fundamental Constitutions" such as those drafted by John Locke for the Carolinas, "Charters of Liberties," and "Concessions." Nevertheless, when in 1775 royal Governors had run away or been expelled and the colonies were confronted by the need of organization, strange to say the very notion of constitutional government seems to have been novel to most Americans. John Adams in his "Autobiography" (Works, iii et seq.) throws light on this and tells what took place.

On the 2d of June, 1775, the President laid before Congress a letter from "the Provincial Convention of Massachusetts Bay," setting forth the difficulties under which they labored for want of a regular form of government, and asking the advice of Congress. Adams had discussed the matter with many of his Massachusetts friends and had given to it much thought. So he was ready to suggest to Congress what its advice should be. "We should probably," he said, "after the example of the Greeks, the Dutch, and the Swiss, form a confederacy of States, each of which must have a separate government. I had looked into the ancient and modern confederacies for examples, but they all appeared to me to have been huddled up in a hurry, by a few chiefs. But we had a people of more intelligence, curiosity, and enterprise, who must be all consulted, and we must realize the theories of the wisest writers, and invite the people to erect the whole building with their own hands, upon the broadest foundation. This could be

[1] *Cambridge Modern History*, iv, chap. xv *passim*.

done only by conventions of representatives chosen by the people in the several colonies, in the most exact proportions. It was my opinion that Congress ought now to recommend to the people of every Colony to call such conventions immediately, and set up governments of their own, under their own authority, for the people were the source of all authority and original of all power. These were new, strange, and terrible doctrines to the greatest part of the members, but not a very small number heard them with apparent pleasure."

A week later Congress passed a resolution advising Massachusetts to elect Representatives and Counselors as usual; "and that such assembly or Council exercise the powers of government until a Governor of His Majesty's appointment will consent to govern the Colony according to its charter."

Although this was no great step, Adams thought it a gain, "for it was a precedent of advice to the separate States to institute governments." He kept on discussing the all-important matter. "Mr. Rutledge," he says, "asked me my opinion of a proper form of government for a State. I answered him that any form that our people would consent to institute, would be better than none, even if they placed all power in a House of Representatives, and they should appoint Governors and judges; but I hoped they would be wiser, and preserve the English Constitution in its spirit and substance, as far as the circumstances of this country required or would admit. That no hereditary powers ever had existed in America, nor would they, or ought they to be introduced or proposed; but that I hoped the three branches of a legislature would be preserved, an executive, independent of the Senate or Council, and the House, and above all things, the independence of the judges. Mr. Sullivan was fully agreed with me in the necessity of instituting governments, and he seconded me very handsomely in supporting the argument in Congress. Mr. Samuel Adams was with us in the opinion of the necessity, and was industrious in conversation with the members out of doors, but he very rarely spoke much in Congress, and he was perfectly unsettled in any plan to be recommended to a State, always inclining to the most democratical forms, and even to a single sovereign assembly, until his constituents afterwards in Boston compelled him to vote for three branches. Mr. Cushing was also for one sovereign assembly."

In October New Hampshire urgently asked Congress for advice in the matter. Adams says: "I embraced with joy the opportunity of haranguing on the subject at large, and of urging Congress to resolve on a general recommendation to all the States to call conventions and institute regular governments.... Although the opposition was still inveterate, many members of Congress began to hear me with more patience, and some began to ask me civil questions. 'How can the people institute governments?' My answer was, 'By conventions of representatives, freely, fairly, and proportionably chosen.' 'When the convention has fabricated a government, or a Constitution rather, how do we know the people will submit to it?' 'If there is any doubt of that, the convention may send out their project of a Constitution, to the people in their several towns, counties, or districts, and the people may make the acceptance of it their own act.' 'But the people know nothing about Constitutions.' 'I believe you are much mistaken in that supposition; if you are not, they will not oppose a plan prepared by their own chosen friends; but I believe that in every considerable portion of the people, there will be found some men, who will understand the subject as well as their representatives, and these will assist in enlightening the rest.' 'But what plan of government would you advise?' 'A plan as nearly resembling the government under which we were born, and have lived, as the circumstances of the country will admit. Kings we never had among us. Nobles we never had. Nothing hereditary ever existed in this country; nor will the country require or admit of any such thing. But Governors and Councils we have always had, as well as Representatives.'"

From time to time Congress continued the discussion. At last a committee was appointed, but they could not be brought to agree and report until November 3, when after another long deliberation and debate Congress decided to advise New Hampshire "to call a full and free representation of the people," to "establish such a form of government, as in their judgment will best produce the happiness of the people, and most effectually secure peace and good order in the Province, during the present dispute between Great Britain and the Colonies."

"By this time," says Adams, "I mortally hated the words, 'Province,' 'Colonies,' and 'Mother Country,' and strove to get them out of the report. The last was indeed left out, but the other two were retained even by this committee, who were all as high Americans as any in the house, unless Mr. Gadsden should be excepted. Nevertheless I thought this resolution a triumph, and a most important point gained."

Next came similar advice to South Carolina, Adams still working in vain to get out the word "Colonies" and substitute "States," but, he says, "the child was not yet weaned." He dared not move the preparation of a plan, for he knew if the motion were adopted, the task would be of long duration, and to get rid of it would be extremely difficult. "And I knew that every one of my friends, and all those who were most zealous for assuming governments, had at that time no idea of any other government but a contemptible legislature in one assembly, with committees for executive magistrates and judges."

All this was leading toward independence, but months were yet to pass before the fruit ripened. In May of 1776 came what Adams considered "an epocha, a decisive event," in the shape of this resolution:

"Resolved, That it be recommended to the respective assemblies and conventions of the United Colonies, where no government sufficient to the exigencies of their affairs has been hitherto established, to adopt such government as shall, in the opinion of the representatives of the people, best conduce to the happiness and safety of their constituents in particular, and America in general."

On the 15th, this with a preamble was adopted. It meant independence. It led to the famous Declaration.

CONVENTIONS

John Adams undoubtedly deserves the chief credit for establishing conventions as the customary device for framing Constitutions in America, but also undoubtedly he drew the idea and also the use of the name from his knowledge of history. We have seen that the Barebones "Parliament," which in 1653 framed the only written Constitution ever adopted in England, was in fact a "Convention." There the name was afterward applied particularly to Parliaments that assembled without the formal summons of the Sovereign, owing to the abeyance of the Crown, as it was termed. Such were those that in 1660 restored Chares II to the throne and in 1689 declared the throne to have been abdicated by James II; and of essentially the same nature was the first revolutionary Convention in America, that to which forty-six Massachusetts towns sent delegates in 1689 when Sir Ed-

mund Andros was charged with tyranny, this body becoming the
de facto government for eight months. It was to be imitated
three quarters of a century later when various revolutionary
bodies were to prepare for and then conduct the Revolutionary
War. Without much precision these were called either "Congresses" or "Conventions," though in general "Congress" came
to signify representation of sovereignties, as the term has been
used in Europe since the seventeenth century for describing the
important conferences of ambassadors of various nations; and
"Conventions" came to be restricted for the most part to meetings of delegates of political sub-divisions.

In the Revolutionary period the functions of all these bodies
were chiefly executive or administrative. Incidentally and almost accidentally some of them added the function of shaping
fundamental law. Not for some time was it commonly agreed
that Constitutions should be written not merely by representatives of the people, but by representatives chosen for that particular purpose. This idea is believed to have been first advanced
by Sir Harry Vane, in a letter to Cromwell in 1656, in which he
recommended that a convention "chosen for that purpose by the
free consent of the whole body" be called to draw up a Constitution for England. Very likely Adams remembered this when he
was goading the American Congress. The first colony to act,
New Hampshire, complied with his view. The members of her
Fifth Provincial Congress, adopting a Constitution January 5,
1776, . et forth in its preamble that they had been "chosen and
appointed by the free suffrages of the people," and had been authorized and empowered "in particular to establish some form of
government." The Congress of South Carolina acting next, declaring itself "a full and free rep.esentation of the people" and
"vested with powers competent for the purpose," adopted a Constitution that turned the Congress into a General Assembly and
in other respects established an adequate government.

In Virginia, third of the colonies to act, the members of the
legislating body did not deem it necessary to justify themselves
beyond saying that they were "the delegates and representatives
of the good state of Virginia." They were in fact styled a "Convention," but clearly they were not a "Constitutional Convention" as we now understand that term, for in accordance with
the vote of the previous Convention they had been chosen in
April to serve for a year, as an executive body to carry on the

war, if Thomas Jefferson's view was correct. Jefferson denied that they had any right to establish a permanent Constitution. He held that the electors, "not thinking of independence and a permanent Republic," could not have meant to grant more authorities than those of an ordinary Legislature. The leading members, however, according to Edmund Randolph,[1] "saw no distinction between the conceded powers to declare independence, and its necessary consequence, the fencing of society by the initiation of government." Jefferson's demur did not keep him from taking a hand in the matter, for he sent down from Philadelphia a draft of a Constitution he had himself written. It came too late for any effect on the Frame of Government, for the tired delegates were unwilling to reopen the discussion, but his Preamble was used, much in the form in which it later appeared in the immortal "Declaration of Independence." In passing it may be noticed that precedent for its use in a Constitution may be found in the "Whereas" introducing the Constitution of South Carolina, in which the grievances of the colonies were set forth three months before the Virginia delegates concluded their labors.

Also in New Jersey the governing body of the time, there called the Provincial Congress, framed a Constitution without having been specially chosen for such a purpose alone. Organized June 10, 1776, as directed by a previous Congress, it received many petitions to frame a government, and on the 21st voted 54 to 3 to follow the recommendation of the Continental Congress, the draft of its committee being confirmed July 2, three days after final action in Virginia.

Pennsylvania, starting next, took the view since predominant, that Constitutions should be framed by bodies authorized thereto. Thomas Paine has told in "The Rights of Man" (part 2, chap. 4,) how his State proceeded. The movement began with a proposal for a conference sent by the committee of Philadelphia to the committees of the other counties. Those who assembled, not having been elected expressly for the purpose of framing a Constitution, felt they could do no more than confer on the matter and advise procedure. On their recommendation each county elected six delegates to a Convention, which framed the document. "They next ordered it to be published, not as a thing established, but for the consideration of the whole people, their

[1] *MS. History of Virginia*, 63.

approbation or rejection." Upon reassembling, "as the general opinion in approbation of it was then known, the Constitution was signed, sealed, and proclaimed *on the authority of the people*," although there had been no popular vote to that effect.

Meanwhile Delaware had captured the honor of being the first to put into effect a Constitution made by representatives chosen for that purpose, the work of her Convention having been proclaimed September 21, 1776, a week before that of Pennsylvania.

Naturally the earliest products of inexperienced constitution-makers were imperfect. Although each group after the first could profit somewhat by the work of its predecessors, not one of the early drafts has stood the test of time to the point of escaping what we somewhat inexactly speak of as "revision." It is needless here to tell the story of each. That can be found in Professor Dealey's "Growth of American State Constitutions." Let it suffice here to go into some detail with the oldest Constitution that survived to our day without complete revision, the Constitution that has most influenced American forms of government — that of Massachusetts.

Although the first to ask how, Massachusetts was the last to perfect a Constitution — barring Connecticut and Rhode Island, which lived under their colonial charters for many years after the Union was formed. Demand for the protection of a "compact" of government had begun months before the Declaration of Independence, in the western part of the province, among the Berkshire Hills. The interesting and little-known story of the Berkshire Constitutionalists may be found in J. E. A. Smith's "History of Pittsfield," vol. i, chaps. 18–20. They were led by the Reverend Thomas Smith, who through four years fought for his particular view of what should be done, visiting every town, persuading and convincing. In December of 1775 Pittsfield adopted a memorial calling for action, but not until September of 1776 did the General Court take the first step, by asking the towns to vote whether they would consent that "the present House of Representatives and the Council, in one Body, with the House and by equal Vote," should agree on and enact "a Constitution and Form of Government." The returns extant from 98 towns show that 72 approved and 26 disapproved the proposal. Yet the opinion was widespread that the work ought to originate with the people. Indeed some went to the point of declaring that the General Court itself ought not to do the work even though authorized. Stoughton, Boston, Attleborough, Concord, Lexington, and Norton, in the order named, declared their views to that effect in October. As far as the records disclose, what honor may attach to priority should go to Stoughton, with its declaration that it was "inadvisable and irrational" to empower the Council and House of Representatives to frame a Constitution. Stoughton also seems to have led with a proposal for the holding of county conventions to be followed by a State Convention or Congress.

Nevertheless the House recommended to the people that they choose their Deputies to the next General Court with the power to adopt a form of government for the State. The Court elected with this understanding gave much time in 1777 to the effort to make a Constitution. The result was submitted to the town meetings in March of 1778. Only 12,000 persons, out of the whole State, answered in any way, and 120 towns neglected to express any opinion at all. Five sixths of those who voted were opposed, under the lead of a unanimous sentiment in Boston. Just why the objection was so general, it is not easy now to learn. It is known, however, that among the reasons were the imperfections of the instrument itself, the lack of a bill of rights or definition of powers, the confusion of the legislative, executive, and judicial departments, and, perhaps most influential of all, the fact that the document had not been the work of a Convention called for that specific purpose. The last reason led the General Court in February, 1779, to ask the people whether they would choose, at this time, to have any new form of government at all; and in case they did, whether they would empower their representatives to summon an assembly for the sole purpose of preparing such a form. Although nearly a third of the towns neglected to give any answer, a majority of the voters in the rest favored, and so a call for a Convention was at once issued.

It met in September and proceeded by appointing a committee of thirty to prepare a declaration of rights and the form of a Constitution. This committee appointed a sub-committee, consisting of James Bowdoin, Samuel Adams, and John Adams, which committee in turn committed the task to John Adams, and accepted his draft, with one or two trifling erasures. It was then reported to the grand committee, which made some alterations. The Convention itself made a few others.

Thirty years later, in a letter to Benjamin Rush, John Adams described his part in the work. "I found," he said, "such a chaos of absurd sentiments concerning government, that I was obliged daily, before that great assembly [of near four hundred members], and afterwards in the Grand Committee, to propose plans, and advocate doctrines, which were extremely unpopular with the greater number. Lieutenant-Governor Cushing was avowedly for a single assembly, like Pennsylvania. Samuel Adams was of the same mind. Mr. Hancock kept aloof, in order to be Governor. In short, I had at first no support but from the Essex junto, who had adopted my ideas in the letter to Mr. Wythe. They supported me timorously, and at last would not go with me to so high a mark as I aimed at, which was a complete negative in the Governor upon all laws. They made me, however, draw up the Constitution, and it was finally adopted, with some amendments very much for the worse. The bold, decided, and determined part I took in this assembly in favor of good government, acquired me the reputation of a man of high principles and strong notions in government, scarcely compatible with republicanism. A foundation was here laid of much jealousy and unpopularity among the democratical people in this State."

By the resolve calling this Convention, whatever Constitution it might submit was to be laid before a regular meeting "of the male inhabitants of each town and plantation in order to its being duly considered and approved or disapproved." (The omission of the property or religious qualifications is significant.) Two years before, the Constitution framed by the Legislature was submitted to the town meetings for their "approbation or disapprobation." Fifteen years later, the submission was, according to the language of the Constitution itself, "for the purpose of collecting their sentiments." On all three occasions the collecting of sentiments was taken to be the thing directed, not merely the casting of ballots that nowadays would be the only procedure. The result was a variety of documents that must have given a hard task to the committee canvassing the returns.

No more vivid light can be thrown on the political capacities of the people of Massachusetts in the last quarter of the eighteenth century than that to be found in the great volumes of "Archives" in which have been bound the reports from the towns giving their votes and their views on the constitutional issues at stake. Many of the town meetings took up the Constitution article by article, discussing each and recording a vote on each. The comments, the objections, the reasons, the suggestions, showed a diffusion of critical intelligence that perhaps had never been equaled before and has never been equaled since. Meetings in towns of but from one to fourscore of voters brought out clear, decided, well-reasoned opinions that would have honored any constitutional convention, no matter how carefully selected. Familiarity with every detail of government was manifest. Of many suggestions for amendment, few were absurd.

The article to receive most criticism was Article III of the Bill of Rights, creating a public religious establishment — the maintenance of public worship at the public expense where not voluntarily provided. Many a town set forth the most liberal of sentiments in objection to this article. Such views did not at once prevail, but the arguments were too strong to be resisted always in a free land, and in 1833 church and state were severed by the Eleventh Article of Amendment, putting an end to the appropriation of public money for public worship, this being supplemented in 1855 by Article XVIII, prohibiting the appropriation of public money to any religious sect for the maintenance, exclusively, of its own school, and in 1917 by Article XLVI still further guarding against sectarian appropriations.

So many of the town returns were conditional or otherwise complicated that the committee thereon had to tabulate them under a dozen headings. The printed Journal says that none of the Reports referred to in connection therewith are to be found on file, so that we must content ourselves with the knowledge that the adjourned session of the Convention declared the Constitution had met the necessary ratification, which was to have been by a two-thirds vote.

New Hampshire took even more pains to try to satisfy everybody. Her first Constitution was quickly found full of imperfections. "The necessity of checks and balances became every day more evident," says Jeremy Belknap.[1] So in 1778 a Convention framed a new Constitution, which the town-meetings forthwith rejected. Another Convention met in 1781. Belknap says it "had more advantage than the former, the neighboring State of Massachusetts having digested and adopted a Constitution which was supposed to be an improvement on all

[1] *History of New Hampshire*, ii, 333.

which had been framed in America." Yet the draft first submitted was met by so many propositions for amendment, and it was found so hard to reconcile opinions, that the Convention had no less than nine sessions and continued for more than two years before the discussion, amendment, and approval in detail by the town-meetings worked out a satisfactory document.

Although in a few of the original States the first Constitution was framed by a legislative body not convened for the sole purpose of drafting such a document, that process has not survived either for framing Constitutions or a general revision. In only one instance since the eighteenth century has a Constitution been successfully drafted by a Legislature. That was in the case of the Territory of Nebraska in 1866. Even that instance was dubious, the courts holding the entire proceeding to be irregular, being cured, however, by the admission of the State into the Union.[1] The thing was attempted in Connecticut in 1905, the Legislature submitting as an amendment a revised Constitution. The revision made no material modifications of any sort, merely incorporating into the main body of the Constitution the amendments that had been adopted since 1828, and increasing the salaries of the members of the Legislature. It was rejected.[2] The Indiana Legislature sought to proceed likewise in 1911, under the theory that the general powers of the lawmaking body would allow it to submit a Constitution to the voters on referendum. The Supreme Court did not accept that theory. Exhaustive treatment of the question may be found in Ellingham v. Dye, 178 Ind. 336 (1912), the majority and minority opinions covering more than a hundred pages. The majority held it was beyond legislative power to submit a Constitution that would be valid if adopted.

Apart from the strictly legal phases of the question, it would on the whole be fortunate if the courts discouraged Legislatures from themselves preparing revisions of Constitutions. Many reasons conspire to unfit a Legislature for constitution-making. The people of Massachusetts were wise when in 1778 they rejected a Constitution largely on the ground that it was prepared by a Legislature instead of by a body called together for the especial purpose.

---

[1] Roger Sherman Hoar, *Constitutional Conventions*, 80, citing Brittle v. People, 2 Neb. 198, 216 (1873).

[2] J. Q. Dealey, *Growth of American State Constitutions*, 102.

The greater part of the original States, and those first added to the Union, went on the theory that the Convention was the embodiment of the people and that its act needed no ratification. Not until well into the nineteenth century did the opposite doctrine become predominant and it is not yet universally accepted. Massachusetts came naturally by the idea that there should be a referendum. When the Reverend John Cotton and the Reverend Nathaniel Ward had prepared separate drafts for the Body of Liberties, we read in John Winthrop's Journal, November 7, 1639, that "the two models were digested with divers alterations and additions, and abbreviated and sent to every town, to be considered of first by the magistrates and elders, and then to be published by the constables to all the people, that if any man should think fit, that any thing therein ought to be altered, he might acquaint some of the deputies therewith against the next court."

It was Puritan theory that the people should be consulted. When John Lilburne's work had produced the "Agreement of the People" at the time of the Puritan Revolution in England, it was asked that the document be submitted for approval, "to be subscribed by those that are willing, as petitions and other things of a voluntary nature are"; and that it should take effect "if upon the account of Subscriptions, there appears a general or common reception of it amongst the people, or by the Well-affected of them, and such as are not obnoxious for Delinquency." There was no formal referendum, but the idea that the people should pass judgment on their basic law got into the public mind on this side of the water and in time its logic began to convince even those who were the opposite of Puritans. For example, when the Maryland Assembly had framed a Constitution, it was submitted to the people for opinion and suggestion. At the next session the Assembly went over the draft again, considering the criticisms, and after amendment enacted it into law.

Possibly in Maryland and in other States where there was no final ratification at the polls, there was fear lest the Tory vote might make trouble.

W. H. Armstrong told the Pennsylvania Convention of 1873 that it was well known that the act authorizing the Convention of 1790 had an express provision by which the work of that Convention was to be submitted to the people for their approval, and yet it was never submitted. The Convention adjourned from

February 26 to August 9, 1790, that the people might examine its work, and then formally proclaimed the new Constitution. The Supreme Court held it became the Constitution by the act of the Convention alone, and without the ratification of the people.

In recent years several States (Mississippi, South Carolina, Delaware, Louisiana, and Virginia) have put Constitutions in force without submitting them to the people. The exceptional problems of the South account in large measure for this. Virginia, in 1902, was sharply criticized for doing it, when the act calling for the Convention distinctly provided for submission and the party platform on which most of the members were elected pledged its supporters to recognize the right of the people to a direct vote on their fundamental law.[1]

Nearly one third of the State Constitutions explicitly require a referendum, and most of the others would undoubtedly provide for it by statute.

The Federal Constitution was not submitted to the people, but some form of ratification was an evident necessity and so it was submitted to Conventions called for the purpose, from which we may infer it was not then universally believed that the legislative assemblies were the embodiment of popular sovereignty. Few episodes in the history of government have been more portentous. Only by the narrowest of margins did the new Constitution win. The fate of a nation hung in the balance. The Union was achieved by stratagems. In some States the day was carried by threats and even by force. In New Hampshire a majority of the delegates were instructed or had made up their minds to vote against ratification. Timothy Walker gave some of them a dinner and then detained them while the Convention was voting. According to tradition, Judge Walker refused to admit the messenger sent to summon the absent members, and when the messenger persisted, threatened to set the dogs on him. In Pennsylvania the necessary quorum was secured with the help of a mob that dragged to the Convention two obstinate members and then kept them from leaving the room. In Connecticut an anti-Federalist delegate who tried to talk out the Convention was silenced by tar and feathers. In Massachusetts victory was secured by a sop to the vanity of John Hancock, who was thereby craftily induced to throw his influence in favor

[1] *The Outlook*, June 14, 1902, 432.

of the Constitution. Hamilton coerced New York with the threat that Kings and Westchester would ratify as an independent State and leave the northern counties at the mercy of foreign enemies and without access to the sea. The charge was believed, if not proved, that the Federalists prevented the circulation of the opposition newspapers in the mails; and in Pennsylvania and Maryland the reports of the debates in the State Conventions were suppressed by purchase and boycott.[1]

[1] Roger Foster, *Commentaries on the Constitution of the U.S.*, i, 4.

CHAPTER VII

AMENDING THE ORGANIC LAW

It has been the habit of men in all ages to think their institutions incapable of substantial betterment. Each generation believes it has reached the apex of development, that it has achieved the *summum bonum*. Of course the few have and always have had and always will have visions of better things, but the many stagnate in self-satisfaction. The few know that change is the law of life, but the many resent the very idea of change. Authors of written forms of government appear to have been particularly confident that their work was the best possible achievement and certain to endure. It brings a smile to read in charter after charter granted to American colonies that the stipulations were to be "perpetual." William Penn seems to have been the first maker of laws for a colony who had any doubts on this score. In his Charter of Liberties of 1682 appears the first provision for a method of amendment. The form or effect of the Charter or any part thereof was not to be changed without the consent of the Governor, his heirs or assigns, and six parts of seven of the freemen in Provincial Council and General Assembly.

It might have been expected that the Revolution would convince all Americans that forms of government do not persist, and indeed their Declaration of Independence and Bills of Rights asserted the right to alter or abolish any form of government, but when it came to making Constitutions they were strangely unmindful of this. About half the original Constitutions of that time contained no provision for change.

Pennsylvania evolved a new idea and Vermont copied. This was a Council of Censors. Two members were to be elected from each county and city in Pennsylvania every seven years, with powers to continue for one year from the date of their election. One of their powers was that of calling, by a two-thirds vote, a Convention for amending the Constitution, and it was on this rock that from factional reasons they came to grief. The first Council met in November, 1783, and adjourned in September, 1784, accomplishing nothing save discussion of the need of amending the Constitution. Partly because they could not agree upon the changes needed, the dispute ended with the decision that there was no absolute necessity for calling a Convention. They never sat again. In September, 1789, a Committee of the Whole of the General Assembly reported that the Council "was not only unequal and unnecessarily expensive, but too dilatory to produce the speedy and necessary alterations which the late change in the political union and the exigencies of the State required." So a Convention was called, and that Convention abolished the Council. It had proved unwieldy and weak.

In Vermont the Censors were elected from the State at large, and not by districts as in Pennsylvania. This made the Council a more homogeneous and responsible body, to which fact Professor Holcombe ascribes in part the better working of the system in Vermont.[1] Furthermore, party lines were less closely drawn there than in Pennsylvania. The Vermont Council proposed amendments every seven years from 1785 to 1869 inclusive, with three exceptions, and Conventions were held. In 1786 and 1793 revised Constitutions followed. No amendments were advised in 1799 or 1806. From 1813 to 1869 the Council made 106 recommendations, 26 of which were adopted by the Conventions. The adoption in 1870 of the proposal of the Council for its own abolition, ended the system.

It is not safe to assume that the omission of reference to Conventions by a dozen States has been due to accident or oversight. Only one of them, Massachusetts, lives under a Constitution framed before Conventions for revising Constitutions became familiar. There is ground for the belief that in some if not all of them it was deliberately intended to leave open only the avenue for change by amendment begun in the Legislature. When in the Massachusetts Convention of 1820 the provision for a method of amendment was under consideration, Daniel Webster said "it occurred to the committee that with the experience we had had of the Constitution, there was little probability that, after the amendments which should now be adopted, there would ever be any occasion for great changes. No revision of its general principles would be necessary, and the alterations which would be called for by a change of circumstances, would be limited and specific. It was therefore the opinion of the committee that no provision for a revision of the whole Constitution was expedient."

[1] A. N. Holcombe, *State Government in the U.S.*, 77.

This is the more significant by reason of the fact that this very Convention sat without constitutional warrant. The Legislature had on its own responsibility submitted to the voters this question: "Is it expedient that Delegates should be chosen, to meet in Convention, for the purpose of revising, or altering the Constitution of Government of this Commonwealth?" The vote having been in the affirmative, the Convention was gathered. One of the amendments submitted by it to the people and adopted, was the Ninth, providing the method of specific amendment now familiar — by action of the Legislature in two successive years and ratification by the voters. This developed the question whether, one method of amendment having been provided, any other was precluded. It was formally asked by the Legislature of the Justices in 1833. Their Opinion (6 Cushing 573) was to the effect that no specific amendment could be made in other than the method prescribed; and that if a Convention were held, it would be limited by the terms of the vote calling it. The Justices did not understand, however, that it was the intention "to request their opinion upon the natural right of the people in cases of great emergency, or upon the obvious failure of their existing Constitution to accomplish the objects for which it was designed, to provide for the amendment or alteration of their fundamental laws." The Opinion, therefore, was not allowed to stand in the way of the Act of 1852, which put the question before the voters in precisely the language used in 1820.

The matter came up again in 1916. A similar act (chap. 98) then changed the question somewhat, making it: "Shall there be a convention to revise, alter or amend the Constitution of the Commonwealth?" It will be observed that by introducing the word "amend" the Opinion of 1833 was even more squarely flouted than it had been in 1852. Possibly the intention was to get a definite declaration of the electorate on that particular point, rather than rely on the legislative authority given to the Convention in another section of the Act, as it had been in 1852 and previously in 1820, empowering the Convention to take into consideration the propriety and expediency of revising or making "alterations or amendments." After the electorate, voting at an election duly authorized by a Legislature, has made orderly provision for a Convention and has specifically authorized it to revise, alter, or amend a Constitution, it is inconceivable that any court would combat proceedings in comformity with such authority.

In the very first paragraph of the Constitution of Massachusetts, it is declared that "the people have a right to alter the government." Should it be held that once they have prescribed a method of exercising that right, no other is "constitutional," well and good. The fact is not changed by the adjective. Call it "revolutionary" if you prefer. However you characterize it, the result will be the same as long as may endure the republican institutions founded on the principles set forth in the Declaration of Independence.

The Rhode Island Senate in 1883 asked the question of the Supreme Court, which answered without reservation (14 R.I. 649) that one method of amendment having been provided, no other was constitutional. It further held that any change must be deemed amendment, the reasoning being that the Constitution of the United States confined each of the States to a republican form of government, that Rhode Island had such a form, and that it was impossible "to imagine any alteration consistent with a republican form of government, which cannot be effected by specific amendment as provided in the Constitution."

On the other hand, the Pennsylvania Court said in Wood's Appeal, 75 Penn. St. Rep. 65, 72: "The calling of a Convention, and regulating its action by law, is not forbidden in the Constitution. It is a conceded *manner*, through which the people may exercise the right reserved in the Bill of Rights."

Remember that in the case of both Massachusetts and Rhode Island, the views of the court were given to the Legislature, in "Opinions" which are recognized not to have the weight of opinions accompanying decisions, for the former are necessarily framed hastily, and usually without the help of either oral argument or briefs. Over against them is to be set the fact that the dozen States containing no provision for Conventions in their Constitutions, have since the adoption of their first Constitution held at least twenty-three Conventions, of each of which it might be said that they were held without constitutional warrant. Some computations make the number nearer thirty. In nearly all these instances, there were provisions for a method of amendment, so that if the maxim, *expressio unius, exclusio alterius*, were to apply, it is singular that no opinions accompanying Supreme Court "decisions" have questioned the results.

No matter where casuistical discussion might lead us, the palpable fact is that the Convention is the established practice for the general revision of Constitutions. The fine-spun arguments of theorists have so far been wholly void of result unless it be that they have kept Rhode Island from holding a Constitutional Convention. Let it not be forgotten that the Convention idea was at the very root of our State institutions. It was the method of organization urged by John Adams on his reluctant associates in Congress in 1775. It was recognized in the first Constitutions of Pennsylvania, Vermont, and Georgia. The first draft of a Constitution for Massachusetts was rejected largely because it had not been framed by a Convention called for that particular purpose.

Georgia in 1777 took the Pennsylvania idea of revision by a Convention, but, in place of initiative by a Council of Censors, substituted the initiative of the people, providing that a Convention should be held on petitions from a majority of the counties, each petition to be signed by a majority of the voters of the county. In the Constitution of 1789 definite provision was made for the election in 1794 of delegates to another Convention, and that one in turn provided for another in 1798, which substituted the method of change by amendment.

Massachusetts in 1780 followed Georgia in recognizing that in time another Convention might be desirable. William Gordon, in an Address to the Freemen of Massachusetts, printed in the "Independent Chronicle," May 4, 1780, said: "I have heard that the Hon. John Adams, Esquire, delivered an excellent speech, soon after the meeting of the Convention, the purport of which was to show, that it was impossible for human wisdom to form a plan of government that should suit all future emergencies, and that, therefore, periodical revisions were requisite." Nevertheless, the draft of the Constitution that Adams prepared contained no provision whatever for either revision or amendment. The want was partly met by the Convention, which inserted an article providing that in 1795 the people should vote "on the necessity or expediency of revising the Constitution, in order to amendments," and that if two thirds favored, a Convention should be held. Little can be learned of what then took place. We know, however, by the "Columbian Centinel" of May 9, 1795, that in Boston "the question was amply discussed at Faneuil Hall; and all parties at first seemed agreed, that such was the perfection of the system, and such the happiness enjoyed under it, that a revision was not necessary: — But as the Constitution pointed out only *one period* (the present) for the discussion of its revisions, fears were apprehended of the consequences which would arise were it left without a period to which the people could look forward, as a time when their right to discuss the question, though always inherent, would be called into active operation." The vote was 78 for to 49 against. "It should be remarked here, as it frequently was in the Hall, that the thinness of the meeting was a strong argument, that our fellow-citizens did not wish the alteration of the Constitution."

It is not easy to find out what was the vote of the State. The Journals of Senate and House do not give the figures, nor have they been found in any contemporary Boston newspaper. The legislative files disclose a report by which it appears that according to the votes "returned," 7999 were for and 8325 against. The report goes on to say that from towns which "made no return of the precepts," 3387 were for and 2542 against. Whether the latter figures were included in the former, is the uncertainty. If not, and if they are to be added together, the totals are 11,386 for and 10,867 against. The "Centinel" of June 20, said by the report of the joint committee "it appeared that there was a majority of votes against a revision." But as a two-thirds vote was required, the word "majority" may have been used to indicate its lack.

It is more edifying than instructive to read in the Inaugural Address of Governor Samuel Adams, June 3: "The citizens of the Commonwealth have lately had before them a question of the expediency of revising, at this period, the form of our present Constitution. The conduct of the citizens on this occasion has given full proof, that an enlightened, free, and virtuous people, can as a body, be the keepers of their own Liberties, and the guardians of their own rights."

The enlightened, free, and virtuous people, however, were not all satisfied that their rights had been guarded, for a committee of the Legislature (according to the "Centinel" of June 20) proceeded to report a series of resolutions for calling on the people again to express their minds on the expediency of calling a Convention to add a clause to the Constitution, establishing a mode for periodically revising the same, if two thirds of the people should at any of the periods, be in favor of such a measure.

"This report," the account says, "was largely discussed — and so far as we can judge from the observations of the members who spoke, the House were generally in favor of the principle of the resolutions, but differed as to the propriety of restricting the people to the appointment of a Convention for a single purpose." The House passed the resolutions, but the Senate non-concurred and a committee of conference could not agree.

Meanwhile New Hampshire in 1784, South Carolina in 1790, Delaware and Kentucky in 1792 had recognized the Convention as a method of revising Constitutions. New Hampshire directed a vote by the people every seven years on the expediency of holding a Convention, two thirds to prevail. South Carolina by indirection put it in the control of the Legislature, saying, "No Convention of the people shall be called, unless by the concurrence of two thirds of both branches of the whole representation." Delaware said, "No Convention shall be called but by the authority of the people," and went on to prescribe that in case of a popular vote, a majority of all the citizens in the State having the right to vote for Representatives should be required. Kentucky directed the people to vote for or against a Convention in 1797. They voted for it, and on its advice the Constitution of 1799 was accepted, with a provision for future Conventions on the initiative of a majority of the members elected to the Legislature, ratified by a majority of all the people of the State entitled to vote for Representatives. Other States followed these examples until now three quarters have provision for Constitutional Conventions.

For the most part it has been presumed or provided that the Legislature shall take the first step toward a Convention. Two States, indeed, make that the only step. Georgia, after incidentally recognizing in 1868 that a Legislature might call a convention without a vote of the people, in 1877 made it clear by a requirement for a two-thirds vote of the two Houses. Maine in 1876 also put it within reach of their two-thirds vote. On the other hand, lest the Legislature might not be willing to give the people a chance to determine the matter for themselves, several States have followed the example of New Hampshire by directing that in any case the question shall be submitted at certain intervals. Indiana (1816) directed a poll every twelve years, but dropped the direction in 1851. New York in 1846 provided for a poll at twenty-year intervals; Michigan in 1850 made it sixteen

years; Ohio in 1851 preferred twenty years. The revision of the
Massachusetts Constitution rejected by the voters in 1853
would have secured submission of the question every twenty
years. Maryland in 1864 chose twenty-year periods. In 1870
Virginia directed a vote in 1888 and every twenty years thereafter, but the provision was dropped when the Constitution of
1902 was framed. Oklahoma in 1907 also specified the twenty-
year period. In several cases there have been failures to live up
to the schedule. This with the fact that only a fifth of the States
have ever looked with favor on the procedure and the further
fact that two of those States trying it have abandoned it, indicates
that it does not well meet the need. By the way, it is interesting
to note that one of the States applying it late and speedily aban-
doning it was Virginia, whose favorite statesman, Thomas Jefferson, was of the strong conviction that society renews itself every
eighteen or nineteen years and ought at such intervals to have
the chance to reshape its institutions.

POWERS OF CONVENTIONS

The problem of political science that has most agitated Constitutional Conventions relates to their powers. Are Conventions
supreme? Are they subordinate to Legislatures? Or are they
coördinate with Legislatures?

It was more common in the earlier Conventions than it is now
for delegates to maintain that the Convention is the embodiment of the sovereignty of the people. For instance, Livingston
declared in the New York Convention of 1821: "The people are
here themselves; they are present in their delegates." Peters in
the Illinois Convention of 1847 averred: "We are the sovereignty
of the State. We are what the people of the State would do if
they were congregated here in mass-meeting. We are what
Louis XIV said he was, 'We are the State.'"

The issue usually becomes of practical importance through
attempts of Legislatures to restrict Conventions in their action.
Can the Legislature tie the hands of the Convention? Can the
people themselves tie the hands of the Convention?

Hours on hours have been given to the issue in various State
Conventions. Not the least interesting of the discussions it has
produced took place in Massachusetts, in the Convention of
1853. Henry Wilson, elected a delegate by each of two towns, resigned his seat from one of them, Berlin. The Convention Act

provided for the election of delegates by secret ballot. After its adoption by the people, the Legislature changed the ballot law so that a voter might enclose his ballot in an envelope, or not, as he pleased. Had the Convention power to fill vacancies? Could it legislate by directing how the vote of Berlin should be taken? Did the old or new election law apply? Could an act of the Legislature subsequent to the embodiment of the sovereign power of the people in a Convention, control that power?

The ablest lawyers in the Convention — and they were some of the ablest in the land — took part in the long debate that followed.

Marcus Morton, who had been Congressman, Governor, and a Judge of the Supreme Court, held the Convention had only the power expressly delegated to it, with by implication, however, a grant of everything necessary to carry that power into effect; but that this grant did not extend to the filling of vacancies. In fact at the outset none of the speakers intimated a belief that the Convention had more than the power expressly delegated, and the debate at first centered upon whether a power to fill vacancies was incidental thereto.

Benjamin F. Butler, afterward General, Congressman, and Governor, took the ground that the Legislature could not modify the act adopted by the people. While maintaining "We are the delegates of the people, chosen to act in their stead," yet he said, "we have the same power and the same right, *within the scope of the business assigned to us*, that they would have were they all convened in this Hall." Two days later he verged on the more vital issue when he asked, "Are gentlemen willing to admit that our charter is from the Legislature, or will they assert that we are here by the will of the people and that alone?"

Rufus Choate also asked questions: "Do you say that this Convention, by virtue of some transcendent power, and so far as its own action is concerned, may annul the law? I deny that you have a grant of power so transcendent from anybody. If you have it, will you permit it to be inspected? I crave *oyer* of the deed, Mr. President, and ask that it may be read to me!"

William B. Greene met the craving for *Oyer* with the paragraph of the Bill of Rights giving the people incontestible, unalienable, and indefeasible right to institute and to change their government; after which he denounced the Legislature for changing the election law subsequent to the adoption of the

Convention Act, declaring their doctrine to be that against which Martin Luther organized the insurrection of human thought and the cannon of Oliver Cromwell thundered, the doctrine of the Czar of Russia and the boy Nero of Austria; and he affirmed that the Legislature had been guilty of treason against the people of the Commonwealth. This appears to have annoyed sundry members of the Legislature who were also delegates to the Convention. Doubtless their disapprobation was not lessened when Benjamin F. Hallett, in language somewhat less trenchant, yet plain enough, said the Legislature had gone out of its jurisdiction. He proceeded to read and endorse the opinion of the New York Judges.

It seems that the New York Assembly had asked the Supreme Court to construe the Convention Act of 1845 in a matter of apportionment of delegates. The Court gave an opinion in the course of which it said: "The Legislature is not supreme. It is only one of the instruments of that absolute sovereignty which resides in the whole body of the people. Like other departments of the government, it acts under a delegation of powers, and cannot rightly go beyond the limits which have been assigned to it. This delegation of powers has been made by a fundamental law which no one department of the government nor all the departments united have authority to change. That can only be done by the people themselves."

The Court went on to hold that no power had been delegated to the Legislature to call a Convention to revise the Constitution; that its Convention Act could operate only by way of advice or recommendation, and not as a law; that its adoption by the people gave it the force of law — "a law made by the people themselves"; with the conclusion "obvious that the Legislature cannot annul it nor make any substantial change in its provisions."

The New York Judges expressed their regret that they had but a few hours to confer and to reduce their opinions to writing, and explained that they had previously given the matter no thought. This and the extra-judicial nature of the opinion may have seemed to the Assembly reason enough for disregarding it. At any rate, such was the outcome, and the people in turn disregarded it by electing delegates under the new apportionment.

Mr. Hallett's presentation of the view of the New York Judges did not by any means end the debate in the Massachusetts Convention. Along came Judge Joel Parker, Professor of the Harvard Law School, with a lengthy and learned speech the other way. He held the Convention Act was a law like any other, and not a charter, something beyond the reach of a subsequent Legislature. Indeed he went so far as to say that a subsequent Legislature could repeal the Act and so abolish the Convention even while it was sitting.

Henry Wilson, afterward Vice-President, declared Judge Parker's notion of the power of the Legislature over the Convention to be extraordinary doctrine to be held at that day in America — a practical denial of the sovereignty of the people, contrary to the opinions of every American statesman, and to the decisions of every judicial tribunal, from the foundation of the government to that moment. He, too, maintained that the Legislature had no right to amend the Convention Act; because, in so doing, it changed the conditions upon which the people gave their assent. The Convention agreed with him, with Butler, Hallett, and the other champions of popular sovereignty, by a vote of 220 to 118, on the motion for reconsideration.

It is true that this debate did not bring up squarely the question of whether the action of the people in their sovereign capacity is final, under all circumstances, but it did record that particular Convention as believing that after the people had acted in deciding upon a Convention, its Legislature could not modify the conditions.

Still farther was it from deciding whether the people themselves bind their Convention by the Act creating it. If a Convention is the embodied sovereignty of the people, is it for the time being the community itself? Is it to be bound by anything that has gone before? Must the result of its action be dependent on anything to follow? In the early years of our national history, many Constitutions went into effect without subsequent ratification by the people, on the ground that the people had acted in the Convention. It was a common view.

In all this the theorists have found an attractive bone of contention. Judge Jameson, who wrote what was long the authoritative book on Constitutional Conventions, reached the conclusion that the New York Justices and the Massachusetts Convention of 1853 were wrong, and that the Massachusetts judges and lawyers who presented the opposing view in the Convention, were right. Some of his critics aver that he shaped his facts to

justify his conclusions, but that may be uncharitable. One episode which he recalled illustrates the difficulties of tracking
sovereignty. In 1857 the two political parties in the Convention
of Minnesota, Republicans and Democrats, disagreeing as to the
organization of the body, formed separate Conventions, which
ran parallel courses, each claiming to be the only legitimate
Convention. Two Constitutions were reported, and it seemed
that the people were to be embarrassed by the necessity of choosing between them, when, toward the close of their respective
sessions, a conference was held between the two bodies, and a
single Constitution was reported to and adopted by them both.[1]

If each had persisted, what would have happened to sovereignty?

Borgeaud, another authority, holds that the Legislature is the
permanent representative of the people, that the Convention is
a special committee of delegates, and that if they have been entrusted with the special task of revising only certain parts of the
Constitution, they are bound absolutely by the act of the Legislature. It follows, of course, that they would be still more firmly
bound by an act of the people, by referendum assigning to them
definite tasks.[2]

Von Holst also found limits to the powers of Conventions. "It
has repeatedly become of the greatest political significance," he
said, "that Conventions — partly by appealing to precedents in
the struggle of the colonies with the mother country, and partly
in imitation of the Convention of the first French Revolution —
have claimed to be the bearers of the people's sovereignty — a
claim that in its final logical results tends to a complete over-
turning of the fundamental principle of American popular government, that is, transforms popular sovereignty into its very
opposite. This doctrine, which rests on the logical absurdity of a
transfer of sovereignty, which is identical with its entire alienation, is constantly losing ground, especially as far as the drafting
of an entire Constitution is concerned." [3]

In the case of Wood's Appeal that followed the Pennsylvania
Convention of 1873, the Supreme Court held (75 Penn. St. Rep.,
65, 72) that the people acting through the Legislature, could
regulate the Convention; that the Convention had no inher-

[1] *The Constitutional Convention*, 263.
[2] *Adoption and Amendment of Constitutions*, 184.
[3] *Constitutional Law of the U.S.*, 263 et seq.

ent rights; that it had powers only, which the people might limit.

Recent thought in the matter tends to take the middle ground, that the Legislature and the Convention is each supreme in its own sphere. For instance, C. Z. Lincoln, whose thorough "Constitutional History of New York" gives proof of long familiarity with the subject and of sage reflection, thinks it is very clear that the Legislature has no power to limit the deliberations of a Constitutional Convention; such a Convention may make or unmake the Legislature itself. While the Legislature represents the people, it represents them for the purpose of exercising the lawmaking power, and not the power to make a Constitution, nor to direct or control the action of other representatives of the people chosen for the express purpose of revising the Constitution. The power to make a Constitution is one thing, the legislative power is quite another.[1]

W. F. Dodd, in his exhaustive work, "Revision of State Constitutions," takes much the same position. The better view, he says (page 80), would seem to be that the Convention is a regular organ of the State (although as a rule called only at long intervals) — neither sovereign nor subordinate to the Legislature, but independent within its proper sphere. Under this view the Legislature cannot bind the Convention as to what shall be placed in the Constitution, or as to the exercise of its proper duties. If then we say that the Convention is independent of the regular Legislature in the exercise of its proper duties, it will be necessary to discuss for a moment what are its proper functions. These are simply to propose a new Constitution or to propose constitutional amendments to the people for approval; or, in States where the submission of Constitutions is not required, to frame and adopt a Constitution if they think proper. In this sphere, and in the exercise of powers incidental to its proper functions it would seem that Constitutional Conventions should not be subject to control by legislative acts.

Of course a Legislature may forbid this or that thing to the Convention it shares in creating. The people may forbid by adopting the act of the Legislature. But it is one thing to forbid and another to prevent. Of what use would be the prohibition if the Convention saw fit to submit to the people for ratification something the Legislature or the people had forbidden, and if the

[1] *Constitutional History of New York*, II, 414.

people then approved? To be sure, the Legislature or the Courts might seek to prevent the use of the election machinery for the ratification of a thing forbidden, but that is altogether improbable. They would resort to almost any expedient for avoiding such an invitation to conflict. They would recognize that the will of the majority of the people in any American State is not likely to be permanently thwarted, and that it would be worse than useless to interpose technical obstacles.

REVISION BY COMMISSION

An elected Convention may not always be the best body to revise a Constitution. Seeking a better method, some of the States have experimented with Commissions. New Jersey appears to have been the first to call in advice after this fashion, and it has followed the plan four times since then, though not with conspicuous success. In 1873, by direction of the Legislature, the Governor appointed a bi-partisan Commission of fourteen, two from each Congressional district. Part of its recommendations were adopted, part rejected. In 1881 another Commission was created, three of its members being named by the Governor, two by the Senate, and two by the House. None of its recommendations were adopted. In 1894 still another was named, consisting of four members at large and two from each of the eight Congressional districts, this time all appointed by the Governor and confirmed by the Senate. None of its recommendations were adopted.

Governor Hoffman of New York in his annual message of 1872, after referring to a recent Convention and the failure of the people to approve its work, recommended that a non-partisan committee of thirty-two eminent citizens, to be selected equally from the two great political parties, should be appointed to propose amendments for ratification by the Legislature and the people. The suggestion won favor and an act was passed authorizing the Governor to appoint such a committee, with four members from each judicial district. The act gave it a free hand, provided no amendments be proposed to the sixth article, that relating to the courts. It sat three months and a half, rewrote or changed many sections, added some and dropped others — in short, made a thorough revision. The Legislature of 1873 embodied in eleven concurrent resolutions such of the changes as it approved, and they were submitted to the people, with the result that all were adopted. In a more limited way the same device was tried a few years later in the matter of municipal reform. On the recommendation of Governor Tilden, May 22, 1875, he received authority to appoint a Commission of not more than twelve citizens to study the subject and report. The amendments it advised were approved by the Legislature of 1877, but failed to secure the endorsement of a second Legislature that was necessary.

Also in 1875 Maine pursued this method, a Commission of ten members being appointed by the Governor at the direction of the Legislature. As a result ten amendments were approved by the people. One of them deserves particular notice, for it directed that after the vote, the Chief Justice of the Supreme Judicial Court should rearrange the Constitution, embodying all amendments then or previously made, and that this rearrangement should stand as the Constitution of the State if approved by the Legislature. As a reasonable, safe, and wise method of getting a systematic presentation of the fundamental law, to be quickly consulted and easily understood, this plan deserves all praise. It was copied in Vermont when in 1908 by joint resolution a Commission of five was appointed to propose amendments. In January of 1910 this Commission made a careful report with eight proposals, and submitted a copy of the Constitution so arranged as to include in the main body all former amendments. Five of the proposals were accepted in substance. The Justices of the Supreme Court were directed to rearrange the Constitution and their revision took the place of the old document. Revision by Commission seems to have been thought useful, for a decade later there was resort to it again. This time there was a Commission of seven. They were appointed by the Governor and five of them were lawyers. The Legislature of 1921 considered nine proposals they submitted, also minority proposals, and others begun in the Senate — to a total of twenty-two. Only four went to the Legislature of 1923, and but three of these came from the Commission.

Constitutional Commissions have been less successful in Michigan and Rhode Island. The Michigan Commission of 1873 prepared a new Constitution which the people rejected. The same fate met the work of the Rhode Island Commission of 1897. The people rejected it in 1898, and when a few verbal changes had been made, rejected it again in 1899, by a larger vote. In

1912 another Commission was appointed, to report in 1915, but as yet no constitutional changes have resulted. Judge Jameson has questioned the constitutionality of amendments originating through the advice of a Commission, but opposition on this score is likely to seem finical to most men. There is nothing in the constitutional history of any State, so far as I have been able to observe, which casts any doubt on the propriety of letting a Legislature ask and take suggestion or advice from whom it will. For it to proceed thus in matters of ordinary lawmaking, has become too common a practice to be questioned. No valid reason suggests itself why it should not pursue the same practice in the matter of fundamental law.

An advisory Commission would be particularly useful for improving the Constitution of the United States. Wonderful though that instrument was, nearing perfection as close as the human mind could get, nevertheless there were omissions in some important matters of detail, and in other respects change of conditions has made modification desirable. Of the hundreds of proposals for amendment that have been submitted to Congress, many have been clearly unwise, some have had sound basis, almost none concerned with machinery have been adopted. Changes of this sort never seem pressing and so by reason of what is thought more urgent business they are postponed from session to session, with now no prospect whatever that they will get Congressional attention in our day. Yet changes ought to be made. No Convention is likely to be called for the purpose. The conservative forces of the country too much fear that once a Convention were assembled, it would try to alter substantially the frame of government, would propose radical changes in what may be called matters of principle, would seek to subvert the established economic and social order. Whether or not such fear is well grounded, it is dominant and bids fair to continue such well beyond our time.

A way out of the dilemma would be to authorize the President to appoint a fairly sizable Commission, directed to consider and propose only technical changes. It should comprise for the most part men who are having or have recently had familiarity with the actual working of the machinery of government, foremost representatives of the legislative, executive, and judicial branches. Together with them might well be a few citizens of such eminent standing that they would be looked on by the people at large as sure to protect their interests and rights. If leading members of Congress, of both branches and both parties, were members, it might be hoped that the resulting recommendations would command Congressional attention and get action, with approval by the State Legislatures surely following.

OTHER METHODS AND DETAILS

Two of the original States, Delaware and Maryland, each acting in 1776, preferred the mode of changing the Constitution by separate amendment, and made no provision for Conventions. Delaware required for an amendment the consent of five parts in seven of the Assembly, and seven members of the Legislative Council. Maryland required a majority vote of two successive Legislatures, with the peculiar addition — "provided that nothing in this form of government, which relates to the eastern shore particularly, shall at any time hereafter be altered, unless for the alteration and confirmation thereof at least two thirds of all the members of each branch of the General Assembly shall concur." Maryland made the first constitutional amendment by providing in 1792 that members of Congress should be excluded from State offices.

South Carolina in 1790 modified the Maryland plan somewhat, requiring a two-thirds vote in the first session, but with no specific mention of a vote at the second session, although requiring that the amendment should then be read three times or on three several days, from which the need of only a majority vote might be inferred. Georgia in 1798 followed South Carolina in requiring a two-thirds vote, and made it clear that in the second session also the vote should be two thirds. Connecticut in 1818 required a two-thirds vote of each House in successive sessions, and added a new requirement, that the amendment should then be ratified by the people. Alabama copied this the next year, but made it more stringent by requiring a majority of all the citizens voting for Representatives. Maine, also acting in 1819, showed less caution, permitting passage by a two-thirds vote at one session only, and then ratification by a majority of the voters voting. Missouri in 1820 provided for a vote by two thirds of each House at two successive sessions, without submission to the people. The Massachusetts Convention of that year found a further variation in requiring approval by a majority of the Senate and two thirds of the House at two successive sessions, with subsequent submission to the people. The change was adopted in 1821, and in that year New York still further modified the idea by requiring a majority of each House at the first session, two thirds at the next, and then submission to the people.

Tennessee, which in 1796 had preferred the convention method, in 1834 changed to the separate-amendment method, with a two-thirds vote by successive Legislatures and then ratification at the polls by a majority of all the citizens voting for Representatives. Michigan in 1835 copied the New York provision of 1821 word for word. Arkansas, in 1836, and Florida, in 1838, contented themselves with the Georgia plan of a two-thirds vote in successive Legislatures without ratification at the polls. Pennsylvania in 1838 showed an advancing liberality by requiring in each of two sessions only a majority of the members elected, and then ratification at the polls by a majority of the voters voting. Rhode Island, in 1842, was not quite so generous, for it modified the Pennsylvania program by requiring a three-fifths vote at the polls. New Jersey in 1844 copied the Pennsylvania provision with but verbal changes. Louisiana in 1845 called for a three-fifths vote of all members at the first session, a majority at the second, and ratification by a majority of all the qualified electors.

It is needless to particularize further. Suffice it to say that this general method is now to be found in all the State Constitutions save those of New Hampshire and Delaware. Fifteen States require affirmative action by successive Legislatures; thirty-two by one Legislature only. A two-thirds vote of each House is required by eighteen States; three-fifths by seven; a majority suffices in seventeen; and in five there are varying combinations of vote requirements. New Hampshire still relies entirely on Conventions.

All the States except Delaware now require what are commonly treated as amendments to be ratified at the polls. About one fifth of them require approval by a majority of the voters voting at the election; in other words, blanks are counted as "No" votes. The vote on amendments usually being small, in effect this proves a serious obstacle. New Hampshire calls for approval by a two-thirds vote, Rhode Island by three fifths. New Mexico calls for three fourths of the electors voting in the State, two thirds of those voting in each county, for changing certain provisions meant to protect citizens of Spanish descent; and on all other amendments an affirmative vote equal to at least forty per cent of all votes cast in the State and half the counties.

After the voters of South Carolina have ratified an amendment, the next Legislature may reject it. In Mississippi, after ratification of an amendment by the voters "it shall be inserted" in the Constitution by the next Legislature. Perhaps this gives opportunity to reject.

Vermont restricts proposal of amendments to once in ten years. The Commission of 1908 recommended eliminating this "time-lock" clause, as it is called, but the Legislature did not submit the recommendation to the people. Like proposal was defeated in 1920, and when coming to the Legislature of 1921 from a Commission of that period, was again rejected, only four Senate votes being recorded in its favor.

Tennessee does not permit proposals of amendment oftener than once in six years; New Jersey, Pennsylvania, and Kentucky oftener than once in five years. Arkansas, Kansas, Montana, and New Mexico say only three amendments shall be submitted at an election; Kentucky, two. Colorado, which up to 1900, permitted but one, now allows six. In Illinois restriction to one was found the most serious obstacle to change of the Constitution. In 1892 the people refused at the polls to make it two. In 1896 a change to three was rejected, for although the "Yes" exceeded the "No" vote by almost a hundred thousand, the total "Yes" vote was not a majority of those voting at the election. In 1924 change to two at last prevailed. While awaiting final action on one amendment, Indiana permits the submission of no other.

The same amendment may not be submitted to the people oftener than once in six years in Tennessee; five years, New Jersey, Pennsylvania, and Kentucky. The Pennsylvania courts have held [1] that the provision precludes submitting a rejected amendment again within that time. Colorado in 1914 refused by 55,667 to 112,537 to allow resubmission of an initiated amendment or measure within six years of its rejection. Ohio in 1915 by 417,384 to 482,275 declined to say that no amendment containing all or any part of a proposal defeated after September 4, 1912, should be submitted within six years of rejection.

Some of the newer Constitutions authorize Legislatures under

[1] Armstrong *v* King, 201 *Penn. State*, 207 (1924).

certain conditions to deviate from or alter the stipulations. For example, Oklahoma after prescribing the duties of the Commissioner of Charities and Corrections, allows the Legislature to "alter, amend, or add to" them. Virginia gives the General Assembly a free hand in sundry particulars after specified dates. This is in line with the views of her great statesman, Thomas Jefferson. Although finding fault because the State Constitution was not framed by a body chosen for that definite purpose, he argued in his "Notes on Virginia" (page 131) that inasmuch as it was framed by an ordinary Legislature, it could be changed by an ordinary Legislature. He held that the Latin words *constitutio*, *constitutum*, *statutum*, and *lex* were convertible terms; that "constitution" means a statute, law, or ordinance; and that a Constitution is not above the usual legislative powers. Presumably he did not mean this would be so in the face of constitutional provision to the contrary. Such provision is now inferred wherever specific modes of amendment are set forth. The question became in effect academic with general recourse to Constitutional Conventions, but has reappeared in a new form as a result of the Initiative and Referendum. Where a Constitution may be amended in either of two ways, may one be used to undo the work of the other? In States without provision regarding this, it may some day perplex the courts.

Of late it has been urged that if Constitutions are to go into matters of statutory detail, some way ought to be provided for changing them without going through the cumbrous procedure of a popular vote. Doctor Whitten in the "New York State Library Review of Legislation" for 1901 suggested amendment by a two-thirds vote of one Legislature or of two successive Legislatures. Professor Dodd, while approving the idea, thinks some popular control should be maintained over even minor alterations. "What may well be done," he says, "is to provide that unimportant constitutional changes may be made by a two-thirds vote of the Legislature, but to permit a popular referendum upon such legislative action if a petition is presented signed by a sufficient number of voters." [1] A popular check upon legislative action would thus be retained, but changes would be made simpler and easier; the electorate would be freed from the burden of passing upon them, except in cases where there was assurance of rather wide popular interest in the matter.

[1] W. F. Dodd, *Revision of State Constitutions*, 290.

The question of whether amendments should be classified with some regard to nature or importance, and be handled accordingly has received some prominence as a result of the contentions produced by the Eighteenth Amendment of the Federal Constitution, prohibiting the manufacture, sale, or transportation of intoxicating liquors. It has been argued that the first ten amendments were in the nature of a Bill of Rights; that the Constitution would not have been adopted but for the assurance that these guarantees would be added; that the agreement to this effect gave the declarations peculiar sanctity. Extremists, holding these rights to be natural, universal, unalienable, say they are unalterable and supreme. Others hold that when one of these declarations may have some bearing on a proposed change in the Constitution, the amendment should be ratified by a vote of the people. Still others, less exacting, would be content with ratification by Conventions chosen for the express purpose of passing judgment. Inasmuch as the basic proposition involved, that Bills of Rights are immutable, gets nowadays no considerable support from authorities on political science and has little or no standing in the courts, the argument need not here hold attention further.

Another problem brought up by the same subject is that of whether ratification within a stipulated time may be made essential to validity. To be sure, the Supreme Court has sustained Congress, holding in Dillon *v.* Gloss (256 U.S. 368–1921) that "as ratification is but the expression of the approbation of the people and is to be effective when had in three fourths of the States, there is a fair implication that it must be sufficiently contemporaneous in that number of States to reflect the will of the people in all sections at relatively the same period." Yet the question was importantly raised for the first time no farther back than the Eighteenth Amendment; there had been no long, continuous, and uniform interpretation; academic discussion had shown belief to be for the most part contrary to the position now taken by the Court; grave doubt still exists; and the Court may change its mind, though probably not.

Akin to this is a third question, that of whether a time limit may be implied in the matter of calling a Federal Convention. The call is to be issued by Congress "on the application of the legislatures of two thirds of the several States." It is argued that inasmuch as twenty-eight States have made such application within the last thirty years, if four more should apply, Congress would be in duty bound to act. In opposition eminent lawyers contend that here too the rule of reason should apply. Some of them also hold that Congress might properly take into account the fact that the States which have acted have been impelled by differing motives. The latter contention strikes me as clearly unsound. A moment's consideration should show the danger of accepting motive as a proper factor in determining constitutional interpretation. Unless definitely expressed in the legislative vote, it would be matter of surmise, for how otherwise could the reason for the vote of the individual legislator be appraised? This would surely develop controversy in Congress, with the result inevitably depending on the judgment of the majority as to the desirability of a Convention, which is just what the framers of the Constitution did not contemplate. They may have been wrong in this particular or others, but whatever the dangers, it is better that the plain meaning of what they said should be followed. Possibly a court may safely interpolate inferences, but not a legislative assembly.

A fourth question, partly vivified by the same Prohibition issue, is whether the ratification of an amendment submitted by Congress ought not to be required from Legislatures elected after submission. Of course the purpose would be to secure an opportunity for expression of the popular will at the polls in the election of legislators known to have before them the exercise of judgment on a pending proposal. More radical advocates of the real end to be accomplished would have the amendment itself submitted to the electorate. In either case the answer involves the whole question of representative as against democratic government, and will be given according to opinion thereon, unless judgment is warped by prejudice resulting from the circumstances of the particular case responsible for the discussion.

The Federal Constitution received such glorification from orators in the early decades of its existence, its principles were at the heart of such great political controversies for three quarters of a century, notably those leading to a civil war, that it became sacrosanct. To suggest altering it in any particular seemed almost impious. Question was even raised as to whether any attempt by Congress to amend would not be itself unconstitutional. The eloquent Edward Everett argued in the House in 1826 that as each member had taken an oath to support the Constitution as it was, no member could propose to alter it without violating that oath.

In a century and a third only nineteen amendments were achieved. In the last hundred years there have been but nine. The bare statement is enough to cast a doubt on the adequacy of the process of amending the Federal Constitution to the needs of changing social conditions. It is, to be sure, a marvelously flexible instrument, and the courts have succeeded in adapting it to many modern necessities; yet one must not be a radical to wish it might be susceptible of somewhat easier change, and to think there would be little danger if this were made possible. From the Civil War to the passage of the income-tax amendment, so many years passed that it was feared the amending process had become quite obsolete. Although it is now seen that with public pressure enough, the thing can be done, yet the difficulty of it still seems needlessly excessive. Why increase that difficulty?

In the States the progress has been toward rather than away from making it easy to change Constitutions. First came the spread of amendment by occasional Conventions; next was added to this the opportunity to change by legislative enactment ratified by the voters; then periodical Conventions grew in favor; the Initiative and Referendum followed. Little by little we are getting away from the fears of our forefathers, the framers of the original State Constitutions, who based their work on the belief that their governments were too unstable.

European countries have given short shrift to such fears, even though most of them have shown far more occasion for worry than exists in the United States. England, the most stable of them all, indeed perhaps the most stable in the world, can justify the omnipotence of Parliament, which unchecked by anything save tradition and opinion can at any moment alter that congeries of charters and statutes, judicial decisions and common law, precedents and usages, which makes up the British Constitution. It remains to be seen whether as much can some day be said of the complete freedom from constitutional limitations with which the Italian Parliament acts, as for example under the leadership of Mussolini. Likewise absence of formal control appears in Hungary.

France puts a little restraint on the National Assembly. The Constitution of the present Republic consisted at first of five laws enacted in 1875. Only three of these had a constitutional form, and one of the three was in 1884 largely separated from what is called the Constitution.[1] The other two, though described as organic laws, may be changed in the same way as any statute. The surviving part of the measures looked upon as truly constitutional, require more procedure for amendment. Each Chamber must first vote that change is desirable. If that is agreed, then the two bodies meet in one Assembly, with a vote for each member, and a majority prevails without further requirement. As a matter of fact this is simpler than the passage of an ordinary bill, for it avoids the dangers and delays incident to separate action by two bodies, often at odds over trivial points.

The Constitution of the German Empire could be changed by the passage of an ordinary law, except that fourteen of the twenty-five votes in the upper branch would defeat the proposal. That of the Republic gives like power, but the vote in each branch must be carried with a two-thirds quorum present and by two thirds of those voting. Although a change approved by the lower branch will otherwise go into effect despite objection by the upper branch, the latter, acting within two weeks, can require submission of the proposal to the electorate. Amendments may also begin by popular initiative, but when so begun, they can be adopted only by majority vote of the whole electorate, which, judging by our experience in Indiana, Minnesota, and other States, makes the opportunity virtually innocuous. It paralyzes progress through this channel. Perhaps such an effect was intended.

In Austria amendments may be made by a two-thirds vote of the lower branch, but they must be submitted to a referendum on demand of one third of the members of either branch, and a complete revision must be so submitted anyhow. In Poland there is to be a general revision every twenty-five years, made by the two chambers sitting jointly, each member having one vote and a majority deciding. In the intervals a motion for amendment must be signed by one quarter of the membership of the lower chamber, and must be approved by a two-thirds vote of the entire membership of each chamber. Czecho-Slovakia required approval by three fifths of the full membership of each chamber.

In Belgium, when the two Houses vote revision necessary, that *ipso facto* dissolves them. The Houses then elected may

---

[1] Joseph Barthelemy, *The Government of France*, tr. by J. Bayard Morris, 21.

amend by a two-thirds vote of a two-thirds quorum, with approval by the King. In Jugo-Slavia if the King proposes an amendment, on the advice of his ministers, there must likewise be a new Assembly, where it may be ratified by a majority of the total membership. If an amendment is proposed in the Assembly itself, it may be adopted by three fifths of the entire membership, which works dissolution, whereupon a new Assembly, chosen within four months, may ratify the amendment by absolute majority. Rumania also applied the dissolution requirement, but modified the method somewhat. If the Chambers acting separately, by absolute majority, decide revision necessary, a joint committee is chosen to agree on the text of the proposed change. Then after two readings in joint session within fifteen days, there is to be approval by two thirds of a two-thirds quorum. Automatic dissolution follows and the newly elected Chambers must approve, again by a two-thirds vote of a two-thirds quorum. In Switzerland an amendment, whether initiated by the people or by the Federal Congress, must be submitted to a plebiscite, and the same requirement appears in Esthonia.

The British North American Act contained no provision for its own alteration by any authority within Canada, and so the Constitution of that Dominion may be changed only by the Imperial Parliament. This, however, is of small consequence, for the Government is always ready to make any change asked for by Canada. Doubtless the Act would have granted power to amend if it had been passed after the development of sentiment for Dominion autonomy that made it possible for Australia and South Africa to get such power. The Constitution of the Irish Free State gives the initiative to its Parliament, with judgment then to be passed at the polls, where for approval a majority of registered voters must vote and either a majority of the registered voters or two thirds of those voting must favor.

It will be seen that of these countries which have framed Constitutions since the World War, four have made provision for direct vote of the people on amendments under certain circumstances, three for indirect vote as a result of dissolution of the Parliament, and none for ratification by the bodies corresponding to our State Legislatures or by Conventions called for the purpose. As Professor Munro points out,[1] it is not that the

[1] W. B. Munro, *The Governments of Europe*, 757.

framers of these Constitutions were unfamiliar with the American methods of constitutional amendment and revision. They had our long constitutional experience before their eyes. But they evidently were not impressed to the extent of giving its results the flattery of imitation.

MODE OF SUBMISSION

The mode of submitting to the people changes proposed by a Convention or Commission is frequently a matter of controversy. The defeat of the proposals of the latest New York Convention was undoubtedly due in part to their submission in the lump, so that every voter had to "take it or leave it." The outcome was that the hostility to single features made an aggregate of opposition which could not be resisted. Anybody who has served in a legislative body must have observed that singular trait of human nature which makes hostility more vigorous than favor. That is the reason why the work of Legislatures is and must be largely of the piecemeal variety, with reforms advanced step by step, little by little. Nothing is harder at the State House than to secure the adoption of a comprehensive, thorough revision of any mass of detail, if it contemplates numerous changes. In all probability this was the reason why the work of the Massachusetts Convention of 1853 failed. It lumped all the important changes in one proposal, submitting as a whole the Constitution thus revised. To be sure, seven other proposals were submitted, but they were of minor significance, and were doubtless swamped by the tide of opposition the big proposal developed. All were defeated by small majorities, not in percentage larger than that proportion of the voters who, having voted "No" on the first item in any list, apparently carry their resentment through the rest of the items.

Ex-Governor Marcus Morton warned the Convention against this, in a strong speech showing why the people ought to have the chance to pass on changes separately, but the Convention voted otherwise, 170 to 73. It was in vain that he called to mind the method adopted by the Convention of 1820. At that time fourteen changes were separately submitted, nine of which were accepted. The largest vote cast on any one was 30,892; the largest majority for any one, 16,282; the largest majority against any one, 12,103. Some inferences are justified if these figures be compared with those of the votes on the proposals of 1853. Then the largest vote was that on the big proposal — 131,372; and the smallest on any proposal was 130,051. The majority against the big proposal was 4,928, and on the others ranged from 401 to 6,713. It would look as if in 1820 the voters gave independent consideration to each proposal, and in evident degree refrained from voting on those about which they were not informed or to which they were indifferent. In 1853, on the other hand, the figures betray the deadening influence of faction. Most men voted either "Yes" or "No" right through the list.

That the fate of a revision may be determined by overshadowing interest in a single proposal is shown by Connecticut experience. There the Constitution of 1902 was rejected probably because of the popular impulse to let the matter of representation predominate. Other issues, perhaps more important, were obscured or ignored. A leading Connecticut lawyer said at the time that the evil of permitting the Legislature to grant special charters to cities and corporations was, practically, far greater than the evil of a misrepresentative Legislature. This was recognized in the Convention, and an attempt was made to deprive the Legislature, by constitutional prohibition, of its power to grant special charters. The attempt attracted little but perfunctory attention, and was dropped almost without comment.[1]

The argument for submitting all or the most important changes in the mass, is evident and logical — it conduces to symmetry and consistency. As a practical matter, however, experience shows that the other method, if less scientific, is likely to be more productive of results.

When changes submitted in the lump have been at first defeated, the usual outcome has been the adoption of many of them by separate amendments afterward or by legislative action securing the same ends. Most of the important changes recommended by the Massachusetts Convention of 1853, and some urged therein without meeting its approval but thereby getting public attention, are now law in that State. C. Z. Lincoln says that about one half of the distinct proposals, including entire articles, submitted by the New York Convention of 1867 have since been incorporated in the Constitution. "Most of those not adopted were of minor importance, and would not now be seriously considered if suggested by independent amendment."[2]

[1] *Outlook*, June 28, 1902, 532.

[2] *Constitutional History of New York*, II, 407.

It is this that makes the educating influence of the Convention a matter of no small importance, and often justifies time and effort that may at first glance have seemed fruitless. Furthermore, even if no change whatever follows, whether at once or ultimately, yet there is the negative value, not to be scorned, of satisfying impatient minorities that their views are not acceptable, and of assuring majorities that their convictions are in fact preponderant. It is well once in a while to get assurance that the situation is sound and satisfactory.

"TINKERING"

How difficult it ought to be to amend a Constitution has long been a subject of earnest discussion, particularly in the matter of the Federal Constitution. That document provides two methods of amendment. At the request of the Legislatures of two thirds of the States, Congress is to call a Convention for proposing amendments, which must be ratified by the Legislatures or Conventions of three fourths of the States. This method has never been used and nothing but a crisis would make it feasible. The other method requires proposal of amendments by two thirds of both Houses and ratification by the Legislatures or Conventions of three fourths of the States. It is interesting to note that the real obstacle in this procedure was quite unforeseen by the statesmen who in 1788 opposed the ratification of the Constitution because of the difficulty of amending. For instance, Patrick Henry, speaking in the Virginia Convention June 5 of that year, asked if it were possible that three fourths of the States could ever agree to the same amendment. He calculated that through the control put within reach of the smaller States, one twentieth of the people might prevent the removal of the most grievous inconveniences and oppression.

It has turned out that this fear was groundless. Once an amendment has been submitted, it has usually proved that in each State there has been about the same proportion between approval and disapproval, or at any rate sectional views have not so widely varied as to produce the results apprehended in the way of blocking action. Furthermore, there has usually been no time limit on ratification by the States. Unless otherwise provided, as was the case with the prohibition amendment, the question may come before Legislature after Legislature until there is an affirmative vote, and once such a vote has been secured, the general opinion is that it cannot afterward be reconsidered. When New Jersey and Ohio tried to reconsider and withdraw their approval of one of the amendments growing out of the Civil War, Congress denied the right. The question came up again in connection with the Prohibition Amendment, but was not pushed to an issue. Jameson maintains that Congress may not recall an amendment it has once submitted. On the other hand it has been held that the action of one Legislature in rejecting does not prevent a succeeding Legislature from ratifying.

This nowadays makes it probable that sooner or later every amendment submitted will be adopted. Of late no group of States numerous enough to prevent approval has long persisted.

The real difficulty has proved to lie in getting Congress to submit amendments. In the first hundred years, according to the exhaustive analysis of Prof. Herman V. Ames, out of 1,736 proposals for amendment made in Congress, only fifteen were submitted to the States.[1] Ten of the fifteen resulted from the discussions of the ratifying Conventions and were proposed at the first session of Congress. From then until the Civil War but two successfully ran the Congressional gauntlet. Three resulted from the Civil War. Then for more than two score years no other amendment was submitted.

The four recent amendments, those for the income tax, direct election of Senators, national prohibition, and woman suffrage, have shown action to be still possible, but its difficulties continue so serious that not a few thoughtful men think the process should be made at least a little easier. The argument against it is that innovation is too strong an impulse in democratic States, and must be regulated; that the organic law should be changed only after long experience and patient deliberation have demonstrated the necessity of the change; and that too great fixedness of the law is better than too great fluctuation. Professor Burgess has voiced the other view by saying it is equally true that development is as much a law of State life as of existence. "Prohibit the former, and the latter is the existence of the body after the spirit has departed. When, in a democratic political society, the well-matured, long, and deliberately formed will of the undoubted majority can be persistently and successfully thwarted, in the amendment of its organic law, there is just as much danger to the State from revolution and violence as there is from

[1] *Am. Hist. Assn. Ann. Report for 1896*, ii, 306–421 (complete list).

the caprice of the majority where the sovereignty of the bare majority is acknowledged." [1] To meet the situation conservatively, as he thought, he formulated this plan: Proposal of amendments by two successive Congresses, Senators and Representatives acting in joint assembly and resolving by simple majority vote; submission of proposals to the Legislatures of the several States, these again acting in joint assembly and resolving by simple majority vote; assignment to each State of the same weight in the count of votes as in a Presidential election, and ratification of amendments by a simple majority of the State votes thus weighted. Such a program while reducing to a simple majority the proportion of votes necessary for proposal and for ratification, would lengthen the period of consideration in Congress; and by requiring the reconsideration of a proposal by a succeeding Congress, give an opportunity to the country to express its opinion in the election of a new House of Representatives. Various other methods of improving the situation have been suggested, but none of then make headway.

In the latter part of his life, after he had been watching Constitutions for forty years, Jefferson delivered himself of some conclusions that are well worth the study and reflection of those who "view with alarm" what they are pleased to call the constant tinkering with the fundamental law. "Some men," he said, "look at Constitutions with sanctimonious reverence, and deem them like the ark of the covenant, too sacred to be touched. They ascribe to men of the preceding age a wisdom more than human, and suppose what they did to be beyond amendment. I knew that age well; I belonged to it, and labored with it. It deserved well of its country. It was very like the present, but without the experience of the present, and forty years of experience in government is worth a century of book-reading; and this they would say themselves, were they to rise from the dead. I am certainly not an advocate for frequent and untried changes in laws and Constitutions. I think moderate imperfections had better be borne with; because, when once known, we accommodate ourselves to them, and find practical means of correcting their ill effects. But I know also, that laws and institutions must go hand in hand with the progress of the human mind. As that becomes more developed, more enlightened, as new discoveries are made, new truths disclosed, and manners and opinions

[1] *Political Science and Comparative Constitutional Law*, i, 151.

change with the change of circumstances, institutions must advance also, and keep pace with the times." [1]

These are the views that have prevailed in the States of the American Union. They have looked on a Constitution as an instrument — as a means and not as an end. A Constitution is not a curio. It is not a relic to be kept inviolate. If it is worth anything, it has life, and anything that lives, either grows or dies. He who deplores the instability of Constitutions, deplores the instability of life. Of course this does not justify trivial, hasty change. Very likely there was ground for the jest of the bookseller who was asked in the course of the Second French Republic, "Have you a copy of the French Constitution?" He replied, "We do not deal in periodical literature." Such a gibe may not be fairly thrown at American Constitutions. Look at the record, remembering that we have grown from thirteen colonies to forty-eight States. Besides the documents with which they started, there have been about seventy-five revisions. (The figure varies according to the treatment of the Constitutions of Vermont, Kansas, and Texas before they were admitted as States.) If every State were to adopt a new Constitution tomorrow, the average interval between general revisions would have been very close to thirty-three years — what is commonly spoken of as a generation. Many Constitutions, however, will not be again revised for years to come; ten of the States have not been in existence thirty-three years; and there were twenty-seven revisions of Constitutions of Southern States brought about by the abnormal conditions of the Civil War. It might be fair to say, therefore, that normally the average life of an American State Constitution is not far from half a century. Of course there are scores of changes by amendment, now averaging not far from one each year for each State, but for the most part these are matters of detail, not going to the essence. Indeed what are called general revisions, have often seen few changes in anything save relatively unimportant machinery.

The injustice of much of the criticism on the score of changes comes from the tendency to exaggerate the significance of action by a few States, often of small population. Idiosyncracies get treated as typical characteristics; the exception is assumed to be the rule.

[1] Thomas Jefferson to Samuel Kercheval, July 12, 1816, *Writings of Jefferson*, P. L. Ford ed., x, 42.

It is not even true that revisions are becoming more frequent. In the second quarter of the nineteenth century there were a dozen; in the last quarter of that century there were a dozen, in the first quarter of the twentieth century less. Yet since 1834 the number of States has doubled, giving, of course, twice the opportunity.

From the time when Pennsylvania concluded that her Council of Censors was "too dilatory" to produce necessary alterations, there has been complaint of the difficulty of amending State Constitutions. Of late years this complaint has grown until it has become one of the sore spots in our political life. It has played no small part in the spread of the Initiative and Referendum. It contributed to the mushroom growth of the Progressive party in 1912. That there was ground for the complaint may be inferred from the fact that many of those who stoutly opposed the Progressive movement, have since conceded the need of some change in this particular. For example, President Nicholas Murray Butler of Columbia University, one of the most earnest opponents of direct legislation and kindred proposals, whose writings had been used in 1912 as campaign documents by the conservative forces, asked the Massachusetts Constitutional Convention of 1917, in the course of an eloquent address, if it might not be said that those who are convinced democrats and believers in constitutional government, have come to a substantial agreement that it is the essence of a sound Constitution for the method for its amendment to be such as to put within the reach of the people opportunity, after adequate consideration and discussion, to readjust it from time to time to new needs and for the solution of new problems. "We are sometimes apt," he said, "to overlook the formula for constitutional amendment, but that, I think on reflection we should all agree, goes to the very essence of a Constitution that is to be a document of advance and of progress and of life, and not merely a fixed formula for a given year and a given generation."

The convention addressed by Mr. Butler agreed later upon so considerable a letting down of the bars as to alarm the more conservative members. By accustomed methods forty-eight amendments had been made to the Constitution since its adoption, which seemed to argue that the methods were not over-rigid. No great need of more rapid change presented itself. The State had been well governed. Its people were as a whole contented and prosperous. On the other hand the radical extremists urged that selfish interests could under the existing system too easily block much needed progress. In the end, after exhaustive debate, what was deemed a compromise between extremes was reached. Besides the method of amendment provided by the Initiative and Referendum, it was agreed that the Legislature might upon majority vote of a joint session in two consecutive years, submit amendments to the people.

If it be thought that such a lessening of obstacles is dangerous, let it be remembered that it is within the power of the Parliament of England to change the Constitution of the British Empire by majority vote at a single session. In France, as we have seen, constitutional revision is accomplished by a majority vote of the two Chambers sitting jointly, after separate resolutions in each. It would probably be agreed in this country that our fathers did well to put barriers between their Constitutions and the whims, passions, frenzies of the people. It does not follow that these barriers may not have been needlessly and injuriously high and wide.

CHAPTER VIII

FUNDAMENTALS AND THEIR FORCE

UNTIL recently it has been the well-nigh universal theory that a Constitution should be a body of fundamental law. Judge Jameson has drawn the accustomed distinctions with probably as much precision as is practicable. "Ordinary laws," he says, "are enactments and rules for the government of civil conduct, promulgated by the legislative authority of a State, or deduced from long-established usage. It is an important characteristic of such laws that they are tentatory, occasional, and in the nature of temporary expedients. Fundamental laws on the other hand, in politics, are expressions of the sovereign will in relation to the structure of government, the extent and distribution of its powers, the modes and principles of its operations, and the apparatus of checks and balances proper to insure its integrity and continued existence. Fundamental laws are primary, being the commands of the sovereign establishing the governmental machine, and the most general rules for its operation. Ordinary laws are secondary, being commands of the sovereign having reference to the exigencies of time and place resulting from the ordinary working of the machine. Fundamental laws precede ordinary laws in point of time, and embrace the settled policy of the State. Ordinary laws are the creatures of the sovereign, acting through a body of functionaries existing only by virtue of the fundamental laws, and express, as we have said, the expedient, or the right viewed as the expedient, under the varying circumstances of time and place." [1]

Comprehensive though on first reading this seems to be, it refers only by implication if at all to what is now generally agreed to be a body of fundamental law that should be in every Constitution, called a Bill or Declaration of Rights. The Convention of Virginia, the first American State to draft such a Bill, adopted it separately, and a fortnight or more later adopted a "Constitution or Form of Government." Maryland and North Carolina followed this classification and terminology. Pennsylvania, however, extended the scope of the word "Constitution,"

[1] *The Constitutional Convention*, 83.

by ordaining, declaring, and establishing a Declaration of Rights and Frame of Government, "to be the Constitution." John Adams copied this for Massachusetts and it has now come to be the accepted American scheme. Although the other original States had no independent Bill of Rights in their first Constitutions, some of the usual principles were embodied.

The need of such a Bill became a cardinal tenet of democratic faith and now it is to be found in every State Constitution. The lack of it in the draft prepared by the Federal Convention was one of the objections to that instrument most strongly urged, and possibly our Federal Constitution would not have been adopted had it not been the understanding that this lack would be supplied by amendments. Presently these were adopted and the first ten Articles of Amendment are commonly taken as the national Bill of Rights. They by no means go the length of duplicating all the declarations to be found in the State Bills. For that matter there is nothing like a consensus of opinion as to what ought to be in Declarations of Rights. Their paragraphs vary from fifteen to forty-five. Unanimity is not found in some particulars that have been thought most essential. For instance, the New York Constitution makes no declaration against search warrants, though it is in every other State Constitution and in the Fourth Amendment of the Federal Constitution. New York has been satisfied to make provision by statute.

The assumption has been that a Constitution should contain none but fundamental laws. This is a purely arbitrary assumption, for which the justification is sought in the fact that the early American Constitutions contained few laws not properly to be classed as fundamental. Those Constitutions invariably provided a frame of government, sometimes set forth what were believed to be natural rights, and rarely contained anything else. They were brief. Using the pages of Thorpe's compilation as the basis of comparison, I find the first of them, that of New Hampshire, covers but two pages. South Carolina, coming next, drafted what fills seven pages, of which more than two were preamble. Virginia followed with a little more than six pages, one of which was given to an arraignment of the King that was soon to appear in another form in the Declaration of Independence; and nearly two pages were taken up with the Bill of Rights.

The fourteen Constitutions drawn in the first decade of constitution-making average about ten and a half pages each, and the thirteen drawn in the next three decades average only about twelve pages, the longest of them, the second Constitution of Kentucky (1799), having less than fifteen full pages. However, what would be called "ordinary" laws were beginning to be incorporated. Indeed, some things that would now ordinarily be handled by Legislatures were put into some of the earliest of the Constitutions. For instance, that of South Carolina in March of 1776 specified the salaries to be paid various officials. Pennsylvania defined the liberty of hunting, fowling, and fishing. Massachusetts devoted a whole chapter to regulating the affairs of Harvard College.

Yet it was not until the land troubles of the newly settled regions vexed their politics that Conventions really engaged in statute-making. Kentucky began it with her Constitution of 1792 in which the Supreme Court was directed what to do in cases respecting certain land titles. Georgia went farther, in 1798, by reason of the Yazoo frauds. It declared certain contemplated purchases constitutionally void, and directed the Legislature to make provision by law for returning purchase money. Ohio in 1802 started what became a long train of constitutional provisions relating to slavery, which at times, especially in the Southern Constitutions, were distinctly in the nature of statutes.

The next step toward special legislation by Constitutional Conventions was that taken by Louisiana in 1812 when it guaranteed to the citizens of New Orleans the right of appointing the officers necessary for the administration and police of the city. Louisiana may thereby boast the honor of being the birthplace of municipal home rule as well as of having first granted special privileges to one community, unless exception is to be made by reason of places designated as State capitals in various Constitutions. Indiana in 1816 prescribed what the General Assembly might do in the matter of banks, and the Convention put in some provisions of its own that were distinctly statutory. Also it legislated about school lands and told the Assembly its duty in the matter. Mississippi in 1817 forbade the incorporation of banks unless the State had the right to subscribe for a quarter of the stock. Alabama in 1819 went into detail on banking matters; made certain statutory provisions about school lands and funds, and declared it the duty of the General Assembly to pass laws for deciding differences by arbitrators, to form a penal code on principles of reformation and not of vindictive justice, to revise and digest the laws at regular intervals, to gather knowledge about navigable waters and roads.

From this time on the practice of making statutes by constitutional provision grew apace. There is no need to detail its progress. The best idea of it is to be secured from the figures showing the steady elongation of Constitutions. From the average of a dozen pages in the generation between 1786 and 1815, they went up to about sixteen pages in the next three decades. The period from 1845 to the War was fertile in Constitutions, and the sixteen framed in it averaged nearly twenty-three pages. In the decade after the War, twenty-one Constitutions averaged to have twenty-eight pages; in the following decade, the average went up to nearly thirty-six; then in the next to more than thirty-eight; and ten Constitutions framed after 1895 had an average of forty-seven pages, Oklahoma having seventy and Louisiana seventy-three.

It has been commonly assumed that the newer States have been responsible for this growth and it is true that the documents which now seem abnormally long were not framed in States that existed before 1800. Yet where the older States have reframed their Constitutions, the growth has been material and significant. Pennsylvania, which began with eleven pages, reached thirty-one in 1873. New York, starting with fifteen, reached thirty-three in 1894. Delaware, starting with six, reached thirty-six in 1897. The enlargements have been due not only to the insertion of statutory provisions, but also to great amplification of the frame-of-government provisions.

The amendments of a legislative character adopted by the New York Convention of 1894 included provisions relating to pool-selling and book-making, damages for injuries causing death, registration of voters, bi-partisan election boards, riders on appropriation bills, contract labor in prisons, the civil service, the forest preserve, the State Board of Charities, lunacy and prison commissions, common schools, the University, sectarian appropriations, city legislation and separate elections, and free passes. The inclusion of provisions on these subjects in the Constitution withdrew them to that extent from the domain of legislative discretion, and this was the controlling purpose of the Convention in adopting them.[1]

[1] C. Z. Lincoln, *Constitutional History of New York*, III, 674.

The Mississippi Constitution of 1890 has nine Sections headed "Injunction," specifying as many kinds of laws that the Legislature shall enact, as, for example, laws to secure the safety of persons from fires in public places; and it has another heading, "Prohibitions," appearing over eleven other Sections that are in addition to the twenty-one classes of forbidden local, private, or special laws, as, for example, that the Legislature shall not authorize payment to any person of the salary of a deceased officer beyond the date of his death.

All this has much grieved those who think a Constitution should be simply the statement of a group of fundamental principles upon which may be erected, as occasion demands, a structure of legislation applying these principles to specific conditions. Note some typical expressions of this belief. President Nicholas Murray Butler said to the Commercial Club of St. Louis in 1911: "A Constitution should contain only those guaranties of civil and political liberty which underlie our whole organized society, and also make carefully drawn grants of power to legislative, executive, and judicial officers, as well as those major political determinations that persist, and are persisted in, through changes of party and of political creed." [1] F. J. Stimson declares: "When a law is unconstitutional, it should ever be only because it violates some great natural right of humanity, personal liberty, property, or the right to common law. When Constitutions go into details which are not substantially connected with these cardinal rights, they bring themselves into contempt, and justify the growing prejudice of our labor leaders against them." [2] William H. Taft when Secretary of War, speaking in Oklahoma City, advised the people of Oklahoma to vote down the Constitution they had framed. "It is not a Constitution, but a code of laws," he declared. Governor Emmet O'Neal of Alabama averred: "The tendency toward making the Constitution a code of statutory laws, instead of a framework of the fundamental principles of government, should be abandoned." [3]

Such instances of objection could be indefinitely multiplied. These will suffice to attest the earnest nature of the criticism. Let us examine the reasons advanced.

[1] "Why Should we Change our Form of Government?" Printed as Senate Doc. 238, 62nd Congress, 2nd Session.

[2] *Popular Lawmaking*, 121.

[3] "Distrust of State Legislatures," *North American Review*, May, 1914.

More than a century ago Count Joseph De Maistre pointed out that "the weakness and fragility of a Constitution are actually in direct proportion to the multiplicity of written constitutional articles." [1] Although the mathematics of this may be open to question, there is truth in it. Everybody will admit that there is more strength in a Constitution than in a Code, that a Constitution commands more respect, indeed more reverence. It follows that the nearer a Constitution is assimilated to a Code, the more it is likely to lose of respect and reverence. There can be no dispute that a great virtue of the Federal Constitution is its brevity. That Constitution, however, created a frame of government which was to exercise powers very few in comparison with the powers of the individual States. Its merits may or may not be those which should be paramount in a State Constitution.

For the States the more serious question may be whether there is gain or loss in putting the more important provisions of law, of ordinary statute law, beyond the possibility of hasty, easy change. There can be no doubt that distrust of Legislatures has been the chief reason for the elongation of Constitutions. The deliberate purpose has been to guard the weightier laws against the follies, the caprices, the passions of the usual lawmaking bodies. Thus the tendency is distinctly conservative and reactionary. The singular thing is that hand in hand with it is developing a tendency of directly opposite nature, radical and almost revolutionary, that of direct action by the people. In the same breath it is said that the Legislatures respond too quickly to the shifting winds of public opinion and that they do not respond quickly enough. As Governor O'Neal pointed out, the incorporation of statutory enactment in the fundamental law puts a check and restraint on the power of the people to govern themselves. Yet the Initiative and the Referendum are meant to give them that power in more ample measure than ever before.

In either case, is there not grave danger that the power of the majority may be unduly increased? On the one hand, by putting statutes into Constitutions in order that they may not be repealed by the next Legislature, the temporary majority shows its fear that its opinions may not stand the test of scrutiny and trial by the people. On the other hand, by enacting laws at the polls, the temporary majority shows it dares not trust its representatives to study and criticize and debate. If government exists for

[1] *On the Generative Principle of Political Constitutions*, 42.

the purpose of protecting minorities, for protecting the weak against the strong, will the supremacy of either extreme be prudent?

If the reader should doubt the tendency of prolix Constitutions to strangle progress, let him read of what happened in California as Samuel E. Moffett tells it. In 1879 that State adopted a Constitution regulating a great variety of the affairs of life in minute detail. When the State government was set to work under it, "at once the elaborate rules prescribed for its guidance began to chafe," Mr. Moffett says. "The Legislature found itself barred on every side. Much bad legislation was prevented, but so was much that was necessary. Then the courts began the process of exposition. Between the statutes that were invalidated, because they conflicted with the elaborate provisions of the new Constitution, and the constitutional provisions that were themselves annulled, on the ground that they did not harmonize with the Constitution of the United States, it began to look as if California had lost the power to do anything at all. Its paper swaddling bands had stopped all growth and movement. Students of political science pointed to the fundamental law of California as an impressive example of the way in which a Constitution ought not to be made. The attempt to provide for everything in advance, it was shown, had led to general confusion and paralysis." [1]

Besides the effect on the body of the law, there is to be considered the effect on the framers of the law. So far as the Convention directs, restricts, or supplants the Legislature, it makes the Legislature less powerful and important. It has been averred that this makes it harder to get able men to serve in the Legislature. I doubt if the criticism is of material consequence. No Constitution has yet taken away from a Legislature enough of its opportunities to leave it without a large field of work. The biggest single class of prohibitions is that of special, local, and private bills. Taking these out of the Legislature ought to make service in that body more rather than less attractive to unselfish, disinterested, public-spirited men. Furthermore, anything that lessens the volume of work, increases the likelihood that busy men of affairs will consent to the sacrifice that membership in a Legislature entails. If all matters of administrative detail were

[1] "The Constitutional Referendum in California," *Political Science Quarterly*, March, 1898.

eliminated, as in the British Parliament, leaving little except policies and programs to be determined, service would become still more attractive to the thoughtful and sincere.

It must be recognized, however, that taking things as they are, the Convention assembles men of a much higher average of intellectual capacity than is to be found in most Legislatures. Membership in a Convention is looked upon as a real honor. Since the opportunity comes only at long intervals, perhaps but once in a generation or two, it arouses the ambition of strong men who see in it the chance for reputation as well as for important public service. Whether or not it confuses the artificial distinctions the theorists would make between fundamental and ordinary laws, the palpable fact is that it results in better work. Since all governmental devices are instruments and not ends, why not accept the fact and make the best of it?

One answer to this might be found in the peril to the balances of our government. The more detail goes into our Constitutions, the more the powers of the legislative branch go down and the powers of the judicial branch go up. For example, take the police power. In these times more serious disputes arise over this than over perhaps any other problem of government. It concerns almost every phase of governmental expansion. How far may the public deprive the individual of his property and his rights for the common good? Already there is grave criticism of the courts for taking unto themselves and denying to the Legislature the decision of what is "a public use," that is, a use of property so important to the common welfare that it transcends individual rights and therefore may be exercised by the lawmaking body. Every limitation on the power of the legislative branch to declare what is for the common welfare adds to the power of the judicial branch in that respect, for one of the two must decide. Read the early Constitutions and you will see that their authors never dreamed of asking the judges to pass upon matters of expediency. Gradually the judicial branch has invaded that field. Is this wisely to be encouraged further?

To this question of basic governmental policy, add the doubt born of the ever-growing burden put upon the courts merely by the need of determining the constitutionality of statutes. Here the strain upon the courts themselves, though no small matter, is after all insignificant compared with what it implies, for every such determination means a plaintiff and a defendant, counsel on both sides, and perhaps a horde of witnesses — in brief, all the laborious and costly essentials and incidents of litigation, with behind the whole complex that uncertainty as to rights and duties out of which litigation springs. Is it wise to invite, to compel, more and more of this?

Judgments based on comprehensive views of the situation vary widely in the matter of general conclusions. Of recent writers who have given the subject thorough study, Professor Dealey thinks that the Constitutional Convention is the great agency through which democracy finds expression. "In its latest form, that of a body made up of delegates elected from districts of equal population, it is one of the greatest of our political inventions. Through it popular rights may be secured in the Constitution, legislative tyranny restrained. These objects have not yet been fully attained, but the Convention is the agency through which public opinion can express itself, as it becomes enlightened in respect to the needs of the times." [1]

Professor Dodd speaks more doubtfully. "Perhaps all that can be said with reference to its use in the several States," he concludes, "is that the Constitutional Convention has in most cases proven a fairly effective instrument for the expression of popular judgment upon important questions, and that the people have often, if not usually, defeated measures, even though relatively unimportant, which should have been defeated. It would be impossible to say that they have always acted wisely or even intelligently in adopting or rejecting measures submitted to them. And under present conditions the amending process is to a large extent ineffective because of the trivial character of many proposals submitted to the people." [2]

It will be generally agreed that in a Convention the emphasis should be on the fundamentals. Judge Denio put it there when he said: "Constitutional provisions are not levied solely at the evils most current at the times in which they are adopted, but, while embracing these, they look to the history of the abuses of political society in times past, and in other countries, and endeavor to form a system which shall protect the members of the State against those acts of oppression and misgovernment which unrestrained political or judicial power are always and everywhere most apt to fall into." [3] This does not deny the Conven-

[1] *Growth of American State Constitutions*, 258.
[2] *Revision of State Constitutions*, 287 (1910).
[3] People *ex rel.* Hackley *v.* Kelly, 24 N.Y. 74 (1861).

tion the right to attack current evils. If in this or that State the conditions are such as to make the Convention the sure and speedy way to attack them, theoretical objections will recall the words of Paul, "The letter killeth."

That the Constitutions should be carried to the point of dwarfing the powers of Legislatures, is a possibility I for one should deprecate. Bryce thought the time might almost seem to have come for prescribing that the Legislatures, like Congress, should be entitled to legislate on certain enumerated subjects only, and be always required to establish affirmatively their competence to deal with any given topic. This would reduce what ought to be the most important and useful of representative institutions, to the level of city councils. They do not deserve such emasculation. It would be a disaster.

More calamitous yet, in my judgment, would be the abolition of the Legislatures. It has been seriously proposed. Professor Dealey, toward the close of his careful analysis, after subtracting all the limitations on legislative powers from the totality, thinks the question naturally arises whether it is worth while to retain large and expensive Legislatures to exercise their small residue of petty powers. He goes so far as to say: "A Convention meeting periodically, and well supervised administrative departments with ordinance powers, might perform all legislative functions with entire satisfaction." [1] With this I cannot agree. Granting that it is eminently desirable to enlarge the ordinance powers of administrative departments and also that Conventions may with ability and without danger determine sundry broad questions of public policy, yet between the two functions will remain a field of no narrow limits that will profitably engage the efforts of Representatives chosen both regularly and frequently, for the purpose of speedily meeting the grievances of the people and steadily bettering the laws of the land.

LEGISLATORS AND CONSTITUTIONS

Deliberate violation of Constitutions is a topic that may here be taken up only as it relates to legislative bodies. The need of keeping lawmakers within the bounds of the fundamental law was felt even in their earliest period. Pericles at Athens deemed it prudent to vest in seven magistrates power of supervision both over other magistrates and over the public assembly. The seven

[1] *Growth of American State Constitutions*, 267.

were called Nomophylakes, or Law Guardians, and doubtless
were changed every year. They sat alongside the Proedri, or
Presidents, both in the Senate and in the public assembly, and
were charged with interposing whenever any step was taken or
proposition made contrary to the existing laws.[1]

Nothing of the sort developed with the growth of the British
Parliament. Indeed it was long before the fundamental law came
to be looked upon by Englishmen with the reverence customary
to-day. The founders of the American colonies were not loath to
evade their fundamental law, the charters. These forbade the
colonists to pass any laws repugnant to the laws of England. Yet
the conditions of life in a new world seemed to compel some devi-
ations from English law, and the preferences of the colonists
urged others. So even the Puritans of New England found in
evasions nothing inconsistent with their striving for righteousness. That the Puritan conscience was not wholly without
elasticity, and that the Puritan brain was shrewd enough to find
a way to violate the spirit without violating the letter of what
was in effect a Constitution, is shown by the course of John
Winthrop, and the magistrates of Massachusetts Bay. By 1636
the people had concluded that their condition was "very unsafe,
while so much power vested in the discretion of Magistrates."
So the General Court raised a committee "to make a draught of
laws." But the wiser men saw that a formal code with provisions
conformed in all respects to the convenience and wishes of the
people, would, as Winthrop said, "professedly transgress the
limits of our charter, which provides we shall make no laws repugnant to the laws of England; and that we are assured we must
do; but to raise up laws by practice and custom had been no
transgression; as, in our church discipline and in matters of marriage, to make a law that marriages should not be solemnized by
ministers is repugnant to the laws of England; but to bring it a
custom by practice for the Magistrate to perform it, is by no law
made repugnant." The magistrates and ministers were able to
stave off for several years the enactment of the code wanted by
the freemen.

Proof of a like spirit is to be found in the history of all the
other colonies. We may be quite sure that if there had been no
occasion, the Charter or Fundamental Laws of West New Jersey,
agreed upon in 1676, would not have contained this provision:

[1] George Grote, *History of Greece*, part ii, chap. 44.

"Chapter XIV. But if it so happen that any person or persons of the said General Assembly, shall therein designedly, willfully, and maliciously, move or excite any to move, any matter or thing whatsoever, that contradicts or any way subverts, any fundamentals of the said laws in the Constitution of the government of this Province, it being proved by seven honest and reputable persons, he or they shall be proceeded against as traitors to the said government."

Pennsylvania in creating a Council of Censors meant to ensure the observance of both constitutional and statute law. The Council was to inquire whether the Constitution had been preserved inviolate in every part; and whether the legislative and executive branches of government had performed their duty as guardians of the people, or had assumed to themselves or exercised other or greater powers than they were entitled to by the Constitution. The Censors were also to inquire whether the public taxes had been justly laid and collected in all parts of the Commonwealth, in what manner the public monies had been disposed of, and whether the laws had been duly executed. They were to have power to send for persons and papers; to pass public censures; to order impeachments; and to recommend to the Legislature the repealing of such laws as appeared to them to have been enacted contrary to the principles of the Constitution.

That the Constitutions did not at once clothe themselves with sanctity is shown by the violations of the Pennsylvania instrument disclosed by the records of the Council. Madison tells of them in No. 48 of "The Federalist." Among them was the passage of a great number of laws without observance of the rule that all bills of a public nature should be previously printed for the consideration of the people. The disregard of the fundamental law appeared in both legislative and executive acts. In part they were to be excused by the circumstances of war, "but the greater part of them," says Madison, "may be considered as the spontaneous shoots of an ill-constituted government," and he might have added that such acts may always be expected when the Constitution is grossly unsuited to actual conditions. Gouverneur Morris was wise enough to recognize this. Writing to Timothy Pickering December 22, 1814, he said: "But, after all, what does it signify that men should have a written Constitution, containing unequivocal provisions and limitations? The legislative lion will not be entangled in the meshes of a logical net. It will always make the power which it wishes to exercise, unless it be so organized as to contain within itself the efficient check. Attempts to restrain it from outrage, by other means, will only render it more outrageous. The idea of binding legislators by oaths is puerile. Having sworn to exercise the powers granted, according to their true intent and meaning, they will, when they feel a desire to go farther, avoid the shame, if not the guilt, of perjury, by swearing the true intent and meaning to be, according to their comprehension, that which suits their purpose." [1]

As the years have passed and Constitutions have hardened into institutions, their observance has become more natural, but not yet by any means universal. Many Legislatures habitually disregard their injunctions. This is especially common in matters of procedure, but also appears in the neglect to enact legislation that has been ordered. The Pennsylvania Constitution of 1873 provided that the Legislature should reapportion the senatorial districts every ten years, but the Legislature of that State has repeatedly violated this provision. Other Legislatures have ignored injunctions on the same subject. The New York Constitution of 1894 declared that there should be no gambling at race tracks and that the Legislature should enact appropriate laws to enforce this provision. Yet gambling was permitted to flourish in that State until the heroic efforts of Governor Hughes secured appropriate legislation in 1909 by convening the Legislature in extra session for that express purpose.[2] Congress, directed in effect by the Constitution to reapportion the members of the House among the several States after every decennial census, did not after 1911 act until 1929.

Occasionally Legislatures, like men, will be swept off their feet by some storm of passion and do things that in calmer moments their members will regret. Such was the case with what was known as the Personal Liberty bill passed by the General Court of Massachusetts in 1855 over the veto of Governor Henry J. Gardner, a veto exercised on the advice of Attorney-General John H. Clifford to the effect that the bill was unconstitutional. It was advice that to-day, with partisan bitterness long allayed, would be generally agreed to have been sound. Gardner had refused to remove Edward J. Loring from the office of Judge of

[1] *Diary and Letters of Gouverneur Morris*, Anne Cary Morris, ed., II, 574.
[2] F. A. Cleveland, *Organized Democracy*, 380.

Probate, which he held in addition to that of United States Commissioner. In his capacity as Commissioner he had outraged the anti-slavery sentiment of the State by his course in enforcing the Fugitive Slave Law against Anthony Burns, handing him over to his master amid scenes of intense excitement. The Legislature sought to remove Judge Loring by address, the peculiar Massachusetts practice by which the Governor removes on request of the Legislature. Upon the Governor's refusal, the Legislature passed a bill that now seems clearly to have transgressed the limits between the branches of government, invading the executive domain by defining grounds for removal, and that of the judiciary by declaring the meaning of statutes relating to habeas corpus. Two years later the attempt to punish Loring was repeated and again the Governor refused. In his statement of reasons he deplored that the unconstitutional law yet remained on the statute books.

It is probably inevitable that in times of great emotional stress, the barriers of Constitutions will be swept aside. So far our government has survived such crises, but of course they spell great danger. We have been preserved by the common instinct of our people that safety lies in respecting the opinions of our judges.

One State seeks that the legislator shall at any rate be conscious of his delinquencies, for by the Mississippi Constitution of 1890 every member is required to declare this in his oath: "I will, as soon as practicable hereafter, carefully read (or have read to me) the Constitution of this State, and will endeavor to note, and as a legislator, to execute all the requirements thereof imposed on the Legislature."

That may be all very well as far as it goes, but it does not reach the real difficulties of the well-meaning lawmaker. It may tell him how he must vote if he is convinced that a proposal is unconstitutional, but it does not help him answer these questions:

How shall I vote if I doubt whether this proposal, however meritorious, is constitutional?

How shall I vote if the position taken by the courts on like proposals makes it reasonably sure they would hold this one unconstitutional?

No less a personage than a President of the United States, himself a veteran lawmaker, had occasion to set forth officially his views on the first of these questions. When President Tyler signed the act for apportionment of Representatives, June 25, 1842, he filed with it an "exposition" of his reasons, in the course of which he said:

"In yielding *my doubts* to the matured opinion of Congress I have followed the advice of the first Secretary of State to the first President of the United States and the example set by that illustrious citizen upon a memorable occasion. When I was a member of either House of Congress I acted under the conviction that *to doubt* as to the constitutionality of a law was sufficient to induce me to give my vote against it; but I have not been able to bring myself to believe that *a doubtful opinion* of the Chief Magistrate ought to outweigh the solemnly pronounced opinion of the representatives of the people and of the States."

If we are to accept Judge Cooley's view, Tyler was in this matter right as a Senator and wrong as President, which, by the way, accords with the impression a good many had at the time about other things. Cooley says: "Whoever derives power from the Constitution to perform any public function is disloyal to that instrument, and grossly derelict in duty, if he does that which he is not reasonably satisfied that the Constitution permits. Whether the power be legislative, executive, or judicial, there is manifest disregard of constitutional and moral obligation by one who, having taken an oath to observe that instrument, takes part in an action which he cannot say he believes to be no violation of its provisions. A doubt of the constitutionality of any proposed legislative enactment should in any case be reason sufficient for refusing to adopt it; and, if legislators do not act upon this principle, the reasons upon which are based judicial decisions sustaining legislation, in very many cases will cease to be of force." [1]

Probably the chief of the reasons Judge Cooley had in mind was that the courts have a right to assume and do assume that legislators have voted according to the best of their judgment as to what the Constitution means. The Supreme Court of the United States, for instance, properly expects that a majority of the 96 Senators and a majority of the 435 Representatives voting have without serious doubt believed that a given measure did not violate the Federal Constitution. This makes a *prima facie* case for constitutionality from the start, a case that is to be overthrown only by powerful and convincing argument. In other

[1] *Constitutional Limitations*, 74.

words the benefit of the doubt accrues to the action of Congress, so that a large share of the responsibility rests on the shoulders of its members. It is wholly unjustifiable for any of them to shirk this responsibility by saying, "Put it up to the Court."

On the other hand, if the Court has spoken first, on substantially the same proposal though in some other form, does it follow that the answer is final and binds the legislator to its acceptance? In answering, bear in mind that confronted again with the same question, the Court may change its mind. The problem was debated in the United States Senate in June and July of 1909, in connection with the income tax.[1] Senator Cummins of Iowa said he had little regard for that sentiment which suggests it is an indelicate and an improper thing for Congress again to ask the Supreme Court to review the Constitution. Senator Root of New York thought the pending proposal not the ordinary case of a suitor asking for a rehearing; he saw in it the beginning of a campaign to compel the court to yield to the force of the opinion of the executive and legislative branches; he deplored the breach between what he called the two parts of our Government, with popular acclaim behind the popular branch, all setting against the independence, the dignity, the respect, the sacredness of that great tribunal, the Supreme Court.

Usually it is vain for lawmaker or executive official to persist in views contrary to those of a Supreme Court, but whether it is always incumbent on him to act in accordance with them is a question on which eminent, sincere, and patriotic statesmen have divided. Thomas Jefferson refused to obey the order of the court in the famous case of Marbury v. Madison. Andrew Jackson vetoed a bank bill because he deemed it unconstitutional, although the Supreme Court had held a like bill to be within the powers of Congress. Abraham Lincoln ignored the opinion of Chief Justice Taney to the effect that suspension of the writ of habeas corpus by proclamation of the President was beyond the authority given to him by the Constitution.

In any case the legislator who sets his own opinion above that of the Court and deliberately votes for a measure the Justices think to be forbidden by the Constitution takes a tremendous responsibility that few prudent men will assume. For this reason our legislative bodies rarely invite a struggle with the courts on

[1] *Congressional Record*, vol. 44, part 4, 3974 *et sqq.*

matters of much importance. Furthermore, these bodies pay
heed to the judiciary not alone as matter of caution and comity,
but also because ordinarily the judiciary can give practical effect
to its views by the use of its formidable powers.

The inevitable antagonism between the branches has at times
driven the judges to extremes in defense, and they have been
unable to resist the temptation to retort. To see the distance to
which a hypercritical jurist can go, read what Judge Stuart of
Indiana said in 1853, in the case of Maize *v.* the State (4 Ind.
342): "The judiciary look to the acts of the Legislature with
great respect, and reconcile and sustain them, if possible.... And
yet there are considerations which might somewhat abate this
blind respect for legislative exposition.... When we further reflect on the manner in which important enactments are often
passed through the forms of legislation, it would seem that our
respect for the construction of the Constitution impliedly given
by such acts, might be profitably qualified. If, for instance, it
appears from the Journals, which are the records of the General
Assembly, that the constitutionality of the act had not been
considered, such a tacit interpretation of the Constitution, even
by so numerous and respectable a body, could scarcely be considered of much weight or pressed upon us as authority. Thus,
in the present instance, bill no. 142 of the house, which subsequently became the act of March 4, 1853, does not appear
to have been referred to the judiciary committee of either
House. The question of its constitutionality was not even
agitated."

If a question of constitutionality presents itself in the course of
the consideration of a bill, that is, occurs to the mind of an ordinarily thoughtful legislator, of course it should be confronted.
But the assumption that it is part of legislative duty to agitate
the question of constitutionality on every measure is unnatural.
In the relations of life we treat most things as normal, or few as
abnormal, and in those matters where habit tells us normality is
to be expected, we do not waste time by hunting for abnormality.
To illustrate: We expect others to tell us the truth. Because
there are liars, we do not pause to weigh every sentence we hear.
Only when something puts us on our guard do we query. So in
legislative work, the rarity with which any legitimate question
of constitutionality can be raised certainly warrants the omission
of any proof or record that it has been invariably raised.

As a matter of fact, under a party system of legislation it is reasonably sure that whenever the question of constitutionality ought to be raised, it will be. Von Holst has pointed out that it is impossible even hastily to turn over the pages of the debates of Congress without being struck by a very important circumstance, to be found in the history of no other constitutional State. Up to the year 1861, there were but few important laws of a general character proposed which, while under discussion, were not attacked by the minority as unconstitutional. The arguments were scarcely ever confined to the worth or worthlessness of the law itself. The opposition in an extraordinarily large number of instances started out with the question of constitutionality. The expediency or inexpediency of the law was a secondary question, and was touched upon only as a confirmation of that first decisive objection.[1]

Very likely the Indiana judge had been led by the prevalence of this state of affairs to think it natural and normal. If such it was then, it certainly is not now. Perhaps because minorities have at last learned the futility of raising baseless questions, perhaps because constitutional channels are better defined, perhaps because the pressure of business no longer permits — whatever the reason, legislators do not now pause to ask if each of hundreds of routine matters does not transgress some paragraph of the Constitution.

This is not inconsistent with the belief that for various purposes, the detection of possible unconstitutionality being one, it would be useful to have expert scrutiny of all measures in the course of enactment. The contention does not go beyond the point of holding that a Legislature is not remiss if it fails to make affirmative record that in respect of every measure constitutionality has been "agitated," to use the word of the Indiana judge, and that the lack of such a record ought not of itself to overthrow the presumption of validity.

Laying aside the extremes of criticism, there remains a great mass of opinion that the situation is unsatisfactory. It is evident, in the first place, that questions of constitutionality take up a great deal of the time and energy of the courts that might to general good be put into other things. Judge Alton B. Parker told the American Bar Association in 1906 that a substantial percentage of the questions brought before the Appellate Courts are

[1] *Constitutional History of U.S.*, i, 70.

related to doubts of the validity of the laws under which actions are brought. Indeed, in the State of New York, in a period covering about twenty years, the constitutionality of more than five hundred statutes was challenged in the Court of Appeals. The dovetailing of new legislation into existing law, and the cost of construing the possible meaning of a legislature, also enter into a considerable part of the annual output of twenty thousand decisions rendered by Appellate Courts.

Judge Baldwin, in "The American Judiciary" (page 107), says that on the average probably one statute out of every three hundred enacted from year to year is judicially annulled. He speaks of the number of Acts of Congress and State statutes set aside by the Supreme Court of the United States as if it were very large. Although the aggregate is indeed big enough to constitute an evil demanding earnest attention, yet on the basis of percentages it seems very small to one with legislative experience. Everybody admits that between "constitutional" and "unconstitutional" there is a borderland of no small width. Remember that the bills which become law are only those believed by the Legislature to be on one of the two sides of a very indistinct line. That it should err only once in three hundred times might well be thought proof of surprising legal instinct on the part of our Legislatures. Perhaps even the judges themselves sometimes forget that every case which reaches a Supreme Court has presented to some trained mind a reasonable chance for difference of opinion on a point of law. The reports now contain thousands on thousands of instances of this. With the apparently limitless chance for opposing views, the marvel is not that Legislatures have erred so much, but that they have erred so little.

Furthermore, the man who dwells on the number of unconstitutional laws the Legislatures have enacted should in all fairness admit that in a hundred, perhaps a thousand times as many instances, they have themselves refused legislation urged upon them as meeting a public need, likely to conduce to the common welfare, rejecting because beyond the powers given by the Constitution.

There is the slightest of ground for thinking Congress has been seriously careless or blameworthy in this matter. Representative C. W. Ramseyer learned through the Legislative Reference service that the sixty-eight Congresses up to March 4, 1925, had

enacted 50,060 laws, and that the Supreme Court, deciding in
that time somewhat more than 30,000 cases, had found unconstitutionality in only forty-seven of these enactments, a small
fraction of one per cent.[1]

[1] *Congressional Record*, February 11, 1925, 3525.

CHAPTER IX

REPRESENTATION

By the foregoing study of the development of lawmaking by Legislatures, it has appeared that in England a body of business agents, gathered to make a bargain with the King, gradually came to acquire the function of making all the written laws; and that in America bodies of men, chosen from the first to make laws, developed into what we now know as Legislatures, or Congress, here also in theory (save as to direct legislation) the sole makers of written laws. This we call representative government. In a general way everybody knows what it means, for all know what it is, but search for scientific definition of it and you will be astonished at the scarcity thereof; or try to frame a definition for yourself, and you abandon the attempt in despair. The difficulty comes in trying to decide what is representation and what is represented. Of the remarkably few concise definitions that have been framed by authoritative thinkers, one is by John Stuart Mill, who wrote a book with "Representative Government" as the title, in which he said:

"The meaning of representative government is, that the whole people, or some numerous portion of them, exercise through deputies periodically elected by themselves the ultimate controlling power, which, in every constitution, must reside somewhere. This ultimate power they must possess in all its completeness. They must be masters, whenever they please, of all the operations of government." [1]

This describes, but it does not define. It discloses one aspect of the relations between the government and the governed. It may cover substitution, but does not cover representation. It leaves unanswered the question — What is representation? It shows that the government is an agent, whose agency may be canceled, but it does not show the nature or extent of the agency.

Take another definition, that of the apostle of minority representation, Thomas Hare:

"Representation itself is a matter of daily occurrence, and common necessity. It is the vicarious performance of duties

[1] *Representative Government*, chap. v.

which cannot be personally executed. It intervenes in commerce, in jurisprudence, in education, and in a thousand other forms. In a multitude of circumstances people are compelled to place themselves and their interests in the hands of others." [1]

This, too, makes of representation nothing but agency. It accords with the early nature of the member of Parliament. It is not adequate in description of the present member of Parliament, Congress, or a State Legislature. It does not identify at all the subject of the function of representation.

Examine next the views of that writer who has made for us the best study of political terminology, Sir G. Cornewall Lewis. Says he:

"A representative government is when a certain portion of the community, generally consisting either of all the adult males, or a part of them, determined according to some qualification of property, residence, or other accident, have the right of voting at certain intervals of time for the election of particular members of the sovereign legislative body." [2]

This, too, is description rather than definition. It portrays the form without revealing the spirit. Skillfully avoiding suggestion of agency, it also avoids all other suggestion of function, save what is contained in the phrase "sovereign legislative body," and this is open to dispute, for if representative bodies in the United States were ever the depositaries of sovereignty, they surely are not to-day in those States that expose every legislative act to the Referendum. Even in England the appeal of a ministry to the electorate raises a doubt as to what is "the sovereign legislative body." In that word "sovereign" is the element of uncertainty on which Hobbes, Locke, Rousseau, Bentham, Austin, and so many others have spent their keenest logic. Is a government representative in which the representatives are mouthpieces? Or does the name imply independent volition? Permit a matter-of-fact illustration from quite another field: Is a representative government like an electric car driven by a current from a central station? Or is it like an automobile, carrying its own motor?

Consideration farther on of certain practical phases of the problem may lead the reader to conclude that these questions cannot be definitely answered, or perhaps that representative

[1] *The Election of Representatives*, xxxv, 3rd ed. (1865).
[2] *Remarks on the Use and Abuse of Some Political Terms*, 96–98 (1832).

government may sometimes be one thing, sometimes the other. For the moment, anyhow, let us assume that no small part of the function of a representative is to interpret the will of the community and put it into written law. Let us accept Burke's view as he gave it in "Thoughts on the Cause of the Present Discontents" — a view, by the way, quite the opposite of that to be found in his famous Speech to the Electors of Bristol, which is to be examined later on, showing once again how consistency is a virtue of weak minds. "The virtue, spirit, and essence of a House of Commons," said Burke when he was not justifying himself, "consists in its being the express image of the feelings of the nation. It was not instituted to be a controul *upon* the people, as of late it has been taught, by a doctrine of the most pernicious tendency. It was designed as a controul *for* the people."

LOT AND BALLOT

How, then, are we to secure through representatives "the express image of the feelings of the nation"?

First, it might be answered, by having the nation elect its representatives. To be sure, this is not beyond dispute.

Simon Sterne has said that the act of voting is not a necessary element of representation. "It is a mere proof that the representative is the deputed authority for those who elect him. Judges who are not elected, administrators who are not elected, are in many respects as truly representative in the power they wield as the members of the legislative body who are directly deputed by the people. Even in monarchies the King may represent, and in most instances does represent, as to his right to reign, the actual will of the people, although the existing generation may have had no instrumentality to express its will on his right to rule."[1] This is true enough and is not to be forgotten, but the fact is that by conventional usage political "representation" implies chosen representatives. In defence of the Lewis definition, it might be said that convention also has given to the word the implication that representatives shall be chosen by vote. But this has not always been the case, and some reformers believe it should not continue to be the case, for they would revive the Greek practice of choice by lot.

Aristotle said in "The Politics" that "the appointment to all offices, or to all but those which require experience and skill,

[1] "Representation," *Lalor's Cyclopedia of Political Science*, III, 581.

should be made by lot." It was the procedure with which he was
familiar. Fustel de Coulanges tells us that for the Athenians the
lot was not chance; it was the revelation of the divine will. Just
as they had recourse to it in the temples to discover the secrets of
the gods, so the city had recourse to it for the choice of its magistrate. It was believed that the gods designated the most
worthy by making his name leap out of the urn. This was the
opinion of Plato himself, who says, "He on whom the lot falls is
the ruler, and is dear to the gods; and this we affirm to be quite
just. The officers of the temple shall be appointed by lot; in this
way their election will be committed to God, who will do what is
agreeable to him." [1] The city believed that in this manner it received its magistrates from the gods.[2]

"It is surprising," de Coulanges also says, "that modern historians represent the drawing of lots as an invention of the Athenian democracy. It was, on the contrary, in full rigor under the
rule of the aristocracy, and appears to have been as old as the
archonship itself. Nor is it a democratic procedure; we know, indeed, that even in the time of Lysias and of Demosthenes, the
names of all the citizens were not put in the urn.... It is worthy
of remark, that when the democracy gained the upper hand, it
reserved the selection by lot for the choice of archons, to whom
it left no real power, and gave it up in the choice of strategy; who
had then the true authority. So that there was drawing of lots
for magistracies which dated from the aristocratic age, and election for those that dated from the age of the democracy." [3]

A curious instance of attempt to revive the lot in more recent
times is to be found in the Fundamental Constitution for the
Province of East New Jersey in America (1683). This provided
that the names of all qualified persons in a county should be put
in a box, from which a boy under ten years of age should draw
fifty. From these he should then draw twenty-five, who would
be those eligible to be sent to the Great Council. The other
twenty-five were to be nominators and were to pick out twelve
from the first twenty-five, if three were to be elected, eight if
two were to be elected: "first solemnly declaring before the sheriff, that they shall not name any known to them to be guilty for
the time, or to have been guilty for a year before, of adultery,

---

[1] Plato, Laws, iii, 690; vi, 759.

[2] *The Ancient City*, Willard Small transl., 246.

[3] *Ibid.*, 240, note.

whoredom, drunkenness, or any such immorality, or who is insolvent or is a fool." Then the three or two were to be elected by ballot.

Those who to-day advocate the lot for the designating of legislators do not, of course, urge the argument of divine direction. They think it would secure the same probability of impartial judgment that is expected of jurors. More important, they think it would be likely to secure a more accurate reflection of the popular will, by bringing together in the work of legislation all sorts and conditions of men. However, their advocacy makes no headway. Not in our time is it likely that there will be any departure from the familiar method of choice by vote.

Thorough treatment of the subject of voting would require a volume by itself. Only some phases of it more directly touching fundamental problems may here be noted.

Certainly the most considerable and perhaps the most important controversy in this connection has been over the question whether the choice of the voter should be made in public or in secret. The dispute goes back more than two thousand years and from the very start has hung on the question whether it is better that the electorate should be guided, even controlled, or be independent. The ballot — remember that in technical discussion the word commonly implies secrecy — the ballot was abolished in Athens by the thirty tyrants when they usurped power. Lysias says in one of his orations that they ordered the suffrages of the Areopagites to be public, in order to manage them as they pleased. When Rome, after the middle of the second century B.C., saw the ballot introduced by laws named from their authors — Gabinius, Cassius, Papirius, Carbo, and Coelius, aristocrats like Cicero bewailed the laws and declared their authors to be men of mean extraction and treasonable purposes. In his essay "De Amicitia" Cicero cited the ballot as among the dangerous measures that good citizens ought not to advocate, even though proposed by their friends. "Mark," he said, "what ruin has already resulted from the ballot, first enacted in the Gabinian law, and two years after in the Cassian. Now I seem to see the people no longer united in the Senate, and the highest interests disposed of at the will of the multitude." He feared the ballot because it would diminish the power of the patricians, and like all aristocrats he felt that safety was to be found only in the supremacy of his own class. In his oration for Sestius he said the people thought their liberty depended on the ballot, but the nobles trembled at the license and daring of the multitude.

Time did not remove the fear. The younger Pliny, in one of his letters written somewhere about the beginning of the second century of the Christian era, notices the restoration of the ballot in the elections as a remedy for the disorder that had prevailed. "But I fear," he says, "that in process of time evils will result from the remedy itself. There is danger that shamelessness may creep into these silent suffrages. For who cares for honesty so much in public as in private? Many regard reputation, but few conscience." Centuries afterward, men writing from the aristocratic point of view found here a potent cause of the downfall of Rome. "The people's suffrages," declared Montesquieu, "ought doubtless to be public; and this should be considered as a fundamental law of democracy. The lower class ought to be directed by those of higher rank, and restrained within bounds by the gravity of eminent personages. Hence, by rendering the suffrage secret in the Roman republic, all was lost; it was no longer possible to direct a populace that sought its own destruction." [1]

Gibbon was of the same opinion. "As long as the tribes successively passed over narrow bridges and gave their voices aloud, the conduct of each citizen was exposed to the eyes and ears of his friends and countrymen. The insolvent debtor consulted the wishes of his creditor; the client would have blushed to oppose the view of his patron; the general was followed by his veterans, and the aspect of a grave magistrate was a living lesson to the multitude. A new method of secret ballot abolished the influence of fear and shame, of honor and interest, and the abuse of freedom accelerated the progress of anarchy." [2]

This was the frame of mind of nearly all educated Englishmen until well into the nineteenth century, when with the Reform Act of 1832 came complaints that the broadening of the franchise was largely nullified by the coercion of voters that was made possible by the publicity of the suffrage. In 1833 Grote the historian began a series of powerful speeches for secrecy, which he continued yearly until 1839, but in vain, for the Chartists took up the issue and that of itself was enough to postpone change. In 1851 a measure for the ballot passed the Commons, but went no farther. It was not until the Ballot Act of 1872 that the use of printed

---

[1] *Spirit of Laws*, Book II, 2.
[2] *Decline and Fall of the Roman Empire*, chap. XLIV.

ballots became compulsory at all national and municipal elections save those of university candidates for Parliament. The Act was not passed without a long and hard fight, and then only as an experimental measure, to remain in force for one year only, unless renewed. It has been renewed annually ever since by the Expiring Laws Continuance Act of each year, but curiously enough, though it was passed more than half a century ago, and though its lapse would throw the whole law of elections into confusion, it has not even yet found its place on the statute book as a permanent measure.[1]

The American colonies were far in advance in this particular, using the ballot almost from the very first. It quickly became the established practice in Massachusetts Bay and was provided for in the Fundamental Orders of Connecticut. Several of the States made it obligatory by their first Constitutions, but voice-voting long after survived in the South, and Kentucky did not finish with it until 1891. It is curious to note the timid and apologetic way in which the first Constitution of New York (1777) approached the matter. The section begins: "And whereas an opinion hath long prevailed among divers of the good people of this State that voting at elections by ballot would tend more to preserve the liberty and equal freedom of the people than voting *viva voce:* To the end, therefore, that a fair experiment be made, which of those two methods of voting be preferred...." Ballot laws were to be passed, and if on trial they were found less conducive to the safety or interest of the State than the *viva voce* method, they might be repealed by a two-thirds vote.

Massachusetts began as a State with constitutional provision for "written votes" for representatives. In 1830 the Supreme Court held (Henshaw *v.* Foster, 9 Pick. 312) that this permitted printed votes. Thereupon half the secrecy of the ballot was speedily lost, because by using colored paper or distinguishing in some other way, each party had its peculiar ballot. In 1839 the Legislature enacted that all ballots should be deposited "open and unfolded." Then came loud complaint of intimidation. Of course a campaign to return to the folded-ballot plan began at once. In 1843 a measure to that end was lost in the House by a single vote. The controversy went on with as much vigor here as the like struggle during the same period in England. Nobody, however, could think how to secure secrecy. A reward

[1] Sir C. P. Ilbert, *Parliament,* 56.

of several hundred pounds was offered in England to anybody who would discover a feasible and effective mode of balloting. The result was an ingenious machine that Amasa Walker saw while abroad. Promptly he remarked it would never do for the Yankees — it had too much machinery about it and would take too much time. But it set him a-thinking, and in 1850 it occurred to him that the end could be achieved by using envelopes, in which the ballots could be put and then sealed. The idea was laughed out of the Senate that year, but in the next year, a change of parties having occurred, the measure met a more fortunate fate, becoming law.[1] Two years later, however, its effectiveness was impaired by an amendment permitting the . voter to use the envelope or not, as he might see fit.

The Australian Ballot Act, adopted by Massachusetts in 1888, replaced all former methods of getting secrecy. Massachusetts was the first American State to enact a State-wide law. So quickly did the system approve itself, that within seven years it had been adopted by all save four of the other States. It appears to have established beyond any likelihood of change in our time, that the electorate shall have all the freedom that secrecy can bring, for expressing the common will without coercion, intimidation, or pressure of any sort.

The belief of Cicero and a thousand other aristocrats that the masses must be guided or else ruin will follow, has found expression in other devices than the public ballot for controlling the electorate. Observe, for instance, how the voters of the Massachusetts Bay Colony were helped to choose the right men for Assistants in 1635. Winthrop describes the election: "The Governor and Deputies were elected by papers, wherein their names were written; but the Assistants were chosen by papers without names, viz: the Governor propounded one to the people, when all went out and came in at one door, and every man delivered a paper into a hat, such as gave their vote for the party named gave in a paper with some figures or scroll in it, others gave in a blank."

Here were the crude beginnings in America of a nominating process destined to grow till it should play a greater part in the choice of lawmakers and executives than the election itself. When the emigrants from Massachusetts founded Connecticut in 1639, their Constitution, the "Fundamental Orders," limited

---

[1] *Debates in the Mass. Convention of 1853*, i, 594 *et sqq.*

the choice of magistrates to the men nominated at some preceding session of the General Court, each town making not more than two nominations and the Court adding as many as it chose. Out of this grew a more elaborate system for keeping well in hand the choice of these dignitaries, the upper branch of the Legislature. In September of each year every freeman was required to nominate twenty men for Assistants. Then the names of the twenty man getting thus the most votes were submitted for the final election, twelve to be chosen. The names on the list were arranged according to seniority of service in the case of those who had previously held the office of "Assistant," and each name had to be voted for separately by each voter according to its place on the list — a rule which subjected the hindmost names to obvious disadvantage. Under this system the advance toward public honors was necessarily slow. Only those who had become the objects of more or less general observation throughout the whole colony could hope to be even nominated for colonial office.[1]

Massachusetts adopted the same plan. On the 19th of October, 1649, it was provided that not exceeding twenty should be nominated for Assistants by the freemen of the towns. On the counting of the ballots, the twenty having the most votes were to be placed before the Court of Election for Assistants. The law further said: "... and as any have more votes than other, so shall they be nominated, except such of their twenty who have been magistrates the year before, who shall have precedency of all others in nomination on the day of election." [2] Since under this plan candidates for reëlection, if among the successful twenty, had their names submitted first for acceptance or rejection, their advantage was such that in practical result life-tenure for the Assistants was the rule.

In 1680 the General Court elaborated this into a system of that experimental type which has never made headway, though still finding apostles here and there. With eighteen Assistants to be chosen in the end, it was provided that each voter should name up to twenty candidates in a general list, without restriction as to residence. The twenty-six getting the most votes should be the nominees, of whom eighteen were to be chosen at the main election following.

[1] James C. Welling, "An Address on Connecticut Federalism," before the N.Y. Historical Society, November 18, 1890, 39.
[2] *Records of the Colony of the Mass. Bay in N.E.*, iii, 177.

There is little doubt that Massachusetts is to be credited with the origin of that nominating device known as the caucus. The word first came into use about 1724. The elder Samuel Adams, a well-to-do Boston brewer, with a score or so of other citizens held meetings "to lay plans for introducing certain persons into places of trust and power." The participants were in part shipwrights and it has been thought that the "calkers" club came to be known as the "caucus." This derivation of the word has been declared fanciful, but nobody suggests one much more plausible. Anyhow the idea throve and grew into a great American institution. Only within the last half-century has it been copied in England.

With the development of the party system after the formation of the Union, the nominating process became elaborate and controlling for all elected officials. A century later free and open conference, the real virtue of the caucus and convention, their paramount justification, had well-nigh disappeared. In the larger cities all pretense of it had been abandoned. Each party kept its caucus polls open for hours, making useful discussion of candidacies impracticable. Committees chosen on the spot could no longer deliberate and advise. Lacking official control, schemers and rascals could intimidate or corrupt the voter, stuff the ballot boxes, vitiate the count. In many places caucuses had become a public scandal. Conventions, too, were often manipulated indecently, but their downfall was chiefly due to the fact that for the most part they no longer served any useful purpose, having degenerated into a piece of machinery that rarely did good and often did harm. This followed because the practice of sending pledged delegates in disputed districts had become general. Where there were but two candidates for one position, the election of pledged delegates made a convention useless, a sheer waste of time. Only with more than two candidates, and no one of them capturing a clear majority of the delegates, could a convention count. Even in that case there was rarely any longer the utility of free and open conference, discussion, deliberation, for the outcome usually depended on powers of endurance or on intrigue or on venal factors.

The evils of all this had become so evident and so serious that proposals to get rid of them by regulating the caucus and eliminating the convention gradually won favor until nearly the whole country had come under the system known as the "direct primary."

No reasonable man ever thought this would prove a panacea. There are no panaceas in politics. What can be fairly said is that it is a system with less evils than those that had debauched the previous system. In their youth the caucus and convention had furnished perhaps most nearly the best method for preliminary selection of candidates that could be devised. Those who want to return to them, forget what they had become in their maturity. Particularly disturbing is the lack of memory in the matter dwelt upon most, that of expenditure. Many have forgotten that it usually cost more to get a nomination through pledged delegates than it now costs by direct voting, assuming like conditions in the campaign.

In point of principle this matter of expenditure raises the issue that furnishes the vital problem in the whole election process, the issue of whether it is better to get the judgment of as large a part of the electorate as possible, or to rely upon that of the few who take a considerable and continuing interest in affairs political. It is the old, old question of government by the many or government by the few. Whatever may be the abstract merits, in point of concrete application to candidacy it may be permitted to one who has had personal experience with both systems, to testify that he would rather entrust his fortunes to the many than to the few.

This is said with no animosity toward political leadership. Until human nature changes, as long as some men have ambition to lead and most men are glad to follow, the expression of the popular will in the choice of representatives and servants will be guided — to greater or less degree as the popular mood of the moment permits — but always guided, and as a rule usefully guided. As far as the direct primary gives chance for wider judgment of the wisdom of specific leadership when the occasion may arise, it surely has merit.

Since all political processes change and develop, it may be confidently asserted that the direct primary is not a finality. It will grow into something better. Some day, though perhaps not short of the millennium, we shall reach the point where political leaders will show such fairness, such wisdom, such patriotism that there will be no need to do other than always follow their advice. Meanwhile the situation is still with us much as it has become in England, according to that vivacious writer, H. G. Wells, who says: "In Great Britain we do not have Elections any more; we

have Rejections. What really happens at a general election is
that the party organisations — obscure and secretive conclaves
with entirely mysterious funds — appoint about 1,200 men to be
our rulers, and all that we, we so-called self-governing people, are
permitted to do is, in a muddled, angry way, to strike off about
half of these selected gentlemen." [1]

INDIRECT ELECTION

Another device for putting the brake on the popular will is
that of indirect election. From the adoption of the Federal Constitution we have used it in choosing the President, and until recently it was the method for choosing United States Senators.
Kentucky put it into her first Constitution (1792), for the choice
of Governor and of State Senators. Every four years the voters
of each county were to elect members of an electoral college, in
number as many as the Representatives to which they were entitled. Doubtless the idea was suggested by the newly adopted
Federal Constitution. It quickly showed its defects and disappeared when a new State Constitution was framed seven years
later.

In France three quarters of the Senators are chosen by electoral colleges, one in each Department, made up of its Deputies,
members of its general council, members of the councils of the
arrondissement, and delegates chosen by the municipal councils
of the communes of the towns. Inasmuch as no city save Paris
can have more than twenty-four members, and each village has at
least one, this usually gives the rural districts overwhelming control, so that Gambetta could call the Senate the Great Council of
the Communes of France. Some of the colleges are very large;
that of the Department of the Seine has more than a thousand
members. This gives to their work much the character of an
American nominating convention, with the same wire-pulling,
bargaining, and manipulation in general. However, the result is
said to be the passage of leading men from the Chamber to the
Senate, and consequently the entry of the most eminent men of
the political world into the higher chamber. [2]

Indirect election is a feature of the soviet form of government
devised by the Bolshevists in Russia upon the overthrow of its
autocracy. At this writing exact and ample information is not

[1] *Social Forces in England and America*, 88 (May, 1912).
[2] Joseph Barthelemy, *The Government of France*, J. Bayard Morris tr., 71.

even yet available, but such as we have indicates that in this respect the revolutionaries have taken a course directly the opposite of that which had been supposed to be the tendency of democracy in our own land. Here we have been removing obstacles from the path of popular power. The Bolshevists began by interposing obstacles. Their system is that of the pyramid. Its base is much narrower than is contemplated by what is commonly thought of as universal suffrage. Only men who work with their hands, it is understood, elect the delegates to the local soviets, which are bodies in the nature of our city councils, but much larger, cities having one delegate for each thousand inhabitants, smaller places for each hundred. These local soviets send delegates to assemblies for larger areas — rural districts, counties, and provinces; also there is a regional assembly of representatives from city and county assemblies. The next higher tier seems to be the All-Russian Congress constituted of dele-gates from the city soviets and provincial assemblies, or if the provincial bodies are not invoked, of representatives from the city and county assemblies, 1400 in number, one for every 125,-000 of population. Apparently at this step one more filtration of the popular will is required in the country districts than in the cities. Next comes the choice of an executive committee of not more than two hundred, made by the Congress. Presumably there is a final step in the choice of the real executive or small group of executives.

It would be hard to imagine a system more likely to fail in giving effect to the will of the masses, or at any rate more capable of perverting that will.

The Turkish Constitution turned over to the National Assembly the task of devising how its 283 members should be chosen and the Assembly decided upon indirect election. Every commune chooses one secondary elector; another if it has from 200 to 300 voters; a third if from 300 to 500; and so on. These secondary electors choose the Deputies. Any primary elector may be a secondary elector if not a domestic servant nor notoriously in bad circumstances. The same plan was followed for the youthful Parliament of 'Iraq, which has 88 members, distributed among the fourteen administrative units (liwa) into which the country is divided, so that each gets several members. The secondary electors, one to each 200 voters, are chosen by the smallest units — villages, groups of villages, or tribal areas.

Usually the voter has to vote for more than one elector. The colleges of secondary electors thus formed are small bodies said to be for the most part composed of comparatively sensible, educated, and intelligent men, fairly representative of the different interests and classes of the community.[1]

What in effect will be indirect election is provided by the electoral law passed in Italy in 1928 at the behest of Mussolini. The syndicalist organizations and others are to nominate candidates for the Chamber of Deputies, to the number of twice those to be chosen. Mussolini's report accompanying the bill when it was laid before the Chamber boldly challenged the belief that the electorate as such can wisely select candidates for office. "The masses by themselves alone," he said, "are incapable of forming spontaneously a collective will of their own, and even less capable of proceeding spontaneously to a selection of men to represent them. This is expressed by the formula: 'Democracy does not exist in Nature.' Where a hundred people are assembled, they are inevitably led by one, two, or three individuals, who guide them in accordance with their own interests and their own opinions.... The problem of the Government, therefore, is never solved by relying on an illusory will of the masses; it is solved by a wise choice of the directing minds.... To place the choice of candidates and Deputies completely in the hands of the electoral body, composed of an inchoate mass of heterogeneous individuals, means in reality placing their choice in the hands of a few intriguers who appoint themselves to be the spiritual guides and teachers of the masses." [2]

On the other hand it would seem inevitable that any form of indirect election will in the long run militate against the theory that the legislative body should, to recall Burke's phrase, be "the express image of the feelings of the nation." It must foster what he called that "doctrine of the most pernicious tendency," the doctrine that the legislature should be "a controul *upon* the people."

If electing is but one of the public duties of the men composing electoral colleges, as was the case when our State Legislatures chose United States Senators, evils become notorious. Huge expenditures, bribery, fraud are not infrequent; trading of votes and the lesser forms of chicanery are common.

[1] "The Working of the 'Iraq Parliament," *Round Table*, December, 1926.
[2] For full text see *Current History*, May, 1928.

On the other hand, where electors are chosen with no other function than that of electing, they become mere dummies, recording the decision that has been reached at the polls between rival groups of would-be electors each pledged to a candidate. So it followed almost at once in the matter of the American President. The framers of the Federal Constitution expected that the presidential electors, picked out as the wisest men in each State, would without preconceived notions canvass the situation and agree on the best man. After the first choice, that of Washington, which was unanimous, parties developed and since then the electoral colleges have been an idle ceremony. No way to make it otherwise has been seriously urged, which would indicate that nobody now thinks a genuinely indirect choice of the President desirable. There is some grumbling about the Senators and there are thoughtful men who wish their election had never been made direct, but return to the old method is wholly improbable. As for the Representatives, no suggestion of indirect choice would get a hearing.

The Voting Problem

Voting has long been urged as a duty by editors, by essayists, and especially by speakers in political campaigns. Of late many other public-spirited persons have joined in the movement to bring home this duty to the electorate, preaching it not only individually, but also through numerous organizations that ought to have wide influence. They had become alarmed by the discovery that whereas of all qualified citizens 80 per cent voted in 1896, only 73 per cent voted in 1900; 62 per cent in 1912; and 49 per cent in 1920. The figures of 1924 showed a turn upward, but only slightly more than 50 per cent of the qualified went to the polls. The patriotic were stirred to new efforts, yet the National Civic Federation, foremost in the movement, was obliged to admit after the election of 1926 that the campaign had failed to secure the hoped-for results, the 1926 vote being less than that of the preceding off-year, 1922, and far below that of the presidential year, 1924.

With the election of 1928 came sharp change. One calculation is that 85 per cent of the electorate voted. This was phenomenal, abnormal. Factors rarely influential in our public affairs stirred the masses. The appeal was to emotion rather than intellect. Prejudice was aroused, passion fanned. This brought to the polls millions who are ordinarily indifferent. It is not to be conceded that this altogether exceptional episode indicates an enduring revival of active interest in public affairs. Whether or not it is repeated in a national campaign, it is not likely to have widespread and prolonged influence on State and local politics in the way of customarily bringing to the polls large numbers of those habitually apathetic. The thoughtful will still have plenty of occasion to ask why citizens do not vote.

In search of an answer to that question, a most admirable inquiry, illuminating and useful, was made after the hard-fought mayoralty election in Chicago, April 3, 1923. The results were published in a book, "Non-Voting," by C. E. Merriam and H. F. Gosnell, which should be studied by anybody who has accepted without question the theory that failure to vote is either inexplicable or inexcusable, or who has without reservations endorsed the Get-out-the-Vote campaign. In this instance with approximately 1,460,000 citizens of voting age, of the 900,000 and more who were registered, 723,000 or so voted — 63 per cent of the men and 35 per cent of the women. About 182,000 failed to vote. The inquiry covered examination of 6000 of the non-voters — a representative cross-section, reaching to all parts of the city and all classes of the people; statistical data as to age, sex, and like factors from the books of the Election Commissioners and census material; some studies of particular districts and individuals; and opinions secured from about 300 persons expert in the election processes.

It was found best to confine the tabulation of the individual examinations of non-voters to 5310 cases, which furnished the following summary of reasons:

	Cases	Percentages
Inertia: general indifference; indifference to the particular election; neglect; intended to vote but failed; ignorance or timidity; failure of party workers	2349	44.3
Physical difficulties: illness; absence; detained by helpless members of families	1351	25.4
Disbelief in voting: of women; objection of husband; disgust with politics or with own party; belief vote counts for nothing; corruption of ballot; disbelief in all political action	944	17.7
Legal and administrative causes: insufficient legal residence; fear of loss of business or wages; congestion at polls; poor location of booth; fear of disclosure of age	666	12.6
	5310	100

Ranking thirteen reasons in their order of importance showed:

	Cases	Percentages
General indifference	1347	25.4
Illness	647	12.1
Absence	589	11.1
Neglect; intended to vote but failed	448	8.4
Disbelief in women's voting	414	7.8
Ignorance or timidity regarding elections	378	7.1
Fear of loss of business or wages	289	5.5
Insufficient legal residence	274	5.2
Disgust with politics	230	4.3
Indifference to particular election	129	2.5
Detained by helpless member of family	115	2.2
Disgust with own party	105	2.
	4965	93.6

Seven other reasons related in each case to less than one hundred persons, two per cent of the whole.

"General indifference" was twice as common among the women as among the men who failed to vote. Three out of four of the indifferent non-voters were housewives. This cause was found to be more common among the young than the old, and least common with the middle-aged. The poor disclosed it more than the well-to-do. Foreign birth was closely related to habitual non-voting; native birth to occasional non-voting or failure to vote in this particular election. Especial interest attaches to nearly four hundred short paragraphs on individual cases. One rises from them with grave doubt as to the wisdom of the "Get-out-the-Vote" programme. Surely very few of these four hundred would have given really useful help in determining the election in question.

Further inquiries of the same sort are much to be desired. They may disabuse us of sundry wrong notions. Take, for instance, the impression that the educated classes are the most remiss in the performance of civic duty. Yet a study of absentees from the election of November 4, 1924, in Delaware, a typical Ohio community, by student interviewers of the Ohio Wesleyan University, showed that of the electors without schoolroom training, only 34.9 per cent voted; of those in the elementary group, 57.2 per cent; in the high school group, 69.6 per cent; and in the college group, 78.1 per cent. Such a showing is worth verification by studies elsewhere.

If this Delaware situation is really typical, what we call the educated classes do not seem strikingly remiss when you remember the Chicago disclosure that one quarter of all absence is due to excusable physical cause. Should the indifference of the classes with less education give us ground for anxiety? Or are there compensations?

Remembering always that schooling and intelligence are not necessarily correlative, yet our most cherished institutions would be vanity were not our educated classes as a whole the more intelligent. Of late we have come to understand that intelligence ranges the scale from 0 to 100 with some approach to even distribution. We always knew there were differences, but we were content with dividing mankind into two classes, the sane and the insane, rather sharply demarked, and with the coming of democracy we allotted to all those above the line an equal share in political powers, privileges, perquisites, rights, and duties. The new psychology has now taught us that the sane vary in their sanity, or at any rate in their wisdom, and it is no longer heresy to recognize that half the sane are wiser than the other half. Indeed it is now almost safe to speak of morons. Taking what risk remains, let it be asked whether it is in fact vital for the public welfare that the morons of the land should be either tempted or driven to the polls. As an ethical principle we have accepted it as established that the State needs and may expect contribution of judgment from every person made an elector by law. But how about the man who has no judgment or none worth while on things political?

May it not be that many such men stay away from the polls with the conscious knowledge or the intuition that they can contribute ncthing to the common stock of wisdom. Men of great intelligence often refuse to vote for candidates of whom they know nothing. Men of less intelligence may think they should enjoy the same privilege.

The really important thing is not that men should express opinions but that they should have opinions to express. Campaign leaders by remembering this would serve the public welfare more and might serve their own interests more if they put the emphasis on instructing rather than on exciting the voter. The informed citizen is the useful citizen. From the public point of view his vote is the only vote worth having. Do not worry about the absence of the uninformed.

One possible help for the situation deserves more attention than it has yet received. Nearly all the States now provide in some measure for absentee voting. The privilege so far has been restricted to those who cannot easily go to the polls. In principle, however, if one man may vote by mail, why not every man? It seems as if this ought to secure not only more general voting, but also voting more informed, deliberate, and thoughtful. It may be worth trying.

In France may be found an expedient that tends, though indirectly, to stimulate voting. If less than half the registered voters go to the polls, the election must be held over again. With us the fear of a resulting expense might incite local authorities to use more pains for informing and reminding the electorate that an election is pending or in progress. Also party committees would not like to have to do their work twice. Framers of election laws might well consider the idea.

They are giving more thought, however, to the theory that the individual voter, rather than the community, should suffer from what is viewed as neglect of duty. It is revival of an ancient principle. In Athens the lexiarchi sent their toxotæ before them to mark with red-powdered cords the white garments of those who tarried, so that they might be deprived of the tickets by which they could draw pay. Nowadays nobody thinks of compensating citizens for voting, and so there can be no forfeiting of pay, but the same end can be secured by penalties. Since 1893 the Constitution of Belgium has said: "Voting is obligatory." Failure to appear at the polls, without adequate excuse to the election officer, is a misdemeanor. After the closing of the polls a list of those who have not voted is sent to a justice of the peace. In the following week every absentee can send a letter setting forth the reasons and the means of proving them, such as a medical certificate. If the excuse is not accepted, the culprit is ordered to appear, and after his explanations have been heard the case is decided without appeal. The penalties are slight — for the first offense a fine of from one to three francs; for the second within six years a fine of from three to twenty francs; for the third within ten years the same fine and the posting of the elector's name on the walls of the City Hall for a month; and for the fourth within fifteen years without good cause, the voter's name is to be dropped from the voting list for ten years and during that time he cannot receive any nomination, decoration, or mark of honor from the public authorities. Professor Léon Dupriez of the University of Louvain, writing a report on the subject for the Massachusetts Convention of 1917, said the system had been very successful. In twenty years the number of registered voters who had failed to vote had never been more than six per cent and there had been adequate causes explaining at least a third of the absences. In Spain, on the other hand, compulsory voting, introduced in 1907, has been a failure; at least one third of those who have the right of suffrage do not vote at all. Dr. Cesar Barja, reporting on the subject, said he did not know of a case where punishment had been inflicted.[1]

Voting is compulsory on cantonal matters in five Swiss cantons, but the obligation is not rigorously enforced, excuses being freely accepted. Theorists are divided as to the merits. In its favor Felix Bonjour, former President of the Swiss National Council, says it "has an unquestionable educational value," in that "it forces the elector to reflect upon the questions presented to him and gives him a vivid realization of one of the most important civil duties." [2] On the other hand a singular result of the law has been its bringing to the polls many persons unwilling to exercise judgment. The report is that sometimes as many as a fifth of the voters cast blank ballots.[2]

Czecho-Slovakia by statute in 1920 provided for compulsory voting, with penalties of fines running from 20 to 5000 crowns, or imprisonment of from 24 hours to a month. A despatch from Hungary in the same year said proceedings had been instituted against 120,000 absentees. By decree of March 3, 1922, penalties were proportioned to taxes paid. In 1923 the Rumanian Constitution prescribed compulsory voting for the election of members of both branches. In New Zealand since 1893 the name of a voter not voting has been stricken from the list; unless his excuse satisfies a court, he loses his vote at the next election. In Tasmania the absentee has his name stricken from the list unless it is there by reason of the fact that he is an owner or occupier of property. The Commonwealth of Australia provided in 1924 that to every man not voting should be sent a form for him to fill out with the reason. If the form is not returned within twenty-one days or the reason is not satisfactory, he is to be fined two pounds. Absence from the polls, which in the election before the law went into effect had been about forty per cent, fell to about nine per cent in the following election.

[1] *Bulletins for Mass. Constitutional Convention of 1917–19*, II, 237.
[2] *Real Democracy in Operation*, 175.

Ambassador Naon of Argentina, asked at a meeting in this country whether there were any features in the governmental system of Argentina to which he attributed any part of its remarkable development, is said to have answered that there were three — compulsory education, compulsory military service, and compulsory voting. The delinquent there is to have his name published as rebuke, and is to be fined ten dollars for the first offence, with the fine duplicated for repetitions.

The scanty colonists of America felt the need of every man's help. So those of Plymouth enacted, according to the revision of 1636: "And for default in case of appearance at the election before mentioned without due excuse each delinquent to be amerced in three shillings sterling." In 1661 the penalty for not attending Courts of Election or else not sending votes by proxy was made ten shillings, "unless some unavoidable impediment hinder such in their appearance." [1] Other colonies had like laws. Virginia maintained hers throughout her colonial history. There the first law on the subject made the fine one hundred pounds of tobacco, and in 1662 this was increased to two hundred pounds. In 1734 Delaware made voting compulsory for all qualified electors, under penalty of a fine of twenty shillings. Some of the New England towns fined freemen who came late to the town meeting.

Georgia in her first Constitution (1777) provided: "Every person absenting himself from an election, and shall neglect to give in his or their ballot at such election, shall be subject to a penalty not exceeding five pounds; the mode of recovery and also the appropriation thereof, to be pointed out and directed by act of the Legislature: *Provided, nevertheless,* That a reasonable excuse shall be admitted." This disappeared with the Constitution of 1789. No other State began with the colonial idea of a money fine and for a long time there was no serious attempt to revive the practice. In 1860 Governor Morgan of New York said in his message that "every effort should be made to encourage, and perhaps compel, the legal voters to exercise the right of voting, which is at once a privilege and a duty." The subject was suggested, but not seriously considered, in the Convention of 1867. Governor Hill, in 1889, said it seemed reasonably clear that it was "the duty of every citizen to take an interest in public

[1] *Laws of the Colony of New Plymouth,* 41, 128.

affairs, and to exercise the elective franchise at each general election," and he recommended to the Legislature the consideration of the subject of making that duty compulsory by statute. In 1891, following a repetition of his suggestion, a bill was introduced, but not passed. Earnest argument was made for the idea in the Convention of 1894, but not successfully.[1]

Agitation of the subject continued and in 1898 North Dakota by amendment authorized the Legislature to prescribe penalties for failing, neglecting, or refusing to vote at any general election. However, the authority has not yet been used. Massachusetts gave like permission to its General Court in 1918. In the Convention the margin was narrow, and at the polls the vote was 134,138 for to 128,403 against — the smallest majority given to any of the nineteen amendments submitted in that year. No action has followed.

Of other ballot problems, that most discussed in the United States at the moment concerns the task imposed on the voter by the multitude of decisions he is asked to make. To meet this, what is known as "the short ballot reform" is earnestly urged. There can be no question that at present even the best-informed voter does not have personal knowledge of the qualifications of a tithe of the candidates between whom at most elections he must choose. The problem, however, bears upon lawmaking only in that present conditions make reliance upon party organizations almost inevitable, and compel the voter to assume that party candidates will favor the enactment of measures commended by party platforms or in harmony with known party tendencies. Woodrow Wilson, before he held office himself, advanced this as one of the explanations of his belief that "our State governments are, many of them, no longer truly representative governments." Said he: "It is impossible for the voters of any busy community actually to pick out or in any real sense choose the very large number of persons we call upon them under our present state constitutions to elect. They have neither the time nor the quick and easy means of coöperation which would enable them to make up the long list of candidates for offices, local and national, upon which they are expected to act. They must of necessity leave the selection to a few persons who, from one motive or another, volunteer to make a business of it. These are the political bosses and managers whom the people obey and affect to despise. It is

[1] C. Z. Lincoln, *Constitutional History of New York*, III, 132.

unjust to despise them. Under a system of innumerable nominations they are indispensable...." [1]

It is quite possible, however, to see in long ballots evils that ought to be avoided, and yet doubt if their correction will make our State governments materially more representative. The candidacies for membership in the State Legislature are usually those about which the voter is best informed. Unless the party system disappears, which does not now seem likely to happen in the near future, these candidacies would with the short ballot be conducted much as they have been with the long ballot. The reform is, in my judgment, likely to affect the administrative more than the legislative department of government.

The technicalities of election have a history of their own, interesting to the curious, but of little practical consequence to-day, for the problems appear to have been solved and the practice has settled down to a routine rarely changed in any matter of principle. We need not concern ourselves here with writs, summonses, and the like, but it may be worth while to remind the student of Legislatures that the return of a member, as the term is commonly used, denotes the election merely; but in its technical sense, it denotes the instrument by which the election is authenticated, or certified from the constituent to the representative body.

[1] *Constitutional Government in the U.S.*, 189 *et sqq.*

CHAPTER X

MAJORITY AND PLURALITY

I⊤ is the custom to proceed as if the will of the greater part of any voting body were the will of the whole. The assumption is that the majority shall prevail. No assumption in all the range of political science gets less question, and none is more important. It is the corner stone of safety. Yet think of what it means. Reflect for a moment on the significance of an assumption, a convention, whereunder the vote of one man, thrown in the wavering scale, may change the course of events so as to affect the destinies of millions of his fellows. Take but one of many dramatic instances that might be cited. Thomas Jefferson labored to prevent the extension of slavery into the new territories, and he very nearly succeeded. In the year 1784 he reported in the Congress of the Confederation an ordinance to organize all the unoccupied territory, both north and south of the Ohio River, in ten subdivisions, in all of which slavery should be forever prohibited. This ordinance failed of adoption by only one vote. Six States voted in the affirmative. Seven were necessary. Only one representative of New Jersey happened to be present, whereas two were the smallest number that could cast the vote of any State. If one other member from New Jersey had been there, the Jeffersonian ordinance of 1784 would have passed; slavery would have been restricted to the seaboard States it then occupied; they would never have drawn the sword against the Union, and the Civil War would not have taken place. Jefferson was cut to the heart by this failure. Commenting on an article entitled "Etats Unis" in the *Encyclopedie*, written by M. de Meusnier, referring to his anti-slavery proposal, he said: "The voice of a single individual of the State which was divided, or one of those which were of the negative, would have prevented this abominable crime from spreading itself over the new country. Thus we see the fate of millions unborn hanging on the tongue of one man, and Heaven was silent in that awful moment." [1]

Is it not strange that a political device pregnant with such possibilities has received so little discussion? When and how it was

[1] Horace White, *Life of Lyman Trumbull*, xxviii.

invented is a mystery that remarkably little attempt has been made to explore or explain. Mr. Justice Stephen graphically said that we count heads in order to save the trouble of breaking them. John Morley cited approvingly the witticism that we must either count or fight, and counting is better than fighting. This epitomizes the common assumption that the basis of majority control is physical force. Tacitus tells us a Germanic assembly rejected a displeasing proposal by an inarticulate murmur; if a proposal proved agreeable, they clashed their javelins. What happened when the noisy javelins of the few drowned the inarticulate murmur of the many, is left to the imagination. The time must have come when somebody doubted the vote. Warriors saw the prudence of giving the decision to those who by reason of superior numbers were likely to be able to whip the rest.

There was nothing abnormal in the establishment of the practice on such a basis by a primitive people, or its continuance when with some degree of civilization voting came. It appeared in Sparta, Athens, Rome. In Sparta there was to be no chance for favoritism or bad faith in deciding elections. We are told that the candidates for office went through the assembly of the people in an order determined by lot. He at whose passing the people raised the loudest cry was held to be elected. The loudness of the cry was judged by men shut up in a house near at hand, from which they could hear the cry, but not see the assembly.[1] The ecclesia of Athens made an actual count when the vote was close, otherwise relying on show of hands, and the majority rule prevailed. Rome introduced the written ballot in the last century of the Republic.

With the Dark Ages such gains as had been made in voting methods were lost. The church almost destroyed the majority principle. In the early Councils unanimity was generally required. That of Nicæa (325) recognized it only to the extent of saying, in the Sixth Canon, that "if two or three oppose the election of a bishop out of a pure spirit of contradiction, the majority shall carry the day." A thousand years later there was an attempt, at the Council of Ferrara, to reach a conclusion by accepting the view of the majority, but the Greeks said this would be a method entirely novel, wholly unknown in practice, and when a formula had been agreed upon to which there was but one

[1] G. Gilbert, *Constitutional Antiquities of Sparta and Athens*, 48.

dissentient, the Pope exclaimed, "Then we have accomplished nothing." Two or three centuries later, speaking broadly, the two-thirds rule had become general for the church. More than a bare majority was also required for election to office in the towns of northern Italy in the twelfth and thirteenth centuries, to which the origins of modern practices are commonly ascribed.

Thomas Baty, discussing the subject learnedly in the "Quarterly Review" for January, 1912, concludes, on the whole, that in England as late as the fifteenth century the general impression was that a body of persons acting in a given capacity must be unanimous; with the practical qualification that the unanimity might take the form of a suppression of discordant elements, and might include a good deal of reluctant acquiescence. To be sure, Magna Charta contained a requirement that the acts of a majority of the twenty-five barons who were to be virtually the guardians of the King, should be binding on the rest. The Provisions of Oxford, rendered necessary by the misgovernment of Henry III, also mentioned a majority. Baty, however, contends that these were in essence veto provisions, and that Redlich, in his "Procedure of the House of Commons," was not warranted in inferring from them that decisions of the Great Council were arrived at by a majority long before the representatives of towns and counties were regularly called to Parliament. There is no record of the passing of a bill by a majority in the House of Commons before the reign of Queen Mary. Baty thinks it the most reasonable supposition that decisions of the House were long unanimous in theory; that divisions were resorted to but seldom, and in comparatively unimportant matters; but that insensibly they came to be accepted as a simple and efficient, if unsatisfactory, means of arriving at a rapid decision on all matters.

For elections majority decision came somewhat earlier. As late as the Reform Act of 1406 returns were to be sealed by all the county electors, but the majority of votes was made decisive in 1430, when the forty-shilling freeholder was introduced. The mediæval history of England, however, furnishes but one or two instances of contested county elections. Borough members were chosen at Worcester, in 1466, "by the most voices."

If in our own day, when speculative inquiry delves into every corner of social activity, nobody questions majority rule and everybody accepts it as axiomatic, it is not surprising that in the past nothing shows that the idea was ever deliberately discussed or consciously adopted. When writers began to give it notice, they assumed its verity. For instance, John Locke held "it is necessary the body should move that way whither the greater force carries it, which is the consent of the majority, or else it is impossible it should act or continue one body, one community, which the consent of every individual that united into it agreed that it should; and so every one is bound by that consent to be concluded by the majority."[1] Locke argued from unsound premises, for it is not true that the consent of the majority is necessarily the greater force. To amend American Constitutions, the usual requirement for the Legislature is a two-thirds vote, and repeatedly a vote of more than half is overbalanced by a vote of less than half. When this happens, the majority gives way to the minority, Locke notwithstanding.

Besides the explanation based on force, two other reasons have been advanced. Dr. Rutherforth in his "Institutes of Natural Law" (II. 1 §1) and Cushing in his "Law and Practice of Legislative Assemblies" (44) set them forth in much the same way, to the effect that the greater number are likely to have more of wisdom and knowledge than the smaller, and that the self-interest of the greater number is more likely to be "consistent with equity," as one says, to "possess the quality of justice," as the other says. Sir G. C. Lewis contests these propositions.[2] He thinks it cannot be affirmed generally, either that a larger number of men is less likely to be mistaken than a smaller number, or that a smaller number is less likely to be mistaken than a larger number. Herein he agrees with the mathematicians, who by their doctrine of chances would destroy the popular delusion that when a red card has been drawn from the pack there is a probability that the next will be black. Nevertheless men still believe it and they still believe that the majority is more likely to be right. If they are in error, it would be a calamitous misfortune to disabuse them, for on their belief rests the safety of republics.

Lewis further says the proposition with respect to the interest of the majority is subject to the deduction that by interest must be understood their true interest as determined by competent judges, and not their interest as conceived by themselves. But here again the really important thing, it seems to me, is not that

[1] *Two Treatises of Civil Government*, ii, chap. viii.
[2] *An Essay on the Influence of Authority in Matters of Opinion*, 170.

the majority shall know what is its true interest, but that the community shall accept the belief of the majority, right or wrong. Without such an acceptance, then chaos. Twice at least history tells us of nations that have perished by reason, in part, of their failure to understand this. In Poland it was the *liberum veto*, the right of a single deputy to prevent or annul the action of the Diet, that produced legislative anarchy. Decided at the Diet of Radom in 1505, this right was based on the principle that a free man cannot be taxed or governed contrary to his own declared will. Of course such a deduction is wholly inconsistent with the representative theory, for the representative must speak for men whose wills may in fact be quite diverse. It is no wonder that the Polish theory became a paralyzing institution. In practice it gave the most serious effect to bribery and corruption. Foreign gold buying but a single vote could thwart any proposal. Holland gives the second instance. One of the three causes to which Doctor Rush, speaking in Congress on the Articles of Confederation (1777), ascribed the decay of the liberties of the Dutch Republic, was the perfect unanimity required on all occasions.

At the opposite extreme would be a system whereunder minorities had no representation at all, power being given over for the time being wholly to the majority. Such a thing was actually tried once in this country. When the Constitution of Connecticut was framed, in 1818, it perpetuated the system of an upper House elected by the people at large on one ticket, representing only the majority of the electorate. Ten years later, however, popular sentiment secured an amendment by which the choice was thereafter to be made by districts. Occasionally in some of our States even with the district method of choice every seat in a House will be controlled by the majority party. It is not a happy outcome. Better by far is the presence of a minority, and a good, strong minority at that, expected to fight as hard as it can, and then accept. Wise observers aver that the greater success of parliamentary institutions among English-speaking peoples is due to the willingness of their minority to yield to the majority in a degree not found in the Parliaments of the Continent.

Decision of proposals by majority vote gets a definite, compelling Yes or No from more than half who vote. Is that result enough? For the immediate purposes of action it may suffice, but there are other purposes in government, secondary, to be sure, yet of no small importance. One is justice. Does the majority system in its simplest form attain the greatest practicable measure of justice for all?

To this it would be replied by not a few that majorities are tyrannous and that minorities have rights which are not respected.

From time immemorial there has been complaint of "the tyranny of majorities." Yet nobody specifies wherein it appears. Even a clear thinker like Lord Acton yields so far to the temptations of generalities as to say, "The most certain test by which we judge whether a country is really free is the amount of security enjoyed by minorities." [1] I am rash enough to question whether there is any certainty whatever to such a test. It is doubtful, indeed, if there can be any such test.

In the first place, it is not established that minorities have any rights which majorities are bound to respect. Some, at least, of the masters of political science have treated the power of the majority as absolute, basing on it the very existence of society. Thus Locke said, "Where the majority cannot conclude the rest, there they cannot act as one body, and consequently will be immediately dissolved again." [2] Hobbes held that the man who does not consent may justly be destroyed by the rest, for he must either submit to their decrees, or be left in the condition of war he was in before.[3] Rousseau's theory of society presumed "the total alienation to the whole community of each associate with all his rights." A curious illustration of actual attempt to apply this theory is to be found in the practice of early days in colonial Massachusetts. After a vote had been taken, an effort was made to secure unanimity. Richard Mather wrote that if the minority "still continue obstinate, they are admonished, and so standing under censure, their vote is nullified."[4] The spirit of the theory has not been abandoned. For example, Speaker Reed frankly said: "There is only one charter of the rights of minorities, and that is the Constitution of the United States. That defines the power of Congress and implies that Congress shall act by its majority. Under that Constitution and within its scope, whatever a majority does is right." [5]

[1] *History of Freedom*, 4.
[2] *Two Treatises of Government*, book II, chap. VIII.
[3] *The Leviathan*, chap. XVIII.
[4] *Church Government and Church Covenant Discussed*, London, 1643, 61.
[5] T. B. Reed, *Century*, April, 1889.

Furthermore, were the majority actually disposed to tyrannize, there would be no preventing it. The will of the stronger part is sure to prevail in the end.

History shows that attempts at tyranny have been more often chargeable to the minority than to the majority. As Elisha Mulford has pointed out, "the tyranny has always been the power of the minority acting with no conformance to a constitutional order, as the despot or dynasty, the hereditary or monetary class, some family or collection of families, bound by a tie among themselves; and these have held the whole as their possession, and subordinated it to their own special ends." [1]

Nevertheless, modern constitutional systems embody the theory that whether or not the individual has any rights that may be superior to the common welfare, it is wise for the sake of expediency if for no other reason to guarantee him the enjoyment of certain privileges. Parliamentary law, too, has developed with this end in view. Its influence is thrown toward giving the minority, however small, at least a chance to be heard. A real cause for grievance is that under our systems a minority has somewhat too much power to impede the will of the majority. On the other hand, it is of the essence of our institutions that a minority shall have unrestricted opportunity to turn itself into a majority if it can. Freedom of speech, freedom of the press, the right to persuade, the right to associate — these are fundamentals.

In Elections

Lewis thinks no explanation can be given of the majority rule, except that it is resorted to as the only possible expedient. Is not that, however, explanation enough in itself? Clearly there must be some rule. This one appears on the face of it more equitable than any other, and therefore comes nearest leaving the minority without any grievance, which may not be the noblest end that could be achieved, but in its relation to the conduct of affairs is the most important, for the business, whether of King or people, must somehow be done.

That it is a rule purely arbitrary and conventional, with no inherent ethical sanction, is shown by the extent to which it has been discarded in the matter of elections. Were some principle of natural right at its base, we should hardly find an absence of legal, philological, or popular agreement as to the use of the word

[1] Elisha Mulford, *The Nation*, 242.

"majority" where election is concerned. In computation that word may mean the amount by which the greater number exceeds the less, if but two numbers are compared; or the amount by which the greatest number exceeds the total of the lesser numbers; or the amount by which the greatest number exceeds the next to the greatest. For the last case we in America customarily use the word "plurality," but in England the normal designation is "majority," and candidates have been elected with regard only thereto from time immemorial. The weight of American usage restricts "majority" to the excess of the greatest number of votes over the total of the rest, and we say that for a majority a total of one more than half is necessary.

Following the American usage, it would be said that members of Parliament have always been chosen by plurality vote. How came it, then, that the requirement of an absolute majority should ever have gained a foothold in the colonies? Once again the explanation is to be found in the fact that they began as trading corporations. It was probably the usual procedure in such corporations to elect what we would now call the directors, one by one, each name being brought forward on motion, with a Yes or No vote thereon. At any rate that is the earliest procedure we find in Massachusetts Bay. Under it of course nobody could be chosen save by majority. When in the course of a few years it had become inconvenient to have everybody travel to Boston for the annual election, and those who were in effect the stockholders were permitted to send in their ballots, this principle of the majority was modified for nomination but survived after a fashion in the election. After 1680, when the nomination ballots came in, the leading candidates to the number of twenty-six were declared the nominees for Assistants. Then the freemen of the towns chose twenty out of the twenty-six — a process under which all the winners were likely to have received the votes of more than half of the electors.

The confusion in the use of the words "majority" and "plurality" leaves some uncertainty as to how far the actual majority was required in other colonies, but it seems clear that it was required in Connecticut and it appears to have prevailed in New York, New Jersey, South Carolina, and Georgia. On the other hand, Rhode Island early provided for election by plurality. Its Assembly enacted in November, 1664, "that whereas there may happen a division in the vote so as the greater half may not pitch directly on one certain person, yet the person which hath the most votes shall be deemed lawfully chosen." [1] Elsewhere as a rule a plurality was enough.

Probably the question was never more thoroughly discussed than in the Massachusetts Convention of 1853. The debate occupied eight days all told and took 259 pages to report. The Constitution of 1780 had provided that in case of failure to choose a Governor or Lieutenant Governor by majority, the House of Representatives should name two out of the highest four candidates, and from these two the Senate should choose one. In the case of failure to elect Senators, candidates having the higher votes to the number of twice those to be elected were the men from whom the Representatives sitting with the Senators already elected, should choose. Towns had to repeat their elections, and that was provided by statute for Congressmen. Under this requirement there were, from the 1st to the 31st Congress inclusive, 201 ineffectual trials in Massachusetts for Congressmen; and the number of votes cast in these attempts was 937,265. [2]

One speaker estimated this had cost the voters five hundred thousand dollars in time wasted. Another declared that in a greater part of the elections since the Constitution was adopted, there had been failure to elect some officers on first ballot. Another showed that each year from thirty to fifty towns failed of representation in the House because unable to elect any candidate under the majority system. Several towns were unrepresented in the Convention itself for this reason. Representation he thought more important than whether a representative had a majority or plurality. John C. Gray said that up to 1834 it had not been necessary to choose a Governor through the instrumentality of the Legislature, but in the last five years the people had not chosen him once.

Marcus Morton pointed out that in seventy-four or seventy-five elections up to that time there had never been an instance when a Governor was elected by a majority of the voters, he meaning thereby a majority of all eligible to vote. He asked: "Why shall a majority govern? Has a majority any natural right to govern? I deny it. In a state of nature, if two men meet, one has no right to control the other. If two men meet another, they

[1] S. G. Arnold, *History of Rhode Island*, i, 312.
[2] *Mass. Convention of 1853*, i, 266.

have no right to control that other person, except in a case of necessity, where their lives depend on immediate joint action. Then it is a matter of necessity that the stronger party shall control. Why is it necessary that a majority shall govern? It is founded in compact; it is not founded in natural right, but because a majority agree that a majority shall govern."

R. H. Dana, Jr., also asked a question: "What is the meaning of the great maxim that majorities shall govern, and majorities only? I understand it to be a maxim aimed at the government of the few, against aristocracy, against oligarchy, against monarchy. I understand it to be a great republican principle the meaning of which really is, that numbers shall govern,... and that the greater number shall prevail. This is perfectly true. Whenever you put a proposition, yea or nay, the greater number prevails. Still further behind lies this question: When you are voting for a number of persons, A, B, C, and D, what do you mean by the term majority then? Why, it means that the greater number should govern. It does not mean that any one man must have more votes than all the others put together."

Henry Wilson, later to become Vice-President, took the opposite view. "I oppose the plurality system," he said, "because I believe it tends to degrade the politics of the country, and to demoralize the politicians of the country. It has increased the power of the caucus, the convention, party organizations, great combinations, great interests, and the influence of political leaders, and it has diminished the power of the people, who follow their higher and better sentiments." His argument was that caucuses and conventions were under the majority system held in check by the knowledge that if they nominated unworthy men, the voters of "moral instincts, liberal tendencies, and unselfish action" who had not attended the caucuses would revolt at the polls; but if a plurality were to elect, if the decision of the first voting were to be final, they would "pause, hesitate, yield, vote for a candidate they knew unworthy, and go home degraded in their own eyes."

Along the same line another speaker held that with plurality choice the vote of a member of a third party has no weight. "He finds himself a political cipher, unless he will resign his honest convictions, and join one of the two great struggling parties. All that is left to him under the plurality system is the miserable alternative of 'choosing between two evils.' The effect is to force upon a large portion of the people a government in which they are compelled to have no choice, or to adopt what their consciences do not approve." Amasa Walker thought they would get, instead of third parties, founded on principle, factions struggling for power. A principle is defined to be "a general law for the guidance of human conduct." If the right of the majority to rule be a fixed principle, a law of our nature, ought we to violate it? Only within a few years have there been more than two parties. We ought not to abandon an important principle for the purpose of meeting a temporary evil, or obviating a temporary inconvenience. On the whole the majority system has worked well. It is a practice prevailing from the foundation of the colony, and a venerable institution not to be lightly changed. It is a distinctively American principle to be accordingly cherished.

To this it was replied that the "great American principle" is that the majority shall have *the power* to rule, not that the majority shall rule.

In the matter of candidacies Benjamin D. Hyde argued for plurality: "We shall be represented by better men. Now the parties understand they must get some man who will secure a majority of the votes, or he will not be made the candidate. The man who is the most popular must be the nominee. They frequently throw aside the man who is best qualified to represent them, and take a man who will command the greatest number of votes. The candidate in the small town is often a negative man, a man who has never done anything to make either friends or enemies." Over against this it was advanced that the greater the number of candidates, the less the chance of electing the best man. The indifferent man has the better chance, and good men will not consent to run.

Likewise in the matter of attendance the predictions were squarely opposed. One man said that with plurality choice and with knowledge that the result of the election would be definitive, attendance at the polls would be larger. Another held that the system would discourage attendance because those who felt that their votes, cast for third party candidates, would not count, would stay away. The speaker who argued for plurality had the advantage in this particular, of being able to point to what had happened under the other system. Experience had shown that after the first election the number attending fell off steadily till the man at last successful was often chosen by less votes than he had received in the first election. Sometimes in the end an election was determined by one tenth as many voters as originally took part. In the nine districts that after the first trial elected by plurality for the Congress then in being, the aggregate vote upon the first trial was 115,638; at the second trial, 74,234. In every case save one, the candidate receiving the largest vote at the first trial was elected at the second; and elected by a much smaller vote than he received at first trial. In the one other case the winner received six hundred and odd less than the vote of the man who led at the first trial. The practical result had been in many cases to put in power men for whom only a plurality of all possible voters had voted.

In this respect the part of the system that threw into the Legislature the election of a Governor or Senators was worse yet. Men had been put into the office of Governor who had received but a few hundred votes from the people — Senators who had received only three votes from the people. The real question is, whether, a majority not existing, you prefer that the election shall be determined by the Legislature, or by a plurality of the people. Elections carried into the Legislature seldom represent, often misrepresent, the will of the majority of the people. As a matter of practical result, the plurality system more often than the majority system secures expression of the popular will. William Schouler argued: "The natural effect of the plurality system is to combine public sentiment and not to scatter it. If every man were to vôte upon his own hook, there could be no government at all — the people would be so divided there could be nobody elected; hence it is desirable that some means should be devised of combining public sentiment and uniting it upon particular individuals, and this is just what the plurality system does."

It was urged for plurality that if a majority cannot be secured, the next best thing is to approximate it as nearly as possible. The party animosity engendered by numerous and repeated unsuccessful contests has given ground for wide complaint. Long-drawn-out contests degenerate into struggles for personal triumphs. The present system has tended to degrade and prostitute the right of voting in the eyes of the people. It is for the interest of politicians to have elections every week in the year, so that the majority system gradually puts the power in their hands.

Miscellaneous arguments on the other side were: We have confidence in our republican government because we know it is made by the many; we lose our confidence in any form of government the moment it comes to be made by the few. In all States where the plurality principle obtains, politics becomes a raffle, the contest of parties and factions a scrub race, in which the one who gets the first start is likely to come out best. The majority principle gives a man his full power; under it his vote always tells, and he feels he has a voice in the government of the State.

The outcome of the great debate was a compromise, providing plurality choice for county and district candidates; majority for the Governor and other State officers, with election by the General Court after first trial; and majority with continued trials in the case of Representatives and municipal officers. Being part of the general revision that constituted the first of eight matters put before the people, their opinion on it as a distinct proposition was not ascertained. The general revision was rejected, the vote being 63,222 in favor and 68,150 against. However, the Legislatures of 1853 and 1854 saw enough good in several of the reforms that lost to warrant putting them before the people in the shape of separate amendments, and in this way plurality choice was adopted, in 1855.

With few exceptions the other States have had the plurality system from the adoption of their first Constitutions. New Hampshire, however, copying the Massachusetts plan for Governor and Senators in 1784, and providing popular election for Councilors in 1792, required majority choice for them until 1912. Maine imitated Massachusetts with a majority vote for Senators, under the same cumbrous system. She replaced this with the plurality vote in 1875. Plurality choice of Representatives had been provided in 1845. When in 1842 Rhode Island framed a Constitution, it specified majority choice, which was changed to plurality in 1893, by a vote of 26,703 to 3,331.

On the Continent of Europe requirement of an absolute majority has been the custom for choice on the first ballot. If no candidate for the German Reichstag got such a majority, at the second election the voting was for the highest two candidates, and in case of a tie the decision was by lot. In France a plurality elects at the second voting, with modification by the law of 1919 that introduced proportional representation to some degree in the election of Deputies. There the system dates back to the election of the States General in 1789, with but two short breaks in 130 years.

Experience shows that the procedure encourages the system of political groups which sharply distinguishes Continental from English and American politics. Lowell explains how it works.[1] Suppose that there are Reactionary and Moderate Republican candidates in the field, and that the Radicals prefer the Republican to the Reactionary, still they have nothing to lose by running a candidate of their own on the first ballot, for if the Reactionary can poll more votes than both his rivals combined, he will be elected in any event; if he cannot, he will not be elected whether the Radicals put up a candidate of their own or not. In this last case, the first ballot will have counted for nothing, and the Radicals will be able to vote for the Moderate Republican at the *ballotage* (second election) and elect him then. They are likely, indeed, to gain a positive advantage by nominating a separate candidate, for if they succeed in polling a large vote on the first ballot, they are in an excellent position to wring concessions from the Moderates as the price of their support.

New Zealand adopted majority choice, in 1908, providing for a second ballot where the first did not develop a majority. At the first trial, in November of that year, twenty-three districts required a second balloting. One result of the act was somewhat unexpected. Where two members of the same party stood against one of an opposing party, and of the two one was defeated, on the second trial the supporters of the unsuccessful candidate were inclined to transfer their votes to the opposition because of the personal feeling that had been engendered.

In our own country a tendency to revert to the discarded practice is to be observed in some of the newer nominating systems. This developed first in the Southern States where there has been virtually but one party, others being negligible in practice from the Civil War to 1928. If a plurality choice should decide in the primary, this would in effect give the voters but one chance to pass judgment, save in the rare case of an independent candidacy at the main election. Therefore majority was required. In the North, where no such peculiar situation exists, there is far less occasion to resume the cumbrous practice. Few would now seriously advocate it for election, and it is not easy to see why the conditions are essentially different in matter of nomination.

[1] *Governments and Parties in Continental Europe*, i, 108, 109.

So very little of utility is accomplished by repeated ballotings, that it seems a pity to saddle our election processes thus with meticulous detail. It is impossible to prove that repeated ballotings would or would not in the end be likely to secure a better man, or one more fairly representing the district. On paper such might seem to be the probability, but the accidents of politics vitiate all reasoning in such a matter.

Another method of accomplishing the same result is strongly advocated by reformers who attach importance to the majority idea. Known as "the alternative vote," it is used in West Australia and was favored by the English House of Commons in the contest with the House of Lords that ended in the compromise on the matter of proportional representation in the Representation of the People Act of 1918. Proportional representation and the alternative vote are quite distinct things, but are easily confused because in the methods most favored resort is had to the same processes, each calling upon the voter to designate more than one choice. In a single-member district this is used to find out what candidate not objectionable to the voters meets with the greatest aggregate of approval. Each voter expresses a second choice. The candidate with the least first choice ballots is thrown out and the second preferences on his ballots are then duly credited. If still nobody has a majority, again the lowest man is thrown out and the second preferences on his ballots likewise credited; and so on until somebody gets an absolute majority.

An odd method evidently having in view somewhat the same purpose was tried in this country, in Delaware, long ago. That State, with only three counties, had but one member in Congress. In 1790 it was provided that each voter should vote for two candidates, one of them a resident and the other a non-resident of the voter's county. The repeal of the law in 1794 leads to the conclusion that this novel scheme did not meet expectations.

An alternative-vote system promises more accuracy in concentrating the popular will than is likely to result from repeated ballotings, and suggests no serious disadvantages. Yet whether it is of much practical consequence, may be doubted. It is true that under present methods a man will occasionally be elected by plurality who could not have secured the support of one more than half his constituents. However, the fact that he is preferred by more persons than prefer anybody else will be thought by

most men who have had experience in government to be enough
for its practical purposes.

Furthermore, the system militates against the strong, virile,
positive, brave man, and helps the colorless, negative, amiable
candidate who makes no enemies. If politics were wholly a matter of principles, this might not count, but in politics personality
is a great factor. Whether we like it or not, we must admit that
with very many voters personality prevails. A system that makes
enmity more powerful than friendship is not without danger.

In the matter of choosing presiding officers the case is somewhat different and there is clear ground for adherence to the
majority rule. A presiding officer ought to have the good will of
the majority of a legislative body whenever possible. That lessens
the chance of friction which might seriously interfere with the
work of lawmaking. The Speaker of the British House of Commons, to be sure, is chosen by what we call plurality vote, but he
is a completely non-partisan presiding officer and political principles are to be in no way advanced by his election. While our
presiding officers are expected to deal fairly by minorities, yet
they are also expected to be partisans in certain important particulars. So it is with us the rule that they shall be chosen by
majority vote.

Deadlocks occasionally compel exceptions to the rule. Two
prolonged contests over the Speakership of the National House
have furnished notable exceptions. On the 22nd of December,
1849, after balloting had gone on for nineteen days, and the 59th
ballot gave no one a majority, it was voted that if after three
more calls of the roll there was no election, the candidate receiving the largest number of votes should be declared to have been
chosen Speaker. On the decisive ballot, with 20 votes scattered
among eight other candidates, Robert C. Winthrop had 100, and
Howell Cobb, with 102, was chosen. In the third Congress after
that, the struggle lasted until February 2, 1856, when likewise
the plurality rule was adopted and on the 133rd ballot, with 11
scattering votes, William Aiken had 100, and Nathaniel P.
Banks, with 103, was elected.

In the course of the proceedings relating to the election of a
President of the Senate *pro tempore*, in May, 1911, Mr. Stone
raised a question of order, that a Senator having received a
plurality vote should be declared elected. Senator Lodge, presiding, decided that under the Constitution, in the absence of

any provision to the contrary, all officers of both Houses must be elected by a majority.

Ohio by statute provides that if in electing officers of either House a choice has not been made by majority vote on or before the tenth ballot, thereupon a plurality shall prevail.

In the matter of the election of United States Senators by the Legislatures, it was always considered that a majority was necessary for a choice, until 1866, when the New Jersey Legislature, in joint session, decided that a plurality should elect. The Senator so chosen was refused a seat in the Senate, and the case led to the passage of a law regulating the mode of election, Congress never having availed itself of its constitutional privilege in the matter. Majority choice was therein stipulated.

ABSOLUTE MAJORITIES

Is a majority the greater part of those who might vote? or of those who attend the polls? or of those who share in the particular vote involved?

In a matter of candidacy, of choice between men, everybody will now at once answer that it is the greater part of those who share in the particular vote. That has not always gone without question. In the matter of general elections the Supreme Court had occasion to meet the doubt by declaring the principle: "All qualified voters who absent themselves from an election duly called are presumed to assent to the expressed will of the majority of those voting, unless the law providing for the election otherwise declares." [1]

As to elections by legislative bodies, the issue was raised when the national House of Representatives chose its Speaker in 1809. It had 141 members. Of the 120 members who voted, 60, one less than a majority, voted for Joseph B. Varnum. A rival candidate, Nathaniel Macon, expressed the opinion that Varnum was elected, but John Randolph strenuously opposed this view, whereupon the House took another ballot, giving Varnum 65 votes out of 119, a majority of those voting, but not a majority of the whole membership. When the Journal was read the next day, showing that the Speaker had been elected by a majority of the votes, Randolph secured its change to read: "Sixty-five votes, being a majority of the whole number of members present, were found in favor of Joseph B. Varnum." The fact that the House

[1] County of Cass v. Johnston, 95 U.S. 360 (1877).

nevertheless accepted the election would seem to have settled the question, but it was brought up again in 1879, when Samuel J. Randall was chosen by a majority of less than the whole number. Omar D. Conger questioned, but the Clerk, presiding, replied that "it requires a majority of those voting to elect a Speaker; as it does to pass a bill."

He voiced what would undoubtedly be conceded to be the general parliamentary law as to ordinary legislation. Early in our history we find the Massachusetts General Court, October 18, 1650, ordering that "the interpretation of the laws, concerning the greater part of the Magistrates and the greater part of the Deputies, are to be understood of the greatest number of those that are present and vote." It is probable that this was the well-nigh universal practice in the colonies, and indeed the framers of our first Constitutions must have assumed its acceptance, for as a rule they took little pains to clarify their reference to votes. New Jersey was an exception, not only being clear, but also adopting a different principle, for its Constitution of 1776 provided: "No law shall pass, unless there be a majority of all the Representatives of each body personally present, and agreeing thereto." With the change of "law" to "bill or joint resolution," the provision was continued by the Constitution of 1844 and still stands.

No other of the older States appears to have thought it necessary to prevent the possibility of lawmaking upon the affirmative vote of only one half or less of the whole membership until New York, in 1846, said: "No bill shall be passed unless by the assent of a majority of all the members elected to each branch of the Legislature, and the question upon the final passage shall be taken immediately upon its last reading, and the Yeas and Nays entered on the Journal." The force of this example may have been what led Michigan, in 1850, to say the same thing, though in other words. Thereafter the idea found quick and wide imitation, Ohio and Indiana taking up with it the next year, and then other States old and new until now it is the rule in about three fifths of the whole number. New England in this matter adheres as usual to old traditions and appears to suffer nothing thereby. West Virginia at first required a yea-and-nay majority of all elected, but dropped the provision in 1872. Instead appeared such a requirement for agreement by one House to amendment by the other. Several States have added the amendment stipulation to the yea-and-nay majority requirement, usually extending it to cover the adoption of reports of conference committees.

A few of the States that do not require the absolute majority on everything, have demanded it on money bills. Wisconsin (1848) required it on bills contracting debts for defraying extraordinary expenditure, but on other debt matters, questions of taxes, claims, and the like, was content in requiring a three-fifths quorum. Kentucky in 1850 stipulated the absolute majority on matters of appropriation or debt. Mississippi in 1890 required it for appropriations. Virginia in 1902 required it in matters relating to finance, and included the creation of new offices.

In the case growing out of Speaker Reed's quorum count, the Supreme Court said: "The general rule of all parliamentary bodies is that when a quorum is present, the act of a majority of the quorum is the act of the body." [1] Whether this general rule covers not only bills, but also matters affected by constitutional requirements, has been a mooted question. In Congress it has risen as to the votes necessary for the passage of bills over the President's veto and for submission of amendments to the Constitution. The House in 1846 established the principle that to pass a bill over the President's veto, a two-thirds vote of those present was enough, in an instance where the vote, standing 127 to 30, had in the affirmative much less than two thirds of the membership. The Senate in 1856, after instructive debate, took the same ground by 34 to 7 on an appeal from the decision of the Chair. The question reached the Supreme Court in a case rising out of the Webb-Kenyon act.[2] Chief Justice White, in a decision supporting the act, said the context leaves no doubt that the constitutional provision relating to the veto was dealing with the two Houses as organized and entitled to exert legislative power; that the veto provision as originally offered was changed into the form in which it now stands after the adoption of the Article fixing the quorum of the two Houses for the purpose of exerting legislative power and with the object of giving the power to override a veto to the bodies as thus organized; and that there is no indication in the Constitutions and laws of States existing before the Constitution of the United States that the

[1] U.S. v. Ballin, 144 U.S. 1 (1891).
[2] Missouri Pac. Ry. Co. v. State of Kansas, 248 U.S. 276 (1919).

legislative body which had power to pass a bill over a veto was any other than the legislative body organized conformably to law for the purpose of enacting legislation. Particularly he referred to the New York Constitution, wherein he found proof of absolute identity of power. Five State courts were cited as holding to the same effect.

The opposite view has not lacked serious expression. Justice Bradley, joining with Justice Miller in dissenting from the opinion in County of Cass v. Johnston (95 U.S. 360 — 1877), believed that in the absence of qualifying or limiting words a constitutional vote of a given body means such a vote of the entire body. When Attorney-General Herbert Parker of Massachusetts was asked in 1904 whether a Soldiers' Bounty bill had been passed over the Governor's veto by a vote of two thirds of those present, but not of the whole membership, he admitted there were authorities holding that the word "House," where context, subject, or condition suggests or induces such conclusion, is to be construed as meaning a quorum of such House. He believed, however, that "peculiar responsibility and gravity attach to that vote which is to nullify an Executive veto, and it is therefore to be distinguished from routine action incident to the mere transaction of ordinary legislative business." By reason of Mr. Parker's opinion that the bill had not received the vote required, the State Treasurer refused to issue certain bonds, and the measure was ineffectual.

Like argument has of late been strongly urged in respect of the provision of the Federal Constitution that reads: "The Congress, whenever two thirds of both Houses shall deem it necessary, shall propose amendments to this constitution." In the First Congress, when proposed amendments came down from the Senate to the House, part of them were agreed to, the record showing "two thirds of the members present agreeing on each vote." The House had 65 members. The first amendment proposed was voted for by 37 and declared to be approved, which was in effect a decision at the very outset that "House" meant a quorum of the House. Nevertheless the question was raised a few years later, when the defect in the Constitution concerning the manner of electing the President had been forcibly brought out by the Jefferson-Burr episode, and what became the Twelfth Amendment was proposed. If the Constitution required the vote of two thirds of all the members, that would have been fatal to the success of the measure, for it was well known no such vote could be had in either House. Senator William Plumer of New Hampshire, opposing the amendment, argued: "If two thirds of those present can propose amendments to the Constitution, it follows that twelve Senators, when only a quorum is present, may propose them against the will of twenty-two Senators." Congress, however, was not alarmed by that view, and it had not changed its opinion when Trusten Polk, presiding over the Senate in March of 1861, ruled that the passage of an amendment required the approval of two thirds only of the members present, for the Senate on appeal sustained him by 33 to 1.

It has become quite the custom to raise the issue whenever a constitutional amendment gives the opportunity. Thus the point of order was made on a suffrage amendment in the Senate in 1869, and not sustained. A like point failed in the House on the amendment for the direct election of Senators, in 1898, Speaker Reed saying the question had been so often decided that dwelling upon it seemed hardly necessary. Nevertheless the doubt was again raised, a score of years later, this time over the Prohibition Amendment. The Senate had passed it by a vote of 65 to 20, and had agreed with the House changes by 47 to 8, the Yeas in neither case being two thirds of the total membership. This was advanced in at least one of the State Legislatures as a reason for not approving the amendment, and since then argument based on it has repeatedly appeared in newspaper and other discussion. When the whole matter was brought before the Supreme Court in National Prohibition Cases (253 U.S. 350 — 1920), allegation on this particular score was thrown in as a make-weight, judging by the scant reference to it in the official synopsis of the arguments. It was summarily rejected by the opinion in which the majority of the Justices joined, citing Missouri Pac. Ry. Co. v. State of Kansas (which, by the way, had concerned an executive veto and not the submission of an amendment). In this particular the two Justices dissenting on other grounds agreed with the majority of the Court. In view of this, even if Eliot Tuckerman is right in his contention that the framers of the Constitution meant to require approval by two thirds of all elected to each body, and that the first Congress erred in construing otherwise, there seems to be very small likelihood that the position of the courts will be reversed or that the practice of legislative bodies will be changed by anything short of another amendment.

The student who would pursue the general subject further, may find it discussed exhaustively, with the arguments on both sides and a learned opinion, in Green *v.* Weller, 32 Miss. 650 (1856).

One of the reasons that have been given in justification of express requirements for an absolute majority, or as warrant for their implication, should have a moment of attention. The Minnesota court in Supervisors Ramsey County *v.* Heenan (2 Minn. 330 — 1858), said the Constitution of that State had required for the passage of any law a majority of all members elected, because of experience in the territorial Legislature. "Laws could be passed by a single member, voting in the affirmative, if no one voted against him; however objectionable this may have been, it was less liable to abuse in bodies composed of a small number of members than in more numerous assemblies." This quite imaginary evil distresses men unacquainted with the details of legislative work, who from the galleries watch with alarm the announcement by the Speaker of vote after vote when in fact no member has opened his mouth. The time-saving process is a favorite butt of ridicule for the muckrakers who hold it up as an awful example of the indifference and negligence of lawmakers. As a matter of fact the citizens may be perfectly sure that in any well-regulated, self-respecting Legislature — and there are such Legislatures — no measure fails to get scrutiny and consideration. While the Speaker is declaring, "The Ayes have it," when there were no "Ayes," a dozen, a score of men are watching the calendar, ready to pounce on anything obnoxious. Party interests, personal ambitions, and a sense of public duty combine to make sure that no bill needing discussion or opposition will fail to be brought to the notice of the assembly. There may be Legislatures of which this is not true, but such Legislatures will find slight embarrassment in requirements for yea-and-nay absolute-majority votes on every measure.

The situation is quite different with respect to measures to be passed upon by popular vote at the polls. There it is nobody's particular business to scrutinize, study, and oppose. No sworn obligation to perform a public duty stirs the conscience of any man. No trust in behalf of others has been formally assumed. Reputation is not at stake. Ambition is not at work. None of the motives impelling a representative assembly are at hand to safeguard the common welfare. For this reason there may very well be requirement of a vote large enough to prove by itself a genuine public interest. Such was the view acted upon by Delaware and Kentucky in 1792, Delaware requiring that the holding of a Constitutional Convention should be contingent on the approval of a majority of all the citizens having the right to vote for Representatives, and Kentucky making it a majority of all who actually voted for Representatives at the same election. Tennessee followed Kentucky; then Ohio and other States.

The Delaware requirement was much more stringent than that of Kentucky, but each of them proved a serious obstacle in the way of constitutional change. Voters know more about men and take more interest in men, than measures, with the invariable result that the vote on any constitutional question or other matter referred to the electorate is smaller than the vote at the same time for candidates — often very much smaller. Ohio devised an ingenious way of meeting the difficulty. In 1910 its Legislature passed a bill permitting political parties to make the question of calling a Convention a part of their tickets, so that a man voting a straight ticket would vote for a Convention. The result was that as the leading parties declared for a Convention, one was called by a nearly unanimous vote. This Convention (1912) submitted a provision that was ratified, to the effect that thereafter amendments might be submitted by three fifths of the Legislature and ratified by a majority of those voting thereon.

Several of the States still require a majority of the whole electorate or of the voters taking part in an election, for the ratification of a constitutional amendment, and a few make like demand in the case of measures submitted to the people by initiative or referendum petition. The Constitution adopted for the German Commonwealth in 1919 prescribed that an act of the National Assembly might be annulled by a popular vote only if a majority of those qualified took part. The requirement of a majority of the whole electorate is excessive. Experience has proved it an unreasonable obstacle in the path of progress. There is much weight to the arguments of those who say it is unfair to require a majority of those taking part in the election. Probably the end worth while will be secured if it is required that a submitted measure shall get the approval of at least a third of those attending the polls and a majority of those voting on the measure itself.

It is better the requirement should be in that form than to make the comparison with the largest number of votes cast in respect to any given office or measure. Justice Brewer for the court, in County-seat of Linn County (15 Kas. 500 — 1875), said that in "cases where two or more questions are submitted at the same election, and more votes are cast upon one question than upon another... the highest number of votes cast upon any one question is clear evidence of the number of voters." Not at all. Whoever watches election canvasses knows that often the highest vote is appreciably less than the total vote. There is no difficulty in the way of returning the total number of voters, and this is the only fair standard by which to gauge interest upon any particular question.

Critics of the Initiative and Referendum have strongly urged that the small votes cast upon referenda, as disclosed even in such important matters as constitutional amendments, are proof of a lack of interest or knowledge that should by itself discredit the system. This does not appeal to me as the strongest of the arguments against plebiscites. Precisely the same phenomenon appears in legislative assemblies. It would hardly do to discredit Parliament or Congress or any State Legislature because a large part of the business is transacted with a bare quorum, or indeed by tacit consent, without any real quorum present. May it not be that whether from assembly or electorate, the really vital thing is to get the opinion of those who have an opinion? Of course the formation of that opinion is quite another matter. Here only its expression is in view. If that expression indicates reasonable volume, with adequate protection against surprise or fraud, possibly the voting-majority test will meet the essential need.

Votes Larger Than a Majority

The States in their Constitutions have never adhered strictly to the doctrine that one more than half should always be enough to prevail. For example, Pennsylvania at the outset required that two thirds of the whole Council of Censors should agree on calling a Convention; Vermont copied the requirement; and in both States that was the rule as long as the Council lasted. Maryland required two thirds of all the members of each branch to concur in any change of the Constitution relating to the Eastern Shore. South Carolina, in 1790, said no Convention should be called "unless by the concurrence of two thirds of both branches of the whole representation." Massachusetts directed that when in 1795 the sentiments of the voters should be collected on the necessity or expediency of revising the Constitution, a Convention was to be held if favored by two thirds of "the qualified voters throughout the State, who shall assemble and vote." The same State devised an odd variant of the ratio in one of the half-dozen plebiscites taken in the District of Maine on the question of separation from the parent Commonwealth, the requirement in 1816 being a vote of at least five to four. An ingenious contention followed. The poll gave 11,969 in favor to 10,347 against, not meeting the requirement, whereupon a Convention shrewdly tried to evade the situation by averring that the affirmative had won because the total affirmative vote in the towns favoring had exceeded the total negative in the towns opposing. The General Court could not see it in that light.

Application of the larger-majority idea was doubtless suggested by the requirement of a two-thirds vote for the passage of bills over vetoes. Probably it was this that led New York in 1821 to put into the Constitution the provision that "the assent of two thirds of the members elected to each branch of the Legislature shall be requisite to every bill appropriating the public moneys or property for local or private purposes." Rhode Island copied this in 1842, Michigan in 1850, Iowa in 1857. The Republic of Texas (1836) made the same requirement, the first State Constitution (1845) changing it to read "No appropriation for private or individual purposes, or for purposes of internal improvement." So it stood until 1876, when the legislative powers of appropriation were harnessed after modern fashion.

In 1868 Georgia said: "No vote, resolution, law, or order, shall pass, granting a donation, or gratuity, in favor of any person, except by the concurrence of two thirds of the General Assembly." Pennsylvania said in 1873: "No appropriation shall be made to any charitable or educational institution not under the absolute control of the Commonwealth, other than normal schools established by law for the professional training of teachers for the public schools of the State, except by a vote of two thirds of all members elected to each House." Mississippi (1890) preferred: "No law granting a donation, or gratuity, in favor of any person or object shall be enacted, except by the concurrence of two thirds of each branch of the Legislature, nor by any vote for a sectarian purpose or use."

From 1821 to 1846 New York also required a two-thirds vote of all members for "creating, continuing, altering, or renewing any body politic." Michigan from 1835 to 1850 and Florida from 1838 to 1868 made like requirement, but the occasion for it passed with the coming of incorporation under general laws. New Jersey in 1844 evidently was still under the spell of that suspicion of banks which had been spread broadcast by Jacksonian politics, for it prescribed the assent of three fifths of the members elected to each House as a requisite for the passage of bank charter laws, but this was stricken out in 1875.

Minnesota requires a two-thirds yea-and-nay vote of the members of each branch, and Delaware, with some exceptions, a three-quarters vote of all elected, for debt bills. Arkansas and South Dakota require other than the ordinary appropriations to be made by a two-thirds vote. Nebraska has the same requirement on appropriations to supply deficiencies.

New York in 1846 devised a shifting scale for the final passage of revenue and appropriation bills. It stipulated that three fifths of the members must be in attendance. Coupled with the absolute-majority requirement for all bills, this meant that if a bare three fifths should be present, it would take approximately five sixths of them to vote affirmatively in order to pass the bill. Kentucky in 1890 applied the principle to all bills, but made the minimum vote in the affirmative two fifths of the total membership and a majority of the members voting. Virginia imposed the same minimum in 1902, including also concurrence in amendments and the adoption of conference reports, as well as discharging of committees. Coupled with the usual majority-quorum requirement, this calls for approximately a four-fifths vote in the affirmative if but a bare quorum is present.

Apart from constitutional provisions, the rules of our legislative bodies show a tendency for more and more departure from the practice of action by majority vote. Some day serious controversy may arise over the question of the binding power of agreements in the shape of rules requiring this or that action to be taken by a two-thirds or four-fifths vote. Justice Shaw held, in French v. Senate, 146 Cal. 604 (1905): "The Senate has power to adopt any procedure and to change it at any time without notice. It cannot tie its own hands by adopting rules which, as a matter of power purely, it cannot at any time change and disregard." If this is sound doctrine, requirements for action by a vote of two thirds or four fifths have no power other than that given to them by acquiescence.

It would be superfluous to cite all the instances in which Constitutions, statutes, or rules have required a vote of two thirds or more. Enough have been given to show that if there is such a thing as the divine right of the majority, its violation is far from small. Is it not the fair conclusion that the majority rule is simply a working hypothesis, to be discarded whenever some other test bids fair to give better results?

At least one of the great political thinkers, Rousseau, has addressed himself to the principles involved in this matter. His was no blind attachment to the simple majority. He thought the requirement for declaring the general will might be fixed at any one of the stages between an equal division of votes and unanimity, according to the condition and requirements of the body politic. "The more important and weighty the resolutions," he said, "the nearer should the opinion which prevails approach unanimity; the greater the despatch requisite in the matter under discussion, the more should we restrict the prescribed difference in the division of opinions. The first of these principles appears more suitable to laws, the second to affairs." [1]

Experience since that was written has shown much of it to be sound, but it may be questioned whether save in time of emergency or crisis, speed should be a factor. Indeed the dangers attaching to hasty, ill-considered action might be advanced as a reason for requiring nearer approach to unanimity. Furthermore the importance of getting sizable approval in order to promise general acceptance and enforcement of law, might well be stressed. More important still, and in the eyes of the conservatives the chief justification for all large-vote requirements, is the fact that nearly all legislation means change. If the benefit of the doubt should be given to the existing status, if the burden of proof should rest upon those who want it changed, then there may be cogent reason indeed for demanding decided preponderance of votes in the affirmative. To this, however, it could be answered that in general the negative has the advantage because by reason of temperament more men instinctively oppose than favor change, and because legislative procedure as a whole furnishes more obstacles than helps to constructive effort.

[1] *The Social Compact*, book IV, chap. 2.

CHAPTER XI

MINORITIES

WE have so far been considering how the will of the larger or largest number has been or should be made to prevail, and some attention has been given to the smaller number, the minority, treated as a unit. The smaller number, however, may be in turn made up of several or many numbers, minorities, which may most conveniently be spoken of here as "groups." The terms are not quite synonymous, for the largest group in the electorate, if more than half the whole, is the majority and not a minority, but inasmuch as adoption of the proposals to be examined would doubtless in many instances affect the size and nature of the majority, a discussion of "groups" will best meet the need.

The doctrine to be studied is that the lawmaking body should contain representatives of all sizable bodies of opinion, whether already formulated or likely to result from the community of interest attaching to occupation, social relationship, or race, to religious, economic, or political creed — in short, anything that inclines men to the same way of thinking on one subject, a few subjects, or many subjects, save only the factor of physical propinquity, residence, which now for the most part determines voting constituencies.

Social or occupational status for several centuries determined. Then came the creation of political parties, not the work of a moment, but a growth that in England covered the greater part of the seventeenth century and on this side of the water did not reach importance until after Washington's service as President. With parties representation shifted from status to opinion.

In English-speaking lands opinion contented itself for a long time with but a single division. On the Continent it quickly split into numerous parts and of late some tendency in that direction has appeared in both the British Empire and the United States.

The representing of different bodies of opinion was at first left to the accidents of preponderance in geographical divisions — towns, wards, cities, counties, States, or artificial districts. This did not long satisfy. In the period of the French Revolution it was suggested by Mirabeau, Condorcet, and Saint-Just that groups holding like views ought to be represented. A generation later the theory began to get consideration. In 1821 an English schoolmaster invented the system now known as proportional representation with the single transferable vote and it was tried out satisfactorily in a literary society. The principle was first applied to public elections in the little colony of Adelaide, South Australia, in 1839.[1] Then in 1844 Thomas Gilpin published in Philadelphia a pamphlet, *On the Representation of Minorities*, which was the first serious work of consequence relating to the subject. Denmark in 1856 saw the first public proportional elections carried out by ballot, the method being devised by C. C. G. Andrae, then Minister of Finance.

Apparently without knowledge of Andrae's achievement, about the same time Thomas Hare in England worked out much the same system, and the publication in 1857 of the first of his several books on the subject led to his being generally accredited as the original inventor. This was helped along by J. S. Mill, who thought that in Hare's idea of "personal representation" he discovered "the greatest improvement of which the system of representative government is capable." Since then the literature of the subject has become voluminous, many plans to accomplish the end in view have been suggested, and progress in their application has been considerable.

Denmark applied proportional representation in 1867 to the election of members of the upper chamber, and in 1908 extended its use to municipalities. By revision of the election law first tested in 1918, an interesting modification was applied to the choice of members of the lower branch. Of its 140 members, 24 are allotted to Copenhagen, to be elected by the list system. The Islands have 42 single-member districts. Jutland has 51. The high man in each of the 93 Island and Jutland districts is declared elected, and then 23 seats are distributed among the less successful parties, 9 to the Islands and 11 to Jutland. Copenhagen does not share in this allotment, but its votes are counted in with those of the rest of the kingdom in determining the allotment for bringing about a closer approximation to a proportional party representation. One person may be a candidate in several districts within a county, in which case it is credited with the total number of votes cast for him within that county.

[1] C. G. Hoag and G. H. Hallett, Jr., *Proportional Representation*, 167.

It is averred that the practical result is to secure representation very nearly proportional to numerical party strength.

Serbia applied the system to local elections in 1888 and to those for the Parliament eleven years later. Swiss cantons began using it in 1891, and in 1918 it was extended to the choice of the lower House of the Federal Parliament. Norway began in 1896 by making it optional for local governments and in 1920 applied it to the election of the single-House Parliament. Belgium in 1899 adopted it for both Houses of its Parliament. Through the remaining fifteen years before the War it gained at least a foothold in Germany, Moravia, Finland, Sweden, Bulgaria, and Austria. Somehow the War gave such impetus to the movement that all the Constitutions adopted on the Continent since (as far as observed) have provided for it to greater or less degree, and several of the countries where some measure of it had been tried, have extended its use.

In France the War was followed by the triumph of a campaign for electoral reform. When the demand for a revival of election by *scrutin de liste* (general ticket) had brought the Chamber of Deputies to set up a committee on the subject in 1907, the report approving *scrutin de liste* combined with it proportional representation. In 1909 the Chamber passed a resolution favoring such a program. It was presented by the Briand ministry of 1910, by the Poincaré ministry, and then by the new Briand ministry, to which it brought downfall in 1913. Three quarters of the Deputies elected in April of 1914 had promised their constituents to support an electoral reform bill embracing proportional representation. Then came the War, and the issue was not again raised until the spring of 1919, when such a bill passed the Chamber by 277 to 138, and then overcame strong opposition in the Senate. The system in use, however, does not commend itself to the friends of proportional representation. They deny that it is the real thing and predict it will not last long.

The War also brought Germany to look on the reform with more favor. Several of the German States had previously used it in limited fashion. Under the provisional government established in November of 1918 the first general election for the national assembly was carried out with proportional representation fully applied according to a list system. The result appears to have been an apportionment of seats fairly in accord with group strength, six groups getting from 22 to 165 seats, 8 seats going to minor parties, and no group having a majority. That the experiment was satisfactory to the dominant forces may be inferred from the fact that the Constitution adopted for the Republic July 31, 1919, directed that delegates should thereafter be chosen "in accordance with the principles of proportional representation."

In Italy proportional representation was provided in 1919 for the election of the Chamber of Deputies. Five years later Mussolini tried a novel experiment. The group that elected the most members was to be given additional seats to such a total that it would have a majority of one in the Chamber. The remaining seats were to be distributed among the other groups in proportion to the votes they cast at the polls. The results of the first test were so disturbing that Mussolini threw the idea overboard and substituted in 1925 the single-district system, which is incompatible with proportional representation. This in turn proved unsatisfactory to the Fascists and in 1928 they substituted another kind of single district, consisting of the whole country. The four hundred members of the Lower House are to be elected at large. Although the preliminary nominations will be made chiefly by occupational groups, nothing like genuine proportional representation appears.

In England the War distinctly helped what many think a reform, for to encourage the masses in patriotic endeavor the leaders of the country decided that concessions to popular demand should be made. So in 1918 the Representation of the People Act became law. Its clauses relating to proportional representation had led to months of controversy between Lords and Commons. Strangely enough the Lords were the more advanced in their ideas, for they stood out in behalf of proportional representation, favoring the plan of districts each electing several members on the Hare system, while the Commons by small majorities repeatedly voted for the alternative-vote plan in single-member districts. Viscount Bryce, Lord Courtney, the Earl of Penwith, H. H. Asquith, Lord Robert Cecil, and A. J. Balfour were among the champions of proportional representation; J. Austen Chamberlain and Walter H. Long were conspicuous on the other side. The outcome was a compromise, with provision for proportional representation of university constituencies returning two or more members, and with permission for the appointment of Commissioners to prepare a scheme under which a hundred members, as nearly as possible, might be returned from other constituencies electing three to seven members each. As might have been expected, the agitation of the subject led to provision for proportional representation, though to but a small degree, in the Act of the following year reorganizing the government of India, and in the year afterward to its inclusion in the Government of Ireland Act, where it went the full length of covering elections to both Houses in both Northern and Southern Ireland. In 1922 it was provided for the Irish Free State.

Other countries in which some measure of the system has been put in force within more or less recent years are Tasmania, New South Wales, Union of South Africa, Iceland, Chile, Uruguay, Argentina, Costa Rica, Cuba.

In the United States

The writings of Hare and Mill awakened American interest in the subject about 1865. The cudgels were taken up in behalf of the reform by two doughty champions, Simon Sterne, Esq., of New York, and Senator Charles R. Buckalew of Pennsylvania, who argued through years, but with small immediate effect. Our first experiment may have been in the choice of thirty-two delegates-at-large for the New York Constitutional Convention of 1867. No elector could vote for more than sixteen. State conventions were held by the political parties, each nominating a ticket of sixteen names. So the whole ticket of each party was chosen, and the system really had no test. Governor David B. Hill of New York wanted minority representation in the Convention he recommended in 1887, to be secured by having 42 delegates at large, with the voter restricted to voting for 15. As the bill was passed, it provided for 32 at large, the elector to vote for only 16. The Governor vetoed it. Governor Flower, in 1892, likewise urged a Convention, and a bill was passed, in which was the provision that in addition to the delegates elected by the people, of whom 32 were to be elected at large, the elector voting for but 16, the Governor should appoint five delegates to represent labor organizations, and three for the Prohibitionists. In his Message of 1893, the Governor said doubt had been raised concerning the constitutionality of such appointments, on the ground that the Legislature could not confer such power. He expressed himself in favor of minority representation, and wanted provision for it in case the plan of appointment should be deemed unconstitutional. Nevertheless, the Legislature in revising the law left out both appointment and minority representation.

Our only test in electing legislators has been in Illinois. The system used is quite different from that favored nowadays by the ablest advocates of the reform and they are doubtless quite justified in asking that a verdict as to proportional representation be not based on the Illinois experience, but for what it may be worth some description of it should be given.

Blaine F. Moore has published (1909) as one of the Studies of the University of Illinois, a monograph on "The History of Cumulative Voting and Minority Representation in Illinois, 1870–1908." It appears to be impartial and judicious, prepared with a care that warrants acceptance of its statements of fact, as well as the attaching of weight to its comments. The Committee of Electoral and Representative Reform of the Illinois Convention of 1869–70, headed by Joseph Medill of Chicago, recommended three Representatives for each district, with permission to the voter to cast his three votes for any one candidate or distribute them as he might see fit. The argument accompanying the report stated that since 1854, with few exceptions, all the Senators and Representatives in the northern half of Illinois had been of one political party; those of the other half of the State, with equally few exceptions, of the opposing party. The Convention adopted the proposal by a large majority, and the people ratified it, 99,022 to 70,082.

The result of the practical test of the plan that had been given by thirty-five years of its use in biennial elections in fifty-one districts when Mr. Moore wrote, was that only three times had all three Representatives of any one district been the regular nominees of one party. Except in one abnormal year, the percentage of the total votes cast by each party in the State was fairly close to the percentage of members of the party chosen to the House. To all save three Houses third-party men were sent, but minor parties received no great benefit from the scheme, as it seldom happens that any minor party has more votes than the weaker of two larger parties in any one district. There had been twenty-four cases in which the minority clearly had an undue share of representation, securing a majority of the Representatives in about two and one half per cent of the total number of elections. "The system has been so seldom subverted in such a manner as to defeat the will of the majority that there can be no serious accusation against the cumulative method in this regard."

Partisans are inclined to assert that great harm may be done the majority by a minority securing undue representation at certain critical times. The occasional extraordinary influence of a small faction holding the balance of power may and does happen under any system of election and is not a defect peculiar to the cumulative system.

To supplement statistical information, Mr. Moore sent letters of inquiry to a varied list of citizens whose aggregate judgment would be worth while. One of the questions was: "Does the system increase or diminish the power of the party machine?" Nine replies asserted that the power was diminished, thirty-five maintained the system had no effect on party organization, while forty-one declared (and most of them were very certain as to the correctness of the answer) that the influence of the party machine was greatly increased. One strong evidence of strict party control was the limited number of real candidates nominated, especially in the Chicago districts. Usually there were but three candidates of the two dominant parties combined. Ordinarily the majority party nominated two and the minority party one. So far as Mr. Moore was aware, no majority party had ever nominated three candidates in order to give its constituents a greater choice at the polls. In Cook County the rule of three candidates between the two larger parties had been almost universally followed; outside Cook County, not so much. "Admitting all the charges, there is no evidence anywhere nor any analogy from which conclusions can be drawn, which would warrant any belief other than that the 'machine' would be just as corrupt and have just as complete control as it now has if the cumulative vote had never been used. It would be useless to deny that the cumulative vote requires strict party discipline and that in this system the political 'boss' found ready-made a means of exercising his control, but all evidence tends to show that if such means had not been furnished he would have found methods of his own to accomplish the same result."

The men interrogated did not supply reasons to believe that the practical difficulties in the matter of counting and recording votes under the cumulative system are considerable enough to be deemed real objections.

One of Mr. Moore's questions was put with the idea of determining public sentiment and ascertaining if minority representation in its somewhat crude and limited Illinois form was regarded as successful enough to lead the people of the State to approve a wider application of the principle. "The answers," he says, "are very significant in indicating how completely the idea of proportional representation has sunk into desuetude and how completely it has been eliminated from the list of live political questions in this country."

Also he made inquiry as to the effect on the personnel of the Legislature. A well-known Chicago lawyer asserted: "I believe that the one-member district plan would be infinitely preferable in its results both as to character and ability of the Representatives secured. This because it would require an actual fight before the people for election." An editor: "In proportion as responsibility is divided, men of less character are chosen for the public service." A prominent official: "I believe the present system secures poorer results in both character and ability than a flat one-vote process. I think the cumulative three-vote plan enables an inferior candidate to be elected in many instances." A member of Congress: "Neither better nor worse candidates are selected on account of it." Out of eighty-four who replied, twenty-four were of the opinion that the method of election had no effect on the character or ability of members; six thought the system bettered the membership in these respects; twenty-one thought not; and thirty-three made the cautious answer that at least the members usually secured were no better than would be elected by other methods. It is to be noted that only six out of eighty-four maintained that any improvement in the personnel had been achieved.

Mr. Moore concludes: "Judging from the opinion of representative citizens whose standing in the community is such that their ideas may be taken as a criterion, public sentiment is either indifferent or opposed to minority representation. The scheme has a few warm friends, but many of those expressing opinions think it has produced but little effect in any direction, while others are squarely opposed, opposition usually being based on the alleged subversion of the system by party organization. All are agreed that one of the principal objects of the introduction of the method, the allaying of sectional strife, has been accomplished. The strongest recommendation for the cumulative system is the fact that at all times it secures representation for a

minor party, thus insuring a strong minority in the lower House
of the General Assembly. The serious objection is the opportunity it affords for 'machine' control and party bossism. If, as
is hoped, the new primary law will check the abuses of the party
organization and give the people as complete a control of their
Legislature as may prevail under the usual majority system,
then the merits of the cumulative methods will greatly outweigh
the defects and furnish ample justification for its existence. But
if the primary fails in its express object in this particular, the
cumulative system, while its defects are no worse than are found
in the ordinary majority system, has so little practical, positive
merit to recommend it, that it can only be regarded as a complication which does not at present justify its continued existence."

Longer experience in Illinois did not remove dissatisfaction
with the system and the Constitutional Convention of 1920–22
recommended its abolition. The proposed Constitution, however, was rejected, for other reasons, so that the judgment of the
electorate was not ascertained in this particular. Another rejected Constitution, that passed upon in Ohio in 1874, would
have imitated the Illinois plan and extended it to Senators as
well as Representatives, in all districts where more than two of
either were to be chosen. Ten years later the principle was considered by the Ohio court in State v. Constantine, 42 Ohio St.
437, and it was held that since no such thing as minority representation or cumulative voting was known in the policy of Ohio
when the Constitution of 1851 was adopted, the elector had a
right to vote for a candidate for each office, and that it was denied by a statute providing for four members of a board of police
commissioners but giving the right to vote for only two.

In 1889 the Michigan Legislature passed an act adopting the
Illinois system, but the court refused to sustain it. Chief Justice
Champlin, in Maynard v. Bd. of Canvassers, 84 Mich. 228
(1890), held the foundation of a representative form of government to be, that, unless the people have otherwise signified by
their Constitution, "every elector entitled to cast his ballot
stands upon a complete political equality with every other elector, and that the majority or plurality of votes cast for any person or measure must prevail." Again: "The Constitution does
not contemplate, but by implication forbids, any elector to cast
more than one vote for any candidate for any office."

Also in 1889 when South Dakota acquired statehood, an article of the Constitution was separately submitted, providing for the Illinois plan of election to the lower House, but it was rejected — 24,161 to 46,200.

Various Systems

Observe that the Illinois plan has customarily secured representation of "the minority" — a loose phrase that may mean all the voters who are not of the greater or greatest part, i.e., those in a plurality or majority, or may mean the one lesser group that is of material size. Equally loose is the phrase "a minority," for it may mean the lesser part viewed as a whole or one of several lesser groups. This helped to make "minority representation" an inexact term as long used. Better understanding may be had if we attempt to classify the various systems that have been devised to accomplish the broad purpose.

All of them presuppose that more than one place is to be filled at a time, as in the case of a City Council to be elected on a general list or of several Representatives from one District, and all require that at least three shall be chosen by one balloting.

The simplest is the single-vote system, where each elector has but one vote and the candidates getting the larger vote are declared elected. This is the method supposed to be justified by the theory that no voter is entitled to be represented in any representative body by more than a single representative. Where the supremacy of party views is the issue, the system is manifestly open to the objection that without an impracticable degree of party machinery and discipline, the majority party, if it has nominated as many candidates as there are places to be filled, may so concentrate its votes that less than half its candidates will be elected, and in any case is not likely to be able so to control its votes as to make sure of a result proportionate to its preponderance. This plan is used for elections to the Japanese House of Representatives and also for part of both the Senate and House of Porto Rico.

Another form of the limited vote system permits the elector to vote for more than one candidate, but not for so many as are to be chosen. Thus in Boston from 1894 to 1898 inclusive, with twelve Aldermen to be elected each voter could vote for seven. It is a system that has been much used for municipal councils in various parts of the world, and prevails for all representative bodies in

Colombia, as well as for judges, county commissioners, and county auditors in Pennsylvania. That it has been discarded in many places would indicate it as having decided imperfections. In operation it has been found that the representation secured to the minority party second in rank has no relation to its numerical importance, and the smaller minority parties get no representation at all. A modification of the idea was embodied in a law enacted in Massachusetts in 1903, providing that each party should nominate eight candidates for the Board of Aldermen in Boston. As thirteen were to be chosen, this was expected to secure that not more than eight would be of any one political party. The results did not satisfy and the scheme was abandoned.

With the next group of systems, known as "cumulative," arithmetical complications grow. These let the voter cast more than one ballot for the candidate he prefers. It was the plan put into effect in Illinois, where with three to be chosen, the voter could cast three ballots for one man, or otherwise allot his three votes as he saw fit. The chief objection to it comes from the temptation for members of the majority party to "plump," that is, cast all their votes for one man, which may result in giving a popular candidate a very large vote and defeating his associates, the minority thus getting more than their proportionate share of the men elected. This invites to contests between party colleagues instead of political antagonists, breeds jealousies, and may lead to party disruption. Evils of such a sort were conspicuous in the choice of English school boards (for which the system was adopted in 1870), since the more men to be elected, the greater the danger from "plumping." The wasteful accumulation of votes for the more popular candidates or those of the more powerful faction, permitted small factions to secure the election of members when not really entitled to them by their numbers, and thus let in weak or mischievous men. Partly for this reason, it is said, school boards in England have been abolished. Elsewhere in several instances the system has been abandoned, but it survives for both Houses and for municipal councils in Chile.

To guard against the evils more conspicuous in the limited and cumulative methods, what are known as "list systems" have been devised, chiefly in order that a vote which would be ineffective if counted for the voter's first choice may help somebody else. This may be accomplished in one of three ways — by having what is known as the transfer of the vote determined by the party, or by the candidate, or by the voter himself.

If parties are to determine, they make up lists of candidates before the election. After the balloting the seats to be filled are divided between the parties in the proportion of the total votes cast by each, the higher men on each list being declared elected to the number their party proportion warrants. With slight exception this is the system used for electing the lawmaking bodies of continental Europe, as far as proportional representation prevails. That the system harmonizes with the habit of political thought on the Continent and stands the test of time, may be inferred from its steady progress through the Swiss cantons, its maintenance in Belgium for now thirty years, and its general adoption in Germany.

The proposal that the candidate, rather than the party or the voter, shall in effect make up the lists, by designating in advance those to whom ineffective votes cast for himself shall be transferred, has had zealous champions but as yet no application.

More important is the third method of transferring votes — by the voter himself. This is known as the Hare system, from its English originator. Under it the voter designates on the ballot the order of his choice. When the ballots have been sorted according to first-choice candidates, and the total found, the smallest number of ballots which for a certainty will secure the election of a candidate, called "the quota," is determined by dividing the total number of valid ballots by one more than the number of candidates to be elected and taking the whole number next larger than the result. The counting proceeds, through the first choices, then the second choices, and so on, with transfers according to the particular variant of the system that may be in force, in a rather complicated fashion that need not be here further described. Suffice it to say that as soon as any candidate reaches the quota figure, he is declared elected, and the other choices on the ballots where he has been given first choice may then go to help somebody else reach the quota.

This is the system that now receives the greatest approval among those who theorize on the subject, as being in their judgment the fairest and most satisfactory. It has made less progress than the list systems, probably because of its complexities, but it is now in use in the Irish Free State, Denmark, some parts of Australia, and in the cities of Cleveland, Cincinnati, and Ashtabula, Ohio, as well as in a few places in Canada and elsewhere. Oregon in 1910 and again in 1912 defeated amendments that would have applied the method to the choice of members of both Houses of the Legislature, and in 1914 defeated an amendment that would have applied it to the lower House, by a vote of 39,740 to 137,116. Also in 1914 California defeated an amendment for its use. An Oklahoma statute of 1925 applying the system to primary elections made certain requirements of the voter as to the number of candidates for whom he should vote, and on this account was nullified by the Supreme Court in Dove v. Oglesby (249 Pac. 798, March, 1926) because obnoxious to the provision of the State Constitution that "no power shall ever interfere to prevent the free exercise of the right of suffrage." The system has also been frowned upon by the courts of Michigan and California, and the courts of New Jersey and Rhode Island have ruled against limited voting, but of course the court decisions do not concern the merits of the methods, only constitutionality being involved.

ARGUMENT AND THEORY

A method of ascertaining the popular will as respects candidates for office that has come to prevail to greater or less degree in the larger part of the countries of the civilized world can no longer be derided nor ignored. It must be studied carefully and without prejudice.

First let us observe the defects averred to exist in an electing process under which a district chooses but one representative — defects the new system is expected to cure, or at least to lessen.

Beginning with certain mechanical results, it is pointed out that in a single-member district all the votes cast for other than the winner are wasted because quite ineffective. On the other hand a big majority and a small majority carry precisely the same weight. If the margin of the winner is small, a shift of but a few votes at the next election may produce altogether disproportionate effect in ultimate influence on legislative action. If party strength is unevenly distributed, as, for instance, in our industrial States, where the bulk of one party is often concentrated in a few cities with the other party controlling by a less margin most of the smaller communities, it may and often does follow that the party which in the aggregate has the fewer votes at the polls will have the greater part of the seats in the Legislature. The likelihood of this is increased by the larger chance that single-member districts give for the gerrymander, that is, the creation of unnatural constituencies, particularly for the election of Senators.

In the single-member district where one party markedly predominates, no man of opposite faith has a chance to embark on a political career. This loses to the community all benefit that might come from public service by strong men there who chance to be of the minority. Furthermore the successful candidates of the majority are likely to be the "good fellows," chosen by reason of qualities that give little promise of legislative usefulness. Were the districts larger, these qualities would count less, with correspondingly greater chance for the modest, unassuming man of real capacity who may not be a good "mixer." For much the same reasons reëlection may be more difficult in single districts, which increases the danger of losing the benefits of experience and sometimes ends the usefulness of statesmen.

When city districts elect each but one member of a Legislature, it may follow that there will be an excess of incapacity for public affairs among those chosen, by reason of the fact that those persons who have such capacity, as shown by prosperity, are wont to dwell together, in a comparatively small neighborhood. No snobbish flavor is to be suspected in the statement that the dwellers in one ward may have had more training and experience than those in another. Government is largely an enterprise, a great enterprise, engaged in administering affairs of common concern, expending vast sums of money, employing large numbers of wage and salary earners. Surely there is nothing supercilious in the suggestion that the directors of the corporation should be the best administrators that can be found. If two chance to sleep in the same block, why prevent more than one from being chosen? At least that obstacle in the way of efficient government would be removed by having large districts in cities. That is one of the reasons why proportional representation is particularly adapted to municipal elections — the field, indeed, where with us it is making the most headway.

Considerations of efficiency will of course have little weight with those who fix their eyes on the other function of government, the political function, that of embodying opinion in law. They would rather base their argument on the fact that minority opinions have no chance whatever for effective expression in the single-member district. As the votes of a minority do not count, its members feel that they are relieved of any of the responsibilities of citizenship. This is thought to increase the volume of indifference, the number of those who stay away from the polls; and to encourage the distrust of government as misrepresentative.

Some of these objections, at least to some degree, also apply to large districts that choose several representatives on one ticket, by what is often called block vote (in France *scrutin de liste*). In any given district this means monopoly for the largest group of voters, with the same results that monopoly brings in single-member districts. Among them is the possibility that although the minority may be close to half of the whole, it will be wholly unrepresented, with the added danger that this may happen in a large district where were it divided into smaller districts, some among them might go the other way. In other words the larger district with the block vote may actually result in more misrepresentation. Inaccuracy may also be increased if the nominating system permits many candidates to divide the support of the majority where the minority strength is confined to just the number to be elected, in which case the minority may carry its whole block to victory.

Proportional representation is expected to meet the defects of both the single-member and the block system. It is believed to hold out sundry other advantages. Primaries will be eliminated. Venality will be lessened. There will be more continuity of governmental policy, for great shifts are less likely. Fair play will be ensured. Good feeling in election periods is more likely to pre-vail. Independent judgment will be encouraged. Most important of all, groups of opinion will be represented in fair proportion to their size.

On the opposite page of the ledger are to be entered certain debits.

The larger the district, the bigger the cost of candidacy. It is already far too heavy. Tripling or quadrupling the electorate means increasing three- or fourfold the cost of circulars, of travel, of rallies — of all the legitimate methods of informing the voters, to say nothing of those outlays commonly looked on as reprehensible, which might well be made more burdensome and dangerous did that not mean also increase of venality.

The larger the district, the less proportionately of personal knowledge of candidates by voters. Candidates for State Legislatures are rarely known beyond a radius of a few miles from their homes. To expose them to the judgment of a widely scattered electorate would surely favor the demagogue and hamper the man of modesty and self-respect. Even now the size of Senatorial districts is often responsible for the success of the inferior man. Candidates for Congress should be men of standing enough to be more widely known, but their reputation too has its limits. Each member of the Federal House represents to-day on the average 275,000 human beings. Trebling this number would mean 725,000; quadrupling, more than a million. Under the Italian law of 1919 not less than ten members were to be sent from each district. With us that would mean constituencies of 2,750,000. In view of the newspaper circulations in the great centers of population, possibly no great harm would there follow from huge districts, but elsewhere the result would in this respect probably be inferior selection, though that is not sure, for in some cases weak men would be deterred, and in others strong men, widely known, would be encouraged.

Offsetting this, however, is the certainty that the larger the district, the greater the power of the party machine to control the event. It would prepare organization lists, in which mediocrities would predominate, for outstanding men make enemies and it would not be good politics to endanger the whole list by the presence on it of anybody inviting attack. To be sure, this would work both ways and lessen the chances of distinctly objectionable men. Anyhow a cautiously selected list, with nobody on it conspicuous for either strength or weakness, would be pretty sure to poll the full party strength. It would be the more likely so to do because independent candidacies are impracticable under most if not all systems of proportional representation. There being no primaries, preliminary contest against the objectionable man is precluded, and once his name is in the party list, it is almost impossible to single him out for defeat. For the same reason the superior man has no chance when he has been rejected by the organization.

Other technical objections spring from the mathematical intricacies of the systems proposed. In those with transferable votes the ballots are harder to mark, and many a voter will have little or no understanding of what he is doing. The count is much harder, with correspondingly greater chance for error. Knowledge of the result is greatly delayed, perhaps theoretically a matter of no consequence, yet annoying to the public and likely to increase dissatisfaction with the election process as a whole. An objection that may arise afterward is based on the lack of an appropriate way to fill vacancies.

The effect on the personnel of the lawmaking body is to be weighed. Whether or not in some or many cases more capable men will be chosen, it is inevitable that proportional representation will introduce into public life a larger number of one-idea men. The candidates of the smaller factions are sure to be men chosen because of their zeal in subordinating everything else to a single purpose. It would be too harsh to classify them as bigots, fanatics, narrow-minded, for that would needlessly emphasize the disagreeable side of their character. Unfortunately it is that side which most impresses itself on the public imagination, and so we have few words to describe them without appearing to blame. In reality such men are of inestimable value to the world. They accomplish all the truly great things. Yet it is doubtful if it would be well to have them preponderate in legislative bodies, or even be numerous.

Be it always remembered that the legislator must vote on an infinite variety of proposals. He does his work best when he has breadth both of knowledge and vision. Equally important is the sense of proportion, which will let him give due attention to each of the activities of government. Furthermore, compromise is of the very essence of legislation, and your zealot is not a man who easily compromises. Of course there are exceptions. It does not always follow that the single-taxer or the prohibitionist or the labor-unionist is unequal to meeting other issues, but the chances are that if he has for years concentrated his mind on one social problem, he will not be well-informed on other social problems and will not handle them so intelligently as will what we call the all-round man. This is the common experience of life. It is notorious that the specialist in any field of knowledge is often a weakling in other fields. Great scholars are usually poor financiers. Great financiers are usually poor scholars. Eminent clergymen, physicians, engineers have made disastrous failures when entering into fields foreign to their training. We speak of them as deficient in common-sense. Note what the term means — the sense that is common to many, the general sense. That is not the forte of the specialist. A Legislature of specialists would come near being a calamity.

Apart from personality, the advocates of proportional representation appear to assume it as axiomatic that the public welfare will be advanced by having champions of the various "isms" on the floor of legislative bodies. This fundamental premise is not easily proved to be valid. We do not put the plaintiff on the jury. That analogy is not wholly sound, but is suggestive.

One practical difficulty lies in the necessity of drawing the line between the enthusiasms clamoring for representation. Clearly they cannot all send a champion, for the voices of reform are multitudinous. To say that a faction shall be championed only when it is large enough to win one member on the quota plan is quite arbitrary. Suppose you saw fit to reduce the size of your Legislature by one half, or double it. Would that rightly vary the privileges of factions?

As a matter of experience it is found that the representation of small minorities on the floor of a legislative body is of insignificant use to its program. I served in Legislatures with two Socialists, one of them a man of culture who had been a clergyman, the other from the ranks of the wage-earners, both earnest, sincere men and good speakers. They made no converts, hardly interested anybody in their beliefs. They aroused more prejudice than approval. They influenced legislation not a whit. They left no trace of their presence. Precisely the same has been my observation of a few Socialists in Congress. Personally genial and congenial, intellectually capable and sincere, not by an inch did they advance their cause. In the routine work that makes up nine tenths of the tasks of government they were handicapped by the repute of their affiliations, and in respect of the remaining tenth their influence on the floor of the House was zero.

Were groups commonly as tenacious of purpose as are the Socialists, group representation would have less of the difficulty springing from the ephemeral character of most movements for reform. Swift fluctuation in the amount of adherence to "isms" is a familiar phenomenon. Often they are but gusts of popular passion. Often they spring from transitory economic causes. Even if occasionally they ought to have opportunity for legislative expression, yet they carry the chance that mass whims and vagaries will take on exaggerated importance. Also at times the issue will disappear before the men chosen have completed their terms of service, sometimes before they have even taken their seats. Some new issue will follow, on which no mandate has been given.

As to the scope of representation, it will not do to disregard wholly the view that at least in some measure the representative should be the agent of his constituents, guarding their interests, advancing their welfare. However much this may have been perverted since the days when Parliament began as an assemblage of agents bargaining with the King, however dangerous may be an exaggerated sense of local responsibility, yet probably we should not, and certainly we cannot, wholly abandon the notion that the representative is to be the spokesman of those who choose him. Indeed this broad principle is of the very essence of proportional representation itself. If that be so, why should not local interests be as much entitled to a spokesman as class interests or any other group interests? The larger the district, the less the possibility of accomplishing this. Furthermore, the wider apart the bounds of a constituency, the less the chance of those personal contacts necessary in order to know the wants and understand the feelings of the citizens represented.

In spite of all these considerations, if minorities really have rights, those rights are to be regarded. Professor Jenks undoubtedly voiced the belief of many advocates of the reform when he said, somewhat bluntly: "If enough fanatics unite upon any one subject to secure a representative in our legislature, they certainly have a right to demand to be heard." [1] The logic of the sequence is dubious. No real connection appears between numbers and a right to demand to be heard, nor has it ever been shown, so far as I am aware, that any form of right attaches to legislative numbers. Yet repeatedly the contrary is assumed. For instance, President Woolsey declared that "a minority fails to get its fair share of influence in a legislature.in nine cases out of ten." [2] Yet on the same page he said "the rule that the majority shall govern is taken by some as a maxim of essential justice, whereas it is simply a means of making business move forward." If justice is not to be a factor for the majority, why should it be for a minority?

Woolsey found injustice in the fact that in an election for a

[1] "Social Basis of Proportional Representation," *Annals of the American Academy*, November, 1895.

[2] *Political Science*, I, 298.

Legislature of 150 members, 100 may be elected by majorities
which all together would not be equal to the minority in a single
district. This is a common argument with the writers for proportional representation. It ignores the fact that ours is a government of parties and that the majority party is held responsible
for legislation. That party may best have definite control, with
a margin of votes large enough to make its responsibility clear.
So long as the minority has representation enough to secure
effective criticism, the real ends of the party system will be accomplished. Minorities are not represented that they may do
things, but that they may make it awkward for bad things to be
done.

One of the stoutest advocates of the proportional idea, Professor J. R. Commons, appears in one place to recognize this.
"The Hare system," he says, "is advocated by those who, in a
too *doctrinaire* fashion, wish to abolish political parties. They
apparently do not realize the impossibility of acting in politics
without large groupings of individuals." [1] Inasmuch as he does
not show why the largest of these groupings should not prevail,
a severe critic might allege that in saying this he gives away his
whole case. In fairness, however, his explanation later on should
be quoted. "All action by government," he avers, "whether
city, State, or nation, is political action. And all action by individuals towards incorporating their views in laws and public
policy must be through associations or groupings of individuals
under their chosen leadership. These groups are political parties,
and this action is the genuine, educational, vital function of
parties in popular government. But where there is freedom and
intelligence, such groupings are not rigidly permanent." [2] He
goes on to argue for proportional representation as facilitating
new alignments.

Perhaps the case for the representation of minorities has never
been set forth more ably than by John Stuart Mill. He held that
Parliament should be an arena in which not only the general
opinion of the nation, but that of every section of it, and as far as
possible of every individual whom it contains, can produce itself
in full light and challenge discussion; where every person in the
country may count on finding somebody who speaks his mind,
as well or better than he could speak it himself — not to friends
and partisans exclusively, but in the face of opponents, to be

[1] *Proportional Representation*, 104.   [2] *Ibid.*, 133.

tested by adverse controversy; where those whose opinion is over-ruled, feel satisfied that it is heard, and set aside, not by a mere act of will, but for what are thought superior reasons, commend-ing themselves as such to the representatives of the majority of the nation; where every party or opinion in the country can muster its strength, and be cured of any illusion concerning the number or power of its adherents; where the opinion which pre-vails in the nation makes itself manifest as prevailing, and marshals its hosts in the presence of the government, which is thus enabled and compelled to give way to it on the mere mani-festation, without the actual employment, of its strength; where statesmen can assure themselves, far more certainly than by any other signs, what elements of opinion and power are growing, and what declining, and are enabled to shape their measures with some regard not only to present exigencies, but to tendencies in progress.[1]

The answer to this might be that whether or not it is a de-sirable ideal, it is quite impracticable, for the reason that the lines which cleave opinion are not parallel. They zigzag through the community with all sorts of curves and angles criss-crossing in hopeless fashion. Just as no two human beings were ever physically alike to the last detail (if the thumb-print experts are to be believed), so no two minds ever worked precisely alike. No two persons agree on every proposition. The most that can be said is that a certain amount of agreement may be secured as to what proposition is for the moment of most importance. Proportional representation would in a general way show the differences of judgment in this one particular, and nothing else. Would it be materially helpful to know that 43 per cent of the voters think peace-at-any-price the most pressing problem of the hour; 29 per cent, universal military service; 18 per cent, pro-hibition; 7 per cent, taxation; 3 per cent, an executive budget? Would demonstration of the changes in these percentages from year to year be of the service Mill expected? Would such figures at any given moment reveal the sentiment of the country on any single problem whatever? How could it be inferred from the pressing of prohibition as of paramount importance by 18 men out of every 100, that more or that less than half the voters wanted prohibition?

Whatever our theories, there is one palpable fact, that pro-

[1] *Representative Government*, chap. v.

portional representation makes slow progress, at least in America. The main reason is not far to seek. It lies in the complexity of the systems urged. They fail at the first critical point, for they cannot get legislative comprehension. It is interesting to watch the mental processes of a committee that listens to an expounder of a quota system. The mathematics of it is beyond the average member. First he is bewildered; then he is bored. Even a clear-headed thinker with training in mathematics finds it hard to follow the reasoning. If by chance the support of a committee is won, then the task of enlightening a House is harder still. In countries where cabinet government prevails and the approval of a few men forming a Ministry suffices, proportional representation has a fair chance. In a country where large legislative bodies must be persuaded, its rejection is well-nigh inevitable.

CHAPTER XII

OCCUPATIONAL REPRESENTATION

DISCRIMINATE between avowed belief and probable belief.

Alignment on the basis of *avowed* belief is contemplated by what is usually called "minority representation" or "proportional representation." That on the basis of *probable* belief, or at any rate common interest, is nowadays much discussed as "occupational representation." "Classes" and "occupational groups" are of course not the same thing, but occupation so often determines class, and the considerations relating to them have so much in common, that for our purpose treatment of them may be combined.

Representation of classes or occupational groups can be secured in full or in part by dividing the whole electorate, directly or indirectly, on broad lines; by forming smaller special group constituencies; by requiring certain varying qualifications from those to be elected; or by combination of any or all of these methods.

Division of the whole electorate into a few defined segments is the oldest way of proceeding, or at least has been the most prominent in political history. Without stopping to discuss the class groupings of ancient times or the caste systems of the Orient, note that from the earliest days of representative bodies men were accustomed to see representation by "estates," that is, classes as determined by status — the clergy, the nobility, the landed gentry, sometimes the citizens of towns, the peasants, or others. Modern Austria sought to apply the principle. After the monarchy was placed under constitutional restraint (1860–61), the election of members of the lower House was put in the hands of the provincial diets, who were to choose them from four classes: the large landowners (save where peasant proprietorship prevailed), the burghers of the cities, the rural communes, and the chambers of commerce and industry. A dozen years later the election itself was turned over to the members of these classes. Then in 1896, in order to let the industrial workers and others have representation, 72 more seats were created, to be filled by the votes of the voters as a whole. The system did not satisfy and in 1907, after long agitation, it was replaced by what was practically manhood suffrage, under a method that in effect secured racial representation in the mixed provinces.

Class representation may to a large extent be secured indirectly by the use of differing rights of suffrage. In the course of the long struggle that in England led up to the Reform Act of 1832, defenders of the old ways urged that they had brought the benefits of what we usually think of as such representation. Later Mr. Bagehot, in his extremely interesting essay on "The Unreformed Parliament," put forward that view. "It gave," he tells us, "a means of expression to all classes whose minds required an expression." And again: "The English Constitution of the last century, in its best time, gave an excellent expression to the public opinion of England." Lilly, discussing the subject in his "First Principles of Politics," was of the same mind. "That the old unreformed House of Commons — to speak merely of that chamber — was truly representative," he said, "is not, I suppose, now denied by any competent authority. The Duke of Wellington — who, although no political philosopher, was 'rich in saving common sense,' beyond, perhaps, any other man who has made a name in English history — declared that unreformed House to be not only 'the most efficient legislative body that has ever existed,' but also 'as complete a legislative body as can be required.'"

There were sure to be members of the nobility in the House, and likewise men who had served in the army or navy; the "landed interests" had their spokesmen; some followers of the learned professions were always elected, and with the era of machinery came a few manufacturers. Since virtually all the burghers were tradesmen, the representation of the boroughs was in effect that of the trading class. The four representatives of the City of London were chosen by the liveried companies down even into the nineteenth century.

Also there was, and there continues to be, distinct recognition of one group meant to be that of the educated, as shown by holding degrees from universities. Men who advocate group representation should not overlook the fact that this notable instance of it is under heavy fire. Attack on it became formidable in 1884, when Sir Henry James, the Attorney-General, took the lead, renewing the assault in the following March. He did not rest his argument on the charge that the institution was an anomaly, for he saw no harm in anomalies if they were practical and useful, but on the ground that the system was bad for the universities themselves, because it took party politics into them, and particularly into their governing bodies. The allegation was that in some cases the evil was carried to the extent of running candidates for academical appointments on purely political grounds, and appointments were made with little reference to the merits of the candidates themselves, but solely from political considerations or to reward political services. The right of voting was confined to those who paid a certain sum per annum to keep their names on the college and university books. Thus the university voters were to a great extent men belonging to the wealthier class, and instead of forming a large body of highly educated men, they mainly consisted of persons not substantially superior to the rest of the upper and middle classes, and by no means of those who had profited most by the university or studies.

Since then the attack has been renewed from time to time, always meeting with stout resistance. Typical argument was that of Sir William Anson, representing Oxford, who asked in 1906: "If university representation were abolished, where would be the representatives in the House whose duty it would be to attend to higher educational interests and watch over their progress?" Sir Henry Craik, member for Glasgow and Aberdeen Universities, spoke to like effect. In Scotland, he said, the university elector regarded himself as voting specially to represent the interests of education and the higher professions. Many electors voted as people charged with the special duty of guarding the interests of science, literature, and education.[1]

The bill passed the Commons, 347 to 92, but the Lords rejected it, 143 to 43.

In the next dozen years sentiment appears to have changed, for when the Representation of the People Act, instead of abolishing plural voting, expanded it in at least one particular, at the same time university representation was broadened, by extension to some of the younger provincial universities, with the vote given to persons having a degree of any kind, and not merely to those having the M.A. degree.

The Constitution of the Irish Free State provides for the election of two Senators by each university. That of Rumania gives

[1] Edward Porritt, "Barriers against Democracy in the British Electoral System," *Political Science Quarterly*, March, 1911.

one to each, chosen from itself by vote of the professors. The only instance of such representation in an American lawmaking body that has come to my attention was in the case of William and Mary College in Virginia, which in 1706 received the right to send a Burgess to the Assembly. No State Constitution permits anything of the sort.

If the university man in England also meets local suffrage requirements, he gets two votes, one by reason of his degree and the other as a unit in the general electorate. This is but one form of what is known as "plural voting," a method of recognizing class interest that in Great Britain has been the subject of much controversy, particularly in the matter of the representation of property, as we shall see when we come to that subject. The principle has been carried much farther in Belgium, though along different lines. There a second vote is allowed to certain landowners and to men thirty-five years of age and older if they pay five francs in taxes and have legitimate children. If a man of twenty-five years or more has received certain educational certificates or held certain offices, he has two additional votes. No one has more than three. In Italy the parliamentary committee to consider the proposed electoral law of 1925 recommended supplementary votes for persons in a large number of categories, based on education, occupation, property, office-holding, and other qualifications.

France is discussing a novel application of plural voting, the basis to be the family. Robert K. Gooch thinks its adoption in a reasonably near future is by no means unlikely.[1] It assumes the monogamous family as the proper basis of society and is pushed by reason of the alarming situation in respect of depopulation. The argument is that a parliament elected by family voting will represent the nation in terms of its true unit; the laws made will have due regard for the family as the basis of society; and in result France will be saved from its threatened destruction. The proposal, first brought into the Assembly in 1871, was renewed thirty years later, and since then has been repeatedly presented, with steadily growing attention. So far there has been no agreement on details, but the general idea is that the head of the family shall cast votes with some relation in number to its size. Attention to some of the principles involved is not confined to France. Opponents of manhood suffrage in Japan argued in

[1] "Family Voting in France," *American Political Science Review*, May, 1926.

both Houses in the debate of 1925 that the family system should be protected by confining the parliamentary franchise to heads of families.

DEFINITE GROUPINGS

The example of the British Parliament was of course familiar to John Adams, and probably he had it in mind when he wrote to John Penn [1] that the representative assembly should be an exact portrait, in miniature, of the people at large. That it might be to the interest of this assembly to do equal right and strict justice, upon all occasions, equal interests among the people should have equal interests in the representative body. Is it not singular and significant, though, that when Adams came himself to write a Constitution, that of Massachusetts, he attempted to put into it nothing of the sort? Other statesmen of the time, however, had not discarded the idea and it was much discussed in the Federal Convention of 1787. Madison there said that the three important classes to be considered were the landed, the commercial, and the manufacturing. It was believed the representation of these was ensured by the very form of the government. Anything more specific was deemed impracticable. Hamilton doubtless voiced the general belief when he said in "The Federalist" (No. 35) that "the idea of an actual representation of all classes of the people, by persons of each class, is altogether visionary." He thought the interdependence of economic groups so great that no distinction in the apportionment of representatives could be made.

Therein Hamilton was wrong. Although he might have drawn some justifiable inference from the fact that the groupings in Parliament were for the most part undefined, not artificial, he should not have neglected another fact, that allotment of representatives to specified classes or groups had long been common on the Continent of Europe. It became familiar in the Middle Ages through the representation of trade guilds. In the Florentine Republic as well as in the cities of the Lombardian and Hanseatic Leagues and in many other cities of the Netherlands, Germany, and France, guilds as corporate bodies elected members of town councils. The revival of the principle in one form or another is one of the most striking developments of our time in the field of political science.

[1] *Works*, IV, 205.

For example, when Lord Morley in the Government of India Act of 1909 allotted the membership of the Indian Parliament, he put the electors into definite categories. Religion was to be the most prominent of several factors. Of the 60 members of the Council of State (the upper branch), 16 were to be elected from non-Mahommedan constituencies; 9, Mahommedan; 2, European Commerce; 1, Sikh; 2, General; and 3 from Mahommedan and non-Mahommedan constituencies rotating. Of the 140 members of the lower branch 100 were distributed in the same way, with the addition of 7 Landholders; 4, Indian Commerce; and 1 non-European (from Burmah). The allotment was largely to regional groups, but, evidently from prudential reasons, was not proportionate, minorities being much over-represented.

Akin to this was the provision of the Rumanian Constitution in 1923, that members of the Chambers of Commerce, of Industry, of Labor, and of Agriculture, meeting in separate colleges, should each elect from among themselves one Senator from each category and for each electoral constituency, these constituencies to be fixed by general law and their number not to be greater than six.

Italian thought has been moving along the same line, and going farther. The plan proposed by the Grand Council of the Fascisti in 1925 was for three corporations in each Province — one representing agriculture, another industry and commerce, the third the intellectual professions. These were to elect the Senators. Somewhat the same principle had appeared in the Constitution furnished by d'Annunzio to the Free State of Fiume in 1920, which provided that of the members of the lower legislative branch, the Council of Provisors, ten should be elected by the industrial and inland workmen, ten by the seafaring people, ten by the promoters of industry, five by agricultural and industrial technicians, five by executive officers of private concerns, five by teachers in the public schools, students in the higher institutions, and others belonging to the sixth Corporation (comprising "the intellect of the land"), five by the followers of liberal professions, five by public employees, and five by coöperative societies of production, labor, and consumption.

The idea ripened in Italy when in March of 1928 a radical and exceedingly interesting change in the electoral system was approved almost unanimously by the Chamber. It contemplated group representation to the extent that nominations of 800 candidates are to be made by groups. Twelve confederations of employers and employees, "syndical organizations," are to name the greater part of the candidates; one fifth are to be named by a thirteenth group made up of professional persons and artists. According to Mussolini's descriptive report, which was laid before the Chamber March 2,[1] chance to nominate is also given to "other organizations whose activities fall outside the professional sphere, provided they have national importance and pursue objects of social utility." This he said would remove the objection that the basis of the new system is purely economic.

Group power is to be held in check by the next step, which consists in the selection of 350 of the 800 by the Fascist Grand Council, and its addition to the 350 of "fifty among the representatives of the moral, spiritual, and political elements of the country." Further control of the situation is given to the Grand Council by empowering it to complete the choice of the men most suitable, "when the insufficiency of the lists of candidates makes it necessary, by the inclusion of other persons." This was expected to bring in, on occasion, persons eminent in science, letters, art, and politics, to which list was added "arms" by amendment in the Chamber.

In spite of these checks, Mussolini may have been over-confident as to results when he said the law did not intend to create a professional or class type of representation. "The designation of the Grand Council, in point of fact," he contended, "takes from the candidate the characteristic of being a representative of the organizations which have proposed him." Should this follow, why have organizations propose unless for the vague and minor purpose of endorsement as to character and capacity? And is it not chimerical to expect that men who owe the start of their political fortunes to this or that group will forget the original source of their power and the interests to which they must look at least in part for its continuance? Furthermore, they will have been named by reason of zeal in support of these interests and it is altogether improbable that group concern will not continue to actuate them. Even a Fascist Grand Council cannot make the leopard change its spots.

The electorate is to have but an illusory part in the programme. The list as perfected by the Grand Council is to be submitted to the voters for approval or disapproval as a whole. Nobody ex-

[1] For full text see *Current History*, May, 1928.

pects they will ever disapprove while the present control lasts. Should it end, this electoral system is likely to end also. Meanwhile if by any chance a list is rejected by the voters, there is provision for a somewhat different system of nomination for a second trial, the complexities of which it is hardly worth while to describe, in view of the small likelihood that they will ever be tested.[1]

Spain, starting earlier than Italy, has moved with more caution. A few months after the Riverist *coup d'état*, the Municipal Statute of March 8, 1924, applied the principle of corporate representation to local self-government. A year later the Provincial Statute did the same thing for the Provinces. Evidently the experiment satisfied enough to warrant carrying the principle up to national affairs, for when the military dictatorship had given way to civil dictatorship and that in turn was ready to revive representative government, a National Assembly was elected on the same basis. This Assembly, meeting October 10, 1927, was the first national representative body chosen in Europe after the World War solely on the corporate group-interest-representation principle. Its members represented municipalities, provinces, the Patriotic Union, the higher administrative departments of the nation, the higher clergy, the higher offices of the army, navy, and judiciary, or were named to be representative of culture, production, labor, and commerce, of farmers, business men, and industrialists. Designed to be a constitutional convention rather than a legislative body, it proposed as part of the permanent form of government to follow, a Chamber of Deputies with 300 members to be elected directly, 150 to be chosen by the various social groups, and an undefined number of royal appointees. A Council of the Kingdom, which is to have in connection with legislation the functions of an upper branch and a constitutional court, though in large part appointed, will represent group interests.[2]

Occupational representation is the basic idea in Soviet Russia. In the cities representatives are elected from shops and factories rather than from districts. The workers in the shops of appropriate size meet therein and make their choice. Smaller factories engaged in the same industry, the smaller shops, and like occupational groups are combined for the same purpose. Housekeepers

---

[1] *American Political Science Review*, February, 1929, 139 *et sqq.*
[2] *Ibid.*, 150 *et sqq.*

get representation by geographical districts, and the independent handicraftsmen generally meet by districts. Although the peasants nominally have geographical representation, as agriculture is virtually the only industry, the representation is in effect occupational, for though homeworkers, teachers, and doctors vote, it is in with the rest and of course the peasants prevail. That it shall be purely peasant control is ensured by the refusal of the vote to any one hiring three or more laborers, to those who live on income not derived from their own labor, and to business men, agents, middlemen, and other traders — the group commonly called the bourgeoisie.

It is singular that this extreme application of radical thought in the course of the biggest governmental revolution of our time should carry out the belief of a great statesman commonly thought of as the personification of reaction. Bismarck toward the end of his days wrote: "The ideal that has always floated before me has been a monarchy which should be so far controlled by an independent national representation — according to my notion, representing classes or callings — that monarch or parliament would be unable to alter the existing statutory position before the law separately, but only *communi consensu*." [1]

In 1893 it was suggested in Belgium that the Upper House should be made up of representatives elected by the great occupational groups. Two years later the same thing was advocated in France by M. Charles Benoist, who suggested voters grouped in seven classes according to their callings. Another publicist of standing, M. Leon Duguit, of the Faculty of Law of the University of Bordeaux, wrote: "If we would secure in the parliament the representation of all the elements of the national life, it is necessary to place beside the assembly elected by the people proportioned according to the numerical strength of the different parties, an assembly elected by the professional groups." His notion was that the lower branch should be representative of the people, and the upper should represent "more particularly the social groups." A League of Professional Representation and Regionalist Action was formed, which presented a scheme of professional representation to the Chamber in 1915, but it was not adopted. In a more recent regionalist bill, however, the group idea was dropped, by reason of failure to agree upon

[1] *Reflections and Reminiscences*, i, 18.

a principle whereby the share of each association in the deliberations of the regional council could be determined.[1]

President Millerand had for a long time been a believer in occupational representation when he was interviewed by Raymond Recouly.[2] The President would have liked the Senate to contain, in addition to the Senators elected under the present system, certain representatives of professional associations, of chambers of commerce, of syndicates of masters and men, of rural and urban syndicates, of the General Confederation of Labor, universities, and academies. "I am convinced," he said, "that if the corporate element entered therein, it would have the happiest effect on the working of public affairs."

MERITS AND DEFECTS

Of late there has been much discussion of the subject, both academic and practical. The theorists begin with dispute over the nature of the social structure, dividing into two camps, monists and pluralists. The monists insist on the unity and absolutism of the state. The pluralists think the state is merely one among many associations into which mankind is divided and to which allegiance is accorded. They say that while the state controls other associations, this does not make them inferior, which is to be questioned, judging by the facts. They say the assumption of inferiority is a fallacy that comes from comparing different immediate purposes, to which it may be retorted that powers, not purposes, control the issue. Pluralists also deny any unlimited sovereign and assert that states as well as all other groups must come within the moral law, which is in essence the doctrine of natural rights. Pluralists wish a federal organization of society, but seem to overlook the fact that even this implies a supreme loyalty, the loyalty to a political sovereignty over and above the federation.

Bringing theory down to application, the problem is whether law should be made by representatives of groups socially formed or of groups regionally formed. Hegel was one of the first to argue that a legislative assembly should represent the people as organic, not as atomistic. He held that classes, expressing the economic and social interests of the community, would furnish the best basis for representation. Herbert Spencer took the same

[1] William Seal Carpenter, *Democracy and Representation*, footnote, pp. 86, 87.
[2] *The Outlook*, January 16, 1924.

ground. Now come the guild socialists of England with like acceptance of what was in essence the belief of Burke and the other ultra-conservatives who defended the class principle against the democratic innovations of their time.

The new form of the old doctrine is well set forth in G. D. H. Cole's "Social Theory." His complaint is that Parliament professes to represent all the citizens in all things, and therefore as a rule represents none of them in anything. "It is chosen to deal with anything that may turn up quite irrespective of the fact that the different things that do turn up require different types of persons to deal with them. It is therefore peculiarly subject to corrupt, and especially to plutocratic, influences, and does everything badly, because it is not chosen to do any particular thing well. This is not the fault of the actual Members of Parliament; they muddle because they are set the impossible task of being good at everything, and representing everybody in relation to every purpose." And further: "To ask me to choose one man to represent me in relation to everything is to insult my intelligence, and to offer me every inducement to choose some one so colorless that he is unlikely to do anything at all — because he will at least do no great harm, and no great notice will be taken of him. This is how parliamentary elections usually work out at the present time. But, if I am asked to choose a different person to represent my wishes in relation to each of the main groups of social purposes of which I am conscious, I shall do my best to choose in each case the man who is most fitted to represent my views and to carry them into effect." Cole goes so far as to argue that real democracy is to be found, not in a single omnicompetent representative assembly, but in a system of coordinated functional representative bodies.

On this side of the water Reinsch has also argued that group representation would give us better legislators. "Each great interest," he holds, "would then be anxious to be represented by its most experienced and able men; and an Assembly composed of the select representatives of the industries, the financial corporations, transportation, commerce, labor, education, etc., would occupy a different plane from so many of the present legislatures in which practical politicians who represent only their lessors play a dominant part. In certain respects our legislatures are indeed representative enough; they are composed of a fair average of men in the various walks of life. But they are indicative rather of that average—a somewhat indifferent mean—than of great ability and experience in social and economic life. Unfortunately the various interests whose power is actually controlling are generally not represented at all in an open and acknowledged manner. They therefore use indirect means of exerting their influence to the endless harm of our political system."[1]

In this matter of diversifying the membership of our legislative bodies, it is also argued that group representation would prevent monopolizing by a few groups, as in the case of the notable preponderance of lawyers at present. This of course would be at the expense of losing many legislators whose work, again as in the case of lawyers, has brought them in contact with a wide range of human interests and made it possible for them to furnish helpful judgment in many directions.

Not all the critics would completely discard regional representation. William MacDonald in his suggestive book, "A New Constitution for a New America," argues (pages 127–139) for representation in the National House based partly on population, partly on occupation. He would have a bare majority from each State — or two members if the total number from the State were four — designated as Representatives of occupational groups, and the rest as Representatives-at-large. He thinks this would be a better guaranty of national stability than is a union of individuals who, outside of their groups, feel little organic relation with each other.

Depreciation or minimizing of community sentiment appears in the writings of many of the sociologists. They declare that there is no distinctiveness of local interests other than that of their local, material wants. They see neighborhood sentiment vanishing through the effect of improvements in transportation and communication. They insist that joint interest is now determined fundamentally by specific vocation. They say the physician living in the eleventh precinct has far more of community of interest with a physician living in the fifth precinct than he has with the broker who lives round the corner; that the natural groupings of our modern world are to be found in the associations of teachers, of merchants, of manufacturers, of physicians, of artisans, and all the other groups that can be isolated vocationally.

On the other hand it is not clear that the source from which

[1] *American Legislatures*, 290.

men derive their incomes shows their chief interest in life. Certainly that is often not the case. Large numbers of men drudge without pleasure in their tasks. Many give more thought to their avocations than to their vocations. In the range from recreation to religion something appeals to them more than the winning of bread.

Whether vocation or something else should be the test, is it certain that making any special interest the test is the wiser course? Already there is ground for thinking that special interests have become too prominent and strong, that they too much affect our social relations. Particularly serious is the power of the occupational organizations, which has come to rival and even sometimes to contest that of the state itself. They are fighting groups, with the primary purpose of advancing their own interests at no matter whose expense. It has been suggested that giving them political status might broaden their views or at any rate compel concession, but inasmuch as their fundamental aim would still be each to advance its material condition in relation to other groups, the danger, if such it be, would persist.

It is, indeed, very doubtful whether self-interest should be encouraged as the mainspring of action. That means competition rather than coöperation. Self-interest breeds antagonism instead of harmony.

Group representation of every variety tends to put self-interest above common interest. Even now self-interest is too prominent in our legislative bodies. With official status for groups, the representative would even more subordinate the common welfare. He would work as an interest and not as a man; and the better he represented his own group, the worse he would represent the rest. Therein lies an important weakness of the proposal, perhaps its futility, for carried to its logical conclusion no man would be qualified, or should be permitted, to vote in respect of any function other than that which he represented.

Were group interest to be enthroned, legislative bodies, already harassed by the lobbies of groups, would find themselves exposed to double the pressure. Already its exercise is a most unfortunate feature of legislative life. Give it official recognition and independent decision with only the common welfare in mind would almost disappear.

In this matter of the common welfare is to be found one of the gravest objections to both occupational and proportional representation, for either would make worse a situation already bad. For example, a palpable weakness of our present method of allotting representatives is that it emphasizes locality interests. Every American legislative body sees the need of continuous struggle against this. It is the chief source of log-rolling, unwise appropriations, sacrifice of conscience. The popular test of a representative is too often not what he does for State or Nation, but what he gets for his district. One argument urged for group representation is that it will lessen this particular evil, but even so its nature is to reappear in worse evils, for while the interests of localities are not necessarily antagonistic, those of occupations are assumed to be competing, or else separate representation would bring no gain. Shall we replace what we now have with the selfish struggles of class, sect, race, occupation, or anything else that allies men for what they think or hope will be their profit, a profit at the expense of others? Will there not be constant impulsion away from harmony and toward discord? Will not the common welfare suffer more than now? Sorry may be the people that builds its institutions with the motto — "Every group for itself and the prize to the strongest."

The prime purpose of representation is to represent persons in the mass, rather than particular ideas or interests. We choose representatives to mirror public opinion as a whole; to voice the general will; to face all the problems of government; to advance the common and not the particular welfare. As President Lowell has well said, "The true conception of public opinion is not a sum of divergent economic interests, but a general conception of political righteousness on which so far as possible all men should unite." [1] The question is primarily one of averages, not of individualities. The task is to reconcile differences, not to accentuate them.

To get some degree of cohesion in political action, English-speaking peoples have discarded the system of factions that long prevailed in England and her colonies, and still prevails on the Continent. In its place we have put the system of parties, usually two in number as far as real importance goes. What would be the effect of either occupational or proportional representation on this? William Dudley Foulke has presented one view, saying: "For my own part I deny that an absolute majority in a de-

[1] *Public Opinion*, 121.

liberative assembly is desirable if there be no such majority in
the people at large. If mere speed and convenience in legislation
were considered, it might be desirable. But we have adopted two
different principles for the two forms of our political action; for
executive action, unity; for legislative action, plurality. Why is
this? Because deliberation, compromises, and the consideration
of different ideas are necessary for the highest form of legislative
action. Our experience in jurisprudence tells us that the best
means of informing the court and arriving at an accurate judgment is to allow each party to set forth its own views, its own
interests, in the most extreme and unfair way, subject to contradiction and refutation by those who have adverse interests
and views. Is it less true that in legislation the best conclusion
will be reached by allowing each phase of thought to be represented by its own advocates, and then, after consideration of all
these, letting that judgment be given which seems to be most fair
and just to all? We merely apply to the legislature the principles
which we have long applied in judicial procedure. The result of
nearly all political action is compromise. In the present system
this compromise is made when parties are organized. When proportional representation is adopted it will be made in the legislative body where all can see more clearly the strong and the
weak points of every claim." [1]

Simon Sterne reached precisely the opposite conclusion about
the effect of transferring compromise from party to legislature.
From his point of view the one formidable objection to the whole
scheme is that it has a tendency to prevent the spirit of compromise and mutual forbearance, which party has a tendency to
create. The same reason which would make minority representation act as a solvent of political parties might result in its acting
as a solvent on constituencies which ought to be held together in
the bands of party, thereby cultivating mutual good will, which
probably would not exist were their parts to be exclusively committed to their own class for political action.[2]

In the course of our experience with the two-party system,
each of the major parties has largely been made up of men with
enough unity of mental habit to permit agreement on most of
the great political problems. This would disappear on substitut-

[1] "Proportional Representation," *Proportional Representation Review*, January, 1915.
[2] "Representation," *Lalor's Cyclopædia of Political Science*, III, 593.

ing the group system. Physicians could have no unity of view on foreign policy, shopkeepers on irrigation, bricklayers on the merchant marine, farmers on States' rights. Inevitably political parties as we have known them would disappear.

The two-party system puts in issue only a few major questions, and each party seeks within its own ranks that degree of harmony without which its success may be endangered. Furthermore each asks for control with the avowed purpose of advantaging all the people. Each argues for its policies as more likely to increase the sum total of prosperity and happiness. We thrive as a country because this is the spirit of our political institutions. Let us think long before we abandon unity and turn to diversity as our goal.

There are serious technical difficulties. Functions are numberless and the persons they engage range from few to many. In theory each function would have the right to representation, and that right would have no relation to quantity, for the self-interest of one group is just as important to its members as in the case of any other group. If representation were confined to the larger groups, as of course it would have to be, where to draw the line would produce constant strife. If it were not arbitrarily drawn on the basis of size, imagine the task of deciding what functions should be deemed essential. And how shall be handled great groups such as those of the unemployed or the retired? Think also of the uncertainties of classification, as suggested by the jurisdictional disputes between labor unions.

Within the group itself there would surely be trouble. Skilled workmen would be classed with unskilled, though their economic interests might widely diverge. Minorities would be without representation however valid the differences of either interest or opinion. You would get only the will of the majority of the group. This in turn would be shaped as much as ever by a few, as we now see in the case of the leaders of labor unions. In fact the power of these leaders, already no small matter, would be importantly increased by the enlargement of their opportunities. Then, too, there are frequent changes of group structure, whether it be formed on social, political, occupational, or economic lines. The constant shifting of the electorate would be an endless perplexity.

If a man were to have a vote for each of his interests, there would still be the impossibility of voting for anybody outside their limits. There could be no "independent" movements. On the other hand, with one vote for each interest men keen to exercise the suffrage would join as many groups as they could. The class of professional "joiners" would grow.

It is in the actual work of representative bodies that the group system develops its greatest weakness. Action is the chief purpose of government. The business must march. It marches best with what we call a working majority, namely, one that can in the end have its way when it is in agreement. In Congress we have seen the mischief that comes when a small third-party group holds the balance of power. Then look out for trades, trucklings, unworthy concessions. Majority rule is replaced by minority rule, and that the rule of the smaller minority. The routine is upset. Business is blocked. The public welfare suffers.

In a legislative body the party having the most votes but less than half the total can prevail at will only by combining with some smaller group or groups. Such combinations are transitory. This is what constantly imperils Cabinet government on the Continent, makes it volatile, ephemeral, futile. So the country is deprived of stable government. The danger is increased by the temptation held out to a minority within a party. Thwarted in its ambitions, it is incited to secede and join some other group or form a quite new party. Everything works for dissension rather than harmony within the group, for resistance rather than concession.

This compels that sort of group discipline which stifles individuality. For example, A. G. Gardiner, veteran English journalist, writing of "The Twilight of Parliament," [1] at a time when there were seventy or so of Labor members in the House of Commons, gives as one reason why they were of singularly negligible influence, the fact that they had entered it committed to a certain collective course on any given issue, regardless of what the debates might reveal.

The other of the two reasons Mr. Gardiner found for the failure of Labor as a Parliamentary factor and for its being the least efficient body in the Chamber was its practice of sending to Westminster trade-union secretaries of third-rate ability and generally without either political training or Parliamentary instinct. This is natural, for the self-centered group inevitably

[1] *Atlantic Monthly*, August, 1921.

wants to be represented by subservient agents, not by trustees who will feel justified in doing their own thinking.

Such effects, both abroad and here, have played a part in impairing the prestige of parliamentary institutions. The less effective these institutions, the less respect for their authority. Mussolini is not an accident; he is a result.

What else can you expect from a structure built on the principle of subdivision? In Belgium after twenty years of proportional representation, forty-five different groups were formed to elect ninety-six members of Parliament. In the German elections of 1924 eleven parties gained seats; in addition thirteen "freak" parties polled 700,000 votes.

Under such conditions, save in the rare instances when one party wins a majority of the seats, party responsibility disappears. Control by minorities takes its place. This is perversion of democracy. At the very heart of self-government is the belief that the greater part shall prevail. It may or may not be the best form of government. Autocracy, aristocracy, monarchy may be better, but if so let it be frankly admitted. The wolf wears sheep's clothing when minorities dominate in a democracy.

CHAPTER XIII

FRANCHISE TESTS

QUALIFICATIONS for the suffrage necessarily imply recognition of classes of human beings. The application of a test involves the use of a standard and that of itself creates classes. Once the standard has been agreed upon, exceptions are manifestly impracticable. Consider the case of a precocious lad who graduates from college at the age of fifteen, perhaps with highest honors in political science, and with phenomenal knowledge of history and economics. He may be measured by his years or by his mental capacity. As a minor he will be excluded under the standard hitherto thought the more important. To admit him would be to make an exception to the predominant rule. Such an exception might be a precedent for others until the twilight zone of uncertainty overwhelmed with its perplexities. Evident as this must be in a field where there is little or no controversy, it is constantly ignored in other fields. We are again and again asked to legislate on the basis of the exceptional. The appeal ought never to carry lawmakers off their feet. Only when it is shown that an existing standard is inferior to some other, should there be change.

The rule should work both ways. Just as a class ought not to be admitted to the franchise because of the fitness of exceptional individuals, so a class ought not to be excluded because of the unfitness of exceptional individuals.

Furthermore the standard must be definite. For example, however desirable it might be to confine the suffrage to men of good character, yet there being no yardstick with which to measure character, it is futile to try to make that quality of itself a test. We can, however, find measurable conditions that indicate the possession of good character or other qualities deemed desirable. Group phenomena may determine.

Of sundry criteria, the most common, because the most natural, presenting self-evident justification, have been those of minority and of mental disease. The exclusion of the insane need but be mentioned. That of children raises no question save as to where the line between child and adult shall be drawn. With

English-speaking peoples the age of twenty-one years has come to be the prevailing rule. Elsewhere there is a variation in views that it would serve no useful purpose here to detail. Two or three oddities, however, may interest. One of them is the provision in some of the newer Constitutions of a higher age limit in the case of voting for members of the upper branch than in that of the lower. Thus in Czecho-Slovakia, though men twenty-one years old may vote for Deputies, only those of twenty-six may vote for Senators. In Poland the limit on the Senatorial suffrage is higher still — thirty years; and Rumania puts it up to forty. On the other hand Russia lets youths of eighteen vote on all questions, and that limit may be lowered by any local soviet with the approval of the central authorities.

Next in generality of application has been the test of citizenship, almost but not quite universal. Tom Paine, to use the familiar form of his name, was elected a delegate to the National Assembly of France in 1792 and took his seat, although still an American citizen. The Assembly, however, had conferred the title of French citizen on "Payne" and eighteen others, including Washington, Hamilton, and Madison. In immature countries like Mexico the report is that foreigners who chance to be at hand are frequently invited to vote by this or that faction. But barring irregular or infrequent exceptions, it may be said that only citizens are expected to contribute their judgment for the common welfare.

Aristotle, writing two thousand years ago, in speaking of the question as to who are the citizens of a state, said: "The answer to this question is different in different States, and depends on the laws and the constitution of each. The whole body of the inhabitants of a country enjoying the protection of its laws, including the young who are still under legal age, and the very old who have passed the time of action, and all others under any species of disability, are, in a certain wide and general sense, citizens. But the full and complete definition of a citizen is confined to those who participate in the governing power, either by themselves or their representatives. This privilege is not attached to mere residence in a place or country, or derived from descent, for the question always recurs, how did the original possessor obtain it? It is a privilege conferred in a legal manner by the act of the estate." [1]

[1] Tremenheere, *Political Experience of the Ancients*, II.

This quotation is worth while because it is so often forgotten that "citizen" and "resident" are not synonymous. At times in the history of government the distinction has been a matter of great importance. So it was in Rome. Remember the significance of Paul's declaration, "I am a Roman citizen." So it was in the early days of the colonies, and particularly in Massachusetts, where the all-controlling wish of the founders for a theocratic government was in constant danger from newcomers with other ideas. Her first "citizens" were "freemen," a term not used in contradistinction to "slaves," but meaning simply members of the corporation.[1] At what has been called the first regular Legislature that met in Massachusetts, May 14, 1634, it was "agreed, that none but the General Court hath power to choose and admit freemen."[2] Two years later we find this in the first revision of laws in Plymouth: "That the laws and ordinances of the Colony for the Government of the same be made only by the freemen of the Corporation and no other."[3] This was followed still two years later (March 5, 1638) by a most interesting vote, providing "that every Township shall bear their Committees charges and that such as are not freemen but have taken the Oath of fidelity and are masters of families and Inhabitants of the said Towns as they are to bear their part in the charges of their Committees so to have a vote in the choice of them."[4] Here was distinct recognition of the fairness of giving a share in the choice of Representatives to those who had to share in their cost, but it is to be noticed that the oath of fidelity, akin to our naturalization process, was required, and that restriction was made to men both masters of families and inhabitants.

The Massachusetts Legislature of 1856, when the Know-Nothing movement was at its height, approved a constitutional amendment providing that no person of foreign birth should be entitled to vote in the Commonwealth unless he had been a resident within the jurisdiction of the United States twenty-one years. This, however, did not get the second passage required before submission to the people, the vote of the House standing 133 Yes to 117 No — short of the necessary two thirds. By the way, the roll-call on that occasion discloses not a single name that would naturally be supposed to be other than Anglo-Saxon.

[1] John Winthrop, *Journal*, April 1, 1634.

[2] *Records of the Colony of the Mass. Bay in N.E.*, I, 117.

[3] *Plymouth Colony Records*, XI, 11.   [4] *Ibid.*, X, 31.

During the period while our Western States were in process of settlement, the question of admitting to a share in government the newcomers from European lands was of no small consequence. Sundry of the States decided to give the ballot to them before they could secure full citizenship through naturalization. With changing conditions the wisdom of this lessened and the need waned. So one by one the Constitutions have been changed and now but a very few let the foreign-born person vote on taking out first papers, those declaring intent to become a citizen.

Religious Qualifications

Religious belief has at times furnished a test of political capacity. It would be necessary to transcribe many chapters of the world's history if the story of the relations between religion and politics were to be told in full, for from the time when the pronunciation of "shibboleth" meant life or death, and doubtless from countless centuries before, men have appraised other men on the basis of religious views, and have admitted them to fraternity or have rejected them on that score. In its bearing on systemized voting, however, there is nothing of consequence to us back of the colonial period. In the early days of some of the colonies Church and State were so interwoven that adequate understanding of the origins of our institutions is impossible if their relations are overlooked.

Massachusetts Bay at its first General Court for election, May 18, 1631, voted: "To the end the body of the commons may be preserved of honest and good men, it was likewise ordered and agreed that for time to come no man shall be admitted to the freedom of this body politic but such as are members of some of the churches within the limits of the same." Thus they established an aristocracy of a description theretofore unknown. "Not birth, nor wealth, nor learning, nor martial skill and prowess," says Palfrey, "was to confer political power among this peculiar people; but goodness — goodness of the highest type — goodness of that purity and force which only the spirit of the Master of Christians can create. The conception, if a delusive and impracticable, was a noble, one. Nothing better can be imagined for the administration of a government than that they who conduct it shall be Christian men — men of disinterestedness and uprightness of the choicest quality — whose fear of God exalts them above every other fear, and whose controlling love of God and man consecrates them in the most generous aims." [1]

The charter had prescribed no conditions for admission to membership. Few members of the corporation were here. More than a hundred men sought a share in the conduct of affairs. If no tests were applied, the determination to establish a theocracy might be thwarted. The natural, the inevitable expedient was the church membership test. It saved the day. For a generation only those who followed the elders could vote. Then came revolt. Men of other faiths had entered the colony. Some who may not have been hostile to the doctrines of the majority, and yet were averse to joining the church, felt themselves unjustly excluded from the franchise. Complaint reached the ear of the King, and he began bringing pressure to bear for liberalizing the conditions of the suffrage. The need of it may be gathered from the perusal of such a vote as that of the General Court, October 21, 1663:

"Whereas it is found by experience that there are many who are inhabitants of this jurisdiction which are enemies to all government, civil and ecclesiastical, who will not yield obedience to authority, but make it much of their religion to be in opposition thereto, and refuse to bear arms under others, who, notwithstanding, combine together in some towns and make parties suitable to their designs in election of such persons according to their ends, it is therefore ordered by this Court and the authority thereof, that all persons, Quakers or others, which refuse to attend upon the public worship of God established here, that all such persons, whether freemen or others, acting as aforesaid, shall and hereby are made uncapable of voting in all civil assemblies during their obstinate persisting in such wicked ways and courses, and until certificate be given of their reformation." [2]

Nevertheless in the next year the colonists, beginning to worry about their charter, saw fit to make what in appearance at least was concession, for the Court voted, August 3, 1664:

"In answer to that part of his majesty's letter of June 28, 1662, concerning admission of freemen, this Court doth declare, that the law prohibiting all persons except members of churches, and that also for allowance of them in any County Courts, are hereby repealed; and do hereby also order and enact, that from henceforth all Englishmen presenting a certificate, under the

[1] *New England,* I, 121.
[2] *Records of the Colony of the Mass. Bay in N.E.,* IV, part 2, 87.

hands of the ministers or minister of the place where they dwell, that they are orthodox in religion, and not vicious in their lives," and having certain property qualifications, shall be "propounded and put to vote in the General Court for acceptance to the free-dom of the body politic by the suffrage of the major part, accord-ing to the rules of our patent."[1] It is believed that not one in a hundred of those not church members could meet the property qualification.[2]

At the May session in 1665 the General Court was greatly disturbed by the demands of the Royal Commissioners, who presented twenty-six changes they desired to have made in the Book of the General Laws and Liberties of 1660. Their principal objects were to substitute for all expressions of the supremacy of the Commonwealth, an acknowledgment of the royal authority; to procure a recognition of the Church of England; and to destroy the long-standing limitation of citizenship to church members. An examination of the edition of the Laws of 1672 shows that only one or two points were conceded by the Court, either then or prior to that issue, and that the recognition of His Majesty's supremacy was allowed in one clause while the power of the local authority was asserted in a score. The right of strangers to be-come citizens was nominally conceded, but on conditions that afforded the minimum of relief to all but church members.[3]

The Code of 1672 reënacted the provision that for admittance as freemen, applicants should be Englishmen, "presenting a Certificate under the hands of the Ministers or Minister of the place where they dwell, that they are Orthodox in Religion, and not vicious in their lives," etc. In 1673 there was more of nominal concession, but it was half-hearted, for the law passed October 15, 1673, said: "Henceforth the names of such as desire to be ad-mitted to the freedom of this common-wealth, not being mem-bers of churches in full communion, shall be entered with the secretary, from time to time, at the Court of Election, and read over before the whole Court sometime that sessions, and shall not be put to vote in the Court till the Court of Election next following."[4]

For the irreligious and those who held to some other than the

---

[1] *Records of the Colony of the Mass. Bay in N.E.*, IV, part 2, 117.
[2] James Truslow Adams, *The Founding of New England*, 331.
[3] W. H. Whitmore, *Introduction to Colonial Laws of Mass.*, 100.
[4] *Records of the Colony of the Mass. Bay in N.E.*, IV, part 2, 563.

orthodox faith, the way was still made hard. In the eleven years before 1677 the franchise was given to only one man not a member of the dominant church as against 875 who belonged thereto.[1] It is believed that by this time the disfranchised outnumbered the recognized church members five to one.[2] In the end the colony lost its charter by reason of its contumacy in this as well as other particulars. William III would not endure the religious franchise, and in spite of the bitter opposition of the Reverend Increase Mather, who had been sent to England to try to save the day, the new charter (1691) put the suffrage in the hands of the "Freeholders and other Inhabitants," having as a freehold an estate in land to the value of forty shillings a year or other estate to the value of forty pounds sterling.

Plymouth never in so many words prescribed church membership as a qualification, but there is little doubt its practice virtually required this. In 1671 it provided that "none shall be admitted a freeman of this corporation, but such as are one-and-twenty years of age, at the least, and have the testimony of their neighbors that they are of sober and peaceable conversation, orthodox in the fundamentals of religion, and such as have also twenty pounds of ratable estate in the government."

Liberal Rhode Island made no demand for church membership. New Haven, more under the influence of the Massachusetts example, excluded those who had not been received into full communion with some church, but the Hartford colony followed the Plymouth plan of refraining from specifically imposing the qualification, though there too the dominance of the clergy makes it probable that men not church members did not easily secure admission to the franchise.

The Connecticut Constitution of 1818 required that every elector "shall sustain a good moral character," and that is still the admirable and altogether futile provision. Ethical standards have not met with favor in the United States. To be sure, men under restraint in our prisons may not vote while there, but can vote afterward. Even when the Federal Senate has by the process of impeachment and trial removed a man from public office, though he is thereby disqualified from holding office again under the United States, he is not deprived of the right to vote. France goes farther. Men who have committed certain offences there

[1] James Truslow Adams, *The Foundation of New England*, 384.
[2] George E. Ellis, *The Puritan Age in Massachusetts*, 203.

are excluded for perpetuity or for five years from taking any part in the direction of society. The rule includes those who have several criminal or correctional sentences, ministerial functionaries dismissed for gross incompetency, and bankrupt tradesmen, but it has now been made more lenient for the bankrupts, the period of deprivation of the vote being for them limited to three years, and there is no forfeiture in the case of judicial liquidation for unfortunate but honest tradesmen.[1]

PROPERTY AS A MEASURE

Property has played a foremost part in the development of franchise qualifications. From the earliest times its possession has been held either to give a claim to a share in government or else to indicate a probability that its possessor could exercise such a share helpfully; and it has been a not uncommon belief that the more property a man may have, the greater his claim or the greater the likelihood of his usefulness. Servius Tullius divided the people of Rome into 193 centuries, which formed six classes. Ranking the rich, who were in smaller numbers, in the first centuries, and those in middling circumstances, who were more numerous, in the next, he flung the indigent multitude into the last; and as each century had but one vote, it was property rather than numbers that decided the election.[2]

Upon the institution of representative government in England, the question did not speedily become of importance. At first it mattered little to any parliamentary borough how its deputies were chosen, for being instructed by the corporation with respect to the precise amount of the supply to be granted, they were only the messengers who declared the will of their principals. In the case of the knights of the shire, as election was incidental work of jurors in the county courts, no question of voting qualification directly arose, but indirectly the practice may have led to important results, for jury duty was part of the feudal system, in which property held a leading place. The full county courts did not include the "common" people, for villeins were not legally qualified to perform the judicial functions for which the courts were held.[3]

[1] Joseph Barthelemy, *The Government of France*, tr. by J. Bayard Morris, 28, 29.
[2] Montesquieu, *Spirit of Laws*, book II, 2.
[3] A. F. Pollard, *The Evolution of Parliament*, 108.

Possibly this may have got Englishmen into the way of thinking that ownership was a natural attribute of an elector. However, we really know very little about it. Without any occasion for arguing qualifications, it is not surprising that the writers of those times ignored the question. Furthermore it was not raised by the changes that at first took place. Indeed Stubbs thinks that the idea of a constitution in which each class of society should, as soon as it was fitted for the trust, be admitted to a share of power and control, and in which national action should be determined by the balance between the forces thus combined, perhaps never presented itself to the mind of any mediæval politician.[1] The immediate object in each case of extension of the franchise was to draw forth the energy of the united people in some great emergency, to suit the convenience of party or the necessity of Kings, to induce the newly admitted classes to give their money, to produce political contentment, or to involve all alike in the consciousness of common responsibility.

It seems to have been established that at least before the reign of Henry VI every resident householder of a borough, capable of paying scot (i.e., his share of local taxation) and of bearing lot (i.e., of discharging in turn the local offices), was sworn and enrolled at the boroughleet, and became a burgess. In the eighth year of Henry VI was passed a remarkable statute, the first disfranchising law on record. Reciting the grievous uproar and disorder at elections, chiefly occasioned by the outrageous and excessive number of people of small substance or none, it enacted, "that for the future knights of the shire shall be chosen by people dwelling and resident in the counties, whereof every one of them shall have free land or tenement to the value of forty shillings by the year at least, above all charges." This operated as a sweeping disfranchisement, for forty shillings then was equal to at least twenty pounds of the present day. Singularly enough at a crisis when democratic notions were in the air, Oliver Cromwell required an estate of two hundred pounds' value to entitle any one to vote. Not for a century yet were signs of revolt against such a spirit to become prominent and the best part of another century was to pass before the agitation against the dominance of wealth would win its first victory.

It was in 1832 that after a most exciting and bitter contest the Reform Bill was passed, admitting to the franchise those of the

[1] *Constitutional History*, II, 158.

middle classes of Englishmen who had not previously shared therein. This was accomplished by lowering the property qualifications. At the same time there was a redistribution of seats in Parliament, what we should call a re-districting. Many rotten boroughs were abolished. These were decayed towns, reduced to a handful of voters, in the control of great landowners, who bestowed their representation as motives of gain or favor inclined.

Radical as was this reform, yet it was partial. It brought no visible benefit to the working classes. Their discontent over this and other matters led to the forming of a social-political party that framed the People's Charter, which gave them the name of Chartists. The Charter was a programme of reform with five articles, the first of which was universal suffrage. In 1839 this programme was presented to Parliament in the shape of a petition bearing 1,285,000 signatures, so bulky that it had to be carried on a wagon. In spite of such a formidable showing the petition was of no avail. After the revolutionary troubles of 1848 that agitated all Europe, an attempt was made to renew the demands of the people in England, with announcement of a petition to have 5,000,000 signatures, but the middle classes arrayed themselves so solidly against the movement that nothing came of it.

No further extension of the franchise was made until 1867, when the property qualifications were still further reduced and seats were again redistributed. In 1884 the property qualifications were carried yet lower, adding more than two and a half million voters. With the impetus given by the Great War to the spread of the democratic spirit and the wish either to recognize or to stimulate the patriotism of the masses, the Representation of the People Act, which received the royal assent February 6, 1918, virtually ended the struggle that had been in progress for a century. This enactment gave the suffrage to all male subjects twenty-one years old, and resident for six months in premises in a constituency; and to every woman thirty years old occupying a home or being a tenant or her husband being a tenant of landed property of an annual value of five pounds. This increased the electorate by about eight million voters, one quarter men and three quarters women.

On the other hand when it came to providing a new suffrage law for India, in 1919, a property qualification was imposed on voting for members of the provincial legislative councils, which though small was large enough to shut out about nine tenths of the adult male population, with a larger requirement in the matter of the Legislative Assembly, and one still higher on voting for the Council of State.

The question has not much vexed the politics of Continental Europe. The right of every man to vote was one of the tenets of the French Revolution and with exceptions not relating to property manhood suffrage prevails to-day in France. It was adopted by Belgium after the World War and is the general provision in the wholly new post-War Constitutions. Italy shows reaction. Manhood suffrage, adopted in 1912, was abandoned by the revolutionary changes of the electoral law of 1928. The electorate was made to consist of married men from eighteen to twenty-one years of age, with children; men more than twenty-one paying 100 lire in taxes or having 500 lire of State consols; civil servants; and Catholic clergy, with ministers of other cults admitted by the State.

Japan abolished the tax-paying qualification in 1925, the electoral law of that year chiefly thereby increasing the electorate from about 3,000,000 to an estimated total of 12,000,000.

The earliest American colonies had no property qualification for the exercise of the franchise. The Virginia charter of 1621 directed that the General Assembly should be chosen "by the Inhabitants." No change came until the period when the Commonwealth was the government in England. Perhaps the Virginia action reflected Cromwell's sentiments in the matter. Anyhow in 1655 the Burgesses decided that none but "house-keepers, whether freeholders, leaseholders, or otherwise tenants," should be "capable to elect Burgesses." The next year the ancient usage was restored, and all "freemen" were allowed to vote, since it was "something hard and unagreeable to reason that any person shall pay equal taxes, and yet have no vote in elections"; but the freemen must not vote "in a tumultuous way." In 1670 the suffrage was again restricted, the reason given being that the "usual way of choosing Burgesses by the votes of all persons who, having served their time," were freemen, produced "tumults at the election." Therefore it would be better to follow the English fashion and "grant a voice in such election only to such as by their estates, real or personal, have interest enough to tie them to the endeavor of the public good." [1] So none but freeholders and house-keepers were to vote.

[1] Hening, *Statutes at Large*, ii, 280.

Bacon's Laws in June, 1676, repealed this, but his laws were in turn repealed after the rebellion had been suppressed, in February of the following year. The instructions of Charles II to Berkeley in 1677 read: "You shall take care that the members of the Assembly be elected only by freeholders."

Notice that "freemen" were those who had served their time. This follows one of the ancient significations of the term, which discriminated a freeman from a slave or serf. The word had, however, other meanings, making it hard to tell just what it delimited in any particular case. "Freeholder" is equally puzzling. In old English law a freeman was a freeholder as distinguished from a villein, i.e. a person attached to a manor, substantially in the condition of a slave. "Freeholder" came to mean the owner of a freehold estate. The inexact use of these terms prevents precision in describing colonial suffrage qualifications. For instance, the Maryland charter of 1632 in the seventh section says that Lord Baltimore is to make laws "with the advice, assent, and approbation of the Free-Men"; the next section provides what shall be done in case of emergency "before the Freeholders of the said province, their delegates, or deputies, can be called together for the framing of laws."

Channing thinks [1] that as practically every person who was not a servant was a freeholder, the words "freeman" and "freeholder" were really synonymous. Such may have been the case for a time after the landing of the first settlers, but of course a landless class developed as soon as towns took shape and careful provision against its having a share in government followed. Thus we find Cecil Calvert in 1670 instructing the Governor to restrict the franchise to those possessing a freehold of fifty acres or forty pounds of visible estate. The experience of the earlier colonies led the men who wrote the later charters to take thought of the matter in advance. The Fundamental Constitutions of East New Jersey (1683) direct that the Great Council shall be chosen by the "freemen," and define freemen as every planter and inhabitant "who hath acquired rights to and is in possession of fifty acres of ground, and hath cultivated ten acres of it"; or in boroughs, a house and three acres; or if only a tenant of house and land, having fifty pounds of "stock" — presumably what we should call personal property. William Penn followed this example, providing in his Frame of Government for Pennsylvania

[1] *History of the U.S.*, I, 266–67.

(1682) that every inhabitant should be accounted a freeman who had bought a hundred acres of land; or who had paid his passage and taken up a hundred acres at a penny an acre, and had cultivated ten acres; or who, having been a servant or bonds-man, had taken up his fifty acres and cultivated twenty; or who paid scot and lot to the government.

The Massachusetts Bay charter of 1629 allowed the members of the Company to admit whom they might see fit, and for a generation the only qualification imposed appears to have been that of church membership. Trouble with the home government over this qualification led to the discreet and conciliatory passage of a law, August 3, 1664,[1] modifying the religious requirement and at the same time requiring applicants to be freeholders, ratable "to the full value of ten shillings." Plymouth, which had also been without charter restriction in the matter, saw fit to follow Massachusetts, stipulating in 1669 that none should vote in town affairs but freemen, or freeholders of twenty pounds' ratable estate; and when in 1671 qualifications were more definitely specified, this amount of property was in the stipulations. When the two colonies were brought together by the charter of William and Mary, it was provided thereby that a voter must be a freeholder to the value of forty shillings a year or have personal estate to the amount of forty pounds. Comparing the market value of labor then with its value to-day, this may have been such a qualification as would be the possession of property worth a thousand dollars now. It has been suggested that this was put in the charter because of the spirit of the times in the mother country, inasmuch as the Revolution of 1688 came about, not through the wish to give the people greater influence or power, but to give greater security and protection to the property held by the minority of the people.

A clause interlined in a different handwriting and at a later date in the Fundamental Orders of Connecticut adopted at Hartford, 1638-39, indicates that towns were to admit inhabitants by a majority vote. In 1658-59 requirement of personal estate in the value of thirty pounds appears, reduced in 1662 one third, but a certificate of honest and peaceable conversation from the major part of the townsmen was required, and even then the candidate might be refused admission to the franchise by the General Court.[2] In the New Haven Colony the voting was to be

---

[1] *Records of the Colony of the Mass. Bay in N.E.*, IV, II, 118.
[2] Edward Channing, *History of the U.S.*, I, 405-06.

done by the "free burgesses" or the "free planters," provided they were church members. The Connecticut charter of 1662 and the Rhode Island charter of 1663, under which government was continued until 1818 in the case of Connecticut and 1842 in the case of Rhode Island, empowered the Assembly to admit such as it might see fit.

New Hampshire copied Massachusetts with a property qualification. At the same period New York, by the charter of liberties and privileges it adopted in 1683, provided that "every freeholder within this province, and every freeman in any corporation shall have his free choice and vote in the electing of Representatives, ... and by freeholder is understood everyone who is so according to the laws of England." Locke's Fundamental Constitutions for the Carolinas (1669) gave the election of parliament men to "freeholders." The royal government began with the principle of "freehold" voting, and though the lower House of the Assembly claimed the privilege of determining the suffrage and qualification laws were enacted from time to time, it does not appear that this principle was violated in South Carolina. The Assembly there in 1716 restricted the vote to white Christians possessing thirty pounds current money, changing three years later to a freehold of fifty acres or the payment of fifty pounds in taxes. In North Carolina the Governors were aggrieved for a score of years because the suffrage had been given to all "freemen," but repeal of the statute in 1735, with a freehold requirement substituted, ended the complaints.

In 1755, the year after an Assembly was provided for Georgia as a royal province, it memorialized the home authorities as to the hardships of the qualifications for electors and Representatives. An elector had to own fifty acres and a Representative five hundred. This shut out holders of town lots that might be much greater in value than the five hundred acres of the planter. Satisfactory modification was granted.

Further details are unnecessary to show that in the middle of the eighteenth century the notion that only property owners might vote was widespread if not universal in the colonies. It took a Revolution to make an inroad on that belief, and even then the belief was at first hardly shaken. To be sure, the abstractions of the Declaration of Independence might be construed as implying a natural right to vote, and Theophilus Parsons in "The Essex Result" (1778) went so far as to assert that "all the members of the State are qualified to make the election, unless they have not sufficient discretion, or are so situated as to have no wills of their own." Yet even the Virginia Declaration of Rights, June 12, 1776, the same Declaration Virginia wanted prefixed to the Federal Constitution a dozen years later, said only that "elections ought to be free, and that all men having sufficient evidence of permanent common interest with, and attachment to the community, have the right of suffrage."

As the colonies became States, one after another they put property qualifications into their Constitutions, Georgia alone making an exception, for there an elector might either be "possessed in his own right of ten pounds value" or be "of any mechanic trade." Vermont, the first State to be added to the original thirteen, was also the first to break away from tradition, for it gave full manhood suffrage (in 1777), deliberately deviating from the Constitution of Pennsylvania, which it copied in most other respects. On the other hand, North Carolina (1776) was less liberal than it had been under royal government, for whereas all "inhabitants" had been voting, now a man had to be a taxpayer to vote for a member of the lower branch, and with a freehold in fifty acres of land to vote for a Senator. Pennsylvania (1776) let taxpayers vote, and sons of freeholders though not taxpayers. New Hampshire (1784) gave the suffrage to taxpayers. The other States had a variety of heavier qualifications not necessary to enumerate here. None were very great, and probably they were thought no larger than was necessary to keep out shiftless persons. Yet as a matter of fact they did keep out a material part of the citizenship. The effect of even a small property qualification may be illustrated by experience in Rhode Island, where still only those assessed on property are allowed to vote for members of city councils. The amount of property required is small, $134, but the vote for the members of the Providence Board of Aldermen, over a period of ten years, averaged only forty per cent of that for the Mayor, who is voted for practically on the basis of manhood suffrage.

Observe that property qualifications were put in the State Constitutions while the rights of man were proclaiming from the housetops. Yet only here and there was a voice raised for the right of a man to vote because he was a man. It is not surprising to find Thomas Jefferson one of the few to remonstrate. In 1782, in his "Notes on Virginia," he pointed out "six very capital defects" in the Constitution of his State, and the very first of them was this: "The majority of the men in the State, who pay and fight for its support, are unrepresented in the Legislature, the roll of freeholders entitled to vote not including generally the half of those on the roll of the militia, or of the taxgatherers."

Only gradually did the idea that this was a defect gain supporters. When the matter came up in the Federal Convention, August 7, 1787, there was earnest discussion of the plan of the Committee by which the qualifications of voters for Federal Representatives should in each State be the same as those of voters for members of its lower branch — an ingenious plan for escaping the issue. Gouverneur Morris did not like it. He wanted some provision to restrain the right of suffrage to freeholders. John Dickinson thought freeholders "the best guardians of liberty; and the restriction of the right to them as a necessary defense against the dangerous influence of those multitudes without property and without principle, with which our country, like all others, will in time abound." Oliver Ellsworth held that taxation and representation ought to go together, but he thought each State the best judge of the circumstances and temper of its own people. Morris took the floor again with a novel argument, based on the fear that the Constitution as it stood threatened the country with an aristocracy. "Give the votes to the people who have no property and they will sell them to the rich, who will be able to buy them." Colonel Mason objected to confining the privilege to freeholders, but only because other things as well as property marked a permanent attachment to the society. Even James Madison believed the freeholders would be the safest depository of republican liberty. Two South Carolina men, Pierce Butler and John Rutledge, spoke against the restriction to freeholders, but judging by Madison's Journal the earnest argument for "the common people" was that of Benjamin Franklin, who held it of great consequence not to depress their virtue and public spirit. Franklin carried the day, for the delegates of only one State, Delaware, voted in favor of the notion of Morris. Furthermore the apportionment of Representatives among the States, "according to their respective Numbers," foreshadowed what was to come.

After the Federal Constitution was adopted, the spread of the democratic spirit and the rise of the Anti-Federalist party, first to be known as the Republican and in later days as the Demo-

cratic party, made easy the keeping of property qualifications
out of the Constitutions of the new States. Only a few of those
admitted since 1789 have recognized property as a factor. Kentucky, the first of them, giving in 1792 the suffrage to all free
male citizens twenty-one years of age, has been credited with
beginning the democratic movement by some writers who have
overlooked Vermont. Tennessee followed Kentucky's example
four years later. Ohio (1802), largely settled from New England,
showed the influence of its origins by restricting the suffrage to
taxpayers, but made it free in 1851. Nearly all the other new
States have been content with omitting reference to property or
taxes in setting forth qualifications, but Idaho (1889) wanted no
misunderstanding, and so she said: "No property qualification
shall ever be required for any person to vote or hold office except
in school elections or elections creating indebtedness."

The original States have shown in this matter how much
harder it is to get rid of a provision that has become obnoxious
than it is to prevent its entrance when starting with a clean
slate. New Hampshire was the first to respond to the change in
public opinion, dispensing with its poll-tax qualification in 1792.
Georgia in 1798 changed its requirement so that nobody of whom
a tax had been required could vote unless the tax had been paid,
provided he might have had the opportunity of paying it. New
Jersey, in 1807, took off her property qualification, and established manhood suffrage by the simple process of an act explanatory of her Constitution. Maryland in 1810 ratified an amendment for manhood suffrage. In the Massachusetts Convention
of 1820, although it was suggested that the payment of a tax as
a prerequisite be abolished, the matter was not pushed and evidently there was then no powerful sentiment for it. Doubtless
George Blake reflected the general opinion when he said the
doctrine of universal suffrage could not be sustained on any
principle. No person who did not contribute to the support of
government was so far a party to the social compact as to have
a right to a voice in the election of the officers of government.
The Convention went no farther than to submit an amendment, which was ratified in 1821, abolishing freehold with an income of three pounds, or any estate of the value of sixty pounds,
as a qualification, substituting the payment of any tax. It was
not until seventy years later that this in turn was abolished.

In New York up to 1821 a man had to have a freehold of

twenty pounds or rent a tenement of forty shillings a year in order to vote for a member of the lower branch of the Legislature; a freehold of one hundred pounds in order to vote for a Senator. The meaning of "freehold" brought more serious trouble than anywhere else by reason of the fact that so much land was leased for 999 years. This made the tenants of Trinity Church in New York City and thousands of tenants of the great Dutch manors, leaseholders instead of freeholders. Furthermore, in the northern and western part of the State much land was sold by the Holland Land Company and others under a system that did not give the buyer his deed until the last instalment of purchase money had been paid. The resulting discontent was one of the chief causes of the Convention of 1821, which gave the suffrage to taxpayers, and also to men who had performed military duty in the militia within the year or were exempted therefrom by reason of being firemen. By amendment in 1826, manhood suffrage was substituted.

The property qualification came very near leading to bloodshed in Rhode Island — indeed, actually did bring what was called rebellion. That State had lagged far behind the other thirteen colonies in adopting a Constitution, contenting itself with living under the Charter it had received from Charles II. From time to time during more than half a century attempts to change were made, but with little strength. The restriction of the suffrage to freeholders and their eldest sons was the chief grievance. In 1829 a committee of the Assembly, reporting on petitions for enfranchisement, defended the freehold qualification, denounced Democracy as the curse of every nation that had ever adopted it, and declared that as their forefathers had seen fit to restrict the suffrage "to the sound part of the community, the substantial freeholders of the State," their descendants had a right to adhere to the restrictions so imposed. A few years later Thomas W. Dorr, college graduate and man of popular manners, belonging to one of the wealthy and influential families, began an agitation for reform. He argued that, upon the Revolution, the sovereignty passed not to the Governor and Company of Rhode Island and the Providence Plantations, but to the people. Theirs was the right to frame a Constitution and this he urged them to do. His propaganda bore fruit in 1841 when a People's Convention framed such an instrument. At the same time a Convention authorized by the Assembly formed the

Freemen's Constitutions on successive days in May, 1842, one at Newport, the other at Providence. Dorr took office as Governor under the People's Constitution. The clash came with his attempt to seize the arsenal. Upon its failure he fled the State, returning to another fiasco in the following month, and again escaping. Upon coming back two years later he was arrested, tried, and sentenced to prison for life, but after a year's confinement he was pardoned, and some years later his civil and political rights were restored. Meantime, in 1843, a Constitution was peaceably adopted, with more liberal franchise, virtually on a taxpaying basis. Manhood suffrage came by amendment in 1888, except that in elections for the city council, or upon any proposition to impose a tax, or for the expenditure of money in any town or city, the voter must have property to the value of $134.

Connecticut dropped the freehold and taxpaying qualifications in 1845. Virginia came to the same step in 1850 — two generations after Jefferson had begun the contest. Oddly enough the Convention of 1864, of delegates from the regions then within the Union lines, put back the taxpaying proviso, but that of 1870 took it out again. North Carolina in 1856 dropped the extra requirement of a fifty-acre freehold to vote for Senators, and in 1868 dropped the taxpaying requirement altogether. Some of the other Southern States give almost the only instances of reaction. South Carolina, which had reached manhood suffrage for residents in 1810, provided in 1895 that the man who cannot read and write must have property assessed at $300 or more in order to vote: a poll-tax was imposed; and all electors must have paid all taxes assessed against them. Mississippi, after having had manhood suffrage since 1832, in 1890 put on the poll-tax. Louisiana, which dropped the taxpaying qualification in 1845, followed along the lines of South Carolina in 1898. Alabama in 1901 required payment of poll-taxes; and when limiting the suffrage to those who can read and write and have been regularly employed during the greater part of the preceding twelve months, exempted owners of forty acres or property real or personal to the value of $300.

Pennsylvania and Delaware have naturally gone along together. Pennsylvania began (1776) with a taxpaying qualification, sons of freeholders exempted. In 1790 it limited such exemption to sons between twenty-one and twenty-two years old,

Delaware doing the same in 1792. Then in 1831 Delaware and in 1838 Pennsylvania let in all men between twenty-one and twenty-two whether taxpayers or not, a singular instance of the decay of privilege. So it stood until 1897, when Delaware came to manhood suffrage. Pennsylvania still requires men of twenty-two or more to have paid a tax of some sort.

THE ARGUMENTS

The arguments for property qualifications fall into two classes. First may be mentioned those based on the belief that the man without property is unlikely to contribute useful judgment. Thus Blackstone said that the true reason of requiring any qualification with regard to property in voters, is to exclude such persons as are in so mean a situation that they are esteemed to have no will of their own. If it were probable that every man would give his vote freely, then every member of the community should have a vote. But since that can hardly be expected in persons of indigent fortunes, or such as are under the immediate dominion of others, all popular States have been obliged to establish certain qualifications; whereby some, who are suspected to have no will of their own, are excluded from voting.[1] Along the same line was the opinion of Guizot who said that capacity exists wherever we meet with the conditions whether material or moral, of that degree of independence and intellectual development which enable a man freely and reasonably to accomplish the political act he is required to perform.

Delegate Trezvant put this phase of it admirably in the Virginia Convention of 1829: "It is no idle chimera of the brain, that the possession of land furnishes the strongest evidence of permanent, common interest with, and attachment to, the community. Much has been already said by gentlemen on both sides, demonstrating the powerful influence of local attachment upon the conduct of man, and I cannot be made to comprehend how that passion could be more effectually brought into action, than by a consciousness of the fact, that he is the owner of the spot which he can emphatically call his home. It is upon this foundation I wish to place the Right of Suffrage. This is the best general standard which can be resorted to for the purpose of determining whether the persons to be invested with the Right of Suffrage are such persons as could be, consistently with the

[1] *Commentaries*, book i, chap. 2.

safety and well-being of the community, entrusted with the exercise of that right."

Such arguments approach the problem from the point of view of the public interest. On the other hand are the arguments based on private interest. Mill, making the usual British assumption that the prime purpose of a representative assembly is financial, declared it to be important, that the assembly which votes the taxes, either general or local, should be elected exclusively by those who pay something towards the taxes imposed. Those who pay no taxes, disposing by their votes of other people's money, have every motive to be lavish and none to economize. As far as money matters are concerned, any power of voting possessed by them is a violation of the fundamental principle of free government; a severance of the power of control from the interest in its beneficial exercise. It amounts to allowing them to put their hands into other people's pockets for any purpose which they think fit to call a public one; which in some of the great towns of the United States is known to have produced a scale of local taxation onerous beyond example, and wholly borne by the wealthier classes.[1]

This is an argument of expediency. In the United States, with the taxation aspects of the controversy that led to Revolution fresh in mind, it had been carried farther, into an argument of right. As late as 1832, more than half a century after the Declaration of Independence, the Justices of the Massachusetts Supreme Court said in an Opinion that it was the intent of an amendment made in 1821 "to give practical force and effect to the maxim, that taxation and representation should go together; and to secure the right of electing those, who are to administer the government, to those who in fact contribute to its support."

This theory, carried a step farther, has been the warrant for the English practice of giving a property owner a vote in every constituency where he has the requisite property. It is the system of "plural voting" that has been attacked so vigorously in England of late. There criticism seems to have been largely in vain, for the Representation of the People Act of 1918, instead of abolishing plural voting, extended it so that a man can acquire a vote elsewhere than the place of his residence by the occupation and use for business purposes of premises worth ten pounds or

---

[1] *Representative Government*, chap. VIII.

more a year. However, a sop was thrown to the critics by forbidding anybody to vote in more than two constituencies at a general election — a restriction of course quite inconsistent with the underlying principle.

In America the system got a foothold in the Southern colonies, which clung more closely to English traditions than the colonies of the North. In Virginia it survived until 1850. In South Carolina at first the voting was all done in Charleston. When in 1716 the Assembly provided for voting in each parish, landowners complained because as the polls were to be open but two days they could not make the rounds of all their estates and vote for all of them. Edward Hooker, who was in the State in 1805, wrote in his Diary: "I understand that serious abuses of the right of suffrage have been heretofore committed by persons who owned property in different districts and parishes, attending the election in these different places, and exercising thereby an undue influence. By this means, the city of Charleston could gain an immense weight in the Legislature: her citizens being accustomed to sally out and carry an election in several country parishes where the number of resident electors is small. The parish of St. Andrews is such an one: Though containing only about fifty families, it sends three Representatives and one Senator to the General Assembly. In some parishes in the low country it is said the disproportion is still greater. The reason is, that the increase of wealth and the multiplication of negroes have diminished the white population." [1] Hooker said that a resolution had passed the Legislature prohibiting the electors from voting in more than one place, but if Thorpe's compilation of Constitutions is to be relied on in this particular, no constitutional change was made until the Civil War, with which the provision for plural voting in North Carolina (in the matter of members of the House of Commons) also disappeared. Georgia, on the other hand, never would have any of it, at least as a State, for in her first Constitution (1777) the rejection was in positive words: "No person shall be entitled to more than one vote." Tennessee in this regard was more influenced by South Carolina than by Georgia, for she began (1796) by permitting the vote to freeholders in any county although they might not live there, dropping the provision, however, in 1834.

None of the Northern States began with plural voting, but in

[1] *Am. Hist. Assn. Annual Report for 1896*, I, 877.

New York it was to be found before the Revolution. A New York statute of 1769 made clear the right, its preamble having stated that doubts had arisen as to whether non-residents could vote in districts where they possessed a freehold.

The idea has of late made no appeal to American sympathies and is now rarely even suggested. It is, however, perfectly logical if in fact property is to be represented for its own protection, whether from unjust laws attacking it, or from the taxes due to appropriations by landless and moneyless legislators. In matters of municipal government it would be particularly defensible by reason of the changes due to modern development in transportation. These have made it possible for large numbers of men with offices or shops or factories in cities to live in suburbs, often miles away. Their interests where they do business and pass their working hours may in respect to nearly everything affected by the administration of law be far greater than those where they sleep. Could they vote where they work, their contribution to good municipal government would be of no small help. Furthermore in these days when so many persons have summer homes in which they pass several months of the year, it is not unreasonable that they should have a share in the government of the towns to which they contribute so much, directly through taxes and indirectly through expenditure. This doubtless is one of the reasons why England continues to let a man vote not only where he resides but also in one other place where he occupies property.

One weakness of property qualifications in matter of technical detail is to be noted. A money requirement is easily evaded, and this is a grave defect in any political system. The process and its ease may be illustrated by an anecdote of Amos Kendall, who became famous by helping Andrew Jackson govern the United States. Kendall's first vote was given in March, 1813, in Groton, Massachusetts, where he was reading law with W. M. Richardson, who had been in Congress. "It was an illegal one," says William Stickney, editing Kendall's Autobiography (page 79). "The election was for Governor. The Constitution of Massachusetts then contained a moderate property qualification for voters, and Mr. Kendall had no property whatever. There was a Federal student in the office who was equally poor. Both of their names had been entered on the list of voters, by what authority Mr. Kendall never knew. The Federal student went up to vote, when Mr. Richardson proposed to Mr. Kendall to go up and 'kill his vote.' He objected that he was not a voter. Said Mr. Richardson, 'I will make you a voter,' and handed him a sufficient sum of money, telling him to show it if his right should be questioned. He voted without being challenged, and returned the money. Of this transaction he says in his journal, 'If I had had time for reflection, I know not what I should have done under the circumstances, but I am satisfied I ought to have declined.' "

In 1812 Ezra Batcheller of North Brookfield was unseated by a Massachusetts Legislature because a voter, to prove his ownership of property enough, presented a note made without consideration, for $200. Other instances could be cited to show the frequency of the offense in the days when property qualifications were common.

In philosophizing on the subject account must be taken of the fact that once a property qualification has been lessened, it has rarely if ever been afterward increased. Once wholly removed, nobody now seriously tries to get it restored. Everywhere since the representative system became systemized, the tendency has been to broaden, not narrow, the suffrage. Nowadays the march is rapid. Take Japan, for instance. Its first electoral law, that of 1889, required voters to pay fifteen yen in direct national taxes; that of 1900 reduced the figure to ten yen; that of 1919 made it three yen; and the fourth, in 1925, removed it wholly. In 1889 the franchise was open to 450,000 men; the latest law raises that to more than fourteen million.[1] Some part of this, however, but comparatively small, comes from the inclusion of priests, religious teachers, primary school teachers, government contractors, and certain classes of teachers previously excluded.[1]

[1] *Political Science Quarterly*, March, 1926.

CHAPTER XIV

THE SUFFRAGE

UPON analyzing the justification for the tests thus far examined, it will be found that the reasons fall into two groups, which may be sufficiently described, even though with some inaccuracy, as those that are subjective, intrinsic, and those that are objective, extrinsic. Reasons from each group may combine in support of any one test. Furthermore a suffrage test involves both exclusion and inclusion, the two here being corollaries. Thus the ownership of property would have as an objective reason the securing of the judgment of persons having an evident and substantial interest in government, a stake in the common welfare; as a subjective reason the granting of a voice in public affairs to persons supposed to need it for protecting the fruits of their labors. On the other hand the landless person may be denied the vote objectively on the ground that having no property of his own, he will use the ballot to get property away from others, or subjectively on the ground that his needs may lead him to sell his vote, thus making him a criminal. In matter of citizenship the vote of the native-born or those long-resident may have objective value because of knowledge of our institutions, familiarity with our habits of thought, and that acceptance of our standards which may be presumed from long usage; subjectively the newcomer may be denied the vote because mere presence, perhaps transient, has earned for him no share in the conduct of our public affairs.

Examining in the light of such analysis the changes in suffrage requirements since representation through the use of the ballot began, the conclusion will be that subjective considerations have had far more weight. To be sure, arguments that this or that enlargement of the electorate would for this or that reason benefit the State, have not been wanting, but they have been secondary, subordinate. The predominating consideration has been a subjective interest, that of the individual members of the group admitted. Furthermore this interest has not been stressed from the point of view of personal advantage of a material nature. The emphasis has been laid on the interest that takes the shape of enjoyment of what is declared a "right." Therefore it becomes a primary importance to determine whether suffrage is or is not a right.

Here once again we find the issue obscured by inadequate terminology. "Right" means many things. Suffrage discussion would be greatly clarified if the word were used only to mean what is often called "natural right." Then we could the quicker conclude whether voting is a function inseparably attached to personality, whether it is an unalienable right of the sort spoken of in the Declaration of Independence. There it was declared that "all men are endowed by their Creator with certain unalienable rights" and that "among these are life, liberty, and the pursuit of happiness." This is not unqualifiedly true. There are no unalienable rights. The very particulars of the Declaration disprove it. Life is held subject to the will of the sovereign power in this as in every other country; we destroy it in the case of traitors and murderers; every able-bodied man of military age must risk his life if called upon in case of war. Liberty is denied at this moment to more than a million inhabitants of the United States who have broken a law or who are deemed of such mental condition that they may not be safely left at large. The pursuit of happiness is thwarted at every turn in the case of those who would pursue what they think happiness, to the injury of others. Everything a man has, everything a man is, the sovereign power may control or destroy as it deems for the common good. At any rate such is the basis of the Constitution and laws of every government in the world. And whatever the theory, the fact rules.

Nevertheless the controversy continues. It has appeared, for instance, wherever woman suffrage has been debated, and there it has taken on great practical importance, for an appeal on the score of right makes many converts. It has confused even the most logical of reasoners. In recent times perhaps there has been no more hard-headed, cold-blooded reasoner than John Stuart Mill. Let me ask you to read rather carefully these sentences from the tenth chapter of his work on "Representative Government," remembering that by "ballot" he meant secret voting:

"The spirit of vote by ballot — the interpretation likely to be put on it in the mind of an elector — is that the suffrage is given to him for himself; for his particular use and benefit, and not as a trust for the public. For if it is indeed a trust, if the public are

entitled to his vote, are they not entitled to know his vote?...
Mr. Bright and his school of democrats think themselves greatly
concerned in maintaining that the franchise is what they term a
right, not a trust.... In whatever way we define or understand
the idea of a right, no person can have a right (except in the
purely legal sense) to power over others; every such power,
which he is allowed to possess, is morally in the fullest force of
the term, a trust. But the exercise of any political function,
either as an elector or as a representative, is power over others.
Those who say that the suffrage is not a trust but a right will accept the conclusions to which their doctrine leads. If it is a right,
if it belongs to the voter for his own sake, on what ground can
we blame him for selling it, or using it to recommend himself to
any one whom it is his interest to please?"

Then turn back to the eighth chapter of the same book and
read:

"In the preceding argument for universal, but graduated suffrage, I have taken no account of difference of sex. I consider it
to be as entirely irrelevant to political rights as difference in
height or in the color of the hair. All human beings have the
same interest in self-government; the welfare of all is alike
affected by it, and they have equal need of a voice in it to secure
their share of its benefits. If there be any difference, women require it more than men, since, being physically weaker, they are
more dependent on law and society for protection. Mankind
have long since abandoned the only premises which will support
the conclusion that women ought not to have votes."

Burke's inconsistency to which I called your attention in
Chapter IX appeared in contradictory views expressed in an
essay and a speech, with an interval of four years between. Mill,
prince of logicians, separates by a single chapter his puncture of
Bright's theory that the franchise is a right, and his own argument based on the assumption that the franchise is a right.

Do you retort that he used the word "right" with different
meanings in these passages? But how can that be reconciled with
his further inconsistency? In the one case he ridiculed the notion
that the ballot is given to an elector for his individual use and
benefit, and not as a trust for the public; and in the other he
said that women needed a voice in government to secure their
share of its benefits.

If it were not profane to suggest mental intoxication in John

Stuart Mill, one would be tempted to appeal from Philip drunk to Philip sober. It was Philip sober who showed that save in the purely legal sense the franchise cannot be a right.

Can the franchise be a privilege?

Not if we use that word with its common implication of favor. The sovereign power gives the franchise to nobody out of kindness, charity, benevolence, anything that prompts a favor; it gives the franchise because it thinks the gift will conduce to the common advantage.

The word "give" adds to the confusion, and more still the word "grant," so often used in connection with franchise laws. Both of them carry a suggestion of privilege and favor. Yet their proper meaning here is that with which they are used in a deed of land, for they are but the formal words of conveyance.

What, then, is the franchise, the suffrage?

Mill, in his tenth chapter, thought it a trust. That usefully emphasizes one phase of it. To my mind, however, a happier because a broader description of it is to be found in calling it a duty. This puts it on all fours with other civic duties to which it is analogous, such as jury duty and military duty. If it be said there is a difference in that jurymen and drafted soldiers must serve whether or no, but that electors need not vote, the answer is that the sovereign power undoubtedly can impose a penalty for not voting, that it has at times imposed such a penalty, and that there is a serious demand in some quarters for it to be imposed in our own time and country.

If the franchise is a duty, why should it be imposed on some persons and not on others?

The question almost answers itself. Clearly it is because the State thinks the judgment of some will help, and that of others will not.

Such has been the opinion of every State that ever existed and it is perfectly safe to say always will be the opinion of every State that exists hereafter. Universal suffrage is a phrase and nothing more. The purest democracy that can be imagined would not establish universal suffrage. To be sure, Aristotle, first to describe a pure democracy, attributed to it "the election of officers by all out of all." [1] He did not mean it. Neither did he mean, nor has anybody else since then meant, that children should vote, or idiots. And once you begin thus excluding classes

[1] Aristotle, *The Politics*, book VI.

of human beings, you have abandoned universal suffrage; your stopping place becomes a matter of expediency, and nothing more or less than expediency. All shadow of right disappears.

If the ballot were a right, either a natural right, if any exists, or an artificial right, like that of owning property, then children and idiots should vote by their parents or other legal guardians as they would in corporations if stock stood in their names. Look back at Mill's argument when he contradicted himself. "All human beings," he said, "have the same interest in self-government; the welfare of all is alike affected by it, and they have equal need of a voice in it to secure their share of its benefits." Children and idiots are human beings. Shall they therefore have a voice in government?

To the logic of Mill I prefer that of Bowyer. "If," he says, "every well-organized society has the right to consult for the common good of the whole, and if upon the principles of natural law this right is conceded by the very union of society, it seems difficult to assign any limit to this right, which is compatible with the end proposed. If, therefore, any society shall deem the common good and interests of the whole society best promoted under the particular circumstances in which it is placed, by a restriction of the right of suffrage, it is not easy to state any solid ground of objection to the exercise of such an authority." [1]

INDIVIDUAL OR COMMON GOOD

In case while treating the various franchise tests I view them in their relation to the common good, it is because of personal conviction that this is the wiser viewpoint. To me they are what is implied in the word "qualifications" rather than what is implied in the word "restrictions." My own judgment is that the franchise exists for the benefit of the State, not for that of the citizen save as he benefits by what benefits all. To me the State is the unit, the citizen is a fraction. Candor, however, demands recognition of the fact that this doctrine is not universally accepted. On the contrary, it is stoutly contested by large numbers of thoughtful persons who are equally convinced that the good of mankind calls for the individual to be taken as the starting point, to be treated as the unit, and who look on the State as an accidental, arbitrary, conventional multiple. Applied to the franchise, their theory leads to the conclusion that each individual

[1] *Commentaries on Universal Public Law*, 260.

has a natural, innate, inherent right to vote because he or she is a human being, or living entity, and that exclusions from the right are to be made only as exceptions on the ground of manifest expediency.

As typical of the argument for this, take the declaration of Charles Sumner in the Massachusetts Convention of 1853. "It is a palpable truth," he said, "that men are not born equal in physical strength or in mental capacities; in beauty of form or health of body. These mortal cloaks of flesh differ, as do these worldly garments. Diversity or inequality in these respects is the law of creation. But as God is no respecter of persons, and as all are equal in his sight, whether rich or poor, whether dwellers in cities or in fields, so are all equal in natural rights; and it is a childish sophism to adduce in argument against them the physical or mental inequalities by which men are characterized. Now, I do not pretend to class the electoral franchise among those inherent, natural rights, which are common to the human family, without distinction of age, sex, or residence; but I do say, that from the equality of men, which we so proudly proclaim, we may derive a just rule for its exercise." [1]

Although Sumner disclaimed the purpose of classing the franchise as an inherent, natural right, the tenor of his notable address was wholly inconsistent with the view that the ballot is an artificial device for furthering the ends of government, to be regulated with only that in view.

The rule that Sumner was at the time seeking did not concern the right of the individual to vote. It concerned the right of the voter to have his vote carry weight equal to that of every other vote. The distinction is of importance. It is often neglected, or not understood. Equality between those within the pale is an altogether different matter from equality between those within and those without. Let me illustrate by the condition of affairs when in 1776 the Declaration of Independence put forth as a self-evident truth the startling and puzzling dictum that "all men are created equal." The estimate of historians is that out of 2,750,000 human beings then in the thirteen colonies, only 150,-000, one in eighteen, met the qualifications for voting. If Jefferson and his fellow-signers meant that all men were created equal in respect of political rights, clearly they never even dreamed of the suffrage as a political right. Nor did their pronunciamento

[1] *Debates in Mass. Convention of 1853*, ii, 593.

lead men at once to dream of it, much less to act on such a notion. From scattered figures it has been concluded that about one third of the adult males were excluded from all participation in the State Government of New York, even in the election of Assemblymen, under the Constitution of 1777. It is estimated on the basis of a careful study that not more than 150,000 out of approximately 600,000 adult white males took part in the elections at which were chosen the members of the State conventions that ratified the Federal Constitution in 1787–89.

If, then, words are to be construed by deeds, what our fathers meant by political equality in the conduct of government was equality between those who were asked to share therein. Such, indeed, if not the only thought, has been the chief thought in the minds of those who have so often and so eloquently extolled equality. For instance, we find Benjamin Kidd saying: "The most fundamental political doctrine of modern Democracy is that of the native equality of all men. It is, in reality, around this doctrine that every phase of the progressive political movement in our civilization has centered for the last two centuries. It is this doctrine which is asserted in the political constitution of every country where the principles of Western Liberalism have been accepted. It is this doctrine which is denied in all other political constitutions. It is the doctrine of the native equality of men that has been behind the long movement in our Western world which has emancipated the people and slowly equipped them with political power; and it is the repudiation of it which constitutes the ultimate fact in every phase and stage of the resistance which this movement has encountered." [1]

Keep this in mind and turn to a later page, where you may read: "Amongst a certain section of modern people, one of the commonest of political assumptions is that of the right of every man of voting power irrespective of position, or of creed, or of opinion; and further, and more important, of the right of every man to *equal* voting power irrespective of the nature or the amount of his interest in the State. If we look closely at this conception, it may be perceived that it is only our familiarity with it which leads us to overlook the fact that not only is it altogether exceptional in the world, but that there is no real explanation of it to be found in any existing theory of the purely political State. It is a conception which has been held by only a comparatively

[1] *Principles of Western Civilization*, 107–08.

small number of people during an insignificant space in recent history. Even by no inconsiderable proportion of persons amongst the advanced peoples of the present day the right of every man to equal voting power, irrespective either of his intelligence, or of his capacity, or of the amount of his property, in the State, is but little understood. Nay, it is often covertly resented, and is outwardly accepted in principle only because the prestige of the results obtained by the advanced peoples amongst whom it has prevailed has created a tendency in affairs against which it is felt to be useless to struggle. But down into the recent past, in the almost universal opinion of the world, the conception would undoubtedly have presented itself, as it has actually done in our time to Nietzsche, and as it still does to the overwhelming proportion of our fellow-creatures in the world, simply as one so inherently absurd as to be beyond the bounds of reasonable discussion." [1]

Kidd is in this neither quite fair nor quite accurate. He is unfair in that he ignores the conception of the suffrage as a means rather than an end, as an adjunct rather than as a purpose of political organization, as a device rather than as a right; and while ignoring this reasonable and important conception, implies that those who question are inspired by prejudice, are guilty of resentment, and are false to conviction, in that they outwardly accept what they inwardly deny, led thereto by the belief that opposition would be futile. The fact is that the doctrine of the native equality of all men as expressed in universal suffrage seems inherently absurd not to an overwhelming proportion of mankind, but to all mankind, for there never was put in practice such a thing as universal suffrage and never will be. The quarrel is over the size of the fraction that shall vote.

He is inaccurate in that he describes the conception of equal voting power as wholly modern, wholly novel. He forgets Greece and Rome, the tribes of ancient Germany, and in the middle ages Ireland and Switzerland. Even the discussion of the vital problem is not new. Cicero shared in it when he held that citizens should be weighed, not counted — "In dissensione civili, quum boni plus quam mali valent, expendendos cives, non numerandos puto." [2]

---

[1] *Principles of Western Civilization*, 368–69.
[2] Cicero, *De Republica*, lib. VI.

Sir G. C. Lewis in quoting this comments:[1] "A remark as applicable to times of domestic discord, as of civil war"; and he might have added — a view calling for reflection under any and all political conditions.

It is to be conceded, however, that the recent revival of the doctrine of political equality has had far more significance and result than all previous instances of its application. Kidd's allotment of two centuries to it was over-generous. A century and a half would be nearer right. The first suggestion of it in modern England is believed to have been made by Major John Cartwright, who in 1776 wrote his earliest work on the subject of reform in Parliament. In it he said: "I would not hastily dissent from a received opinion, especially one supported by great authorities; but yet my own conceptions of truth oblige me to believe, that personality is the sole foundation of the right of being represented."[2]

Parliament by that time had so widened its functions, as to warrant Major Cartwright in advancing the novel proposition, but he would have given a more precise idea of his contention if he had said, "Personality should now be the sole foundation of the right of being represented." Originally it was nothing of the sort. Remember that the election of men to represent localities in Parliament began as an incidental and occasional attribute of jury duty. Every voter was first a juror; he was a voter only because he was a juror. The vote of a juror was not a matter of individual right, but of duty to the community. Furthermore, as Pollard observes,[3] representation was not the offspring of democratic theory, but an incident of the feudal system. Suit and service were due from all, but if the lord or his steward went to the county court, their presence would "acquit" the tenants; if neither lord nor steward was present, there must come the priest and the reeve, with four best men of the township on behalf of their fellows.

Men were no more anxious then than they are now to serve on the jury. To have told them that by so serving they would get the precious right of voting for a representative would have seemed to them ridiculous. The boon of representation was not in the right to go to the polls, but in the privilege of staying away.

[1] *The Use and Abuse of Some Political Terms*, 95, note.
[2] *Life and Correspondence of Major Cartwright*, 92.
[3] *The Evolution of Parliament*, 109, 154.

With the broadening of men's thoughts in the last third of the eighteenth century, came a point of view directly the reverse. Men began to think of themselves as citizens, not as subjects. It was no mere coincidence that in the year when Thomas Jefferson pronounced the equality of men, Major John Cartwright should have declared personality the sole foundation of the right of being represented. The rights of the individual were in the air on both sides of the Atlantic.

It was to be on this side that Cartwright's doctrine would first bear fruit. We have seen how the abolition of property qualifications spread. Inevitably the next great step was the granting of the suffrage to women. This indeed came nearer to being coincident with the early extensions to men than is generally known. Women voted in New Jersey through a generation after its Constitution was adopted, for that document gave the ballot to "all free inhabitants of the State" who were twenty-one years old and owned fifty pounds proclamation money, clear estate. The law of 1807 which restricted the franchise to free white males, declared in its preamble that this limit was made because women, negroes, and aliens had been permitted to vote. Probably the latitude of the original proviso was not deliberately intended. Doubtless it was due to the haste with which the Constitution was drawn.

The time was not ripe. In those days nobody would have seriously argued for woman suffrage had the question been raised. A century of controversy must follow, throughout the land, before the greater part of the men would grant the appeal. To narrate the details of the change in sentiment that came about would call for a volume by itself. To try to epitomize the copious literature on the subject or to enter upon the considerations advanced, might be a fruitless invasion upon space that can otherwise be given to less familiar aspects of the suffrage. Suffice it, therefore, to say that in a large part of both America and Europe the duty of the ballot has been imposed on women; in other words, it has been decided that women may helpfully be asked to share in voicing the common will.

On the Continent, by reason of the democratizing effect of the World War, the inclusion of women in the electorate was accompanied by the extension of the suffrage to large numbers of men hitherto voiceless. A typical step was that of Germany, which, announcing itself a republic in its Constitution adopted

July 3, 1919, declared that "the representatives of the People must be elected by the universal, direct, and secret suffrage of all German citizens, both men and women." In England also the same period that saw women win their fight saw the volume of men voters increased.

The fight for the ballot always has been more exciting in England than on this side of the water, because the battles of English democracy are fought in Parliament, that political arena on which all eyes are focused. Here the suffrage was long held to be a matter for the States, and the battle grounds were as many as there were Legislatures. Only by the prosaic process of aggregating results do we come to realize what has taken place. Start with the fact that about four per cent of the population, one inhabitant in twenty-five, exercised the right to vote not long after the Revolutionary period. A generation later we have the first figures of the popular vote for Presidential electors that approach completeness, those for 1828, only South Carolina then continuing to have the Legislature choose. In the States other than South Carolina almost exactly ten per cent of the population voted. In 1900 about eighteen per cent voted; in 1920 a little more than twenty-five per cent; in 1928 a little more than thirty per cent. Those formally qualified to vote in 1928 were estimated at not far from thirty-five per cent of the total population. Speaking relatively, therefore, the legal electorate has grown about nine-fold in a century and a half.

How many have the theoretical right to vote, it is impossible to say, partly because of Southern conditions, partly because of incomplete statistics in all of the States as to the numbers who would be excluded because of insanity, confinement for crime, or other causes. Possibly about one half of the population now have the legal right to vote upon complying with the registration laws.

Such extension of the suffrage alarms those who have little faith in democracy. It gratifies those who feel that all arbitrary social classifications are tainted by fallacy, those who draw from history the conclusion Freeman drew. "Ignorance and prejudice," he held, "are the monopoly of no particular social class and no particular social party. Really wise men and good citizens are to be found scattered up and down among all classes and all parties. No system has yet been found which will make them, and none but them, the sole possessors of political power. No class has any real right to despise any other class, whether above or below it in the social scale." [1]

These considerations are beside the mark. The question is one of group capacity, and its answer depends not on the estimated merit of classes, but on their actual or potential contributions to the utility of government. Thus viewed, measured by results, it is by no means clear that each and every extension of the suffrage has brought gain.

Indeed, let no man confidently aver that what we call universal suffrage has come to stay. There are tides in political science. Now that the electorate has almost everywhere reached its flood, it may ebb. Time alone can tell whether real significance attaches to the reaction started in Italy with the abolition of general suffrage, in 1928. This may or may not be the conspicuous beginning of a slide down the hill that suffrage has been climbing for a century and a half. That period is but a brief hour in the history of mankind, and all institutions change. Although we of the United States have had the longest experience in this newest of political institutions, it would be vain to call the experience determining. Few thoughtful observers would say positively that broad suffrage is a success in the governing of our big cities. Many are uncertain about its results in some of our more populous States. Perhaps in the course of another century or two growth alone will drive the nation to some other and still better resort for securing the greatest measure of liberty, and the greatest measure of achievement in the pursuit of happiness.

LITERACY AND INTELLIGENCE

Indeed, we of the United States, where Democracy scored its first notable triumphs of modern times, may have begun, quite unconsciously, to lessen its perquisites in a way fraught with momentous possibilities. We may have started toward capacity as a qualification for a share in declaring the public will. This may prove the most useful and the most important of qualifications. In any case if fully applied it will materially diminish the electorate.

Its origin will be traced to educational qualifications, which have made thus far the only noteworthy exception to the general tendency toward broadening the suffrage. The idea was first applied in New England, undoubtedly as a result of the growing

[1] *History of Federal Government*, I, 86.

apprehension caused by the flood of immigrants from across the sea. This led to the organized agitation that became for a time politically powerful as the Know-Nothing party. Under its influence Connecticut in 1855 applied the first literacy qualification by a constitutional amendment reading: "Every person shall be able to read any article of the Constitution, or any section of the Statutes of this State, before being admitted an elector." Two years later, under the same influence, Massachusetts followed Connecticut, and went farther by requiring the applicant to be able to write his name. Maine in 1892 closely imitated the Massachusetts provision, and so did New Hampshire ten years afterward.

The example of the two New England States that led the way was first copied in the Far West. When Colorado was admitted, in 1876, its Constitution authorized the Legislature to prescribe an educational test to take effect after 1890. North Dakota in 1898 more than authorized, it directed the Legislature to prescribe an educational test. Meanwhile Wyoming in 1889 had required the elector to be able to read the Constitution. California in 1894 required him to be able to read in the English language and write his name. Washington in 1896 said the Legislature should enact laws "defining the manner of ascertaining the qualifications of voters as to their ability to read and speak the English language." Then the East again took up the matter, Delaware in 1897 requiring that a voter should be able to read the Constitution in the English language and to write his name.

In the Southern States it was seen that this kind of a qualification might be effectively employed to keep the ignorant colored man from voting. Mississippi first applied it, in 1890, with a requirement that after January 1, 1892, every elector should be able to read any section of the State Constitution; and "be able to understand the same when read to him, or give a reasonable interpretation thereof" — a provision that to everybody away from the influence of the Southern negro problem seems open to serious criticism because of its evident chance for abuse. South Carolina in 1895 imposed substantially the same requirement, to stand until January 1, 1898, after which all applicants for registration were to be able to read and write any section of the Constitution, unless paying taxes on property to the value of $300 or more. Louisiana in 1898 made the requirement the ability to read and write, either in the English language or the mother tongue, unless paying taxes on $300 or more. North Carolina, in 1900, made it ability to read and write any section of the Constitution, except in the case of persons or the descendants of persons entitled to vote January 1, 1866, and registered before December 1, 1908, an exception that has come to be known as "the grandfather clause."

Alabama in 1901 provided that after January 1, 1903, electors must be able to read and write in the English language, and have been regularly employed in some occupation during the greater part of the preceding twelve months, or physically unable to work; excepting owners of forty acres of land or property assessed at three hundred dollars or more, etc. In 1921 it was added that the electors must "be of good character and must understand the duties and obligations of citizenship under a republican form of government." Virginia in 1902 had required ability to read and give a reasonable explanation of any clause of the Constitution; or if the applicant was unable to read, ability to give a reasonable explanation of a section read to him; except in the case of persons paying as much as a dollar in taxes on property owned, and of certain others.

Oklahoma, in 1910, stipulated that no person shall be registered as an elector "unless he be able to read and write any section of the Constitution," and added "the grandfather clause." This clause came before the Supreme Court in the case of Guinn v. U.S. (238 U.S. 347), decided in 1914, and it was declared to be void as in violation of the fifteenth amendment. The court (speaking through Chief Justice White) held that the standard made the period of time before the enactment of that amendment the controlling and dominating test of the right of suffrage, and that the amendment was in view when the clause was drafted. Myers v. Anderson, 238 U.S. 368 (1914), applied the reasoning of Guinn v U.S. to a Maryland statute imposing the "grandfather" test in the municipal election of Annapolis.

Texas in 1923 more frankly sought to achieve the well-understood purpose of these Southern illiteracy laws. It enacted: "In no event shall a negro be eligible to participate in a Democratic primary election to be held in the State of Texas, and should a negro vote in a Democratic primary election, such ballot shall be void." As in Texas the primaries have almost inevitably determined the election, this meant the exclusion of the negro as such. The matter was taken to the Supreme Court of the United States, in the case of Nixon v. Herndon and Porras (273 U.S. 536 — 1926), and the Court upheld the plaintiff in his right to sue the Judges of Election for refusing to let him vote. Thereupon the Legislature repealed the obnoxious law and enacted another in which nothing was said about the negro, but power was given to every political party to prescribe the qualifications of its members. This was an attempt to meet the objection that the original law constituted a meretricious union between the State and the Democratic party, quite improper, it was argued, inasmuch as the State has no right to interfere with such business as that of political parties. In the case of Waples v. Marrast (108 Tex. 11), it had been held that the objects of political organizations are intimate to those who compose them. "They do not concern the general public." Agreeing with this view, the District Court of the Southern District of Texas, in 1928, in the case of Grigsby et al. v. Morris et al., supported the new statute and refused to enjoin the enforcement of a resolution of a State committee providing that only white qualified voters of the part should take part in its primary. On the other hand, in Virginia, Judge D. Lawrence Groner of the Federal District Court, handing down an opinion June 5, 1929, held that a negro had been deprived of the rights given to him by the Fourteenth and Fifteenth Amendments of the Constitution, when he was refused the privilege of voting as a result of a resolution adopted by the Democratic State Convention forbidding any but white persons from taking part in Democratic primaries. Judge Groner's view was that the statute regulating primaries erred in giving political parties the power to impose requirements inconsistent with the spirit of the constitutional provisions concerned. It is, indeed, hard to follow the reasoning of those Judges who have held that while a negro may not be prohibited by law from taking part in a primary, a committee may be permitted by law to prohibit him from so doing.

Up to the time of our entry into the World War, this generation of Americans had complacently supposed that the amount of illiteracy within our borders was of small consequence. Then in the course of the application of the army tests it was disclosed that a quarter of the 1,552,256 men between the ages of twenty-one and thirty-one who were examined were illiterate. The test in this particular was the ability to read and understand newspapers and like printed matter, and to write letters home in English.[1] Possibly this revelation had something to do with action in New York. There in 1918 the Legislature gave the first of the two votes necessary toward amending the Constitution to meet the situation. The people ratified the amendment in 1921, whereupon the Legislature started an innovation by providing that in place of examination the election officers might accept a literacy certificate issued by school officials. In 1923 this was modified by requiring the applicant to present a certificate that he had completed the eighth grade in the schools, or a certificate of qualification from the Board of Regents. This was taken to the Court of Appeals where it was upheld.[2] Thus New York was the first State to place the power solely in the hands of the educational authorities. The committee of the Regents decided to set the test tentatively at the requirements of the fourth school year. Their purpose was to be sure the would-be voter could read and write intelligently. Not mere penmanship, but the ability to convey meaning in writing is the object of the examination. In 1924 there were 48,888 who passed the Regents' test and 12,255 who failed; 15,136 were qualified by school credentials. In New York City in 1927 there were 26,702 applicants who could not present the eighth-grade certificate, of whom 4,472 failed to pass satisfactorily the test corresponding to the requirements of the fourth grade. The test consisted of eight simple questions calling for the restatement of facts relating to Decoration Day, set forth in a hundred words or so which the applicant could read as many times as he wished. Nobody would imagine that a man who could not meet this test would contribute useful judgment or opinion by the use of the ballot.

A score or more of the States now have some form of literacy test as a result of Constitution or statute, or have specified that the Legislature may enact. The indications are that many if not all the rest will sooner or later follow suit. New Mexico, however, will have to reverse her position to do this, for she put into the Constitution adopted in 1910 the unique provision that the right of any citizen to vote, hold office, or sit on juries, should never be abridged on account of inability to speak, read, or write the English or Spanish languages; and stipulated that this could not be amended save by a vote of three fourths of the

---

[1] William Seal Carpenter, *Democracy and Representation*, 104–05.

[2] Matter of Chadbourne *v.* Voorhis, 206 N.Y. Appellate, 374.

voters of the State voting, and at least two thirds of those voting in each county.

The literacy test is rare in the rest of the world. Japan applies one indirectly by having each elector write the name of the candidate, and perhaps that might be found elsewhere. The Hungarian man who would vote must have had at least four years of primary education; the woman, if thirty years of age or more, six years of schooling, with the exception that if she is the mother of three children or earns her livelihood, four years of it will suffice. Graduates of the higher institutions of learning may vote irrespective of age or sex, a provision that has much to be said in its favor.

At the other extreme from excluding the illiterate is the granting of additional weight to the man of more than ordinary education. John Stuart Mill was of the opinion that "until there shall have been devised, and until opinion is willing to accept, some mode of plural voting which may assign to education, as such, the degree of superior influence due to it, and sufficient as a counterpoise to the numerical weight of the least educated class; for so long the benefits of completely Universal suffrage cannot be obtained without bringing with them, as it appears to me, a chance of more than equivalent evils." [1] This theory has received no important application save in Belgium, where another vote was given to the citizen who held a diploma from an institution of higher instruction, or a certificate showing secondary education of the higher degree; or if he held a public office, or a position, or practiced a profession that presupposed a like degree of education. Plural voting, however, was abolished in Belgium in 1921.

The chief argument advanced for the literacy test has been that if a man cannot read, he is not likely to be well enough informed about candidates and policies to make his judgment useful. It will have been seen that with the second constitutional provision on the subject, that of Massachusetts in 1857, another element was introduced, for the ability to write one's name involves quite different considerations. It may serve to show a degree of education desirable on general principles, or it may prove to a degree the possession of mental capacity. That education in and of itself was for some time the uppermost thought in the Northern States, might be inferred from the phrase used

[1] *Representative Government*, chap. VIII.

by Colorado, "an educational qualification for electors," and that used in North Dakota, "an educational test as a qualification." It was in the South that mental capacity began to be thought of, judging by the Mississippi requirement of 1890 that an elector must be able to understand any section of the State Constitution, or give a reasonable interpretation thereof. Whether or not this provision and like provisions in some of the other States of the South had an ulterior purpose, on the face they call for tests of mental capacity.

Clearly such a test was the outcome of the action of the voters in New York in 1921, for there now the applicant for registration who has not gone through eight school grades must show that he has intelligence enough to have passed at least the fourth grade. Thus the largest State in the Union definitely makes the possession of a certain degree of intelligence a prerequisite for the exercise of the suffrage, and makes the school either directly or indirectly the medium through which it is to be ascertained.

No more significant step has been taken since the history of the suffrage began. If generally copied and if carried to its probable conclusion, it may reduce the American electorate by from one quarter to one third. It may radically change the character and conditions of our public life. The warrant for it should be studied.

Within a generation a new science has developed, that of psychology. It concerns knowledge of the mind and is new in so far as our time has seen the first statistical studies and systematic inquiries, the first application of scientific methods in this field. Binet and Simon made the first intelligence tests in 1905. The theory is young, immature, and therefore the conclusions thus far reached are not to be accepted implicitly, without question, but at least to the extent that they tally with what have been the common beliefs of mankind in all ages, they may be welcomed as scientific verifications of ancient truths. For example, men have always appraised their fellows by the use of such words as *brilliant, bright, ordinary, slow, dull, stupid, crazy*. The implication of these seven words shade into each other like the seven colors of the spectrum, but everybody understands what in general they signify. What the psychologists have done has been the devising of ways to allocate men as individuals into groups of intelligence with what is argued to be a reasonable amount of accuracy. There are critics who deny that the thing can be done at all, but he who scans impartially even a tithe of the literature on the subject, already voluminous, will find it hard to conclude that these critics are right and that Science cannot vindicate the universal practice of mankind.

In this field, however, as in every other, Science can and does not only vindicate but also refute. In common thought we have been accustomed to divide men into two classes, the sane and the insane, with a fairly sharp line between them, drawn at the point where some measure of care or restraint becomes necessary. We are now learning that there are all degrees of mental deficiency, and that a much larger part of the population than we had supposed lacks that degree of intelligence which may be necessary for the performance of this or that task or duty. Application of this to the suffrage is what concerns us here, and the particular question is the validity of school accomplishment as a test.

This must first meet the assertion of some critics that there is no necessary relation between mental capacity and book learning. The answer is that many examinations, conducted independently, in various parts of the country and under varying conditions, have shown that there is a high correlation between a student's IQ (as the result of an intelligence measurement is called) and his success in school. N. J. Lennes, in his interesting, informative, and suggestive book, "Whither Democracy?" says all the investigations tell the same story and that dozens could be quoted. He tells us that 90 per cent of the retardation of students is due to mental inferiority, and that a low grade of mentality, as revealed by the tests, practically precludes the possibility of success in school.

The startling thing is the disclosure of the proportion of human beings so deficient in mental equipment that they are not likely to perform the duties of citizenship usefully, to exercise wise judgment in public affairs, to have wills of their own, as our fathers used to say in discussing some phases of the suffrage. Lennes finds that scarcely any of the group lowest in the scale of intelligence, comprising one quarter of our people, would be able to graduate from a modern high school, even if they used their best effort. Three fourths of this group are so dull that they would probably fail to graduate from the eighth grade. Three fourths of one fourth figures out 18.75 per cent. The use by the New York Regents of requirements corresponding only to those of the fourth school year resulted in rejecting almost exactly 20 per cent of the applicants for registration without eighth-grade certificates, or 16 per cent of the total. Lennes would seem to have been not far out of the way.

No warm reception is likely in our time for any proposal that the intelligence tests as applied by the psychologists be used in determining qualification for the suffrage. The idea is too new. Furthermore it is still stoutly contended in some quarters that intelligence is not inborn, native, and that it is not static. There are those who argue for environment against heredity, who believe that even the fundamental qualities of the mind can be changed by surroundings or by education. As matter of science the situation is too confused to be accepted as a basis for action by men who enact laws and submit constitutional amendments. The practical consideration is that the public does view schooling as somehow indicative of capacity. Perhaps without overmuch inquiry into reasons, it will widely adopt schooling tests that after all will accomplish the results which the men of science would advise.

CHAPTER XV

PLACES OR POPULATION

IF it is borne in mind that the change from regional to numerical representation has been in progress less than a century and a half, various differences between present and past will be clarified. Previously for six hundred years representation had been almost wholly geographical, sometimes called organic, with reference to organic or administrative divisions of the State. Such were the towns of Aragon, which in 1162 received equal representation, the first recorded instance of representation other than by status. Castile copied the device in 1169. In Sicily Frederick II, in 1232, assigned to each place two representatives. In the French States General and in the German Diet, cities were equally represented. The principle appears again in the Union of Utrecht in the Netherlands, and the Swiss Confederation.

Meantime it had become firmly implanted in the English Constitution. The basis of English representation originally, and through centuries, was always organic, never personal. Parliament represented land rather than men. As long as the feudal system persisted, the agents of the communities came to Westminster as vassals.[1] Electors voted not because they were men, nor even because they were Englishmen, but because they were freeholders of a particular county, or because they were citizens or burgesses of a particular city or town. It was representation not of interests nor of opinions, nor of population as a mere aggregate of individuals, but of population organized. Men were regarded not merely as men, but as neighbors.[2]

This was the inevitable result of the circumstances under which Parliament began. We have seen that the House of Commons grew out of the representation of the communities, not the people, for dealings with the King. The members were agents of groups of persons territorially defined — counties and boroughs. As originally each community bargained through its agents about its own taxes, without regard to other communities, it was of no consequence to any one of them that another, perhaps

[1] A. F. Pollard, *The Evolution of Parliament*, 157.
[2] W. E. Hearn, *The Government of England*, 470.

smaller and poorer, sent the same number of agents. When creditors send lawyers to represent them in a bankruptcy proceeding, no creditor expects to employ lawyers in number proportionate to the size of his claim, and no group of creditors retains lawyers in proportion to their own number. So here at the outset there was no occasion whatever for any question of population or apportionment.

The same conclusion will be reached if adhesion is given to another theory of the origin of English representative institutions, that advanced by Professor H. J. Ford in his book on "Representative Government." Combating vigorously the theory that these institutions were of Teutonic origin, and going to an extreme in rejecting suggestions of Anglo-Saxon influence, he held that we must look to the church for the source, and particularly to the monastic orders, which developed rapidly in England in the same century when Parliament took shape. At first, on the Continent, these orders were without organic bond, but as they grew in numbers and power, and spread through various countries, they felt the need of united action. It chanced that this led to definite, organized representation on an important scale in matters religious at the same period in which it appeared in England in matters political. Professor Ford saw in this much more than a coincidence.

Especially in the Dominican order did he find origins. To the yearly meeting of the provincial chapter, the national parliament of the order, each house at first sent with its own prior a varying number of representatives. In 1265 the number was restricted to two — the prior and one chosen by the community. Simon de Montfort had Dominican advisers, and the summons to the Parliament of 1265 called for two representatives from each borough. When the victor over de Montfort ascended the throne as Edward I, he also had Dominican advisers and for the Parliament of 1282 he sent to each city, borough, or merchant town a summons to send two representatives. Hence Professor Ford reasoned: "The church originated representative institutions; the state adopted them." The deduction may or may not be sound, but anyhow it is clear that through centuries representation was based on community or other associations as units and not as aggregates.

That it was a community affair is shown by the attitude of the communities themselves. Torrington thought itself lucky because it got a charter giving it perpetual exemption from representation in Parliament. Men looked in the same way on the work of representing. The two knights for Oxfordshire fled the country when they were elected to Parliament. Centuries were to pass before the service became a privilege, the burden an object of envy and source of pride.

Another feature of the original conditions was the lack of any motive for being represented save the selfish interest of the community concerned. If any locality saw fit to acquiesce in whatever the King might demand, without negotiation, that locality did nobody else any harm if it saved the costs of sending agents to Parliament. Many instances of this took place in early times. It was explained and justified when in the reign of James I the borough of Agmondesham was restored to what had now become the privilege of sending members, more than three centuries after it had stopped sending. Wendover and Marlow were restored at the same time. In an abstract of the case drawn in 21 Jac. I it was said: "Thirdly, the use in these ancient times being, that the burgesses, attending in Parliament, were maintained at the charge of the boroughs; when the boroughs grew poor, the boroughs only for that reason neglected to send their burgesses to the Parliament; therefore, now seeing they were contented to undergo that burthen, or to choose such burgesses as should bear their own charges, there was no reason to deny that petition."

The argument went on with a proposition significant as showing that by the seventeenth century, men had begun to think of reasons why the sending of members had taken on new aspects of duty: "Lastly, it was urged in behalf of the burgesses, that the liberty of sending burgesses to Parliament is a liberty of that nature and quality, that it cannot be lost by neglect of any borough; for every burgess so sent is a member of the great council of the kingdom, maintained at the charge of the borough; and if such a neglect may be permitted in one borough, so may it be in more, and consequently in all the boroughs in England; and then it might follow that, for want of burgesses, there would be no Parliament." [1]

This recognized that Parliament was necessary to the welfare of the kingdom as a whole. The idea was brought to America by the colonists. In 1670 the Virginia Assembly enacted that any

[1] John, Earl Russell, *Essay on the History of the English Government and Constitution*, ed. of 1866, 173, 174.

county which failed to send two burgesses should be fined 10,000 pounds of tobacco.[1] The Plymouth records have this entry, October 20, 1646, "Committees" being the name used then for Deputies: "It is enacted that if any township being orderly thereto required shall neglect or refuse to elect and choose Committees according to the two former orders, the town so neglecting or refusing to be fined to the government's use 40s. and every Committee so chosen and makes not his personal appearance in the Court at the day appointed there to do his service, be fined 20s. unless he can show a reason approved by the Court."[2]

As time went on the importance of a full representation dwindled and the practice grew of omitting the election of some or all representatives in towns that could ill afford to pay their charges. In fact up to Revolutionary times representation in the General Court of Massachusetts was looked on rather as a burden than as a right. In 1745, before any troubles with the mother country arose, out of 132 towns, only 71 were represented, so that nearly half were without spokesmen. And long after the Revolution towns omitted the sending of representatives whenever they saw fit to take the chance of a fine that the State Constitution empowered the House to impose. At first it was naturally thought unconstitutional for a town to pass a solemn vote not to do what the Constitution seemed to require, and for not doing which a town would be liable to punishment. So we find the memorialists in the case of Josiah Puffer of Westminster (1790) asserting that "the principle held out and acted upon, that every town has a right to vote they will not send a member to the General Court, strikes at the very nerves of the Constitution, and throws the people into anarchy at once." Decisions of the House, however, were to the contrary, and in 1815 the Justices gave their opinion that although to send a representative was a corporate duty as well as a corporate right, for the neglect of which the House might impose a fine, yet this neglect they were under no obligation by the Constitution to punish, and "if the House may excuse the delinquency, we think it clear that a town may constitutionally vote not to send, and so incur the risk of a fine, or trust to the clemency of the House." The practice continued beyond the middle of the century. Here is a typical entry in the Resolves of 1851: "Resolves abating fines

[1] Hening, *Virginia Statutes at Large*, ii, 282.
[2] *Plymouth Colony Records*, xi, 54.

to towns for not sending representatives. Whereas, the towns hereafter mentioned were fined in the several sums annexed to their respective names, for not sending a representative to the General Court the last year — that is to say — Hamilton, $49.23; Holliston, $64.00," and so on for about fifty towns. Few things in our political history are more curious than the complete change in this regard since then. It would to-day astonish most men if they were told that within the lifetime of some of us communities still evaded the election of members of the Legislature.

In England numbers began to be recognized by the Reform Act of 1832, but only to a small degree. The agitation for that Act had begun long before with demand for representation wholly by numbers. After Major Cartwright had advanced the new theory in 1776 and Dr. John Jebb had taken it up in 1779, the Duke of Richmond followed, in 1780, propounding in the House of Lords a comprehensive scheme of reform, in a bill which the brief record of that day states occupied an hour and a half in reading. This measure, after declaring the right of suffrage to be in male persons of twenty-one, went on to prescribe that a list of the number of voters should be taken in every parish, and returns of them made to the Lord Chancellor. The total was to be divided by 558 (the number of members then in the House), and the quotient should be the number by which one member of Parliament was to be elected. Every county was to be divided into as many districts as it contained quotients of this nature, and these districts were to be called boroughs.

Assuming that numbers should be a factor in representation, there was certainly good ground for the Duke's demand of reform. He found that not more than 6,000 men returned a clear majority in the House of Commons. It was alleged in the petition of the Society of the Friends of the People, in 1793, that 84 individuals absolutely returned 157 members to Parliament; that 70 influential men secured the return of 150 members; and that, in this manner, 307 members — being the majority of the House before the union with Ireland — were returned to Parliament by 154 patrons; of whom 40 were peers. The author of No. 56 of "The Federalist," giving Burgh's "Political Disquisitions" as authority, said: "The number of inhabitants in the two kingdoms of England and Scotland cannot be stated at less than eight millions. The representatives of these eight millions in the House of Commons amount to 558. Of this number one ninth

are elected by 364 persons, and one half, by 5723 persons." In
1821 Mr. Lambton stated he was prepared to prove by evidence,
at the bar of the House, that 180 individuals returned, by nomination or otherwise, 350 members.

Accustomed as we are to numbers as the predominant factor
in representation, inevitably at first blush we wonder how anything more than a mere statement of these things was necessary
to procure change. Yet reform did not come until after the most
bitter parliamentary struggle England ever saw. This is intelligible only by remembering that England had never known
representation by numbers. Furthermore, many thoughtful,
sincere, disinterested men believed numbers ought not to be a
factor in representation. Study their arguments without prejudice and you will find that these did not lack logic and strength.
Indeed he must be sanguine and easily satisfied who thinks that
even yet the wisdom of the revolution is established beyond
dispute.

The Reform Bill of 1832 but indirectly recognized population.
It did not give any town representation simply because it was a
town with inhabitants who ought to be represented. However,
it extended the limits of small boroughs to take in surrounding
parishes, it formed unions of boroughs, it divided counties into
sections, and in other particulars made population a factor. Sir
C. P. Ilbert, the best present-day authority on Parliament, gives
a much more recent date to the change. "As to the distribution
of seats," he says, "the Act of 1885 made a departure from the
principle of local representation, and approximated to the principle of electoral districts with equal population. The ancient
idea of the representation of communities, or organized bodies of
men, has thus given way to that of representation of a number of
men, grouped only for the purpose of election." [1]

Our forefathers brought here the idea of organic or geographic
representation. When the first legislative assembly in the new
world was summoned to meet, at James City in Virginia in 1619,
nothing was more natural than that each of the eleven plantations, towns, and hundreds should send two Burgesses. It is not
so easy to understand how it came about that to the Assembly of
1629, of the twenty-three places represented, some sent two, some
four, and some as many as six Burgesses; though "for the Eastern
shore no Burgesses did appear." Yet since apparently the num-

[1] *Parliament*, 60.

ber to be sent, if any, was left to the discretion of each place, the circumstance is not to be held as an indication that numbers were yet taken into account. In 1634 the hundreds and plantations were grouped in eight shires, to be governed as the shires in England, the designation being "counties" after 1643. At times after the shires were formed, plantations were represented, and from 1629 to 1645 some sent as many as six Burgesses. On one occasion a shire or county sent eight. For the sake of greater regularity an act was passed in 1645 limiting county representation to four Burgesses, except that James City should send five for the county and one for Jamestown, and this may have been the first recognition of numbers in Virginia. In 1660–61 to save expense the representation was reduced from four to two.

In 1666 we find proof that the rights of the colony at large had come to be thought superior to those of the district. Several of the counties sent but one member; only Isle of Wight had three; the others had two each. At the October session Isle of Wight County proposed to dismiss its extra member, but the Assembly refused to allow it, because after "legal and deliberate examination of his return,... it cannot consist with the honour of the house to dismiss him from attendance." [1] This, it will be seen, was a renunciation of the doctrine of agency. It was a step toward the modern view that once representatives are chosen, they become merged in the general assembly and are to serve for the general welfare.

Three years later, in 1669, all discretion of choice was taken from the counties, by a law compelling each to send neither more nor less than two Burgesses. This established the system of representation by counties that was to last until long after the Revolution.

Massachusetts early began to pay some attention to the comparative size of constituencies. At a General Court, September 8, 1635, it was ordered that thereafter, no town in the plantation that had not ten freemen resident in it should send any deputy to the General Courts; those that had above ten, and under twenty, not above one; betwixt twenty and forty, not above two; and those that had above forty, three, if they would, but not more.[2] On the 13th of March, 1638–39, it was ordered that no town should send more than two deputies.[3]

[1] Hening, *Virginia Statutes at Large*, ii, 253.
[2] *Records of the Colony of the Mass. Bay in N.E.*, i, 178.   [3] *Ibid.*, 254.

It will be noticed that an element of discretion entered into these orders. This is more clearly shown by an entry of May, 1642: "The Court left it to the liberty of the towns to send but a deputy apiece, if they please, to the next session of this Court." For two centuries and more Massachusetts in practice held to this view that representation was primarily a privilege to be exercised in some degree at the pleasure of the places represented, the old English view. Sometimes when towns were incorporated, as in the case of Palmer (1752), permission was asked and granted to be exempt from sending a Representative. As in England, so here, expense was the practical consideration. It appears, indeed, that as early as 1644 this led to an attempt to revise the system of representation. The General Court voted, November 13, to lay before the people a new plan for the lower House: "Whereas we having found by experience that the charge of this General Court groweth very great and burdensome, in regard to the continual increase of deputies sent into the same, and further foreseeing that as towns increase the number will be still augmented, to the unsupportable burden of this commonwealth," the shires should choose deputies — Suffolk six, Middlesex six, Essex and Norfolk together eight. No record of the result appears.

When the various ordinances respecting Representatives were formed into one in 1658, the provision stood: "No town shall send more than two deputies and no town that hath not to the numbers of twenty freemen shall send more than one deputy; and such plantations as have not ten freemen shall send none, but such freemen may vote with the next town, in the choice of their deputies, till this court take further notice." The larger places no longer had the right to three Representatives. It was returned to them, however, by an act of March 16, 1680–81, only to be again taken away by the province charter of 1691. By this each town and place was "empowered to elect and depute two persons and no more, to serve for, and represent them respectively." The charter also gave authority to the General Court, "from time to time, to direct, appoint, and declare, what number each county, town, and place, should elect and depute to serve for, and represent them respectively." The use of the word "county" was probably unintentional. At any rate it had no result, for counties have never been represented as such in the Massachusetts House. The Act of 1692 provided, "That henceforth every town within this province, consisting of the number of forty freeholders, and other inhabitants, qualified by charter to elect, shall, and hereby are enjoined to choose and send one freeholder for their representative; and every town consisting of the number of one hundred and twenty freeholders and other inhabitants, qualified as aforesaid, or upwards, may send two such representatives; and each town of the number of thirty freeholders and other inhabitants qualified as aforesaid, or upwards, under forty, are at liberty to send one or not. And all towns under thirty freeholders, may send one to represent them, or join with the next town, in the choice of their representatives, they paying a proportionable part of the charge." [1]

An exception was made for Boston, giving it four Representatives, and the ratio of representation was subsequently changed, but no new provisions were introduced through the life of the Province respecting the union of towns and districts in the election.

In various instances, under the provincial charter, the Legislature incorporated districts, and invested them with all the power of towns, except that of sending a Representative. Some of these districts were left entirely without a voice in the choice of a member of the General Court — for instance, Ware and Natick. Others had liberty to join with neighboring towns.

The creation of new towns with Representatives proved a more serious matter, for it developed one of the causes of friction between the province and the Crown. Governor Shirley in 1742 complained to the Lords of Trade that the enlarged membership of the House, due to the continual division of townships and the settlement of new territory, rendered it unwieldy and caused it to overshadow the Council, thereby destroying the proper balance between the two bodies established by the charter. To be sure, he reported that the 160 towns, most of them entitled to send two each, generally did not send more than 120 all told, but he pointed out that they had it in their power to double or treble their number in case of what might seem to them an emergency. The Board concurred in these views and instructed him not to pass any further act erecting a new township or dividing an old without insisting upon a suspending clause, that is, a clause suspending the operation of the act until approved by the King in Council. Massachusetts held that under the charter it was exempt from suspending clauses, and rather than establish a prece-

[1] Stat. 4 of William and Mary, c. 19.

dent or come to an open break, it refrained from adding to the membership of the House for several years.

In 1761 the Board admitted that the restriction was in conflict both with the charter and with an act of the General Court that had been confirmed. So it withdrew the instructions and advised the Governor to get, whenever possible, incorporating acts without the privilege of sending Representatives. This, however, was far from ending the trouble. Disputes continued, and when the province had thrown off its shackles one of the early acts of an independent General Court, July, 1775, had this preamble: "Whereas there are divers acts or laws heretofore made and passed by former general courts or assemblies of this colony for the incorporation of towns and districts, which against common right, and in derogation of the rights granted to the inhabitants of this colony by the charter, contain an exception of the right and privilege of choosing and sending a representative to the great and general court or assembly." The act went on to provide that every town with thirty or more freeholders and other inhabitants qualified by charter to vote in the election of a Representative, should have the right "to elect and depute one or more persons, being freeholders and resident in such town or district, to serve for and represent them."

Connecticut, starting with equal representation of towns, was throughout the colonial period more consistent than Massachusetts in adhering to the principle. Rhode Island, on the other hand, had recognition of comparative numbers almost from the start. The charter of 1663, under which she lived until 1843, directed that the Deputies should not exceed six for Newport, four each for Providence, Portsmouth, and Warwick, and two for each other place, town, or city. In New Hampshire as late as the year 1773, of one hundred and forty-seven towns, forty-six only were represented. They had thirty-four members, several towns being classified together, for the choice of one. Nottingham and Concord, though populous and more than forty years old, had not once been admitted to the privilege of representation; and this was the case with many other towns, which, though not of so long settlement, yet contained more inhabitants than some others that had always enjoyed the privilege. No uniform system of representation had been adopted. None could be established by law, because the Governor claimed it as part of the royal prerogative to call Representatives from new towns; and this prerogative was exercised without any regard to the rights, the petitions, or the sentiments of the people.[1]

Penn's Charter of Liberties of 1682 left the allotment of Pennsylvania Representatives to the Council to propose and the Assembly to resolve, but it was to be "most equally to the Division of the Hundreds and Counties which the Country shall hereafter be divided into." The Charter of Privileges of 1701 allotted four to each county, "or a greater number at any Time, as the Governor and Assembly shall agree."

Maryland began with the hundred as the unit of representation, changing to the county in 1654, and so continuing, with the addition of one city in 1671. Trouble rose from the action of Lord Baltimore in 1670 in directing that though each county should elect four Delegates, only two should be summoned to attend. Although this was put on the score of expense, the advantage it gave to the Lord Proprietor was clear and the freemen vigorously protested, with the result that the Governor promised to fix the number to be chosen, summon all elected, and issue writs to fill vacancies. Five years later he broke his word, summoning only two from a county and refusing to have vacancies filled. The dispute ended with concession on both sides — vacancies to be filled and only two from a county to be summoned. In 1692 the representation was made four from a county, and it so continued until the Revolutionary War.

Locke's "Fundamental Constitutions" contemplated dividing Carolina into precincts, with one "member of parliament" from each. The division into precincts was not at once made, and at the outset twenty members at large were elected at Charleston. In 1695 the freemen were called together to decide about the number of Representatives. Twenty was the number fixed upon for Berkeley County and ten for Colleton, while Craven was omitted altogether. Dissatisfaction grew. In 1716 election by parishes was enacted. These had been created as a result of an act passed in 1704 establishing the church of England in the colony and dividing the colony into parishes, each to contain a church presided over by an Episcopal clergyman. It does not appear that there was originally any idea of using these as a basis for political action, but the convenience of such a step commended itself, and so the parish became the political as well as the religious unit of South Carolina. The colony had trouble with

[1] Jeremy Belknap, *History of New Hampshire*, III, 192.

the Proprietors over the election act of 1716 and it was modified somewhat by following acts, but in substance it continued until the Revolution. In 1716 the number of members of the Assembly was put at thirty, which was increased to thirty-six in 1719. By the division of old parishes and the creation of new, the number had reached forty-eight in 1775, with a very unequal distribution of Representatives.

In the first attempt at confederation made in America, that of the "United Colonies of New England," in 1643, each of the four colonies was represented in its council by two delegates, although the burdens of taxation and military service were allotted by population. Five years later Massachusetts demanded another Representative on the score of her numbers, or an equalization between taxes and representation. This was denied in the reorganization of the confederacy. The formation of the Province of Massachusetts by the charter of 1691 had one characteristic of a federation in that the twenty-eight Councilors or Assistants were allotted respectively to the four regions combined, and some regard was paid to numbers by giving eighteen to the territory formerly that of Massachusetts Bay, four to that of Plymouth, three to that formerly called the Province of Maine, and one to the territory between the Sagadahoc River and Nova Scotia. Benjamin Franklin submitted to the commissioners from seven colonies who met at Albany in June, 1765, a "plan of union" under which the membership in a general council with legislative powers should be distributed every three years among the colonies, by the "proportion of money arising out of each colony to the general treasury."

Such in general was the situation in the colonies at the approach of the Revolution. Nowhere did representation bear any uniform relation to the number of electors. Here and there the factor of size had been crudely recognized. It took the travail of the birth of a nation to make men think they had rights as men, as individual men, and that each was entitled to a share in government equal to that of his neighbor. Although like every other political idea, this was a development, a step on from something that had been before, it came nearer than most political ideas to being an invention, a discovery.

NUMBERS IN THE STATES

If before the revolutionary epoch anybody anywhere had proposed an apportionment of representatives in strict ratio to population, the proposal had attracted no attention nor any support, much less any attempt at execution. Perhaps Patrick Henry should have the credit of first urging the idea publicly. At any rate he was the first man of prominence to get a hearing for it. At the first session of the Continental Congress, in Philadelphia, September 5, 1774, James Duane of New York proposed a committee to prepare regulations "particularly on the method of voting, whether by colonies, by poll, or by interests." Patrick Henry, declaring that he sat "not as a Virginian but an American," urged a "national" system of representation based on free citizens, excluding slaves; but the Congress, as John Adams reminded it, had accurate information neither as to the wealth nor the population of the colonies, and it was at length voted "that in determining questions in this Congress each colony or province shall have one vote, the Congress not being possessed of or able to procure materials for ascertaining the importance of each colony." The precedent thus established of necessity was accepted in practice and became the rule of procedure in the Continental Congress, first by consent and later by the Articles of Confederation. Proportional representation was urged by Virginia, but steadily voted down by the smaller states.[1]

The idea next appeared in Massachusetts, and now was full-grown. After the General Court in 1775 had declared that every town had a right to be represented, the inequality of the old system became more apparent than ever and the number of Representatives became what was then thought too large, although the total, 260, twice what it had ever been before, would be doubled, almost trebled, in years to come. The grievance led a convention of delegates from the towns of Essex County, at Ipswich, April 25, 1776, to adopt a memorial to the Legislature in which it was declared: "If representation is equal, it is perfect; as far as it deviates from this equality, so far it is imperfect, and approaches to the state of slavery; and the want of a just weight in representation is an evil nearly akin to being wholly destitute of it. An inequality of representation has been justly esteemed the cause, which has, in a great degree, sapped the foundation of

[1] Talcott Williams, "Apportionment," *Lalor's Cyclopædia of Political Science,* I, 103.

the once admired, but now tottering fabric of the British empire; and we fear that if a different mode of representation from the present is not adopted in this colony, our Constitution will not continue to the late period of time which the glowing heart of every American now anticipates.... We cannot realize that our honors, our wise political fathers, have adverted to the present inequality of representation in this colony, to the growth of the evil, or to the fatal consequences which will probably ensue from the continuance of it."

Probably in part as a result of this memorial, a law was passed beginning, "Whereas, The present representation of this Colony is not so equal as it ought to be, and this Court being desirous to have the same as proportionate as it can in the present state of the Colony be made"; and going on to give three members to each town with two hundred and twenty freeholders, with one more for each additional hundred. Then followed the effort to frame a Constitution in 1777, which failed partly by reason of dissatisfaction with its handling of this very matter. Again was the county of Essex influential, for another convention at Ipswich put forth the document now known as "The Essex Result," powerfully presenting the defects of the Constitution that had been submitted, and supposed to have been the chief influence in its defeat. Here we read: "The rights of representation should be so equally and impartially distributed, that the representatives should have the same views and interests with the people at large. They should think, feel, and act like them, and, in fine, should be an exact miniature of their constituents. They should be, if we may use the expression, the whole body-politic, with all its property, rights, and privileges, reduced to a smaller scale, every part being diminished in just proportion. To pursue the metaphor, if, in addition to the representation of freemen, any ten are reduced into one, all the other hundreds should have just the same reduction.... Let these representatives be apportioned among the respective counties, in proportion to their number of freemen."

Strong arguments to the contrary must have also been presented, for we find that when Samuel Cooper sent from Boston to Benjamin Franklin a copy of the proposed Constitution, Cooper wrote: " ... which has been rejected in a very full meeting of this Town, and is like to be by many others for different reasons; particularly, because in the opinion of the maritime towns,

Representation is too unequal, while in the opinion of others it is too nearly equal."

At first it looked as if the Essex reasoning might make the more headway, for when Mount Washington was incorporated, in 1779, it was denied a Representative. In the same year the town-meeting of Boston, voting instructions to its Representatives in regard to the proposed Convention for framing a Constitution, recommended "that in order to avoid so numerous an Assembly as will take place if each Town and District send Delegates in proportion to their numbers,... the General Assembly fix upon a Competent number, and call upon the Several Counties to send Delegates to form this Convention in proportion to their respective numbers." Such an attack on the ancient prerogative of every village could not be endured. The small towns rallied to each other's support, and in the Convention itself succeeded in securing constitutional assurance of one Representative to every existing town, no matter how little. Almost humorously they prefaced this gift by saying "in order to provide for a representation of the citizens of the commonwealth, founded upon the principle of equality." That must have been intended for the provision later in the Article, giving an additional Representative to towns with more than 375 ratable polls, with one more for every 225 above that. Furthermore, no town thereafter incorporated was to get a Representative unless it had 150 polls.

The conception on which the main provision was based, found expression in various Opinions of the Justices of the Supreme Court. In 1811 they said (7 Mass. 526): "The right of sending Representatives is corporate, vested in the town; and the right of choosing them is personal, vested in the legal voters. Because the right of sending a Representative is corporate, if the town, by a legal corporate act, vote not to send a Representative, none can be legally chosen by a minority dissenting from that vote." This was reiterated in 1815, the question then being whether a town could constitutionally vote not to send a Representative, and whether such vote would be binding on a minority of the voters. The Court held (15 Mass. 537) that a town might constitutionally so vote, and that the vote would be binding. In an Opinion in 1826, given in answer to a question about filling vacancies in the House, the Court went so far as to say (3 Pick. 519): "Every town, having the number of polls required by the Constitution, has a right to be represented in the popular branch of the Legislature, and this is a valuable and important right, of which the inhabitants ought not to be deprived without their own consent."

The Convention of 1820 had proposed that towns with less than 1,200 inhabitants should elect every other year, except in the year when the valuation of estates was to be determined, but the amendment was rejected by a vote of 9,904 to 20,729. The system of having each town represented was destined to prevail just two hundred years — from 1636 to 1836. By amendment ratified in 1836, in the case of towns with less than three hundred ratable polls, the number of their polls was to be multiplied by ten, the product divided by three hundred, to determine in how many years of each decade they should have a Representative. The weak point in this was that during some years of each decade the small towns were wholly unrepresented in the lower branch, unless they chose to unite with others, which they never did.

Here was a departure from the old theory, but that theory had by no means been abandoned. When Robert C. Winthrop, as Speaker of the House of Representatives, had occasion to give an exhaustive ruling on the votes of interested members, February 19, 1840, he said the real question before the House was, whether the city of Boston should be deprived of two of its members legally chosen and duly qualified, and the town of Dorchester of one third of its rightful representation, on an allegation that the private interests of the members referred to were inconsistent with a faithful discharge of their duty to their constituents. It was the right of the towns and cities, and not of the members themselves, which was really at stake in this and all similar cases. And gentlemen would do well to bear in mind, that though the controversy might now relate to a city and a town which perhaps could afford to spare a vote or two, it might next be raised in relation to such as had but one Representative, and thus disfranchise them altogether on particular questions.[1]

Note the whole atmosphere of this was one of town representation as such. Arrayed against it was the theory of individual equality, as set forth, for instance, by Charles Francis Adams at Quincy in 1853. "I maintain," he said, "that the moment a majority in a republic assumes to draw a distinction with the intent that certain men shall be enabled to enjoy twice or thrice the amount of political power which an equal number of other

[1] *Addresses and Speeches*, i, 274.

men are to possess, that is the hour when tyranny begins." The Adams theory was destined soon to prevail, for in 1857 the towns at last were vanquished and the district system, based as nearly as practicable on numerical equality, was put into effect. This was not, however, numerical equality of inhabitants, for the Know-Nothing movement was at its height and the hostility to the unnaturalized foreign-born kept them out of the count, "legal voters" being made the basis and to this day continuing so to be. Otherwise the only officially recognized inequalities since then have been the allotting of one Representative each to the islands of Martha's Vineyard and Nantucket (under the guise of counties). The decennial division has given the chance to show a little mercy to counties growing slowly or dwindling, but the favoritism has been of no great consequence.

No other New England State has followed Massachusetts in making every man's vote carry weight equal to that of every other man. New Hampshire has come nearest. Her original Constitution, brief and crude, the first framed by an American Commonwealth, apportioned the members of the upper branch by counties. The Constitution of 1784 allotted her twelve Senators to her five counties, evidently in a general way corresponding to population. It permitted the Legislature to rearrange, with the proviso that there should never be more than ten nor less than five districts. In 1792 came the substitution of twelve single districts, changed in 1902 to twenty-four. In the Constitution of 1784 it was directed that in assigning the number of Senators to be elected by the respective districts, the General Court "shall govern themselves by the proportion of public taxes paid by said district." In 1792 this was changed to "direct taxes," and the provision was preserved in the Constitution of 1902. In 1912 the voters rejected an amendment increasing the Senate to thirty-five members and dividing the State into senatorial districts on the basis of population. Representatives have always been allotted by towns; those larger than the standard getting additional Representatives in proportion to population; those smaller being at first classed with other little towns, and now having representation for a proportionate part of the time. Each ward of a city is for purposes of representation treated as if it were a town.

Maine comes next in paying regard to population. She has always apportioned her Representatives by counties, but this has no great significance, since there is further apportionment to towns and groups of towns. As at the start, she still gives one to each town of 1500 inhabitants, and up to seven if the town has 26,250; but no town is to have more than seven, with the result that the larger places deem themselves partly disfranchised. Senatorial districts are to conform as near as may be to county lines. In 1869 it was provided that towns might be divided for the election of Representatives.

When Rhode Island framed her first Constitution, in 1842, although it specified that apportionment was to be by population, yet it stipulated that each town and city should have at least one Representative, and no town or city should have more than one sixth of the total; and that no town or city should be divided in the choice of Representatives. Since 1909 the provision has been that no town or city is to have more than one fourth the total number, which is limited to one hundred. Single districts were authorized in 1909. Apportionment is to be with population in view, but each town is to have at least one Representative. Each town and city has one Senator.

Chester Lloyd Jones has said that in Rhode Island there are twenty towns with a combined population of 41,068. "Their representatives control the Senate. The total population of the State is 542,610. Consequently, a majority vote drawn from seven and one half per cent of the population controls the policy of the Upper House." [1] This is a good example of the *post hoc, propter hoc* argument frequently used in discussing not only apportionment problems, but also many others relating to suffrage and representation. Once in a million years, seven and one half per cent of the population of Rhode Island might control the policy of her Senate, but it would be a result of the doctrine of chances, not of the apportionment system. All we can safely say is that the rural vote counts for more than the city vote.

Vermont has always apportioned Representatives by towns. The Constitution of 1786 directed that for seven years towns with eighty or more taxable inhabitants should send two Representatives, smaller towns one; and after "the said septenary" all should send one each. The provision was repeated in the Constitution of 1793. From the beginning of the nineteenth century, one each has been the rule. When the Senate was created, in 1836, each county was to be entitled to one Senator, and the rest

[1] "Rotten Boroughs of New England," *North American Review*, April, 1913.

of the thirty Senators were to be allotted to the counties on the
population basis after each census.

Connecticut is the notorious example of town representation.
Quires, reams of paper, and gallons of ink have been used in denouncing its inequities. Yet it persists, to the horror of those who
make a Bible out of the arithmetic, and to the contentment of
some who think government exists for results rather than to make
sure that the individuals composing a fraction of the population
known as the electorate carry equal weight. Connecticut has always apportioned its Representatives by towns. Starting with
two apiece, after the Revolution it gave but one each to various
newly incorporated towns that are now sizeable places. In 1874
it graciously gave two to each town of more than five thousand
inhabitants, without disturbing the existing representation of
smaller places. The large cities writhe, but the people will not
change the old system. In 1902 they rejected a revised Constitution that had been submitted as the result of four and a half
months of Convention deliberation. It was designed principally
to rectify inequalities of legislative representation. It would
have increased the Senate from thirty-six to forty-five members,
and have given to towns of two thousand population two Representatives instead of one, to towns of fifty thousand three Representatives, and to those of one hundred thousand four.

New York has never accepted the numerical theory *in toto*.
Joseph H. Choate, informing the Convention of 1894 to this
effect, argued that the counties had been formed as political
divisions for the very purpose of being the centers of home rule,
if you please, of local government — and that every one of them
had the right, and the equal right, of representation. If there
were sixty counties, and but sixty Representatives, the Representatives must be distributed among these sixty counties, upon
every doctrine that has ever prevailed in the State. As a result of
such views, no county in New York is to have more than a third
of the Senators; no two counties adjoining, or "separated only
by public waters" (a provision aimed at the metropolis), are to
have more than half the total. Every county but one is to have
at least one Assemblyman. Nevertheless even in New York
population is not without defenders. In 1918 the Court of Appeals, in the case of People *v.* Voorhis (119 N.E. 106), laid down
the rule that when a Legislature reapportions Congressional districts after a decennial census, it does not thereby exhaust its

power or completely discharge its duty, but is under a continuing obligation to keep on redistricting the State as often as the shifting of population may make it necessary or advisable.

New Jersey reached the population basis in 1844, when the Legislature was directed to apportion among the counties on the basis of population. The original Constitution (1776) had assigned three members of the Assembly to each county, permitting the Legislature to add to or diminish the number, when they might judge it "equitable and proper, on the principles of more equal representation." The Senate has always consisted of one from each county.

In Delaware from 1776 to 1897 both Senators and Representatives were chosen by counties, with no regard to population. The constitution of 1897 created thirty-five Representative districts with boundaries minutely set forth, one county getting fifteen, two ten each. One county got seven Senatorial districts, the others five each, likewise specified in detail.

PENNSYLVANIA FIRST

To Pennsylvania belongs the credit of first establishing apportionment on the basis of numbers. The Convention of that Province held in Philadelphia January 23, 1775, following the example set by the Continental Congress in the preceding September, had given one vote to the "committee," or what we should now call the delegation, from each county and the city of Philadelphia.[1] Cumberland County with two delegates carried as much weight as Philadelphia with fifty-five. The injustice of this was speedily felt and when in the following year a Constitution for the new State was framed, provision was made for numerical apportionment. For three years Philadelphia and each county should choose six persons to represent them in the General Assembly. "But as representation in proportion to the number of taxable inhabitants is the only principle which can at all times secure liberty, and make the voice of a majority of the people the law of the land," a census should be taken, with the results reported to the Assembly elected in 1778, who should appoint a representation to each county, "in proportion to the number of taxables in such returns." This was to continue for seven years, when there should be another census and apportionment, "and so on septennially forever." In the Constitution of

[1] Hazard, *Register of Pennsylvania*, IV, 133.

1790 we find that after every seven-year census, the number of
Representatives (not less than sixty nor more than one hundred)
was to be fixed by the Legislature, "and apportioned among the
city of Philadelphia and the several counties, according to the
number of taxable inhabitants." The combination of population
and taxable property as the basis for representation lasted until
1873. Why the change was made to population alone by the Convention of that year is not clear. There was little or no debate in
reference thereto. Without serious objection, the long-established practice was swept away.

Maryland began as a state (1776) by allotting four Delegates
to each county. In 1799 it made a specific allotment roughly
corresponding to population, with separate provision for the
city of Baltimore. With minor changes this stood until 1851.
For many years apportionment was one of the chief issues in
State politics, kept at the front by those impatiently seeking a
Constitutional Convention. When they at last got their Convention, apportionment was its knottiest problem. The contest
was long and strenuous, compromise in the end being reached
with difficulty. It provided that the whole number of Delegates
should not be more than eighty-five nor less than sixty; each
county should have at least two; population should be the basis;
and Baltimore should have four more than the most populous
county. In the course of this Convention, Mr. Dashiell, of Som-
erset county, moved to amend the preamble by inserting after
the word "Maryland" the words, "representing the counties,
and city of Baltimore." The object of the amendment was to
assert the theory that the counties and the city of Baltimore
were parties to the compact in their municipal capacities. This
theory of political individuality of the counties had been urged
many times in the Legislature, in the course of the reform agitation, and was referred to in the Convention. Mr. Dashiell's view
of the government of Maryland was that of a confederation of
counties: each county being a separate and distinct community.
He did not regard the counties as sovereignties, because the
State herself had scarcely a principle of sovereignty left after the
formation of the Federal Government.

The basis of this view of the political individuality of the
counties was historical. In the Convention of 1776, which
framed the original Constitution of the State, the counties were
represented equally. In that Convention the voting was by

counties, and not by individuals, except in certain cases, and on
the final adoption of the Constitution. Mr. Dashiell argued that
the right to political existence and equal representation was reserved to each county, and whenever this equal representation
was to be changed, modified, or abolished, it must be done by the
free consent, or acquiescence, of the counties; that it was under
this agreement of equal representation that the counties entered
into the compact of government in 1776.[1] Dashiell's amendment
did not prevail, but his contention has interest. The Constitutions of 1864 and 1867 revised the apportionment on the population basis, with separate provision for Baltimore.

Virginia (1776) gave two Representatives to each county and
the district of West Augusta, one for the city of Williamsburg,
one for the borough of Norfolk, "and a Representative for each
of such other cities and boroughs, as may hereafter be allowed
particular representation by the Legislature." But should a city
or borough dwindle to half the size of any one county, it should
lose its Representative, after seven successive years of being below the mark. As might be expected in the author of the Declaration of Independence with its notion of political equality,
this did not suit Thomas Jefferson. When he came to write his
"Notes on Virginia" (1782), the second of the six "very capital
defects" in her Constitution, which he thought time and trial had
discovered was that "among those who share the representation,
the shares are unequal," because of the distribution of seats by
counties. A short time afterward he prepared a draft of what he
thought would be a better Constitution, in which he provided
that "the number of delegates which each county may send
shall be in proportion to the number of its qualified electors; and
the whole number of delegates for the State shall be so proportioned to the number of qualified electors in it, that they shall
never exceed three hundred, nor be fewer than one hundred; and
if any county be reduced in its qualified electors below the number authorized to send one delegate, let it be annexed to some adjoining county." Even Thomas Jefferson, however, could not
then get such an heretical notion adopted in Virginia. Yet he
doubtless helped largely toward fanning the controversy over
apportionment that lasted for half a century.

The inequality grew as population ratios changed. By 1815
the four Senators from the western part of the State represented

[1] J. W. Harry, *The Maryland Constitution of 1851*, 51.

a white population of about 233,000; while the eastern part, with about 343,000 white voters, had twenty Senators. Attempts for a Convention failed, but the Legislature itself gave some relief by an apportionment made by the Assembly of 1816–17, on the basis of the census of 1810. After a time, further population changes renewed the controversy and at last brought the Convention of 1829–30. The great fight therein was over the question of apportioning on the basis of the white population, or on the so-called Federal basis, that of the United States Constitution. It ended in a compromise, meant to get an average of the two systems.

This did not stop the controversy, for it speedily sprang into vigor again and had much to do with bringing about the next Convention, that of 1850–51. The Constitution of 1830 had allotted a specified part of the delegates to the region west of the Alleghany Mountains; another part to that between the Alleghanies and the Blue Ridge; and the rest to the region between the Blue Ridge and tidewater. This disappeared in 1850–51. Both Senators and Delegates were then allotted by districts separately, and there followed a singular provision for the future. In 1865 if the two Houses could not agree on a scheme of apportionment, the people were to vote on whether they preferred apportionment on the "suffrage basis," i.e., according to the number of voters; or on the "mixed basis," i.e., white inhabitants and taxes paid; or with the Senate on the basis of taxation and the lower branch on the "suffrage basis"; or the Senate on the "mixed" and the House on the "suffrage" basis. The Civil War kept us from knowing how such a complicated referendum would have resulted. The Constitution of 1864 specified the districts, as did that of 1870, leaving reapportionment to the General Assembly without instructions. That of 1902 approved the apportionment just made by the General Assembly, and directed it to reapportion every ten years.

North Carolina began as a State (1776) with one Senator from each county and one from each of six specified towns. This in time led to serious jealousies between the eastern and western parts of the State. By 1835 the counties of the western part, somewhat fewer than those of the eastern, were much the more populous. Since the election of the Governor and other important officials, the judges and the militia officers, was in the Assembly, the predominance therein of the East embittered the

West. The conflict brought the Convention of 1835, which provided that Senators should be elected from districts formed on the basis of public taxation, and that the members of the House of Commons should be apportioned among the counties on the basis of Federal population. This helped the richer East in the Senate, the more populous West in the House. So it stood until in 1857, after a contest of nine years, the property qualification for Senators was abolished. In 1868 the districts were specified in the Constitution, being counties single or grouped, with no reference to taxes; in 1876 population was made the basis for framing districts, with no county to be divided unless entitled to two or more Senators.

The South Carolina Constitution of 1778 after apportioning Senators and Representatives by parishes and districts enumerated in detail, directed that reapportionment seven years later, and then after every fourteen years, should "be proportioned in the most equal and just manner according to the particular and comparative strength and taxable property of the different parts of the same, regard being always had to the number of white inhabitants and such taxable property." No provision on the subject appears in the Constitution of 1790, which again set forth an apportionment specified in detail. In 1808 an amendment introduced a novelty in the shape of a combination of white population and of taxes paid on account of property, as the basis for the assignment of Representatives to the various districts. In 1868 the tax factor was dropped and also the restriction to "white" inhabitants. In 1895 it was definitely set forth that each county should constitute one election district; from two to nine Representatives and one Senator were assigned to each.

Georgia's development of an apportionment system has been interesting. Her first Constitution (1777) contained a unique survival of the ambassador principle in the Council, the body that served as a quasi-Senate for a dozen years. There were two Councilors from each county (except those not yet entitled to send ten members to the Assembly), and it was required that they should not vote individually, but by counties. More advanced views, however, prevailed in the matter of Representatives. They were allotted to counties on a population basis, with these curious additions: "The port and town of Savannah shall be allowed four members to represent their trade. The port and town of Sunbury shall be allowed two members to represent their trade." In 1798 special provision for Savannah and Sunbury disappeared, and allotment was made to counties on the basis of their population, no one to have more than four. In 1843, by amendment, a novel method appeared; the thirty-seven counties having the most population were to have two Representatives each, the others one, with redivision to be made on the same plan after each enumeration of the inhabitants. In 1868 this was modified to give the largest six counties three Representatives each; the next thirty-one, two each; and the rest one apiece. In 1877 this was further changed to give the largest six, three each; the next twenty-six, two each; and the remaining one hundred and five, one each.

CHAPTER XVI

APPORTIONMENT UNDER THE UNION

THE Articles of Confederation adopted by the States in 1777 provided that the cost of government should be defrayed out of a common treasury, to be supplied by the States in proportion to the value of all land, buildings, and improvements within each State. The Congress was to provide a mode of estimating the value thereof, but this was found impracticable by reason of differences as to assessment, and in 1783 the Congress urged the States to authorize their delegates to provide for a census of population that should serve as a basis for apportioning the contributions required. The States refused so to do and the Confederation became more and more embarrassed by the inability to extract from the States anywhere near enough money to meet the public need. This was probably the most serious cause for the Convention of 1787.

The Convention quickly divided into two camps — one made up of the men who feared that if in the Congress to be created each State had a vote equal to that of every other, as had been the case under the Confederation, the small, poor States would fleece the few large, wealthy States — the other of the men who feared that if the States were represented in proportion to their numbers, the larger States would take undue advantage of the smaller. This threatened to be a fatal obstacle. Only by compromise and concession could it be escaped. After weeks of dispute, in the darkest hour, when the outlook seemed hopeless, the basis of a bargain was proposed, seemingly in large part through the conciliatory efforts of Doctor Benjamin Franklin. The States should have equal representation in the upper branch, representation by numbers in the lower. Many days were to pass before this could be fully worked out, but the result of this trade was the legislative framework of the Nation as it exists to-day.

Nowhere in the discussion, as far as it is recorded, did any one urge the representation of men as men. Be it remembered that was a new idea in the world, born only eleven years before, in London, and not yet familiar on this side of the ocean. There can be no shadow of question that populations were accepted as a measure of material interests — landed, agricultural, industrial, commercial, in short, property. This appears in the quite arbitrary grant of representation proportionate to three fifths of the number of slaves. They were not to be represented because they were human beings; their owners were to be represented in the ratio of ownership of human property. Again, only taxed Indians were to be counted, for they alone of the red men had any property. Most convincing of all, "representatives and direct taxes" were coupled in the paragraph providing for apportionment among the States "according to their respective numbers."

In view of all this, it would seem indisputable that citizens and aliens were not as such in the minds of the men who wrote the Constitution nor of those who were delegates to the ratifying conventions. Our fathers meant to apportion the membership of the House on the basis of all who dwelt within the respective States. Property was the basis, not humanity. Such political philosophy might not prevail to-day were the Constitution to be written anew, but until the Constitution is changed, it must be construed as it was meant to be construed.

Representative Homer Hoch, of Kansas, brought the subject into the seventieth Congress.[1] Proposing that by a constitutional amendment "aliens" be coupled with "Indians not taxed," and so excluded, he showed that in reapportionment on the basis of the 1920 census, seventeen States would either gain or lose members of the House, New York losing as many as four. Of course this instantly brought New York members to their feet in expostulation. The effect on Presidential elections might be more serious, since the electors correspond in number to Congressional representation and the change proposed might easily result in altering the balance of the totals. In general it would lessen the power of those States where immigrants most gather, the States with large urban centers, and increase agrarian influence in national affairs. At the moment the matter was not put forward in a manner to secure a vote, nor was there at first any test when it was brought up again, in the seventy-first Congress, this time by Representative Henry St. George Tucker, of Virginia, a former President of the American Bar Association and an authoritative expounder of constitutional law. His recognized eminence in that

[1] *Congressional Record*, December 15 and 20, 1928.

field would earn respect for his argument despite the fact of its novelty and that it would upset an interpretation of language accepted for a century and a half. The Constitution had said that "numbers" should be determined by adding to the whole number of free "persons," including those bound to service for a term of years, and excluding Indians not taxed, three fifths of all other persons. Mr. Tucker contended that the word "persons" did not include unnaturalized foreigners, aliens. When the Constitution was framed, he averred, there were practically no aliens in the country. Beginning the document with, "We, the people of the United States," the framers could not have meant to include aliens as part thereof. Mr. Tucker held it was never intended to give aliens any part in the government of our country.[1]

The contention was so powerfully presented that sympathizers plucked up courage enough to disregard the question of constitutionality and try to accomplish the object in view by an amendment to the pending census and apportionment bill. To the general surprise they won, in spite of the opposition from the cities and regions where there are large alien populations, as well as on the part of members who believed a constitutional amendment necessary. However, the vote was quickly followed by a motion to amend the bill further for the purpose of giving effect to the requirement of the Fourteenth Amendment that when the right to vote is denied or abridged, the representation of the State shall be reduced proportionately. It is, of course, well known that in the Southern States the vote of the colored man has been virtually eliminated, but Congress has never set the Constitution at work in this particular. Year after year Representative George Holden Tinkham of Massachusetts had sought vigorously but vainly to get a vote in the matter. At last his chance came. To retaliate for the vote about aliens, enough members supported Mr. Tinkham's motion to give it a majority. This was a blow that sobered the Southerners. By the next morning the full significance of the two motions had worked a decisive change of sentiment and both provisions were stricken from the bill.

The allowance made for slaves in the compromise of 1787 was purely arbitrary. Nobody could find a logical reason for making five slaves rather than four or six the equivalent of three free men. The conjecture disappeared when the Fourteenth Amendment

[1] *Congressional Record*, May 3, 1929.

was adopted. To-day, whether men and women of color in the South vote or not, the representation of the Southern States in the national House of Representatives complies exactly with the main purpose of the framers of the Constitution, that is to say, a representation of property interests as indicated by numbers of inhabitants. It follows that the political suppression of the negro, while a serious enough question by itself, has no bearing on apportionment except that resulting from the special provision of the Fourteenth Amendment for reducing representation in proportion to denial of the vote.

Although many Northern members of Congress have long resented the political treatment given to the colored citizens of the South, no practical way to meet the difficulties suggests itself. One obstacle is the possibility that the Fifteenth Amendment nullified the Fourteenth in this regard. Since by the Fifteenth any State statute denying or abridging the vote by reason of race, color, or previous condition of servitude would be unconstitutional, and therefore a nullity, some authorities aver that avenue to be closed. When negroes are shut out in some way other than by the operation of a statute, the offense is hard to prove and its extent would be beyond the power of census enumerators to determine with any accuracy. The remedy must be sought in some other direction. Perhaps the time will come when the South will be content to rely on such a literacy test as that of New York, which by indirectly measuring intelligence will legitimately exclude all persons, both white and black, who cannot vote usefully.

The implanting of numerical apportionment in the Federal Constitution gave great impetus to its advocacy everywhere. Dr. James Currie, who took up parliamentary reform in 1793, told Englishmen the system had been "carried into practice pretty exactly in the Constitution of America." [1] On this side of the water it naturally influenced the conventions that framed the Constitutions of the new States. Kentucky came first, in 1792, directing her Representatives to be apportioned according to the number of free male inhabitants above the age of twenty-one years in each county, as found by an enumeration every four years — a significant deviation from the precedent of Virginia, whence came so many of the settlers of the new State. By the way, the apportionment of the delegates to the Convention so providing was unique in American history, for it was on the

[1] *Memoir of James Currie*, ii, 308.

basis of a delegate to every company of militia in the Kentucky district. In 1850 another singular device appeared. The State was divided into ten groups of specified counties. After a census taken every eighth year, the Representatives were to be apportioned to these groups according to the number of qualified voters in each; and then within each group, to the counties, towns, and cities on a sliding scale of qualified voters. In 1890 a straight-out single district plan was substituted, on a population basis.

Tennessee began (1796) with Representatives to be "apportioned among the several counties according to the number of taxable inhabitants in each," and taxable inhabitants were also to be the basis for the formation of Senatorial districts. Ohio (1802) apportioned Representatives by counties on the basis of white male inhabitants, and Senators by counties or districts to be established by law. The Constitution of 1851 set forth the senatorial districts, made up of counties or groups of counties, one Senator to each, save one district allotted three. Because her Constitution had not been revised since the Civil War, Oregon continued restriction to "white population" until 1927, when the anachronism was removed.

Readers who are familiar with only the more populous counties of the East or those of the West and South in which the sizable cities are located, will get a wrong conception of the use of counties as a basis of apportionment unless they take notice of certain averages. There are a little more than 3000 counties in the United States. Eliminating about 130 with a population of 100,000 or more leaves a trifle above 2900 with an average population to-day of not far from 25,000. Our State Representatives average to represent about 21,700 each. Were those in the large Houses of some of the Eastern States to be left out of account, the average represented in the rest of the country would be strikingly close to the average of the population in 95 per cent of the counties. In other words that many of the counties, barring variations in size, would be normally single-member districts anyhow. So unless constituencies are to be larger in area than counties, which is rarely urged, with us the problem is chiefly urban, to some extent suburban, and very little rural.

The acceptance of numbers as the basic factor has become general; but agreement as to what should constitute "numbers" has not been fully reached. A few States still exclude from the count aliens, or even the native-born who are not qualified to vote. The question has perhaps been more discussed in Massachusetts than anywhere else. There, in the allotment of Representatives to towns, the Constitution, adopted in 1780, used for a basis "ratable polls," i.e., those assessed to pay a poll-tax. At that time, and presumably long before, the designation covered all male inhabitants between the ages of sixteen and seventy. In 1843 "above the age of twenty years" was substituted; and in 1844 the seventy-year maximum was dropped. Meantime, in 1811, was raised the question whether aliens were ratable polls within the meaning of the Constitution. In answering it (Opinion of the Justices, 7 Mass. 439) the Supreme Court said:

"We assume, as an unquestionable principle of sound national policy in this State, that, as the supreme power rests wholly in the citizens, so the exercise of it, or any branch of it, ought not to be delegated by any but citizens, and only to citizens. It is therefore to be presumed that the people, in making the Constitution, intended that the supreme power of legislation should not be delegated, but by citizens. And if the people intended to impart a portion of their political rights to aliens, this intention ought not to be collected from general words, which do not necessarily imply it, but from clear and manifest expressions, which are not to be misunderstood.... It may, therefore, seem superfluous to declare our opinion, that the authority given to *residents* and *inhabitants* to vote, is restrained to such inhabitants and residents as are *citizens*." Although the Court went on to hold that aliens might constitutionally be included in estimating the number of ratable polls, to determine the number of Representatives any town might be entitled to elect, yet it was not of the opinion that by being so included they acquired any political rights.

Among resolutions reported by committee to the Convention of 1820 was this: "Resolved, That it is proper and expedient so to alter and amend the Constitution as to provide that every corporate town containing twelve hundred *inhabitants*, and also all towns now united for the purpose of electing a Representative, and having together a like number of inhabitants, may elect one Representative." When this came up for debate, a substitute proposition was presented, for the use of ratable polls rather than population as the basis. Objecting to this, Luther Lawrence, of Groton, presumed ratable polls never would have been adopted, if there had been at the time of the framing of the Constitution any provision for the periodical enumeration of the inhabitants. Polls did not before that time form the basis of representation. By the laws of 1692 and 1776, the number of freeholders was the basis. It would be found that, from particular causes, the number of ratable polls was not proportioned to the number of inhabitants. In the county of Suffolk, for instance, there were two thousand more ratable polls than in Berkshire, though in the latter county the population was greater. The Legislature also may alter the number of ratable polls, but cannot the number of inhabitants. They may provide by law for taxing all polls over ten years of age, or that only those over twenty-one or fifty should be taxed. The determining the number of polls is left to the towns, and is liable to fraud.

The Journal goes on to say: "The question on the amendment was taken and decided in the negative."

The view of the Committee in this particular — as to "inhabitants" — was embodied in Article V of the Amendments submitted to the people. The address accompanying the Amendments said: "We have found great difficulty in amending the representative system in a satisfactory manner. We have all agreed that whether the representatives are few, or many, representation should be according to population, in this branch."

The people rejected this Amendment, 9,904 to 20,720, though undoubtedly not because of this particular provision, but because the amendment covered the whole system of representation and was obnoxious in other details.

Inasmuch as many who were assessed the poll-tax were not citizens, but were foreign-born and not naturalized, or were newcomers from other States, presently there came discussion of the equity involved, but Massachusetts did not accept the newer theory until 1840, when by amendment it replaced "ratable polls" with "inhabitants." In the Convention of 1853 this chanced to be the first amendment considered and three days were given to its discussion. The influx of foreigners, settling chiefly in the cities and the mill towns, had made the question of importance. In 1850, of 973,715 inhabitants of the State, 245,142 were polls, and of these 183,128 were voters. It was the unequal distribution of the 62,014 who were polls but not voters, together with the excess of women in the mill towns, that made the trouble.

Henry Wilson, afterward Vice President, presented the report favoring population as the basis. He and other friends of the masses talked of "taxation without representation," the right of every man to count one in ascertaining the popular will, no matter where he might have been born, the right of every woman and every child, every pauper and every idiot, to be counted, though júst that phraseology was not used. It was shown that in some places there were three times as many "voters" to every one hundred inhabitants as there were in others, and that therefore to measure by "voters" was unfair. A few voices were raised in remonstrance, but the Know-Nothing movement, about to sweep the board in Massachusetts, had not quite yet developed its strength, and when the votes were counted, one hundred and sixty-six stood by the Committee and only four recorded themselves the other way. As the Convention had more than four hundred delegates, evidently many dodged. So for a while longer, Representatives were allotted on one basis and chosen on another. By 1857 the anti-Catholic influence had twice prevailed in the Legislature and once at the polls, on this particular proposition, and the Constitution was accordingly amended. Since then Representatives in Massachusetts have been distributed in proportion to "legal voters."

That term had one costly result. For more than threescore years it was supposed to be a dominant reason for taking a State census every decade, midway the Federal censuses. Then (in 1924) the Supreme Court told the Legislature, in answer to inquiry, that it did not go beyond "registered voters," the number of whom can of course be ascertained from the city and town clerks at trifling cost. At the same time the Opinion ended the giving of any weight to the eligibles who do not value the suffrage enough to go to the trouble of registering.

The first Constitution of New York (1777) directed that at the expiration of seven years "a census of the electors and inhabitants in this State be taken." If it should then appear that the arbitrary allotment of Representatives made by the Constitution to the various counties be "not justly proportioned to the number of electors in the said counties respectively," a reapportionment should be made. When amendment of the system was made in 1801, the apportionment was still to be "according to the number of their respective electors." The Constitution of 1821 made a significant change, directing that "each Senate district shall contain, as nearly as may be, an equal number of inhabitants, excluding *aliens*, paupers, and persons of color not taxed," and a like exclusion was made for the apportionment of Representatives. "Inhabitants, excluding aliens" is still the provision. Tennessee in 1834 substituted "qualified electors" for "taxable inhabitants," and that continues. Texas, using "free population" as the basis for Representatives, made it "qualified electors" for Senators. The Maine census preliminary to apportionment is to exclude "foreigners not naturalized and Indians not taxed." North Carolina excludes "aliens" and Indians not taxed. New Hampshire in 1920 would have secured the same result in apportionment for Representatives had the amendment reducing the size of the House been adopted. In California the end is accomplished in part by the exclusion of persons not eligible to become naturalized citizens, a provision of course aimed at Orientals.

RURAL AND URBAN

Although nearly all the States created in the last hundred years have used numbers as the chief or only factor in apportionment, so many have given concessions to the less populous localities that of all the States in the Union, only about two fifths can be said to have numerically equitable apportionment. The most common bar to it has been the practice of giving at least one Representative to each town or each county, no matter how small. Frequently coupled with this have been provisions limiting the number of Senators or Representatives from centers of population, no matter how large. To detail the variations of this policy here would be tedious and useless. Let one illustration suffice, taken at random: Iowa, which in 1904 provided that each county should have one Representative, with one extra in the case of counties having a certain excess of population above the ratio, but not to the number of more than nine counties — the largest, of course. One reason for the policy is found in the contention that territory as well as population should be a factor in apportionment. Another may be the stubborn tenacity with which the communities growing less rapidly have clung to old privileges. But the most powerful motive has been jealousy, suspicion, and fear of the cities.

This motive began to be effectual about a hundred years ago. When Maine was set off from Massachusetts, the delegates to

her Convention of 1819 were thoroughly familiar with the pre-
ponderating influence of Boston in Massachusetts politics. Most
of them believed they had themselves suffered therefrom. Theirs
was chiefly a farming region, and the farmers wanted no city
domination. So they put a maximum on the number of Representatives any one place could have. In the New York Constitutional Convention of 1821 Chancellor Kent strongly urged
a provision of like purpose, but was voted down. New York,
however, has in a measure accomplished the result sought by the
Chancellor, and tenaciously holds to it in spite of the protests of
her great city. Elihu Root in the Constitutional Convention of
1894 gave the argument. Defending provisions that discriminated in favor of the country and against the cities, by fixing a
smaller ratio for the country counties than was fixed for the
larger counties and the cities, and providing that no city having
more than a specified number of Senators should have another
Senator, except upon a full ratio, he stated that there were two
reasons for not applying a strict rule of representation according
to absolute population to the whole State, first, that territorial
extension, variety, and separation of interests required a representation not necessary when there was a condensation in the
great centers of population; and, in the second place, that the
great increase of effective force which comes from the election of
a large number of representatives of one city — representatives
who represent, not, in fact, their separate districts, but the
whole city, representatives who are responsible to the same
public opinion, and, in fact, represent but one combined interest
of the citizens of that city — the great accumulation of power
created by that combination so far outweighed the effective
power of a great number of scattered representatives of widely
divided centers of population, small centers of population, that
a difference in the ratio, such as was preferred in the amendments under consideration, went but a small way toward equalization. "Every man who is sent to the Legislature from a great
city," said Mr. Root, "represents not this artificial territory,
this territory artificially defined; that is but a means of determining what voters shall pass upon the question of whether he
or another man goes to the Legislature. But he represents the
whole city; every representative of every part of the city represents the whole city, and no special part of it.... I insist, sir, upon
the principle which has been adopted in a large number of the

States of this Union, in almost every State which has had to deal with the problem of a great city within its borders, and the relations of that city to an agricultural community, that the problem which they have had to deal with shall be dealt with by us upon the same principle; that the small and widely scattered communities, with their feeble power comparatively, because of their division, shall, by the distribution of representation, be put upon an equal footing, so far as may be, with the concentrated power of the cities. Otherwise we never can have a truly representative and a truly republican government."

For a presentation of the argument on the other side of the question, take an extract from a speech of Nathan Hale in the Massachusetts Constitutional Convention of 1853: "In whatever part of the Commonwealth persevering industry and skill, in any commercial, manufacturing, or other enterprise, has led to the accumulation of property, for the benefit of its individual proprietors, and at the same time of all the inhabitants of the town, in all those places without exception, the growth of improvement and of population has marked those towns for the exclusion of their inhabitants in the proposed system of representation for an equal share in the power of government; and it is only to the inhabitants who have limited their efforts to the cultivation of the soil, or to pursuits which have exempted their particular towns from those great improvements which have so signally changed the face of the Commonwealth within the last thirty years, that the privilege is reserved of controlling the affairs of the Commonwealth by means of an undue share in the representation.... The very reason why so large a number of inhabitants concentrate in these large cities is because the great interests of business are concentrated there, and those interests require legislation in proportion to their novelty, magnitude, and importance. They require to be regulated by legislation, with the aid of men acquainted with them. The magnitude of those interests is precisely in proportion to the number of inhabitants. ... There is no reason why a population, having the most important interests of business, should be represented in inverse proportion to their property." [1]

It is to be feared that such considerations, somewhat theoretical and academic on each side, have not really determined the issue in the many Constitutional Conventions where the ques-

[1] *Debates in Mass. Convention of 1853,* i, 840.

tion has been fought. More human and personal considerations prevail. Chief among them is the wish of the political leaders in every county and district to hold what they have. That is said to be the real reason for the survival of the Senatorial apportionment in New York. In so far as jealousy of the big cities arouses the prejudice of country delegates in Constitutional Conventions, probably the fear of being outvoted in the Legislature is not the chief factor. More potent is the conviction that, numbers for numbers, there is more of capacity, honesty, and patriotism in the country than in the town.

The controversy has by no means been confined to the United States. Lord Brougham, discussing it from the English point of view in his book on the British Constitution, in 1860, presented an argument particularly applicable where the lawmaking body meets in a large city. If London had a representation in proportion to its size, he thought so large a body always on the spot, and representing constituencies so numerous in the immediate neighborhood of the Parliament and the government, would have an influence exceedingly dangerous to the balance of the Constitution and the independence of the legislature.

Russia under the soviet system takes the opposite view. It gives the city voter about two and a half times as much representation as the country voter, defending this on the ground that the industrial workers are both more intelligent and more class-conscious than the peasants.

As it actually works out in practice with us, big-city representation rarely results in throwing into the scale a solid, determining mass of votes. City delegations are usually divided on party lines, and the larger half will be coherent only on party questions or, sometimes, on measures of particular consequence to the city itself; and in regard to these it is logical that the will of the majority of those particularly concerned should have weight. Furthermore, the bigger the city, the less of civic pride, the less of blind loyalty or what passes therefor. Often there is more of acquaintance and fellowship and solidarity in a rural county covering a large area than in a big city of few square miles. Men know each other better in the country than in the city. They seek to know each other. To illustrate by small things, it is a custom for members of the Massachusetts Legislature from the remoter counties to dine together at intervals during the session, without regard to party lines; the members from Suffolk County (mostly Boston) never sit down together. By coöperation the members from the western part of the State, having about one eighth of its population, often get more than their share of public benefits, while Boston with a fifth of the population of the State, and more, almost never accomplishes anything by definitely organized effort of all its Representatives.

Furthermore, the members from all the cities in a State never join in support of what might be called an urban programme or policy. Members from the country districts, however, often help each other from sympathetic motives. What class feeling appears in the State Legislatures is chiefly agrarian.

The fears that have made State Constitutions handicap the more populous communities are of much the same nature as those that in the Federal Convention of 1789 led to the framing of the United States Senate on the basis of two Senators from each State. In matter of size time has greatly increased disparity, until now the extremes show two Senators for Nevada with a population of about 77,000 and two for New York with a population of about 11,600,000. Complaint of this occupies the professional critic when he has nothing else to do. Of course it has ridiculous features, but really any serious effect on a great part of legislation is hard to find. Occasionally, however, there comes along a measure where the equality of representation enures much to the benefit of the smaller States, of course at the expense of the larger.

A striking instance of this appeared in that same special session of the seventy-first Congress in which the House came so near trying to amend the Constitution by excluding aliens from the basis of apportionment. The Senate voted to attach to the Farm Relief bill what was known as the debenture plan, a provision for export bounties on staple products of the farm. On the basis of average exports thereof in the preceding three years, this would cost the Treasury $150,000,000 a year. Analysis of the Senate vote shows that of the delegations of thirty-seven States not divided in opinion, nineteen favored the debenture and eighteen opposed, but that the population in 1920 of the nineteen States favoring the debenture was less than thirty-seven million, of the eighteen opposing, more than forty-four million; and that of the total of income taxes paid by the thirty-seven States in question, seventy-five per cent is coming from the States opposed, twenty-five per cent from the States in favor.

Perhaps we are too near this and other like episodes to get the right perspective; perhaps we are too far from regional conflicts of the past to remember their intensities and their effects; but it does seem as if there is a growing tendency for the smaller, poorer States to combine for using their power in the Senate to the disadvantage of the States with larger populations and much larger wealth.

To see if definite conclusions were possible in the matter, Carroll H. Wooddy analyzed the votes of the Senate for fifty years.[1] He found that in ten of the twenty-five Congresses covered, misrepresentation of the total population of the country probably had no effect on the results; in ten the changes on that account would be few; in five a fair number of votes would be "unrepresentative"; and in four a distinct percentage of all votes and a large percentage of contested votes were, in all probability, "contrary to the popular will." This assumes, however, certain standards that may of themselves be questioned, and numerous uncertain factors crop up in such an inquiry.

Many of the ablest and most useful Senators have come from the small States. It would be hard, indeed, to show any ratio whatever between the value of individual Senators and the size of their constituencies.

Oddly enough, regional rivalries make more mischief in some of the States than in Congress, and they are said to be fostered by the representation of counties as such. Governor Carey of Wyoming told the Governors' Conference of 1913 that in his State the fight in every Legislature is between counties. "If an institution is to be established, every county is fighting for it, and the question of locality governs, and not the real merits of the location. If the State could be districted so the question of counties could be eliminated, I know from my own experience, and what I have seen in the State, there would be great benefits derived from it." [2] The remedy of course is to unite for purposes of representation counties with few inhabitants and divide those with many, as the ratio may justify. The tendency is in this direction. For instance, Kansas in 1873 ordered that each county with less than two hundred legal voters should be part of the representative district to the east. Texas in 1876 provided that

[1] "Is the Senate Unrepresentative?" *Political Science Quarterly*, XLI, June, 1926.

[2] *Proceedings*, 311, 312.

for a surplus of population a county might be joined in a representative district with any contiguous county or counties. Illinois in 1848 permitted cities or towns with the requisite population to be erected into separate districts, and in 1870 permitted counties to be divided.

Mississippi put three novel provisions into her Constitution in 1890. In counties divided into legislative districts, any citizen of the county might represent any one of its districts. Secondly, the counties were classified in three groups, with the provision that each group in any future apportionment should never have less than forty-four Representatives. Thirdly, a reduction in the number of Senators and Representatives might be made by the Legislature provided it should be uniform for each of these three divisions.

In California the problem has been exceptionally difficult by reason of the abnormal massing of population in centers. More than one half of the total is contained in the counties of Los Angeles, San Francisco, and Alameda. Equal allotment would give these three more representation than the other fifty-five. Sectional feeling has complicated the situation; there have even been threats of secession. Successive Legislatures refused to obey the constitutional mandate to reapportion. At last, in 1928, the matter was settled, at any rate for the time being, by the adoption upon referendum of what is known as the "federal plan," whereunder the Senate is to be apportioned by counties, the Assembly by population.

Little argument is necessary to show that representation on the geographical rather than the numerical basis is the normal procedure for loose federations, where each member retains sovereignty as to at least its internal affairs. This responds to the group-consciousness out of which springs patriotism. Naturally it was embodied in the programme for a League of Nations that followed the Great War. In the United States some reluctance developed at the prospect of standing on an equality with smaller nations such as those of Central America, and really serious criticism sprang from the allotment to the British Empire, but on the whole it was recognized that unless the world is to be amalgamated, equal voice for homogeneous peoples, regardless of their number, will continue to be demanded and in many respects to be justified.

With close federations, such as that of Germany, the question continues to perplex. It is significant that the new German Constitution (1919), though specifying that each State should have at least one vote in the National Council, yet directed that the larger States should have one vote for each million of inhabitants, with one in addition for any excess equal to the population of the smallest State. At the same time it safeguarded the smaller States by saying that no State should be credited with more than two fifths of the total of votes. Such combination of the geographical and numerical principles, though of course in some degree artificial, is probably the wisest solution of a vexatious problem.

REAPPORTIONMENT

All the States except Delaware provide in their Constitutions for a periodical reapportionment. In early years they varied much in their times for this. Gradually they accepted the recurrence of the Federal census as the most convenient period, but not always has the argument for it convinced. Iowa was certainly looking for trouble when in her first Constitution (1846) she directed that the General Assembly should apportion the House at every regular session, and the Senate at every second regular session. The ten-year basis was not reached until 1875.

In most of the States constitutional provisions for reapportionment are to be carried out by the Legislature. Since 1851 the Ohio provisions have been carried out by the Governor, Secretary of State, and Auditor; since 1867, those of Maryland by the Governor. Missouri provided in 1875 that if the Legislature failed to allot Senators, it should be done by the Governor, Secretary of State, and Attorney-General. The minority party charged that three successive reapportionments by these officials were among the worst examples of gerrymandering. Their power was held by the courts to have been taken away by the adoption of the Initiative and Referendum. Thereupon the Convention of 1923 proposed to rectify the situation by entrusting reapportionments to the Governor, Secretary of State, Attorney-General, Auditor, and Treasurer. Their action was not to be subject to the Referendum and they were to be impeached if they did not act. The electorate rejected the proposal. Pennsylvania in 1873 directed that "townships and wards of cities or boroughs shall form or be divided into election districts of compact and contiguous territory, in such manner as the court of quarter sessions of the city or county in which the same are located may direct," with certain provisions of detail. California in 1928 directed that if the Legislature fails to act, the work shall be done by a Commission made up of the Lieutenant-Governor, Attorney-General, Surveyor-General, Secretary of State, and Superintendent of Public Instruction.

The Union began with a specified allotment of Representatives to the States, meant to correspond to relative population, but admittedly conjectural. Within three years a census was to be taken, and then one every ten years, to furnish a basis for accurate apportionment. As at first agreed upon the provision contained one clause quickly to be made superfluous by the growth of population, but which gave rise to an interesting incident, for it furnished the only occasion on which George Washington, presiding over the Convention, entered into its debates. At the very last, although the work of the Convention had been virtually completed, Nathaniel Gorham, of Massachusetts, rose to express the wish that thirty thousand, instead of forty thousand, might be the basis for representation in the House. Thereupon Washington said that although his situation had hitherto restrained him from offering his sentiments on questions depending, and, it might be thought, ought now to impose silence on him, yet he could not forbear his wish that the alteration proposed might take place. It was much to be desired that the objections to the plan recommended might be made as few as possible. The smallness of the proportion of representation had been considered, by many members of the Convention, an insufficient security for the rights and interests of the people. He acknowledged that it had always appeared to himself among the exceptionable parts of the plan; and, late as the present moment was for admitting amendments, he thought this of so much consequence, that it would give him much satisfaction to see it accomplished.[1] This, the only request of the foremost man of the Convention, was without debate unanimously granted.

The Constitution did not specifically state that Congress should reapportion after every census, but through thirteen decades the language was construed as imposing a duty. Then, after the census of 1920, it was first importantly argued that the provision was declaratory and not mandatory, so that Congress might reapportion or not as it saw fit. In four Congresses the

[1] *Elliot's Debates*, v, 555.

House refused to act; in one the Committee on the Census made no report. It was argued that the Census of 1920 had been unfair, because it was as of the 1st of January of that year, when the effects of the World War in abnormally disturbing populations had not disappeared, and because it was taken in the winter season, to the disadvantage of the agricultural regions. The real reason for inaction, however, was the fact that a considerable number of States would lose members if the size of the House should not be increased — a dozen of them if the 1920 figures were taken as the basis, twenty-three if the estimated figures for 1930 should be used. Of course the members from these States felt it necessary to prevent losses if they could, and on the other hand a large part of the membership, probably a majority, strongly felt the size of the House should not be increased. The dilemma proved insoluble for the time being.

Unprejudiced men can hardly fail to conclude that the House avoided a constitutional duty. The practice of much more than a century, the holdings of courts, the rulings of Speakers, and the contemporary explanations of the Constitution — all these combine to convince that the direction is mandatory. Indeed, No. 58 of the Federalist would seem to make it clear that it is more than a technical duty, that it is an ethical duty, for the original provision was a bargain between the big and the little States, one of the compromises that alone made the adoption of the Constitution possible.

The refusal of the House to act gave ground for just complaint. The disproportionate growth of population in such areas as those of which Detroit and Los Angeles are the centers had produced manifest unfairness. Even where reapportionment would give but one more member, as in Texas, the matter was held to be serious. To assert its rights Texas saw fit to elect a member-at-large to the Sixty-Eighth Congress. His application for admittance was rejected, but the injustice had been emphasized.

As the decade wore on and action on the basis of the 1920 census became more and more unlikely, attention was turned to the desirability of anticipating the situation after 1930 by providing for some agency outside Congress to do the ministerial work of apportionment upon a basis that, set forth in advance, might avoid some of the difficulties inevitable when members must pass judgment on changes that in the immediate future will affect their personal fortunes. To this end the bill voted upon by the

House in March, 1927 (rejected by only twelve votes), would have directed the Secretary of Commerce to make the apportionment on the lines laid down, immediately upon receipt of the data from the Census Bureau. One objection raised was that Congress would have no chance to interpose unless by repeal or amendment of the law, and that this avenue might be closed were the Secretary to act promptly or were the figures first known toward the end of the short session, when filibustering is easy. To meet this the measure was changed before coming up for debate in 1928, and still further before the debate of January, 1929, so as to require the figures to be reported to Congress, on the first day of the session following the taking of every decennial census, the Secretary of Commerce to act after the end of the session unless Congress had itself made an apportionment. This was intended to overcome the argument that one Congress cannot bind a successor, as it was urged would be the case were that successor deprived of the opportunity for performing a constitutional duty. Perhaps the change contributed toward passage of the bill by the House in January of 1929, but to no immediate avail, for it was blocked in the Senate.

When Congress met in special session the following April, it was agreed that one of the imperative duties was the passage of a census and apportionment bill. This was at last accomplished through compromise of conflicting views. The enactment provided that after the census every ten years, the President shall lay before the House a statement showing what will respectively be the result if Representatives to the existing number are apportioned by three different methods, (1) the method last used, (2) and (3) methods differing according to the treatment of fractions. (So the law provides, though as a matter of fact either the second or third is likely to be identical with the first.) Then if the Congress to which this statement is submitted, fails to act, apportionment shall take place automatically, so to speak, in accordance with the method last used. This postponed the puzzling mathematical problem of fractions. Also it secured to Congress the chance to thwart attempt by anybody in the executive branch to handle the figures unfairly; and it avoided any shadow of executive discretion. If this programme works satisfactorily, it would save future Congresses a great deal of controversy and time.

The argument that the original proposal of the House for apportionment by the Secretary of Commerce contemplated an improper delegation of ministerial duty does not seem to me consistent with what the courts have held to be ministerial functions. Surely it is to be hoped that no such argument will anywhere prevent the ultimate adoption of some method of this sort for escaping the difficulties that are becoming so serious. It was conspicuous that every year of delay by Congress in the performance of its duty, made it harder, for by reason of constantly changing economic influences every year brings greater variation in the distribution of population, with more and more exposure to loss of representation upon reapportionment.

This effect has appeared in various States where Legislatures have neglected to comply with similar requirements for reapportionment at periodic intervals. For example, Illinois has failed to reapportion since 1901, with the result that Chicago has come to be grossly under-represented in the Legislature. The quarrel over rectifying the situation was largely responsible for the deadlock that prolonged a Constitutional Convention from January, 1920, to late in 1922, and the conclusion reached in this particular matter was in turn largely responsible for the overwhelming rejection of the new Constitution proposed. In Cook County (which is mainly Chicago), it was favored by only about one voter in seventeen. Some think the chief reason was the proposal to restrict the representation of the county in the Senate to one third of its membership. There were other reasons, but undoubtedly this one had much weight.

One unfortunate feature of such situations is that successful recourse to the courts is difficult if not impossible. A Cook County voter tried it in vain. He sought to have the State Treasurer enjoined from paying salaries to the members of the Assembly, on the ground that as the apportionment required by the State Constitution had not been made, the members were not legally holding office. When denied by the Supreme Court of the State, he asked the Supreme Court of the United States to review the decision, but was refused the necessary writ of certiorari, which means that the court would not take jurisdiction. No reason was given, but presumably it was on the ground that this is a political question, outside the province of the Court. This position is not easy to circumvent. When, not long afterward, it was brought to the attention of Congress while the apportionment bill was under discussion, in connection with the proposal to eliminate aliens from the basis of apportionment, Senator Borah expressed the belief that if Congress should violate what he (and many others) thought the intent of the Constitution in this particular, a way could be found to secure the intervention of the Court, but he did not suggest a method. The trouble is that in such a case no one citizen can show that he has an interest apart from that of other citizens, and what interests all citizens is a political matter, to be handled by the legislative rather than the judicial branch. It would be interesting to see what the Supreme Court would say if some State Legislature instructed its Attorney-General to represent to the Court that the interests of the State in question, as distinct from those of other States, had been injured by an enactment of Congress in which some provision of the Constitution relating to the States as such had been violated.

The struggle in Illinois, in various other States, and of late in Congress, has been between urban and rural populations, between city and country. It bids fair to keep on vexing. At the outset agricultural interests made up nine tenths or more of the whole. Now only about one quarter of the workers make their living by agricultural and allied pursuits. With the improvement of farm machinery and of agricultural processes, the ratio of the farmer to the rest, numerically speaking, bids fair to become smaller and smaller. It is natural, it is inevitable, that the farmer will resist, and with him will be the sympathy of the dwellers in the towns and small cities that look to the farmer chiefly for support.

This is the chief reason nowadays underlying the contentions about apportionment. Apart from it the only reason with any broad interest is that characteristic of Democracy which Nietzsche described as "this mania for counting noses." The epithet may not be inappropriate in the instances furnished by the zeal with which fractions have been pursued. Note the painstaking of Oklahoma. There, after each decennial census, the population is to be divided by 100 to get the quotient that shall serve as a ratio. Each county with half the ratio gets one Representative; each county with the ratio and three fourths over gets two; after the first two an entire ratio is necessary for each additional Representative. A county with a fractional excess above one fifth of the ratio is to get a proportionate number of Representatives in specified years of the decennial period. No county is to be divided except to make two or more complete districts. If the mathematics of this does not satisfy your appetite, try to grasp the proposal made to the Illinois Constitutional Convention of 1869–70, by the committee of which Joseph Medill was Chairman, to the effect that any district with a fraction of population above the ratio so large that being multiplied by the number of regular sessions of the Legislature in a decade the result equalled one or more ratios, should elect an extra Representative or Senator in those years in which the fraction so multiplied should produce a whole ratio. Fortunately the Convention escaped a chance to pass judgment thereon.

The anxiety of some of the States to care for fractions has resulted in the creation of what are called "floating" or "flotorial districts." These have been defined as "a grouping of counties, at least one of which is already separately represented, for the purpose of combining fractions of the representative 'ratio,' and thus securing, for the group as a whole, an additional Representative." The discovery that under existing constitutional provisions this device was permissible seems to have been made first either in Kentucky or Illinois. Its vogue has been greater in the South than in the North. It was forbidden in Illinois in 1848, in Iowa in 1857.[1]

Without special knowledge, one would be mystified by such a provision as this in the Mississippi Constitution: "The counties of Harrison and Jackson each shall have one Representative and a floater between them."

This matter of fractions gave George Washington the occasion for his first veto, singularly enough connected with the only provision in the draft of the Federal Constitution that he had asked should be changed. He sent the veto reluctantly. After the first census it was found that dividing the total by thirty thousand gave one hundred and twenty for the possible number of Representatives. It was proposed to divide the population of each State by thirty thousand, and to take care of the fraction by allotting the excess to the various States, beginning with the largest fraction, until the number of one hundred and twenty had been exhausted, which we have seen to be the "major fraction" principle. As each fraction would represent less than thirty thousand, Washington vetoed the bill. The difficulty was

[1] A. Z. Reed, "The Territorial Basis of Government under the State Constitutions," *Columbia University Studies*, 40, 553 (1911).

met by making the divisor thirty-three thousand. The principle upon which Washington's objection was founded was not importantly questioned until after the census of 1830, when a special committee of the Senate, headed by Daniel Webster, gave it serious study. Webster's report argued that a fraction larger than one half should give a State another Representative. That view did not then prevail, but was adopted for the apportionment after the census of 1840. Ten years later a modification known as the Vinton method was preferred and this was used for six apportionments. It was supposed to accomplish the same end that Webster sought, but a weak spot developed in the way of a queer mathematical paradox whereunder it was possible for some State to lose a member if the size of the House were increased by one, and so after the census of 1910 return was made to the Webster method.

The puzzle faced the House again in May of 1928 when it came to debate the proposal for reapportionment that the Committee had reported. The mathematicians had fought a battle over the question of whether it should be made with the use of the system of "major fractions" or that of "equal proportions." Most of the members of the House had scant idea of what either meant. Without trying to explain here their intricacies, suffice it to say that under the system the Committee preferred, each State would get one Representative for each full quota and each major fraction thereof, the "full quota" being the number found by a somewhat elaborate computation to be that number which will produce this result for a House of predetermined size. So it is called the method of "major fractions." The other method, that of "equal proportions," also gives an idea of its result by its name, the purpose of calculation being to secure for the various States as nearly equal a proportion as possible between its total population and its total number of Representatives. The curious may find it explained by its chief sponsor, Professor Edward B. Huntington, in remarks extended by Representative F. W. Dallinger in the Congressional Record for May 16, 1928, and further discussion of it in "Science," May 3, 1929. The practical bearing of the controversy is that the method of equal proportions gives some advantage to the smaller States, a few of them losing less than they would under the method of major fractions.

There are also known to be at least three other methods by which the figuring could be done, and one reason advanced for leaving the matter open in the compromise of 1929 was the possibility of discovering still more, which will surprise those who may have supposed that in such matters as this the mathematicians had reached the ultimate.

It is to be feared that these meticulous anxieties for perfect proportion have more often had their origin in personal ambitions and party interests than in any high regard for scientific accuracy or any exalted wish for collective justice. The new apportionment that lessens representation lessens by so much the chance to gratify individual aspirations and by so much may endanger party control. Yet the truth is that constituencies worry little over the matter. A representative may by reason of illness be absent from his seat for a long time without anybody being much disturbed because the district is unrepresented in debate and votes, but let him die and then individual interest agitates the political waters instantly. The demand is to have the vacancy filled at the earliest possible moment. Yet as a matter of fact the need is of no great importance. The chance that delay will adversely affect the constituency is remote. Generally it is the same with reapportionment. As far as the general welfare of State or Nation may be concerned, one vote more or less in Legislature or Congress rarely makes any difference.

Of course the situation may be quite otherwise when shifts of population are taken into account only once in twenty or thirty years. Then injustices to large groups of population may be of serious consequence. For this reason, and because whatever the basis of representation constitutionally provided, it should on general principles be complied with as closely as practicable, delays are unfortunate. If, however, apportionments are conducted at the proper intervals, they seldom warrant the controversy they arouse.

CHAPTER XVII

DISTRICTS

THE most difficult and most controverted problem of apportionment concerns the number of members to be elected from a district. Is it wisest to elect the whole membership at large, on a general ticket? or to have a few districts, each with several members? or to have many districts, with but one member from each?

Before the question gained vigor anywhere, Montesquieu laid down this general proposition: "The inhabitants of a particular town are much better acquainted with its wants and interests than with those of other places; and are better judges of the capacity of their neighbors than of that of the rest of their countrymen. The members, therefore, of the legislature should not be chosen from the general body of the nation; but it is proper that in every considerable place a representative should be elected by the inhabitants." [1]

This was the early practice in England, which was the country whose institutions most commended themselves to Montesquieu. It has been generally the practice in the election of lower Houses or their equivalent. Trouble began with elected upper Houses in populous countries or States. Comparatively small electorates such as those of the American colonies could without difficulty and with quite satisfactory results choose by general ticket such of their little Councils as were elected. As population grew, it became harder to select intelligently, with personal knowledge of candidates. Furthermore, men began to ask why members of an upper branch should not as well as members of a lower branch have local attachments, responsibilities, and knowledge. So when our first State Constitutions were framed, most of them allotted Senators to counties. The Federal Constitution, giving two Senators to each State, confirmed in general the theory of Senatorial districts, and since then that theory has until of late not been seriously contested.

Doubt remained, however, as to whether more than one State Senator should be chosen for any one district. New Hampshire in 1792, Kentucky in 1799, decided for single districts. Most of

[1] *Spirit of Laws*, book XI, chap. 6.

the other States have since then come to the same decision,
where it had not been already reached in effect by giving one
Senator to each county. Only in New York has the change been
stoutly and persistently contested. At the outset that State
was divided into four great districts for the election of Senators,
with nine allotted to one, six to each of two, and three to the
fourth. This distribution was to be changed from time to time
as population changed. "Under this arrangement," says J. D.
Hammond,[1] "as many times very obscure men were put in
nomination for that important office, it was impossible for an
immense majority of the electors to have any personal knowledge
of the candidates for whom they were called upon to vote." In
1821 the State was divided into eight districts, composed of
groups of counties, each to choose four Senators. In 1846 single
districts came, with counties still recognized in the scheme of
allotment. In the Convention of 1867 the committee upon legislative organization unanimously proposed dividing the State
into eight districts as established in 1821 but abandoned in 1846.
The chairman gave the committee's opinion when he said that in
his belief the large district plan would "invite into the Legislature the ablest minds in the State." Horace Greeley suggested
fifteen districts, each to elect three Senators on the cumulative
system. In the end the Convention decided on the single-district
plan then in force. The Constitutional Commission of 1872–73
recommended eight districts, each to elect four Senators, but the
Legislature did not approve this nor submit it to the people.

Single districts for Assemblymen were provided in New York
in 1846, and it appears thereby to have been the first State
to apply the system in full. In the preceding year, however,
Louisiana had divided that part of New Orleans on the left bank
of the Mississippi into nine Representative districts, and it is
said this was the first breaking up of a populous district in the
United States. The New York Convention committee of 1867
wanted also to abolish single districts for Assemblymen, and its
proposal to substitute election by counties was sustained by a
vote of 64 to 43. All the work of the Convention, however, was
rejected by the people.

Few American politicians have had a longer or more intimate
experience with State Legislatures than Thurlow Weed, for half
a century a journalist and party manager in New York. In his

[1] *History of Political Parties in the State of N.Y.*, II, 14.

"Autobiography" he said (page 410): "What was regarded as beneficial in respect to single Assembly districts has proved the reverse. It would be better any way to return to the general ticket system. With a reasonable compensation for legislative services, and the selection of members from counties instead of districts, we should have improved Houses of Assembly. Nor has the popular idea of brief terms for Senators worked well. The Senate would be stronger, and more independent and useful, by enlarging the districts and extending the term to four years."

In Louisiana the experiment of 1845 does not appear to have encouraged the extreme application of the single district plan, for the Louisiana Constitution of 1864 apportioned from one to eight Representatives to a district, and from one to five Senators. Three Constitutions in that State since then have followed the same course, but the latest allots not more than two Senators or three Representatives to any one district.

Wisconsin in 1848 went further than either New York or Louisiana. Single districts, formed "according to the number of inhabitants," were directed for both Senators and Representatives — in the case of members of the Assembly "such districts to be bounded by county, precinct, town, or ward lines, to consist of contiguous territory, and to be in as compact form as practicable." Inasmuch as there was no mention of apportionment to counties, as there had been in New York, Wisconsin may claim the credit of being the first to apply completely the single district system in the election of Representatives.

Two years later Michigan adopted the system, but not in its entirety, for though single districts were specified for Representatives, the proviso was added "but no township or city shall be divided in the formation of a Representative district." A general ticket was to be used by township or city if entitled by population to more than one. In the same year single districts for Senators were ordered. Previously upon each decennial enumeration of the inhabitants, the State was to be divided into not less than four nor more than eight Senatorial districts.

Pennsylvania reached single Senatorial districts in 1857, but only for Philadelphia. When as a State it had first created a Senate, in 1790, it directed that Senators should be chosen by districts, "each to elect not more than four Senators." Philadelphia was not to be divided, nor was any county. In 1838 this was changed so that no district should elect more than two, un-

less of such size as to call for more; and was in no case to elect
more than four. By amendment in 1857 the restriction as to
Philadelphia was removed and provision was made to divide
that city into single Senatorial districts. In the Convention of
1873 the matter received instructive discussion. "It has always
seemed to me," said Wayne MacVeagh, "that if we could elect
the Senate on a general ticket, we should take a longer step possibly toward the extirpation of the evils under which we suffer
than in any other single method. Your great hope of a pure
government lies in the character of the men who are in office;
and it does seem quite clear to my mind that upon a general
ticket you would be much more likely to get men of the highest
character, of recognized ability, and of eminent fitness and integrity in these positions." Andrew G. Curtin, Pennsylvania's
war Governor, said he would vote most heartily for election by
general ticket. He named strong men who under the old system
in New York, of four Senators to a district, had been elected in
that State. "No one of that class of men," he said, "could go
into the Senate of New York now from any single district. Then
they represented the whole State, and men of that type could
get into the Senate, and were only too glad to receive such an
honorable distinction." William H. Armstrong made a forcible
appeal for diversity between the bases of Senate and House.
"Local interests," he declared, "have everywhere become so
predominant that the struggle in our Legislature every year is
to adjust the rivalries of conflicting local interests.... At the root
of this monstrous evil lies the pernicious system which organizes
both branches of the Legislature upon a plan which makes them
both practically identical, and subjects them equally to local
prejudices and influences — and makes them equally dependent
upon local favor for election, and by consequence responsible to
a local constituency alone. Under such circumstances it is not
surprising that our legislation has been so often perverted — nor
will the restrictions which we have placed upon legislative power
be, in my judgment, sufficient to correct the abuse unless we
constitute the Senate upon a basis which will remove its responsibility to a merely local constituency."

On the other hand Jeremiah S. Black, Attorney-General and
Secretary of State in Buchanan's cabinet and one of the ablest
men in Pennsylvania, said he could imagine nothing more
demoralizing. "One House of the Legislature is then elected

entirely by a political oligarchy." This argument against entrusting the choice of the Senate to a State Convention of the predominant party seems to have been persuasive, for the proposal mustered only thirty-one votes. In passing, it should be noted that the general substitution of direct nomination for nomination by conventions has altered the premises on which many of the Pennsylvania arguments of 1873 were based.

In the matter of Representatives the original provision (1776) was that until the system of choice directed should begin, "each county at its own choice may be divided into districts, hold elections therein, and elect their Representatives in the county," etc. The Constitution of 1790 said: "No person residing within any city, town, or borough which shall be entitled to a separate representation, shall be elected a member for any county," etc. Each county was to have at least one Representative. The Constitution of 1838 said: "The Representatives shall be chosen annually, by the citizens of Philadelphia, and of each county respectively," etc. The only reference to districts was the provision that a Representative should be "an inhabitant of the district in and for which he shall be chosen a Representative."

By amendment ratified in 1857 references to the city of Philadelphia and counties were stricken out, and it was provided that in 1864 and every seventh year thereafter apportionment should be made by districts, "in proportion to the number of taxable inhabitants," with the proviso that any county having 3500 taxables might be allowed separate representation, that no more than three counties should be joined, that no county should be divided, and that any city with taxables enough to entitle it to two Representatives should have separate representation, in which case it was to be divided into single districts. The Constitution of 1873 directed apportionment by counties, after every United States census, each to have at least one Representative. Cities with a population equal to a ratio should elect separately. Every city entitled to more than four Representatives, and every county with more than one hundred thousand inhabitants, should be divided into districts, no district to elect more than four Representatives.

Massachusetts also in 1857 came to single Senatorial districts, but went farther than Pennsylvania, applying the system to the whole State. At the same time reorganizing its House of Representatives, on the numerical basis, it provided that no district

should choose more than three members. The allotment is first
to counties, and then each county is subdivided. Whether a
district shall be single, double, or triple depends on the county
commissioners, who are restricted by provision that wards and
towns shall not be divided, and who must make the best groupings they can to approximate equality. It is to be feared that
partisanship too often inspires the arithmetic of the process.

In 1859 Kansas said: "In the future apportionments of this
State, each organized county shall have at least one Representative; and each county shall be divided into as many districts as it has Representatives." Missouri in 1865 provided for
a sub-apportionment by single districts of counties, in the case
of both Senators and Representatives. California in 1879 applied the single district system to both Senators and Representatives. However, it cannot be said that the system has yet established itself. Ohio, in 1857, 1889, and 1893, refused at the
polls to accept amendments creating single legislative districts.
Even the newer and presumably more radical States have not
all taken up with the idea. Two of those organized in 1889
avoided it: Montana provided that no county should be divided
in the formation of Representative districts; and North Dakota
directed that Representatives should be elected "at large" from
each senatorial district.

The merits and demerits of the single district system became a
matter of national controversy in 1842. The Federal Constitution had said: "The House of Representatives shall be composed
of members chosen every second year by the people of the
several States." An unprejudiced reader, coming fresh to this
with no knowledge of what has happened, would in all probability say that it contemplated the election of Congressmen by
each State on a general ticket. The Constitution, however, also
said: "The times, places and manner of holding elections for
Senators and Representatives, shall be prescribed in each state
by the Legislature thereof." This came to be interpreted by
State after State as warranting them in providing for the election of Representatives by single districts. The general ticket
had resulted in throwing the whole delegation of each State into
the control of the political party dominant therein. What was
thought the injustice to minorities that this system worked led
to its downfall.

Francis Lieber, in his Manual of Political Ethics (II, 348), gave the prevailing view. "The members of the House of Representatives," he said, "are the direct representatives of the people, hence they are, in justice, apportioned according to population all over the land. That those from one State will act in many instances unitedly is natural, for the interest and public opinion of their constituents will lead them to do so; yet that they do not do so in a thousand cases, and ought not to do so, we all know. I hold it to be a principle of last importance, that the representative in Congress is a national representative. If this position of ours is correct, it appears that it is not acting upon the true principle of the Constitution of the United States if members of the House of Representatives of Congress are elected by general State ticket."

Six States out of the twenty-six yet adhered to the general ticket when the apportionment to be made on the basis of the census of 1840 came up for discussion, in 1842. Aiming chiefly to break up the delegations from New York and Pennsylvania, William Halstead, of New Jersey, moved that the States be required to elect by districts. Supported by the Whigs and opposed by the Democrats, this was passed, 101 to 99, in the House, and 29 to 19 in the Senate. It was opposed as unconstitutional, because it directed the State Legislatures to lay out districts, and deprived the citizen from voting for the entire congressional representation of his State. John Tyler was President, becoming such on the death of Harrison. Elected as a Whig, he had quarreled with the leaders of the party that chose him, and had reverted to Democratic sympathies. This Whig measure displeased him. He signed the bill, but filed a paper in the Secretary of State's office giving his reasons for entertaining deep and strong doubts of the constitutionality of the law. A resolution was adopted by the House calling upon the Secretary of State for a copy of this paper, which was sent to the House. It caused much feeling in that body. John Quincy Adams, as chairman of the committee to which it was referred, made a report condemning the act of the President as unwarranted, wholly unprecedented, of evil example for the future; and declaring that the House solemnly protested against its ever being repeated or adduced as a precedent. The committee stated that they considered the mandate to the States, to provide for electing Representatives to Congress by single districts, as the most important and useful feature of the act. Mr. Tyler, they said, was, by the course he had taken, only inviting such States as preferred to elect their members by general ticket to violate or refuse to comply with the law. As it turned out, four States refused for a short time to comply. Their contumacy brought the question before the House Committee on Elections. Its majority, reporting by Stephen A. Douglas, held the apportionment act unconstitutional. For the minority Garrett Davis held the other way. Neither report was adopted, but the House refused to unseat the members from the stubborn States. Presently these States fell in line with the others.

France has led the world in controversy about the matter. The quarrel is over election by *scrutin d'arrondissement*, sometimes called *scrutin uninominal*, that is, one member from each of the arrondissements (minor administrative districts), of which there are now 362; or by *scrutin de liste*, that is, a group chosen on general ticket by each of the Departments, of which there are now 86. For more than a hundred years the country has shifted from one system to the other and then back again. To enumerate all the changes would be futile, but the circumstances attending some of them may be instructive. *Scrutin de liste*, provided by the "Moderate" government in 1817, was replaced by *scrutin d'arrondissement* three years later as a result of the Royalist reaction, one member to a district being thought to the advantage of the country gentlemen and their tenants. The general ticket system prevailed when Louis Napoleon was elected Emperor by a plebiscite, but the new Constitution substituted the single ticket. After another crisis, that brought by the Franco-German war, the general ticket was put in force in the belief that it would give full expression to national sentiment, but the single ticket was revived in 1875, this time the hope being that it would safeguard the Republic against shocks.

Ten years later the general ticket came in again, at the suggestion of Gambetta, who thought it would accrue to the benefit of his party. It proved a boomerang. General Boulanger saw in it the chance to bolster up his fortunes, and he came near making it the means to annihilate his political foes. This was attempted through the French practice of letting a candidate stand in any Department, regardless of his residence. When a vacancy came, Boulanger was a candidate and by reason of his popularity easily won. He held the seat only till there was a vacancy in some other Department, when he resigned and became again a candidate, again winning. This he repeated, getting himself more and more vindicated and endorsed, until it looked as if he would succeed in his plan to be a candidate in all the Departments at the next general election, perhaps in the end making him another Napoleon. This would be virtually impossible under the single district system and so the *scrutin d'arrondissement* was hastily restored, before the general election of 1889.

The return to the old system brought a revival of familiar evils, which in time led to renewed agitation for the general ticket. The Briand ministry in 1909 championed the reform and in the following year went to the people with it at the head of its programme. Only one twelfth of the Deputies then chosen were openly hostile to the proposal and in 1912 by a large majority the Chamber passed a bill combining *scrutin de liste* with proportional representation. This came to grief in the Senate, in 1913, causing the resignation of Briand. Then the war interrupted the agitation, but it was successfully renewed, and at the election in November, 1919, the electors voted for as many Deputies as were allotted to any one Department.

Forthwith agitation began for change once more. The system not at the moment in use seems to be always the one preferred. By 1925 practically everybody was agreed upon return to the single ticket, but there was dispute over details not straightened out till two years afterward, when still once more it was decided that each voter should vote for one Deputy.

Italy too has swung back and forth, though nothing like so frequently as France. The general ticket was tried there from 1882 to 1891. Then there was return to the single ticket, which in turn was after the war, in 1919, replaced by *scrutinio di lista*, just as in France at the same time. As each district chose but from two to five Deputies, that sort of a ticket did not prove general enough to satisfy Mussolini and his Fascist following, and in November of 1927 authoritative proposal was made for one ticket covering the whole country.

In England the Representation of the People Act in 1918 provided that a borough entitled by its population to return either three or four members of Parliament should vote for them on general ticket; if entitled to five or more, it should be divided into districts electing not less than three nor more than five. To meet the demand for proportional representation, the result of a sharp contest between Commons and Lords was provision for commissioners to prepare a plan whereunder a hundred members should be elected from town and country areas combined into constituencies returning from three to seven members, the plan to be approved by Parliament.

The Japanese Reform Bill of 1902 gave to each of forty-seven rural constituencies from four to twelve seats, according to population; and to each of sixty-one urban constituencies either one or two seats, except that the largest three cities were to have eleven, six, and three seats respectively.

These are indications that the tendency is away from single districts, but it may be reversed at any time. The fact is that there are evils in both systems. They are of course supposed to be worse in the case of that system which happens at the moment to be in effect. So there are always reformers who want to change to the other. Of late both abroad and at home a return to the general ticket system has been particularly urged by the believers in proportional representation, who can carry out their most promising plan only if several men are to be elected at the same time. That is probably the chief impulse behind the British programme. On this side of the water in 1914 extremists went so far as to put before the voters of Oregon by means of the Initiative a proposal combining proportional representation with election of the Legislature at large, and it actually received 39,740 votes, but fortunately 137,116 voters saw its folly.

ARGUMENTS

The most common argument for the general ticket is that it will tend to make the legislator put the interests of State or nation as a whole above those of a particular district. It is believed that when he is chosen by a comparatively small electorate, he thinks himself its agent rather than a co-trustee for a State or nation of which the district is but a fraction. It is interesting to notice that Lieber in the quotation given above based his argument for single districts on this very proposition, and that Professor Duguit of the University of Bordeaux, one of the abler exponents of the opposite theory abroad, uses precisely the same proposition in support of the general ticket. Ogg quotes Duguit [1] as contending that the scheme of *scrutin de liste* (general ticket) harmonizes better than does that of *scrutin*

[1] F. A. Ogg, *The Governments of Europe*, 320.

d'arrondissement (single district) with the fundamental theory of representation in France, which is that deputies who go to Paris do so as representatives of the nation as a whole, not of a single locality.

Duguit and Lieber can be reconciled. Lieber's general ticket was that of an American State; Duguit's, that of a French Department. Our States have always had far more individuality than French Departments, which are mere administrative divisions of a highly centralized government. The representative of a Department would not deem himself called upon to advance its interests primarily, even if thereby getting some advantage over other Departments, but in Lieber's time the representative of a State was its ambassador, with its interests at heart and its welfare more important than any other consideration. As things are now in this country, it is quite probable that the general ticket would tend to lessen local influence; and few voices are raised to deny that such a result would be a gain. Most men of legislative experience would agree with the opinion expressed by the Bureau of Municipal Research in a document prepared to help the New York Constitutional Convention of 1915: "The acceptance of the purely fortuitous boundary lines of county and town has more than a negative importance. It places representatives in the attitude of local competition and reduces the Legislature as a branch of the government to the plane of a commercial exchange in which local representatives bicker for advantage. A second result has been to pit the country against the town in a contest of strength, which not infrequently defeats measures necessary to the highest welfare of the people of the State. A third result is that it causes the Legislature to retain control over many local matters that could best be left to county or municipal government." [1]

The second result mentioned is peculiar to New York and possibly two or three other States. Elsewhere it is not a conspicuous evil. The first and third results appear in the Legislature of every State in the Union.

The Bureau points out in the same document (page 3) that in organizing the legislative body "the principle of the representation of geographical districts, which was equitable enough in a time when rural communities and towns were fairly equal in population and possessed of substantially identical interests,

---

[1] *The Constitution and Government of the State of New York*, 61 (May, 1915).

has obtained to-day to vitiate the very essence of representation, namely, the accurate reflection of the will of all important groups of people in a highly complex society." One specific evil resulting from this was brought to the attention of a committee of the Convention itself, June 3, 1915, by President Goodnow of Johns Hopkins University. "There is," he said, "an irresistible tendency, which is to my mind one of the most dangerous tendencies of popular government, toward useless expenditures in localities for the purpose of influencing locally the standing of the Representative in the Legislature. There is not any use enlarging upon it. Any of you men who have been members of the Legislature know what pressure is brought to bear, and how difficult it is to resist." [1]

The evil is widespread, indeed is well-nigh universal, wherever representative government exists, and attempts at remedy do not yet appear efficacious. President Lowell, who speaks with authority on the governmental experience of Europe, says that general tickets in France and Italy accomplished no radical cure, for although local interests became larger, they were not effaced. [2]

England also feels the need of remedy. In proof let me quote from two recent writers who think. First, Sidney Low: "The device of using the local division as an electoral unit is so convenient that it is never likely to be abandoned, since it is a method of getting the legislature chosen, which cannot easily be bettered for simplicity and rough practical effectiveness. Yet it is both imperfect and unscientific, if the object be to bring together an assembly, in which the various elements of the population, and the leading activities and occupations of all classes, are fairly represented. It can hardly be pretended that, in these days, persons living in local juxtaposition have interests necessarily identical, or are in any but a purely physical and geographical sense the members of a community. This might possibly have been the case when difficulties of communication made men everywhere dependent on their immediate neighbors. These conditions have changed. Localities have weakened; the intercourse between persons of the same profession and the same class can be pursued easily enough on a national scale. The modern Englishman may love his neighbor; but he is not bound to have anything to do with him. On the other hand,

[1] N.Y. Convention, Document No. 13, 7.   [2] *Public Opinion*, 120.

those with whom he is associated, in sentiment and interest, and with whom indeed he is in frequent contact, may have their place of residence many miles away.... It is undoubtedly a defect in the House of Commons that it takes no account of the interests which have grown up irrespective of locality." [1]

Next, H. G. Wells, writing in 1914: "The world is passing rapidly from localised to generalised interests, but the method of election into which our fathers fell is the method of electing one or two representatives from strictly localised constituencies. Its immediate corruption was inevitable. If discussing and calculating the future had been, as it ought to be, a common, systematic occupation, the muddles of to-day might have been foretold a hundred years ago. From such a rough method of election the party system followed as a matter of course. In theory, of course, there may be any number of candidates for a constituency, and a voter votes for the one he likes best; in practice there are only two or three candidates, and the voter votes for the most likely to beat the candidate he likes least. It cannot be too strongly insisted that in contemporary elections we vote against; we do not vote for." [2]

The damage done by the single district system is greater here than it is abroad because of our practice in restricting choice to residents of the district. This is particularly noticeable in the large cities, where a few wards are likely to contain most of the men of intellectual capacity, special training, and large experience. The representation of these wards, however, is no greater than that of others having very few residents especially qualified by study or otherwise to make laws. This gives force to the suggestion of Albert Shaw that the group system be applied to cities. "In the choice of practically half the Legislature from the great metropolis of New York," he said, "it is plain that this system of small districts does not give us a kind of representation at Albany that is suited to the actual conditions. There are hundreds of measures coming up at Albany that affect the city of New York as a whole. There is no measure that affects the particular Assembly district, whether on the lower East Side or in one of the outlying boroughs. A group system, where members of the Legislature come from a large city, would probably give better representation. The time will come, I am confident,

---

[1] *The Governance of England*, 243.

[2] *Social Forces in England and America*, 304.

when we shall elect members of the Legislature from our great cities upon the plan of large districts from which a group of members are to be elected, with some system of cumulative voting or minority representation." [1]

Besides the undue importance given by the single-district system to the accident of sleeping place, at any rate in cities, there is another reason for preferring the group system. To elect but one man from a district lessens the chance of bringing into public life men with no talent for electioneering. That lack is often the case with studious men, men who are a little shy, perhaps conscious of lack of experience in public speaking, perhaps over-modest. A legislative body made up wholly of such men would be a sorry affair. It would be neither representative nor efficient. Yet the presence of some such men is desirable. They stand a better chance of getting drafted if several places are to be filled at the same time.

Also it is probable that on the whole the group system makes it easier to keep in office during a series of terms men especially qualified for the work of lawmaking — one of the most important needs of our public life. Single districts favor the rotation plan.

Furthermore, candidates who descend to the lower methods of getting support, such as the promise of help in procuring public contracts or appointment to office, or who buy votes outright, find it much harder to profit thereby when running on a ticket with others than when running alone. William Lilly was not much out of the way, at any rate so far as the big cities are concerned, when in the Pennsylvania Convention of 1873 he said of the single-district system: "It perpetuates in power the smallest kind of small politicians and of the corruptest possible stripe."

These various considerations have led sundry critics to deplore the change from large to small districts. James Schouler has written sharply of what he thought the effects of this change in Massachusetts. "Representation," he says, "now came much under the control of intriguers and petty seekers for place; instead of centurions in politics were the leaders of tens and twenties; while towns, cherishing local pride no longer, had to be content with bargaining that the common deputy of the geometrically arranged district for the time being should be put up at one locality for one Legislature, and at another for the next.

[1] Albert Shaw, "The Problems of the Constitutional Convention," Address as Presiding Officer of the Academy of Political Science, November 19, 1914.

Deterioration of ideals and of personal character comes as a necessary consequence of all this nicety in fractional representation, though other causes of political degeneracy may doubtless be sought elsewhere." [1]

In view of Mr. Schouler's belief that small districts brought representation under the control of intriguers, it is edifying to find President Lowell telling us that "in Italy as in France the organization and power of the local wire-pullers grew with the increase in the number of deputies elected in a district." [2]

Apparently change produces the same result either way.

Such differences of judgment do not extend to one consideration that must be thrown in the scale on the side of the single district. It is beyond question that every enlargement of the electorate lessens the degree of personal knowledge about candidates on the part of the electors. In an argument for the single district plan of electing Senators, Delegate Morris told the New York Convention of 1846 that he knew of a young man sent from New York City whom the voters elected supposing they were voting for either his uncle or grandfather. They never discovered their mistake until he came to Albany to be sworn, when it was found the voters had elected a very clever boy of twenty-one instead of a man of experience. Ex-Governor J. F. Fort of New Jersey said to the Economic Club of Boston, November 29, 1915: "I have lived in Essex County in my State for forty years. We now have a system that is bad. We used to elect our Assembly by Assembly districts. Then I voted for only one and I knew him. But now they elect a general ticket throughout the whole county and we each vote for twelve. That is a mistake. If there is only one you can find out about him. Now we may do injury to one for the sins of others."

It is certainly true that some of the strongest arguments for the short-ballot reform militate against electing groups of Representatives. They lose much of their force, however, if the group idea is not carried so far as in New Jersey, or as in Australia, where for the election of Federal Senators the country has been divided into some half-dozen gigantic electoral districts. No serious difficulty is caused by the lessened chance of acquaintance in the double and triple districts that elect a good part of the Massachusetts House of Representatives. My personal ob-

[1] James Schouler, *Constitutional Studies*, 250.

[2] *Governments and Parties in Continental Europe*, i, 158.

servation of and share in the politics of a city that had all told six Representatives in the Massachusetts House, elected in two districts with three each (the largest permitted by the Constitution), lead me to think even better results might have been secured by electing all six on one ticket; that such men as ought to have been sent to the Legislature would have been known throughout the city; that there would have been somewhat less of those features of electioneering least to the liking of men who approach public office as an opportunity for public service rather than private advantage. On the other hand, the perfectly legitimate expense of campaigning would have been twice as great, its other burdens twice as irksome. In the matter of the relative sense of local and State obligation on the part of the men elected, it would not have made the slightest difference. That factor is constant as long as districts are either municipalities or parts of municipalities. It changes when districts become larger. This makes it worth while to note a suggestion of Governor O'Neal of Alabama. He said: "The practice of giving representatives to each county should be abandoned. With a certain number of the members representing the State at large, the other members should be elected from districts, according to population." [1] Such a system ought to result in a representation of both local and general interests with happy results. On the face of it I see no reason why it might not work out usefully. It ought at any rate to insure the presence in the Legislature of more men of high standing, wide experience, and tested capacity than are now found frequently in the Legislatures of the land.

THE GERRYMANDER

Constitutional provisions have frequently been framed with the hope of preventing gain of partisan advantage in apportionment. The chance of such gain early suggested itself. Elmer C. Griffith thinks that Pennsylvania began the questionable practice. In his scholarly monograph on "The Rise and Development of the Gerrymander," he attributes its birth to the action of Penn's colony in 1705 when the Delaware counties had been allowed to withdraw. The Assembly had consisted of four from each county and two from the city of Philadelphia. Now the number from each county was made eight. Doctor Griffith, recognizing that this caused little if any injustice at the begin-

[1] "Distrust of State Legislatures," *North American Review*, May, 1914.

ning, finds its harm in the later refusal of the counties to revise
the apportionment as Philadelphia grew in relative importance.
It seems to me this takes the case out of the class of transactions
that later came to be known as gerrymanders, which are better
treated as premeditated attempts to obtain unjust advantage.
The real spirit of the evil appears more clearly in the prevalence
of attempts in Virginia to change county lines for political gain.
Governor Spotswood of that colony, writing in 1710, said the
voters frequently considered the attitude taken by the various
candidates for the House upon this question, and it was often
the sole issue on which the election turned. The Governor of
North Carolina was engaged as early as 1732 in dividing precincts for his own political ends, and the device was not unknown in other colonies.

It was, however, with the beginnings of political parties as we
now know them that the practice took on serious importance.
Parties were the product of the Federal Constitution, which
divided the people into two groups, its friends and its foes,
speedily to become those favoring and those opposing a strong
central government. While it was a matter of friends and foes,
the vital issue was the adoption of amendments, notably those
designed to be a Bill of Rights. In Virginia the advocates of such
amendments, led by Patrick Henry, strongly opposed the election of James Madison to either branch of Congress, partly because he was supposed to object to amendments. First they prevented his election to the Federal Senate. Two thirds of the
members of the Legislature were hostile to the Constitution and
so Madison was defeated, though a change of five votes would
have elected him. Then he turned to the House as his chance to
help start the machine in framing which he had played so great
a part. His friends then claimed and very likely he himself believed that at this juncture the opposition, under the lead of
Patrick Henry, resorted to unfair expedients. Rives, the biographer of Madison, says that in laying off the State into districts,
ingenious and artificial combinations were made for the purpose
of securing his defeat. The county in which he lived was thrown
into association with seven others, five of which, through their
delegates to the State Convention, had given an undivided vote
against the adoption of the Constitution. If there was a plot, it
failed, for Madison was elected by a handsome majority.[1]

[1] *Life and Times of James Madison,* II, 651–57.

Most writers have accepted this view of it and have held Henry responsible for the real introduction of the gerrymander in American politics. Doctor Griffith, however, has come to the rescue of Henry's reputation with a careful study of the case, from which he draws the conclusion that adequate proof of a gerrymander is lacking, but that possibly the attempt was made by Henry to include such other counties in that district as would have kept his rival from Congress.

There were a dozen or more clear instances of the practice, and constitutional provisions seeking to restrict it, in Pennsylvania, Tennessee, and Kentucky, before it found a name. It was christened in Massachusetts, in 1812. The Constitution of that State directed forty Senators to be chosen in such districts as the General Court might designate, with not more than six Senators to any one district. At the start counties were taken as the basis. When the Republicans got control of the State in 1810, they determined to arrange matters if possible so they might keep their grip on the State Senate. Early in 1812 they revised the districts without regard to county lines, overcame Federalist strongholds, and in the next Senate had twenty-nine Senators out of forty. Elbridge Gerry was then Governor. Austin says in his biography of Gerry that the districts for election of members of Congress had always been arranged by the Federal party, as far as it could be done, with the same object and on the same system, but previously the intention was less easily fastened on the authors than in the present instance, where it was too apparent to be denied. To Gerry the project was extremely disagreeable. He urged to his friends strong arguments against its policy as well as against its effects. After it had passed both Houses he hesitated to give it his signature, and meditated returning it to the Legislature with his objections to its becoming a law, but being satisfied that it conformed to the Constitution, he doubted whether the private opinion of a Governor on a mere question of propriety or policy would justify the interposition of his negative.[1]

It is odd indeed that a law signed under such circumstances should have made the name of the signer part of a word that now for more than a hundred years has been used as an epithet of opprobrium and bids fair to carry that significance for many a generation yet to come. The story has been told in different

[1] J. T. Austin, *Life of Elbridge Gerry*, II, 347.

ways. The one thing sure seems to be that a map of the two districts of Essex County was printed in the "Boston Weekly Messenger" of March 6, showing one fairly compact district half encircled by another of distorted outline. Some say it was at a dinner party, others say it was in the office of the "Columbian Centinel," that somebody noticed the resemblance of the outer district to a prehistoric monster. One story is that the artist Stuart added a head, wings, and claws with his pencil and turning to the editor said, "There, that will do for a Salamander." This version has it that the editor, punning on the Governor's name, retorted: "Better call it a Gerrymander." John Ward Dean, however, thinks the artist was Elkanah Tisdale and that it was probably Mr. Alsop who suggested the name now universally used.[1] A huge cut of the monster was prepared and spread over the State as a broadside, with such effect that in the spring of the next year the people overthrew the Republicans, and gave the control of the Senate again to the Federalists, who repealed the obnoxious law.

In that same year of 1812 when the practice got its name, the other side, the Federalists, resorted to the same device in New Jersey. The Republicans had a majority of twenty-five hundred of the votes of the people, but the Federalists controlled the Legislature, and so they applied the gerrymander to the arrangement of congressional districts. Their six Representatives had been chosen by general ticket. Now three districts sending two Representatives each were so arranged that two of the districts were Federalist and one Republican.

So rapidly did the practice spread that Constitution-makers everywhere began trying to check it. For instance, Missouri in 1820 provided that when a Senatorial district was composed of two or more counties, one should not be entirely separated from another. Many other States since then have searched for adequate restraints, the remedies developing until in 1907 Oklahoma provided that no district, whether Senatorial or Representative, should contain a greater excess in population over an adjoining district in the same county than the population of a town or ward, constituting only one voting precinct therein, adjoining such district. Nevertheless gerrymandering has become so general and familiar a procedure that it may fairly be called a characteristic of American politics. So Bryce looked

[1] *N.E. Historical and Genealogical Register*, xlvi, 374–83 (1892).

upon it. He found a district in Mississippi (the so-called Shoestring District) five hundred miles long by forty broad, and another in Pennsylvania resembling a dumb-bell. And in Missouri a district had been contrived longer, if measured along its windings, than the State itself, into which as large a number as possible of the negro voters had been thrown. Although these were the extremes naturally pounced upon by a critic, it is not to be denied that he might have compiled a long list of gerrymanders, with a picturesque assortment of nicknames.

America, however, no longer has a monopoly of the practice. Perhaps hereafter foreign critics, having begun to acquire glass houses of their own, will desist from throwing stones. In 1927 a committee of the French Assembly, the Commission on Universal Suffrage, flagrantly gerrymandered France. To the general rule that no district was to have less than 40,000 or more than 100,000 population, itself an inequitable rule, it made forty-nine exceptions, creating seventeen constituencies with less than the minimum of the rule and thirty-two with more than the maximum. The result was that 588,000 persons had an average of one Deputy to 34,600, and 3,536,000 had one to 110,500. The published excuse was the necessity of maintaining "an equilibrium between the representation of the cities and the countryside," but an American observer of the bitter debates on the electoral bill in the Chamber read between the lines "the sordid story of bargaining for individual and party advantage." [1]

JUDICIAL AND OTHER VIEWS

Doubtless because of the difficulty in coping constitutionally with evils of this class, many years passed before our courts were called on to help, and then it was found that they were most reluctant to question legislative judgment. Thus in Prouty v. Stover, 11 Kas. 233 (1873), Justice Brewer, speaking for the Court, said: "An apportionment cannot be overthrown because the representatives are not distributed with mathematical accuracy, according to the population. Something must be left to the discretion of the Legislature, and it may without invalidating the apportionment make one district of a larger population than another. It may rightfully consider the compactness of territory, the density of population, and also we think the

---

[1] Walter J. Shepard, "The New French Electoral Law," *American Political Science Review*, August, 1928.

probable changes of the future in making the distribution of representatives."

However, after the census of 1890 the injustice of apportionments in some of the States became so glaring that the courts felt they must interfere. In Michigan the new arrangement of Senatorial districts was held to be unconstitutional because "an honest and fair discretion was not exercised." In concurring opinions gerrymandering was severely denounced in very plain language by three of the Justices.[1] In Wisconsin an apportionment of both Senate and Assembly districts was upset, the Court declaring that the differences between the districts bore "upon their face the intrinsic evidence that no judgment or discretion was exercised." [2]

One of the objections in Wisconsin was to the dismemberment of counties. The same objection prevailed in Indiana, where it was held that the splitting of counties to form Senatorial districts was obnoxious as constituting a gerrymander, and likewise the union of three counties in Representative districts, this being "an attempt to do indirectly that which could not be done directly, namely form districts of counties not contiguous." [3] County division also brought to grief the New Jersey apportionment act of 1891 with its supplements of 1892, most remarkably, for the Court saw fit to invalidate a practice acquiesced in through forty years. The Constitution of 1844 had required the election of members of the Assembly "by the legal voters of the counties respectively." Under this provision members were chosen at large by counties until a statute was enacted in 1852 dividing the counties into districts. Much gerrymandering followed but not until 1893 was constitutionality invoked.[4] Rarely has a situation so long accepted been disturbed by the judicial branch.

In the same period the question was taken to the higher courts of New York. In 1892 a law involving numbers rather than geography was upheld.[5] In the following year, when a county districting was voided, the Court laid down an intelligible rule: "It must be a grave, palpable, and unreasonable deviation from

[1] Giddings v. Blacker, 93 Mich. 1 (1892).
[2] State v. Cunningham, 81 Wis. 440 (1892).
[3] Parker v. State, 133 Ind. 178 (1892).
[4] State v. Wrightson, 56 N.J.L. 126 (1893).
[5] People v. Rice, 135 N.Y. 473 (1892).

the standard, so that when the facts are presented argument would not be necessary to convince a fair man that very great and wholly unnecessary irregularity has been provided for." [1] A year later a second apportionment was supported on the ground that irregularity of a city district does not necessarily show inconvenience.[2]

The Constitution of New York does not require compactness. In Illinois, on the other hand, districts must be "compact," and about this time the meaning of that word there became important. The Court sustained an apportionment act, saying: "The provision that districts shall be formed of contiguous and compact territory means that the counties or subdivisions of counties (when counties may be divided), when combined to form a district, must not only touch each other, but must be closely united, territorially." [3] Another aspect of the same problem came to the front in the contested election case of Parsons v. Saunders in the Sixty-First Congress (1909–1911), the majority of Elections Committee No. 2 recommending that the contestant should be seated because of the outrageous character of a gerrymandering of districts in Virginia. The contention was that when the Legislature transferred Floyd County from one district to another, the requirement of contiguity was violated, because though there remained a ten-mile strip of contiguity as shown by the map, in reality a mountain ridge prevented travel by road between the inhabitants of one half of the district and those of the other half. The report was made late in the session and was sent back to the committee, with the result that in the end no action was taken by the House.

The extent to which the gerrymandering abuse was carried after the census of 1890 gave President Benjamin Harrison occasion to discuss the matter in his third annual message, December 9, 1891, by reason of the action of Michigan concerning the method of choosing presidential electors. "For nearly sixty years," he said, "all the States save one have appointed their electors by a popular vote upon a general ticket, and for nearly thirty years this method was universal. After a full test of other methods, without important division or dissent in any State and without any purpose of party advantage, as we must believe, but

[1] Baird et al. v. Supervisors, etc., 138 N.Y. 95 (1893).
[2] Matter of Baird, 142 N.Y. 523 (1894).
[3] People v. Thompson, 155 Ill. 451 (1895).

solely upon the considerations that uniformity was desirable and
that a general election in territorial divisions not subject to
change was most consistent with the popular character of our
institutions, best preserved the equality of the voters, and perfectly removed the choice of President from the baneful inference
of the 'gerrymander,' the practice of all the States was brought
into harmony. That this concurrence should now be broken is,
I think, an unfortunate and even a threatening episode, and one
that may well suggest whether the States that still give their approval to the old and prevailing method ought not to secure by a
constitutional amendment a practice which has had the approval
of all. The recent Michigan legislation provides for choosing
what are popularly known as the Congressional electors for
President by Congressional districts and the two Senatorial
electors by districts created for that purpose. This legislation
was, of course, accompanied by a new Congressional apportionment, and the two statutes bring the electoral vote of the State
under the influence of the 'gerrymander.'

"These gerrymanders for Congressional purposes are in most
cases buttressed by a gerrymander of the legislative districts,
thus making it impossible for a majority of the legal voters of
the State to correct the apportionment and equalize the Congressional districts. A minority rule is established that only a
political convulsion can overthrow. I have recently been advised that in one county of a certain State three districts for the
election of members of the Legislature are constituted as follows:
One has sixty-five thousand population, one fifteen thousand,
and one ten thousand, while in another county detached, non-
contiguous sections have been united to make a legislative district. These methods have already found effective application
to the choice of Senators and Representatives in Congress, and
now an evil start has been made in the direction of applying
them to the choice by the States of electors of President and
Vice-President. If this is accomplished, we shall then have the
three great departments of the Government in the grasp of the
'gerrymander,' the legislative and executive directly and the
judiciary indirectly through the power of appointment....

"Nothing just now is more important than to provide every
guaranty for the absolutely fair and free choice by an equal suffrage within the respective States of all the officers of the National Government, whether that suffrage is applied directly, as

in the choice of members of the House of Representatives, or indirectly, as in the choice of Senators and electors of President. Respect for public officers and obedience to law will not cease to be the characteristics of our people until our elections cease to declare the will of majorities fairly ascertained without fraud, suppression, or gerrymander. If I were called upon to declare wherein our chief national danger lies, I should say without hesitation in the overthrow of majority control by the suppression or perversion of the popular suffrage. That there is a real danger here all must agree; but the energies of those who see it have been chiefly expended in trying to fix responsibility upon the opposite party rather than in efforts to make such practices impossible by either party."

This is the conventional view, the view taken by every writer on the subject whose opinions have come to my notice. Now for an unconventional view. Since written judgments are unanimous that gerrymandering is reprehensible and odious, it would not be safe to put forward a statement of the other side of the case as a defense. Rather call it an explanation. Surely there is some need to explain how it happens that hundreds, yes, thousands of legislators, sworn to maintain a Constitution, have proceeded to violate its spirit if not its letter by apportionments palpably meant to advance the interests of their party. This they could not have done without public consent. But how can the public consent to an unfair and dishonorable practice? The answer is that fairness and honor are conventions, with standards determined by the many and not by the few. The many look upon partisanship as in the nature of war. Whatever helps toward victory is right until proved wrong. This is the result of neither whim nor indifference. On the contrary it springs from an earnest conviction that party purposes are of gravest consequence and call for the utmost endeavor. Every party urges with all the strength at command that on its success depends the public welfare, the general happiness, perhaps the common safety. Once in our history such convictions led to Civil War, a struggle transferred from legislative halls to the battlefield. It was partisanship carried to an extreme but perfectly logical conclusion.

So it comes about that a device like the gerrymander may be detested by the few through a century and yet be permitted by the many — more than that, may be accepted or even encouraged. If to you or me it seems an undesirable device, likely to work many kinds of mischief, ours is the duty to try to persuade others to that effect. Therein we shall not quickly succeed by starting from the assumption that there are not two sides to the matter, or by using epithets instead of argument.

CHAPTER XVIII

CORRUPT PRACTICES IN ELECTIONS

A SKETCH of the part played by the suffrage in representative government would be incomplete without a reference to vitiating the expression of the public will by what have come to receive the name of "corrupt practices." Manifestly the more votes are bought, the less accuracy can be assumed in the result as a reflection of public opinion. Corruption in elections is therefore a serious evil and should be earnestly combated by all good citizens. Yet he who to-day turns the pages of history can find no reason to think that duty in this respect is more pressing than it ever was before. Freeman wrote wisely about it. "Under any conceivable electoral system," he said, "many votes will be given blindly, recklessly, and corruptly. Men who are careless about political differences, if well to do in the world and not devoid of a conscience, will not vote at all; if they are at once poor and unprincipled, they will sell their votes. Many again who are not corrupted will be deceived; a hustings speech has become almost a proverb for insincerity. This ignorance, carelessness, and corruption among the electors appears to be the inherent vice of representative government on a large scale. There is probably no form of government under which bribery can be wholly prevented. It is a vice which comes everywhere in some shape or other, but which varies its shapes infinitely. If bribery appears in a despotism or in a city-commonwealth it commonly takes the form of bribery of the rulers; in a representative government, it takes the form, the really worse form, of bribery of the electors." [1]

In Rome as wealth grew, corruption grew. Long before the Republic fell, the evil called for penalties. In 181 B.C. appeared the first of numerous laws against bribery at elections, declaring any one found guilty thereof incapable of being a candidate for the next ten years.

In England corruption began when seats in Parliament came to be desirable. Bishop Burnet tells us that on the occasion of the choice of Queen Mary's first Parliament, Gardiner, Bishop of Winchester, was sent to the Emperor "to inform him that

---

[1] *History of Federal Government*, I, 83.

unless great sums of money were sent over for carrying the elections the opposition would be such that the Queen must lay
down all thoughts of marrying his son." [1]

The first record of punishment for bribery in English elections
is that of a fine imposed on the borough of Westbury in 1571, for
receiving a bribe of four pounds from Thomas Long. Westbury
seems to have been blamed, however, not so much because it
took a bribe as because it was so thoughtless as to receive the
four pounds from one "being a very simple man and of small
capacity to serve in that place." The evil appears to have first
developed into a system in the reign of Charles II. It grew apace
after the Revolution of 1688 made seats in Parliament more
desirable. Sir Walter Clarges was alleged to have spent two
thousand pounds at the Westminster election of 1695, unsuccessfully. Defoe tells us, in a pamphlet published in 1701, that
there was a regular set of stock-jobbers in the City (of London)
who made it their business to buy and sell seats in Parliament;
that the market price was a thousand guineas; and that Parliament was thus in a fair way of coming under the management of
a few individuals.[2]

Under George I action was felt to be necessary and in 1728 a
bill was passed imposing severe penalties and making a corrupt
election void. Little good it did. Much more bribery took place
in the election of 1747 than ever before, and from then on it was
a notorious scandal. In 1754 Sir J. Barnard actually moved the
repeal of the bribery oath, in the interest of public morals, on the
ground that it was the occasion of general perjury. With the
reign of George III comes the acknowledgment of a property
right in boroughs, which were held capable of sale or transfer,
like any other property. In 1764 Lord Chesterfield advises his
son how best to get a thousand pounds for the surrender of a seat
that had cost him two thousand. Prices rise, by reason of the
competition of the nabobs, the newly rich from the East or West
Indies, the great Lords, the commissaries. The market rate
ranges from twenty-five hundred to four thousand pounds.
Sir George Selwyn sells Ludgershall for nine thousand pounds.
In 1767 the Mayor of Oxford and other magistrates write a letter
to their two members of Parliament offering to reëlect them for a

[1] *History of the Reformation*, II, 261.
[2] "The Freeholder's Plea against Stock-jobbing Elections of Parliament,"
Wilson, *Life of Defoe*, I, 340–41.

specified amount. The letter being produced in the House, the writers are arrested and committed to Newgate, stay there for some time, and then are released upon petitioning the House, having been first reprimanded, while on their knees, by the Speaker. Meantime, while in Newgate, they sell the representation of their city to the Duke of Marlborough and the Earl of Abingdon. The town clerk carries off their books, with the evidences of the bargain, and the business is laughed at and forgotten.

The sale of seats went on for half a century longer, until the Reform Bill destroyed the system of rotten boroughs. Professor Pryme says: "I have seen an advertisement offering a borough for sale (Westbury), as not only to be sold, but to be sold by order of the Court of Chancery. A short time before the Reform Bill, Lord Monson paid one hundred thousand pounds for Gatton, which contained about twenty-five houses, and rather more than one hundred inhabitants."

Lord Palmerston described in his Journal the manipulation of constituencies by the Grenville Administration in 1806. The Ministers bought seats from their friends at a low price, making up the deficiency probably by appointments and promotions. These seats they afterward sold out at the average market price to men who promised them support; and with the difference they carried on their contested elections. "The sum raised in this manner was stated, by a person who was in the secret, to be inconceivably great, and accounts for an assertion afterwards made by Lord Grenville in the Lords', that 'not one guinea of the public money had been spent in elections.'" This observation seems to indicate that the spending of public money for party elections would not have been deemed, on the part of any Government, an extraordinary occurrence.

In Scotland matters were even worse than in England. The Lord Advocate in 1831 told a grotesque instance in the matter of the county of Bute, with a population of fourteen thousand and but twenty-one electors, of whom only one resided in the county. Only one person attended the meeting, except the Sheriff and the returning officer. "He, of course, took the chair, constituted the meeting, called over the roll of freeholders, answered to his own name, took the vote as to the Preses, and elected himself. He then moved and seconded his own nomination, put the question as to the vote, and was unanimously returned."

Along with the sale of seats came an enormous increase in the costs of election. From Lord Chesterfield's letters to his son we learn that the contest for the borough of Northampton was stated to have cost the candidates at least thirty thousand pounds a side. Lord Spencer is said to have spent seventy thousand pounds in contesting this borough, and in the proceedings upon an election petition that resulted. The rivalries of great families in the counties led to the wildest extravagances. The Duke of Portland is supposed to have spent forty thousand pounds in contesting Westmoreland and Cumberland with Sir James Lowther in 1768, and Lowther must have spent at least as much. Lord Brougham notes that the committee which conducted Mr. Wilberforce's election for Yorkshire in 1807 put their expenses at fifty-eight thousand pounds, "with every resource of the most rigid economy, and great voluntary assistance in labor." An election for the county of York is known to have cost nearly one hundred and fifty thousand pounds.

May tells in his "Constitutional History of England" (i, 277 et sqq.) of an episode that will interest those who fear the extension of governmental activities by public ownership or otherwise may involve us in political troubles heretofore unknown on this side of the water. The Seven Years' War had increased taxation, and consequently the number of officers employed in the collection of revenue. It was quite understood to be part of their duty to vote for the candidate who hoisted the colors of the minister of the day. In the cities and ports troops of petty officers of custom and excise were driven to the poll, and, supported by venal freemen, overpowered the independent electors. In 1768 Mr. Dowdesdell tried in vain to insert a clause in a bribery bill for disqualification of such officers. In 1780 a like clause was again rejected, and once more in 1781. In 1782 the ministry felt compelled to meet the issue. Its imperative necessity was proved by Lord Rockingham himself, who stated that seventy elections chiefly depended on the votes of these officers; and that eleven thousand five hundred officers of custom and excise were electors. In one borough he said that one hundred and twenty out of the five hundred voters had obtained revenue appointments, through the influence of a single person. The measure was now carried by large majorities, though not without remonstrance against its principle, especially from Lord Mansfield. "It is not to be denied," says May, "that the disqualification of any class of men is, abstractedly, opposed to liberty, and an illiberal principle of legislation; but here was a gross constitutional abuse requiring correction; and though many voters were deprived of the rights of citizenship, — these rights could not be freely exercised, and were sacrificed in order to protect the general liberties of the people."

All this means bribery in many forms and on the largest scale. Pages might be filled with instances, but to give a few will suffice. Note, for example, the ingenious device of a majority of the electors of New Shoreham in 1771. They had formed an association, called "The Christian Club," which, under the guise of charity, had been in the habit of selling the borough to the highest bidder. The members divided the spoil among themselves. They all fearlessly took the bribery oath, as the bargain had been made by a committee of the club, who refrained from voting, and the money was not distributed until after the election. In 1782 it appeared that out of two hundred and forty-three electors of Cricklade, eighty-three had already been convicted of bribery, and actions were pending against forty-three others, whereupon the House mildly met the situation by extending the franchise to the freeholders of the adjoining hundreds. In 1819 Sir Manasseh Lopes was sentenced to pay a fine of ten thousand pounds and to be imprisoned in Exeter Gaol for two years, for bribing several of the electors of the borough of Grampound. The freemen of Grampound were known to have boasted of receiving three hundred guineas a man for their votes at one election. Respecting the general election of 1826, the "Times" of June 20 said: "At Sudbury, four cabbages sold for ten pounds, and a plate of gooseberries fetched twenty-five pounds; the sellers where these articles were so dear being voters. At Great Marlow, on the contrary, things were cheap, and an elector during the election bought a sow and nine young pigs for a penny."

A story told of the Irish borough of Cashel shows how the voters usually scored. The electors, fourteen in number, always sold their votes. The favorite candidate at one election, anxious to win the seat honestly and not to spend a penny in corruption, got the parish priest to preach a sermon at Mass, on the Sunday before the polling, against the immorality of trafficking in the franchise. The good man went so far as to declare that those who betrayed a public trust by selling their votes would go to Hell. Next day the candidate met one of the electors and asked what

was the effect of the sermon. "Your honor," said he, "votes
have risen. We always got twenty pounds for a vote before we
knew it was a sin to sell it; but as his reverence tells us that we
will be damned for selling our votes, we can't for the future
afford to take less than forty pounds." [1]

Feeble attempts to meet the evil by legislation appear from
time to time, in 1762 pecuniary penalties for bribery, in 1782 and
1783 bills unsuccessfully proposed by Lord Mahon to check corruption at elections, and other occasional evidences of an uneasy
public conscience, but for the most part the situation was accepted as natural and the offenses were generally viewed as more
venial than venal. Upright statesmen found ways of excusing
themselves for their share in the system. For instance, Sir
Samuel Romilly, who bought his seat for Horsham from the Duke
of Norfolk for two thousand pounds and yet is characterized by
May as "the most pure and virtuous of public men," wrote in
1805: "One who should carry his notions of purity so far, that,
thinking he possessed the means of rendering service to his
country, he would yet rather seclude himself altogether from
Parliament, than get into it by such a violation of the theory of
the constitution, must be under the dominion of a species of
moral superstition which must wholly disqualify him for the
discharge of any public duties." [2]

Only after the Reform Act did public opinion begin to raise
its standards, with a new conception of the relation between
representatives and constituents, a new ideal of civic morality;
but the purifying of the public conscience is a slow process and
no exception is to be found here. In 1841 Lord John Russell
introduced an act changing the rules of evidence in bribery cases,
so that committees were required to receive evidence generally
upon the charges of bribery, without prior investigation of
agency. This was followed in the next year by an act providing
for the prosecution of investigations into bribery after an election committee had closed its inquiries, or where charges of
bribery had been withdrawn. These measures not having proved
effectual, in 1852 another act was passed, providing for the most
searching inquiry by commissioners appointed by the Crown, on
the address of the two Houses of Parliament, when corrupt
practices were alleged. Other acts followed, but bribery per-

[1] Michael MacDonagh, *The Pageant of Parliament*, i, 27.
[2] Diary; *Life*, ii, 122.

sisted. At Canterbury 155 electors were bribed at one election, 799 at another; at Barnstable, 255; at Cambridge, 111; at Kingston-upon-Hull, 847. In 1858, 183 freemen of Galway received bribes; in 1859, 250 of Gloucester; and in Wakefield, a borough created by the Reform Act, 98 persons were concerned in bribing 86 electors.

Public opinion was not ripe for thoroughgoing reform until 1881. Then Mr. Gladstone set himself the task and his ministry produced the Corrupt Practices Act that became law in 1883. It did not end corruption and it did not make elections costless, but it wrought wonders.

Another step was taken when the Representation of the People Act in 1918 transferred the burden of the official election expenses from candidates to the government. At the same time the limit of a candidate's outlay for county constituencies was made sevenpence an elector, and in boroughs fivepence. The act also provided that every candidate for Parliament must deposit one hundred and fifty pounds, which will be returned to him if he gets one eighth of the votes cast. This at first blush might seem a step away from relief for candidates, but as a rule it is likely to lessen their expenditures, by hindering insincere opposition, conceived with money profit in view — what in the parlance of American politics are known as "fake candidacies." No genuine candidate is likely to forfeit his deposit.

AMERICAN ADVANCE

In America the proof is equally clear that society has advanced to a higher stage of public morals. Those who worry see in the prevalence of an evil at any given time or place evidence of degeneracy. Corruption in elections does exist, lamentably, in various parts of the United States, but we may at any rate console ourselves with the knowledge that our ancestors found occasion for drastic laws against corrupt practices even in Puritan Commonwealths where the standards of morals are commonly presumed to have been both unusually high and unusually observed. The General Court of Massachusetts Bay ordered, October 17, 1643, "that if any freeman shall put in more than one paper or bean for the choice of any officer, he shall forfeit ten pounds for every offence; and any man that is not free, putting in any vote, shall forfeit the like sum of ten pounds." This did not suffice or else the evil grew, for the law as it appears in the revision of 1660 had been expanded into: "It is ordered by this Court and the Authority thereof, That for the yearly chosing of Assistants, the freemen shall use Indian Corn and Beans, the Indian Corn to manifest election, the Beans contrary, and if any freeman shall put in more than one Indian Corn or Bean for the Choice or refusal of any public Officer, he shall forfeit for such every offence, Ten Pounds, and that any man that is not free, or hath not liberty of voting, putting in any vote shall forfeit the like Sum of Ten Pounds."

After Massachusetts became a State the first "corrupt practices" case reported is that of John Pratt of Mansfield, charged in 1784 with having obtained his election "by bribery, and by corrupting the minds of as many as he could by spirituous liquors," and by other improper and illegal methods. On the advice of the committee the House suspended him till the matter could be heard, but the propriety of this was questioned, and another committee unanimously reported, "that for the House to proceed to suspend a member duly returned, merely on the allegation of a number of individuals, be that number greater or less, is altogether repugnant to the principles of the Constitution, and the spirit of all free governments, and, in its consequences, might deprive every member of the Legislature of those essential rights, which, by the Constitution, are secured to every citizen of this Commonwealth." So the House reversed its action and Mr. Pratt, after a two days' hearing by the full House, was permitted to retain his seat, although the committee had reported the election to be illegal.[1]

To the Massachusetts Convention for ratifying the Federal Constitution in 1788 seven inhabitants of the town of Sheffield presented what in the Journal is spoken of as "a paper called a remonstrance." In it Zadok Loomis did solemnly affirm and declare that he saw, clearly and plainly, a certain person put two votes in the hat at the meeting to choose delegates. "I, Isaac Salburgh, saw a certain other person than that which Zadok Loomis saw, put two votes into the hat at said meeting. And I, Anthony Austin, saw Jacob Johnson put a vote into the hat at said meeting, which said Jacob Johnson had not been an inhabitant of the town of Sheffield more than eight months.... We think it further our duty to inform your honors, that the said John Ashley, Jr., Esq., being one of the Selectmen, presided in

[1] *Reports of Election Cases in Mass.*, 17.

the meeting, and held the hat for receiving the votes. But instead of sitting it fair and open on the table as usual, held it in his left hand, pressed close to his breast, receiving the votes from the voters, in general, in his right hand, and putting (or pretending to put) them into the hat himself, at the same time suffering others to put their hand, *shut* into the crown of the hat, so that it could not be known whether they put in one vote or ten." Farther on: "When we see a certain set of men among us not only ravenously greedy to swallow the new Federal Constitution themselves, but making the greatest exertions to ram it down the throats of others, without giving them time to taste it — men, too, whom we have reason to imagine expect to have a share in administering the new Federal government — when we see such men fraudulently and basely depriving the people of their right of election, threatening, awing, deceiving, cheating, and defrauding the majority in the manner above-mentioned, it is to us truly alarming." [1]

In 1806, where it appeared that Thomas Keeler, returned a member from Sanford, had furnished numbers of the electors, both before and after the election, with refreshments of victuals and drink, at his own expense, the election was not thereby invalidated, even though the memorialist declared among other things "that the meeting was tumultuous and disorderly, and conducted with an unusual and unpardonable degree of spirit and acrimony, probably from the cause above mentioned." [2]

In 1810, in order to influence the inhabitants of Gloucester to elect six representatives, and to indemnify the town for any expense that might arise beyond the legal expense of two, fourteen individuals executed a bond, and the election was contested "because the precedent if established by the House of Representatives, would prove fatal to the liberties and independence of the country; and the period might not be far distant, when a legislature would be assembled, under the pay and influence of a foreign country." [3] The committee found the act highly reprehensible and not to be countenanced by the House, but since the members-elect were in no way concerned, it was recommended not to disfranchise the town by unseating them. The House in the end decided otherwise and did unseat them. The Treasurer's office on this occasion certified that the whole pay for

[1] *Journal of Mass. Convention of 1788*, 52.
[2] *Reports of Election Cases in Mass.*, 55.   [3] *Ibid.*, 97.

the six representatives for Gloucester at the May session, 1909, amounted to eighty dollars, being four dollars less than for the attendance of two members every day in the session. At the winter session of forty-two days, the pay-roll for six was only eighty-two dollars. The bond was conditioned on the election of the "federal republican ticket."

In 1839 George Williams of Hubbardston invited those who had taken part in the caucus that nominated him to drink at his expense, and there was evidence that some of the persons who drank at the bar became excited, "not so much as to prevent them from walking, but enough to prevent them walking straight." In its report on the contest of the election that followed, the committee said: "The committee cannot reprobate, in too strong terms, the practice of treating, either before or after an election; and, while a penalty is attached to this at all *military* elections, they cannot perceive any good reason why the same or increased penalties should not be attached to the same practice at elections of members of the General Court. The frauds that are practiced *at* the ballot boxes, and *on* the ballot boxes, are believed to originate, in a great measure, in the free use of ardent spirits." Yet not believing bribery had been shown, they advised that the member be allowed to keep his seat, and the advice was accepted.[1]

Massachusetts typifies the Puritan colonies. For the others we naturally turn to Virginia, the oldest and in its influence on the political institutions of the country the most important. Here, too, we find early proof of corrupt practices. Laws against bribery appeared in 1699. Then it was provided that any gift of money, meat, drink, or provisions, for votes, would make the election void. Even a promise to give anything to influence a vote, disqualified the promisor to sit as a burgess.[2]

Nevertheless the customs aimed at were still in full vogue and evidently supported by general opinion long afterward. George Washington's great-grandfather, father, and elder brother sat in the Virginia House of Burgesses, and naturally on becoming the head of the family he had the ambition to do likewise. As early as 1755, when on the frontier, he wrote to his brother at Mount Vernon to find what chance there might be, but the county magnates evidently disapproved. In 1757 he offered

---

[1] *Reports of Election Cases in Mass.*, 1839.
[2] E. I. Miller, *The Legislature of the Province of Virginia*, 76.

himself as a candidate, and was defeated at the polls, getting
only 40 votes to 270 for Captain Thomas Swearingen, whom
Washington later described as "a man of great weight among
the meaner class of people, and supposed by them to possess extensive knowledge." Washington had written to the Governor
denouncing the number of tippling houses at Winchester as a
great grievance and he had declared war on the publicans. He
whipped his soldiers when they became drunk, kept them away
from the ordinaries, and even closed by force one especially culpable tavern. The saloon element of his own county wanted no
such man in the Assembly and the liquor forces united against
him. The next year he fought the Devil with his own weapons.
The statute forbade all treating or giving what were called
"ticklers" to the voters, and declaring illegal all elections thus
influenced. None the less, the voters of Frederick County enjoyed at Washington's expense strong drink to the value of more
than thirty-five pounds. The chief beverage was rum punch,
there being items of one hogshead, one barrel, and forty gallons.
Besides, nearly thirty gallons of wine were consumed, with
lesser delectations. After the election was over Washington
wrote Colonel John Wood, the county boss, whose friendly aid
he had secured: "I hope no Exception was taken to any that
voted against me, but that all were alike treated, and all had
enough. My only fear is that you spent with too sparing a hand."
It is hardly necessary to say that such methods reversed the
former election. Washington secured 310 votes; Swearingen, 45.
What is more, so far from now threatening to blow out his
brains, there was "a general applause and huzzaing for Colonel
Washington." From that time until he took command of the
army he was a Burgess. He spent between forty and seventy-five
pounds at each of the elections, and usually gave a ball to the
voters on the night he was chosen. Some of the miscellaneous
election expenses noted in his ledger are, "54 gallons of Strong
Beer," "52 Dro. of Ale," "£1.0.0. to Mr. John Muir for his
fiddler" and "For cakes at the Election, £7.11.1." [1]

A decade after Washington entered politics, Thomas Jefferson
announced himself a candidate for the county of Albemarle; and
during the winter of 1768–69 he canvassed his county for votes,
visiting each voter, asking him for his vote and influence, getting
his promise if possible, keeping open house and full punch-bowl

[1] Paul Leicester Ford, *The True George Washington*, 294 *et sqq.*

as long as the canvass lasted. "During the three election days the candidates supplied unlimited punch and lunch, attended personally at the polls, and made a low bow as often as they heard themselves voted for." [1]

After being a member of the first Assembly under the Virginia Constitution, James Madison, at the election of 1777, his biographer tells us, was outvoted by candidates who brought to their aid a species of influence unfortunately not uncommon in that day, but against which he was firmly principled. "The practice of *treating* at elections was one which in England, had long and rankly flourished in spite of prohibitory enactments; and it had been transplanted, with the representative institutions which it tended to vitiate and corrupt, to the virgin soil of the new world. Mr. Madison, believing, to use his own language, that 'the reputation and success of representative government depended on the purity of popular elections,' resolved to give no countenance to a practice which he deemed so destructive of it; and he declined therefore, to follow the example of his competitors in courting the suffrages of the electors by offering them treats. He fell a victim, as others have done before and since, to the inflexibility of his principles; but his self-respect raised him above the mortification of defeat. In a paper containing some reflections on the importance of maintaining the purity of popular elections, he has incidentally given an account of this early experience of his political life, which we cannot do better than present in his own words to the reader.

"'In Virginia, where the elections to the colonial Legislature were septennial, and the original settlers of the prevailing sentiments and manners of the parent nation, the modes of canvassing for popular votes in that country were generally practiced. The people not only tolerated, but even required to be courted and treated. No candidate who neglected these attentions could be elected. His forbearance would have been ascribed to a mean parsimony, or to a proud disrespect for the voters. The spirit of the Revolution and the adoption of annual elections seeming to favor a more chaste mode of conducting elections in Virginia, my way of thinking on the subject determined me to attempt, by an example, to introduce it. It was found that the old habits were too deeply rooted to be suddenly reformed. Particular circumstances obtained for me success in

[1] James Parton, *Life of Thomas Jefferson*, 88.

the first election, at which I was a candidate. At the next, I was outvoted by two candidates, neither of them having superior pretensions, and one particularly deficient in them; but both of them availing themselves of all the means of influence familiar to the people. My reserve was imputed to want of respect for them, if to no other unpopular motive.'" [1]

A petition that the election be set aside by reason of corrupt influence proved unavailing, for want of definite proof.

Southern elections in those days were indeed vivacious affairs. You may find a lively description of their characteristics in the speech by Representative Smith of South Carolina upon the contested election case of Preston v. Trigg, coming to the third Congress from Virginia in 1793.[2] Commenting on the charge that a man had gone to the Court House with a club under his coat, Smith said he supposed at his own election five hundred men had clubs under their coats. "A man of influence came to the place of election with two or three hundred of his friends; and, to be sure, they would not, if they could help it, suffer anybody on the other side to give a vote as long as they were there." As to liquor, "if the committee are to break up every election where persons were seen drunk, they will have a great deal of work upon hand, sir."

"The Concessions and Agreements of the Proprietors, Free-holders, and Inhabitants of the Province of West New-Jersey, in America" declared (1676): "That no person or persons who shall give, bestow or promise directly or indirectly to the said parties electing, any meat, drink, money, or money's worth, for procurement of their choice and consent, shall be capable of being elected a member of the said Assembly." The man guilty of such an offense was to be disfranchised and be incapable of holding office for seven years.[3] By the New Jersey election law of 1725 bribery and corruption were prohibited, and any candidate practicing them was to be disabled from sitting. Any one who slandered the opposing candidate or influenced votes by indirect means was to forfeit twenty pounds, one half to the Crown and one half to the person who sued for the same.

William Penn's Frame of Government for Pennsylvania (1682) provided that "the elector, that shall receive any reward or gift,

[1] W. C. Rives, *Life and Times of Madison*, I, 179–81.
[2] Clarke & Hall, *Election Cases*, 82, 83.
[3] *Grants and Concessions of New Jersey*, Leaming and Spicer ed., 405.

in meat, drink, monies, or otherwise, shall forfeit his right to elect; and such person as shall directly or indirectly give, promise, or bestow any such reward as aforesaid, to be elected, shall forfeit his election, and be thereby incapable to serve as aforesaid." The Frame of Government made by Governor Markham and the people in 1696, to remain in force unless Penn should object to it, added to these offenses an offer to serve for nothing, or for less wages than the law prescribed, and reduced the penalty for the elected member to incapacity to serve in Council or Assembly that year. The brief Charter substituted by Penn in 1701 omitted provisions on the subject.

In South Carolina, where the division into parishes for religious purposes came to be adopted for political purposes as well, elections were put in the hands of church officers. The churchwardens had entire charge of the balloting. They were obliged to be present during the hours of voting, and if from the existence of a law inference of occasion for it may be drawn, there is curious significance in the fact that they were to be heavily fined for stuffing ballot-boxes or for opening ballots before the close of the polls.

As the States came to draft their Constitutions, some saw fit at once to recognize therein the dangers of bribery, and by this time most of the rest have come to the same course after one fashion or another. Pennsylvania began (1776) with saying that "any elector, who shall receive any gift or reward for his vote, in meat, drink, monies, or otherwise, shall forfeit his right to elect for that time, and suffer such other penalties as future laws shall direct." The briber was to be incapable to serve for the ensuing year. Vermont copied this in 1777. Tennessee did likewise in 1796, but made the term of the briber's ineligibility two years, extending it in 1834 to six years. Massachusetts, in 1780, made permanently ineligible to a seat in the Legislature or any office of trust or importance under the government of the Commonwealth, anybody convicted of bribery or corruption in obtaining an election or appointment. New Hampshire said the same in 1784. Georgia in her first Constitution (1777) required members-elect to swear "I have obtained my election without fraud or bribe whatever." In 1789 this was enlarged to read "I have not obtained my election by bribery, or other unlawful means." The phraseology seems to have proved not specific enough, for in 1798 it was amplified into: "I have not obtained my election by bribery, treats, canvassing, or other undue or unlawful means, used by myself, or by others with my desire or approbation, for that purpose." That word "canvassing" has interest. It must have taxed the conscience of Georgia legislators of the next two generations, for not until 1865 was this replaced by the more reasonable requirement that the oath or affirmation should be to the effect that "he hath not practiced any unlawful means, either directly or indirectly, to procure his election." Three years later there was again amplification, this time to cover bribery, but it stood only until 1877, when the subject disappeared altogether from the oath of office.

Kentucky's first Constitution (1792) contained this provision: "Each Senator, Representative, and Sheriff, shall, before he be permitted to act as such, take an oath or make affirmation, that he hath not directly or indirectly given or promised any bribe or treat to procure his election to said office, and every person shall be disqualified from serving as a Senator, Representative, or Sheriff, for the term for which he shall have been elected, who shall be convicted of having given or offered a bribe or treat, or canvassed for the said office." This was dropped in 1799 and in its place laws were directed to be made to exclude from office and from the suffrage those who should be convicted of bribery, perjury, forgery, or other high crimes or misdemeanors.

Maryland, in 1851, put the denial of bribing into the oath to be taken by every person elected or appointed to any office of trust or profit, and it stayed there until 1867. What Maryland thus rejected, Illinois picked up, for in 1870 it began requiring that every member of the General Assembly should swear or affirm that he had not bribed in order to get elected. Then came Pennsylvania, with a long discussion of the subject in the Convention of 1873, resulting in a provision of the same purport as that in Illinois. Half a dozen other States have since adopted the idea.

Such provisions are ineffectual. Men who will bribe will falsify. There was a time when oaths embarrassed falsehood. They may still be of some use in courts, where the judge can caution witnesses and the perils of perjury can be emphasized. Taken on entering office, oaths now accomplish little else than to bring home to some men the seriousness of their responsibilities. Not much more is to be said for the provisions to be found in many Constitutions, disqualifying men who have been found guilty of bribery, usually for the term, sometimes permanently. Bribery proves to be one of the things hard to establish in court. Convictions are very rare. In practical effect, therefore, such provisions do not go much beyond contributing to spread and strengthen the belief that bribery is iniquitous. The need of this in many regions is all too evident, and anything that helps is not to be scorned.

Of course the real remedy is to be found in an enlightened public opinion. What can be hoped from oaths or laws in such an atmosphere, for example, as that of Nevada in 1864 when her Constitution was framed? Bribery was actually defended in the Convention. Said a member: "This clause seems to strike at the glorious privilege of electioneering for a man's friends. If I have a friend whom I believe particularly fitted for a particular office, and I have a desire for the sake of the public good to get him into that office, I have a right to use all honorable means to that end, and, if it is necessary, to buy a little whiskey, too." The Convention seemed to agree with the speaker, as the bribery clause was rejected.[1] Instances of such frank championship of ancient privileges are not plentiful, but it is to be feared that the spirit of the Nevada delegate would not even now lack sympathy in some parts of the land. Yet on the whole the standards of the people are much higher than they were two or three generations back.

The New York Constitution of 1846 authorized the Legislature to pass laws "for depriving every person who shall make, or become directly or indirectly interested in any bet or wager depending upon the result of any election from the right to vote at such election." From 1865 to 1875 Missouri by constitutional provision directly disfranchised for this cause. Florida in 1868 directed the Legislature to "enact the necessary laws to exclude from every office of honor, power, trust, or profit, civil or military, within the State, and from the right of suffrage, all persons ... who shall make, or become directly or indirectly interested in, any bet or wager, the result of which shall depend upon any election." Such provisions will doubtless strike anybody unfamiliar with practical politics as a singular invasion of personal liberty, as extreme instances of censoriousness. Yet there is in fact ample justification for them. Shrewd manipulators have seen and used the chance to give large numbers of men a pecuniary interest in election results by means of pools in which shares

[1] F. H. Miller, "Legal Qualifications for Office in America," *Am. Hist. Assn. Ann. Report for 1899*, I, 144.

are sold. The ownership of such a share may very easily vitiate the judgment of the indifferent or thoughtless. That, too, may be the effect of an individual wager. The prospect of making money by an election, if openly countenanced, may inject self-interest into politics to a pernicious degree. In various localities this unfortunate effect is notorious.

Do not suppose this particular form of electoral vice to be peculiar to the United States or a natural product of the American temperament. In 1838 an election committee of the British House of Commons took a whole day in considering whether the vote of James Browne should be thrown out because he had bet a new hat on the Youghal election, by which act it was contended that he had become interested in the event, and had consequently rendered himself utterly incompetent to exercise the franchise with which he had been entrusted. The case excited the deepest interest throughout the day, and so nicely were the arguments on both sides balanced, so nearly equal the weight of authority adduced, that it was not until about three minutes before the Speaker was at prayers that the committee was able to come to a decision, that as Browne was offered the bet from a fraudulent motive, his vote should be held good. It appeared that an unscrupulous non-elector had basely betrayed Browne into the business in order to invalidate his vote, which alone induced the committee to come to this favorable decision.[1]

CAMPAIGN EXPENSES

The startling growth of the use of money in elections has made the evil one of the most serious problems in our public life. To be sure, it is not a new problem. When Martin Van Buren was inaugurated as Governor of New York, January 1, 1829, he attacked "the practice of employing persons to attend the polls for compensation, of placing large sums in the hands of others to entertain the electors," and other devices by which the most valuable of all our temporal privileges "was brought into disrepute." If the expenses of elections shall increase as they have lately done, he said, the time will soon arrive "when a man in middling circumstances, however virtuous, will not be able to compete upon anything like equal terms with a wealthy opponent." In long advance of a modern agitation for reform, he proposed a law imposing "severe and enforcible penalties upon

[1] Francis Lieber, *Manual of Political Ethics*, 2nd ed., II, 250, note.

the advance of money by individuals for any purpose connected with the election except the single one of printing." [1]

The evil was, however, then sporadic. In fact as late as 1858 President Buchanan wrote: "We never heard until a recent period of the employment of money to carry elections." George S. Boutwell has said of the conditions in Massachusetts: "From 1840 to 1850 I was the candidate of the Democratic party of Groton for representative of the town in the General Court. The party in the town met its moderate expenses by voluntary contributions. I contributed with others, but never upon the ground that I was a candidate. We paid our local expenses. We paid nothing for expenses elsewhere, and we did not receive anything from outside sources. In 1844–46 and 1848 I was the candidate of the Democratic party for the National House of Representatives. I canvassed the district at my own charge. I did not make any contribution to any one for any purpose, and I did not receive financial aid from any source. The subject was never mentioned to me or by me in conversation or correspondence with any one. Again, I may say the subject was not mentioned in my canvass for the office of Governor in the years 1849–50 and 1851. In 1862 I became the candidate of the Republican party for a seat in Congress. After my nomination the District Committee asked me for a contribution of one hundred dollars. I met their request. The request was repeated and answered in 1864, 1866 and 1868. On one occasion I received a return of $42 with a statement that the full amount of my contribution had not been expended." [2]

Soon after the Civil War conditions everywhere changed much for the worse and the English Corrupt Practices Act of 1883 found plenty of occasion for the copying here. Still the States were slow to act and it was not until 1890 that the first step was taken, by New York, with a law requiring candidates to file statements of campaign expenses. Colorado and Michigan followed to like effect in the next year. Massachusetts proceeded somewhat more elaborately in 1892, and in 1893 Michigan added to her law a specification of what her Legislature thought to be proper objects of expenditure, forbidding all else. Most of the other States have followed with partial and insufficient borrowings from the English law; and Congress, hesitating to go beyond

[1] Edward M. Shepard, *Martin Van Buren*, 145, 146.
[2] *Sixty Years in Public Affairs*, II, 14.

their example, has enacted for Federal elections a statute equally futile.

Nowhere have the results been what was hoped. The experience strikingly illustrates the singular and well-nigh inexplicable difference between the English and American way of reforming, or for that matter between the two ways of handling almost every problem in political science. When once England attacks an evil, she is likely to go the whole distance. American Legislatures and the American Congress are likely to cut off the dog's tail by inches. So it was with what we call the Australian ballot. In its home and wherever in the English dominions it has been adopted, unless some exception has escaped my notice, it has not carried party designations. We took part of the system, but omitted that feature and are only now, in a few States, approaching the genuine thing. So it has been in the matter of corrupt practices.

England achieved a reasonable degree of gain because at one stroke it accomplished five purposes: (1) publicity as to expenditures; (2) a scale of maximum expenditure; (3) prohibition of a substantial number of useless or undesirable classes of expenditure, with restriction of others within narrow limits; (4) adequate penalties; (5) the enlistment of self-interest or party interest as a motive for securing the enforcement of the law.

We have copied the first and second with varying success. We have gone nowhere nearly so far as we ought in the prohibition of certain specific classes of expenditure or the limitation of others. We have not provided adequate penalties. And we have made it of personal importance to nobody to enforce the law.

The result is that our corrupt practices acts are a good deal of a farce, a pretense of virtue that may appease the clamor of righteousness, but satisfies nobody who comes in actual contact with their operation. The trouble is that these laws embarrass the honest man, who is not the man we want to hit; and do not embarrass the lawless man, who is the man we are after. Their only considerable effect has been to attract some attention to the larger uses of money in politics. It is not even clear that they have created censorious opinion to any influential degree. Although they have been on the statute books for years, the aggregate of expenditure has grown strikingly, perhaps alarmingly. From the figures in the admirable study of "Party Campaign Funds," by James J. Pollock, Jr., it appears that the Republican and Democratic National Committees disbursed $2,211,396.87 in 1912; $3,967,860.95 in 1924. In the latest campaign, that of 1928, the Republican National Committee reported receipt of $3,814,815.45, disbursement of $3,529,178.25. The Democratic National Committee reported receipt of $3,844,958.43, disbursement of $5,342,349.89. This made the total of disbursement in 1928, $8,871,528.14, considerably more than twice as much as four years before.

To this is to be added an unknown number of millions received and disbursed by State and local committees, as well as the expenditure by the horde of candidates. The State Committees of Ohio reported in 1914 disbursements of $81,166.32; in 1922, $186,239.74. Those of New York reported in 1914, $219,-812.18; in 1922, $453,620. (These were the "off-years," with no Presidential campaign.) Comparative figures in the matter of expenditure by or in behalf of individual candidacies are not to be had, but even rumor never attributed to American campaigns in the nineteenth century anything like what we have learned of recently. In 1926 the campaign funds for five candidates seeking nomination for Governor or United States Senator in Pennsylvania totaled almost $2,800,000. That same year almost a million dollars is known to have been spent in the Illinois campaign for the Republican nomination for United States Senator.

Such figures, taken by themselves, do not necessarily prove delinquency on the part of any one, nor should they necessarily cast odium on those concerned. In view of the size of the electorates in Pennsylvania and Illinois, every dollar may have been spent within the law as it now stands, and spent for what has hitherto been held a commendable purpose. This consideration makes it gravely doubtful whether the United States Senate was warranted in the dictum it attached in January of 1922 to its resolve that Truman H. Newberry had been duly elected Senator from the State of Michigan. Whether or not the amount expended in his behalf had been a few thousand dollars in excess of the $195,000 fully reported or openly acknowledged, the Senate declared: "The expenditure of such excessive sums in behalf of a candidate, either with or without his knowledge and consent, being contrary to sound public policy, harmful to the honor and dignity of the Senate, and dangerous to the perpetuity of a free government, such excessive expenditures are hereby severely condemned and disapproved."

Sturdy, brave words these, but perhaps beside the mark. More than a million persons vote in Michigan, and twenty cents apiece for their enlightenment may not be so very excessive a sum. To be sure, that is a good deal higher than Congress has since made the maximum, for in 1925 it said a candidate for the Senate should not spend more than three cents for every vote cast in the previous election and in no case more than $25,000. Three cents would hardly pay for one circular, in a sealed envelope, to every voter. However, no attempt was then made to put a limit on what others might spend in a candidate's behalf, and though in the following year a bill was reported to close that door, it did not become law.

The real question is not how much money shall be spent, but who shall contribute the money necessary to have an interested and informed electorate.

At present the money comes from private sources and in their privacy lies one of the serious dangers. Some of the motives are innocuous, or even praiseworthy, such as party zeal or personal friendship. More ominous are the motives springing from mercenary interest. With the tremendous growth of wealth and particularly because of its concentration in the conscienceless corporate form, the menace here has become vital. The public awoke to it when the New York committee investigating insurance committees reported in 1906 that these companies had been making large contributions to political campaigns. That was, to be sure, not a new thing, for it had been understood ten years before that "frying the fat" out of corporations had become a common practice, but it seemed a particularly offensive thing that the money of life insurance policy holders should be used for such purposes and there was quick response in the way of prohibitions by States and the nation. It was supposed that the evil had been virtually suppressed, but twenty years later it cropped up in the shape of large contributions made by men in control of great corporate interests, ostensibly out of their own pockets, but presumably at the ultimate expense of stockholders, and anyhow from purely mercenary motives, for the contributions were made to the funds of both parties at the same time and manifestly for the purpose of buying favors and good-will.

Judging by party platforms, academic writings, and the floundering of legislators, there are still many who think publicity the panacea. To my mind it is at most a palliative. As such it deserves some intelligence of application. Those of us who have been making reports might be consulted. We would come near being unanimous in saying that their visible consequence is almost *nil*. The detail of the reports that must be filed by candidates before the voting, whether at primary or election, rarely if ever reaches the observation of the voters. Those filed after the voting are forgotten before the next campaign comes round. Only in the rare cases of contested elections or legislative investigations are they ever examined by other than the officials with whom they are filed. They are not worth the pains as things now go.

Perhaps they would accomplish more were it required, as in New Hampshire and Georgia, that they be published in several newspapers. There is something in the suggestion of Doctor Pollock [1] that they be put into a public document after every campaign, though as a matter of fact all such public documents get very small circulation, interesting only students and the curious. As far as they told the truth about items of expenditure, they would be without effect, for there would be no serious criticism of legitimate items. Men are not going to incriminate themselves by reporting things the law forbids. Probably this could be met by nothing short of requirement that all expenditure be made through some agency presumably above perversion, as in New Jersey, where no campaign manager may authorize an expenditure unless the amount required is on deposit in some national or State bank or trust company, and no expenditure is to be made by any one unless on a written order made on a required form by a campaign manager.[2]

Honest information about the source of campaign funds would be harder to ensure. The palpable fact is that under present laws the disclosure of reprehensible sources is accidental. The man who breaks the law from venal motives or even those he feels may be questioned is likely to lie about it, or to evade.

In view of these considerations, after personal contact with the operation of Corrupt Practices Acts during the greater part of the time since one was adopted in Massachusetts, after sharing in various attempts to improve the Massachusetts law and watching others, after observing the futility of the Federal law, I am coming to the belief that there is only one way to stop the

[1] *Party Campaign Funds*, 213.
[2] *New Jersey Laws*, 1920, cited by Pollock.

excessive and dangerous use of money in elections, and that is to stop its contribution or expenditure by individuals, whether candidates or others, in any individual capacity.

Recognize that there are two purposes for spending money in politics. One is to advance principles; the other is to elect men to embody the public will in law, or to administer the law. Contribution and expenditure for the first of these, which may be otherwise called the shaping of public opinion, presents a problem by itself. It has recently been brought to the front by the disclosure of large and systematic outlay in connection with public utilities, as well as with the battle over prohibition. The topic is interesting and may become vital, but to discuss it at this point would take us too far away from the immediate issue, that of the use of money for the election of men to carry out opinions which we may assume to have been formed. Of course the line cannot be sharply drawn. There is contribution and use with the advancement of a principle the larger motive, but it is found to an unimportant degree in that half of the process which concerns nomination, and equally unimportant is it in the other half as far as concerns contribution by candidates and their friends. Furthermore, self-interest often masquerades under the guise of principle.

Taking all the factors into account, it is safe to conclude that genuine public spirit, disinterested, altruistic, accounts for but a relatively small part of campaign contribution, and not enough to turn the scale against stopping the selfish use of money. It should not prevail against the consideration that the election of men to office in order to embody the public will in law, and to carry out that will, is primarily a public interest and concern, not a private interest and concern. The stake of the public is far greater than that of any of its parts. Self-interest should not control. There are, indeed, those who think that the best government will result from the competition and conflict of self-interest, but that is not the conception now prevalent.

John Stuart Mill declared it to be his fixed conviction that a candidate ought not to incur one farthing of expense for undertaking a public duty. Said he: [1] "Such of the lawful expenses of an election as have no special reference to any particular candidate ought to be borne as a public charge, either by the State or the locality." Presumably Mill had in mind the official expenses

[1] *Autobiography*, 280.

that with us are met out of the public treasury, but in England then fell on the candidates. His statement, however, was broad enough to cover much of the expenditure of central committees, and whether he meant that or not, it should commend itself to anybody who believes that parties exist for public ends rather than private interests.

Mill went on to say: "If members of the electoral body, or others, are willing to subscribe money of their own for the purpose of bringing, by lawful means, into Parliament some one who they think would be useful there, no one is entitled to object." Is that really the case? Keeping always the personal phase in mind, why may there not be sound objection if the result is to favor the candidate with wealthy friends to the detriment of the candidate whose friends have not been equally fortunate in one particular field of endeavor, namely, the amassing of money? Is there nothing to be said on the ground of the obligations a candidate, thus helped, may feel he must recognize? What public gain can come from making elections a contest between check books? Only one suggests itself — the greater enlightenment of the voters. This, however, is a public concern that ought not to be left to the accidents of private interest.

Mill's next proposition seems to me irrefutable. "That the expense, or any part of it," he says, "should fall on the candidate, is fundamentally wrong; because it amounts in reality to buying his seat. Even in the most favorable supposition as to the mode in which the money is expended, there is a legitimate suspicion that any one who gives money for leave to undertake a public trust, has other than public ends to promote by it; and (a consideration of the greatest importance) the cost of elections, when borne by the candidate, deprives the nation of the services, as members of Parliament, of all who cannot or will not afford to incur a heavy expense."

Leaving the general proposition, and looking for a moment at details, how many forms of expenditure can you find that, as things now go, accomplish any direct benefits save those that accrue to the advantage of the man or party with the longer purse? Separate from the rest the forms of expenditure that directly benefit the public as a whole, and it will be seen that they almost exclusively concern the enlightening, the informing, and the instructing of the voter. These things are now accomplished, to greater or less degree, by the spoken word through meetings and the radio, by the printed word through the columns of the press and the mails.

To furnish at the public charge places of assembly for public purposes is fast coming to be legitimate and desirable. The principle has already been recognized in many urban "community centers," where cities have provided spacious buildings partly that neighborhoods may have meeting-places for purposes of just this sort. As for the radio, the tentative suggestion might be hazarded that sending stations could be prohibited from receiving payment for time used in discussing matters of a political nature, in which case the owners would probably find it to their own advantage to put prominent speakers "on the air," just as they now do sundry entertainers. If they were not fair to all sides, they would quickly get into trouble.

Political advertising has become a serious and dubious method of outlay. The public may reasonably look to the news columns of the journals for a fair presentation of facts, and to the editorial columns for judgments unbiased by money considerations. Political advertising imperils these things. Fortunately our publishers as a class have hitherto kept apart the counting room and the editorial room, but they may not always resist temptation, and even now there is ground for fear that in some instances the dollar counts. Billboard and street car advertisements go in damage beyond giving unfair advantage to the larger bank account, in so far as they present the catchword and the slogan instead of argument. Photographs make a costly appeal that should have no place in public affairs. They are both irrelevant and adventitious. Physiognomy may be one of the fine arts but it is not one of the exact sciences. Ought the choice of a Senator to vote on our entry into the World Court depend on whether he is shown to part his hair in the middle or to be delightfully bald?

The money now spent on wasteful and sometimes harmful uses of printer's ink could for the public benefit be better spent on submitting information and argument directly to the individual voter through the mails. At present they are costly avenues of instruction when constituencies number tens or hundreds of thousands of voters. Why should not the post-office be opened in this particular for a public service at public expense? In England any candidate can send, free of postage, to each registered elector in his constituency one postal communication containing only matter relating to the election and not exceeding two

ounces in weight.[1] By the suffrage measure enacted in Japan in
1925, a candidate may send one letter gratis to each voter in his
district. If election is a public concern, what is more logical than
for the public to pay the cost of conveying the necessary information to itself?

Go a step farther and ask why the public, rather than the
candidate, should not pay for the cost of printing that information. Looking in that direction is the Oregon "candidates'
pamphlet," which has been issued by the State since 1908, but
only the binding and distribution are paid for out of the public
treasury, the cost of the printing being borne by the political
parties at the rate of $50 a page.[2] There can be no excuse for this
except illogical thrift. If part of the cost is properly a public
charge, so is the rest.

It is this matter of expense that Doctor Pollock holds responsible for the repeal of publicity laws in some States where they
have been tried. Yet it is arguable that in this particular, as in
all other matters of campaign expenditure, the system of private
expenditure is in the long run more burdensome to the community than would be that of public expenditure. All outlay diffuses
itself more or less and individual wastes become a general loss.
The thing will be done anyhow. It ought to be done. The way
we do it now is terribly wasteful. As good as a guess as any is
that we are spending $20,000,000 in every national campaign.
The total may be more or less than that, but at any rate is huge.
Another guess is that from quarter to half of this is wasted, that
is, produces no effect reasonably proportionate. Of course nothing but a guess is possible, but anybody who has had a share
in the activities of a campaign knows the waste would wring the
heartstrings of any business man.

Much of this could at once be saved by prohibiting those expenditures that clearly accrue to the benefit only of the wealthier candidate or the party with the larger campaign fund, such
as transportation to the polls, checkers and other workers at the
polls, unnecessary employees at headquarters, banners, buttons,
bands. It is argued, to be sure, that some of these things have
important value through arousing interest in campaigns and
issues, but we seem to have suffered nothing through the general
abandonment of the torchlight procession and the great lessening

---

[1] 8 Geo. V, ch. 64, sec. 33. Cited by Pollock.
[2] James K. Pollock, Jr., *Party Campaign Funds*, 104.

in the use of flags. Furthermore a good part, or rather a bad part, of the outlay for workers is nothing but an indirect form of bribery. The sooner these things are cut out, the better.

Already some of our States have recognized this. When Earl K. Sikes published his thorough study of "State and Federal Corrupt-Practices Legislation" in 1928, thirteen States had made it unlawful to pay for the conveyance of voters to the polls. If this should be extended to cover payment of railroad fares, this in itself would end what is no small drain on party chests and on the pocketbooks of sundry over-anxious candidates.

In various ways the public treasury has taken over a material part of campaign expense, such as that for the printing of ballots, the furnishing of polling places and officials, the guarding of the polls. There is no reason to suppose we have reached the end of the march. If it goes as far in the next half-century as it has gone in the latest, the country will have come near taking over all the load.

The progress may be the faster in one of two directions, that immediately concerning candidates, or that concerning committees. The simpler and easier step would be to prohibit entirely any outlay by candidates, other perhaps than that now recognized by statutes as distinctly personal, such as traveling expense. With committees the case is different. The legitimate performance of their useful functions costs money. Is there any logical reason why it should not be supplied by the governmental unit concerned? Proposal of this was made to Congress by President Roosevelt in his annual message of 1907. He said he was well aware that it would take some time for people so to familiarize themselves with such a proposal as to be willing to consider its adoption. It has in fact been winning approval but slowly, yet not a few thoughtful men of high standing and of long experience in affairs political have given it their support. Perhaps like many reforms that have been long in the incubating, when some day it breaks through the shell, it will grow fast.

Mr. Roosevelt met one of the arguments for old ways by suggesting that no party receiving campaign funds from the treasury should accept more than a fixed amount from any individual subscriber or donor. Of late years the principle this involves has been recognized in sundry systematic attempts to finance campaigns, at least in part, by a large number of small subscriptions.

No serious objection to this presents itself, but on the other hand it has the manifest benefit of giving the electorate at large a chance to show its interest in this or that platform or candidate by a share that can have no mercenary implication, but will helpfully attest sympathy or conviction. Our experience with many kinds of social undertakings has shown that there is no better way of arousing and continuing interest in them than the widespread canvass for money support. It may well supplement reasonable contribution from the public treasury.

Perhaps the problem of new parties and independent candidacies could be solved by having the public treasury match what might be raised through moderate private subscription. This, however, should be strictly limited, as in a country where the two-party system is the accepted order, it would be inconsistent to stimulate insurgencies. A multiplicity of candidates, though, is not much to be feared. That was predicted when the primary election system was in the making, but it has not so turned out. The prospect of wounded pride or loss of prestige that would be brought by overwhelming defeat has proved enough to keep the number of aspirants within bounds.

Colorado set a laudable example by statutory recognition of the theory that justifiable election expenditures may properly be a public charge. In 1909 at the instigation of Governor Shafroth it enacted a law [1] declaring that "the expenses of conducting campaigns to elect State, district, and county officers at general elections shall be paid only by the State and the candidates." Under this Act the State was to give to each political party twenty-five cents for every vote cast by it at the last preceding election for its candidate for Governor. Candidates for salaried offices might give and expend in the aggregate not to exceed forty per cent of the first year's salary; those for fee offices not more than twenty-five per cent of the fees for the last calendar year. Contribution by any other person or by a corporation to or for any party committee or any candidate, and the acceptance of any such contribution, was made a felony punishable by imprisonment in the penitentiary for not exceeding two years, or a fine not exceeding five thousand dollars, or both. Unfortunately the country lost the benefit of what would have been a most interesting experiment, for the Supreme Court of the State declared the law unconstitutional, in the case of People *ex rel.*

[1] Courtright, *Colorado Statutes*, 2401–A.

Galligan, State Treasurer, *et al.* It is to be regretted that no opinion was filed. By one of the Justices I am informed that the chief objections were to the unequal treatment of parties and the lack of provision for any new party. It would not seem impossible to meet these as well as sundry defects in matters of detail. Some State would do a service by testing the idea with a law more carefully drawn.

The importance of the matter has been doubled by the granting of the suffrage to women. Coming on top of the growth in population, this has brought the cost of what are looked upon as legitimate expenditures, in many contests for the higher offices, to a point almost prohibitive for any save the man of independent means. The less wealthy candidates must too often put themselves under unfortunate obligations to contributors of campaign funds. Some feel themselves justified in recouping their outlay by methods inconsistent with honorable public service. All suffer. The situation is demoralizing and dangerous. It ought to be met.

CHAPTER XIX

THEORIES OF REPRESENTATION

It is unfortunate that our language furnishes no terms that may be used to set forth clearly and precisely the different conceptions of representative government. Perhaps "deputy" comes nearest to conveying accurately one of the contrasted ideas; "representative," the other. The lawyer may see in "deputy" the notion of agency; in "representative" the notion of trusteeship. The expounder of political science may prefer to think of a "deputy" as an ambassador; of a "representative" as a plenipotentiary. The man in the street may feel that the postman is a "deputy" or may think priest or pastor to be his "representative." At best these are all inexact applications, but taken together they may differentiate accurately enough.

The two opposing ideas have been struggling with each other for centuries. First one wins the more acceptance, then the other. Just at present in English-speaking countries the deputy idea is winning and we are back where we started, six or seven hundred years ago. It is beyond question that Parliament began as a matter of agency and not of representation. Its members gathered as agents to declare the will of their principals, not to consult about the good of the whole. At what time they became representatives rather than agents, deputies, delegates, nobody can say with precision. Yet it would be reasonable to set the time as that of the disappearance of wages, for the members, being looked upon as agents, were originally and long afterward paid as such by their principals, that is, those who sent them. The last member known to have received wages regularly was Andrew Marvell, the poet. Through the first eighteen years of the reign of Charles II he was returned by the mayor and aldermen of Hull. We find him asking for instructions as to how he should act. "I desire that you will, now being the time, consider whether there be anything that particularly relates to the state of your town, or of your neighboring country, or of yet more public concernment, whereof you may think fit to advertise me, and therein to give me your instructions, to which I shall carefully conform."

It was about this time that authoritative writers began to declare against the doctrine of agency and to assert that members of Parliament represented all the people of England, not the particular constituencies that chose them. Sir Bulstrode Whitelocke averred in his "Notes upon the King's Writte for Choosing Members of Parlement XIII Car. II" (II, 330): "The citizens and burgesses are to have the same power with the knights; and the knights with them, when they are met in Parliament. They are not citizens and burgesses only for the places for which they serve; but they are then members of Parliament, serving for every county, city, and borough, in England, for the whole kingdom; and are obliged by the duty of Parliament men, to take equal care of the good and safety of every other county, city, and borough of England, as they are to take of those which particularly chose them. So that now they are become 'knights, citizens, and burgesses of England.' And a defect of power in them, or an improvident choice of them, may hinder the business of the whole kingdom, wherewith every one of them is intrusted."

Such doctrine carried little weight with the corporations of the boroughs. For example, in 1681 the freemen of the City of London instructed their four members of Parliament to refuse assent to money grants until security against Popery had been obtained. Perhaps it was this episode that led Algernon Sydney, in "Discourses concerning Government" (published in 1698 but written at least before 1683), to draw the distinction between members of the English Parliament and the delegates of the United Netherlands and Switzerland, going on to say: "It is not therefore for Kent or Sussex, Lewis or Maidstone, but for the whole nation, that the members chosen in those places are sent to serve in Parliament; and though it be fit for them as friends and neighbors (so far as may be) to hearken to the opinions of the electors for the information of their judgements, and to the end that what they shall say, may be of more weight, when every one is known not to speak his own thoughts only, but those of a great number of men; yet they are not strictly and properly obliged to give account of their actions to any, unless the whole body of the nation for which they serve, and who are equally concerned in their resolutions, could be assembled. This being impracticable, the only punishment to which they are subject, if they betray their trust, is scorn, infamy, hatred, and an assurance of being rejected, when they shall again seek the same power."

Dicey holds that the Septennial Act passed in 1716, lengthening the term of Parliament from three to seven years, proved to demonstration that in a legal point of view Parliament is neither the agent of the electors nor in any sense a trustee for its constituents.[1]   Nevertheless, whatever the legal point of view, the pendulum had begun to swing the other way, and within a generation of the time that act was passed, the agency idea was again conspicuous. Most of the boroughs sent instructions to their members to oppose Walpole's unpopular Excise Bill of 1733. Lecky tells us that when Walpole resigned, in January, 1742, statesmen observed with concern the great force the democratic element in the country had almost silently acquired in the course of his long and pacific ministry. The increasing numbers and wealth of the trading classes, the growth of the great towns, the steady progress of the press, and the discredit that corruption had brought upon the Parliament, had all contributed to produce a spirit beyond the walls of the Legislature such as had never before been shown, except when ecclesiastical interests were concerned. Political agitation took new dimensions, and doctrines about the duty of representatives to subordinate their judgments to those of their electors, which had scarcely been heard in England since the Commonwealth, were freely expressed.

Lecky goes on to cite "Faction Detected by the Evidence of Facts," a remarkable pamphlet that went through many editions and was ascribed to Lord Egmont. He had been an ardent opponent of Walpole, but was so much terrified at the aspect the country assumed after Walpole's fall that he drew a lively picture of what he termed "the republican spirit that had so strangely arisen." He notices as a new and curious fact the "instructions" drawn up by some of the electors of London, of Westminster, and several other cities, to their representatives, prescribing the measures that were required, and asserting or implying "that it was the duty of every Member of Parliament to vote in every instance as his constituents should direct him in the House of Commons," contrary to "the constant and allowed principle of our Constitution that no man, after he is chosen, is to consider himself as a member for any particular place, but as

[1] A. V. Dicey, *Law of the Constitution*, 44.

a representative for the whole nation." He complains that "the views of the popular interest, inflamed, distracted, and misguided as it has been of late, are such as they were never imagined to have been"; that "a party of malcontents, assuming to themselves, though very falsely, the title of the People, claim with it a pretension which no people could have a right to claim, of creating to themselves a new order in the State, affecting a superiority to the whole Legislature, insolently taking upon them to dictate to all the three estates, in which the absolute power of the Government, by all the laws of this country, has indisputably resided ever since it was a Government, and endeavoring in effect to animate the people to resume into their own hands that vague and loose authority which exists (unless in theory) in the people of no country upon earth, and the inconvenience of which is so obvious that it is the first step of mankind, when formed into society, to divest themselves of it, and to delegate it forever from themselves." [1]

Historically this was all wrong, but its vehemence throws light on the aspect the question had then taken and suggests that the issue was very much alive. The conservative view of it was presented in more temperate language by Onslow, who was Speaker of the House of Commons from 1727 to 1761, and who has ever since been looked on as an authority on all parliamentary matters. Onslow said: "Every Member, as soon as he is chosen, becomes a representative of the whole body of the Commons, without any distinction of the place from whence he is sent to Parliament. Instructions, therefore, from particular constituents to their own Members, are or can be only of information, advice, and recommendation (which they have an undoubted right to offer, if done decently; and which ought to be respectfully received, and well considered), but are not absolutely binding upon votes, and actings, and conscience, in Parliament." [2]

Blackstone, writing in 1765, naturally took the same view. "Every member," he held, "though chosen by one particular district, when elected and returned, serves for the whole realm; for the end of his coming thither is not particular, but general; not barely to advantage his constituents, but the *common wealth*; to advise his majesty (as appears from the writ of summons) '*de communi consilio super negotiis quibusdam arduis et*

[1] W. E. H. Lecky, *History of England in the Eighteenth Century*, I, 429.
[2] Hatsell, *Precedents*, II, 76n.

urgentibus, regem, statum, et defensionem regni Angliæ et ecclesiæ Anglicanæ concernentibus.' And therefore he is not bound, like a deputy in the United Provinces, to consult with or take the advice of his constituents upon any particular point, unless he himself thinks it proper or prudent to do so." [1]

Should it be thought that this was all theoretical, casuistical, of no practical importance, let the impression be dissipated by recalling it was the very heart of the quarrel between the colonies and the mother country that ripened into the War of the Revolution. "Taxation without representation" was the cry that roused the colonists to battle. And ever since then, even to this day, the same cry has been sounded again and again to stir men for this or that cause. Recently we heard it in discussions of woman suffrage. Rarely is it correctly applied. Rarely is its meaning understood. Yet there are few phrases in the literature of political science that more importantly demand adequate conception and clear thinking.

Mr. Speaker Onslow said: "That every Member is equally a Representative of the *whole* (within which, by our particular constitution, is included a Representative, not only of those who are electors, but of all the other subjects of the Crown of Great Britain at home, and in every part of the British empire, except the Peers of Great Britain) has, as I understand, been the constant notion and language of Parliament." [2]

If this was the case, then a British subject in Massachusetts Bay or Virginia was represented in Parliament just as much as if he were living in London. The accident of voting or not voting had nothing to do with the question. As a matter of fact only a small part of the men actually in the British Isles themselves took any part in electing members of Parliament. In theory, election and representation were different things. One was the mechanical device by which the other was brought into action.

Otis and the Adamses and the other American remonstrants did not view the case in that light. They held they were not represented in Parliament inasmuch as they had no share in sending anybody there. So they believed they were victims of "taxation without representation." This was one of those happy phrases that make a strong popular appeal, but will not bear critical inspection. Often, however, such phrases have their source in right. Often they guide the mind to a just conclusion,

[1] *Commentaries*, I, 159.   [2] Hatsell, *Precedents*, II, 76 n.

although by paths not those of logic. In this particular instance, the defect in theory may be suggested by the fact that nowhere in the world then prevailed, and nowhere to-day prevails, such a thing as taxation with representation, that is, a general tax levied upon only those persons who are directly represented in the taxing body. Always the tax falls upon some persons who are represented only indirectly, and often they outnumber those who are represented directly. There would not be taxation with representation even if only those who voted were taxed, unless they all voted for the same man. The minority, those who vote for the losing candidate, are unrepresented in the sense that their nominal representatives are not their choice and are not presumed to express their views.

Furthermore, the colonists were taxed by a Parliament in which the House of Lords had an equal voice with the House of Commons. It could not, indeed, originate money bills, but it shared in their enactment. Surely the Lords represented the colonists as much as they represented any other Englishmen. Of course it might be said that they represented nobody but themselves, yet in theory they too have spoken for England. They have been representatives chosen by the accident of birth instead of the accident of ballot.

The Doctrine of Instructions

It is to be noted that the most eloquent friend of the colonies, Edmund Burke, preached a doctrine of representation quite inconsistent with the colonial view. That was not the main point in his famous "Speech to the Electors of Bristol," but was a logical corollary. In 1774 he was asked to be a candidate for Bristol. In the course of the poll, an opponent raised the issue of instructions to representatives. Upon the announcement of Burke's election, that statesman addressed his constituents in a speech ever since held to set forth so well the representative relation that the part of it referring thereto may usefully be here quoted in full:

"Certainly, gentlemen, it ought to be the happiness and glory of a representative, to live in the strictest union, the closest correspondence, and the most unreserved communication with his constituents. Their wishes ought to have great weight with him; their opinion high respect; their business unremitted attention. It is his duty to sacrifice his repose, his pleasures, his satisfactions, to theirs; and, above all, ever, and in all cases, to prefer their interest to his own. But, his unbiased opinion, his mature judgment, his enlightened conscience, he ought not to sacrifice to you; to any man, or to any set of men living. These he does not derive from your pleasure; no, nor from the law and the constitution. They are a trust from Providence, for the abuse of which he is deeply answerable. Your representative owes you, not his industry only, but his judgment; and he betrays, instead of serving you, if he sacrifices it to your opinion.

"My worthy colleague says, his will ought to be subservient to yours. If that be all, the thing is innocent. If government were a matter of will upon any side, yours, without question, ought to be superior. But government and legislation are matters of reason and judgment, and not of inclination; and, what sort of reason is that, in which the determination precedes the discussion; in which one set of men deliberate, and another decide; and where those who form the conclusion are perhaps three hundred miles distant from those who hear the arguments?

"To deliver an opinion, is the right of all men; that of constituents is a weighty and respectable opinion, which a representative ought always to rejoice to hear; and which he ought always most seriously to consider. But *authoritative* instructions; *mandates* issued, which the member is bound blindly and implicitly to obey, to vote and to argue for, though contrary to the clearest conviction of his judgment and conscience; these are things utterly unknown to the laws of this land, and which arise from a fundamental mistake of the whole order and tenour of our constitution.

"Parliament is not a *congress* of ambassadors from different and hostile interests; which interests each must maintain, as an agent and advocate, against other agents and advocates; but parliament is a *deliberative* assembly of *one* nation, with *one* interest, that of the whole; where, not local purposes, not local prejudices ought to guide, but the general good, resulting from the general reason of the whole. You chuse a member indeed; but when you have chosen him, he is not a member of Bristol, but he is a member of *parliament*. If the local constituent should have an interest, or form a hasty opinion, evidently opposite to the real good of the rest of the community, the member from that place ought to be as far, as any other, from any endeavour to give it effect. I beg pardon for saying so much on this subject. I have been unwillingly drawn into it; but I shall ever use a respectful frankness of communication with you. Your faithful friend, your devoted servant, I shall ever be to the end of my life; a flatterer you do not wish for. On this point of instructions, however, I think it scarcely possible, we can ever have any sort of difference. Perhaps I may give you too much, rather than too little trouble."

Nevertheless contrary views were making headway. The general election of that very year appears to have been the first occasion on which the custom of exacting pledges from candidates at elections prevailed so far as to attract public notice. Many popular questions, May tells us, especially the differences with America, were then under discussion; and in many places tests were proposed to candidates, by which they were required to support or oppose the leading measures of the time. Wilkes was forward in encouraging a practice so consonant with his own political principles; and volunteered a test for himself and his colleague, Sergeant Glynn, at the Middlesex election. Many candidates indignantly refused the proposed test, even when they were favorable to the views to which it was sought to pledge them.[1]

By the way, it is related of Wilkes that when asked how it was possible to allow his judgment to be fettered by such a rabble as had instructed him, he answered, "Oh, as to that, I always take care to write my own instructions."

As the years went by, the views of Burke appear to have won more supporters than those of Wilkes. If the personality of the men had anything to do with it, your true conservative would say it was because Burke was a statesman and Wilkes was a demagogue. Whatever the cause, the first half of the nineteenth century saw at any rate the masters of English political thought united on the side of Burke. Typical of their position was the attitude of Sir G. C. Lewis. According to the unquestionable theory of representation, he said, in 1832, a representative is neither an advocate to plead the cause of his constituents, nor is he merely their organ, obeying their instructions with just so much discretion as a lawyer exercises on behalf of his client: but he is a member of the sovereign legislative body, acting by no delegated authority, entitled to form an independent judgment,

[1] *Constitutional History of England*, i, 418.

legally answerable to none for his conduct, but bound by a moral obligation to vote for the good of the whole community.[1]

About the middle of the century the pendulum had begun to swing back. A critic in the "Edinburgh Review" for October, 1852, lamented over what was happening: "In place of selecting men, constituencies pronounce upon measures; in place of choosing representatives to discuss questions and decide on proposals in one of three coördinate and coequal bodies, the aggregate of which decree what shall be enacted or done, electors consider and decree what shall be done themselves. It is a reaction toward the old Athenian plan of direct government by the people, practised before the principle of representation was discovered."

The heresy was not to spread without protest from high places. Lord Brougham came out with a weighty restatement of the Burke doctrine. It was in his work on "The British Constitution," published in 1860. "The essence of Representation," he declared, "is that the power of the people should be parted with, and given over, for a limited period, to the deputy chosen by the people, and that he should perform that part in the government which, but for this transfer, would have been performed by the people themselves. It is not a Representation if the constituents so far retain a control as to act for themselves. They may communicate with their delegate; they may inform him of their wishes, their opinions, their circumstances; they may pronounce their judgment upon his public conduct; they may even call upon him to follow their instructions, and warn him that if he disobeys they will no longer trust him, or reëlect him, to represent them. But he is to act — not they; he is to act for them — not they for themselves. If they interfere directly, and take the power out of his hands, not only is the main object of Representation defeated, but a conflict and a confusion is created that makes the representation rather prejudicial than advantageous....

"Nothing can be more inconsistent, or indeed more absurd, than for men to meet in order to vote as they have been ordered; nor can anything be more preposterous than for those men to be selected with care in order to perform this mechanical task. It is not of the least importance who are chosen for the purpose. Nay, it is not of the least importance by whom they are chosen. Men appointed by any other power in the State would be just

[1] *Remarks on the Use and Abuse of Some Political Terms*, 104.

as capable of giving the prescribed votes, as the representatives the most carefully selected by the people themselves.

"Some have with little reflection maintained that a general discretion may be given to the deputy, but that on occasions of extraordinary importance he must obey the instructions of his constituents. Who is to determine what is and what is not an important occasion? Do we not know that the important measure always means the present measure, and that the people ever give that name to the matter in hand, ever confine their attention exclusively to the affair of the day? Besides, suppose we had any test of relative importance, the very occasions of highest moment are precisely those upon which it is the most inexpedient that the direct interference of the people should be allowed." [1]

And farther on: "He represents the people of the whole community, exercises his own judgment upon all measures, receives freely the communications of his constituents, is not bound by their instructions, though liable to be dismissed by not being reëlected in case the difference of opinion between him and them is irreconcilable and important. The people's power being transferred to the representative body for a limited time, the people are bound not to exercise their influence so as to control the conduct of their representatives, as a body, on the several measures that come before them." [2]

Brougham and all the other theorists of like belief could not check the tide. In the last fifty years it has set steadily back toward the original idea of agency. Burke's view, says Sidney Low, writing of things as they have become in recent years, is not at all the view of a representative's functions taken by the members of a modern Liberal or Conservative Association. They do not send him to Parliament to exercise his independence; they would be particularly annoyed and irritated if he did; and they scrutinize his votes with jealous care, in order that they may take him to task speedily, and with no superfluous delicacy or reserve, if he shows any dangerous tendency in that direction. A member of Parliament is elected to vote for a particular ministry, or to vote against it. He is the delegate of his constituents, or rather of that active section of his constituents which assumes the local management of political affairs. [3]

[1] *The British Constitution, Works*, vol. XI, 35, 36.
[2] *Ibid.*, XI, 94.   [3] *The Governance of England*, 63.

The question has reached the courts. When the Labor Party gained strength enough to send numerous members to the House of Commons, the need of their support led to the levying of assessments on union members to provide wages. The right to do so was brought in question and was at first decided in favor of the unions. The court of appeal reversed this. One of its members, Lord Justice Moulton, took the ground that the rule of the society was void as against public policy. It was in November, 1908, that he said a member of Parliament "has accepted a trust toward the public; and any contract, whether for valuable consideration or otherwise, which binds him to exercise that trust in any other way than as on each occasion he conscientiously feels to be best in the public interest, is illegal and void." Nor would it make any difference if before or at the election the candidate avowed his intention to be thus contractually fettered, for the majority who elected him could not waive the rights of the minority in this respect. An appeal to the House of Lords (the five law lords sitting) was unanimously dismissed. Lord James said: "The effect of this rule and others that exist is that a member of the trade union is compelled 'to answer the Whip of the Labour Party.' I construe this condition as meaning that the member undertakes to forego his own judgment, and to vote in Parliament in accordance with the opinion of some person or persons acting on behalf of the Labour Party. And such vote would have to be given in respect of all matters, including those of a most general character — such as confidence in a Ministry or the policy of a Budget — matters unconnected directly at least with the interests of labour." He held that support of a member under such conditions was not within the powers of a trade union, but he did not take up the broad constitutional question affecting the general support of members. Lord Shaw said a member who accepted a seat in the House of Commons under such conditions had put himself under a contract to place his vote and action in subjection to the Labor party, as against what he might judge to be the real interest of the constituency that elected him, or against what he might regard as the true line of service to the whole realm. Such subjection was not compatible with the spirit of the parliamentary constitution or with the independence and freedom that had hitherto been held to lie at the basis of representative government in the United Kingdom.

Nevertheless members chosen by the Labor party continued to endure leading strings. Likewise in Australia, where the Labor party is still more formidable, its candidates make a formal pledge to do their utmost to carry out the principles embodied in the party platform. They promise on all questions affecting that platform to vote as a majority of the party members in Parliament may decide. Substantially the same has been the policy of the Socialists of the United States.

The Imperative Mandate

On the Continent of Europe the doctrine of instructions, or what is frequently there spoken of as the imperative mandate, has met with little favor. The notion that a man was to represent only his constituency, and therefore be nothing but its mouthpiece, was resisted at the very outset of genuinely representative institutions, when in France the States General became a single Assembly. The Grand Master of Ceremonies, at the order of Louis XVI, came to command the delegates of the Third Estate to leave the Throne Room, where they persisted in sitting. Mirabeau proudly replied: "Go tell those who sent you that we are here by the will of the people." The Constitution of 1795 read (52): "The members of the legislative body are not representatives of the departments which have elected them, but of the whole nation, and no specific instruction shall be given them."

The principle disappeared in the Constitutions established under Napoleon, wherein the terms national representative and national representation were carefully avoided. When the Emperor was greatly dissatisfied with the Deputies (convoked, in 1813, in consequence of his disastrous campaigns, after the Deputies had been disregarded during his imperial reign), he said to a deputation of them: "And who are you? Not the representatives of the nation, but the deputies of the departments." The original principle did not reappear in France until the Constitution of the Republic of 1848. It was put into the Constitution of the Third Republic and continues to be the declared policy. However, it is not uncontested. Of late years the electors have been attempting more control and many a French Deputy now looks on himself as an agent. The struggle between this and the trustee idea is one of the causes for the alternations between *scrutin de liste* and *scrutin d'arrondisse-*

ment, for of course election of a single Deputy brings greater chance of accountability to the particular electorate than election by general ticket.

The political philosophy of the French Revolution spread to neighboring lands. The prohibition of specific instructions appeared in the Constitution of the Cisalpine Republic of 1797. The Constitution or "Edict" of the Grand Duchy of Hesse, of 1820, said that no member of the first or second chamber could exercise his vote by proxy (which would have been as an agent), nor should he receive instructions. Belgium incorporated the principle in her Constitution of 1831. Then with the revolutionary agitations of 1848 the theory gained a wider foothold. It appeared in the Sardinian "Statuto" of that year, which became the Constitution of the Kingdom of Italy; in the Swiss Constitution of the same year as to the members of the Federal Assembly; in the Hungarian constitutional acts of the same period; and in the Constitution drawn up by the Parliament of Frankfort.

In 1850 it was embodied in the Prussian Constitution, from which it was copied by the Constitutions of the North German Confederation and then by the German Empire. Germany said: "The members of the Reichstag are the representatives of the people as a whole, and shall not be bound by orders or instructions." With the Bundesrath (the upper House) it was different. The delegates there voted according to the instructions of their home governments, and the Constitution expressly declared that votes not instructed should not be counted. This was on the theory, of course, that they were ambassadors. Lowell tells us this provision did not mean that a delegate must produce his instructions before being allowed to vote. On the contrary the Bundesrath appears to have taken no cognizance of his instructions, which might, indeed, be of any kind, including an authority to vote as the delegate thought best; and it was even asserted that a vote was valid whether it was in accord with the instructions or not. The provision in the Constitution was probably a mere survival; but it has been suggested that its object was, on the one hand, to allow a delegate to excuse himself from voting on the plea that he had not been instructed, and on the other to make it clear that a vote could be taken, although the delegates had not all received their instructions, thus taking away an excuse for delay that might otherwise have been urged.[1]

---

[1] *Governments and Parties in Continental Europe,* i, 262.

The Constitution of the German Commonwealth adopted July 31, 1919, declared that the delegates to the National Assembly (the lower branch) are representatives of the whole People. "They are subject only to their own consciences and are not bound by any instructions," the article reads. Nothing on the subject appears in the provisions relating to the upper branch.

The Fundamental Laws of Austria (1867) said: "Members of the House of Representatives shall receive no instructions from their electors." The principle was carried forward into the Constitution of the Austrian Bund in 1920. That of Denmark reads: "Members of the Riksdag shall be bound by their own convictions alone and not by any instructions from their electors." That of Greece: "The representatives represent the nation and not only the electoral district by which they are returned." That of Portugal: "The members of Congress are representatives of the nation and not of the colleges which elect them." That of Belgium: "The members of the two Houses shall represent the nation, and not the province alone, nor the subdivision of the province which elects them." Czecho-Slovakia is particularly emphatic: "Members of Parliament shall execute their functions in person. They shall not receive orders from anybody." Poland and Esthonia speak to the same effect. The principle was put in the Constitution of Egypt and appears in that of Japan.

Italy said: "Deputies shall represent the nation as a whole, and not the several provinces from which they are chosen. No binding instructions may therefore be given to the electors." One of Mussolini's purposes in revolutionizing the Electoral Law was to nullify this. In his long Report accompanying the new draft that was submitted to the Chamber of Deputies March 2, 1928, he declared: "Vainly does the Constitution admonish that the Deputy represents the whole Nation and not merely the electoral district in which he has been elected. In practice it is just the contrary that takes place, and must inevitably take place, for the local limitation of the polling cannot fail to concentrate the attention of the electors and the elected alike primarily upon local problems." He went on to say that this limitation intensifies local disputes; stirs up controversies between individuals of the same region; often leads to the exclusion of the best minds from public life. Granted that this is so, yet in substituting group interests as the basis of representation, he may be jumping out of the frying pan into the fire. He may find the group better organized, more powerful, and more selfish than the district.

INSTRUCTIONS IN AMERICA

On this side of the water opinion in this matter has had just as marked fluctuations as on the other. In the beginning, at any rate in Massachusetts Bay, complete independence for the representative seems to have been contemplated, if we may judge by the seventieth paragraph of the Body of Liberties, that remarkable code of 1641. It declared: "All Freemen called to give any advice, vote, verdict, or sentence in any Court, Council, or Civil Assembly, shall have full freedom to do it according to their true Judgments and Consciences, So it be done orderly and inoffensively for the manner." In 1651 this was amplified into a form that appears in the codification of 1660 as follows:

"It is ordered and by this Court declared, that all & every freeman and others Authorized by Law called to give any advice, vote, verdict or sentence, in any Court, Council or Civil Assembly shall have freedom to do it according to their true judgment and Conscience, so it be done Orderly and inoffensively for the manner, and that in all cases where any freeman or other is to give his vote, be it in point of election, making Constitutions and Orders, or passing sentence in any case of judicature or the like, if he cannot see light or reason, to give it positively one way or other, he shall have liberty to be silent, and not pressed to a determinate vote, which yet shall be interpreted and accounted, as if he Voted for the Negative."

Nevertheless, along with this came the beginnings of a practice quite inconsistent with it, the practice of instructing Representatives. As early as March 14, 1652–53, at a town-meeting of Boston it was ordered: "That the Commissioners for the Town and the Select men are desired to draw up instructions for the deputies against the General Court they or any five of them are to do it." Robert Treat Paine, Jr., has found[1] that beginning with 1661 Boston, according to its town records, gave instructions to its Representatives in forty-five different years before the adoption of a Constitution in 1780. Six of these were be-

[1] "Massachusetts' Historic Attitude in regard to Representative Government," *Arena*, July, 1907.

tween 1660 and 1670. There were but seven further instances until 1718, when the practice began to obtain with regularity, prevailing in almost every year until after 1739. Then until 1764 it was followed only twice, but from 1764 on it was again almost continuous. The subject matter of these instructions covered pretty nearly the whole field of legislative activity both as to general principles and as to special topics, including education, morality, political conduct, agriculture, manufactures, trade and commerce, the fisheries, taxation, debt, military affairs, slavery, and constitutional questions relating to the mother country and to the other colonies. The instructions of any one year varied from a single subject to a dozen, and in length covered often two pages, in one instance as many as six pages. Among those receiving instructions were John Hancock, Samuel Adams, James Bowdoin, James Sullivan, James Otis, Oliver Wendell, John Lowell, and William Phillips. Among men on the committees framing the instructions were John and Samuel Adams, Samuel Eliot, Joseph Warren, Richard Dana, and Edmund Quincy.

The wording shows the point of view. For instance, that of 1764 read: "By this choice, we, the freeholders of the town, have delegated you the power of acting in our public concerns, in general, as your prudence shall direct you; reserving to ourselves the constitutional right of expressing our minds and giving you such instructions upon important subjects as at any time we may judge proper." In 1766: "Although it is not customary for us to give instructions to our representatives for their conduct in all cases, or upon all occasions, yet we hold the right of so doing, whenever we think fit, to be sacred and unalienable." In 1773, Samuel Adams being on the committee: "It is our unalienable right to communicate to you our sentiments, and when we shall judge it necessary or convenient, to give you our instructions on any special matter, and we expect you will hold yourselves at all times bound to attend to and to observe them."

From this it would appear to be beyond question that for a century and more the citizens of Massachusetts towns looked on their Representatives to the General Court as their agents, each a delegate or ambassador of his own town. This was the logical result of the nature of the town. At the outset that was primarily ecclesiastical rather than political. The town-meeting was long more of a parish meeting than anything else, an assembly of the congregation for business ends. Church discipline could not permit delegates to be independent. They must be under control. So when problems purely political became the most important, old habits of authority continued and controlled. John Fiske has observed that it was especially characteristic of men trained in the town-meeting to look with suspicion upon all delegated power, upon all authority that was to be exercised from a distance. "They believed it to be all important that people should manage their own affairs, instead of having them managed by other people; and so far had this principle been carried that the towns of Massachusetts were little semi-independent republics, and the State was like a league of such republics, whose representatives, sitting in the State Legislature, were like delegates strictly bound by instructions rather than untrammeled members of a deliberative body." [1]

Perhaps this overstates what actually took place. Hosmer has pointed out that whatever may have been the New England theory, there is no doubt that, in practice, the men who sat in the Assembly, if they really had ability and force, were as free as need be. Such men as Joseph Hawley at Northampton, Elbridge Gerry at Marblehead, James Warren at Plymouth shaped the opinions of the communities in which they dwelt. According to the form, they spoke simply the views of the town, and regularly after election listened respectfully to the instructions which prescribed to them a certain course of conduct, sometimes with great minuteness. They themselves, however, had led the way to the opinions that thus found voice; for, with their natural power quickened by their folk-mote training, they usually had tact and power enough to sway the town to propositions near their own. Practically, with all the independent thinking, the able men shaped opinion. In theory, however, all proceeded from the town-meetings, and those who stood for them were deputies, who could only do the people's will. [2]

It is well known that this characteristic of the town-meetings has fixed upon them the responsibility for the break between Massachusetts and the mother country. The enemies of the Province in the home government knew whence the danger came. In 1774, too late, they tried to stifle the source of their troubles by an Act of Parliament "for the better regulating the govern-

---

[1] *Critical Period of American History*, 317.
[2] J. K. Hosmer, *Samuel Adams*, 54–58.

ment of the province of the Massachusetts Bay in New England." It declared that henceforth no meeting should be called "by the selectmen, or at the request of any number of freeholders" without the leave of the Governor, or in his absence of the Lieutenant-Governor, in writing, expressing the special business of the meeting, except the annual meeting, "and also except any meeting for the election of a representative or representatives in the General Court, and that no other matter shall be treated of at such meetings, except the election of the aforesaid officers or representatives, nor at any other meeting except the business expressed in the leave given by the Governor, or in his absence by the Lieutenant-Governor." The reason given in the act itself was that "a great abuse has been made of the power of calling such meetings, and the inhabitants have, contrary to the design of their institution, been misled to treat upon matters of the most general concern, and to pass many dangerous and unwarrantable resolves." It was these resolves, passed for the guidance of Representatives, that led to Lexington and Bunker Hill.

Massachusetts was not alone in the practice of instructing Representatives. You may read in the "Pennsylvania Chronicle" of October 24, 1768, that the town of New London, Connecticut, had instructed its Representatives to take the most effectual measures to keep up a union with all the American colonies; and in the same paper a week later that the town of Windham, Connecticut, had instructed its Representatives, October 10, to move for measures to bring about a general Congress from the several English governments upon the continent. The people of Portsmouth, New Hampshire, gave instructions to their Representatives in July, 1776, "that they nor any other Representative in future shall consent to any alteration, innovation or abridgment of the Constitutional form that may be adopted without first consulting their constituents in a matter of so much importance to their Safety." [1]

The "Instructions for the deputies appointed to meet in general congress on the part of the colony of Virginia," that is, the Continental Congress of 1774, may be found in Niles' "Principles and Acts of the Revolution in America" (page 201): "That they may be better informed of our sentiments, touching the conduct we wish them to observe on this important occasion, we

[1] *N.H. State Papers*, VIII, 301.

desire they will express," etc. Not until within a decade had
such procedure been put into common practice in southern or
middle colonies. Organized on the county rather than the town
basis, with general assemblage only for election purposes, they
lacked the machinery to give instructions. There had been almost no formal recognition or assertion of the right to instruct.
In only one document in the nature of a Constitution that ever
went into effect does it come to my notice. The Concessions and
Agreements of West New Jersey in 1676 said that the proprietors
and freeholders at the time of choosing "deputies or trustees,"
were to give them "their instructions at large, to represent their
grievances, or for the improvement of the province." If this was
ever done in the early days, it made no impress on history.
Surely nothing came of a provision in what is thought to have
been an early draft of a Constitution for Pennsylvania, by William Penn, in which he is supposed to have been helped by
Algernon Sydney. Had this draft not been modified into the
actual "Frame òf Government," [1] there might have been an interesting trial of something more drastic than America has ever
known. Each Deputy was to bring to the Assembly the written
instructions of the electors, duly signed by them and accompanied by an acceptance in his own handwriting. A copy was to
be registered in "every respective tribe." Should he act contrary
to it he was never more to presume to stand for election "unless
the people, sensible of his repentance, shall forgive and choose
him." Furthermore in the Assembly itself the Deputies were to
make or abrogate no law and were to raise no money "without
first consulting their Principals or Tribes, that depute them, that
they may always remember they are but deputies and men intrusted to the good of others and responsible for that trust."

The efficacy of instructions for uniting the people to rebel encouraged the idea that instructions were an inherent attribute of
representative government and led to inclusion of the principle in
the Bills of Rights that were put into many of the State Constitutions. Virginia was the first to frame such a declaration of the
inalienable rights of man, adopting it June 12, 1776. New Hampshire and South Carolina had acted earlier and their Constitutions had been framed without a Bill of Rights. New Jersey in
July drew its very brief Constitution hastily and likewise
omitted such a Bill. Since then most of the State Constitutions

---

[1] *Pennsylvania Magazine of History and Biography*, xx, 283 (1896).

have used the Virginia Bill as a model, frequently copying much of its language without change.

The second paragraph of the Virginia Bill declared: "That all power is vested in, and consequently derived from, the people; that magistrates are their trustees and servants, and at all times amenable to them." Two months later Maryland varied this to read: "That all persons invested with the legislative or executive powers of government are the trustees of the public, and, as such, accountable for their conduct." As in the case of Virginia, the Maryland Bill did not specify the right of instruction, but the doctrine, based in those days on the principle of accountability, was at work even in the Convention that framed the Maryland document. We are told that Worthington, Carroll, Barrister, and Chase, the latter two undoubted leaders and members of the committee to prepare a form of government, resigned from the Convention because they had received "instructions from their constituents, enjoining them, in framing a government for this State, implicitly to adhere to points in their opinion incompatible with good government and the public peace and happiness." [1]

Pennsylvania, acting in September, was the first to declare explicitly the right of instruction. It said — "That the people have a right to assemble together, to consult for their common good, to instruct their representatives, and to apply to the legislature for redress of grievances, by address, petition, or remonstrance." North Carolina (December, 1776) followed Pennsylvania word for word, except that it omitted "by address, petition, or remonstrances," evidently for the sake of brevity. Vermont (July, 1777) copied the Pennsylvania wording without change. When John Adams came to draft the Constitution that Massachusetts adopted in 1780, he rewrote both the Virginia paragraph about accountability and the Pennsylvania paragraph about instructions. His language about accountability was as strong a statement of the doctrine of agency as he could frame. "All power," he said, "residing originally in the people, and being derived from them, the several magistrates and officers of government, vested with authority, whether legislative, executive, or judicial, are their substitutes and agents, and are at all times accountable to them." Such a doctrine was palatable to a community that had approved the words of the patriot preacher,

---

[1] *Proceedings of the Convention of Maryland*, 222, 228, as quoted by W. F. Dodd, *Revision of State Constitutions*, 12.

William Gordon, who on the first anniversary of the Declaration of Independence, July 4, 1777, in a sermon before the General Court, exhorted his hearers thus: "Let us mould the governments of the respective States... so as not only to exclude kings, but tyranny, and, as ever, to retain the supreme authority in the people, together with the power, no less than the right of calling their delegated agents to account, whether they sit in the assembly, the council, the chair, or the Congress." [1]

In rewriting the Pennsylvania article, Adams specifically stated that "the people have a right... to give instructions to their representatives." The article containing this appears to have gone through just as he wrote it, without alteration either in committee or in the Convention itself. It had long been his faith. In 1765 he drew up instructions to the Representatives of Braintree concerning the Stamp Act, and they so suited the views of other places that forty copied them. And he adhered to his faith, probably to the end of his life. At any rate as late as 1808 he wrote: "The right of the people to instruct their representatives, is very dear to them, and will never be disputed by me." But he had then come to think this a very different thing from what he called "an interference of a State legislature," for he could upon principle "see no right in our Senate and House to dictate, nor to advise, nor to request our Representatives in Congress. Congress must be 'the cloud by day and the pillar of fire by night' to conduct this nation, and if their eyes are to be diverted by wandering light, accidentally springing up in every direction, we shall never get through the wilderness." [2]

The right of the people themselves to instruct, so long familiar in Massachusetts and explicitly recognized in the new Constitution, continued to be used. Boston gave instructions in October, 1780, and in following years. In 1785 John Hancock, the leading citizen of the State, was one of the seven Representatives thus instructed.

New Hampshire (1784) copied the Massachusetts declaration. Then, singularly enough, Pennsylvania (1790) dropped it. Tennessee, however, declared (1796) that the citizens have a right "to instruct their representatives," and so did Ohio (1802), Indiana (1816), Illinois (1818), Maine (1819), and Michigan (1835)., Arkansas said it in 1836 and stopped saying it in 1874.

[1] *Patriot Preachers of the American Revolution*, 183, 184.
[2] John Adams to J. B. Varnum, December 26, 1808, *Works*, IX, 605.

When in 1844 New Jersey adopted a new Constitution, a Bill of Rights was put in, with a new and half-hearted way of meeting this particular issue, for it said "the people have the right to make known their opinions to their representatives." Iowa copied this two years later and in 1870 Illinois substituted it for the original declaration.

California (1849) contented itself with the familiar phrase, "to instruct their representatives." Oregon (1857) found new phraseology: "No law shall be passed restraining any of the inhabitants of the State from assembling together in a peaceable manner to consult for their common good, nor from instructing their representatives, nor from applying to the legislature for redress of grievances." Kansas in her contesting Constitutions (1855, 1857, 1858, 1859) used each time the old phrase, "to instruct their representatives." Nevada (1864) and Idaho (1889) said the same. On making new Constitutions, Florida inserted it in 1868 and West Virginia in 1872.

Notice that something less than half the States now see fit to include the right of instruction in their declarations of the fundamental rights of citizens of a republic. In the case of a mooted question of this sort, widely debated, with one theory put conspicuously into many of the early Constitutions, it is fair to attach almost as much significance to omission as to insertion, and to conclude that a majority of the States may not believe in the principle. Yet the respectable array of States supporting it and the really vital nature of the issue call for further illumination, which may best be found in the more important incidents of its history since this country became independent.

Our first Congresses were distinctly gatherings of ambassadors, of agents who felt themselves dependent on the will of their principals. The embarrassments and dangers thereof early presented themselves. When the Articles of Confederation were debated in 1777, Doctor Rush called attention to three causes to which he attributed the decay of the liberties of the Dutch republic, one of which was the obligation of the delegates of the provinces to consult their constituents.[1]

As the war progressed, the weakness of Congress from a like cause became more and more evident. When after the war it was urged that the right to the Mississippi should be surrendered to Spain, if it were made the condition of an alliance, Virginia, in

[1] *Elliot's Debates*, i, 77.

deference to her neighbors, proposed that Mr. Jay should be re-instructed accordingly. James Madison was then a member of the Congress and was of the opposite conviction. He yielded to the prevalent view that representatives must implicitly obey instructions, but not till he had appealed to the Assembly to reconsider its decision. A biographer tells us that two years later (1783) he refused to accept a position of inconsistency in obedience to instructions which his State attempted to force upon him. At the moment when debate upon the revenue law was the most earnest, and the prospect of carrying it the most hopeful; when a committee appointed by Congress had already started northward to expostulate with, and, if possible, conciliate Rhode Island: at that critical moment came news from Virginia that she had revoked her assent of a previous session to the impost law. This was equivalent to instructing her delegates in Congress to oppose any such measure. The situation was an awkward one for a representative who had put himself among the foremost of those who were pushing this policy, and who had been making invidious reflections upon a State which opposed it. The rule that the will of the constituents should govern the representative, he now declared, had its exceptions, and here was a case in point. He continued to enforce the necessity of a general law to provide a revenue, though his arguments were no longer pointed with the selfishness and want of patriotism shown by the people of Rhode Island. In the end his firmness was justified by Virginia, who again shifted her position when the new act was submitted to her.[1]

The episode is of importance because of the light it throws upon the position taken by one of the men who had most to do with framing the Federal Constitution. When as an author of the Federalist he came to defend his work, this was his argument as to representatives:

"A pure democracy, by which I mean a society consisting of a small number of citizens, who assemble and administer the government in person, can admit of no cure for the mischiefs of faction. A common passion or interest will, in almost every case, be felt by a majority of the whole; a communication and concert result from the form of government itself; and there is nothing to check the inducements to sacrifice the weaker party or an obnoxious individual. Hence it is that such democracies have ever

[1] S. H. Gay, *James Madison*, 34–36.

been spectacles of turbulence and contention; have ever been found incompatible with personal security or the rights of property; and have in general been as short in their lives as they have been violent in their deaths.... A republic, by which I mean a government in which the scheme of representation takes place, opens a different prospect.... The effect [of the delegation of government] is to refine and enlarge the public views, by passing them through the medium of a chosen body of citizens, whose wisdom may best discern the true interest of their country, and whose patriotism and love of justice will be least likely to sacrifice it to temporary or partial considerations. Under such a regulation, it may well happen, that the public voice, pronounced by the representatives of the people, will be more consonant to the public good than if pronounced by the people themselves, convened for the purpose." [1]

Hamilton's ideas ran in the same channel. "The republican principle," he wrote in "The Federalist," "demands that the deliberate sense of the community should govern the conduct of those to whom they entrust the management of their affairs; but it does not require an unqualified complaisance to every sudden breeze of passion, or to every transient impulse which the people may receive from the arts of men, who flatter their prejudices to betray their interests. It is a just observation that the people commonly *intend* the *public good*. This often applies to their very errors. But their good sense would despise the adulator who should pretend that they *always reason right* about the *means* of promoting it. They know from experience that they sometimes err; and the wonder is that they so seldom err as they do, beset as they continually are, by the wiles of parasites and sycophants; by the snares of the ambitious, the avaricious, the desperate; by the artifices of men who possess their confidence more than they deserve it, and of those who seek to possess rather than deserve it. When occasions present themselves, in which the interests of the people are at variance with their inclination, it is the duty of the persons whom they have appointed to be the guardians of those interests, to withstand the temporary delusion, in order to give them time and opportunity for more cool and sedate reflection. Instances might be cited in which a conduct of this kind has saved the people from very fatal consequences of their own mistakes, and has procured lasting monuments of their gratitude

[1] *The Federalist*, No. 10.

to the men who had courage and magnanimity enough to serve them at the peril of their displeasure." [1]

Notice, however, that he began this by making the conduct of representatives subject to "the deliberate sense of the community." This will explain how he could say in the New York Convention, June 21, 1788: "If the general voice of the people be for an increase [in the number of Congressmen], it undoubtedly must take place. They have it in their power to instruct their representatives; and the State Legislatures, which appoint the Senators, may enjoin it also upon them." [2]

In the same convention John Jay said, two days later: "The Senate is to be composed of men appointed by the State Legislatures; they will certainly choose those who are most distinguished for their general knowledge. I presume they will also instruct them, that there will be a constant correspondence supported between the Senators and the State executives, who will be able, from time to time, to afford them all that particular information which particular circumstances may require." [3]

In the Virginia Convention of the same year, James Monroe said, referring, of course, to the Congress of the Confederation: "Being amenable, upon the principles of the federal compact, to the Legislature for my conduct in Congress, it cannot be doubted, if required, it was my duty to obey their directions; but that honorable body thought best to dispense with such demand." [4]

Also in that Virginia Convention, Patrick Henry, carping at the proposed Federal Constitution, said: "At present you may appeal to the voice of the people, and send men to Congress positively instructed to obey your instructions. You can recall them if their system of policy be ruinous. But can you in this government recall your Senators? Or can you instruct them? You cannot recall them. You may instruct them, and offer your opinions; but if they think them improper, they may disregard them. If they give away or sacrifice your most valuable rights, can you impeach or punish them? If you should see the Spanish ambassador bribing one of your Senators with gold, can you punish him? Yes, you can impeach him before the Senate. A majority of the Senate may be sharers in the bribe. Will they pronounce him guilty who is in the same predicament with

---

[1] *The Federalist*, No. 71.   [2] *Elliot's Debates*, ii, 252.
[3] *Ibid.*, ii, 283.   [4] *Ibid.*, iii, 334.

themselves? Where, then, is the security? I ask not this out of triumph, but anxiously to know if there be any real security." [1]

In the Massachusetts Convention held for the same purpose, that of ratifying the Federal Constitution, General William Heath declared: "It is a novel idea that representatives should be chosen for a considerable time, in order that they may learn their duty. The representative is one who appears in behalf of, and acts for, others; he ought, therefore, to be fully acquainted with the feelings, circumstances, and interests of the persons whom he represents, and this is learnt among them, not at a distant court. How frequently on momentary occasions, do the members of the British Parliament wish to go home and consult their constituents, before they come to a decision. This shows from what quarter they wish to obtain information." [2]

Of more significance was the assurance given to the wavering delegates by Rufus King, who had been one of the delegates to the Convention that framed the Federal compact. Explaining and defending it, he declared: "The State Legislatures, if they find their delegates erring, can and will instruct them. Will not this be a check? When they hear the voice of the people solemnly dictating to them their duty, they will be bold men indeed to act contrary to it. These will not be instructions sent them in a private letter, which can be put in their pockets; they will be public instructions, which all the country will see; and they will be hardy men indeed to violate them." [3]

The division over the question of ratifying was in Massachusetts very close, and had the vote gone against ratification it is doubtful if any such Union as we now have would have been formed. It might, therefore, be alleged with some ground that one of the promises which made the Union possible was the promise of Rufus King that the delegates of a State in the national Congress might be instructed.

[1] *Elliot's Debates*, III, 355.
[2] *Debates of Mass. Convention of 1788*, 110.   [3] *Ibid.*, 146.

CHAPTER XX

INSTRUCTIONS IN CONGRESS

MASSACHUSETTS took Rufus King at his word. In the very first session of the new Congress, the principle of instructions was maintained by one of her Representatives, Elbridge Gerry, who had himself been a member of the Federal Convention, although not signing its report. It was on the 15th of August, 1789, when the House was in Committee of the Whole on amendments to the Constitution, that Tucker of South Carolina moved to insert: "to instruct their representatives." Clymer of Pennsylvania hoped this might not be adopted, though he wished that if constituents chose to instruct their representatives, they might be at liberty so to do. "If they have a constitutional right to instruct us, it infers that we are bound by those instructions. This is a most dangerous principle, utterly destructive of all ideas of an independent and deliberative body." Gerry thought nevertheless that a Representative would still be at liberty to act as he pleased. He also thought the people had a right both to instruct and to bind. Madison pointed out it was not true the people could bind. A Representative would not be at liberty to obey instructions to violate the Constitution. He opposed the proposition. Gerry retorted by inquiring, "Can we conceive that our constituents would be so absurd as to instruct us to violate our oath?" After a general debate in which nearly a score of the members took part, the motion was defeated, 10 to 41.[1]

Senator William Maclay of Pennsylvania, who was bitterly opposed to the assumption of State debts by the Federal Government, gives in his Journal under date of April 12, 1790, a particularly venomous description of the attitude and aspect of the Massachusetts delegation in the House when at one stage the measure met an adverse vote. Here we may be concerned with only one portrait: "Gerry exhibited the advantages of a cadaverous appearance, at all times placid and far from pleasing. Through an interruption of hectic lines and consumptive coughs he delivered himself of a declaration that the delegates of Massa-

[1] *Annals of Congress*, first session, I, 761–76.

chusetts would proceed no further, but send to their State for instruction."

The practice had already begun in Massachusetts. On the 24th of February its General Court had "directed" the Senators "to lay the Representation relative to the Cod and whale fishery before Congress and to use their Influence that the same be taken up and duly considered." On the 2nd of March the Representatives were "requested" to move for compliance with a request regarding pensions. In February of 1791 Senators were "instructed" on the same matter and Representatives again "requested." In September, 1793, was reached the formula that became customary, the vote being to the effect that the Senators "hereby are instructed, and the Representatives requested" to adopt the most speedy and effectual measures in their power to obtain certain amendments to the Constitution. The discrimination was of course no accident. It followed the theory that the Legislatures were the constituents of the Senators, but that the Legislatures had no control over the members of the lower House.

In the Senate itself, however, there was by no means agreement to concede the claims of the Legislatures. The question was there first brought up February 24, 1791, when the Virginia Senators moved a resolution that the doors of the Senate should be opened on the first day of the next session, and mentioned their instructions. Maclay writes: "This brought the subject of instructions from the different Legislatures into view. Elsworth [so he spelled Ellsworth] said they amounted to no more than a wish, and ought to be no further regarded. Izard said no Legislature had any right to instruct at all, any more than the electors had a right to instruct the President of the United States. Mr. Morris followed; said Senators owed their existence to the Constitution; the Legislatures were only the means to choose them; and was more violently opposed to instruction than any of them. We were Senators of the United States, and had nothing to do with one State more than another. Mr. Morris spoke with more violence than usual. Perhaps I may be considered as imprudent, but I thought I would be wanting in the duty I owed the public if I sat silent and heard such doctrines without bearing my testimony against them. I declared I knew but two lines of conduct for legislators to move in — the one absolute volition, the other responsibility. The first was tyranny, the other in-

separable from the idea of representation. Were we chosen with
dictatorial powers, or were we sent forward as servants of the
public, to do their business? The latter, clearly, in my opinion.
The first question, then, which presented itself was, were my
constituents here, what would they do? The answer, if known,
was the rule of the Representative." [1]

In the next year the House took a stand on the principle involved. In the course of an address by it to the President
February 10, 1792, appears this passage: "It is not more essential to the preservation of true liberty that a government should
be always ready to listen to the representations of its constituents and to accommodate its measures to the sentiments and
wishes of every part of them, as far as will consist with the good
of the whole, than it is that the just authority of the laws should
be steadily maintained."

This could hardly have been congenial doctrine to Washington, for he was one of those who stood for the independence of
the representative. Sparks tells us that when it was a practice in
Virginia to form societies for discussing political topics, examining public measures, and instructing delegates to the Legislature,
Washington expressed strong disapprobation of these societies
in letters to a nephew, who belonged to one of them. "Nor was
he in any case friendly to positive instructions from electors,
believing that the representative, who is of course acquainted
with the sentiments of his constituents among whom he resides,
should be left to act according to the judgment he shall form,
after being enlightened by the arguments and collected wisdom
of a deliberative assembly." [2]

For half a century and longer after Madison had met the
issue, Virginia made more trouble in the matter than any other
State, but the controversy was by no means confined to her
borders. New Hampshire furnished a stout opponent of instructions in the person of Senator William Plumer. After the bitter
controversy in Congress over the choice between Jefferson and
Burr for President, what became the Twelfth Amendment was
proposed. Plumer told the Senate that four or five State Legislatures, including his own, had instructed their Senators to favor
the amendment. "When we have done it," he said, "the Legislatures throughout the Union will be told that they must adopt

[1] *Journal of William Maclay*, February 24, 1791.
[2] *Life of Washington*, *Writings of Washington*, I, 491.

them, because Congress, in its wisdom, has seen fit to propose
them. We, because they have done it; they, because we have;
with no independent action in either case. If such instructions
are obligatory, we are mere machines; and our votes must be
governed, not by the convictions of our own minds, but by the
sovereign mandates of our Legislatures. I do not so understand
the nature of my office, nor my duty in it. The people themselves established the Constitution, giving us certain rights under it, and these we are bound to exercise, according to our own
judgment, without interference from others. In so doing we
obey, in the highest sense, the voice of the people." [1]

The amendment when submitted did not receive the vote of
New Hampshire, and the biographer says: "so that, though my
father voted against instructions in this case, his constituents
came round and voted with him in the end against the amendment." [2]

Massachusetts furnished the next noteworthy episode, and it
is interesting to note that the man who suffered was the son of
the man who had put the doctrine of instructions into the Massachusetts Constitution. In 1808 John Quincy Adams was a
United States Senator, his term to expire in March of 1809. The
General Court was so dissatisfied with his course that it took the
unusual step of electing a successor ahead of time, James Lloyd
being chosen by a vote of 248 to 213 for Adams. On the same
day anti-embargo resolutions were passed in both branches by
like majorities. The next day Mr. Adams addressed a letter to
the Legislature, in which he stated that it had been his endeavor, he deeming it his duty, to support the administration of
the general government in all necessary measures to preserve
the persons and property of our citizens from depredation, and
to vindicate the rights essential to the independence of our
country; that certain resolutions having passed the Legislature,
expressing disapprobation of measures to which, under these
motives, he had given assent, and which he considered as enjoining upon the representatives of the State in Congress a sort
of opposition to the national administration in which, consistently with his principles, he could not concur, he, therefore, to
give the Legislature an opportunity to place in the Senate of the
United States a member whose views might be more coincident
with those they entertained, resigned his seat in that body.

[1] William Plumer, Jr., *Life of William Plumer*, 268. [2] *Ibid.*, 272.

James Lloyd was immediately chosen by the Legislature for the unexpired term also.[1]

In 1811 Timothy Pickering, another Massachusetts Senator, received instructions from the Legislature on the bill for the recharter of the Bank of the United States. On the 19th of February he spoke thereon, holding instructions to be erroneous in principle; that they infringed the rightful independence of representatives; and in respect to members of Congress, that they violated the Constitution of the United States. Quoting the first sentence of the Constitution he said: "If State Legislatures undertake to dictate, by their instructions, or by requests which are intended to operate equally with instructions, what votes shall be given by their Representatives in Congress, they so far assume the powers vested by the Constitution exclusively in Congress. And if their instructions or requests are obeyed, then the State Legislatures, and not Congress, enact laws for the United States."

The history of the doctrine now returns to Virginia. Its Legislature had instructed Senators Giles and Brent to vote against the recharter of the Bank. They refused to obey. On the 20th of February, 1812, the Legislature passed a long "Preamble and Resolutions, Asserting the right of the State Legislatures to instruct their Senators in the Congress of the United States; and disapproving the conduct of the Senators from this State in Congress, in relation to the instructions given them at the last session, on the subject of the Bank of the United States." This document gives a full page of instances proving that the instruction of members of Parliament had been common. Coke was quoted as saying: "It is the custom of Parliament, when any new device is moved for on the King's behalf, for his aid, and the like, that the Commons may answer, they dare not agree to it without conference with their counties." And Sydney as maintaining "that many members, in all ages, and sometimes the whole body of the Commons have refused to vote, till they consulted with those who sent them — that the Houses have often adjourned to give them time to do so." It was pointed out that notwithstanding a most splendid display of warm and touching eloquence, the people of Bristol would not reëlect Mr. Burke, for this very offense of disobeying instructions. The abstract reasoning that followed in the preamble deserves attention:

[1] Josiah Quincy, *Life of John Quincy Adams*, 40, 41.

"The representative must, in the nature of things, represent his own particular constituents only. He must, indeed, look to the general good of the nation; but he must look also, and especially to the interests of his particular constituents as concerned in the common weal; because the general good is but the aggregate of individual happiness. He must legislate for the whole nation; but laws are expressions of the general will; and the general will is only the result of individual wills fairly collected and compared; in order to which collection and comparison (that is, in order to express the general will, in order to make laws) it is plain, that the representative must express the will, and speak the opinions, of the constituents that depute him."

The *reductio ad absurdum* was used: "If the right of the constituent to instruct the representative be denied, a law might be enacted, according to all the forms of the Constitution, and yet contrary to the express will of every man in the community, the individual representatives themselves only excepted."

After demonstrating that it was not improper for the Legislature to take on itself the duty of instruction, the Preamble essayed to meet the objections to the general proposition. One retort was particularly clever. It had been said that the constituents do not hear the debates and so cannot judge the merits of the matters. This was the reply: "If this objection have force enough to defeat the right of instruction, it ought to take away, also, the right of rejecting the representative at a subsequent election."

To this was added a somewhat cumbrous proposition: "The truth is, that our institutions suppose, that although the representatives ought to be, and generally will be, selected for superior virtue and intelligence, yet a greater mass of wisdom and virtue still reside, in the constituent body, than the utmost portion allotted to any individual."

So it was "resolved" that the Assembly disapproved the action of Senators that raised the issue; declared instruction an indubitable right, with, as a consequence, bounden duty of obedience, provided the instruction did not require a violation of the Constitution or an act of moral turpitude; and proclaimed that no man who did not hold himself so bound ought thereafter to accept the appointment of a Senator of the United States from Virginia.[1]

[1] *Acts of Virginia*, 1812, 143 *et sqq.*

In 1814 Senator David Stone of North Carolina fell into disfavor with the Legislature of his State by reason of his voting with the New England Federalists. Upon being informed that the General Assembly had by a large majority resolved that he had incurred its disapprobation, he at once resigned.

Henceforward for a generation the relation between Senators and Legislatures was a great political issue. Governor Thomas Ford, in his "History of Illinois," says (page 25) that in the election of delegates to the first Illinois Convention, that of 1818, "the only questions made before the people were, the right of the constituent to instruct his representative, and the introduction of slavery, which were debated with great earnestness during the canvass." When the Tariff Bill of 1828, "the Tariff of Abominations," reached the Senate, John Rowan of Kentucky made a speech against it, and then observed it might be inferred from what he had said that he would vote against it. He did not wish any doubts entertained as to the vote he should give upon this measure, or the reasons which would influence him to give it. He was not at liberty to substitute his individual opinion for that of his State. As the organ of the State of Kentucky, he felt himself bound to surrender his individual opinion, and express the opinion of his State.[1] Martin Van Buren, though he sat still during the debate, cast for the bill a protectionist vote, with Benton and several others whose convictions were against it, but who yielded to the supposed public sentiment or the peremptory instructions of their States, or who did not yet dare to make upon the tariff a presidential issue. Van Buren felt constrained by a resolution of the Legislature of New York passed almost unanimously.[2]

Two English women who traveled in America have told about the experiences of men who disobeyed instructions. "I remember," wrote one whose book was published in 1821, "the case of a distinguished member from the west of Pennsylvania (Mr. Baldwin), who once voted in decided opposition to his received instructions. At his return home, he was summoned to give an explanation or apology, under risk of being thrown out. The member replied that, at the time of his vote, he had expressed his regret that his opinion differed from that of his electors; but that he should have been unworthy of the distinguished office he

[1] Benton, *Thirty Years View*, i, 95.
[2] Edward M. Shepard, *Martin Van Buren*, 122, 123.

held, and of the public confidence which he had for so many years enjoyed, if he could apologize for having voted according to the decision of his judgment; that his fellow citizens were perfectly right to transfer their voices to the man who might more thoroughly agree with them in sentiment than in this case he had done; that for himself, he could not only promise to consider every question attentively and candidly, to weigh duly the wishes of his constituents, but never to vote in decided opposition to his own opinion. His fellow citizens received his declaration with applause, and, as his whole political life had been in unison with their sentiments, they took this one instance of dissent as an additional proof of his integrity, and unanimously reëlected him." [1]

The other writer was Harriet Martineau, who arrived at Washington on the 13th of January, 1835. "We joined a party of highly esteemed and kind friends," she says, "a member of the House of Representatives from Massachusetts, his wife and sister-in-law, and a Senator from Maine, at Mrs. Peyton's boarding-house. The Senator happened, from a peculiar set of circumstances, to be an idle man just now. The gentleman's peculiar and not very agreeable position arose out of the troublesome question of Instructions to Representatives. Senators are chosen for a term of six years, one third of the body going out every two years; the term being made thus long in order to ensure some stability of policy in the Senate. If the government of the State from which the Senator is sent changes its politics during his term, he may be annoyed by instructions to vote contrary to his principles, and, if he refuses, by a call to resign, on the ground of his representing the principles of the minority. This had been the predicament of our companion; and the question of resigning or not under such circumstances had become generally a very important and interesting one, but one which there was no means of settling. Each member in such a scrape must act as his own judgment and conscience dictate under the circumstances of the particular case. Our companion made a mistake. When the attempt to instruct him was made, he said he appealed from the new Legislature of his State to the people who chose him. He did appeal by standing candidate for the office of Governor of the State, and was defeated. No course

[1] *Views of Society and Manners in America*, by "An Englishwoman," New York, 1821, 264, note.

then remained but resigning; which he did immediately, when his senatorial term was within half a session of its close. He had withdrawn from the Senate Chamber, and was winding up his political affairs at the time when we joined his party." [1]

The Senator in question must have been Peleg Sprague of Hallowell, who resigned January 1, 1835. He was a Whig; had been elected Senator in 1829; and became U.S. District Judge in Boston, holding the position from 1841 to 1865. It was in January, 1834, that the Maine Legislature instructed the Senators and requested the Representatives to oppose the restoration of the government deposits and the renewal of the charter of the United States Bank. The quarrel over this matter, one of the bitterest quarrels in the history of American politics, led in one way or another to the most notable incidents in the history of instructions.

These incidents centered about the fight led by Benton to get expunged the Senate censure of President Jackson. John Tyler and William C. Rives were the Senators from Virginia. The General Assembly of that State passed resolutions condemning the dismissal of Duane and the removal of the deposits. Thereupon Rives, a supporter of Jackson, promptly resigned. B. W. Leigh was elected in his place. Then Benton's expunging resolution was made an issue in the State election. Jackson's friends won the next Assembly and in February of 1836 that body commanded Tyler and Leigh to introduce and vote for an expunging resolution. It declared that the right of instruction was one of the vital principles of our free institutions, and that it was the duty of the representative to obey or resign. Governor Tazewell refused to transmit the resolutions, whereupon they were sent by the presiding officers of both branches of the Legislature.

John Tyler had begun his public career by taking his seat as a member of the Virginia House of Delegates in December, 1811. It was he who in 1812 had moved the vote to censure Giles and Brent because they had refused to obey instructions to oppose the recharter of the United States Bank. It was Benjamin Watkins Leigh who had drawn the resolutions of instructions. Now, a quarter of a century later, these two men were to be put to the same ordeal. Leigh's election to succeed Rives was in effect an express command to oppose expunging. This he used with ability and power in defense of his refusal either to obey the new

[1] *Retrospect of Western Travel*, I, 143–46.

instructions or to resign, but he never recovered party standing.

Tyler took a different course. He wrote to the Legislature February 29, 1836, a long letter in the course of which he said: "I now reaffirm the opinion at all times heretofore expressed by me, that instructions are mandatory, provided they do not require a violation of the Constitution or the commission of an act of moral turpitude." [1] He held that the instructions in question called upon him to violate the Constitution, but in the end, after consulting his friends, concluded not to stand on that contention. His friends, and particularly Judge White, advised him that he had no choice and it was most politic to resign.[2]

His resignation was read in the Senate February 29, 1836. Rives was elected in his place. In the Assembly session of 1838–39, the two were opponents for the Senate. A contest of many days, with thirty-eight ballotings, ended in an agreement that if Tyler's friends would yield Rives' election to the Senate, Tyler should be the nominee for Vice-President in 1840. Tyler's friends would not vote for Rives, but leaving their seats, lessened the majority necessary to elect, giving Rives the victory.[3] In due course Tyler was nominated for Vice-President and elected. The death of Harrison made him President. So it came about that one man's adherence to the doctrine of instructions helped him to the highest place in the Republic, just as the rejection of the doctrine by John Quincy Adams, may have helped him to the same position, though not so directly.

Berrien of Georgia disobeyed in the matter of expunging. King of Alabama took the opposite view. Presenting resolutions from his State assembly entreating its Senators to use their "untiring efforts" to cause the censure to be expunged, he said that never having doubted the right of a Legislature to instruct its Senators in Congress, he should consider himself culpable if he did not carry its wishes into effect, when properly expressed.

North Carolina in 1834 instructed Senator Mangum to vote for Benton's expunging resolution. He refused and would not at once resign, but gave in his resignation in 1836. Robert Strange succeeded him. Bedford Brown was the other Senator. In 1838 it was their turn to disobey, for the Whigs, getting control of the Legislature, passed resolutions disapproving the policy of the administration and condemning the expunging of the Jackson

[1] Niles' Register, 50, 25.
[2] Henry A. Wise, Seven Decades of the Union, 138.   [3] Ibid., 157, 158.

censure. When the Senators asked whether they should consider these resolutions as instructions, the Legislature declared it had spoken clearly enough. Thereupon Brown and Strange gave reasons to the Senate for not obeying "these instructions," saying they would have obeyed had these been mandatory. That roused the ire of Henry Clay and on the 14th of January he castigated the North Carolina Senators in a fiery speech. In the course of it he asked: "What is the basis, and what the principle of the doctrine of instruction? Sir, to a certain extent, I have always believed in this doctrine, and have been ever ready to conform to it. But I hold to the doctrine as it stood in 1798; that in general, on questions of expediency, the representative should conform to his instructions, and so gratify the wishes, and obey the will, of his constituents, though on questions of constitutionality his course might be different.... And what is the doctrine of instruction, as it is held by all? Is it not that we are to act, not in our own, but in a delegated character? And will any who stand here, pretend, that whenever they know the wishes or will of those who sent them here, they are not bound to conform to that will entirely? Is it not the doctrine, that we are nothing more than the mirror to reflect the will of those who called us to our dignified office? That is the view which I take of the doctrine of instruction." [1]

Evidently the political climate of North Carolina became too warm for the recalcitrant Senators. Anyhow they resigned in 1840.

This episode brought out clearly the weakest point in the argument for instructions. When a Representative or Senator of known convictions has been chosen by an electorate by reason of agreement with those convictions on the part of a majority of the electorate, and then that majority shifts to the opposite view, the Representative or Senator is to change his convictions, which would be unethical, perhaps dishonorable, or he is to resign, which is inconsistent with the constitutional provision for fixed terms. Senator Southard of New Jersey discussed the point intelligently in the Senate, February 22, 1835. "It may, it often does, happen," he said, "that the political character of the Legislature is frequently changed. Upon this theory there must be a new Senator upon every change. In Rhode Island, if I recollect correctly, the changes have been such that she might

[1] Mallory, *Life and Speeches of Henry Clay*, ii, 351.

have had, nay, ought to have had, six Senators in two years. So in Ohio; last year she instructed her Senators: one of them disobeyed; if he had resigned, the present Legislature, which is of a different political aspect, would have instructed his successor, and we should have had two new Senators upon the floor, and the State had five in a little more than one year. The rebellious one of last year might have been restored; unless indeed the Legislature should, as they ought under the circumstances, spurn him from their confidence for his servility, as destitute of that moral courage and independence of character without which a public agent is a public curse. The history of my own State is not destitute of facts to illustrate this doctrine. The changes which have taken place in the political parties there since 1824 would have given to us some six or eight different members, and this resulting from no versatility or changeableness in the character of her people. The number of our counties is small — only fourteen. The parties throughout the State have long been nearly balanced. In several of the counties the change of a few votes, or the neglect of a small number to attend the poll, would not only give a new representative in the Legislature, but change its political character; a little more than one hundred votes, in one or two of several counties, would have changed the late instructions."

It was at this period that Abraham Lincoln, then a young man, pronounced himself upon the relation of a representative to his constituency. When he was a candidate for reëlection to the Illinois Legislature in 1836, he began his canvass with a platform containing this:

"If elected, I shall consider the whole people of Sangamon my constituents, as well those that oppose as those that support me. While acting as their representative I shall be governed by their will on all subjects upon which I have the means of knowing what their will is, and upon all others I shall do what my own judgment teaches me will best advance their interests." [1]

Governor Ford in his entertaining history of Illinois tells us that among the members of the Legislature who voted for the disastrous internal improvement law in 1837, were Stephen A. Douglas, Ninian W. Edwards, James Shields, and — for so Ford spelled the name in 1850 — "Abram Lincoln." Ford says (page 196): "These gentlemen have been excused upon the ground that

[1] Nicolay and Hay, *Abraham Lincoln*, i, 129.

they were instructed to vote as they did, and that they had
every right to believe that they were truly reflecting the will of
their constituents. But it appears to me that members ought to
resign such small offices, to sacrifice a petty ambition, rather
than become the willing tools of a deluded people, to bring so
much calamity upon the country."

The Tariff Act of 1846 was carried in the Senate by the vote
of Spencer Jarnagin of Kentucky, a declared protectionist, who
had spoken against the bill. He acted under instructions from
the Kentucky Legislature, and disinterestedly, for it was already settled that he would not be reëlected.

In 1848 Thomas H. Benton, then nearing the end of his fifth
term as a Senator from Missouri, found himself in the clutches
of the doctrine that had so greatly helped him in winning his
contest to expunge the resolutions that censured Jackson.
Benton took issue with Calhoun and the slavery extremists in
the matter of the legislation following the Mexican War that
related to the newly acquired territories. In the middle of his
fight against extending slavery into them, his enemies won
control of the Missouri Legislature and passed resolutions
truculent and disloyal in tone, demanding that slavery be permitted to exist in all the new States to be admitted, and instructing the Senators from Missouri to vote accordingly. Benton's colleague Atchison presented them in the Senate. Benton,
a doughty man, full of courage, did not hesitate. On the 9th of
May, 1848, he addressed a letter "To the People of Missouri."
He refused to obey the instructions. "From this command I appeal to the people of Missouri, the whole body of the people —
and if they confirm the instructions, I shall give them an opportunity to find a Senator to carry their will into effect, as I
cannot do anything to dissolve this union, or array one half
of it against the other." [1] They took him at his word and defeated him for reëlection. So he was hoist by his own petard.

In January, 1849, the Legislature of Michigan passed a joint
resolution repudiating squatter sovereignty, and asserting that
Congress had the power, and that it was its duty, to prohibit by
enactment the introduction of slavery into the West. The Senators were instructed and the Representatives requested to use
their efforts to accomplish such an object. Lewis Cass was
elected to the Senate but a few days after these resolutions were

[1] *Niles' Register*, May 23, 1849.

approved, and he therefore began his second term with the knowledge on both sides that his own beliefs on the great questions were different from those of a majority of the Legislators and of his constituents.

He spoke on the subject in the Senate January 21 and 22, 1850. His closing sentences were: "I will endeavor to discharge my duty, as an American Senator, to the country and to the whole country, agreeably to the convictions of my own duty and of the obligations of the Constitution, and when I cannot do this I shall cease to have any duty here to perform. My sentiments upon the Wilmot proviso are now before the Senate, and will soon be before my constituents and the country. I am precluded from voting in conformity with them. I have been instructed by the Legislature of Michigan to vote in favor of this measure. I am a believer in the right of instruction when fairly exercised, and under proper circumstances. There are limitations upon the exercise; but I need not seek to ascertain their extent or application, for they do not concern my present position. I acknowledge the obligations of the instructions I have received, and cannot act in opposition to them. Nor can I act in opposition to my own convictions of the true meaning of the Constitution. When the time comes, and I am required to vote upon this measure as a practical one, in a bill providing for a territorial government, I shall know how to reconcile my duty to the Legislature with my duty to myself, by surrendering a trust I can no longer fulfill." [1]

Webster's famous 7th of March speech, in which he deplored unnecessary agitation, advocated compromise, and lamented sentiment, had direct effect at the North. It was itself the expression of reaction and conservatism. It aided the growing desire to settle the question and to restore harmony, and seems to have influenced the Legislature of Michigan to reconsider its instructions and requests to the Congressmen of the State. On the 11th of April Cass exultingly read to the Senate resolutions freeing him from any obligation to vote contrary to his judgment. [2]

But his experience with instructions was not to end thus happily. In February of 1855 resolutions from the Legislature of Michigan were presented in the Senate, by Stuart, the col-

[1] *Appendix to the Congressional Globe*, vol. XXII, part I, 74.
[2] A. C. McLaughlin, *Lewis Cass*, 263–73.

league of General Cass, instructing them, and requesting the Representatives, to vote for an act prohibiting slavery in the Territories, and for the repeal of the Fugitive Slave law. Cass replied at length, refusing to obey the dictates of a party that had suddenly and, as he believed, temporarily become possessed of the government of the State. When instructed before, he had acknowledged that such instructions were valid "under proper circumstances," but asserted that there were "limitations upon the exercise." He now thought these limitations in force. He was fully persuaded that the adoption of the measure proposed "would be the signal for the breaking up of the government and the dissolution of the Confederacy." Stuart followed the example of his senior colleague.[1] In the following January Cass received only sixteen votes for reëlection to the Senate.

There are those who assume that the importance of the doctrine of instructions, reaching its height in the exciting struggle over Jackson's policies, ended with the bitter partisanship that preceded the Civil War. Not so. To be sure, the recurrences of the controversy since then have not been of great consequence in themselves, but its continuance shows that the question is not yet dead. At the special session of Congress in March, 1869, Senator Reuben E. Fenton of New York, under instructions of the New York Legislature, favored the repeal of the tenure of office act. Roscoe Conkling, a member of the Judiciary Committee that reported a bill amending the act, disregarded the dictates of a body that did not elect him.[2]

In 1877 Senator Eaton of Connecticut, a Democrat, when instructed to vote for the Electoral Commission Bill, declared his purpose to disregard his instructions and to vote according to his convictions. He had no idea of resigning. The Legislature afterward rescinded the instructions.

In February of 1878 the Mississippi Legislature instructed the Senators and requested the Representatives from that State to vote for the act remonetizing silver. Senator L. Q. C. Lamar laid his instructions before the Senate and declined to comply with them, saying: "I cannot and will not shirk the responsibility which my position imposes." To a member of the Legislature he wrote: "I recognize the right of a Legislature to express its opinion upon questions of Federal policy, and I think

[1] A. C. McLaughlin, *Lewis Cass*, 306.

[2] A. R. Conkling, *Life and Letters of Roscoe Conkling*, 318.

such expressions of opinions are entitled to the most respectful and patient consideration of the Federal Representatives; and if there be any doubt in the mind of either a Senator or Representative as to what his course ought to be, he should give to the sentiment of his people, as expressed by the Legislature, the full benefit of that doubt, and vote in accordance with their wishes. But in this particular case their wishes are directly in conflict with the convictions of my whole life; and had I voted as the House of Representatives directed, I should have cast my first vote against my conscience." In the following December Jefferson Davis wrote an open letter defending the right of instruction. Discussion followed in Mississippi. Lamar declared: "No Senator should depart in his votes from an opinion thus expressed or given, unless in case of a clear and conscientious conviction that in following such instructions he would be violating the Constitution or injuring the interests of the whole country." He stumped the State on the issue and converted it to his view.

On the 27th of January, 1898, the Legislature of Kentucky asked Senator Lindsay to resign, on the ground that he was misrepresenting his party and State on the money question. In refusing he said: "I do not exercise my senatorial duties subject to legislative supervision, nor hold my place at the legislative will. I represent, not merely a party or faction, but all the people of Kentucky. My term of service is fixed by the Constitution of the United States. It cannot be abridged by the action of the Kentucky Legislature, and an attempt by certain members of that body to abridge it is the assertion of a right which does not exist and could not exist without imperiling the independence of this great branch of the Federal Legislature. Resolutions emanating from State Legislatures touching matters pending in the Federal Congress, are entitled to most respectful consideration, and always receive it; but they cannot determine the duty of a Senator or relieve him from the responsibility of his position. I am a Senator from Kentucky, but I am also a Senator for the United States. When great public interests affecting alike every portion of the Union are to be acted upon, they are to be considered from the standpoint of the broadest patriotism." [1]

These are by no means all the cases of instructions to United States Senators and Representatives that could be cited, but

[1] *Congressional Record*, vol. 31, part 2, 1433.

they suffice to show the vitality of the doctrine, whether it be erroneous or not. Therefore I cannot share the confidence of Professor Charles A. Beard, who says in "Readings in American Government and Politics" (page 233): "It is a principle of our constitutional law that Senators and Representatives are not to be instructed by their constituents." And in view of the express declaration of the right in about two fifths of the State Constitutions I query the implication of his further statement that the principle he sets forth "is constantly violated in practice by State Legislatures." It has indeed been held by able statesmen that the doctrine is obsolete. Such has been one of the arguments presented against so-called "Public Opinion Bills" as they have been urged on various Legislatures, bills meant to facilitate the formal expression of public opinion on matters of broad public concern. It is quite true that of late years there has been little attempt to instruct Representatives, whether State or Federal. Yet even in Massachusetts, where the independence of the lawmaker has had almost complete sway, instructions have not disappeared. At the annual meeting of the town of Lincoln, March 8, 1915, it was voted, on the motion of Charles Francis Adams, "That the attention of our Senators and Representatives in the Great and General Court and of all other officials of the Commonwealth be called to the fact above stated [the increase in the cost of government]; and they be requested, and, when representative, be instructed rigidly to systematize and revise all items of public expenditure," etc. This was the last public act in the life of a student of government whose great-grandfather, the most learned man of his time in that science, had penned the Braintree instructions which led the way to Revolution and who had put the doctrine into the Massachusetts Constitution; whose grandfather had resigned a seat in the United States Senate because he could not conscientiously voice the views of the Legislature of his State.

A combination of plebiscite and legislative action has recently appeared in Massachusetts. On the ballot at the election in 1928, in thirty-six out of forty of the Senatorial districts, appeared this question: "Shall the Senator from this district be instructed to vote for a resolution requesting Congress to take action for the repeal of the Eighteenth Amendment to the Constitution of the United States, known as the Prohibition Amendment?" In all but two of the districts the vote was in the affirmative; the total favoring was 707,352; in the negative, 422,655; and of those voting at the election 310,244 did not vote on the question. The following Senate complied with the instruction and requested Congress to act accordingly. What became the duty of a Massachusetts Congressman? It will be noticed that less than half those who went to the polls, voted in the affirmative. It was known that the leaders of the forces favoring prohibition had urged its friends not to vote on the question. It was probable that a majority of the party that elected thirteen out of the sixteen Representatives, opposed the resolution. Ours is a two-party form of government, under which the party for the time prevailing is responsible for legislation, and that party in turn is to be controlled by a majority of its membership. On the other hand many more than half the citizens voting on the question had declared for the resolution. It would have been interesting to see how the Massachusetts members would have met the embarrassing problem, but as the question did not come before Congress they were saved perplexity.

In a somewhat similar situation, Senator Copeland of New York, previously listed as a supporter of prohibition, was in November of 1926 reported in the press as announcing that henceforth he would espouse the cause of liquor law modification because he held the referendum vote in his State on the "wet-and-dry" question to be a mandate, binding on him and every other Congressman from his State. It looks as if with the spread of the Initiative and Referendum legislators will be increasingly confronted with the need to decide whether they will shape their course to correspond with the votes of the electorate.

VARIOUS VIEWS

Our writers on political science have of course not failed to address themselves to a problem that has had such prominence in the political life of this country, and as their judgments may be presumed to have been reached with the maximum of deliberation and the minimum of bias, they should be considered. Francis Lieber, the first of our theorists not in public life to earn a wide hearing, published his "Manual of Political Ethics" when the controversy was at its height, in 1838, and naturally gave thorough treatment to the subject. In part he said: "The doctrine of instruction, as it is now presented by its advocates in the United States, may be stated thus: The representative ought, as far as he is able, truly to represent the wishes of his constituents, and if on any important question the views and desires of the majority of his constituents are made known to him in any manner which convinces him that it is really the voice of the majority, he ought either to obey, or, if he cannot conscientiously do so, to resign. An attempt is thus made to give to the representative a character between that of a representative and a deputy. The chief arguments urged in favor of the above doctrine, and in fact, as far as my knowledge extends, the only ones, are these: That, could the people meet, as in ancient times, in the market, they would act for themselves, each according to his interest and views, and that now, when the number of inhabitants or extent of country prevents them from meeting in a general and primary assembly, it is clear that those who are sent for the mere sake of expediting the business, instead of the people's convening themselves, must speak as the people themselves would have spoken. The representatives are the speaking-trumpets of their constituents, and nothing more. Secondly, which in fact is but the above in other terms, the representative is the servant of his constituents; and how can he be called a servant if he does not their will?... If the representative is merely the speaking-trumpet of the people who can no longer assemble, it appears to me perfectly clear that consistency would actually demand that he should speak say three hours for the measure and one against it, if he has been elected by six thousand votes against two thousand, for these two thousand would or might have spoken in the general assembly and laid their views before the assembly. I beg to observe that this is not advanced in a sportive sense, but gravely. If we are to have absolute democracy with agents who do not speak for the minority, this minority loses all the right which it had in the primary assembly." [1]

Another authoritative writer, T. D. Woolsey, President of Yale, has taken this view of the matter: "Each representative is to consider the whole State first, and then each part of the State as far as its apparent welfare does not collide with that of the whole. He can, therefore, lawfully place himself under no pledges nor receive any instructions which are binding upon him, for to do so would imply that he is bound, after being convinced that the general good requires a certain course, to take directly

[1] *Manual of Political Ethics,* 2nd ed., II, 310–11.

the opposite. It would place the citizens, who cannot know the reasons which appear after full deliberation, in the position of giving orders to one who has carefully listened to the deliberation, and of controlling his actions, although they ought to be of the same mind with him, and although he was sent to the assembly to find out what was best and to vote after deliberation upon that conviction. It would in fact be deducible from the same premises that the representative is bound to follow the will of his constituents in all cases whatever, only with more certainty when they give him direct instructions, with less when they do not. And thus it would follow also that deliberation is a mere farce, and that the great power actually put into the hands of the representative to vote as he thinks best ought to be abridged." [1]

Our chief authority on parliamentary law, Luther Stearns Cushing, wrote in 1856: "In this country, the right of instruction has been contended for, on the one hand, independent of constitutional provision, and, on the other, has been denied to exist, even where it is expressly conferred, in any other sense, than as declaring the right of constituents to make known their views and wishes to their representatives. Both propositions are equally untenable. A right of instruction, to which the duty of obedience is not correlative, is entirely inconsistent with the constitution and functions of an independent, sovereign legislative power; and it is equally impossible to suppose that the right of instruction is restricted, in those of the Constitutions in which it is declared, to signify a mere expression of opinion, on the part of constituents, with which representatives are at liberty to comply or not at their pleasure. It may be stated, therefore, in regard to the right of instruction in this country, that it exists only in those States in which it is expressly reserved by constitutional provision; and that where it exists it is an absolute right, to be implicitly obeyed, when exercised, so far as it is authoritatively expressed.

"Where the right of instruction exists by constitutional provision, or is admitted as obligatory, it is important to ascertain in what manner it may be exercised, for which a few remarks will be sufficient. In the first place, if the constituency is a municipal corporation, competent to express itself by a corporate act, that is clearly the only authentic mode of giving binding instruc-

[1] *Political Science*, i, 296.

tions to its representatives; so if the constituency is a sovereign State, as is the case with reference to the Senate of the United States, it can only give binding instructions by means of a legislative act, passed in the ordinary form. If the constituency is not a municipal corporation, as is the case with the greater number of districts for the election of representatives in the Congress of the United States, there is no other mode of instructing their representatives than by the signatures of individuals, or by their attendance at a public meeting called for the purpose. In a case of this kind, the member, to whom the instructions are addressed, must determine for himself, whether they express the opinions of a majority of the constituency (for no smaller number certainly can be competent to instruct) and, therefore, whether they are to be implicitly obeyed, or only respectfully considered. Lastly, if the instructions are sufficiently expressed, and the obligation of obedience exists or is recognized, the member addressed has no alternative but to obey, and cannot relieve himself from his obligation by resigning his seat; a proceeding which, in most cases, would as effectually destroy the right of instruction as direct disobedience." [1]

Another technical author, Judge Jameson, who has written the authoritative book on Constitutional Conventions, touches on instructions as related to delegates to such bodies. Before the Ohio Convention of 1850 a meeting of "the democracy of Butler County" passed resolutions instructing the delegates who might be chosen from that county to support the doctrine that charters of incorporation may be repealed. Mr. Vance, a candidate for the Convention, in a communication published before the election, refused to subscribe to the platform thus laid down for him, but nevertheless was elected by a large majority. After the Convention had assembled, his course on this topic not being agreeable to the "democracy of Butler County," a meeting thereof repeated and emphasized the instructions, and requested the delegates of the County to adhere strictly to the instructions or resign. Mr. Vance chose to resign, not distinctly admitting the instructions to be binding on him, but being unwilling to be placed in a position which would carry with it even the appearance of disobedience to the will of his constituents.

In commenting on this, Judge Jameson submits that as a Convention is an advisory body, it would be an act of absurd

[1] *Law and Practice of Legislative Assemblies*, 286, 287.

inconsistency to instruct. "It would be simply to ask advice, but first to dictate to the advising body what its advice should be!" Furthermore he says: "Whatever the delegates to the Convention represented, they certainly did not represent the 'democracy of Butler County,' who, therefore, had no more right to instruct them than had the milkmaids or the barbers of Butler County. If those delegates represented anybody within the county, it was the electors there residing, without distinction of party, of whom the election expressed the collective will. If the right of instruction were conceded to any designated section of the electors, acting, not as electors, but in a party or other private capacity, it could not be denied to every individual voter." [1]

In supplement to these views, it is worth while adding the judgment of a statesman of our time, a man with exceptional grasp of the problems of government, Henry Cabot Lodge, long Senator from Massachusetts. "The use of instructions has died out," he said, speaking with direct reference to a proposal in his own State, "although they are still employed occasionally, simply because improved means of communication and the growth of commercial, labor, and trade organizations have made other modes of reaching the same result quicker, easier, and more practicable. But this fact does not impair the rights of a constituency in the least, and any constituency can avail itself of this right if it so desires, for it is one of which no constituency could be deprived except by constitutional amendment. Every constituency, I repeat, has the right now, as always, to issue instructions to its representative if it can agree upon them, just as it has the right of petition; but that is a very different thing from the final determination by ballot of every possible abstract question by a popular vote. It is worth while to emphasize this difference, for it throws light upon the whole question. The constituency, in the first place, instructs only its own representatives. It does not undertake to instruct the representatives of other constituencies, but only its own, thereby recognizing the representative character of the member or Senator or Congressman whom it has chosen. The instructions, moreover, are passed by a meeting where they can be discussed, amended, and modified, and where the arguments of both majority and minority can be heard. The constituency in passing instructions is not

[1] *The Constitutional Convention*, 342.

confined to a blind, categorical 'yes' or 'no' upon a question where neither amendment, discussion, nor modification is possible. They act themselves only with the same safeguards which have been thrown about the passage of laws in the legislature. They are not the helpless instrument of a plebiscite, but freemen setting forth their opinions in the manner which the history of free government has consecrated. Instructions from a constituency are the very antithesis of the 'mandate' which it is proposed to extort or cajole from the people by such a scheme as this Public Opinion Bill." [1]

As to the course a representative should pursue on the receipt of instructions or after a plebiscite, I am not willing to dogmatize, nor am I inclined to be censorious. Nearly all the work of every legislative body nowadays is matter of expediency, without any ethical content. Where no question of right or wrong is involved, and a vote contrary to the evident opinion of a district would be likely to end the political career of its representative, he might with some logic conclude it better for his district, quite apart from his own fortunes, that he should waive his judgment in this one thing rather than through the stubborn exercise of independent decision end such usefulness as he might have acquired by long training and experience. So constituted as to insist on the right to do my own thinking and believing that the majority of the citizens of my district wish me so to do, I stand for independent judgment, ready to take the risks. If my colleague takes the opposite view, he is within his rights and will get no blame from me, but in my judgment independent decision works for better legislation.

After all is that not the real test? The purpose of legislation is government. We all want the best government. Those legislative practices are wisest that bring the best government. It is the philosophy of expediency, of pragmatism, but what is there in the history of mankind to show it is not sound?

This does not necessarily mean the renunciation of democracy. The mind of the many may be on the whole wiser than the mind of the few. Yet there are times when the few are better informed, can give more study and reflection, can hear and weigh all the arguments. The representative who conscientiously decides as he believes his constituents would decide were they in his place,

[1] Henry Cabot Lodge, *The Democracy of the Constitution and other Addresses and Essays*, 10.

with all its advantages of knowledge and enlightenment, will not go far astray.

This course is the easier to follow when it is remembered that the formalities of instruction do not of themselves prove either authority or importance. Any one who has served in a State Legislature knows, for example, how scant the attention there given to proposals for memorializing Congress or otherwise affecting Congressional action. These proposals usually prevail with little or no debate. Somehow the legislators feel no responsibility for positions taken in regard to them. Inasmuch as many members of Congress have served in State Legislatures and understand all about this, it is not surprising that the hundred and more memorials sent by the Legislatures to every Congress are ignored. They are that much waste paper.

Plebiscites carry somewhat more weight, but the man with experience enough in affairs political to have become a member of Congress well knows how often votes have been cast at the polls without knowledge of all the arguments, how often they are in reality manufactured by a prejudiced or self-interested few, how often they are not the product of calm, prudent, informed judgment. Unsupported, they ought not to dominate.

Pledges, Censure, and Recall

Pledges are akin to instructions. They differ, of course, in that a pledge is a promise and an instruction is a command, so that normally they proceed from the opposite parties — the elector instructs, the elected pledges. The two things have been much confused in discussion. Burke's speech to the electors of Bristol, for instance, would apply to either, but as a matter of fact both he and Wilkes were chiefly concerned with pledges.

A pledge may be purely voluntary, an independent declaration of purpose; or it may be given in response to demand. Very few critics have ever gone so far as to suggest that a preëlection announcement of belief is reprehensible. Perhaps that might be inferred to have been the notion of Whitelocke, who said, a century before Burke and Wilkes took sides: "The members of Parliament are not, beforehand, to make any compacts, or undertakings, what they will do, or not do. But what shall be propounded among them, when they are met together; that is to be considered by them, that they are to deliberate upon. And after a free debate in full Parliament; as their judgments shall be swayed by reason, and as God shall put into their hearts, so they are to ordain; and therefore it is said, 'shall happen to be ordained.' The members come not to Parliament prepared, or bespoken beforehand; but as free counsellors, to give their votes, as their reason shall be satisfied; as they judge will most conduce to public good." [1]

Assuming that Whitelocke would have gone as far as to say that a candidate ought not to open his mouth before election, his theory would call for no discussion here inasmuch as it would nowadays be held chimerical. It is wholly inconsistent with party government, which requires that the opinions of candidates shall be known to be those of the party they would represent. Mill voiced well the view of our times. "A man of conscience and known ability," he says, "should insist on full freedom to act as he in his own judgment deems best, and should not consent to serve on any other terms. But the electors are entitled to know how he means to act; what opinions, on all things which concern his public duty, he intends should guide his conduct. If some of these are unacceptable to them, it is for him to satisfy them that he nevertheless deserves to be their representative; and if they are wise, they will overlook, in favor of his general value, many and great differences between his opinion and their own. There are some differences, however, which they cannot be expected to overlook. Whoever feels the amount of interest in the government of his country which befits a freeman, has some convictions on national affairs which are like his life-blood; which the strength of his belief in their truth, together with the importance he attaches to them, forbid him to make a subject of compromise, or postpone to the judgment of any other person, however greatly his superior. Such convictions, when they exist in a people, or in any appreciable portion of one, are entitled to influence in virtue of their mere existence, and not solely in that of the probability of their being grounded in truth." [2]

De Tocqueville was less tolerant and judicial. He wrote his "Democracy in America" just when the controversy over instructions was coming to a head, and perhaps that was what he had in mind, but it will be noted he used the word "pledged" (if the translation is accurate) when he wrote this: "A proceeding

---

[1] *Whitelocke's Notes Uppon the King's Writte for Choosing Members of Parlement,* ii, 294.

[2] *Representative Government,* chap. x.

which will in the end set all the guarantees of representative democracy at naught is becoming more and more general in the United States: it frequently happens that the electors, who choose a delegate, point out a certain line of conduct to him, and impose upon him a certain number of positive obligations which he is pledged to fulfill. With the exception of the tumult, this comes to the same thing as if the majority of the populace held its deliberations in the market-place."

A more recent writer, who evidently thinks along the same lines, declares: "To hold that the delegate should be fettered by pledges is, so far, to prevent the working of free thought. The popular assembly is not free in its action unless each one of its members is free to think his own thought, to utter it in his own way, and to change his opinions when convinced by reasonable argument. It is of the very essence of free democratic institutions that the thought and action of the delegate should be as free as that of the citizen." [1]

This probably goes beyond what would prove to be the consensus of belief. It certainly goes beyond everyday practice. Platforms of political parties would lose what little utility they yet possess if all candidates standing on them felt perfectly free to ignore them *in toto* after election. On the other hand, it is not common expectation that a representative will blindly abide by every plank in his party platform. Furthermore, when it comes to applying principle, there must be leeway for the exercise of judgment, otherwise committee hearings and debate on the floor would be quite superfluous.

Pledges given by a candidate in response to demand may or may not be blameworthy. If they harmonize with the convictions of the pledger, no direct harm is worked, but even then they cannot escape the suspicion of interest, no matter though it be unjust. Any pledge given before election in response to demand appears to bring in the element of what the lawyers mean by consideration, *quid pro quo*, a bargain. The law would undoubtedly declare such a pledge unenforceable as contrary to public policy. It would be regarded as an indirect violation of the principle that secures to a representative freedom from coercion by his constituents. Specific prohibition of such a pledge was asked of the Illinois Legislature in 1915. A bill imposing a fine of from $200 to $1000, or imprisonment not exceeding sixty days, for

[1] Albert Stickney, *The Political Problem*, 123.

giving a pledge with respect to legislation, was amended in the House to add the vacating of the seat of any member guilty thereof. It passed the House by a vote of 89 to 41, but I find no record of action by the Senate.

Of late years England has had more occasion than the United States to worry over the matter of pledges: Their extensive use among all parties in the general election of 1906, committing candidates to support of legislation that would put back the trades unions where they were before the decision in the Taff Vale case, forced the Campbell-Bannerman government to pass the Trades Disputes Act; and two years later the same method of constraint drove the Asquith government to change its attitude on woman suffrage. In the United States tendencies are toward going over the heads of the Legislatures with the Initiative and Referendum; in England they have not yet passed the stage of coercing legislators by extorting promises in advance.

The candidate who indulges in specific pledges invites trouble for himself later. He shuts the door to whatever help may come from committee study and from debate on the floor, as far as concerns principles. Yet he may find that after being fully informed and hearing all considerations, his honest judgment would be against the course he has promised. Furthermore the measure may take a shape he cannot approve, may contain details that will thwart the wish of those to whom the pledge has been given. It may prove most embarrassing to try to explain a vote under such circumstances, whichever way it is cast. Again and again have I heard legislators privately express regret that they ever committed themselves. The prudent course is to avoid making any definite promise whatever. When it is necessary to take a stand upon some specific campaign issue, assurance may both cautiously and honorably be couched in general language that will leave open the chance to modify views if occasion comes.

Censure is another menace threatening those representatives whose constituents view the relationship as one of master and servant. Fortunately it is rarely bestowed by formal action, for it is the most ineffective and useless form of influence that can be exerted. The mischief, if mischief it be, has been done and rarely can be undone. Censure humiliates, embitters. Far better it is to punish by the accustomed method of defeat for reëlection. There is a lesson in the story of the most noteworthy instance of censure in our political history. It is the pathetic story of the last years of Charles Sumner. George W. Julian says in his Political Recollections (p. 350) that after the election of 1872, when in Washington, he called on Sumner, and found him in a wretched state of health, which was aggravated by the free use of poisonous drugs. He had lost caste with the great party that had so long idolized him, and which he had done so much to create and inspire. He had been deserted by the colored race, to whose service he had unselfishly dedicated his life. He had been degraded from his honored place at the head of the Senate Committee on Foreign Relations, and for no other reason than the faithful and conscientious performance of his public duty. He had been rebuked by the Legislature of his own State. Sumner had introduced in the Senate this bill:

"Whereas, the national unity and good-will among fellow citizens can be assured only through oblivion of past differences, and it is contrary to the usage of civilized nations to perpetuate the memory of civil war: Therefore, — *Be it enacted,* That the names of battles with fellow citizens shall not be continued in the Army Register, nor placed on the regimental colors of the United States."

It happened that in December, 1872, as Moorfield Storey tells it, the Legislature of Massachusetts was holding an extra session. A country member introduced a resolution condemning the Senator's bill, and the committee to which it was referred gave the introducer a private hearing. On the last day of the session this resolution was reported by half the committee, and after a debate, in which Sumner's purpose was wholly misrepresented by those who favored the resolution, it was passed. The legislators feared the anger of the veterans, and this fear carried the resolution. As adopted it described Sumner's bill "as an insult to the loyal soldiery of the nation" and as "meeting the unqualified condemnation of the people of the Commonwealth." The leaders of Massachusetts rallied to Sumner's support, and when the new Legislature met in January, 1873, an attempt was made to have the resolution of censure rescinded. A very strong petition was presented, supported by energetic speech and action; but the movement failed, owing largely to the efforts made by members of the previous Legislature, who wished not to be discredited so promptly and who argued that one Legislature could not reverse an expression of opinion by another. Party feeling, fear of "the soldier vote," desire to propitiate the administration, with which Sumner was at war, carried the day. Such action from his own State, coming when he was prostrated by disease and discouraged by the political situation, naturally hurt Mr. Sumner, but did not change his purpose. He was determined to persuade Massachusetts. Unhappily his strength was not enough for the undertaking. During the whole winter he suffered from recurring attacks of *angina pectoris*. It was another year before the Legislature rescinded its resolution of censure.[1]

Recall is a weapon for constituents much commended to-day in certain quarters. It is not a new idea. On the contrary it is as old as the country itself. When at a General Court of the Massachusetts Bay Colony, May 18, 1631, the law relating to the election of Assistants (the magistrates who came to constitute the upper branch of the Legislature) was amplified, to the effect that they should be chosen by a General Court, with a poll in case of doubt, it was added: "The like course to be holden when they, the said commons, shall see cause for any defect or misbehavior to remove any one or more of the Assistants." When Plymouth created Representatives, March 5, 1638, calling them "committees" of the towns, its vote read: "But if any such Committees shall be insufficient or troublesome that then the Bench and the other Committees may dismiss them and the Town to choose other freemen in their place." [2]

The provincial charter of Massachusetts Bay in 1691 provided: "And that the said Councillors or Assistants or any of them shall or may at any time hereafter be removed or displaced from their respective Places of Trust of Councillors or Assistants by any Great General Court or Assembly." The Constitution drafted for Pennsylvania by the convention over which Benjamin Franklin presided, in 1776, directed that delegates to represent the State in Congress should be chosen annually by the General Assembly, and said: "Any delegate may be superceded at any time, by the General Assembly appointing another in his stead." Vermont copied this provision in her Constitution of 1777. When on the 15th of November of that year Articles of Confederation were adopted by the Continental Congress, at Yorktown, Article V read in part: "For the more convenient management of the general interests of the United States, dele-

---

[1] Moorfield Storey, *Charles Sumner*, 419 *et sqq.*

[2] *Plymouth Colony Records*, x, 31.

gates shall be annually appointed in such manner as the Legislature of each State shall direct, to meet in Congress on the first Monday in November, in every year, with a power reserved to each State to recall its delegates, or any of them, at any time within the year, and to send others in their stead, for the remainder of the year."

Rehoboth, a Massachusetts town, proposed, June 1, 1778, a law "enabling each town in this State, at any time, to elect a Representative or Representatives to represent them in the great Convention or General Court, and thereby to recall their former Representative or Representatives as the pleasure of any town may be, or to add to their present number, similar to the power of this State, of sending or recalling their Delegates to or from the honorable Congress." [1]

Advocacy of the idea must have been widespread, for when the Federal Constitution was submitted to the States for ratification, the absence of a provision for recall aroused criticism that had to be seriously met in the Conventions. Theophilus Parsons, one of the most eminent of the eminent men who have been Chief Justices of the Supreme Court of Massachusetts, was a member of the Convention of that State. "It has been objected," he said, "that in the old Confederation the States could at any time recall their delegates, and there was a rotation. No essential benefit could be derived to the people from these provisions, but great inconveniences will result from them.... What is the effect of the power of recalling? Your representative, with an operating revocation over his head, will lose all ideas of the general good, and will dwindle to a servile agent, attempting to secure local and partial benefits by cabal and intrigue." [2]

In the New York Convention G. Livingston moved a resolution, June 24, 1788, providing that the Legislatures might at any time recall their Senators. Lansing said in support of it that the power of recall under the Confederation had been an excellent check, though it had, in fact, never been exercised.[3] Chancellor Robert R. Livingston believed that the power of recall would have a tendency to bind the Senators too strongly to the interests of their respective States; and for that reason he objected to it. "It will destroy that spirit of independence and free deliberation which ought to influence the Senator. Whenever the interests of

[1] *Continental Journal and Weekly Advertiser*, February 4, 1779.
[2] *Debates of Mass. Convention of 1788*, 191.   [3] *Elliot's Debates*, II, 289.

a State clash with those of the Union, it will oblige him to sacrifice the great objects of his appointment to local attachments. He will be subjected to all the caprices, the parties, the narrow views, and illiberal politics, of the State governments, and become a slave to the ambitions and factions at home." [1] Melancton Smith rejoined: "As the Senators are the representatives of the State Legislatures, it is reasonable and proper that they should be under their control. When a State sends an agent commissioned to transact any business, or perform any service, it certainly ought to have a power of recall." [2] Alexander Hamilton replied to Smith: "That a man should have the power, in private life, of recalling his agent, is proper, because, in the business in which he is engaged, he has no other object but to gain the approbation of his principal. Is that the case with the Senator? Is he simply the agent of the State? No. He is an agent for the Union, and he is bound to perform services necessary to the good of the whole, though his State should condemn him." [3]

Thirty-three Pennsylvanians from a dozen or more counties convened at Harrisburg, September 3, 1788, resolved that sundry amendments to the newly adopted Federal Constitution were "essentially necessary" — among them one giving Legislatures the power to recall Senators. [4]

Rhode Island, in ratifying, May 29, 1790, proposed twenty-one amendments, and among them this: "That the State Legislatures have power to recall, when they think it expedient, their federal Senators, and to send others in their stead." In 1803 the Legislature of Virginia proposed a like amendment. Five years later it renewed the proposal with an amendment that Senators might be removed by a majority vote of the whole number of members of their respective State Legislatures. This called out resolutions of disapproval from the Legislatures of Maryland, New Jersey, Tennessee, Georgia, Massachusetts, and Vermont.

No such amendment has ever been made. Now that Senators are elected by direct vote, it is likely that from time to time agitation will spring up for power to recall them likewise, but the value of the structure of the Senate in ensuring the delay that brings calm consideration has so often demonstrated itself that no speedy success for such agitation seems probable. It is notice-

---

[1] *Elliot's Debates*, ii, 296.   [2] *Ibid.*, 311.
[3] *Ibid.*, 320.   [4] *Ibid.*, 543.

able, indeed, that in the great volume of recent advocacy of the recall, very little is aimed at the legislative branch of government, Federal, State, or local. It is the executive and judicial branches that have been under fire. The greater part of the citizens serving in State Legislatures sit in but one regular session, and there would seldom be time enough to put in motion the recall machinery and carry through the process before the session ended. Federal and municipal elections come so often that national and local legislators can be displaced soon enough to prevent much damage.

In England, where terms average to be longer than here, from time to time a claim has been made by some local political organization that it is entitled to call upon its member of Parliament to resign when he ceases to act with his party. In the course of the South African War the claim was put forward in several cases. President Lowell says its validity cannot be said to have been on that occasion universally admitted or denied.[1]

[1] *Public Opinion and Popular Government*, 124.

CHAPTER XXI

INDEPENDENCE *v.* RESPONSIBILITY

CLASSIFY, summarize, analyze the foregoing facts and the conclusion is irresistible that the outstanding problem of representative government is the degree to which power should be delegated. Call it the case of Independence *v.* Responsibility. Let witnesses be summoned and arguments be heard.

First for Independence. Begin with English views, for it has been in England that the stoutest fight for self-reliant representatives has been made.

Sir H. S. Maine may lead the attack: "On the complex questions of politics, which are calculated in themselves to tax to the utmost all the powers of the strongest minds, but are in fact vaguely conceived, vaguely stated, dealt with for the most part in the most haphazard manner by the most experienced statesmen, the common determination of a multitude is a chimerical assumption; and indeed, if it were possible to extract an opinion upon them from a great mass of men, and to shape the legislative and administrative acts of a State upon this opinion as a sovereign command, it is probable that the most ruinous blunders would be committed, and all social progress would be arrested. ... What is called the will of the people really consists in their adopting the opinion of one person or a few persons.... The ruling multitude will only form an opinion by following the opinion of somebody — it may be, of a great party leader — it may be, of a small local politician — it may be, of an organized association — it may be, of an impersonal newspaper. The process of deciding in accordance with plausibilities (in the strict sense of this last word) goes on over an enormous area, growing ever more confused and capricious, and giving results even more ambiguous or inarticulate, as the numbers to be consulted are multiplied." [1]

Let Lord Brougham answer the browbeaters: "Any proceedings on the part of the people tending to overawe or unduly to influence their representatives upon any given question, though no outrage should be committed, and only an exhibition of

[1] *Popular Government*, 89–92.

numerical force be displayed for these purposes, are contrary to the whole nature of representative government, and in themselves revolutionary, being criminal in the people, and doubly criminal in any of their representatives, who thereby commit a flagrant breach of duty." [1]

John Stuart Mill is more conciliatory: "Superior powers of mind and profound study are of no use if they do not sometimes lead a person to different conclusions from those which are formed by ordinary powers of mind without study: and if it be an object to possess representatives in any intellectual respect superior to average electors, it must be counted upon that the representative will sometimes differ in opinion from the majority of his constituents, and that when he does, his opinion will be the oftenest right of the two. It follows that the electors will not do wisely if they insist on absolute conformity to their opinions as the condition of his retaining his seat." [2]

Jeremy Bentham for once is diplomatic: "Ought the legislator to be a slave to the fancies of those whom he governs? No. Between an imprudent opposition and a servile compliance there is a middle path, honourable and safe. It is to combat these fancies with the only arms that can conquer them — example and instruction. He must enlighten the people, he must address himself to the public reason; he must give time for error to be unmasked. Sound reasons, clearly set forth, are of necessity stronger than false ones. But the legislator ought not to show himself too openly in these instructions, for fear of compromitting himself with the public ignorance. Indirect means will better answer his ends." [3]

W. E. Hearn theorizes: "The primary principle upon which [the value of the representative system] rests is the same principle which regulates the exercise of the Royal will. The people require checks and limitations and enlightenment no less than the King. An aggregate assemblage of individuals must be restrained and informed no less than each individual unit of that aggregate. If a monarchic absolutism be liable to infirmities, democratic absolutism is liable to other and not less dangerous infirmities. For the Sovereign Many therefore, as well as for the Sovereign One, the law assigns a specific and exclusive power of

---

[1] "The British Constitution," *Works*, xi, 94.

[2] *Representative Government*, chap. xii.

[3] *Theory of Legislation*, Transl. by R. Hildreth, 77.

expression. The object of this form is the same in both cases. It is designed to secure the deliberate and well-weighed opinion of the utterer. For popular utterances a suitable organ is found by the aid of the principle of Trusteeship." [1]

Barring the parallel with monarchy, that has been the conception also of sundry American thinkers. For instance, Francis Lieber holds: "It is the trusteeship that gives so high a value to representative government.... Every one feels his responsibility far more distinctly as a trustee than otherwise. Let a man in an excited crowd be suddenly singled out and made a member of a committee to reflect and resolve for that crowd, and he will feel the difference in an instant. How easy it would be to receive the most lavish and most dangerous money grants from an undivided and absolute multitude! Is it necessary to remind the reader that liberty has been lost quite as often from false gratitude toward a personally popular man as from any other cause? Trustees, carefully looking around them, and conscious that they have to give an account of themselves, are not so easily swayed by ravishing gratitude. The trusteeship in the representative government is the only means yet discovered to temper the rashness of the democracy and to overcome the obstinacy of monarchs." [2]

Next listen to a few men of more recent authorship, selected at random, not necessarily the men who have best argued the question, but who may present typical points of view. Thomas B. Reed trenchantly declared: "The danger in a free country is not that power will be exercised too freely, but that it will be exercised too sparingly; for it so happens that the noise made by a small but loud minority in the wrong is too often mistaken for the voice of the people and the voice of God." [3]

William H. Taft, with wise counsel abundantly given serving his country even more usefully than as its President, spoke the word of caution: "No one ought to minimize the danger there is of corrupt corporate control of legislatures and obstruction to the popular will. There are serious evils to be provided against, I fully admit, but, on the other hand, I think that the slavish subordination of the representative, against his better judgment, to temporary, popular passion is also a serious evil. The disposition of politicians to coddle the people, to flatter them into

---

[1] *The Government of England*, 465.
[2] *On Civil Liberty and Self-Government*, 167.   [3] *Century*, April, 1889.

thinking that they cannot make a mistake, and to fail to tell them the truth as to their own errors and tendencies to error, is a growing difficulty in the matter of successful popular government." [1]

Governor O'Neal of Alabama flouted the masses. Said he to the Governors' Conference of 1911: "That the Government of our States is the government of the numerical majority, I deny. There is nothing in the Constitution of any State that warrants such an assertion. The warning lessons of history had taught the framers of both National and State Constitutions that no republic based upon a numerical majority without constitutional limitations on power had ever survived a single generation. It was the introduction of the representative principle, instead of direct action by the numerical majority, which was the most distinguishing characteristic of both National and State Constitutions, and it was the absence of the representative principle which proved fatal to all the so-called republics of ancient and modern times. A Government without limitations is a monarchy, and there is little difference between the rule of a despot and the unlimited and unrestricted tyranny of a majority. When our fathers constituted this government, the whole purpose of our written Constitution was to establish certain constitutional guarantees which should constitute a shield and bulwark of defense to every citizen, however humble and obscure." [2]

Professor Henry C. Emery also remembered history: "The constitutional safeguards were originally adopted very largely to prevent a too hasty response to the immediate will of the people. Do not allow yourselves to be deluded by the phrases of some orators with the idea that a more direct response of the legislative body to the popular desire is a 'restitution of the government to the people.' It is not a question of restitution because the founders of the Republic carefully provided against hasty and impulsive action. If their judgment was in error we may adopt a new system, but remember that it will be a new system, not a return of something that has somehow been stolen from the people." [3]

Another Professor, Henry Jones Ford, presented more concrete argument. "What," he asked, "is wrong with the proposition that it is the business of representative government to reflect the community, which makes it so mischievous in practice?

[1] *Popular Government*, 62.   [2] *Proceedings*, 53.
[3] *Politician, Party and People*, 154.

Is it not plain that such terms as the people, the community, connote an ideal unity, whereas the actual situation is one of endless multiplicity, great inequality, and continual variation? The notion of institutions as a reflection of such instability is as vain and impossible in politics as it is regarded to be in every other kind of business." [1]

Senator George F. Hoar gave the personal application: "I have throughout my whole public political life acted upon my own judgment. I have done what I thought for the public interest without much troubling myself about public opinion. I always took a good deal of pride in a saying of Roger Sherman's. He was asked if he did not think some vote of his would be very much disapproved in Connecticut, to which he replied that he knew but one way to ascertain the public opinion of Connecticut; that was to ascertain what was right. When he found that out, he was quite sure that it would meet the approval of Connecticut. That in general has been in my judgment absolutely and literally true of Massachusetts. It has required no courage for any representative of hers to do what he thought was right. She is apt to select to speak for her, certainly those she sends to the United States Senate, in whose choice the whole Commonwealth has a part, men who are in general of the same way of thinking, and governed by the same principles as are the majority of her people. When she has chosen them she expects them to act according to their best judgment, and not to be thinking about popularity. She likes independence better than obsequiousness. The one thing the people of Massachusetts will not forgive in a public servant is that he should act against his own honest judgment to please them. I am speaking of her sober, second thought. Her people, like the rest of mankind, are liable to waves of emotion and of prejudice. This is true the world over. It is as true of good men as of bad men, of educated as of ignorant men, whenever they are to act in large masses. Alexander Hamilton said that if every Athenian citizen had been a Socrates, still every Athenian assembly would have been a mob. So I claim no credit that I have voted and spoken as I thought, always without stopping to consider whether public opinion would support me." [2]

Speaking purely as a witness, and not as counsel, let me testify. As House Chairman of the Committee that pushed through the

---

[1] *Representative Government*, 147.

[2] *Autobiography of Seventy Years*, ii, 112, 113.

Massachusetts Legislature the primary election reform, I was held responsible for the law, my name was attached to it. At least once, therefore, I was at the very core of a substantial change in law and should be able to speak with authority as to what took place. In the case of few measures would a wider public interest and understanding be expected. Yet it is within bounds to say that not one half of the voters of the State knew or cared anything about the bill, not one in a hundred understood the bill. Of two hundred and eighty members of the legislature itself, not a score had any real appreciation of the changes it would work in our politics. Certain palpable arguments carried the day. To say that this law was enacted in conformity with any widespread public judgment is absurd. It was enacted in response to a very general but very vague demand for improvement in the nominating process, and how that might best be accomplished was in reality determined by a very small part of the citizenship, really acquainted with the problem. Out of more than a million adult men and women in Massachusetts it is safe to say that not 100,000 ever are informed about any single proposition coming before the Legislature, or give any thought to it at all. If indeed the estimate were put at 10,000 it would not be ludicrously far from the mark, save in the case of such exceptional questions as woman suffrage or prohibition.

In summing up this side of the case, counsel might also point out that the ordinary legal conception of the relation between principal and agent is not to be found in the relation between constituency and representative. There are no legal duties and penalties. There is nothing enforceable by courts. An agent can do only what his principal can do, but our Constitutions permit to a representative many things not legally within the immediate power of the constituency. Ordinarily the appointment of an agent may be revoked, but thus far members of lawmaking bodies have not been made subject to recall or to any revocation of powers during their terms of office.

Counsel might go on to describe the position American judges have taken when Legislatures have tried to shift their responsibilities on the people, citing, for instance, Barto *v.* Himrod, 8 N.Y. 483 (1853). Its head-note reads: "Laws must be enacted by the legislative bodies to which the legislative power is committed in the Constitution. They cannot divest themselves of the responsibility of their enactment by a reference of the

question of their passage to their constituents." Two sections of
the Free School Act of March 26, 1849, provided for a referendum vote by the people of the State. "Without contradicting
[their] express terms," said Ruggles, C. J., "it cannot be said
that the propositions contained [in the Act], in relation to free
schools, were enacted as law by the Legislature. They were not
law or to become law, until they had received a majority of the
votes of the people at the general election in their favor, nor unless they received such a majority. It results, therefore unavoidably from the terms of the act itself, that it was the popular
vote that made the law. The Legislature prepared the plan or
project and submitted it to the people to be passed or rejected."
So the law was held unconstitutional. "On this question of expediency," the court further said, "the Legislature must exercise
its own judgment definitively and finally. When a law is made to
take effect upon the happening of such an event, the Legislature
in effect declares the law inexpedient if the event should not
happen, but expedient if it should happen. They appeal to no
other man or men to judge for them in relation to its present or
future expediency. They exercise that power themselves, and
then perform the duty which the Constitution imposes upon
them."

Five years later, in Geebrick v. State, 5 Ia. 491, Justice
Stockton said: "The position seems to us too clear to admit of
any doubt, that if the act of January 29, 1857, receives its vitality and force from a vote of the people, such vote is an exercise
of legislative power, and the law is unconstitutional and void."
To be sure, there are decisions the other way, but they depend
mainly on the question of what is a contingency that will suffice
to bring into operation a completed law. Almost nowhere can be
found any expression of judicial belief that under our form of
government the legislator can legitimately avoid his duty to
make law by the exercise of his own judgment.

A concluding appeal to the jury might be after this fashion:
"When you have heard testimony and argument from both
sides, you are to go behind closed doors and there reach a verdict
by means of the exercise of your own judgment, uninfluenced,
without fear or favor. For more than a thousand years Anglo-
Saxons have believed that thus justice will be most likely to be
achieved. Why should the body that makes the laws proceed
differently from the body that applies the laws? Will not a legis-

lature be more likely to determine what is wise and right if it, too, is independent?"

Now for the case of Responsibility.

Here the testimony will be mainly American. As a modern theory, the idea is so young in England that none of the authoritative writers there yet defend it. In France, however, its merit was proclaimed from the very start of the new political philosophy. Rousseau pushed it to its extreme, saying: "He who frames laws has or ought to have, no legislative right, and the people themselves cannot, even if they wished, divest themselves of this incommunicable right, because, according to the fundamental compact, it is only the general will that binds individuals, and we can never be sure that a particular will is conformable to the general will until it has been submitted to the free votes of the people." [1]

Bear that doctrine in mind while reading the words of President Woodrow Wilson in vetoing the Immigration Bill, January 28, 1915: "If the people of this country have made up their minds to limit the number of immigrants by arbitrary tests and so reverse the policy of all the generations of Americans that have gone before them, it is their right to do so. I am their servant and have no license to stand in their way. But I do not believe that they have. I respectfully submit that no one can quote their mandate to that effect. Has any political party ever avowed a policy of restriction in this fundamental matter, gone to the country on it, and been commissioned to control its legislation? Does this bill rest on the conscious and universal assent and desire of the American people? I doubt it. It is because I doubt it that I make bold to dissent from it. I am willing to abide by the verdict, but not until it has been rendered. Let the platforms of parties speak out upon this policy and the people pronounce their wish. The matter is too fundamental to be settled otherwise. I have no pride of opinion on this question. I am not foolish enough to profess to know the wishes and ideals of America better than the body of her chosen representatives know them. I only want instruction direct from those whose fortunes, with ours and all men's, are involved."

For judicial opinion to offset that cited above for Independence, let Justice Oliver Wendell Holmes speak. When he wrote his learned book on "The Common Law," he said (page 41):

[1] *Social Compact*, book 2, chap. VII.

"The first requirement of a sound body of law is that it should correspond with the actual feelings and demands of the community, whether right or wrong." Later, when he went on the Massachusetts Supreme Bench, he found occasion to dissent from the views of a majority of his associates upon three questions asked by the House of Representatives: if it would be constitutional to make an act for woman suffrage in town and city elections take effect (1) upon acceptance by the voters of the State, (2) in any city or town upon its acceptance by the voters thereof, (3) upon acceptance by the voters of the State including women specially authorized to register and vote on that question alone. Four of the Justices answered No to each question; one answered No to the first and third, Yes to the second. Justice Holmes, answering all three questions in the affirmative, saw no evidence that the first question ever occurred to the framers of the Constitution. "It is but a short step further to say that the Constitution does not forbid such a law. I agree that the discretion of the Legislature is intended to be exercised. I agree that confidence is put in it as an agent. But I think that so much confidence is put in it that it is allowed to exercise its discretion by taking the opinion of its principal if it thinks that course to be wise. It has been asked whether the Legislature could pass an act subject to the approval of a single man. I am not clear that it could not. The objection, if sound, would seem to have equal force against all forms of local option. The difference is plain between that case and one where the approval required is that of the sovereign body. The contrary view seems to me an echo of Hobbes's theory that the surrender of sovereignty by the people was final. I notice that the case from which most of the reasoning against the power of the Legislature has been taken by later decisions states that theory in language which almost is borrowed from 'The Leviathan.' Rice *v.* Foster, 4 Harringt. (Del.) 479,488. Hobbes urged his notion in the interest of the absolute power of King Charles I, and one of the objects of the Constitution of Massachusetts was to deny it. I answer the first question, Yes. I may add, that, while the tendency of judicial decision seems to be in the other direction, such able judges as Chief Justice Parker of Massachusetts, Dixon of Wisconsin, Redfield of Vermont, and Cooley of Michigan, have expressed opinions like mine." [1]

Justice Holmes might have found in the earliest history of rep-

[1] *Opinions of the Justices*, 160 Mass. 594.

resentative government in Massachusetts warrant for the theory that the Legislature as an agent may consult its principal. For instance, it was ordered May 29, 1644, "That it shall be lawful for the deputies of the Court to advise with their elders and free-men, and take into serious consideration whether God do not ex-pect that all the inhabitants of this plantation allow to their magistrates, and all other that are called to country service, a proportionate allowance,... and that they send in their deter-minations and conclusions to the next General Court." [1]

Next throw into the scale the most noted instance in American history where a statesman changed his position on a vital ques-tion because his constituents had changed. He was one of our greatest statesmen, some would say our greatest — Daniel Webster. That there may be no suspicion of bias in telling the story, let it be in the words of one of his biographers, Henry Cabot Lodge, who has since become known as one of the most earnest and able defenders of Independence in legislative action. The famous speech on the Tariff of 1828, Mr. Lodge tells us, marks an important change in Mr. Webster's views and in his course as a statesman. He now gave up his position as the ablest opponent in the country of the protective policy, and went over to the support of the tariff and the "American policy" of Mr. Clay. This change, in every way of great importance, subjected Mr. Webster to severe criticism, both then and subsequently. When Mr. Webster first entered Congress he was a thorough-going Federalist. But the Federalists of New England differed from their great chief, Alexander Hamilton, on the question of a protective policy. Coming from exclusively commercial com-munities, they were in principle free-traders. They regarded with disfavor the doctrine that protection was a good thing in itself, and desired it, if at all, only in the most limited form and purely as an incident to raising revenue. With these opinions Mr. Webster was in full sympathy. In a reply to Calhoun in 1814 for instance, he said: "It is the true policy of government to suf-fer the different pursuits of society to take their own course, and not to give excessive bounties or encouragements to one over another. This, also, is the true spirit of the Constitution. It has not, in my opinion, conferred on the government the power of changing the occupations of the people of different States and sections, and of forcing them into other employments." In his

[1] *Records of the Colony of the Mass. Bay in N.E.*, II, 67.

speech of 1828 he said: "Finally, after a winter's deliberation, the act of 1824 received the sanction of both Houses of Congress and settled the policy of the country. What, then, was New England to do?... Was she to hold out forever against the course of the government, and see herself losing on one side and yet make no effort to sustain herself on the other? No, sir. Nothing was left but to conform herself to the will of the others. Nothing was left to her but to consider that the government had fixed and determined its own policy; and that policy was *protection*."

Mr. Lodge goes on: "Opinion in New England changed for good and sufficient business reasons, and Mr. Webster changed with it. Free trade had commended itself to him as an abstract principle, and he had sustained and defended it in the interest of commercial New England. But when the weight of interest in New England shifted from free trade to protection, Mr. Webster followed it.... As to the want of deep conviction, Mr. Webster's vote on this question proves nothing. He believed in free trade as an abstract general principle, and there is no reason to suppose that he ever abandoned his belief on this point. But he had too clear a mind ever to be run away with by the extreme vagaries of the Manchester school. He knew that there was no morality, no immutable right and wrong, in an impost or a free list.... Mr. Webster never at any time treated the question of free trade or protection as anything but one of expediency.... He rested the defence of his new position upon the doctrine which he had always consistently preached, that uniformity and permanency were the essential and sound conditions of any policy, whether of free trade or protection." [1]

In further support of Responsibility, a thousand other witnesses could be brought from American public life, but why cumulate? Everybody knows it is the firm conviction of a large part of the Americans and their public men that a representative should be the mouthpiece of his constituents. Let their view be summed up by a typical editorial expression in that year of ultra-democratic triumph, 1912. It was not, however, the expression of an editor who wished Democratic triumph with a big "D," for it was the view of the "Outlook," as printed on the 7th of September in that year: "The great political issue in this country to-day is whether the representatives of the people shall devote themselves to managing the details of great questions which are

[1] H. C. Lodge, *Daniel Webster*, 156–69.

determined by the people, or whether the representatives shall decide the fundamental questions for the people.... 'Boss' government differs from popular government in one character-istic essential. The bosses believe that they, instead of the peo-ple, should determine the fundamental questions of government. It is for that reason that they are called by the people 'bosses.' When they cease to be 'bosses,' and sincerely and effectively endeavor to ascertain and to carry out the will of the people, it is then, and then only, that they become truly the representatives of the people."

The jury in the case of Independence *v.* Responsibility would surely disagree, and in so doing they would but apply the fact that a "Yes" or "No" applicable at all times and under all circumstances is here an impracticability. In this I must differ from that eminent authority, Sir G. C. Lewis, who held: "Either a representative is a mere delegate, empowered only to act ac-cording to the instructions of his constituents, and not concerned about the general expediency or inexpediency (as it may seem to him) of the course which he is pursuing; or he is morally bound, no less than he is legally able, to follow that line of conduct which he considers most conducive to the public welfare. Besides these two alternatives, there is no third: a representative must be either a delegate or a free agent; he must either follow the opin-ions of others, or his own: nor is it possible to distinguish between cases in which he should be his own master, and in which he should be the servant of his constituents." [1]

Over against this I would set the views of three eminent Americans, two of whom have been Presidents of the United States, and the third of whom is the President of Harvard Uni-versity. After service in the Assembly of New York, Theodore Roosevelt wrote: "As a rule, and where no matter of principle is involved, a member is bound to represent the views of those who have elected him; but there are times when the voice of the people is anything but the voice of God, and then a conscien-tious man is equally bound to disregard it." [2]

After he had been President William H. Taft said: "Undoubt-edly when a man permits his name to be submitted to the people as a candidate for their suffrage, with the announcement, either by himself or through a party, that he is in favor of certain gov-

[1] *Remarks on the Use and Abuse of Some Political Terms*, 103.
[2] "Phases of State Legislation," *Century*, April, 1885.

ernmental policies to be embodied in executive or legislative action, he is bound to conform to those policies or is guilty of deceit. But in the discharge of the functions of a representative, it often occurs that issues arise which were not the subject of discussion at the time of the election, and it often occurs also that even though the general object was the subject of discussion, the particular means to be selected furnished so complicated a question that it played no part in the election. Under such circumstances, I conceive that the representative is to act on his own best judgment, even though it may differ from that of many of his constituents.... The representative ought not to be the mere mouthpiece of his constituents. He is elected because he is presumably well-fitted to discharge the particular duties in respect to which he is to occupy a representative capacity, and he knows more about them than his constituents. In carrying out their general purpose, he is still within his authority if he selects his own means of executing that promise according to his conscience." [1]

After exhaustive study of the government of many lands, A. Lawrence Lowell, now President of Harvard University, wrote: "In a legislature elected by the people neither view does, nor in the nature of things can, wholly prevail; for, on the one hand, a representative is presumably in general accord with the opinions of his constituents, and is in fact more or less sensitive to their desires; while, on the other hand, if he has self-respect he never feels absolutely bound to follow their directions in all matters. He is no doubt selected because the voters approve of his attitude on the leading public issues, but special questions often arise on which he must be free to act according to his own opinion." [2]

These three views would corroborate Lewis to the extent of their agreement that on any given question a representative must act either as he thinks best or as somebody else thinks best, with apparently no third course open. But is that quite adequate? Does it wholly agree with the constant experience of everyday life? Arithmetically it is as clear as that one and one make two. Yet human nature and human conduct do not always conform to arithmetic. Sometimes they are to be discussed in the terms of the higher mathematics, of algebra, with the un-

[1] *Popular Government*, 28, 29.
[2] *Public Opinion and Popular Government*, 124.

known factor "x"; or in the terms of those computations that take in variables. Men are ever turning to each other for advice. Of what good would advice be if independent judgment were the only thing ethically proper? Or why ask advice rather than instructions if obedience is the alternative? Every day, almost every hour of our lives we permit our opinions to be modified by those of others. In the little things of social intercourse we are constantly modifying our own views. For the sake of amity and harmony, more than that, for the sake of getting results, we are conciliatory, we compromise. Nobody thinks such a course unmanly or dishonorable, for everybody follows it. Are conditions really different when it is a matter of making laws? If they were, then there could be no such thing as a political party and there could hardly be such a thing as legislation. The making of a law often means that a majority of several score of men, sometimes two or three hundred men, must combine on a group of propositions, though no single one of these propositions may meet the approval of every supporter. How ruinous it would be, then, to insist invariably upon individual independence! How dangerous, to say that the best legislator is the stubborn, uncompromising, self-sufficient man who deifies his own judgment!

And on the other hand, how inadequate would be unquestioning subserviency! To accept blindly and without scrutiny the dictates of others is as blameworthy as to play the dictator.

It is the middle course that I champion as wise, expedient, and right, the course followed by the man who feels it as much of a duty to try to modify in others opinions with which he disagrees, as to try to let his own opinions be modified by the wisdom of others. Such a man gets out of parties the good they possess, and avoids their evils. Such a man deals fairly both by his constituents and by himself. Such a man deems it necessary to break with party or with constituency only on those very rare occasions when Judgment must step aside and let Conscience rule. The great mass of legislation is matter of expediency. Not once in a thousand times is it matter of right and wrong. Only when right and wrong are at stake may the legislator refuse to concede, to compromise, or to yield.

Whom Does the Representative Represent?

Whether we decide that the representative is to be trustee or agent or sometimes one and sometimes the other, there remains a question just as difficult — For whom does he act? Is it for those who elected him, commonly called his constituency? Or is it for the larger body — the State or the Nation as a whole — of whose legislating assembly he is a member?

Here the bulk of theoretical opinion is decidedly one way, favoring the idea that the representative is to act for State or Nation. In England the practice wholly conforms to that idea. In the United States, the practice, though divided, goes mainly against it. As a practical matter, it is of grave consequence, for to the belief that a representative is to represent his district may be traced some of the most serious evils of Congress and all the State Legislatures. Many Congressmen and State Representatives live up to the belief that their first duty is to get all the favors they can for their districts. Many districts reward or punish their representatives according as they have succeeded or failed in getting appropriations for public buildings, roads, bridges, river and harbor improvements, or in getting appointments, pensions, or other local benefits. Thus it becomes of personal advantage to the representative to put the general welfare in second place. The evils are so apparent and their denunciation by all sorts of reformers, critics, and theorists is so emphatic and sweeping, that one hesitates even to suggest the possibility of two sides to the question lest he be denounced as a traitor to righteousness even before he has been heard. Yet the words "practice" and "custom" necessarily involve approval by somebody, for it is inconceivable that a people should steadily and persistently follow a course reprehended universally or even without some considerable degree of support. And to convince that a course is bad calls not only for exposure of its evils, but also for refutation of the arguments advanced in its behalf.

Senator Tazewell of Virginia declined President Jackson's offer of a place in his Cabinet, and said: "Having been elected a Senator, I would as soon think of taking a place under George IV, if I were sent a Minister to his Court, as I would to take a place in the Cabinet." [1] This notion that a representative is an ambassador would not to-day be so strongly expressed, but the spirit of it still pervades our public life. A delegate to the New Hampshire Convention of 1902, whose name the stenographer did not catch (more's the pity, as he ought to be immortalized for his frankness), put the case in a nutshell when he said: "I had

[1] J. A. Woodburn, *The American Republic*, 240.

just as soon not be represented at all as to be represented by a man not from my town. What good does it do me to be represented by a man whose interests belong to another town, and who does not help our town?"[1]

It is of no use denying that this man said what thousands of Americans think. It must be recognized, too, that their belief is justified by men of no mean ability and no small experience. For example, Governor Byrne of South Dakota said to the Governors' Conference of 1913: "What I mean by representative government is a lawmaking body representing localities, representing constituencies, and I believe that the best results in legislation in the end will be secured from the meeting of many minds of many views, from the gathering together of people representing localities and constituencies of diverse interests, and coming together and working out the problems. The best, the safest results will be had from the common judgment of average men."[2]

Those who hold to this doctrine argue that the best government is secured through the conflict of the interests of localities. If each individual really knows what is best for him, he will work to secure that end. Thus, within any given district, each man voting intelligently for his own interests, the expression of the majority will inevitably be an expression of what is best for that community. Then let each district be represented in the national council and let each representative work solely for the interest of his particular district, and likewise inevitably the result of majority action must mean the adoption of such legislation as is for the best interests of the community as a whole. Professor Henry C. Emery, who thus sets out the theory, says he once heard it very forcibly stated by Thomas B. Reed, one of the greatest Speakers the House of Representatives has ever had. Professor Emery points out that the theory involves two premises: first, that every man does know what is best for him; and, secondly, that he knows best how to get it. "I do not believe," he says, "that the 'agency theory' is carried out even in practice to-day as much as it was a dozen years ago, or as much as many people believe it to be, and I believe that one reason for this lies in the control of the individual representative by his loyalty to party or by the presence of the party caucus."[3]

[1] *Journal of New Hampshire Constitutional Convention of 1902*, 172.
[2] *Proceedings*, 286.   [3] *Politician, Party and People*, 108 *et sqq.*

And farther on: "Whatever theory we may hold regarding the relation of the representative toward public policies in the matter of independence and freedom of judgment, he is really a *representative;* that is, he represents the particular district from which he is elected and the men who vote for him have not done so solely from the idea that he should be a great statesman exercising his mind all the time on the problems of national welfare. They want part of his mind and part of his time themselves and, what is more, they have a right to expect a certain amount of attention from him. It is sometimes possible for a man practically to disregard his constituency and tell them that he will pay no attention whatsoever to their demands in the matter of patronage or appropriations, or their requests for assistance in personal matters, however legitimate. Such men, however, if they are to keep their positions in Congress at all, must have already achieved such a commanding position that their districts take sufficient pride in the power of their representative to offset their dissatisfaction at the neglect of their interests." [1]

It is worth recalling that one of the most celebrated of statesmen, Edmund Burke, did not feel it beneath him to be an errand boy for his constituents. Six years after his famous speech "To the Electors of Bristol," he addressed them again, in 1780, at the Guild Hall in Bristol, this time "Upon Certain Points Relative to his Parliamentary Conduct." Said he: "Most of you have heard that I do not very remarkably spare myself in *public* business; and in the *private* business of my constituents I have done very near as much as those who have nothing else to do. My canvass of you was not on the change, nor in the county meetings, nor in the clubs of this city. It was in the House of Commons; it was at the custom-house; it was at the admiralty. I canvassed you through your affairs, and not your persons. I was not only your representative as a body; I was the agent, the solicitor of individuals; I ran about wherever your affairs could call me; and in acting for you I often appeared rather as a shipbroker, than as a member of Parliament. There was nothing too laborious, or too low for me to undertake. The meanness of the business was raised by the dignity of the object."

Great man that he was, this breathes somewhat too much of obsequiousness and servility to suit the temper of self-respecting Americans. To be sure, there are familiar instances of Congress-

[1] *Politician, Party and People,* 114.

men with very ordinary capacities who have kept their seats through many years by running errands. In the end they have sunk into oblivion, unregretted even by most of those with whom they have curried favor. Far happier the man who can leave his period of service with the consciousness that he has really served his country! And if it was beyond him to be like Burke, at the same time statesman and slave, yet will his declining years bring him more content if he can recall that he chose the nobler course.

President Woolsey succinctly puts the case for general welfare. "The object of a deliberative assembly," he says, "is to find out first of all what is the highest good, within the reach of political measures, for a whole community, and not what will suit the greatest number of constituents. The delegates are sent to advise with one another, and are not, in a proper sense, delegates of parts or parties, but belong all to the whole country. It is the whole, the organized community, which appears in the halls of legislatures." [1]

In their most abstruse form the arguments have been given by Elisha Mulford, always profound, not easy to understand, but stimulating to those who are willing to think hard and study out his meaning (whence some of us who as youths came in familiar touch with him, reverently called him Socrates). "The representation of the Republic," he argued, "is of a person by a person. It is not of one person in substitution for another, but in community with another. To regard one person as in the place of another would be the negation of personality, the representation of a person by a form or symbol. The representative violates his own personality, if instead of standing in his own free and conscious self-determination, he aims to follow a constituency and to stand in identity with that. Then he is no longer free in his own will and knowing his own mind, and the result can be only the weakness and instability of government. The representative is a person, and is the representative of the moral personality of the nation, and therefore in the realization of that acts immediately only in relation to the nation and to God. It is the law and the majesty of the nation, in its unity and freedom, and as a government over the whole, that is to be realized in his determination. He is not the blind and mechanical instrument or exponent of an external will, as a constituency or a party, but

[1] T. D. Woolsey, *Political Science*, II, 108.

stands in the will and determination of the State, which is not external to him, but is to be realized in him; but every formal notion of the nation forbids this, since then the representative has only a formal relation to the nation, and is representative only of separate parties or certain persons in it." [1]

In spite of the fact that most of the theorists are on this side of the case, I am inclined to think that President Lowell is wiser in taking the middle course, and that his view is practical and reasonable. It is impossible, he says, to determine whether a modern legislature represents the whole country, on the ground that each of its members, although elected by one district, holds a national office; or whether it does so because, while each member represents only his own district, they reflect in combination the opinions of the country as a whole. Neither principle can be asserted absolutely and neither can be entirely denied; for in fact the representative has two duties and performs two functions. He does not keep them distinct in his own mind, and fortunately they are not contradictory enough to oblige him to do so; but we may observe that it is considered a mark of larger patriotism to talk in public about his duty to the nation. [2]

The topic should not be dismissed without a word on the special phase of it that is sometimes brought in issue when home rule for cities is discussed. For example, take the argument of C. C. Binney. The idea of representative government, he holds, is, properly, government by those who, in whatever capacity they serve, are elected to represent the people who are affected by the acts done or measures adopted. To entrust a Legislature with power over matters which concern exclusively districts which the majority of the members do not even profess in any way to represent, and to the people of which they cannot be held responsible, is, therefore, strictly speaking, not representative government at all. That the officers of a city should be appointed by the State executive would not be more at variance with the representative principle. [3]

This gives short shrift to the theory that a Legislature represents the State as a whole, and therefore all its fractions. It is peculiarly inexact, like much argument for municipal home rule, because it ignores the overlapping of interests. The business of

[1] *The Nation*, 249.
[2] *Public Opinion and Popular Government*, 117.
[3] *Restrictions upon Local and Special Legislation in the U.S.*, 16.

all cities feeds on a large surrounding district, suburban and rural. Furthermore, half the business men and owners of real estate not used for dwellings in such a city as Boston may live and vote outside its arbitrary limits. The welfare of Providence is a matter of greater or less concern to every citizen of Rhode Island. Nearly every State has one large city where bad government will hurt thousands on thousands who can reach it only through the State Legislature. Modern methods of transportation and communication have knit our interests together, and the modern newspaper makes us one huge community. More than ever before, the city and the town are fractions, not units. More than ever before is it vital that the State and not the municipality should be the master.

ANTICIPATING THE PEOPLE

Of the same genus as the foregoing problems, though not of the same species, is this question: Ought a member of a Legislature to vote on the merits of a constitutional amendment proposed for submission to the electorate, or should his vote be determined by his judgment as to whether or not the people may wisely be asked to decide?

In principle the question is the same as to the duty of a Congressman when he is to vote on submitting an amendment to the Legislatures.

In practice, most legislators allow their votes under such circumstances to be affected by their view of the merits. Are they right?

John Koren, discussing "Government and Prohibition" in the *Atlantic Monthly* for April, 1916, brought out the great practical importance of the question. He showed the attitude of the Anti-Saloon League toward Congress by quoting William H. Anderson, State Superintendent of the League for New York, as follows: "The Anti-Saloon League is not asking any member of Congress to declare that he is in favor of National Prohibition, but simply that he shall not become an avowed exponent and protector of the liquor traffic by refusing to vote to allow the people of the nation, by States, through their representatives, to determine this question in the manner provided therefor by the framers of the Constitution."

Upon this Mr. Koren commented: "Nothing less is contemplated than a *de facto* reversal of the process by which amendments to the Federal Constitution are intended to be made. The provision of the Constitution that the Congress, by a two-thirds vote in both Houses, has power to propose amendments to the Constitution, which become effective when ratified by the Legislatures of three fourths of the States, necessarily implies a deliberative act on the part of the Congress and imposes a solemn obligation for the nature of the amendment proposed. The requirement that an amendment must be submitted to the several States for ratification is merely in order that there may be a sufficient check upon any action of the Congress. But the Anti-Saloon League would have the nation's chosen representatives abdicate as a deliberative body, efface personal conviction, and forego their greatest responsibility, so that 'the people of the nation' may determine the question of national prohibition, under threat that he who refuses becomes an 'avowed exponent and protector of the liquor traffic.'"

Humorously enough, the interests for which Mr. Koren seemed to hold a brief, went to the other extreme as soon as the Prohibition Amendment had been ratified by enough Legislatures to give it effect. Then they declared that both Congress and the Legislatures ought to have received specific mandates. Wherever the Referendum had been adopted, they declared it ought to be used. They began an agitation to change the Federal Constitution so that it cannot be amended without a vote by the people. They denounced every Congressman who in the exercise of his own judgment had voted for the first step toward constitutional suppression of the liquor traffic.

Both extremes are untenable. The legislator who votes against submitting an amendment does not thereby become an avowed exponent of anything, and does not necessarily defend what is aimed at by the amendment. On the other hand, if he votes for submitting an amendment, he does not abdicate the deliberative function, and does not necessarily forego what Mr. Koren means by responsibility, nor avoid what he means by solemn obligation. It need not be dishonorable, nor even inconsistent, for a legislator to vote to submit an amendment, while intending to vote against it at the polls. If it seems to him a pure question of expediency, on which judgments may well vary, with an evident demand for a vote by the people, he may with perfect propriety waive his own inclination. Likewise he may honorably and consistently think the time is not opportune for a plebiscite on a proposition he himself favors, or he may think the same end would better be accomplished in some other way. Indeed, he may hope to secure by legislation what he fears he would lose were an amendment submitted.

It is palpable that the requirement of a two-thirds vote does contemplate serious deliberation and emphatic decision, but this does not touch the real question. Little light is shed on that by the discussions in the Federal or State Conventions. Randolph's plan with which the debate in the Federal Convention began, expressly declared that the assent of the national legislature ought not to be required to amendments. Pinckney's draft contained the provision for Congress to act, much as it was adopted, with the addition of power to amend by a Convention. Colonel Mason held "it would be improper to require the consent of the national legislature, because they may abuse their power, and refuse their assent on that very account." [1] Three months later, Mason still thought the article "exceptionable and dangerous," fearing that as Congress would have a hand in the process, "no amendments of the proper kind would ever be obtained by the people, as he verily believed would be the case." [2] Thereupon Gouverneur Morris and Elbridge Gerry moved to amend by making provision for a Convention, and this was agreed to without opposition. The fact that Congress must call a Convention — the language is mandatory — if the Legislatures of two thirds of the States call for it, shows that it was not meant to leave all avenues for amendment at the mercy of Congress. That body is to propose amendment whenever two thirds of both Houses shall "deem it necessary." The word "necessary" may mean any one of many things. Evidently each member must decide its meaning by himself, and no member is to be criticized if he acts upon any reasonable meaning.

Yet it can hardly be denied that regardless of theory, the legislator will in fact receive some degree of blame or praise based upon the critic's view of the main question. The probability of this he will disregard at his peril. On the other hand he will appease his conscience only if he votes as he thinks right. So the dilemma is much the same as in the case of an ordinary bill.. The attempt to escape being impaled on either of its horns adds interest to legislative life.

[1] *Elliot's Debates*, v, 182.   [2] *Ibid.*, v, 551.

CHAPTER XXII

THE RIGHT OF PETITION

LEAVING the relation of the individual representative to his constituency, turn to that between the public at large and its representative bodies. First may be considered the influence brought to bear by means of petitions.

The right of petition goes back beyond history. Subjects have petitioned rulers ever since there were subjects and rulers. The right was implied in that reluctant promise extorted from King John with the rest of Magna Charta, a charter of ancient liberties — "*Nulli negabimus rectum aut justitia*" — "To no man will we deny right or justice." Most petitions to the monarch were for redress of personal or local grievances, and the remedies prayed for were such as would not be found in courts of equity or sought from a legislative body in the shape of private, special, or local bills. For centuries petitions were a necessary method of relief from oppression that could not be met by the slow and cumbrous machinery of the courts of justice then provided. As the judicial system developed, bringing more protection to private rights, this class of petitions to the Crown lost importance.

At the same time Parliament was gradually absorbing petitions for change of laws. At first Parliament itself was a petitioner. That was how lawmaking by statute began. No sooner had Parliaments been summoned than they grasped the opportunity of laying common grievances before the King by mass petition. Naturally localities saw the convenience of having their agents transmit their prayers; individuals saw the strength their petitions would get if endorsed by Parliament. So in the reign of Henry IV they began to petition the Parliament to petition the King. Stubbs tells us [1] that such private petitions as seemed to merit the consideration of the Commons were after examination sent up to the Lords with the note prefixed, "*Soit baillé aux seigneurs*," and there passed through the further stages before receiving the King's assent: "*Soit fait comme il est désiré.*" All these were of the nature of what are now called private bills — a proceeding half legislative and half judicial.

[1] *Constitutional History*, III, 460.

The result may be termed an act of Parliament, but it was not a statute, and instead of appearing among the laws of the realm, was certified by letters patent under the great seal.

The theory that it was for the King to redress grievances prevailed even after Parliament became in fact the real and only maker of laws. As late as the Stuarts we find it said by Sir Robert Filmer, who wrote in defence of absolutism: "The benefit which accrues to the subject by Parliaments is, that by their prayers and petitions Kings are drawn many times to redress their just grievances, and are overcome by their importunity to grant many things which otherwise they would not yield unto; for the voice of a multitude is easier heard. Many vexations of the people are without the knowledge of the King, who in Parliament seeth and heareth his people himself; whereas at other times he commonly useth the eyes and ears of other men." [1]

To this day private bills constitute a great part of the work of both English and American legislatures. In view of their origin, in view of the Great Charter promise that to no man shall be denied right or justice, it may be wondered if those American Constitutions that forbid private bills, that forbid the Legislature to redress grievances the courts cannot meet, have altogether wisely abandoned the customs of our ancestors in the mother country. Documents with such prohibitions would have had little sympathy from the men who drew the Bills of Rights for our early Constitutions. Note, for instance, what Pennsylvania said in 1776: "The people have a right to apply to the Legislature for redress of grievances, by address, petition, or remonstrance." North Carolina copied this in the same year, with the omission of "by address, petition, or remonstrance." The next year Vermont used the whole of the Pennsylvania provision. Massachusetts improved on it in 1780 with: "The Legislature ought frequently to assemble for the redress of grievances, for correcting, strengthening, and confirming the laws, and for making new laws, as the common good may require." New Hampshire set forth the principle still more clearly in 1784: "The people have a right to request of the legislative body, by way of petition or remonstrance, redress of the wrongs done them, and of the grievances they suffer." The right of petition is now guaranteed by every State Constitution except in the case of Virginia, Minnesota, and New Mexico.

[1] *Patriarcha*, chap. III.

In the early days of Parliament, genuine statutes, changes in the law, went through much the same process as the provisions in special cases, for it was long the fact, not merely the pretense, that the laws were enacted by the King, upon the petition of his Parliament. Throughout the fourteenth century it was declared that a statute was made with the assent of the earls, prelates, and barons, and at the request of the knights of the shires and Commons in Parliament assembled. The Commons presented their petitions. It was for the King, with the aid of those nearest him, to decide whether legislation was required and if so what form it should take.

The people began to use political petitions in earnest in the seventeenth century. Many on political subjects, largely signed, were presented both to Charles I and to the Long Parliament. The dangers of this kind of intimidation were not overlooked by Charles II. His first regular Parliament enacted (13 Car. II, c. 5) that no petition to the King or either House of Parliament, for alteration of matters established by law in Church or State (unless the contents thereof had been previously approved, in the country by three justices of the grand jury of the county, and in London by the Lord Mayor, Aldermen, and Common Council), should be signed by more than twenty names or delivered by more than ten persons, under penalty, in either case, of a fine of a hundred pounds and three months' imprisonment.

Nevertheless petitioning on a large scale was not thereby ended. In December, 1679, in consequence of the dissatisfaction of the nation at the repeated prorogations of Parliament, great exertions were made to get up numerously signed petitions to the King for its assembling. Thereupon a royal proclamation was issued, forbidding all persons to sign such petitions, under pain of punishment. Even this, though it checked, did not entirely stop their presentation. Counter addresses were therefore sent up to the throne from grand juries, magistrates, and many corporations, expressing their *abhorrence* of such things, whence the two principal parties in the country, afterward distinguished as Whigs and Tories, received for the time the names of Petitioners and Abhorrers.

Meanwhile occasion had arisen in Parliament to discuss thoroughly the right of petition. In 1668 one Thomas Skinner presented a petition to the House of Lords, complaining of certain oppressive acts of the East India Company. The Company thereupon presented a petition to the House of Commons, complaining of the House of Lords, and denying their right to proceed in the premises. The Lords took umbrage at this petition, as libelous and scandalous, as a breach of their privilege and an encroachment upon their prerogative, and proceeded to punish Sir Samuel Bernardiston and other members of the Company by fine and imprisonment. A long and angry dispute forthwith arose between the two branches. Elaborate reports were made on both sides, and sundry resolutions were adopted. In those of the Commons were the following declarations: "That it is an inherent right of every commoner of England to prepare and present petitions to the House of Commons, in case of grievances and of the House of Commons to receive the same. It hath been always, time out of mind, the constant and uncontroverted usage and custom of the House of Commons to have petitions presented to them from commoners, in case of grievance, public or private; in evidence whereof, it is one of the first works that is done by the House of Commons, to appoint a Grand Committee to receive petitions and informations of grievances."

This view was not to remain uncontested. In 1701 the grand jury and other freeholders of Kent presented to the Commons a petition imploring them to turn their loyal addresses into bills of supply (the only phrase in the whole petition that could be construed into disrespect) and to enable His Majesty to assist his allies before it should be too late. The Tory faction was wrought to fury. They voted that the petition was scandalous, insolent, and seditious, tending to destroy the constitution of Parliament, and to subvert the established government; and ordered that Mr. Colepepper, who had been most forward in presenting it, and all others who had been concerned in it, should be taken into custody of the serjeant, whereupon five were imprisoned until the end of the session. Among resolutions passed that were directed against Colepepper was one declaring the undoubted right of the people of England to petition *the King* for the redressing of grievances, etc. To petition Parliament was a different thing. One critic said: "For the law declares that a general consultation of all the wise representatives of Parliament is more for the safety of England than the hasty advice of a number of petitioners of a private county, of a grand jury, or of a few justices of the peace, who seldom have a true state of the case represented to them." [1]

[1] Hallam, *Constitutional History of England*, chap. XVI.

The Bill of Rights, one of the first acts passed after William of Orange took the throne in 1689, and justly held to be one of the bulwarks of English liberty, had declared — "That it is the right of the subjects to petition the King, and all commitments and prosecutions for such petitioning are illegal." The Tories of 1701 were wholly wrong in drawing the inference that Parliament could not be petitioned with equal propriety. As Fox said many years later, "no man could question the subjects' right to present petitions to their representatives; because, it was idle to suppose, that when a stipulation has been made by the Bill of Rights that the subjects should, in all cases, have a right to petition the crown, they had not an equal right to petition the House of Commons, their own representatives." [1]

Hatsell expressed it more emphatically: "To receive, and hear, and consider the petitions of their fellow-subjects, when presented decently and containing no matter intentionally offensive to the house, is a duty incumbent on them, antecedent to all rules and orders that may have been instituted for their own convenience. Justice and the laws of their country demand it from them."

Notice that the petitions are to be presented "decently." This was the condition ignored by Lord George Gordon, president of the Protestant Association, when in 1781 he presented in the House of Commons a petition for the repeal of the bill removing penalties from Romanists. It bore thousands of signatures, and he went to the House at the head of a large mob he had collected. His followers attacked several members and tried to intimidate. The motion was, however, rejected almost unanimously, and the rabble, after rioting several days, subsided. In Gordon's case Lord Mansfield said that the Statute of 13 Charles II limiting the number of petitioners was still in force.

It was about this time that the modern system of agitation by petition began. The start of systematic petitioning is attributed by May to an extensive organization in 1779 to promote measures of economics and parliamentary reform.[2] As yet, however, the number of petitions was comparatively small, bearing little proportion to the vast accumulations of later times. In 1782 there were about fifty petitions praying for reform in the representation of the Commons in Parliament; and also a consider-

[1] *Parliamentary Register*, xxiii, 113.
[2] *Constitutional History of England*, i, 412 *et sqq.*

able number in subsequent years. The great movement for the abolition of the slave-trade soon followed. The first petition against the infamous traffic was presented from the Quakers in 1782, but it was not supported by other petitions for some years. In 1787 and 1788, a greater number of petitions were presented for this benevolent object than had ever been presented to Parliament upon any other political question.

After development of pressure by mass petitions, the next step was their use within the House itself as a basis for contest. For instance, when at the end of the Napoleonic wars it was proposed to stop the income tax, the campaign was conducted by means of petitions: For five or six weeks from four o'clock in the afternoon till two or three in the morning, petition after petition was presented and each was debated. It was one of the most extraordinary episodes ever seen in the House of Commons. After the Reform Act of 1832 the debating of petitions threatened to become the sole business of the House. In 1839 that body was forced to the drastic expedient of prohibiting all debate upon their presentation. Other means to get publicity have, however, been devised. A thousand or more petitions are now printed annually in full; and all petitions are so classified as to exhibit the number, with the signatures, relating to every subject.

The American history of petitions begins almost with the coming of the colonists. It is by no means one-sided. In Massachusetts, at least, the earliest legislators wanted to do their own thinking. In 1637 a petition signed by nearly all the members of the Boston church was presented to the General Court, praying that proceedings in judicial cases should be conducted publicly, and that matters of conscience might be left for the church. This paper was at once ordered to be returned to those from whom it came, with an endorsement upon it to the effect that the Court considered it presumptuous. Sundry entries on the records of the Court are illuminating. For instance: — "November 2, 1637: — "Mr. William Aspinwall being questioned in regard his hand was to a petition or remonstrance, and he justified the same, maintaining it to be lawful; the Court did discharge him from being a member thereof.

"Mr. John Coggeshall affirming that Mr. Wheelwright is innocent, and that he was persecuted for the truth, was in like sort dismissed from being a member of the Court, and order was given for two new deputies to be chosen by the town of Boston." [1]

"Mr. Willi: Aspinwall being convented for having his hand to a petition or remonstrance, being a seditious libel, and justifying the same, for which, and for his insolent and turbulent carriage, he is disfranchized and banished, putting in sureties for his departure before the end of the first month next ensuing." [2]

On the 15th of November six others were disfranchised for having put their hands to the same writing, and two of them were also fined, one for justifying the same and using contemptuous speeches. Besides, the noted Captain Underhill was discharged from his place of Captain and disfranchised for the same thing. Nine others acknowledged their sin in subscribing the seditious writing and desired to have their hands crossed out, which was yielded them. [3]

Possibly it was this episode that John Winthrop discussed in his Journal, May 22, 1639. The Court, he said, finding the number of deputies to be much increased by the addition of new plantations, thought fit, for the ease of both the country and the court, to reduce all towns to two deputies. "This occasioned some to fear, that the magistrates intended to make themselves stronger, and the deputies weaker, and so in time, to bring all power into the hands of the magistrates; so as the people in some towns were much displeased with their deputies for yielding to such an order.... A petition was brought to the court from the freemen of Roxbury to have the third deputy restored.... The hands of some of the elders (learned and godly men) were to this petition, though suddenly drawn in, and without due consideration, for the lawfulness of it may well be questioned: for when the people have chosen men to be their rulers, and to make their laws, and bound themselves by oath to submit thereto, now to combine together (a lesser part of them) in a public petition to have any order repealed, which is not repugnant to the law of God, savors of resisting an ordinance of God; for the people, having deputed others, have no power to make or alter laws, but are to be subject; and if any such order seem unlawful or inconvenient, they were better prefer some reasons, etc., to the court, with manifestation of their desire to remove them to a review, than peremptorily to petition to have it repealed, which amounts to a plain reproof of those whom God hath set over

[1] *Records of the Colony of the Mass. Bay in N.E.*, i, 205.
[2] *Ibid.*, 207.   [3] *Ibid.*, 207–09.

them, and putting dishonor upon them, against the tenor of the fifth commandment." [1]

Observe that here Winthrop set forth almost the extreme view of legislative independence. To be sure, he condescended to admit that the people might prefer some reasons to the court, but a petition was an insult. Once the power had been entrusted to representatives, then to question their decisions savored of resisting an ordinance of God. This was the belief of an educated man, unusually well-informed for his time, a clear thinker, serious and earnest.

His view did not long prevail. More democratic instincts soon got the upper hand in the colony. The Body of Liberties in 1641 laid down opposite doctrine. "Every man," it said, "whether Inhabitant or foreigner, free or not free shall have liberty to come to any public Court, Council, or Town meeting, and either by speech or writing to move any lawful, reasonable, and material question, or to present any necessary motion, complaint, petition, Bill or information, whereof that meeting hath proper cognizance, as it be done in convenient time, due order, and respective manner."

The broad scope of this permission brought embarrassments, as you may see by a vote of the General Court, October 27, 1648:

"Whereas, by sad experience, it is found very burthensome unto this Court that many petitions of inconsiderable concernment are in every Court presented, which occasion much expense of time, and tend greatly to the exhausting the estate of the country:

"It is hereby ordered, that all petitions which are of a common and ordinary nature, the petitioner shall, on the delivery thereof, pay unto the secretary or clerk where the same shall be delivered two shillings six pence for each petition."

The order went on to establish a scale of fees for other petitions, regarding fines, controversies, debts, appeals, etc. [2]

It is to be borne in mind that not for a long time to come was there to be complete separation of legislative and judicial functions, and that the General Court would long concern itself with administrative details, a practice indeed even surviving perniciously to-day. Petitions were granted for license to keep

[1] John Winthrop, *Journal*, May 22, 1639.
[2] *Records of the Colony of the Mass. Bay in N.E.*, ii, 261.

ordinaries or sell liquor, for permission to carry on such business as that of salt-making, for grant of lands, for confirmation of sales, for permission to buy or sell lands, for bounding towns, for probate of wills, for remission of fines and penalties, for the redress of grievances of all kinds. A century later the harm of all this had become so evident that attempt was made to stop it by enactment. The first act passed at the session of 1741 began: "Whereas Persons are frequently put to great Cost and Charge in making Answer to Causeless Petitions preferred to the General Court of this Province." It went on to provide that upon the dismission of vexatious and causeless petitions, the adverse party could recover reasonable costs and damages; furthermore, that no petition was to be received after fourteen days from the Court's first sitting unless the cause arose within the sitting.

This did not end the evil. We find Governor Hutchinson saying in his speech to the two Houses May 31, 1770: "A multitude of petitions came before the General Court the last year, some of which seemed to be of very small importance and I thought it hardly consistent with the dignity of the Court, to take cognizance of them. The Assembly then passed one act, which had a tendency to lessen private petitions; and I should be glad if further expedients could be agreed upon to like purpose." He speaks of private petitions; the language of the law of 1741 shows it was aimed at matters that would now come before trial courts; and the law to which Hutchinson referred concerned what would now be treated as court procedure. This phase of the situation was met by the Constitution of 1780, which sharply separated the three branches of government, and in 1790 the Legislature repealed the act of 1741.

Much the same process of development went on in Virginia. The right of petition, at first used without formal recognition, in 1664 was systemized. It was then provided that a notice should be given in the parish churches and that days should be appointed for the people to meet in their election places and present their grievances to the Burgesses. This was a legal provision for petitions to the government for redress of grievances. It gave rise to all sorts of complaints and unsigned petitions that did more evil than good. The law was amended in 1680, so that the sheriff was to appoint a time and place for the meeting and all petitions had to be signed, or they could not be presented in the Assembly. The right to petition continued throughout the colonial era and was much used. Occasionally, however, at the end of a session a limit was put to the time within which petitions would be received. This was only to prevent their coming in during the last few days of the session, when there was no time to act on them. The enactment of 1680 was renewed in 1705 and again was reënacted in 1762 under the head of a provision for a court of claims in each county, where claims, grievances, and petitions to the Assembly might be presented.[1]

It is unnecessary to trace the growth of kindred practices in the other colonies. Suffice it to say that by the time trouble with the mother country began, the custom of bringing influence to bear upon legislative bodies by the use of petitions was thoroughly entrenched. Of course it grieved the royal Governors, who met in it a powerful influence hostile to their own. With dismay they watched the authority of the crown eaten away by the tireless agitators whose petitions and instructions kept the colonial legislatures ever pugnacious. It was the efficacy of the procedure that made it doubly dear to the American people.

When the passage of years had dimmed the memory of colonial precedents, and men had somewhat forgotten the lessons of revolutionary times, the right of petition again came in question. John Adams had put it into the Constitution of Massachusetts. His son was to vindicate its presence in the Constitution of the United States. There it had been placed, in the very first of the amendments insisted upon by the people as virtually a condition of their acceptance of the work of the Federal Convention. John Quincy Adams was to fight for it at two widely separated periods. The second struggle is famous, the first almost forgotten. You may find the story of the first in his Diary under date of April 21, 1806. Memorials had been presented to the United States Senate by Samuel G. Ogden and William S. Smith, praying for relief because of their treatment by the Judge of the District Court of New York. It was a matter of politics and Senator Wright led the excitement. Adams began by presenting the memorials. "Wright," says Adams, "as usual, raved like a bedlamite, and, amidst a torrent of personalities, for which he was repeatedly called to order by the President and several other members, threatened once and again to move for my expulsion, but he could not inspire his own rage into any other bosom, though some members would have been glad to censure

[1] E. I. Miller, *The Legislature of the Province of Virginia*, 155.

me could they have found it possible. He first made a motion to *reject* the memorials; but that could not be obtained, it being without precedent, and inconsistent with the unanimous vote to receive them. Another motion was then made to reconsider the vote for receiving the memorials. But it was impossible to reconsider a vote already carried into effect. Dr. Mitchell moved that the memorialists should have leave to withdraw their memorials; but Wright could not be satisfied with that. He insisted upon rejecting the memorials. After repeated declarations from the Chair that it could not be done, Dr. Mitchell withdrew, and renewed, and altered, and renewed again his motion to suit Wright upon every return of his paroxysms. At last Wright produced a motion, for which Baldwin quoted a precedent in the other House, to return the memorials to the memorialists on account of highly exceptionable matter contained in them. But Dr. Mitchell's motion for simple leave to withdraw the memorials was before the Senate, and they would not give him leave to take it back. In order therefore to get at the question of *censure*, Wright moved to amend the motion of simple leave to withdraw by striking out the words 'the memorialists have leave to withdraw their memorials,' to insert 'the memorials be returned to the memorialists.' I then called for a division of the question, which was first taken on the striking out. The votes upon this question were eleven and eleven, besides the President pro tem. who declared *against* the striking out; and the question upon simple leave to withdraw was taken, and passed without opposition. Here the matter rested for that time; but the same memorials had been presented by Mr. Quincy to the House of Representatives, and had raised there a much more violent flame than in the Senate. There it resulted in votes of 'return of the memorials,' and of censure upon their being presented."

Adams came again to the defense of petitions thirty years later, and began that memorable contest which was waged in Congress from January 4, 1836, to December 3, 1844. Two years after his failure to secure reëlection as President, he was elected to the lower branch and there he served until his death in 1848, a conspicuous example of the public service that can yet be given by one who has received the highest honors of a republic. In all his long and eminent career he brought his countrymen no achievement of more enduring benefit than that which accrued from his nine years of battle for the right of citizens to lay their requests before legislative assemblies. He fought single-handed, only the smallest of help coming to him during much of the contest. Perhaps never for so long was one legislator the target of so much virulence, denunciation, censure, ridicule, abuse. Perhaps never did one legislator display more courage, tenacity, patience, fortitude.

The right of petition would not have been put in such jeopardy if the subject matter at issue had not aroused the bitterest animosities. The representatives of the slave-holding States saw in the petitions for the abolition of slavery a concrete opportunity to combat the steadily growing sentiment of the North. Goaded by the attacks on what to them had now become a sacred institution, they exhausted the arsenal of invective. It was accident that the right of petition was involved. Yet if the vindication of that right seemed at the time but incidental, by itself it was of vast importance.

So far as the contest related to the slavery question, it need not here concern us beyond explanation that of the hundreds and hundreds of petitions presented by Mr. Adams around which the battle raged, all involved slavery or his own relation with the subject. A petition to abolish slavery in the District of Columbia began the struggle, January 4, 1836, by bringing a motion that the petition be not received. Before this motion was determined, the question was broadened somewhat by a resolution declaring that the House would not entertain any petitions for the abolition of slavery in the District. At the outset the main contention was that Congress had no constitutional power in the premises and that it ought not to entertain petitions to do an unconstitutional act. Before final action ground was again shifted, new petitions of like tenor being met by a motion that the motion not to receive be laid on the table, which was referred to a select committee. In May this committee, after averring that Congress had no power to interfere with slavery in a State and ought not to interfere with it in the District of Columbia, met the technical issue by advising that whereas the agitation of the subject was disquieting and objectionable, "all petitions, memorials, resolutions, or papers, relating in any way or to any extent whatsoever to the subject of slavery or the abolition of slavery, shall, without being either printed or referred, be laid upon the table, and that no further

action whatever shall be had thereon." When the resolution to
this effect was read, and the call of the Yeas and Nays had begun, Mr. Adams, as soon as his name was called, rose and said:
"I hold this resolution to be a direct violation of the Constitution of the United States, the rules of this House, and the rights
of my constituents." He was interrupted by shrieks of "order"
from every side, but their only effect was to make him speak the
louder and his obstinacy carried the sentence to its end. Of
course the resolution prevailed.

So began the famous "gag-rule." With the opening of every
Congress thereafter, Mr. Adams regularly moved its repeal, only
to be as regularly voted down. At intervals through every Congress he presented the petitions, now a few, now a score, now
hundreds. Again and again was the battle renewed, always in
appearance to the discomfiture of the doughty old warrior, always in reality to his gain, for every defeat made for him more
friends among the people.

Once a new twist to the question threw the House into wild
excitement. It was in February, 1837, that after presenting
about two hundred petitions, he said he had in his hand a paper
concerning which he would wish to have the decision of the
Speaker before presenting. It purported to be a petition from
twenty-two slaves, and he would like to know whether it came
within the rule of the House concerning petitions relating to
slavery. The Speaker, manifestly confused, said the circumstances were so extraordinary that he would take the sense of the
House. Members were hastily brought in from the lobbies; many
tried to speak; cries arose — "Expel him! Expel him!" The
infuriated Southerners outvied each other in their proposals for
punishment of one who had so insulted the dignity of the House
as to bring within its walls a petition from slaves. Censure,
expulsion, criminal prosecution were in turn threatened. At last
the culprit got a hearing. Then he confounded his assailants by
disclosing that the prayer of the petitioners was that slavery be
not abolished. The next day he had the chance to defend himself at greater length, in a masterly speech, so convincing that in
the end the idea of even censure was abandoned by his enemies,
and all that came out of it was a resolution that slaves did not
possess the right of petition secured by the Constitution to the
people of the United States.

In 1842 there was again high talk of censure or worse, this

time because the irrepressible member from Massachusetts presented a petition from citizens of Haverhill in that State, praying the House "to adopt measures peaceably to dissolve the union of these States," for the alleged cause of the incompatibility between free and slave-holding communities. While one outraged member said the petition should never have been brought within the walls of the House, and another wished to burn it in the presence of the members, Mr. Gilmer, of Virginia, offered a resolution, that in presenting the petition Mr. Adams "had justly incurred the censure of the House." This was presently laid on the table. The next day a substitute was offered in the shape of long and careful resolutions prepared in a caucus of forty members of the slave-holding party. The preamble recited that a petition proposing to Congress to destroy that which its members had solemnly sworn to support, was a "high breach of privilege, a contempt offered to this House, a direct proposition to the Legislature and each member of it to commit perjury, and involving necessarily in its execution and its consequences the destruction of our country and the crime of high treason"; wherefore it was to be resolved that Mr. Adams, in presenting a petition for dissolution, had "offered the deepest indignity to the House" and "an insult to the people"; that the House deem it an act of grace and mercy when they only inflict on him their severest censure; that so much they must do "for the maintenance of their own purity and dignity; for the rest they turned him over to his own conscience and the indignation of all true American citizens." Nevertheless in the end the House voted to "lay the whole subject on the table forever."

By this time the majorities against the motions of Mr. Adams to strike out the "gag-rule" had begun to dwindle. In 1842 they had come down to four; in 1843 the majority was but three. On the 3rd of December, 1844, he made his usual motion, and this time a motion to lay it on the table did not prevail. On the main question he won the long-delayed victory by 108 to 80. With warrantable exultation when recording the event, he wrote, "Blessed, forever blessed, be the name of God!" [1]

Much the same problem was forced on at least one of the State Legislatures, that of Massachusetts. George S. Boutwell recalls that when he was a member, the House was made indignant one morning by the introduction of a petition by Mr.

[1] John T. Morse, Jr., *John Quincy Adams*, 249–307.

Tolman, of Worcester, asking that the clergy who approved of capital punishment should be appointed hangmen. A motion was made to reject the petition without reference. Boutwell interposed and called attention to the similarity between the position the House was thus taking and the position occupied by the National House of Representatives in regard to petitions upon the subject of slavery. The suggestion had no weight with the House. The petition was rejected without a reference. "The next morning," Boutwell relates, "the messenger said Mr. Garrison wished to see me in the lobby. I found Mr. Garrison, Wendell Phillips, and William Jackson with bundles of petitions of the kind presented by Mr. Tolman. They assumed that as I had advocated the reference of the Tolman petition I would present others of like character. I said, 'Gentlemen, when petitions are presented by a member upon his personal responsibility I shall always favor a reference, but as to the presentation of petitions, I occupy a different position. I must judge of the wisdom of the prayer. In this case I must decline to take any personal responsibility.' The petitions were presented by Mr. Tolman and the House retreated from its awkward position." [1]

It will be noticed that from the technical point of view the real issue in these controversies was whether the right of petition precludes a legislative body from raising the question if any given petition is fit to receive. The House of Commons in 1668 passed on that point. A resolution was moved to the effect, "That it is the undoubted right and privilege of the House of Commons to judge and determine touching the nature and matter of such petitions, how far they are fit or unfit to be received." Before this resolution was adopted, the word "received" was stricken out, upon formal motion, and the word "retained" inserted in its place.

In the next century two rules giving effect to this principle were adopted by Parliament. One was to the effect, "that they would receive no petitions against a bill, actually pending, for imposing taxes or duties"; the other, "that they would receive no petitions for grants or appropriations of money relating to public service not recommended by the Crown." Robert C. Winthrop told Congress these were the only rules of the kind ever known to the parliamentary proceedings of England; and that all the cases in which petitions, respectful in their terms,

[1] *Sixty Years in Public Affairs*, i, 74.

had been refused a reception, are found to be ranged under the authority of these two rules.[1]

Italy has gone so far as to provide by its Constitution (Art. 57), a procedure that would seem to compel not only the receiving of all petitions, but also some attention to them. "Every person," it says, "who has attained his majority shall have the right to send petitions to the Houses, which shall order them to be examined by a committee; on report of the committee each House shall decide whether such petitions are to be taken into consideration, and in case of an affirmative decision they shall be referred to the competent minister or to one of the sections of the House for action." (The House of Deputies is divided into nine sections, among which legislative business is divided by the President of the House.)

The Declaration of Rights prefixed to the French Constitution of June 24, 1793, read: "32 Le Droit de présenter des pétitions aux dépositaires de l'autorité publique ne peut, en aucun cas, être interdit, suspendu ni limité." This was construed to mean that petitioners should not be confined to the presentation of their requests by a member of the Assembly. They were allowed to come within the House in person, until disorder and even crimes were committed by intruders who pretended to appear before the Assembly for this purpose. In the Constitutions of 1795 and 1799 the evil was checked by the provision that only persons single, and not societies, should appear on such occasions.[2]

Both in England and the United States petitions are privileged. In the time of Charles II, Edward King in a petition to a committee of Parliament charged one Lake with "many horrible and gross abuses." Lake brought an action for libel and the case had most deliberate investigation, depending twelve terms. In the end the petition was held lawful, although the matter contained in it was false and scandalous. A like case came up in Vermont in 1802 when petitioners had alleged that Ebenezer Harris, Justice of the Peace, was a peace-breaker, guilty of quarreling, threatening, and fighting on the Sabbath and other days, as well as of other shortcomings. Judge Tyler in the opinion (2 Tyler 129) said the case was more interesting to the people of Vermont than any theretofore agitated in that

[1] *Addresses and Speeches*, I, 401..
[2] T. D. Woolsey, *Political Science*, I, 271.

court. Lake *v*. King was followed. "No action can be maintained for a libel, upon a petition for redress of grievances, whether the subject matter of the petition be true or false, simply on its being preferred to either branch of the General Assembly, or disclosed to any of its members." Four years later in Reid *v*. Delorme, 2 Brevard (S. Ca.) 76, it was held that though the conduct of a petitioner may have been unreasonable and malicious, yet in petitioning the Legislature against a public officer of the State he was in the exercise of a constitutional right. "Every citizen has a right to petition the Legislature for a redress of grievances, and even on account of grievances which do not exist, although in doing so, the feelings of individuals, or their reputations, should be wounded."

The right of petition has in our time come in reality to be only a right to an idle form, a waste of time and energy for both the petitioner and the petitioned. The reasons are clear. First may be named the uncertainty as to genuineness. This is no new defect, for Lord Clarendon tells us that in 1640, when a multitude of hands was procured, the petition itself was cut off, and a new one framed suitable to the design in hand, and annexed to the long list of names, which were subscribed to the former.[1] By this means many men found their hands subscribed to petitions of which they before had never heard. Frauds of this sort as well as forgeries are so easy that the chance of them casts a doubt on all bulky petitions.

If the signatures are all genuine, there is the further doubt of their meaning what they purport to mean. Everybody in public life knows perfectly well how easily petition signatures are obtained, how carelessly they are given, how little weight they really deserve. The result is that when they reach an American legislative body, they get scant courtesy. Only the purpose of the petition is disclosed to the House itself, for it is not read at length, so that the House does not hear any information or argument it may contain. Usually the name of only the first signer is read, the rest being disposed of by "and others," so that the number of signatures has then no weight. Summarily referred to a committee, the document gets no further attention. Usually it is never even spread out before the committee, and rarely are the signatures scrutinized. Notice is taken only of the arguments presented in committee hearings or advanced by committee members from their independent knowledge.

[1] *History of Rebellion*, ii, 357.

President Woolsey has given two other reasons, which would not seem valid to most men of practical legislative experience.[1] He says the representatives think that in all important matters they understand the opinions of their districts better than the petitioners do. That may be true of a part, but on the other hand there are many representatives who look to their constituents for guidance and would be glad of some accurate way to learn their opinions. The second reason Woolsey gives is even farther from the facts, for he says that all important measures "are judged from the standpoint of party and not from that of public interest." This is open to criticism from several directions. Many important measures are not made party issues. In some legislative bodies, as for instance the Massachusetts General Court, party lines are rarely drawn. Even where partisanship dominates, it would be of importance for party advantage if for no other reason, to have a trustworthy gauge of public sentiment. And furthermore if political parties have any virtue, it lies in their belief that party interests and public interests are identical.

Whatever the reasons, the palpable fact is that petitions are to-day wholly discredited. The continuance of the system leads thoughtful legislators to deplore the waste of effort it shows. Many well-intentioned persons persist in resorting to it, however. They have their trouble for their pains. One earnest word spoken to a Representative by a constituent whose judgment inspires confidence is worth a yard of petition signatures.

The Massachusetts Legislature continues the practice of the fathers in receiving every petition and giving every petitioner an answer. With the growth of the State and the general increase in the desire for legislation, this practice has become burdensome. It is one of the causes for the length of the annual legislative session, and so when in 1914 a recess committee was created to consider how the session might be shortened, naturally the subject of petitions was conspicuous. The only requirement in the matter of presentation had been that each petition should carry on the back the name of the member presenting it, not as endorsing its prayer, but as an indefinite sort of guarantee of good faith. As no real responsibility attached to the member, it had been very rare that a petitioner had not found some one to present his petition, no matter how absurd or otherwise hopeless

[1] T. D. Woolsey, *Political Science*, I, 271.

it might be. The Senate of 1914 adopted a proposal that would limit the number of petitions which might be sponsored or filed by each member. It was thought this would lead a member to use his right with some care, and would result in his choosing the more important measures. The House rejected the proposition. The Recess Committee said it undoubtedly had merit, but in view of its rejection by the House declined to recommend it for immediate adoption, hoping, however, at some future date it might be resurrected.[1]

There was the suggestion, also, that every petition should have a certain definite number of signatures, or not be received. The Committee thought it an open question whether there would be any great reduction in the number of petitions thereby. There would be no improvement in quality, for certain well-known "hardy-annual" petitioners would unquestionably go out and get the necessary signatures. It would therefore seem to be an imposition upon the worthy petitioner without corresponding gain.

It was believed by some that if the name of the petitioner and of the party introducing the bill were omitted from the records, much-sought publicity would be discouraged, and hence, indirectly, there would be a curtailment of some kinds of petitions from some kinds of petitioners. The Committee thought that undoubtedly some sensationalists would refrain from petitioning if there was no likelihood of their names appearing in print, but the difficulty of indexing the petitions and bills would more than offset the good to be gained. It would mean considerably more work on the part of the clerks at a time when they are overworked. Furthermore, it would be hard to get information relative to specific bills, and their course of passage through the various stages in the Legislature. Then, too, these persons are always able to secure publicity in some way, and there are always newspapers ready to assist them, whatever obstructions are put in their way.

A suggestion of little value in the reduction of business, but of some importance in facilitating it, was that petitioners be required to sign address as well as name. While the Committee did not think a rule ought to be adopted shutting out entirely the petitioner not giving his address, it did believe that the committees having such petitions should not try to give notice of any

[1] Mass. House Document 280 of 1915.

hearing, nor hold any hearing, thereon. The report said: "If the petitioner does not keep in touch with his petition, and fails to sign his address, the committee would seem to be justified in disregarding the petition entirely. This ought to be established in some way, if not as a written rule, at least as an unwritten law, in view of the fact that it is custom only which compels committees to give hearings and notices thereof. We have been informed that last year the clerk sending out notices found it difficult to locate a large number of petitioners, and much time was wasted in trying to look them up. Let the petitioner bear this burden."

Many acquainted with the situation hoped the Recess Committee would advise one simple and justifiable change that in the belief of expert observers might shorten the session by a month or two. This would be in the nature of a rule requiring the payment of a nominal fee for filing a petition. That would not be without precedent. By the Massachusetts Bay law of 1648, as we have seen, the payment of fees was required from petitioners. To be sure, that was done in the days when the redress of individual grievances was a far greater part of the business of the General Court than it is now, and the trial of causes had not been wholly relegated to the judiciary, but is not the principle the same? To-day the General Court is the only court in the Commonwealth that does not require even a nominal fee.

The primary object of fees in the trial courts is not to help meet the cost of the courts, but to discourage trivial litigation and to give an earnest of serious purpose. The Legislature, however, not only receives every petition without charge, but also prints free the accompanying bill and makes a certain number of copies available for distribution. This lets any and every enthusiast, crank, fanatic ride his hobby at the public expense. It puts the cumbrous and costly machinery of the legislative process at the command of whim or cupidity, for custom requires a hearing, rules require a report, on every petition, and the procedure means both direct outlay by the State and indirect expense through prolonging the session. It adds to the labor of committees. It facilitates "strike bills" — the chicanery of the lobbyist who lives by exploiting corporations and business men. No legitimate petition would be embarrassed by the requirement of a nominal fee. It might head off many petitions, illegitimate or nonsensical or useless. Nevertheless the Committee declined to advise such a requirement. They held it would be an actual curtailment of the right of petition; that it would place a burden upon the worthy and the unworthy alike; and that it would probably not improve the quality, though it might lessen the quantity of the petitions, for, said the report, "when we find persons determined upon certain kinds of legislation, they are usually willing to pay the price. The crank with his freak legislation, while protesting violently, would pay the fee before he would lose his chance to expound his doctrines."

The Committee further said: "There is one class of petitioners that would feel the effect and justly, namely, those members of the Legislature who believe that only by filing a large number of bills, and securing the passage of a lot of new legislation, can they appear in a proper light before their constituency. These men would oppose this suggestion, therefore, and we believe that an enlightened public opinion and a realization of the displeasure of their colleagues will accomplish the same result in a more sensible way without causing unnecessary expense to legitimate petitioners."

This last sentence is an excellent example of the tendency not alone of legislators, but of public men generally, to throw on somebody else or on the public at large a responsibility that they know perfectly well will never prove onerous, if indeed ever felt. There is not the remotest chance that either an enlightened public opinion or the displeasure of legislators will in our day interpose a straw to check this evil. The fact probably is that the extreme conservatism of Massachusetts legislators will delay logical reform until the evil becomes unendurable.

Something is to be said in defense. The Massachusetts Legislature following ancient practices has preserved its reputation as the best lawmaking body in the United States, perhaps in the world. Change may endanger this proud position. That alone is enough to account for the rejection of such a reasonable reform. It will also account for the fact that of the very mild and harmless proposals for improvement which the Committee brought itself to advise, not one of real importance has been adopted by the General Court.

CHAPTER XXIII

PUBLIC OPINION

THE greatest of all the forces that influence the legislator is public opinion. The outstanding feature of the political history of the last century and a half has been the growth of this force on both sides of the water. In England the reigns of the first two Georges had been an era of dull, stupid prosperity. Under Walpole, ruling by corruption, the progress of liberty had stagnated. In France Louis XV maintained almost unshaken the absolutism that Louis XIV had brought to its highest pitch. In America the period from Anne to the Seven Years' War was less eventful than any other in our history — the happy youth of an apparently contented people. Then came out of a clear sky first the clouds and speedily the storm.

If the responsibility is to be individualized, it might be laid at the door of three men. In 1762 that strange misanthrope, Jean Jacques Rousseau, wrote "The Social Contract." In 1763 John Wilkes, the dissolute demagogue, published Number 45 of the "North Briton." In 1764 Samuel Adams, a busybody of Boston, drafted the instructions of that town to its representatives in the General Court, containing the first public denial of the right of Parliament to put in operation the Stamp Act, and the first suggestion of a union of the colonies for redress of grievances. From that time on the power of the people grew apace.

It is, of course, very far from true that the people began to think for themselves only when Rousseau and Wilkes and Adams appeared. The forces those men helped so greatly to stimulate had long been gathering strength. Lecky observes that although early in the eighteenth century the people had little power of controlling or directly influencing Parliament, yet whenever their sentiments were strongly expressed on any particular question, either by the votes of the free constituencies or by more irregular or tumultuous means, they were usually listened to, and on the whole obeyed. The explosions of public indignation about the Sacheverell case, the Peace of Utrecht, the commercial treaty with France, the South Sea Bubble, the Spanish outrages, the Bill for naturalizing the Jews, the Hanoverian

policy of Carteret, foolish as in most instances they were, had
all of them a great and immediate effect upon the policy of the
country.[1]

It was not, however, until after George III came to the throne
that the people learned how to voice their will with systemized
efficiency. Another English historian tells us it is from the quarrels between Wilkes and the House of Commons that we may
date the influence of public meetings on English politics.[2] The
gatherings of the Middlesex electors in support of Wilkes were
preludes to the great meetings of the Yorkshire freeholders in
which the question of Parliamentary reform rose to importance;
and it was in the movement for reform, and the establishment of
corresponding committees throughout the country for the purpose of promoting it, that the power of political agitation first
made itself felt. Political societies and clubs took their part in
the creation and organization of public opinion; and the spread
of discussion, as well as the influence that now began to be
exercised by the appearance of vast numbers of men in support
of any political movement, proved that Parliament would soon
have to reckon with the sentiments of the people at large.

By 1782 statesmen had begun to accept the revolution in
British politics that had accompanied, at least in point of time,
the revolution costing England her best colonies. In that year
Fox, addressing Parliament in the matter of expunging the
records of the controversy with Wilkes, recognized the new
situation. Said he: "If the people of England, sir, have at any
time fully and explicitly declared an opinion respecting a momentous constitutional question, it has been in regard to the
Middlesex election." Although he opposed the motion, he felt
very little anxiety for the event of the question; for when he
found the voice of the people was against the privilege, as he
believed was the case at present, he would not preserve the
privilege. The people had associated, had declared their sentiments to Parliament, and had taught Parliament to listen to
the voice of constituents.

Without reviewing the details of the further rise of popular
power, for its next stage take the judgment of that learned and
sagacious observer, Henry Thomas Buckle, who informs us how
things stood in 1857, when his notable work was published.

[1] *England in the Eighteenth Century*, i, 491.
[2] J. R. Green, *Short History of the English People*, 738.

"The rapid progress of democratic opinions," he said, "is a fact which no one in the present day ventures to deny. Timid and ignorant men are alarmed at the movement; but that there is such a movement is notorious to all the world. No one now dares to talk of bridling the people, or of resisting their united wishes. The utmost that is said is, that efforts should be made to inform them as to their real interests, and enlighten public opinion; but every one allows that, so soon as public opinion is formed, it can no longer be withstood. On this point all are agreed; and this new power, which is gradually superseding every other, is now obeyed by those very statesmen who, had they lived sixty years ago, would have been the first to deny its authority, ridicule its pretensions, and, if possible, extinguish its liberty.

"Such is the great gap which separates the public men of our time from those who flourished under that bad system which George III sought to perpetuate. And it is evident, that this vast progress was brought about rather by destroying the system than by improving the men. It is also evident, that the system perished because it was unsuited to the age; in other words, be- cause a progressive people will never tolerate an unprogressive government. But it is a mere matter of history, that our legis- lators, even to the last moment, were so terrified by the idea of innovation, that they refused every reform until the voice of the people rose high enough to awe them into submission, and forced them to grant what, without such pressure, they would by no means have conceded." [1]

Half a century more brings us to our own time, and concerning this there is no more competent, judicious witness in England than A. V. Dicey. "The close and immediate connection," he says, "which in modern England exists between public opinion and legislation is a very peculiar and noteworthy fact, to which we cannot easily find a parallel. Nowhere have changes in popu- lar convictions or wishes found anything like such rapid and immediate expression in alterations of the law as they have in Great Britain during the nineteenth century, and more especially during the last half thereof.... In 1804 George the Third was on the throne, and English opinion was then set dead against every legal or political change, yet there is now [1905] hardly a part of the English statute-book which between 1804 and the present

[1] *History of Civilization in England*, Am. ed. 1865, I, 36.

day has not been changed in form or substance; and the alterations enacted by Parliament have been equalled or exceeded by innovations due to the judge-made law of the Courts."[1]

It has come to be established, on the highest authority, that Parliament cannot legislate on a new question of vital importance without instructions from the people. Mr. Balfour refused to grant time for a debate on free food, on the ground that it would be constitutionally improper for Parliament to act on the question until it had been submitted to the people at a general election, and that it would be unwise for the House to discuss a subject on which it could not act.[2] This conception introduced what is much like a referendum. When Lloyd George put to the test his great financial measure in 1909, with its clauses imposing a tax on the unearned increment of land in the centers of population, a tax on the monopoly value of liquor licenses, and a super-tax on incomes of more than five thousand pounds a year, every member of the Asquith ministry who was in the House of Commons, took to the platform in order to argue the question before the country. Members of the rank and file of the Government party in the House of Commons followed the precedent set by Cabinet Ministers, and the Conservatives had necessarily to go into the constituencies or to use the newspapers to explain the grounds for their opposition at Westminster to the financial proposals of the Government. From April to September more was thus done for the direct education of the people than in any year since members of Parliament had to woo constituencies; and not since the House of Commons began to levy taxation were the common people so well informed as to why a particular tax was levied or as to the possible alternatives.[3]

Doubtless the general impression would be that the change in America has not been so revolutionary as in England, for there is a widespread belief that the Declaration of Independence created a full-fledged Democracy, and that from 1776 the people ruled. To find anything farther from the truth would be hard. Restrictions left the suffrage to about one inhabitant in eighteen when the Colonies became States. The leadership of the few was at that time at least as conspicuous as it ever has been in our history. It is supposed that one third of the people

---

[1] *Law and Opinion in England*, 7.
[2] A. L. Lowell, *The Government of England*, i, 426 (1908).
[3] *The Outlook*, September 18, 1909, 85.

were Tories, partisans of England in the quarrel. Figure out, then, how extensive was the demonstrated "consent of the governed" that the Declaration proclaimed. As a matter of fact, the government was an aristocracy, differing from the aristocracy of England only in that within the aristocratic class the variations of wealth were not so great here as in the mother country. Charles Pinckney gave a wrong impression when he told the Federal Convention he did not suppose that in the Confederation there were one hundred gentlemen of sufficient fortune to establish a nobility, and when he said: "There is more equality of rank and fortune in America than in any other country under the sun.... I lay it therefore down that equality of condition is a leading axiom in our government," [1] he took no account of the thousands on thousands of landless men who had no vote. He ignored the influence of the clergy, waning yet still strong. He forgot the power of the planters of Virginia, the landlords of New York, the merchants of Boston and Philadelphia. Alexander Hamilton was nearer right when he told that same convention: "In every community where industry is encouraged, there will be a division of it into the few and the many." [2]

The record of the debates abounds with fear of the many. Roger Sherman said: "The people, immediately, should have as little to do as may be about the government." Elbridge Gerry, though he was to win fame as their champion, yet declared: "The evils we experience flow from the excess of democracy." [3] Hamilton averred: "The voice of the people has been said to be the voice of God; and, however generally this maxim has been quoted and believed, it is not true in fact. The people are turbulent and changing; they seldom judge or determine right." Later he was to charge: "The people, sir, the people is a great beast!" Over against him was to be Thomas Jefferson, proclaiming with his followers that the maxim *vox populi, vox Dei* is an eternal verity. Hence came political parties in the United States.

Hamilton lost. Jefferson won. With a rush the doctrine of popular supremacy swept through the land. Federalism disappeared. Yet as usual power and responsibility sobered the newcomers in leadership. Reaction followed. Even such an idol of democracy as Andrew Jackson turned out to be a despot.

[1] Yates' Minutes, *Elliot's Debates*, i, 443.
[2] Madison's Journal, *Elliot's Debates*, v, 202.   [3] *Ibid.*, 136.

Nominally the humble servant of the people, in reality he ruled
with an iron hand. Not long after his time the use of instructions to members of Congress began to dwindle. Representatives
became more and more important. After the Civil War attempt
at popular control of representatives almost disappeared. Then
the pendulum began again to swing the other way. The initiative
and referendum came into action. With the Progressive movement of 1912 the rights and powers of the people once more were
brought uppermost. Public opinion was once more paramount.

To describe all this as a growth may not be accurate, and
certainly is not adequate. If sundry masters of political science
have brought here their usual perspicacity, these phenomena
indicate a change in the manifestation of a force already existing,
rather than the development of something new. Long ago David
Hume, historian and philosopher, came to the conclusion that
on opinion only is government founded. "Nothing," he said,
"appears more surprising to those who consider human affairs
with a philosophical eye, than the easiness with which the
many are governed by the few; and the implicit submission,
with which men resign their own sentiments and passions to
those of their rulers. When we enquire by what means this
wonder is effected, we shall find, that, as Force is always on the
side of the governed, the governors have nothing to support
them but opinion." [1] This he held to be true of the most despotic
and most military governments as well as of the most free and
popular. Lord Pembroke has put the same idea in another way.
"Law," he says, "is nothing but public opinion organized and
equipped with force, however grave the questions affecting such
organization may be; and so far from law being always a worse
thing than private action, the difference between them is in
many cases simply the difference between civilization and barbarism." [2]

Rousseau, too, found law and public opinion identical. After
describing three other kinds of law, he added a fourth, "the most
important of all," he declared, "which is graven neither on mar-
ble nor on brass, but in the hearts of the citizens; a law which
creates the real constitution of the State, which acquires new
strength daily, which, when other laws grow obsolete or pass
away, revives them or supplies their place, preserves a people in

[1] *Essays* (1742), I, 109, 110, Green and Grose ed.
[2] *Liberty and Socialism*, 40.

the spirit of their institutions, and imperceptibly substitutes the force of habit for that of authority. I speak of manners, customs, and above all of opinion — a province unknown to our politicians, but one on which the success of all the rest depends; a province with which the great legislator is occupied in private, while he appears to confine himself to particular regulations, that are merely the arching of the vault, of which manners, slower to develop, form at length the immovable keystone." [1]

Bryce has developed the thesis at length in his great book on "The American Commonwealth," devoting a whole Part (IV.) to it, and he who would ponder the conclusions of one of the wisest students of government, should study his argument in full for the light it throws on the most important group of problems confronting the republic. A few sentences here must suffice to show the course of his logic. "Opinion," he says, "has really been the chief and ultimate power in nearly all nations at nearly all times.... Governments have always rested and, special cases apart, must rest, if not on the affection, then on the reverence and awe, if not on the active approval, then on the silent acquiescence of the numerical majority.... The difference therefore between despotically governed and free countries does not consist in the fact that the latter are ruled by opinion and the former by force, for both are generally ruled by opinion. It consists rather in this, that in the former the people instinctively obey a power which they do not know to be really of their own creation, and to stand by their own permission; whereas in the latter the people feel their supremacy, and consciously treat their rulers as their agents, while the rulers obey a power which they admit to have made and to be able to unmake them — the popular will."

He shows the nature of the change that has taken place. Even where the machinery for measuring or weighing the popular will from week to week or month to month has not been, and is not likely to be, invented, there may nevertheless be a disposition on the part of the rulers, whether ministers or legislators, to act as if it existed; that is to say, to look incessantly for manifestations of current popular opinion, and to shape their course in accordance with their reading of those manifestations. Such a disposition will be accompanied by a constant oversight of public affairs by the mass of the citizens and by a sense on their

[1] *The Social Compact*, book 2, chap. XII.

part that they are the true governors, and that their agents, executive and legislative, are rather servants than agents. Where this is the attitude of the people on the one hand and of the persons who do the actual work of governing on the other, it may fairly be said that there exists a kind of government materially, if not formally, different from the representative system as it presented itself to European thinkers and statesmen of the last generation. And it is to this kind of government that democratic nations seem to be tending.

Farther on: "The phrase 'government by public opinion' is most specifically applicable to a system wherein the will of the people acts directly and constantly upon its executive and legislative agents.... This is the goal toward which the extension of the suffrage, the more rapid diffusion of news, and the practice of self-government itself, necessarily lead free nations.... Of all the experiments which America has made, this is that which best deserves study, for her solution of the problem differs from all previous solutions, and she has shown more boldness in trusting public opinion, in recognizing and giving effect to it, than has yet been shown elsewhere."

NATURE AND EFFECT

Evidently it is of high importance to know what public opinion is, how it is formed, what are its virtues and defects, and how it should be treated.

Elwood says that "by public opinion we mean a more or less rational collective judgment formed by the action and reaction of many individual opinions upon one another." [1] If by "rational" he means the product of conscious reasoning, the definition is open to dispute. Instinct and impulse are at the base of much public opinion. For example, how small a part has reason played in such public opinion as exists on the subject of capital punishment! Or take the matter of what are called trusts, and note how little of the collective judgment is based on any rational conception of the merits and demerits of monopoly.

Furthermore, it has of late been denied that the influences shaping government are "collective" in the sense that they have an element of harmony or unity. Arthur F. Bentley has written a long and learned book, "The Process of Government," to prove the contrary. Opinion he thinks to be but one differenti-

[1] *Sociology in its Psychological Aspects*, 334.

ated agency to represent the process of control, and not at all
the most accurate expression of it, at that. There is no public
opinion that is unanimous. Public opinion is an expression of,
by, or for a group of people. It is always directed against some
activities of other groups of men. It has just the value of the
group to which it gives expression. Pressure indicates the push
and resistance between groups. Government is a network of
activities, an adjustment or balance of activities. Law is not a
resultant of government, but *is* government — the same phenomenon stated from a different angle. It is a forming, a system-
ization, a struggle, an adaptation, of group interests, just as
government is. The law is what the mass of the people actually
does, and tends to some extent to make other people do, by
governmental agencies.

Log-rolling, says Mr. Bentley, is the most characteristic
legislative process. When one condemns it "in principle," it is
only by contrasting it with some assumed pure public spirit
which is supposed to guide legislators, or which ought to guide
them, and which enables them to pass judgment in Jovian calm
on that which is best "for the whole people." Since there
is nothing which is best literally for the whole people, group
arrays being what they are, the test is useless, even if one could
actually find legislative judgments which are not reducible to
interest-group activities. And when we have reduced the legislative process to the play of group interests, then log-rolling, or
give and take, appears as the very nature of the process. It is
compromise, not in the abstract moral form, which philosophers
can sagely discuss, but in the practical form with which every
legislator who gets results through government is acquainted.
It is trading. It is the adjustment of interests.

Mr. Bentley applies his views to the problem of representative
government. "There is a theory," he says, "that all acts of
government ought to be the product of clear, cold reasoning, and
that the maximum of detachment on the part of the legislator
from the interests at stake will get the best results. We may say
that this is 'the' theory of political science, as it certainly is the
professed point of view of most criticisms of government and of
the theoretical statement of most schemes of reform which do not
get into too close contact with immediate application. According to it every point at which government gets away from the
purest and freest reasoning is an abnormal point. According to

it also the standards of justice and desirability are matters which reason alone, if left undisturbed, can solve." Our modern legislatures, he further says, are often disparaged in contrast with the good old times, and their lack of wise reasoning is made the mark of their degeneracy. Yet because they yield to pressures, he holds that they are representative bodies in their way.

So far as such a theory of group pressures emphasizes the fact that public opinion is rarely if ever the opinion of the public, the whole public, and nothing but the public, it is helpful; but once it is conceded that what we call public opinion is really the opinion of a group, then where there are conflicting groups the success of one of them merely means that its opinion predominates, which is what in common parlance we mean by public opinion. If one group wants a high tariff, another a low tariff, and a third free trade, and if high tariff carries the day, we say it is supported by public opinion, meaning thereby prevailing opinion. The same thing is true if there are no adverse groups of opinion, or none with cohesion and energy enough to make opposition felt. In that case, also, we speak of the group that demands, secures, or enforces a law as "public opinion," although of itself it may be insignificant in size or substance.

After having tracked public opinion from the public to a group of the public, the search for its origin has but begun. Sometimes the source, the spring, from which it wells, appears to be a book of originality and power. Very likely most American free traders would ascribe their inspiration to Mill's "Political Economy." The doctrine of executive responsibility, now so prominent, might be traced to Wilson's "Congressional Government," the first volume to catch the American ear with the theory that our fathers were wrong in separating the three powers, and that the British cabinet system is the better. Great ingenuity has been spent on giving all the credit for the basic ideas of the Federal Constitution to Pelatiah Webster. Equally ingenious and equally failing in conviction has been the attempt to credit to Holland and the Dutch all our institutions that are worth while. Take any one of these alleged origins and behind them you may find traces of still other origins until the train is lost in the mazes and mists of antiquity. And so it is if you look for the first impulse in what would be called an epoch-making speech or any human utterance. Behind the word is the brain, and what impelled the brain, who can tell?

Suppose, however, you do at last place the germ, the seed, how explain why it fell on fertile ground, why it ripened and fructified while many other seeds sown at the same time failed of their purpose? Or how explain the speed of growth? The oldest abolition society in the world was "The Society for the Relief of Free Negroes unlawfully held in Bondage," and it was formed by a score of men who gathered in the old Sun Tavern at Philadelphia five days before the battle of Lexington. From that hour to Lincoln's Emancipation Proclamation, eighty-eight years passed, and the result came about only as an incident to a great war. Meantime England had freed all the slaves in her dominions without firing a gun.

It is all a mystery. Sometimes it seems the work of a divine Providence, sometimes that of blind Chance — in either case inscrutable. Whether theist or atheist, explain if you can the episode Harriet Martineau described after her travels in America from 1834 to 1836.[1] "Lotteries," she said, "were formerly a great inducement to gaming in Massachusetts. Prudent fathers warned their sons against lotteries; employers warned their servants; clergymen warned their flocks. Tracts, denouncing lotteries, were circulated, much eloquence was expended — not in vain, though all sober people were already convinced, and weak people were still unable to resist the seduction. At length, a young man drowned himself. A disappointment in a lottery was found to be the cause. A thrill of horror ran through the community. Every man helped to carry his horror of lotteries into the Legislature; and their abolition followed in a trice."

Of course it is easy to see in this instance what instrument caused the explosion, just as you can see the hammer of a rifle strike the cartridge, but why did the explosion this time when the gun had missed fire a hundred times before? Or turning to another question, when every rational man in the country knew from his own observation the terrible effects of the abuse of intoxicating liquor, in poverty, suffering, misery, crime, death, why did public opinion so long delay the attempt to stop that abuse?

If, however, we were to yield to the belief that whatever the causes and the forces, they are wholly beyond human influence or control, then would the reformer live in vain, then would the legislator be a mere puppet in the hands of destiny. Fortunately

[1] *Society in America*, I, 26.

most men do not abandon the struggle. Most men are convinced
by experience and observation that the will of the individual
counts and can help. We know enough of the history of changes
in opinion to nurture confidence that we too in our turn can har-
ness fate.

Study of any revolution in public opinion is likely to disclose
the powerful influence of the imitative faculty. Some lead and
the many follow. Bagehot has given us an acute description of
this trait of human nature. The truth is, he says, that the pro-
pensity of man to imitate what is before him is one of the strongest parts of his nature. We must not think that this imitation is
voluntary, or even conscious. On the contrary, it has its seat
mainly in very obscure parts of the mind, whose notions, so far
from being consciously produced, are not even felt at the time.
Scarcely any one can help yielding to the current infatuations of
his sect or party. For a short time — say some fortnight — he
is resolute; he argues and objects; but, day by day, the poison
thrives, and reason wanes. What he hears from his friends,
what he reads in the party organ, produces its effect. The plain,
palpable conclusion which every one around him believes, has an
influence even greater and more subtle; that conclusion seems so
solid and unmistakable; his own good arguments get daily more
and more like a dream. Soon the gravest sage shares the folly of
the party with which he acts, and the sect with which he wor-
ships. The mere presentation of an idea, unless we are careful
about it, or unless there is within some unusual resistance, makes
us believe it; and this is why the belief of others adds to our belief so quickly, for no ideas seem so very clear as those inculcated
on us from every side.[1]

No more striking and saddening illustration of the truth of
this can be found than in the wretched story of the Salem witchcraft delusion. Read there how even the clergy and the magistrates, the wisest and best men of their time, were engulfed by
the tide of belief. Read the confession offered by Judge Samuel
Sewall on the occasion of the public fast appointed by the General Court, "that God would pardon all the errors of his servants
and people in a late tragedy, raised amongst us by Satan and his
instruments." Imagine the foremost magistrate of the Commonwealth standing in the church while the minister reads: "Samuel
Sewall, sensible of the repeated strokes of God upon himself and

[1] *Physics and Politics*, chap. III.

family, and being sensible that as to guilt contracted upon the opening of the late commission of Oyer and Terminer at Salem (to which the order for this day relates) he is upon many accounts more concerned than any that he knows of, desires to take the blame and the shame of it, asking pardon of men and especially desiring prayers that God who has an unlimited authority, would pardon that sin and all his other sins." Recall how Giles Corey suffered horrible death by the common-law judgment of *Peine forte et dure*. "As his aged frame yielded to the dreadful pressure, his tongue protruded from his mouth. The demon who presided over his torture, drove it back again with the point of his cane." Ponder all this and then decide for yourself whether public opinion should sway uncontrolled.

Such revelations of the weakness of humanity have led profound thinkers to see in the mob spirit the greatest menace to the safety of society. Fortunately public opinion goes mad only at rare intervals. Even in ordinary times it by no means gets the admiration of all observers. On the contrary, it is ever viewed with suspicion by those who mistrust the masses, and sometimes by those who are not without popular sympathies, as, for instance, Sir Robert Peel, who in a letter written in 1820 described "public opinion" as "that great compound of folly, weakness, prejudice, wrong feeling, right feeling, obstinacy, and newspaper paragraphs." In the same generation Hegel said: "In public opinion are contained all sorts of falsehood and truth." But he went on to add: "To find the truth in it is the business of the great man. He who tells his age what it wills and expresses, and brings that to fulfillment, is the great man of the age." [1]

Rousseau, with a more generous confidence in the people, saw the duty and opportunity of leadership in the same light. Of themselves the people always desire what is good, but do not always discern it, he said. The general will is always right, but the judgment which guides it is not always enlightened. It must be made to see objects as they are, sometimes as they ought to appear; it must be shown the good path that it is seeking, and guarded from the seduction of private interests; it must be made to observe closely times and places, and to balance the attrac-

---

[1] *Plut. des Rechts*, 318, p. 404; quoted by D. G. Ritchie, "On the Conception of Sovereignty," *Annals of the American Academy of Political and Social Science*, January, 1891.

tion of immediate and palpable advantages against the danger of remote and concealed evils. Individuals see the good which they reject; the public desire the good which they do not see. All alike have need of guides. The former must be compelled to conform their wills to their reason; the people must be taught to know what they require. Then from the public enlightenment results the union of the understanding and the will in the social body; and from that the close coöperation of the parts, and lastly, the maximum power of the whole. Hence arises the need of a legislator.[1]

Here Rousseau seems to recognize that law itself is a creator of opinion — a point of vast importance. In arguing that the legislative body should reflect the public will, we are apt to forget that such is not its only function. It has a double duty — it should lead as well as follow. Dicey has excellently explained the seeming paradox. Every law or rule of conduct must, whether its author perceives the fact or not, lay down or rest upon some general principle, and must therefore, if it succeeds in attaining its end, commend this principle to public attention or imitation, and thus affect legislative opinion. Nor is the success of a law necessary for the production of this effect. A principle derives prestige from its mere recognition by Parliament, and if a law fails in attaining its object, the argument lies ready to hand that the failure was due to the law not going far enough, i.e. to its not carrying out the principle on which it is founded to its logical consequences. The true importance, indeed, of laws lies far less in their direct result than in their effect upon the sentiment or convictions of the public.[2] "Legislative opinion is itself more often the result of facts than of philosophical speculation; and no facts play a more important part in the creation of opinion than laws themselves."[3]

It is this that justifies the legislator in constructive thought. Were it otherwise, he need never concern himself with more than trying to determine what the people want. Limited to a matter of interpretation, the task would never attract men of originality and genius. The race of statesmen would disappear. It will be a sad day when representatives are forbidden to think of what the people ought to want, a sad day when leadership becomes an offense.

[1] *The Social Compact*, book 2, chap. VI.
[2] *Law and Opinion in England*, 41.   [3] *Ibid.*, 463.

The skillful combination of the two functions makes the most useful legislature, and is the end at which the representative bodies of England and America really aim. The very scope and object of representation, well observed Lord John Russell, is to obtain a select body, who may not only have a sympathy with the people, but who may, by the habits of business which their number permits, and the judgment which their election implies, manage the interests of the country somewhat better than each town and county could do by petition and public meeting. "If you render the House of Commons a mere echo of the popular cry, you lose, on many questions, all the benefit of having a body in some degree capable of directing public opinion. I am aware that this argument may be easily pushed too far. I can only repeat, to explain my meaning, that the House of Commons ought to make such decisions as are either agreeable to the people at the time, or when they are not so, the weight of argument should be so great as to convince the country, within a short time afterwards, that the resolution or vote was adopted, not from any corrupt or sinister motive, but from an enlarged and sagacious view of the public interest." [1]

In our own time another English statesman, Morley, who sat in the House of Commons for quarter of a century, has voiced a like view. "Great economic and social forces," he observes, "flow with tidal sweep over communities only half conscious of that which is befalling them. Wise statesmen are those who foresee what time is thus bringing, and try to shape institutions and mould men's thought and purpose in accordance with the change that is slowly surrounding them." [2]

An American view of like purport is that of Professor Willoughby who says the test of good government is the facility it affords for the formulation of an intelligent and enlightened General Will, and the nearness with which its action harmonizes with such will when so formulated. [3]

It would seem self-evident that men engaged in the affairs of state are more likely than anybody else to conceive wise changes. For the time being their prime purpose, their vocation, is the observation and study of the machinery of government. They

---

[1] *An Essay on the History of the English Government and Constitution*, ed. of 1866, 186.

[2] John, Viscount Morley, *Recollections* (1917).

[3] *The Nature of the State*, 140.

best know why and where the machinery creaks and what new devices are needed. It is more than their passing privilege, it is their instant duty, to improve the processes where possible in order that the condition of society may be ameliorated. Therefore it is logical that those who write laws shall at times decide what public opinion ought to be, and inevitable that they will. Furthermore, as all bodies of men must be and are guided and usually dominated in important matters by a few of their number, the responsibility in the end attaches to those who for the time being are what we call the leaders. In reality, therefore, public opinion is in no small part the judgment of the few accepted by the many.

The legislative functions of leadership and what may be called followship tend to act against each other, like the centrifugal and centripetal forces in nature. Failure to understand this sometimes gets innovators into artificial, illogical, inconsistent positions. Such is the case of the man who with one breath argues that President or Governor should be a real leader, and with the next argues for more of popular control over lawmaking. Fortunately no great harm will come from emphasizing either function, provided the other is not altogether suppressed.

Ascertaining and Reflecting

Remembering, then, that there are two functions of a legislature, each to play its due part, let us consider how the one that concerns itself with reflecting the General Will may work the most efficiently.

Bryce has pointed out, in his chapters on Public Opinion, that one of the chief problems of free nations is to devise means whereby the national will shall be most fully expressed, most quickly known, most unresistingly and cheerfully obeyed. The obvious weakness of government by opinion is the difficulty of ascertaining it. If at any time the people desire measures which do not merely repeal a law or direct an appropriation, but establish some administrative scheme, or mark out some positive line of financial policy, or provide some body of rules for dealing with such a topic as bankruptcy, railroad or canal communications, the management of public lands, and so forth, the people must decide for themselves what they want and put their wishes into practical shape. In other words, public opinion must hammer out a project, and present it to Congress or to the State

Legislature (as the case may be), with such a voice of command as to compel its embodiment in and passage as an Act. But public opinion has no machinery available for the purpose.

Bryce meant, of course, "no adequate machinery," or else he would have had to find some other than the natural explanation of parties and their platforms, as well as all the rest of the electing process. In theory the very purpose of an election is to express the public will and give it effect. In practice, an election is a crude, lumbering, awkward machine that most imperfectly and inadequately carries out its purpose. Its fundamental weakness comes from its attempt to do more than one thing at a time. By it legislators are chosen to decide a thousand questions. Party platforms often include a score of more or less unrelated propositions. The Progressive party platform of 1912 contained nearly sixty. As a matter of fact an election never clearly demonstrates the public will on more than one question, that which has been uppermost in the public mind. Even then there is no certainty unless the issue has been outstanding, for if there have been other issues important though not predominant, they may have determined enough votes to make the apparent majority deceptive.

Although this does not regularly take place, it is extreme to hold with Professor Sumner that public interest cannot be active on more than one question at once. Sumner's propositions were that the uneducated man cannot embrace in his attention a number of subjects at the same time; the educated man can embrace a large number, but his doubts are more numerous as to them all; there is never but one platform plank that is direct and clear; this is the one on which party coherence depends for the time being; the other planks are transparent attempts to say something which two men of opposite opinions may understand each to suit himself.[1] The argument gives too much weight to platforms, assumes too much of them, ascribes to them an influence that in fact is not invariable. Sometimes, as in the presidential campaign of 1928, voters are powerfully influenced by issues ignored in the platforms, or glossed over, which the electorate nevertheless forces to the front by reason of the personality of candidates or their known views.

Yet it is true that usually one issue is paramount, never do more than three or four issues play a part of consequence, and

[1] *Collected Essays on Political and Social Science*, 114.

always the presence of more than one influential issue brings uncertainty as to what in fact is the preponderance of public opinion. For these reasons President A. Lawrence Lowell well builds his "Public Opinion in War and Peace" on the postulate that as election is a choice between alternatives, the fewer of them the better. "When a new decision is made by a large body of men among alternatives presented to them, the more they are limited, the more real and intelligent the choice will be."[1] And further: "The presenting of a single pair of alternatives is not a perfectly accurate method of ascertaining collective opinion, but it is on the whole less imperfect than any other."[2]

Professor Sumner declared that the theory of elections, when tested by experience, proves false in four of its most important assumptions: (a) the voters have not their opinions already formed whenever the election day comes around; (b) they will not deliver their opinions without fear or favor whenever the election day comes; (c) they will not decide their votes purely in view of the public welfare; (d) the mechanism of the ballot is not a simple and adequate means of expressing the public will.[3]

Such criticisms seem to me extreme in some particulars. They really do not help much so far as they call attention to weaknesses of human nature that would in greater or less degree impair any method of ascertaining the general will. Fear and favor are somewhat less conspicuous in the secret ballot of a large electorate than they are in most other governmental devices. To say that the people will not decide their votes purely in view of the public welfare, imputes to them motives that at any rate are not universal. All and even many of their opinions are indeed not formed before election day, but some of them, and those in fact the most important, usually are. Yet there is no disputing his last charge, that the ballot is not a simple and adequate means of expressing the public will.

How can you express your own will on a dozen public questions by voting for a man with eleven of whose views you may differ, your vote being determined by a chance agreement on the twelfth? And how shall the man you have elected know that he has been chosen because any one particular opinion he holds is held by even a majority of those who voted?

If government were a matter of isolated problems that could

[1] *Public Opinion in War and Peace*, 169.   [2] *Ibid.*, 170.
[3] *Collected Essays on Political and Social Science*, 136.

be handled separately, one at a time, political parties would function more accurately in the disclosure of public opinion, but that is so inconsistent with their nature and the facts of the situation as to make the idea visionary. Lowell rightly holds that the question is not whether political parties are good or evil, for a consideration of the way public opinion is formed and made politically effective in a democracy, as well as the actual experience of all large democratic countries, shows that they are inevitable.[1] He thinks that if they present perfectly clear, definite alternatives on every political question, they are performing their function to the fullest extent. Yet it seems to me that without harm to themselves or loss to the public they would perform their function far better if they ignored a multitude of minor matters that now crowd their platforms, where declarations change an insignificant number of votes, and if they have any effect on the election at all, secure it at the expense of the major issues.

In passing, however, it should be noted that although the minor planks of party platforms do little in the way of bringing out the opinion of the masses, they do disclose the judgment of a serious group of men who take a real interest in public affairs, a judgment expressed, too, with some element of responsibility. Burton Y. Berry has made an illuminating study of the result in one of the States, Indiana.[2] He found that of sixty-seven platform planks presented by the successful parties in the twenty years from 1900 to 1920, forty-one met the approval of the Legislature; thirty-six were accepted by the Governor and made administration measures. Of those supported by him seventy per cent became law; of those not supported by him, fifty per cent. Although less than three per cent of all the legislation in that period could be traced to conformance with platforms, that three per cent was of the policy forming type and so was highly important. Berry thinks the tendency is to give the platform a more important place in politics, and to increase its prestige by introducing more specific planks. "The political platform and the Governor's message," he says, "have a greater influence on legislation in Indiana than all other factors combined."

Returning to the election system, we further find it proceeding

[1] *Public Opinion in War and Peace*, 187.

[2] "Influence of Political Platforms in Indiana," *American Political Science Review*, February, 1923.

on the theory that the man who fails to represent his constituents, that is, fails to judge rightly what they want, will be punished by defeat when he comes up for reëlection, and thus by anticipation will somehow be kept in the right path. Of course the fear of punishment may make him more assiduous in studying public opinion and trying to find which way it inclines. But is not reliance on that by the community very much like locking the stable door after the horse is stolen? As a matter of fact, however, few things are more futile than the academic theory that the people do at the polls seriously pass judgment on the votes of their representatives. Occasionally by reason of a "salary grab" vote or some other that arouses public wrath, a representative will be defeated, but such cases are most exceptional. Generally the punishment is unfair, for it is inflicted without giving any credit for the scores of times the representative has voted as his constituency wished.

Worrying legislators who try to anticipate retribution sometimes resort to amusing precautions. Governor Thomas Ford in his "History of Illinois" (p. 284) tells of the origin of a system of voting devised for his own guidance by John Grammar, a man who despite his name could neither read nor write, yet was shrewd enough to keep himself in the Legislature for a quarter of a century. He set the example for those politicians who make it a rule to vote against all new measures, about which the opinions of the people are unknown; shrewdly calculating that if such a measure passes and becomes popular, no one will inquire who had opposed it; but if it turns out to be unpopular, then they can show by the Journal that they voted against it. And if the measure fails of success and becomes popular, the members who opposed it excuse themselves to the people by pretending ignorance of the will of their constituents and by promising to be in its favor if again elected. Fortunately so clumsy a process as this has not much commended itself.

When defeat comes, it is often the work of a small fraction of the electorate, that fraction which is said to hold the balance of power and is called the independent vote. From election to election this vote sways back and forth between the parties, accomplishing indeed a purpose desirable in many aspects, yet quite inconsistent with the theory that election results normally show the will of the majority in regard to a particular question. The balance of power is never held by a majority; its very name implies a minority. Suppose 45 per cent of the electors vote by reason of approving in general the greater part of one set of party principles, and 45 per cent by approving in general the greater part of an opposing set. Then if the 10 per cent controlling the result are moved by a single principle, all the election proves is what one voter in ten thinks on any particular question. Surely this is no demonstration of the popular will.

Instances have not been unknown in our public life where a representative has seemed to cater deliberately to this independent vote, establishing a favor with it that has kept him in office long after his own party would gladly have replaced him with a man more loyal to party principles. The party has not dared attempt the change lest the independent representative accept a nomination from the other side and so with the help of the independents keep his seat. The practical effect in such cases has been to make the result a matter of tactics and give the real representation to a tithe or less of the voters.

Another fallacy of the theorists is to be found in the notion that candidates are preferred because of their pronounced support of specific opinions. Sometimes this happens, but far from often enough to prove that opinions are commonly reflected in the choice of candidates. If ever this had been the case surely it would have been in the New England town-meetings, famed for their deliberative qualities. Yet Francis B. Crowninshield of Boston said to the Massachusetts Convention of 1853: "I know something of the proceedings of a town-meeting, and I must confess that I was a little astonished when the gentleman for Manchester [R. H. Dana, Jr., of Cambridge] alluded to the debates and deliberations which take place in these town-meetings as to the qualifications of Mr. A. or Mr. B., or of the qualifications of this candidate or that for the office of representative. Why, Sir, such a thing, I apprehend, was never heard of at any town-meeting for the choice of representative, in the Commonwealth of Massachusetts, as for a debate to arise upon any subject touching that election, unless it were the subject of whether they should send a representative or none at all." The situation is even more pronounced to-day, for the growth of cities and the mechanical development of the nominating process have made consideration and discussion of particular opinions held by candidates almost impossible, at any rate in the primary itself. These opinions are disclosed only in the comparatively few cases where a candidate invites support on the ground of a specific, particular issue.

There was a time when town-meetings did discuss questions of State-wide concern. It was long ago, in the Revolutionary period. As a matter of historical interest it may be worth while to describe a typical instance, taken at random from the returns of action on the Massachusetts Constitution. The record begins: "At a legal meeting of the Freeholders and other Inhabitants of the Town of Granville on May the 8th, 1780, the Selectmen of said Town laid before them the Constitution or Form of Government framed by the Convention of the State of Massachusetts Bay, they taking the same into consideration passed the following votes on the several articles in said Constitution." Then follow the figures of 99 separate votes, one on each of the 99 articles. The total vote on the first article was 45. By the time they reached the 25th, the attendance had risen to 86. There were 71 men still voting when they reached the 93rd article, but probably it was getting late, for only 42 stayed through the 99th. Fourteen of the articles met with substantial opposition. Two (articles 2 and 3 of Ch. 6, Pt. 2) were unanimously disapproved. Less than two thirds were unanimously favored.

The objections and reasons were set forth in three cases. Let me quote one to show the old-time capacity of a New England town for passing deliberate judgment on serious matters of principle. Remember this was one of the remote towns of the State, far from the center of learning. Here is the entry:

"1st. Christ himself is the only Lord of Conscience and King and Lawgiver in his Church. Teachers of religion are officers in his kingdom, qualified and sent by him, for whose maintenance he hath made sufficient provision, by the laws which belong to his own kingdom. Therefore no supplementary laws of human legislatures are necessary.

"2nd. The interference of the magistrate in matters that belong to the Christian Church, is, in our view, an encroachment on the kingly office of Jesus Christ, who stands in no need of the help of any civil legislature whatever, consequently is an affront to him.

"3rd. The interference of the civil magistrate in matters that belong to Christ and conscience, ever has been and ever will be productive of oppression to mankind. There could be no persecution if the civil magistrate did not support the power and cruelty of men of narrow and ambitious minds.

"4th. True religion has evidently declined and been corrupted by the interference of statesmen and politicians. Church history proves this to have been the case from the days of Constantine down to our own day."

Save for punctuation and capitalization, this is as written. But one error in spelling is found — "currupted" — and very likely this was a slip of the pen. The episode is typical, not exceptional.

The plan of government first drawn up by the New Hampshire Convention that met in 1781 was printed and sent to every town. The inhabitants were requested to state their objections distinctly to any particular part, and return them at a fixed time. The objections were so many and so various that it became necessary to alter the form and send it out a second time.[1]

The early democrats saw in such episodes ground for their insistence that, as Walter Lippman happily puts it, "a reasoned righteousness welled up spontaneously out of the mass of men."[2] If, however, the exceptional conditions of a revolutionary period stirred the public intellect into a spasm of creative activity, it was not to persist. No longer do we see such discussion as that in New Hampshire or like discussion both when the Massachusetts Constitution was shaping and when fifteen years after its adoption the appointed time came for considering revision. That sort of thing is all gone. Anything like community discussion of matters having more than local concern is nowhere to be found. Even the Initiative and Referendum does not so much as contemplate it, judging by the machinery provided. Nowadays, without concerted discussion, without systematic argument, without deliberative procedure, public opinion is mainly left to its own resources for means of shaping and expression.

The first result is to raise a doubt as to whether such a thing as a definite, concrete body of public opinion exists at all beyond a very, very few matters having what may be called a social interest, such as prohibition or sectarianism. If it does exist in respect of political problems in general, how are you going to explain such an outcome, for example, as that of the attempt of the Richmond, Va., "Times-Dispatch" in 1925, to learn what was the preference of the people for Governor and also how they stood on five important issues to confront the next General

[1] Jeremy Belknap, *History of New Hampshire*, ii, 335.
[2] *Public Opinion*, 257.

Assembly? A hundred thousand ballots were sent out. Only 7654 voters returned their ballots, and of these voters only about four fifths had an opinion on the legislative problems at issue. Even when the inquiry takes the simplest possible form, with but a single question to be answered and that by "Yes" or "No," the result is not essentially more significant. When the payment of a soldiers' bonus perplexed Congress, Representative Allen T. Treadway of Massachusetts sent letters to about 79,000 voters of his district asking them to fill in an enclosed card by saying whether they were for or against a bonus. It was the livest sort of an issue, the subject of great interest and wide discussion. Yet only about 10,000 voters returned the cards.

Large-scale episodes of this sort are not exceptional. On a much smaller scale I myself made an illuminating experiment. Puzzled by a technical problem before one of my committees, I sent a request for opinion and advice to a score and more of leading men in the vocational group concerned, a group in which might be expected intelligence of a high order as well as complete familiarity with the principles involved. Not one gave me a definite answer or a helpful judgment.

If, however, there are public opinions more generally than such experiences indicate, can they be deliberately extracted? Lippman, speaking of the democrats of the post-Revolutionary period, says one thing was certain: if public opinion did not come forth spontaneously, nobody in that age believed it would come forth at all. It seems to me that to-day there is even more ground for such a belief, by reason of the growth of population as well as its disintegration into groups with clashing interests. Anyhow, studied ascertaining of the popular will is a far more perplexing matter than it was in the simpler days of our fore-fathers. As I have said elsewhere,[1] the most difficult task that confronts the legislator is to find out what may be the preponderance of public opinion on any given topic. I incline to think that the harder he works to find this out, the less he accomplishes. At every turn of his activity he invites deception. He can safely put reliance on no popular vote. Lack of information is the predominant and sufficient cause. Rare, very rare, is the voter who has acquainted himself with all the facts and who has read or heard thorough argument from both sides. Few, very few, are the men and women who study public questions and reflect upon

[1] Robert Luce, *Congress — An Explanation*, 48 et sqq.

what they learn. Most persons have not the leisure, the patience, the training, or the inclination for such tasks.

Response to individual inquiry is misleading. Suppose a Representative in Congress should write, asking an opinion, to each of the 100,000 or so of persons qualified to vote in his district. Experience shows he could not get response from one tenth. How about the other nine tenths and more? Of them it might be said by way of paraphrase, you can lead a man to logic, but you can't make him think. Supposing the dumb can give an opinion if they want to, what likelihood is there that the few who can be induced to respond will give a fair sample of the judgment of the whole, in view of the fact that some will be the zealots, some the men who give snap judgment on anything, and most will have heard but one side of the question?

Petitions are even more untrustworthy. In the secrecy of the polling booth the voter will exercise his own judgment, if he has any, but when with many others he signs a petition, there is no warrantable presumption that he knows what he is asking or expresses his own view. So many men sign petitions because they are asked and for one reason or another do not want to refuse, that no experienced legislator will dare to put trust in them. Resolutions are almost as futile. When they have been the subject of earnest, informed discussion, they count, but the argument has usually been one-sided and the perfunctory factor is large.

The newspapers are more helpful. Editorials are the studied work of men more or less informed, who have had some training in the ascertainment and interpretation of the popular mind. It is their business to gather the raw material of public opinion, manufacture it, and sell the product to a public willing to pay for seeing its own ideas in print — sometimes, to be sure, ideas the readers never knew they had, but the ownership of which they will not disavow. Yet editors are no more nearly infallible than legislators, and though they help, they do not suffice.

Where, then, shall the lawmaker turn to know what the public really wants? Nowhere, and yet everywhere. If he but talks and listens and reads, a thousand influences will gradually mould his judgment, and presently he will find himself voting as the greater part of his constituents would vote if they had the information and were in his place.

Mysterious though its processes, public opinion somehow

dominates. Gradually legislators who get out of harmony with
it, are supplanted. Constant changes in the membership of our
legislative bodies are ever bringing in men fresh from the centres
of social activity where it is in the making. During the term of
service it is at work all the time through the newspaper, the
pulpit, the platform, the club, through all sorts of societies and
associations, and through the personal interplay of ideas that
goes on wherever men converse. Since no legislator isolates himself, no legislator escapes. For the most part unbeknownst to
himself, these things usually make him a real representative of
public opinion.

Of late what may prove to be a problem of the first magnitude
has grown out of the selfish origin and artificial propagation of
influences. The manufacture of public opinion has become an
industry. "Propaganda" is the name for it that was implanted
in the dialect of public affairs by the World War. So successfully
was it then used in developing and shaping the popular will for
purposes of thrift, sacrifice, loyalty, all the ends essential to
united and enthusiastic support of the national interest in the
great struggle, that class, group, and corporate interests recognized in it an effective device for increasing power and securing
advantage. A decade had not passed after the Armistice before
it was found that the science of creating opinion had been developed most skillfully and to what alarmists thought the danger
point. So far, however, as legislators are concerned, apprehension need not be unbounded. Your Congressman is not easily
deceived. Should you watch him run through his bulky mail and
observe the speed and accuracy with which he throws much the
greater part of it in the waste-basket, you would be reassured.
Most of the propagandists overdo the thing. The mere volume
of one-sided argument, evidently of self-interested origin, puts the
legislator on his guard. Not only with him but also with the public,
incessant repetition of half-truths becomes tiresome, and not infrequently breeds more of hostile prejudice than sympathetic
support. In politics as in Nature, pests are their own undoing.

Nevertheless propaganda must be included among the influences that have some share in determining the legislator's
course. For the most part, however, he is thereby affected unconsciously, and it is hardly fair to attach to him overmuch
responsibility, whether in this instance or in the other cases
where covert influences shape his judgment. The real issue is

whether he should knowingly yield to them or even deliberately
invite them. So many legislators are believed to follow this
course that critics lament. Bryce, for example, has said that
nothing is more remarkable about our State Legislatures than
their timidity. "No one seems to think of having an opinion of
his own. In matters which touch the interests of his constituents,
a member is, of course, their humble servant. In burning party
questions — they are few, and mostly personal — he goes with
his party. In questions of general public policy he looks to see
how the cat jumps; and is ready to vote for anything which the
people, or any active section of the people, cry out for, though of
course he may be secretly unfriendly, and may therefore slyly
try to spoil a measure." [1] This is altogether too severe. It may
be true of many representatives, but my own observation at
close range leads me to contest it stoutly when applied to legislators as a whole. Even if it were true of a numerical majority,
which I very much doubt, it is not often true of that small group
of men who really determine legislation. In every Legislature
the bulk of the work is done by from a fifth to a tenth of the
members, who by reason of excelling ability or longer experience
naturally control. These men are for the most part men of
courage and seriousness, men accustomed to do their own thinking, men who by nature are more used to lead than to follow. It
has not been my experience that such men are unduly attentive
to popular impulses, or that they "keep their ears to the ground"
more than is legitimate and expedient where a republican form of
government prevails.

Bryce is more just when he says "experience shows that good
men are the better for a sense of their responsibility and ordinary
men useless without it." And he recognizes the true situation
when he recalls what Lincoln said in his famous contest against
Douglass: "With public sentiment on its side, everything succeeds; with public sentiment against it, nothing succeeds."
Lieber has forcibly shown why the legislator must remember
this, if his work is to have any value. Public opinion, he says,
is not only an opinion pronounced upon some subject, but it is
likewise that which daily and hourly interprets laws, carries
them along or stops their operation, which makes it possible to
have any written laws, and without which the wisest law might
be made to mean nonsense. It is that which makes it possible to

[1] *The American Commonwealth*, chap. 44.

prescribe and observe forms without their becoming a daily
hindrance of the most necessary procedures and actions; it is
that mighty power which abrogates the most positive laws and
gives vast extent to the apparently narrow limits of others; according to which a monarch ever so absolute in theory cannot do
a thousand things; which renders innocent what was most
obnoxious, and at times makes useless the best intentioned
measures, protecting sometimes even crime.[1]

What, then, is the task of the statesman? Mulford has admirably answered.[2] The statesman must learn to estimate the
strength and the weakness of public opinion, and when and how
to disregard it. It is always to be considered and weighed as a
positive force in the conduct of affairs, and those who acted in
indifference to it, would expose their measures to the unnecessary
risk of disaster. It is to be regarded in any course of action, with
respect to what it may indicate in the mind of the people. But so
far from any immediate representation of it, it is always to be
held as a force which has not even a law of discrimination, whereby its own thought and purpose may become clear. The disposition to overestimate it is a characteristic of weakness. It is more
often not itself clear, and instead of being the guide of the State,
needs a firmer intelligence to guide it. He who would have even
its support in the long run, must be strong alike to lead and resist; he must learn to apprehend the enduring purpose of the
people, and to hold it against betrayal. The danger is that men
who are untrue to themselves, and thus without a self-respect or
rectitude, will listen for it blindly, and follow its uncertain
voices, until in their weakness they lose their foothold, and are
swept away by its current. Public opinion cannot and is not to
govern. To regard the government as only its representative,
would argue a defect of will. There would be in it the subversion
of personality. The power which became its exponent to indicate its courses and the shift in its changes, would be no longer
a real government. It would open the way to "unstable slight-
ness." It would yield in the panic of unformed thought. It
would be the regiment of those who start at the shaking of the
leaves. In the agitation and surging of its crowd, they that
would aim to follow it must leave the place of leaders, and become lost in its multitude as their call is drowned in the tumult.
If they rise for a moment upon it, it is only to be swept away by
the tide.

[1] *Manual of Political Ethics*, 2d ed., I, 223.　　　　[2] *The Nation*, 240.

CHAPTER XXIV

THE INITIATIVE AND REFERENDUM

In tracing the growth of representative government we have seen that the making of laws by mass vote, a characteristic of the city republics of the ancient world, virtually disappeared with those republics. Something of the sort probably existed in the Germanic tribes from which Western civilization sprang, but when their records began to be set down on paper, the common practice was for the chieftain to make the laws, which were then approved or rejected by the people or their spokesmen. Thus the famous capitularies of Charlemagne were at least nominally submitted to popular judgment. For example, in 803 after the great Emperor had made certain additions to the Salic Law, he instructed the *missi dominici* — the staff officers sent into every province — as follows: "Let the people be interrogated touching the articles which have recently been added to the law; and after they have all consented to them, let them affix to the said articles their signatures in confirmation."

In Saxon and Danish England, and even after the Conquest, we read of the share of the Witenagemot in the creation of law, but the early Norman monarchs found this little to their liking and presently the practice gave way to that ordered representation of the kingdom which came to be known as Parliament. From then on there was in England nothing suggestive of mass voting on measures until Parliaments came to be dissolved in order that by a new election of members the popular will on a disputed measure could be directly manifested.

On the Continent, unless it was in such primitive communities as those making up Switzerland or in such tiny republics as those of Andorra and San Marino, mass voting on laws was for many centuries unknown. It came to the surface again with the revolutionary ideas that inspired the French in their National Convention of 1793. The impotent Constitution then framed would have given to the primary assemblies of the communes the opportunity to pass judgment on any law proposed by the national legislative body. If within forty days after submission one tenth of all the primary meetings of more than half the

Departments had not protested, the bill was to become law. In case of the required amount of protest, the primary meetings were to be called together for a mass vote. Framed by the Robespierre party, the fall of its leader prevented any test of this programme, and nothing of the sort was provided in the Constitution of 1795.

The idea was akin to that of the Swiss method of lawmaking, but with one distinct difference, for although in each case decision was to be with the people, in France the law was to come down to them, whereas in Switzerland, at any rate in part, it went up from the people. From its beginning as a defensive league in the thirteenth century, Switzerland was a federation of democracies, and in some of these the people have never ceased to make their own laws and vote their own taxes. The solemn conclaves for this purpose, known as Landsgemeinde, held once a year or oftener, with attendance sometimes running up to ten or eleven thousand, have often been proclaimed by lovers of democracy as the finest type of self-government — an honor, however, to which the New England town-meeting has equal right.

Federation, whether of communes in a district, or of cantons in a league, compelled acceptance of representation, but the Swiss were so loath to let their rights go beyond control that they instructed their delegates, and required that if a delegate would deviate from his instructions or if a new question arose, he should come back to his constituents for their approval. So the councils or diets or whatever they were called, voted *ad referendum*. That phrase, familiar in this connection at least four centuries ago, has given to the world the name for a lawmaking process that to-day is one of the most interesting topics of political science.

It will be observed that in so far as the Swiss instructed their delegates, thereby the people themselves began the lawmaking process, in other words, took the *initiative*. When in modern time this method was developed and formulated, "initiative" was the word adopted for its description. The combination of the two names, "initiative" and "referendum," into "the Initiative and Referendum," has given us a clumsy phrase, inexact in its significance, often loosely applied, wholly unsatisfactory whether for scientific description or everyday use. More attractive is the term "direct legislation," but this is far from synonymous with "the Initiative and Referendum" and may add to confusion. However, taking the terms as we find them, we shall approach clear thinking if we try to restrict "initiative" to that independent process whereby an electorate begins the making of a law; "referendum" to that process whereby an electorate completes or prevents the making of a law; and "direct legislation" to that process of lawmaking wherein a representative body plays either a subordinate part or no part at all.

Taking modern form, the Swiss Referendum first appeared in the German-speaking canton of Saint Gallen in 1831. A Constitution being in process of revision, the opposing parties, one favoring pure democracy, the other representative government, compromised on a system whereby laws enacted by an assembly should take effect unless within forty-five days the people had refused to sanction them, a communal assembly to pass judgment being necessary within that time if demanded by fifty citizens. A majority of all registered electors was required in order to reject.

It will be seen that this was in the nature of a permissive veto. In 1839 the Valais adopted a variant by which the meeting of the communal assemblies was made compulsory, an absolute majority of the registered voters still being required to reject. This was modified in 1844 by substituting a majority of those voting. Other cantons copied the idea, the progress being rapid after 1860, until the Referendum, either compulsory or optional, became general. In some of the cantons the absolute majority is required in order to reject, in others a majority of those voting. Where the Optional Referendum prevails, the time within which it must be requested is usually thirty days, and the number of signatures required varies from five hundred to a thousand, according to the size of the canton.

It is not without significance that the Referendum was embodied in the Swiss Constitution after it had received thorough test in the cantons. Its compulsory application to constitutional amendments has nothing of novelty for us of America, who are quite accustomed to its use in like matters, but with its application to federal laws we are not yet familiar. In Switzerland by Article 89 of the Constitution federal laws are to be submitted to the people for adoption or rejection on the demand of 30,000 citizens, or eight cantons. The same requirement is made in the case of federal decrees of a general bearing and not of an urgent nature.

Both for the cantons and the confederation the Initiative came into use years after they respectively adopted the Referendum. The first canton to apply the Initiative was that of Vaud in 1845, its use spreading to the others until now every canton but one has it for amendment of the Constitution and all but three have it for ordinary cantonal laws. Amendment of the Federal Constitution may begin with a demand of 50,000 voters, either expressing their desire in general terms or putting it in concrete form. If the desire has been expressed in general terms and the Federal Assembly favors, that body submits a draft to the people; if the Assembly does not favor the proposal, it asks the people whether the desired amendment shall be made, and if the vote is in the affirmative, then puts the proposal in proper and final shape, reliance being placed on the Assembly to carry out fairly the wish of the petitioners. However, the petitioners may by submitting their proposal in final shape require that it shall be submitted in such form to the people and cantons for adoption.

In other European lands after the World War the turn to democracy naturally led to study of the Swiss example. Germany and Prussia put the Initiative and Referendum into their new Constitutions, and several of the smaller countries of the Continent proceeded likewise. The Irish Free State did the same, but there the dangerous possibilities of the system have aroused a strong sentiment for taking it out of the Constitution and its life may be short.

IN AMERICA

Both the Referendum and the Initiative appeared very early in the New England colonies. These colonies were federations of towns and it is instructive to note that instinctively they balked at complete delegation of lawmaking power to representative assemblies. The little democracies that gathered in town-meetings resented the idea of letting their delegates pass beyond their control. Probably they knew nothing about the custom of the Swiss cantons. Quite independently they worked out their own theory of democracy.

The first provision for the Referendum in America is to be found in the history of Plymouth Colony. The law arranging for representation in the General Court, March 5, 1638, contained this most interesting stipulation: "Provided that the laws they

THE INITIATIVE AND REFERENDUM

do enact shall be propounded one Court to be considered upon
until the next Court, and then to be confirmed if they shall be
approved of (except the case require present confirmation) And
if any act shall be confirmed by the Bench and Committees
[Representatives] which upon further deliberation shall prove
prejudicial to the whole that the freemen at the next election
Court after meeting together may repeal the same and enact any
other useful for the whole." [1]

Five years later when the New England Confederation was
formed, for defense against the Indians, by representatives of
Massachusetts, Connecticut, New Haven, and New Plymouth,
the delegates from Plymouth referred the Articles of Confederation to the people of their colony and refrained from signing
until the Articles had received the popular assent.

The Massachusetts Bay colony never went to the same length
as did Plymouth in exposing all the legislation of its General
Court to popular disapproval, but it early recognized that certain of the more important measures might well require the
general acceptance. When in 1639 a joint committee of the
Magistrates and Deputies was charged with drawing up into one
model those models that might be presented "concerning a form
of government and laws to be established," it was further directed to "take order that the same shall be copied and sent to
the several towns, that the elders of the churches and freemen
may consider of them against the next General Court." [2] This
was not a referendum in the modern sense, for evidently the last
word rested with the General Court rather than with the people,
but it showed at any rate a belief that the electorate should be
consulted in as grave a matter as that of drafting a fundamental
code resembling in some particulars a Constitution. From this it
was no long step to the submitting of laws for popular approval
and we find the General Court declaring, November 13, 1644,
when a new plan for choosing that body was proposed, that "if
the freemen shall accept thereof," a trial of it is to be made for a
year. "Every town shall forthwith, namely, by the last of the
next month, send in under the hands of their late deputies their
vote, assenting or dissenting to this proposition." [3] Unfortunately the records make no further reference to the matter, but if

[1] *Plymouth Colony Records*, x, 31.
[2] *Records of the Colony of the Mass. Bay in N.E.*, i, 279.
[3] *Ibid.*, ii, 88.

the vote was actually taken, it must have been in the negative. Complete record of a referendum begins in the Court of November 11, 1647, when a law reducing the number of deputies of each town from two to one, was suspended, and a referendum upon it ordered. In the following March this entry was made: "The most of the freemen desiring their former liberty of sending one or two deputies to the General Courts from time to time, the former wonted liberty is continued, and the former act in suspence is repealed." [1]

Still more interest attaches to the early experiment in Rhode Island, where the Initiative and Referendum were combined in a system that for elaboration and complication almost matches the intricate methods of to-day. When the loose form of government sufficing for a decade and more after Roger Williams settled Providence in 1636, was supplanted by the General Assembly in Portsmouth (1647), a unique method of passing laws was provided. The right to originate laws, the Initiative, was primarily vested in the towns, then four in number. Any proposed law was first to be discussed in a town-meeting, and if there approved was to be sent to the other towns for like discussion and vote. Then the matter was to be handed over to committees of six men from each town, who were to meet in a General Court; and if therein assembled they found the proposal had been favored by a majority of the colony, it was to be promulgated, without revision by the Court, and was to stand as a law until what we would now call the Obligatory Referendum had been applied, for the next general assembly of all the people was to decide whether it should continue as a law or not.

The Initiative did not rest exclusively in the towns. If the General Court, having disposed of the matters for which it was called, found anything else seeming to require action, it might debate and decide what to recommend to the towns. Here, it will be seen, was the Referendum precisely as of old among the Swiss cantons. A proposal thus reported to the Rhode Island towns was to be debated and voted upon in the town-meetings. The votes were sealed and sent to the General Recorder of the colony, who opened and counted them in the presence of the President. If a majority of the voters had favored, the proposal was to stand as a law until confirmed or repealed by the next General Assembly.

[1] *Records of the Colony of the Mass. Bay in N.E.*, II, 209, 217, 231.

The towns kept their share in the Initiative only three years. Presumably it was found too cumbrous. Whatever the reason, a revision of the system in 1650 confined the Initiative to the "Representative Committee," as the assembly of the town committees was to be called. Any laws that this body might enact were to be sent to the towns within six days after adjournment, there to be read in town-meeting within three days. Any freeman who disliked the laws thus submitted, or any one of them, might send his negative vote, with his name upon it, to the General Recorder, and if that official found the majority in any town to be against a law, it was thereby annulled.

This extreme application of the Referendum is to be explained by the reluctance of the little democracies to give up their independence. Only piecemeal did they accept federation. The next concession was in 1658 when it was agreed that a law should not be annulled unless the majority in each of the towns was against it. This did not meet the need and two years later another modification required disapproval by a majority of all the votes from all the towns put together, in order to nullify. At every change more time was allowed for deliberation and report, until at the last "four score and six days" were permitted in which to make the return. The system disappeared with the charter of 1663, the General Assembly of March 1, 1663–64, passing a resolution that deprived the people of their right to vote for general laws after approval by their deputies.

Perhaps Connecticut was the first to accomplish anything like a constitutional amendment by the use of the Referendum. The Fundamental Orders had forbidden the immediate reëlection of a Governor. John Winthrop, Jr., son of the famous John Winthrop of Massachusetts Bay, was chosen Governor in 1657, and served with so much satisfaction that the people wanted him again. So toward the close of his term the General Assembly ordered the Secretary to insert in the next warrant for the choice of Representatives an article removing the restriction on reeligibility. The amendment was carried and a "liberty of free choice yearly" was thus provided.

These early colonial instances of lawmaking shared by the people bore no fruit of consequence at once. Development was along the lines of strengthening representative government rather than toward pure democracy. It was not the case, however, that the powers of the General Courts and Assemblies passed beyond control. Notably in Massachusetts, as we have seen, the people became accustomed to make known their will by an indirect form of Initiative in the shape of instructions. The next step was for the lawmaking body to ask them. In the beginning of the Revolution the Massachusetts House of Representatives resolved to recommend to the towns that might send a member or members to the next General Assembly, "to possess him or them with their Sentiments relative to a Declaration of Independence of the United Colonies of Great Britain to be made by Congress and to instruct them what Conduct they would have them observe with regard to the next General Assemblys Instructing the Delegates of this Colony on that Subject." The Council voted not to concur, but the House adhered to its resolve, which was accordingly printed in the newspapers for the benefit of the towns. The record of the returns is incomplete, but it is known that of thirty-eight towns, only one voted against the proposed Declaration, and in most of the towns the vote for it appears to have been unanimous.

Here, it will be seen, the process was in the nature of a Referendum rather than of the Initiative. It was natural that the democratic spirit of the time should bring each into play. How far that spirit carried the radical men of the day can be gathered from the resolution of the town of Ashfield, in Hampshire County: "That all Acts passed by the General Court of the State respecting the several towns be sent to the several towns for their acceptance before they shall be in force." The proposal of such an innovation was premature. In ordinary matters the people were still willing to put complete trust in their representatives. However, the Constitution they presently adopted not only recognized the right of the people to initiate legislation by instructing their Representatives or by petitions to their legislative body — a right also recognized in other Constitutions — but also gave formal countenance to the principle of the Referendum by saying: "No subsidy, charge, tax, impost, or duties ought to be established, fixed, laid, or levied, under any pretext whatsoever, *without the consent of the people* or their representatives in the legislature." [1] In the application and extension of this principle Massachusetts led the other States. Its first use in a matter of high importance came in the course of the agitation of thirty-five years for setting off the District of Maine as an

[1] *Bill of Rights*, Art. XXIII.

independent State. Six times the people of the District were called upon to vote whether they would or would not ask for separate existence. It is to be noted that in not one of these instances were all the people of the State consulted. Only those who might leave were asked, the question being whether they wanted to go.

In the Convention of 1820, Massachusetts set another example destined to have wide imitation. It began the giving of some measure of self-determination to municipalities. Towns might receive city charters "with the consent and on the application of a majority of the inhabitants of such town present and voting thereon." The object primarily in mind was the incorporation of Boston, which had grown to be too unwieldy for the town form of government. As soon as the constitutional amendment had been adopted, the General Court passed an act establishing the city of Boston, subject to the condition that within twelve days it should be approved by the voters of the town. Although the principle cannot be said to be universally established, it has in the course of a century become a common practice throughout the land to submit to the voters of a municipality questions relating to the fundamentals of their organization.

When John Adams put into the Massachusetts Bill of Rights the declaration that taxes ought not to be levied without the consent of the people or their representatives, he entered a field where the Referendum was to have abundant growth. The extravagances of the period that culminated in the panic of 1837 taught the danger of public finance inadequately controlled. So when Rhode Island came to frame her first Constitution, in 1842, she put into it this provision: "The General Assembly shall have no power hereafter without the express consent of the people, to incur State debts to an amount exceeding fifty thousand dollars, except in time of war, or in case of insurrection or rebellion." Four years later New York took similar ground, declaring that no law creating debt (with certain exceptions) should go into effect until it had been submitted to the voters. The question on the passage of the bill was to be: "Shall this bill pass, and ought the same to receive the sanction of the voters?" Illinois in 1848 made like provision, with an exception of debts below fifty thousand dollars, as in Rhode Island.

California (1849) began with a requirement for the referendum on laws creating State debt. Kentucky in 1850 made like provision. Nebraska (1866) followed the example. North Carolina in 1868 made a similar requirement in the matter of giving or lending the credit of the State. Arkansas put in her Constitution of 1868: "The credit of the State or counties shall never be loaned for any purpose without the consent of the people thereof expressed through the ballot box." With the Constitution of 1874, however, the provision disappeared. South Carolina in 1873 required a vote of the people, with two thirds in the affirmative, for creating any new debt, guaranty, endorsement, or loan of credit. Montana in 1889 forbade passing a limit of one hundred thousand dollars without a majority vote of the people.

The practice of submitting local questions for local approval has steadily gained favor. By 1908 the tide had reached such a pitch that Michigan put into her Constitution: "No local or special act shall take effect until approved by a majority of the electors voting thereon in the district to be affected." The validity and utility of this practice are to-day alike unquestioned.

Until toward the end of the nineteenth century the State-wide use of the Referendum on other than questions of finance was rare. Occasionally the location of a State capital would be determined by popular vote, or some other question peculiarly appropriate for a plebiscite would be submitted, but for the most part it was not thought desirable to let the Legislatures evade their responsibilities. The popular Initiative had even less advocacy. To be sure, it had appeared very early in a State Constitution. That of Georgia in 1777 had said: "No alteration shall be made in this Constitution without petitions from a majority of the counties, and the petitions from each county to be signed by a majority of voters in each county within this State." This provision, however, survived for only a dozen years, and found no imitators.

In the period immediately after the Civil War, representative government seemed to be so powerful that nothing was likely to impair its vitality. Yet it was breeding within itself evils that presently would curb its strength, if not threaten its existence. Many of our lawmaking bodies gave too much occasion for loss of public respect. The standards of Congress were at their lowest level; in some of the State Legislatures venality went unrebuked, in others the machine and the boss were usurping power. Large numbers of the people became convinced that somehow their will was thwarted, their confidence abused. The result was that in the third-party movements which followed one after another in response to a blind impulse toward better things, they sought some way to free themselves from the controls, the restraints, what they thought the perversions, of the prevailing legislative system. Probably descriptions of the Swiss procedure turned the aspirations of the reformers toward the Initiative and Referendum as a remedy for political ills. It was a remedy not inconsistent with experiments and tendencies in our own experience, but we had hardly gone far enough in this direction to warrant saying now that the new programme was a natural step in our own development. On the other hand it cannot fairly be called an innovation foreign to our institutions.

The first proposal of the reform by an American political party is believed to have been made by the Socialist Labor party in 1889. Two years later the Knights of Labor declared for it, and in 1892 it was championed by the newly organized People's Party, with endorsement shortly afterward by the American Federation of Labor and the National Grange. As in the case of most of the proposals for political change in which the latest generation has been fruitful, this one found the greater favor in the West and there achieved its first victories. In 1897 the municipalities of Nebraska were empowered to petition for the use of the Initiative and Referendum in local affairs, the system to go into effect if approved by a majority of those voting. In the same year the Legislature of South Dakota decided to submit a constitutional amendment that would bring about the reform, and at the next election, in 1898, the amendment was adopted. Utah adopted a like measure in 1900, Oregon in 1902, Nevada in 1904, and then other States at the rate of about one a year.

Impediments of one sort or another, thrown in the way of the early attempts to introduce the system, delayed actual test of it until 1904, when two measures were voted on in Oregon. Two years later eleven measures were submitted in that State. Then other States began putting the system into use, with the result that in the ten years after 1906, 337 measures in all were submitted by petition for popular vote. By the twentieth year after the first test eighteen States had adopted the system. In that year seventeen measures were referred to the people by Legislatures, fifteen were so referred upon petition, eighteen were measures proposed by initiative petition, and five constitutional amendments were proposed by initiative petition.[1]

CONSTITUTIONS AND LAWS

The possible shapes and combinations of the Initiative and Referendum are many. Each or both may be applied to either changes in Constitutions or to ordinary laws. The Initiative may be direct, i.e., may work without including the Legislature in its course; or by requiring some degree of action on the part of that body, may be indirect. The Referendum may be compulsory, after the fashion long familiar in the case of constitutional amendments, a method usually applied under the new system to amendments or statutes that have been initiated by mass petition; or it may be optional, which means that it may be applied at the will of a sizable part of the electorate, as shown by mass petition, to specified laws that have been passed by the Legislature. The variations put into practice by combining these possibilities in different degree make digest and classification so elaborate and intricate as to confuse more than to enlighten. Lest by reason of the trees we may miss seeing the forest, let us avoid overmuch detail and examine certain general considerations.

In the first place it may be observed that it is common under the Initiative and Referendum to handle somewhat differently constitutional changes and ordinary laws. Most of us still feel that there is something almost sacred about a Constitution, that it is something not to be lightly profaned. Only about half the States that have adopted the new system permit the Initiative to reach the Constitution at all. In the others it is common to require more signatures in the case of a petition for constitutional amendment, and a few insist that an amendment shall be adopted only by a majority of all the votes cast at the election, thus compelling as much support for measures as for men — a requirement far from unimportant in practical effect. Also a few States permit only the controlled Initiative when the Constitution is concerned. For instance, in North Dakota an amendment that has been approved by the people must then go before the Legislature; if approved by that body it at once goes into effect; if not so approved, the people vote on it again, whereupon it takes effect if thus for the second time they favor. Massachu-

[1] *Political Science Quarterly*, vol. XL, no. 1, Sup., 80, 81.

setts is yet more cautious. An Initiative amendment proposed by petition is first passed upon by the Legislature; if it gets the support of one quarter of the members in joint session, it goes to the next Legislature; and if there it again gets one quarter of the votes, it then goes to the people.

A few of the States have given evidence of confronting the very interesting question presented by the declarations in Bills of Rights. If such a declaration sets forth a natural, inalienable right common to all mankind, can it be legitimately subverted even by the electorate itself? In times past not merely closet philosophers, but also statesmen among the most eminent in our history, have held these declarations of rights to be among our chief contributions to the science of government. With pride it has been pointed out that we alone among all the nations of the earth have set certain things beyond the reach of autocrats, whether they be monarchs or legislative assemblies; have said they should not be disturbed by sovereignty itself; have denied ourselves. Now State after State has renounced the sacrifice, saying in effect that nothing is beyond the will of the majority. Thus with one sweep modern Democracy disposes of an age-old problem.

Not all the States have been willing to go the full distance. Massachusetts, while refusing to protect the whole of the Bill of Rights, saved freedom of speech, freedom of the press, freedom of elections, trial by jury, and certain other specified rights. Also it put up a barrier, as several of the other States have done, by forbidding the people to exercise any legislative powers refused to the Legislature by the Constitution. Such a barrier, however, is not insurmountable, for the Constitution itself can now be changed by popular vote, save in particulars excepted as in Massachusetts.

This leads to the interesting question of whether the people can prudently be permitted to change by mass vote the constitutional provisions for the Initiative and Referendum itself. The fundamental purpose of our Constitutions, the reason for their existence, was to define and prescribe the powers of the three branches of government. To no one of the three did we give permission to change by itself the definition or the limitation of its powers. That was supposed to be another of the great merits in our contribution to political science. Now we are transferring to a fourth agency, the electorate, part of the powers hitherto confined to the representative legislature, and in greater or less degree permitting their independent exercise. As Professor Holcombe has well pointed out,[1] the electorate is not the people. It functions through a majority of the minority of the people. An electorate is itself a representative body, created by certain quite arbitrary qualifications. Logically if one type of representative body, a Legislature, ought not to be able to define its own powers, why should another?

That this is no mere matter of idle speculation, but may at any time prove of great practical consequence was shown by what took place in Arizona in 1914 when it was proposed that by the use of the Initiative and Referendum the electorate should deprive the Legislature of the right of amending or repealing any law enacted by the electorate. In spite of the inconvenience and worse that this might cause, the electorate adopted the proposal. It will be seen that this opens wide the door to the oppression of minorities whenever the electorate may be moved by some gust of passion. In periods of great religious, racial, or social prejudice, the most sacred rights of the individual may be swept by the board. It is answered that in such periods laws will not restrain anyhow. This may be true, and yet it does not follow that because all restraints go down before Revolution in hours when might makes right, there should be no restraints.

Our Constitutions are in and of themselves restraints. With variations in form, they all have at the core essentially the same system of checks and balances, designed to protect each great agency of government not only against the others, but also against itself. When one of these great agencies is divided into two parts, the representative legislature and the mass legislature, the newly recognized part cannot assert to itself independence without endangering the whole system.

Critics of the new device have seen particular menace in the possibility that the mass legislature may claim the power to dominate the other branches of government, especially the judicial. By passing upon constitutionality the courts have exercised restraints deemed salutary by all those who prefer the doctrine of John Marshall to that of Thomas Jefferson, and they have been the great majority of thoughtful Americans for more than a century. If it should prove that by the Initiative and Referendum the electorate can in fact supplant the judiciary

[1] *State Government in the U.S.*, 442.

as the arbiter of fundamental rights, then indeed the barrier that now protects the people against their legislatures, may be carried by flank attack. It does not yet appear, however, that the courts will be unable to protect the people against themselves. If there are such things as inalienable rights, either they will be maintained by the courts or else our ancient liberties will disappear.

Experience thus far has not shown that the Initiative and Referendum help any toward checking the tendency to break down the time-honored distinction between Constitutions and statutes. On the contrary the new system makes it easier to imbed in the organic law provisions that ought to be open to speedy changes possible by the action of a Legislature. Men who will go to the trouble of working the cumbersome machinery of the Initiative and Referendum usually think their hobbies are of supreme importance and ought to be lifted above the possibility of desecration. With sense of proportion dulled by their enthusiasm, they would interpolate a by-law in the Ten Commandments if they had the chance. So it has come about that in Oregon, for instance, the critics find ground for saying there is no longer any Constitution. There and in not a few other States what was a Constitution is fast becoming a glorified statute-book.

One result of the new opportunity seemed to be a race between the Legislatures and the electorates to see which could get the most changes made in the Constitutions, for the two processes go on side by side. In 1914, for instance, in eleven States, forty-five amendments were proposed by the use of the Initiative and Referendum, fifty-four by the Legislatures. Apparently the Legislatures used the more judgment, for twenty-five of their proposals prevailed, against only eleven successes initiated by part of the electorate. A decade afterward, amendment by way of popular initiative had so lost favor that, if the tabulation of the "Political Science Quarterly" was accurate, only five of 163 constitutional amendments submitted were proposed by initiative petition.

DRAFTING

The drafting of measures to be submitted by use of the Initiative presents a debatable problem. Through centuries of experiment and experience we have built up a process of lawmaking by assemblies to the point of universal assumption that it is desirable to expose every measure to the moulding of com-

mittees and to scrutiny, discussion, and amendment in the
assembly itself. Rarely does any important measure emerge as
it entered. Often the changes are so numerous that the original
draft would hardly be recognized in the finished product. All
this disappears under the Initiative. In most of the States, as the
measure comes from the petitioners, so it must be accepted or
rejected by the electorate. An episode in California shows the
extreme to which results may go, indeed actually have gone.
Section 31 of Article IV of the Constitution of that State contains two clauses, forty words, repeated in succession. The
Constitution is printed in the Statutes of 1915 with the comment: "The repetition of the words indicated by parentheses in
the above section occurred in the resolution by which the amendment of the above section was proposed to the people. As no
change could be made thereafter the section was voted on and
adopted in the above form." (It was adopted in 1914.)

When even a clerical error cannot be corrected, there is no
need of debating on the importance of having the original draft
satisfactory.

Mere blemishes in point of form would be no very grave
matter. Serious trouble begins when the form fails to express
the intent. Even the most carefully drafted statutes, after all
the labor spent on them in the processes of a legislative assembly,
are constantly vexing our courts with problems as to their
meaning. Indeed the interpretation of statutes is a field of law
already of no small proportions. These proportions may be
greatly enlarged if the accustomed safeguards are removed from
the lawmaking process.

More dangerous still is the possibility that the form may
express and yet conceal the intent. A skillful draftsman, perverting his capacities to base ends, can by the adroit use of
language achieve purposes that the words would never suggest
to the ordinary voter, whose ballot may therefore accomplish
precisely the opposite of what he intends. Even though the
men who drew the measure may have been inspired with no
selfish or otherwise unworthy motive, they have had an unfair
advantage that may on occasion lead to serious results. When a
legal document is to be drawn in a controverted matter, every
lawyer seeks to have the drawing of it rather than let it be drawn
by his adversary. That is an advantage corresponding to position in sport or war.

In spite of these palpable possibilities of harm, friends of the Initiative assert that it actually produces better results in point of workmanship than the old system. This they explain by saying that the superiority of laws passed under the Initiative, in point of technique, results naturally from the fact that they have mostly been drafted by a rather large committee of persons having a lively interest in the matter in hand and some practical knowledge of it, besides what knowledge they may have of the general requirements of legislation; and that the framers are aware that their measure once launched must go as it is, for better or worse. The perfecting work that a legislative committee would do, is in the case of an initiated law done in the course of many conferences, which are supplemented by much correspondence with friendly critics. If no lawyers are in the group of men most interested, legal help from outside is called upon to put the measure in proper form. The result is that it is likely to be in far better shape than the ordinary bill when introduced into a Legislature.

The argument is plausible and not without force, but is unfair in ignoring the fact that the more important measures introduced in our lawmaking bodies have often received just as much preliminary study. Indeed if it were not for the coöperation of public-spirited, self-sacrificing men, who with no wish for advertisement and no motive save that of the desire to be of service put arduous labor into the preparation of bills, the legislative product would be far more open to valid criticism than it is to-day.

It may very well be that in some if not all of the Western States where the Initiative first gained approval, better work results from it on the whole than from the legislative methods there in vogue. It does not follow that at its best the legislative method may not be superior. To be sure, careful amendment in advance, so to speak, might be thought always preferable to the ill-considered, hasty, off-hand amendment of a legislative chamber, but even in this particular the question is not altogether one-sided. Striking proof of this was given by the Massachusetts Convention of 1917 that framed the amendment for the Initiative and Referendum itself. A group of exceptionally capable men, some of them legislators of long experience, had through many months worked to get their measure in perfect shape. Yet the Convention made many changes, of all degrees of importance, and it is probable that now the men who presented the original draft would admit that far the greater part of the changes were wise. At any rate every one of these changes commended itself, after thorough discussion, to a majority of a Convention where more than half of the delegates had been chosen as favorable to the principle.

Even in the West there have been in the use of the Initiative instances of workmanship as poor as any that comes out of the Legislature. The anti-pass law submitted in Oregon on an Initiative petition in 1906 was so badly worded that, construed literally, it prohibited a railroad company from giving passes to its own employees and allowed it to issue passes to the employees of other roads. This finally failed to become law in spite of its approval by 57,281 votes to 16,799, because the petitioners had neglected to insert an enacting clause. Allen H. Eaton, a not unfriendly critic, in his book on "The Oregon System," said in 1912: "A further discouraging result of our new plan is that some of the more recent constitutional acquisitions have been so complex and confusing in terms that no one knew just what was meant." Governor Ammons of Colorado said to the Governors' Conference of 1913: "We had two utilities bills submitted at the last election. One was an absolute fake, and the other had in it provisions for which no good citizen, if he read it over, would like to vote. There was an irresponsible preparation of that bill, or there was a definite purpose to job the whole matter; and so I tell you, that while no one has been more enthusiastic for this measure than I, we have much to learn before we can make it bring about the best purposes. We must provide some safeguard under which measures shall be prepared with greater care so as to cover the subject properly." [1]

Those who framed the Initiative and Referendum for Massachusetts were groping in the right direction when they embodied in their programme a new idea in the shape of provision that the original petition shall have ten signers. Of itself this amounts to little, for some or all of the ten may be "dummies," but the implication may develop a custom of having the public look to these ten men as those really responsible not only for the idea but also for the workmanship. In that case the friends of the proposal will be anxious to get ten names that will command public confidence. Such men will not be likely to be willing to stand sponsors for poor work.

[1] *Proceedings*, 279.

In the same direction the Massachusetts Convention took another step, commendable though short, by a provision that a measure shall be submitted to the Attorney-General for certification that it is in proper form for submission to the people. This ensures against palpable defects in structure, but it does not go far enough to meet the really serious dangers. My belief has been that a satisfactory solution of the difficulty will not be reached until it is conceded that no amateur, no group of amateurs, no legislative assembly, no electorate is best fitted to construct the machinery of law. John Stuart Mill told Parliament half a century ago that sooner or later legislatures will realize they are incapable of making laws — of course meaning thereby the best laws. Assemblies or electorates may well agree upon principles, determine policies, but the task of furnishing the technique of execution, the task of drafting the bill, the task of providing the administrative details, ought to be turned over to some agency created for that particular kind of work.

With this in mind I suggested to the Massachusetts Convention that "a proposed law shall be confined to a specific, concrete proposition, unaccompanied by administrative or technical detail, but may direct what agency of government shall administer it." This would have let the people say what ends they want to accomplish, but would have left to experts the determination of how those ends should be accomplished. For example, the people may well be trusted to say whether or not they want an old-age pension law, but after the people have decided that they want old-age pensions and perhaps have decided whether they want them contributory or non-contributory, then experts ought to say whether the payments should be made at the rate of five, eight, or ten dollars a month, whether the age should be sixty-five, seventy, or seventy-five; in other words, the details of the law may wisely be entrusted to somebody in whom the people have confidence.

The proposal was defeated, by a vote of 114 to 126. The time was not quite ripe for such an innovation. Too jealous of their privileges are those who enjoy the petty power of handling minutiæ. Too common is the distrust of all experts. Specializing has not yet won general respect. Everybody still thinks himself quite equal to the making of laws. Furthermore the zealous advocates of direct legislation see danger in even remote possibilities of obstructing the popular will. Thus one of them said in the debate on this proposal: "If you do not give the people a chance to complete their law and make it workable but provide that the Legislature must complete it, therefore wherever this takes effect it throws the legislation finally into the hands of the Legislature and takes it out of the hands of the people." This assumed that the Legislature would provide the machinery, but such in fact would not be the most desirable recourse. Far better would it be to have a small body of makers of administrative law continuously employed in expert application of principles laid down for their guidance, whether laid down by Legislature or electorate.

If nothing short of delegating detail will remove the underlying cause of the chief defect in all the legislative bodies of the land, how can it be thought prudent to put detail within the reach of the electorate, which by its very nature is even less competent to handle detail? Every additional complexity will add to the improbability of comprehension by the untrained voter, and will correspondingly lessen both his interest and his confidence. Already experience shows that he soon feels his incompetence to deal with technical detail and tends to meet the situation by voting against what he cannot understand. The result is that fair decision is given only on simple, brief proposals relating to clear-cut moral and political issues which have had long and thorough discussion by the public. If it proves impossible to provide that only such questions shall go on the ballot, yet in time the desirable end may be brought about through recognition of the futility or folly of submitting any others to the electorate.

INFORMATION

It is idle to expect that the mass of voters will profit by even such scanty and one-sided opportunities for information about methods and details as may be open to them. As DeLolme wisely observed long ago,[1] men seeing themselves lost, as it were, in the crowd of those who are called upon to exercise the same function with themselves, will not enter upon a laborious task when they know it can scarcely answer any purpose. With equal wisdom President Lowell, in our own time, has observed that no device except a popular assembly has ever been invented whereby the mass of the people can be made to expend consider-

---

[1] *The Constitution of England* (1784), book II, chap. 5.

able effort on mastering facts that do not touch their imagination or affect clearly their daily lives.[1] Elihu Root, thinking along the same lines, concludes that in ordinary cases the voters will not and cannot possibly bring to the consideration of proposed statutes the time, attention, and knowledge required to determine whether such statutes will accomplish what they are intended to accomplish; and the vote usually will turn upon the avowed intention of such proposals rather than upon their adequacy to give effect to their intention.[2]

Advocates of the Initiative and Referendum do not deny that these considerations have weight, but they insist that the incapacity and indifference of the voter are overestimated. Give the voter a chance, they say, and he will make a genuine effort to inform himself and to reach a wise conclusion. Their first step in giving him a chance is to supply him with an official bulletin, setting forth the measures that are to go on the ballot, with arguments for and against each. There is dispute as to whether these publicity pamphlets are widely read, but the probability is strong that those who deny it are nearer right. It is not reasonable to suppose that the greater part of the voters will carefully read a pamphlet of perhaps one or two hundred pages — some have even been longer — with the text of laws that may run up to twenty or thirty thousand words and be highly technical in character. The statement of arguments for and against each proposal may be scanned, for they are necessarily brief, say five hundred words on a side, but this brevity, which is enforced by law, of itself prevents adequate explanation and discussion of complicated measures. Furthermore, if Professor Barnett is right in what he tells us about the Oregon system, downright misstatements of fact in the pamphlets constitute an abuse which it seems impossible to correct.

Yet on the whole the publicity pamphlet helps, and should be a feature of any Initiative and Referendum system. It must not be forgotten that under any system of lawmaking the few will furnish the information and the opinion for the many. The publicity pamphlet will at any rate help enlighten the few.

The voter's chief inspiration will come from the newspaper press. Much of this inspiration will be honest; little of it will be impartial. However sincere the editor, he is no more free from

[1] Public Opinion, 53.
[2] Experiments in Government and the Essentials of the Constitution, 32, 35.

bias than other men. If a partisan, he is likely to share the views of his party and see no good in anything favored by the other side. If an independent, he is likely to be more partisan than the partisans, with the difference that his partisanship will be variegated and inconsistent. If having an eye to the main chance, he will extol or condemn according as he thinks praise or blame will please advertisers or subscribers. This all means that editors are as human as yourself, and as little likely to have the judicial qualifications necessary for a fair review of the facts and a fair weighing of the arguments. In the courts there are many attorneys, few judges. The editor is usually of counsel.

When counsel are matched in court, judge and jury hear both sides. The newspaper reader, however, as a rule gets only one side, for he seldom reads two papers. He is fortunate indeed if he gets one side of any public question fully and accurately. Success in journalism comes to be more and more dependent on the ability to give readers what they want, and publishers seem to find more and more reason for believing that readers do not want information or advice upon what they think the minor phases of government. It is palpable that voters take far more interest in men than measures. The personal side of politics helps to sell newspapers much as the sporting page helps, but who buys a newspaper nowadays with the hope or expectation of finding in it an adequate report of the latest debate in Congress or Legislature? The press is not to be blamed for giving the public what the public wants. If there be blame, it attaches to the public. Blame or no blame, it is indisputable that the newspaper cannot be counted on to inform the electorate fairly and completely about questions that are to appear on the ballot.

It can, however, be counted on to play a steadily growing part through the development of political advertising. We have seen the outlay for this become an important feature of campaigns for office. It is sure to become important in the use of the Initiative and Referendum. The regrettable thing is that this means more power to the pocket-book. It means that the public will be informed as to the arguments making for the advantage of selfish interests. Rarely can these interests affect a Legislature, easily can they affect an electorate, by paying for advertising space. Likewise they will have the advantage in the circulation of booklets, circulars, letters. The plebiscite invites to the use of money.

As far as all this tends to vitiate the ground-work for the framing of public judgment, it is unfortunate, but it is not necessarily fatal. If with the new system we may have a revival of public discussion, that can overcome the danger. Other things being equal, the printed word will never prevail over the spoken word. The Initiative and Referendum may work to the public good if they can bring to their help that which made a success of the Swiss landsgemeinde and the New England town-meeting — free and full debate among the electorate. The opportunity to hear and be heard gives both dignity and vitality to citizenship.

It is, however, altogether improbable that oral debate will determine the decision of any but a few of the questions on the ballot. There may be widespread discussion of the matters that will be the natural successors of prohibition, woman suffrage, and like problems, but for the great mass of questions brought forward by the new system, the voters are sure to seek direction rather than rely on their own judgments shaped by debate. They will look to societies and associations organized as a medium for leadership, or furnishing it ready-made. They will look to their party councils. They will still have representative government, but it will be unofficial. They will still ask and accept the judgment of other men, but those men will be more often self-appointed than chosen for the purpose. It will be the autocracy of the zealot. Perhaps there might be worse autocracy, but it will not be democracy.

EXCLUSIONS

These considerations give much weight to the argument that there are certain classes of statutory as well as constitutional matters which may well be excluded from the scope of the Initiative. Some critics who admit the utility of allowing the people to secure a mass vote on simple, broad questions of public policy on which many voters are likely to be informed and to have intelligent opinion, deny the wisdom of exposing to their direct action certain other classes of questions which it is averred can be handled better by the representative system. Among these are appropriations. It is argued, for instance, that in States without State Universities, the people might wisely declare by their votes whether or not they want such an institution, but that how much shall be expended to establish it can be more wisely determined by the Legislature. Not only is that a matter for expert study, but also it should be determined with some regard to the finances of the State as a whole, in accordance with one of the principles for which many advocates of the budget system stoutly contend. Naturally those who fear that a Legislature may abuse any power of control left to it, object to refusing the people the right to say just how much of their money shall be spent for any specified purpose, but it is hardly reasonable to suppose that any representative body would long try to thwart the popular will in such a matter, by refusing to appropriate, unless for reasons so clear that the electorate itself would on further information and consideration, approve. Furthermore there is peculiar danger in putting appropriations on the ballot, because of the opportunity this would give the demagogue to appeal to cupidity. At every stage of the world's history there have come to the front men who, by appealing to the cupidity, the venality, or the selfishness of their fellows, have acquired political power. The people in the mass have ever been ready to receive largess. Groups have ever been willing to profit at the expense of other groups. It is a matter of record that measures indulging cupidity are those that get the heartiest support at the polls. Voters take a keen interest in whatever may advance their individual fortunes. The prospect of gain will bestir the voter more than the fear of loss when the gain is definite and direct, the loss indefinite and indirect.

This is not inconsistent with the fact that numerous instances seem to give ground for the allegation that the people when voting in the mass lean toward parsimony. Such has been the Swiss experience and the same thing has been shown by the vigor with which American electorates commonly reject proposals for increase of salaries. The phenomenon is to be explained by remembering that self-interest is the chief motive of human action. In the secrecy of the voting-booth self-interest is unchecked. If personal advantage to the voter is clear, he will be extravagant; if the advantage is to accrue to another, the voter will be stingy.

Because of the dangers attending appropriations, legislative bodies have found it prudent to surround them with exceptional precautions. They must get more study by committees or receive a larger vote or in other ways be harder of enactment than the ordinary statute. It is felt that special caution must be used in regard to whatever transfers money from the pockets of some men to the pockets of other men. With all these considerations in mind the Massachusetts Convention of 1917 listened to the appeal that no specific appropriation should be proposed by an Initiative petition; and contented itself with providing that if a law approved by the people is not repealed, the Legislature shall appropriate the money necessary to carry such law into effect.

The same Convention recognized the undesirability of having a State-wide vote on matters of purely local concern, and so it excluded measures that in operation would be restricted to one locality. The cognate proposal that special and private matters should be excluded, met with less sympathetic reception. Despite the fact that their evil has been so serious as to lead about four fifths of the States to try by constitutional provisions to keep special and private bills out of the legislative halls, the Convention insisted on leaving their possibilities for mischief within the scope of the Initiative. The argument probably turning the scale was that the people ought to be able to get at any obnoxious public-service corporation. This way lies gross injustice. Does anybody believe a public service corporation in disfavor with the people could ever get fair play at the polls?

The reverse of the argument might well have given pause, for an unrestricted Initiative lets the public-service corporation reach the people, and if the corporation has not incurred ill-will, its resources give it dangerous power when it asks for favors and privileges. With the recollection of what happened when railroad promoters could reach the credit of towns, counties, and States, building their roads with bonds backed by the taxpayer, it might have been more prudent not to open the door.

Special legislation is the curse of our Legislatures, the source of nine tenths of the log-rolling and graft and corruption, the very root of our troubles. Out of it, however, come few bad laws that are bought, for it is very hard to buy the approval of a bad law from both Houses of a Legislature and also from the Governor. Probably it would be even harder to buy such a law from the electorate of a State, through debauching the voters, but were the money skillfully spent on unscrupulous leaders and in deceitful publicity, it is by no means sure that special privilege could not more easily be secured from an electorate than from a Legislature and Governor.

Special legislation is almost always matter either of privilege or of equity, for by its very nature it is an exception to the general rule. The dispensing of either favor or justice by a popular assembly has always been notoriously bad. Is there any reason to suppose that it will be done any better in the polling-booth than in the forum?

We must take into account that singular trait of human nature which blinds men in the mass to the appeal of justice, where singly or in small groups they would deal fairly with each other. Acting as a body, the people have no ethical conceptions. They are unjust and they are merciless. They look only at their own welfare and they ignore individual rights. Oregon gave a clear illustration of this in 1910 when by popular vote it prohibited fishing except with hook and line in Rogue River, an excellent trout stream, very attractive to sportsmen. This meant the virtual destruction of a canning and fishing industry representing an investment of probably a quarter of a million of dollars, and the throwing out of work of many men. It is contrary to the individual instinct of justice, though not to the mass instinct, that men shall be deprived of their property without due compensation. Realizing the possible application of the police power, men have engaged at their peril in such occupations as those connected with the liquor business or various noxious trades. Fish hatching and canning would hardly be classed therewith. In such a juncture it is altogether probable that a Legislature would work out some way of securing the public interest with due regard to private right.

Another objection to the use of the Initiative for special, private, and local measures is that they are often too trivial for a place on a State-wide ballot. Perhaps vastly important to a few individuals, they are of no interest to tens of thousands of voters who are asked to pass upon them. Yet we find among the measures put before the whole electorate of a State numerous proposals for creating counties, changing county lines, or removing county seats; together with such matters as, for example, a contribution by a county for an exposition, abolition of justice courts in a specified city, creating an additional judgeship for a specified district, raising the debt limit of a specified city, changing the name of a blind asylum, establishing another normal school, fixing the course of study at a specified normal school, empowering specified towns to assess abutting property for permanent improvements. Also we find in the matter of general laws an abundance of changes that are either trivial or of minor consequence, not deserving the ponderous machinery of a plebiscite, such as, for example, provisions against the sale of game, for extra sessions of district courts of appeal, for establishing a child-welfare commission, regulating fruit commission merchants, raising a Governor's salary, changing the day for his inauguration, regulating dentistry, merging certain State offices.

State-wide voting on many of these things was necessary because they involved constitutional changes. The blame, of course, lies at the door of a governmental system which puts administrative details into Constitutions. Professor Dodd was justified in his conclusion that the amending procedure has in many cases become a mere farce because of the triviality and multiplicity of questions submitted. Upon unimportant matters a popular verdict is obtained which is worth little or nothing, and the amending procedure is so cumbered with unimportant questions that matters of importance — matters on which the people may have a real judgment — are obscured.[1] Massachusetts saw fit to hamper the putting of trivial things into the Constitution and the proposal of trivial changes in that document, as well as to discourage the ill-considered agitation of any constitutional change whatever, by requiring any Initiative amendment to get the support of at least a quarter of all the members elected to two successive General Courts, before its submission to the people. In the matter of ordinary enactments no device has yet been adopted to prevent the harassing of the electorate with trivial proposals.

CONFLICTS

Another field where restriction, or at any rate control, is desirable is that of conflicting proposals. Suppose one petition is to the effect that incomes shall be taxed, another to the effect that incomes shall not be taxed, and suppose each is adopted. Of course this would rarely happen and the result, being a nullity, could do no harm, but much labor would have been wasted. The difficulty becomes more serious when the proposals, without contradicting each other, are inconsistent. By instance of what has actually taken place, understand the problem. In Oregon in 1912 there was conflict between the single tax proposal and the proposal for exemption of household goods from taxation, and

[1] W. F. Dodd, *Revision of State Constitutions*, 288.

another, apparently, between this household exemption bill and a taxation amendment. There was conflict between three sets of road measures, one of them a constitutional amendment; two "majority rule" amendments appeared; the proposal as to the office of Lieutenant-Governor conflicted with a provision in another measure for an election in case of a vacancy in the office of Governor; and the university and agricultural college mileage-tax bill was really a substitute for the university appropriations referred at the same election. In 1914 the two amendments abrogating the rule of "equal and uniform" taxation were in direct conflict with another amendment which retained this rule, and the latter amendment contained a tax exemption provision which conflicted with the fifteen-hundred dollar exemption amendment. Moreover, the tax-code commission bill submitted at this election was really the rival of all the tax administration bills submitted.[1]

On the California ballot of 1914 measure no. 5 was an Investment Companies Act, creating a State corporation department, and amendment no. 9 was for Regulating Investment Companies, apparently meant to secure the same result in another way; no. 19 was for the Consolidation of City and County, and Limited Annexation of Contiguous Territory, while no. 21 was for City and County Consolidation, and Annexation with Consent of Annexed Territory — a different way, probably, of attempting the same result; amendment no. 26 was for the Legislative Control of Irrigation, Reclamation and Drainage Districts, and no. 30 was in regard to Irrigation Districts Controlling International Water Systems.

The presence of conflicting measures on the same ballot may thwart the will of a large majority of the people, even when the measures have been initiated in perfect good faith and their purposes are substantially identical. The majority may divide their support, and their "No" votes on the measure not preferred by one group or the other, combined with those of voters opposed to both measures, may result in the defeat of both. Suppose a group of men favoring proportional representation puts on the ballot a proposal embodying the preferential system and another group petitions for a measure embodying the cumulative system. It can be shown mathematically that al-

[1] J. D. Barnett, *The Operation of the Initiative, Referendum and Recall in Oregon*, 48.

though four fifths of the voters wanted proportional representation, if half of them voted for one plan and against the other, and the other half reversed that vote, the remaining one fifth opposed to both plans would see their view prevail.

Hence comes the direct invitation to subvert the popular will by insincerely putting forward a proposal conflicting with one that is obnoxious to the schemers. It has been found in the West that it is no difficult matter to devise and place before the electorate what is for convenience called a "fake" proposition. Honest men seek some improvement in the law; the improvement is objectionable, perchance, to certain moneyed interests, perhaps to some sectarian interests, perhaps to some labor interests. The opposition immediately starts up a rival petition, designed to confuse the voters, and differing from the first proposition only enough to make wise choice by the people practically impossible.

Again, selfish interests may employ the expedient to fight each other. An instance is the Columbia River episode. The upper river fishermen use the fish wheel, the lower river fishermen the gill net. Each group saw advantage in getting prohibition of the method used by the other. Each initiated a measure to carry out its own selfish purpose. Both measures prevailed and each method of fishing was prohibited. Allen H. Eaton concluded the significance of the case to be that the Initiative was used by each fish party "not for the benefit of the whole people or for the perpetuation of such an important industry as that involved, but to put the other fellow out of business in order that the selfish interest might be able to pile up its profits." [1]

In the United States Senate Jonathan Bourne told the story more favorably for the Initiative. For a great many years, he said, there had been efforts to secure adequate laws for the protection of salmon, but because of the conflicting interests between the upper river and the lower river, the Legislature could not be induced to enact laws that would protect the fish. As a consequence the salmon fisheries were being destroyed. There was wide discussion of both bills, and the suggestion was freely made that both should be adopted. The people, disgusted with the failures of the Legislature to enact suitable laws for the protection of fish, followed this suggestion, and both bills were enacted. With fishing practically prohibited, the Legislature of 1909 responded to the popular demand by enacting, in con-

[1] *The Oregon System*, 68.

junction with the State of Washington, a fishery law that provided adequate protection. The Senator believed he was safe in saying that this would not have been done but for the popular adoption of the two fishery bills.[1]

In spite of this ingenious argument, even friends of the system will admit that this is hardly a desirable way to accomplish desirable results, and they recognize that it can produce very undesirable results. Some have thought it useless to attempt a remedy, believing either that the people should be trusted to meet the situation or else that any remedy would do more harm than good. Others have proposed various methods of choice in case of conflict. It has been suggested that the conflicting measures go on the ballot in turn, at successive elections, in such order as may be directed by the Governor or the Legislature, until one has been adopted or all have been rejected. Another way would be to have the order determined by the relative number of signers to the petitions. More favor has come to methods whereby conflicting proposals shall be grouped on the ballot, the voter to designate which one he approves, if any. Massachusetts chose this plan and also directed that if in any judicial proceeding provisions of constitutional amendments or laws adopted at the same election are held to be in conflict, those of the measure that received the largest number of affirmative votes shall govern.

Professor W. F. Dodd doubts the efficacy of all provisions for competing or alternative proposals. He says they must necessarily be somewhat complex. The voter can with some intelligence answer "Yes" or "No" upon one definite and concrete question, but few have the time and patience to deal successfully with two competing measures upon the same subject. This difficulty alone he thinks enough to condemn the plan of competing proposals.[2] The criticism is well grounded, but it remains to be seen whether an attempt at remedy, even if imperfect, may not be better than no remedy at all.

DESCRIPTION

It is particularly desirable that fairness and wisdom shall combine in a matter very small as measured by words, very

[1] *Congressional Record*, May 5, 1910.
[2] "State-Wide Initiative and Referendum," *Annals of American Academy of Political and Social Science*, September, 1912.

large as measured by effect — that of description of the proposal. Rarely is a law short enough to go on the ballot in full. So there must be resort to description. That by itself will decide a great part of the voters. It is hard in a few words to describe any measure fairly, intelligently, and completely; in the case of long and complex measures it is impossible. This is shown by many instances in the Western States, including much of deceptive and even fraudulent misrepresentation. A typical case was that of the Arizona law of 1915 represented to be for a system of old age and mothers' pensions. In accepting it the people incidentally voted two to one to abolish their county hospitals and poor farms, leaving without care their indigent sick and other victims of poverty. Of this the Supreme Court of Arizona thought it not too strong to say that not one voter in a hundred knew that all the county hospitals were to be abolished. "It was the generous and philanthropic title of the act that caught the eye and mind and heart of the voter." [1]

The mischief has not been unknown in even so cautious a State as Massachusetts. To illustrate, a law for party enrollment at primaries there proved so distasteful to certain elements in the community that it was repealed upon referendum. Return to the old abuses not being to the taste of the Legislature, it submitted the matter again, this time adroitly framing the question to read: "Shall an act passed by the General Court in the year 1916, entitled 'An Act to prevent the voters of one political party from voting in the primaries of another political party,' be approved and become law?" So described, the measure appealed to the voters and they reversed their position. Again, take the case of Ch. 688 of the Acts of 1914, which put on the ballot the question of a Saturday half-holiday for State employees, with the blind addition — "and otherwise to regulate their employment." The "otherwise" prescribed day-work instead of piece work as far as possible, a matter, it will be seen, not related at all to the proposal set forth in the question, which did not even fairly put the voters on their guard.

In this particular case, both proposals concerned the general subject of State employment, and no great harm would have come from coupling them in a legislative bill, exposed to the scrutiny of lawmakers presumed to be more or less expert; but under conditions preventing amendment, where the voter must

[1] Board of Control v. Buckstegge, 18 Ariz. 277 (1916).

accept or reject *in toto*, the impropriety, the unwisdom, the
danger of the procedure are all evident. It invites log-rolling,
the swapping of support and votes, which alone should suffice for
its condemnation. Worse yet, it prevents an accurate expression of the public will. For example, the first law submitted to
popular revision in Switzerland, that on marriage and the civil
rite, contained proposals with regard to marriage and divorce,
believed by many likely to have an injurious effect on family
life, together with clauses relating to the civil ceremony, for
which the need was obvious. It has been declared that a great
many citizens, forced to vote "Yes" or "No," voted "Yes" in
spite of the obnoxious part.

If a popular proposal is cleverly put at the head of other
proposals like a locomotive at the head of a freight train, it may
drag into the Constitution weighty amendments to which the
people are indifferent or even actually opposed. In 1908 the
people of Oregon by a vote of almost two to one rejected an
amendment announced as a step in the direction of the single
tax. At the next election the measure was adopted because, as
is generally admitted, it was reframed so as to start off with
the declaration — "No poll or head tax shall be levied or collected in Oregon." Poll-taxes are always unpopular with farmers and wage-earners. As to that, they are unpopular with
almost everybody, for only a very few reflect upon the utility of
having the governmental relation brought home to each citizen
by some direct tax, however small. So when the first thing to
catch the eye of the Oregon voter was the disliked poll-tax, that
was enough. It made no difference that the important part of
the poll-taxes had been abolished years before.

Allen H. Eaton says of the working of the system in Oregon
that "often important provisions not understood will be decided
by some unimportant provision which the uninformed voter
readily recognizes." [1] This danger must exist whenever Initiative measures carry many details, even though all are related to
one general purpose. It becomes the more serious when unrelated topics are combined. In one Initiative measure in Oregon
were found thirty-two distinct subjects. Thirty of our State
Constitutions in one form of language or another require that no
bill passed by the Legislature shall embrace more than one subject. Seven others restrict a bill to one subject and matters

[1] *The Oregon System*, 152.

properly connected therewith. Two others confine the requirement to private and local bills. Thus nearly forty States recognize the danger of omnibus bills. Surely this danger ought to be
recognized in every provision for the Initiative.

AMENDMENT

Thoughtful friends of the system admit that one of its grave
defects lies in the absence of the amending power. Legislative
experience has taught that very few bills are incapable of improvement in point of technique or detail at the hands of a committee or when exposed to the scrutiny of a critical assembly.
For example, see what happened in the case of a comparatively
simple matter before the Massachusetts Constitutional Convention of 1917, that of preventing appropriations for sectarian
institutions. Three delegates of experience and capacity prepared with great care drafts of an amendment that each no
doubt thought perfect. After study of the matter for days and
weeks a committee drew out of the three proposals a new form of
which it was willing to say: "Here is something that is perfect.
Every line, every word, every punctuation mark is right." Then
the Convention set to work on the perfected draft and made
changes. The Committee on Form and Phraseology made
changes. The original committee itself made changes. In the
end thirty-one changes were made from the time of the receipt
of the three original drafts, which were presumably supposed by
their authors and friends to be each in the best form for submission to the people.

Even the best-intentioned and broadest-minded of men,
working by themselves or in a small group, may fail to foresee
all the bearings of a measure that is to have general and wide
application. No city man fully understands the farmer's point
of view. No farmer fully understands the complexities of urban
life. The mechanic and the shopkeeper, the physician and the
miner, the lawyer and the trench-digger, approach many a problem from different angles. What is one man's meat is another
man's poison. This makes government a series of compromises,
and representative government can accomplish them because it
provides for a system of concessions, worked out by the processes
of redrafting and amendment. In the course of debate men learn
each other's viewpoints. Every corner of the State, nearly every
group in the community, may have its interests represented, its

opinions voiced. Thus we apply the principle uppermost in our courts of justice, that all parties in interest shall be heard. The Legislatures, like the courts, dispense justice in so far as they determine rights. In each the spirit of arbitration prevails, but in the Legislatures more often than in the courts it is necessary to depart from the absolute right and conclude what may be expedient, the course that at the same time will bring the most good and the least harm.

For this reason a Legislature must often decide which is the best of several possibilities. The general purpose can usually be met with a "Yes" or "No," and if lawmaking went no farther than that, some of it could be done by an electorate as well as by an assembly. Therein, however, is not where the chief difficulty lies. The real task is not to determine what shall be done, but to determine how it shall be done. There are generally two ways of doing a thing, sometimes twenty ways. Nothing has yet been devised to enable a voter to know to the extent that a legislator may know, whether a proposed law is adequate to meet the need or is the best method of meeting the need.

Some of the States have sought to meet the difficulty by providing that when a measure has been submitted to the Legislature by Initiative petition, the Legislature may if it sees fit prepare a measure of its own to accomplish the same general purpose, in which case both measures will go to the people for their choice. In Massachusetts this plan has been carried farther by providing that the initiated measure is not to go to the people without additional signatures secured after the Legislature has had opportunity to act, thus giving a chance for the men behind the measure to drop it if they think the Legislature has passed a satisfactory bill. If, however, they think the legislative bill unsatisfactory or if the Legislature has not acted, they can proceed, in which case they are furnished with the chance to profit by whatever weaknesses the legislative discussion has developed, for they are allowed to amend their measure if with the certificate of the Attorney-General that the amendments are perfecting in nature and do not materially change the substance. If it is a constitutional change that is in question, the Legislature itself may amend by a three-quarters vote in joint session. This may in part meet the difficulty, perhaps fully obviate it in practice, but it remains yet to be proved whether any adequate substitute can be found for the hammering, shaping, polishing processes of committee study and legislative debate.

Amendment after enactment is commonly necessary in the case of all but the simplest laws. As in the case of new machines, only use can disclose what is weak and what needs adjustment. Human foresight is not equal to anticipating all the bearings of any complicated measure. Even a simple measure may have results that will surprise and disappoint its friends. This raises the delicate question of whether a Legislature should be permitted to repeal or change a law that has been enacted by popular vote. Here those who distrust Legislatures will hesitate to give them any chance to nullify the popular intent, and will prefer that measures adopted by the Referendum should be repealed or changed only by the Referendum. For the most part, however, it has been thought that the difficulties and dangers of such a requirement make it wiser to assume that a Legislature will have a wholesome respect for an enactment by the people, and will not lightly undertake to thwart their desire.

The courts had occasion to face the question long before the modern form of Referendum came into vogue. In accordance with the requirement of the Illinois Constitution, a General Banking Law was duly ratified by the people in 1851. Then in 1857 an amendment of the law relating to the taxation of banking corporations was not submitted to the people. Was it valid? The Supreme Court upheld it on the ground that the Constitution placed taxation and revenue in the hands of the Legislature alone.[1] Judge Jameson thought that the decision might have been placed upon broader and more solid ground by holding simply that the Constitution of the State required only the question of the expediency of incorporating banking institutions to be passed upon by the people, leaving all questions of details to the General Assembly, to which, as involving only the exercise merely of a legislative discretion, they belonged.[2]

After the Initiative was introduced, the matter came up again, in the case of Kadderly v. Portland, 44 Ore. 118 (1903), the court holding that "laws proposed and enacted by the people under the initiative clause of the amendment are subject to the same constitutional limitations as other statutes, and may be amended or repealed by the Legislature at will." Of course this can be prevented by the Constitution itself, and some States have gone to that extreme. California and Michigan forbid change by the

[1] Bank of the Republic v. County of Hamilton, 21 Ill. R. 53.
[2] J. A. Jameson, The Constitutional Convention, 379.

Legislature unless the law itself permits, but in Michigan the Legislature may propose to the people alteration or repeal. Arizona changed to that position in 1914, by the narrow margin of 83 votes. Nevada takes a middle course by forbidding amendment or repeal by the Legislature within three years following enactment, and Washington likewise, save that the time is two years — a provision that can be criticized only because it prevents immediate rectification of a mistake. North Dakota was more prudent when in 1918 it provided for amendment or repeal by a two-thirds vote of all members elected to the Legislature. Most of the States are probably yet wiser in leaving the Legislature without restraint in the matter, relying upon the Referendum to defeat any repealing or amending law enacted in bad faith.

CHAPTER XXV

THE REFERENDUM

THE Referendum is now so commonly coupled with the Initiative in current thought and expression that we are apt to forget the two things are not necessarily dependent on each other. The Initiative might not go beyond what would in effect be a mass petition to the Legislature. The Referendum has long been used without the popular Initiative, notably in the case of the requirement for the submission of constitutional amendments. In certain aspects the Referendum used by itself is quite a different thing from the Referendum in sequence with the Initiative, and so in regard to these aspects it should be examined separately. (Of course it will be understood that by the Initiative is here meant the proposal of laws, and the petition for the application of the Referendum to a law the Legislature has enacted is not included.)

The Referendum independent of the Initiative may be applied at the will of the Legislature or a body of petitioners. We may conveniently call these processes the Voluntary and the Optional Referendum.

As applied by a Legislature voluntarily, the Referendum was long contested as an unauthorized delegation of legislative power. The argument was that an agent may not delegate the performance of his duty without the express consent of his principal. The first clash in the courts came over local option laws, measures depending for vitality upon acceptance by localities. To one of these the Supreme Court of Delaware phrased the objection perhaps as succinctly as it has been put: "The powers of government are trusts of the highest importance; on the faithful and proper exercise of which depend the welfare and happiness of society. These trusts must be exercised in strict conformity with the spirit and intention of the Constitution, by those with whom they are deposited; and in no case whatever can they be transferred or delegated to any other body of persons; not even to the whole people of the State; still less to the people of a county." The argument with which the Court continued may be assumed to set forth the reasons why the

Constitution did not permit delegation: "If the legislative functions can be transferred or delegated to the people, so can the executive or judicial power. The absurd spectacle of a Governor referring to a popular vote whether a criminal, convicted of a capital offense, should be pardoned or executed would be the subject of universal ridicule; and were a court of justice, instead of deciding a case themselves, to direct the prothonotary to enter judgment for the plaintiff or defendant, according to the popular vote of a county, the community would be disgusted with the folly, injustice, and iniquity of the proceeding. All will admit that in such cases, the people are totally incompetent to decide correctly. Equally incompetent are they to exercise with discernment and discretion collectively, or by means of the ballot-box, the power of legislation, because, under such circumstances, passion and prejudice incapacitate them for deliberation."[1]

Not all the courts took this extreme view. On the contrary many of them conceded the right to submit local questions, and by the time Cooley wrote his "Constitutional Limitations," the clear weight of authority, he believed, supported this class of legislation. It was, however, held to be governed by exceptional considerations, and ordinary legislation was still controlled by the rule against delegation. Judge Jameson, writing in 1866, said: "No position is better established in American law than that ordinary legislation belongs exclusively to the Legislature proper, and cannot be delegated even to the people or electors, who are in one sense superior to both Legislatures and Conventions." With their regard for precedents, courts would doubtless almost everywhere hold this still to be the case, in want of constitutional provision to the contrary, but all along it has been denied by able jurists. Thus when in 1894 a majority of the Massachusetts Supreme Court told the Legislature (160 Mass. 586) that it might not submit to the voters of the State an act granting women the right to vote in city and town elections, Justice Oliver Wendell Holmes, Jr., thought so much confidence is put in the Legislature as an agent that it is allowed to exercise its discretion by taking the opinion of its principal if it thinks that course to be wise.

Constitutional declarations on this point appeared in Ohio and Indiana in 1851. Ohio said: "All laws, of a general nature,

[1] Rice v. Foster, 4 Harr. 479 (1847).

shall have a uniform operation throughout the State; nor, shall any act, except such as relates to public schools, be passed, to take effect upon the approval of any other authority than the General Assembly, except as otherwise provided in this Constitution." Two such exceptions related respectively to acts creating or changing counties, and to acts authorizing associations with banking powers. Indiana thought the matter serious enough to put into her Bill of Rights: "No law shall be passed, the taking effect of which shall be made to depend upon any authority, except as provided in this Constitution." Oregon in 1857 and Kentucky in 1890 provided to the same effect, specifically exempting certain familiar classes of local legislation. Save in these instances, the tendency has been wholly in the opposite direction. Already a quarter or so of the States have expressly authorized their Legislatures to submit laws to the electorate at large for its judgment.

Any thoughtful man who has served in a Legislature must have serious doubts about the wisdom of permitting the voluntary Referendum. It is the resort of the coward. No safer way of shirking duty, of evading responsibility, was ever devised. Yet it must be admitted that however brave, conscientious, and confident a legislator may be, sometimes when confronted by a proposal that peculiarly depends upon the public will for its wisdom, he wishes the ballot might come to his help. Then, too, there are measures urged by a noisy faction of zealots who may not really have the approval of a majority of the people, but inasmuch as in such cases the majority is usually silent, the legislator is put in an awkward predicament. If he refuses to yield to the zealots, they will scourge him, with little likelihood that the silent majority will awaken to his support. May he not be justified in feeling sometimes that the majority ought to be compelled to vindicate his position?

Were it possible to confine the voluntary Referendum to measures of these classes, it might be a salutary expedient, but if left wide open to abuse, as seems unavoidable, it threatens a lamentable weakening of the self-reliance, the stamina, the morale, of our legislative bodies.

Should it be applied in countries where the system of ministerial responsibility has prevailed, it might work a revolutionary change. Suppose that in England whenever a dangerous issue threatened the Prime Minister with a vote of want of confidence, he could escape by sending the matter directly to the people, how many Ministries would ever perish before their allotted time? Might not ministerial responsibility disappear? There are, indeed, those who think this would not be wholly a misfortune. They point out that it would protect men who want to serve their country in the making of laws but are unwilling to compromise their principles. The voluntary Referendum, transferring particular decisions to the electorate, would increase their own likelihood of long and useful service, through lessening the chance of having their careers cut short by some fortuitous and passing issue.

If the issue is one on which the leaders of the majority have no conviction as a matter of principle, it presents another aspect of the Cabinet system, with more influence in turning English thought toward favorable consideration of the Swiss idea. Sooner or later the fate of a Cabinet may rest on a single cast of the die. In other particulars the work of its members may be satisfactory, but they may be thrown out of power if in this one respect they misread public opinion. In such a crisis a mandate from the people would solve the problem and save the day. To get that mandate by a general election is really a rather clumsy way, and very costly at that, for apart from the expense of the poll, no small matter of itself, there is the much greater waste that comes from the defeat of many experienced and capable legislators.

Doubtless it was with these considerations in mind that Mr. Chamberlain, in the House of Commons, May 18, 1904, expressed great admiration for the Referendum, and regretted that England had no such expedient for finding out the popular will on a single important issue of policy. Two years later, when the Liberals returned to power after eleven years in the minority and the Lords were stirred into fresh assertion of their rights, serious consideration was given to the Referendum as an expedient for solving deadlocks between the two Houses. The Marquis of Lansdowne took up the proposal and gave it prominence in a speech in the House of Lords in November, 1909. On the 25th of that month, in the campaign then waging, Mr. Balfour said to nearly ten thousand persons in the Royal Albert Hall in London: "I have not the least objection to submitting the principles of tariff reform to a referendum." This momentous utterance put the issue squarely into English politics. The arguments pro and

con, the discovery of obstacles, the prediction of benefits —
everything proceeded much on the same lines as with us, except
that as England has no State Legislatures, there was no occasion
to consider anything like our complex systems for making laws
directly. With the Great War, discussion of all such questions
went into abeyance.

In the English dominions and colonies, it was long thought
undesirable, or at any rate unimportant, to poll the people on
even their fundamental laws. Our use of the referendum on
Constitutions, and changes therein, found no early counterpart
in the domains under control of Great Britain. In the federating
of Canada there were no referenda at all and only in New Bruns-
wick was there a general election on the question. In the case of
the Union of South Africa, only in Natal was a referendum held.
In Australia, on the other hand, referenda were held in all six
States, and it was not until all the six States had concurred that
federation was adopted.[1] In order to confirm the action of the
Australian Parliament on amendments to the Constitution, the
people must vote.

Australia also prescribes referenda for deadlocks between the
two Houses in case of disagreement as to the Constitution. The
new Constitution of the German Commonwealth (1919) gives
resort to the principle when the National Council and the National Assembly cannot agree as to proposed laws, for in such
case the National President may within three months refer the
subject of the dispute to the people.

When Optional

The optional Referendum, optional with the electorate, is
quite another matter. In this form it consists of permission to
a specified number of voters to require that any bill passed by
the Legislature shall be submitted to the electorate for approval
before it can become law. In essence this is the Roman veto put
into the hands of the people, for use at their pleasure. It is
grounded on the belief that the people have a right to correct the
errors of their agents, to annul false judgments, to prevent injuries. In theory this is admirable; in practice its dangers are
few. There are those who fear it will weaken the legislator's
sense of responsibility, but are they not confounding the situation with that where the Referendum is at the command of the

[1] A. B. Keith, *Responsible Government in the Dominion*, i, 370–71.

legislators themselves? If it is to be applied only at the will of outside petitioners, how can the course of the legislator be affected, save possibly in those rare instances where he has reason to be confident that the Referendum will follow anyhow? It is to be doubted if any lawmaker will be made timid or fearful by a remote possibility that his work will be exposed to the judgment of his constituents. Indeed it is not at all unlikely that he would rather have the popular judgment thus expressed than have his own reëlection made the test, and if that be so, the contingency of the Referendum may fortify rather than lessen his courage.

The argument that legislators will lose in dignity and self-respect if they are told that their decisions may not be final, is somewhat far-fetched. Judges of the lower courts are not demoralized by having their findings subject to appeal. On the other hand, that makes them careful and cautious. More serious is the contention that the Referendum is an appeal from the judgment of the instructed to the opinion of the uninstructed — from knowledge to ignorance. In this there is enough truth to make it unanswerable directly. It must be set down on the debit side of the ledger.

Other debit entries may be drawn from experience. In Switzerland it is said that the Referendum is just as likely to kill good measures as bad. Furthermore it is charged that useful measures have been defeated merely because the country was dissatisfied with its representatives and rulers.[1] In some of our own States desirable laws have been kept from going into effect for many months, held up by reason of petitions engineered by selfish interests with no expectation that they would in the end prevail, but solely to secure delay. This suggests possibilities of blackmail. Also the door is opened for some other of the baser of human motives — resentment, rancor, jealousy, spite.

Over against these things may be set certain gains. It seems clear that the tendency of the device is to lessen the use of money in the Legislatures. In the States where the system has been adopted, corporations are said to hesitate to pay anything for the passage of bills that may be easily killed by the Referendum. Not too much weight should be attached to this, for corporations spend their money mainly to prevent rather than to secure legis-

[1] W. E. Rappard, "The Initiative and Referendum in Switzerland," *American Political Science Review*, vi, 361 (August, 1912).

lation, but if the fear of the Referendum lessens their venalities at all, so much the better. In one direction at any rate this probably results, for the menace of the "striker" has been blunted. No longer can he with much effect threaten the corporation with the passage of an obnoxious bill unless he is bought off, for the corporation itself can resort to the Referendum for protection.

It is unlikely that the reformers who have agitated for the application of the Referendum in this country knew about one of its results in Switzerland, else their zeal might have been dampened. There, to the confusion and dismay of its strongest advocates, Boyd Winchester tells us,[1] the measures which they most prized, when in spite of them put on the ballot after enactment, have been negatived. Contrary to all expectations, laws of the highest importance, some of them openly framed for popularity, have been vetoed by the people after they have been adopted by the federal and cantonal legislatures. This result is intelligible enough. It is possible, by agitation and exhortation, to produce in the mind of the average citizen a vague impression that he desires a particular change, but when the agitation has settled down, when the subject has been thrashed out, when the law is before him with all its detail, he is sure to find in it something that is likely to disturb his habits, his ideas, his prejudice, or his interest, and so he votes "No." Thus the system serves as a guarantee against precipitate legislation in matters of vital concern to the community; and is deemed thoroughly successful by those who wish that there should be as little legislation as possible.

The referendum in Geneva on the old-age pension law has been described by Edwin E. Slosson, writing on the spot. Within three months of the passage of that law by the Grand Council, it was annulled by the people of Geneva, by a vote of 2,458 in favor to 9,276 against. Although fewer than half of the registered voters took part, there was no room for doubt that the result was a fair expression of the opinion of the whole electorate. The percentage voting was greater than at any other referendum in the preceding ten years. Rich wards and poor, Catholic and Protestant, German and French speaking, rural and urban populations, agreed in rejecting the law. Only one precinct out of the fifty-two in the canton voted "Yes," and that was a small precinct of 48 votes.

[1] *The Swiss Republic,* 169.

Although the adoption of the Referendum is generally advocated by the radicals, says Mr. Slosson, it seems from this, as from many other instances, that when the Referendum really works as it is intended to work, that is, when it elicits an expression of opinion from a considerable proportion of the electorate, it is more likely to err in conservative than radical directions.[1]

The same result has begun to appear on this side of the water. A notable instance is that of the Full Crew Bill in Missouri in 1914. Organized labor had for some time in various parts of the country been waging a campaign to compel the railroads to put more men on each freight train than the roads thought necessary. The pressure of the unions was felt in the Legislatures, but when a statute that had been enacted in Missouri was held up by referendum petition and put before the people, they rejected it by a vote of more than two to one. Episodes of this sort give ground for thinking it far from impossible that the Referendum may block more than the Initiative can advance.

Certain details of the optional Referendum should be noticed. One concerns what are known as emergency measures. Manifestly some measures may be of such pressing and immediate importance that they ought not to be exposed to chance of delay by referendum petitions. On the other hand it is almost impossible to provide for this without giving undue opportunity to escape the Referendum. If the Legislature may declare what of its bills are emergency measures, the temptation is strong to go far beyond reason. Thus in South Dakota of 2,573 acts passed in twenty years, 1,039 were passed with the emergency clause. With great variety of phrasing, most of the States have tried to stop the loophole, but with doubtful success. The South Dakota Supreme Court came to the rescue in 1915 with a decision [2] to the effect that the emergency clause cannot prevent a referendum unless there exists an actual emergency, as defined by the Constitution. Perhaps in time other decisions will combine with higher standards of legislative honor to lessen the cause for criticism.

About half the States, viewing the Referendum as a veto, have applied to it the new idea that it ought to be possible to veto part of a measure without annulling the rest. This is open to some

[1] "The Referendum in Action," *Independent*, October 6, 1910.
[2] State *ex rel*. Richards *v*. Whisman, 36 So. Dak. 260.

grave objections. The situation is quite different from that when a Governor is concerned, for if a Governor vetoes part of a bill, at any rate before the end of a session, the Legislature may override the veto. In such case the Governor has not a free hand in changing the whole purport of a measure by vetoing part of it. If the popular veto be unrestricted, the people, by taking out one word, might even change a negative to an affirmative. Should it be retorted that they ought to be able to do this or anything else they please, one rejoinder would be that in a legislative body measures containing more than a single simple proposition are often worked out wisely by compromise. To remove this or that concession by the Referendum might work injustice and would at any rate throw the scheme out of balance. If it be granted that an electorate is unfitted for compromise and adjustment, the objection has weight. Yet it is to be admitted that if parts of bills cannot be reached what are known as "jokers" are protected. This so nearly balances considerations as to make the question one of much difficulty.

Poland has a novel form of the optional referendum, the option resting with the Cabinet, if we may presume that is meant by the translation which says the "Government" by unanimous vote may refer to the electorate a Government bill that has been rejected by the Parliament.

NUMBER OF QUESTIONS

The number of measures, constitutional and statutory combined, brought to the ballot by the Initiative and Referendum or the Referendum alone, has given ground for much discussion. The charge is that it has put on the electorate a strain to which the voters are altogether unequal. There can be little question that in some instances this has been the case. For example, no unprejudiced man can seriously contend that when forty-eight questions confronted California voters in 1914, the task was within the capacity of any but a very few. Even the most experienced legislator would be appalled at having to determine within a few minutes the merits of forty-eight unconnected proposals for legislation. To be sure, there was opportunity for decision in advance and doubtless many voters earnestly tried to reach a wise conclusion before entering the booth, but such preparation cannot be imagined of the greater part of the electorate. It must have been largely an unintelligent vote.

However, exceptional cases of this sort must not get too much weight. In fairness it should be set forth that in the first dozen years of the actual use of the system at fifty-one elections where measures were submitted as a result of Initiative petitions, three hundred and fifty measures were placed on the ballots, an average of almost exactly seven at an election. The opportunity was used excessively in Oregon, California, Colorado, and Arizona. In the dozen other States where measures were so submitted, the average was three and a half. Furthermore it has not been uncommon for the people to use the system as a child would a new toy, at first with joyous zeal, then tiring of the sport. In some States the reaction took the form of spontaneous revolt after a few years, the word going about to "kill everything," with the result that proposals good, bad, and indifferent were slaughtered *en masse*. Doubtless after a while we shall reach equilibrium in the matter. It is not likely, though, that we shall get down to the Swiss level. There only two federal measures were enacted in a score of years as the result of the Initiative. In the cantons the showing is even more discouraging to those who look to this device for the regeneration of government. For a like period the average was less than one measure to a canton.

Americans are more active than the Swiss politically, and such averages are not likely to be duplicated here. It is more probable that even after the novelty of the system has worn off we shall use it to a perplexing degree, made all the more perplexing by the steady increase in the number of ballot questions from other sources. To illustrate, in that year when California had forty-eight questions on the ballot, only twenty-one were initiated by petition, the other twenty-seven being put on by the Legislature. Then there are the questions coming as a result of the optional Referendum, beside a host of purely local questions. This is all on top of the necessity of choice between an inordinate number of candidates, for we still insist upon electing a great variety of administrative officers who ought to be appointed, and the short-ballot reform, a most commendable proposal, makes slow headway.

Something will have to be done about it if we are to get reasonably intelligent use of the suffrage. Voting by mail, with the ballots distributed some time in advance, would help the situation if a way to prevent frauds could be devised. An arbitrary limit is not impossible. In the Massachusetts Convention of

1917 it was suggested that as petitions there were to go first to the Legislature, the right of way might be given to the five getting the larger votes in Senate and House combined, the others to be referred to the following Legislature. This was objected to on the ground that it would invite the filing of petitions for trivial objects, which would be supported by legislators hostile to vital reforms — a possibility still thought by the author of the proposal to be somewhat remote. Another suggestion was that the petitions having the larger number of signatures should get the right of way, to which it was objected that the result would be an alarming expenditure of time and money by rival groups of signature hunters. The problem is not simple. Extreme advocates of direct legislation see no danger in the prospect — on the contrary they enjoy it — but most men versed in suffrage processes will agree that it is a problem worth study.

Something is to be gained by preventing the same question from reappearing on the ballot year after year. Several of the States have forbidden the resubmission of a defeated proposal for three years. On the other hand it must be admitted that nearly all reforms worth while have been the result of long agitation, reaching success after repeated defeat. Only from practical considerations can the reformer be wisely denied the chance to present his views as often as he pleases. Two straws indicate that the electorate itself may not favor repressing the reformer. Colorado, by a vote of 55,667 for to 112,537 against, defeated in 1914 a proposal that a rejected measure should not be submitted again for six years, and Ohio in the following year defeated a like proposal, by a vote of 417,384 to 482,275. Perhaps, though, the decision was on the score of the length of the delay.

One way to discourage putting too many questions on the ballot is to require a large number of signatures to the petitions. Partly for this purpose, partly to get a guarantee of good faith and of a reasonably large public interest, it has been common to require the signatures of a specified percentage of the electorate, the figures running from three to ten per cent in the case of proposed statutes, from five to fifteen per cent in the case of proposed constitutional amendments. A few States have added minima or maxima, and some by requiring that a certain proportion of the signatures shall come from a specified number of counties or fraction of all the counties, try to ensure that the demand for the measure shall be reasonably widespread. To put the requirement in percentages has proved to have the objection that as population grows the number of signatures necessary becomes unduly large, and the defect was developed from another angle by the doubling of the electorate as the suffrage was given to women. Of late, therefore, the tendency has been to stipulate for a fixed number of signatures.

SIGNATURES AND EXPENSE

This matter of signatures is one of the perplexing things in putting the system into effect. It is purely arbitrary, and therefore invites heated controversy altogether out of proportion to its importance, between friends who want to make the machinery work easily and foes who want the machinery to be as cumbersome as possible. As far as convenience goes, that of not only the officials but also of everybody else concerned, the argument is all on the side of having the requirement as low as may be safe. On the other hand a large requirement has some merit in the way of securing greater attention for the proposal, developing wider discussion, encouraging study. In and of themselves the signatures are really of slight significance or consequence. Everybody knows that good nature and the dislike of saying "No" incline most men to sign anything in the way of a petition that is laid before them. Often they pay no attention to its nature, and this makes deceit easy.

In the scandalous case of the attack on the University of Oregon by use of the Referendum, said to have begun in the spite of a disappointed labor-union organizer who determined to be revenged because he was unable to organize a Carpenters' Union in the place where the University is located, respectable men testified on the stand that they had signed the petitions because these had been represented to them as favoring a municipal paving plan for the city of Portland. "Others stated that they had signed the petition because the circulators had represented it to be for the purpose of giving the University its money and not holding the money up." [1]

More objectionable still, at least in some ways, is that feature of the process which is presented by payment for getting signatures. It has become customary to pay five or ten cents a name and this has developed an entirely new occupation — that of signature-getting. Burton J. Hendrick has described in lively

[1] Allen H. Eaton, *The Oregon System*, 147.

fashion what goes on in Oregon.[1] He avers that at all times these "signature-getters" keep busy, though they are most active during the April and May following a legislative session. They are found in practically every part of the State. They invade the office buildings, the apartment-houses, and the homes of Portland, and tramp from farmhouse to farmhouse. Young women, ex-book-canvassers, broken-down clergymen, people who in other communities would find their natural level as sandwichmen, dapper hustling youths, perhaps earning their way through college — all find useful employment in soliciting signatures. The canvasser bustles into an office, carrying under his arm a neat parcel of pamphlets, the covers perhaps embellished with colored pictures of the American flag. He gives his victim a few minutes to read the printed matter, and then, placing his finger on a neatly ruled space, says, "Sign here."

The same sort of thing is reported from California. It is averred that in Los Angeles, for example, there are many persons who do nothing else for a living but circulate petitions. One man is said to maintain an office there the year round, and to have many men in his employ; he will enter into a contract with a customer to circulate successfully any Initiative petition that the customer may want. Governor Byrne of South Dakota told the Governors' Conference of 1913 of an instance where the daily papers of his State contained for some weeks an advertisement telling of a certain law to be initiated and calling for agents to circulate petitions at ten cents a signature. He told of two instances where "for purely commercial purposes, frankly and openly expressed, without attempting to hide it, interested people referred a law, paying ten cents each for signers, for the definite purpose of suspending a salutory law for two years, not expecting to defeat it in the end."[2] At the same gathering Governor Ammons, of Colorado, sounded a note of warning: "Be sure of all things you do, to provide penalties for the securing of names to petitions for pay, because with that feature we have had a great deal of trouble."[3] Returning to the subject at the Conference of 1914, he said: "We had thirty-four measures that went to the people two years ago for their vote. Sixty-five per cent of all the signatures for the submission of all these were secured in the city of Denver, between the Union depot and Stock

[1] "Law-making by the Voters," *McClure's Mag.*, Aug., 1911.
[2] *Proceedings*, 289. [3] *Ibid.*, 279.

Street, about six squares away, and between 14th and 20th Streets in consecutive order. We had pages and pages right along together that were apparently forgeries." [1]

Worse than that kind of fraud is the blackmail the system has here and there developed. J. D. Barnett says that in Oregon in the case of at least one measure circulators of petitions were bought off by opponents of the proposed legislation, and in another case a promise was made, with apparent power to make it good, that a referendum would be dropped upon payment, the first offer being for $1500, followed by other offers down to $400. Less blatant, but even more pernicious, is the evil resulting from the temptation put before the professional petition-circulator to stir up agitations in order that he may have employment. [2]

Various ways to prevent such evils have been suggested. Governor Byrne went at the problem in South Dakota on the theory that in signing a petition the voter was exercising a right of franchise, and that paying him or his receiving pay was bribery. He wanted a law making this a misdemeanor. In this he failed, but he did get a provision for a return with the petition, in which the circulator makes affidavit that he did not receive pay. Allen H. Eaton, after studying the situation in Oregon, thought the evil would be eliminated by making it a crime to give or receive money for signatures. [3] The Massachusetts amendment directed only that provision should be made by law for penalties for signing or refusing to sign for money. In the Convention framing the amendment other remedies were also discussed. One suggestion, buttressed by the assertion that in California it costs $7500 to circulate an Initiative petition, was that it might be just as well to have the money paid over to the State, in a lump, as a filing fee, doing away with signatures altogether. More stress was laid on the proposal that, as in Switzerland, the voters should go to some official in order to sign. In Switzerland it is also permitted to cast votes for a petition in the gatherings that correspond to the New England town-meetings, and a like method of endorsement was suggested for use here. The suggestion that voters should present themselves at some office was met with the answer that in America this would be fatal to the system, because our people would never go to that trouble, to which it was rejoined that if the voters did not care enough about

---

[1] *Proceedings*, 232.   [2] *Initiative, Referendum and Recall in Oregon*, 68.
[3] The Oregon System, 148.

a measure to take some trouble in its behalf, it could not be worth much. The Convention came near adopting a compromise under which the Secretary of State would send signature cards to the voters, to be returned if the voter saw fit.

The cost of signatures is not the only expense accompanying the I. and R. Governor Pierce of Oregon asserted in his message of 1925 that the repeal of the income tax law "was accomplished by the prodigal use of a lavish campaign fund spent very largely in the repeated publication of false and misleading propaganda." A committee reporting to the California Legislature in 1923 on expenditure in 1922 had found $1,081,784 to have been spent on seven strenuously contested measures, which was of course less than the real total, for such things are never fully disclosed. The side that had spent the most money, won.

It seems unfortunate that when so much effort is being directed toward lessening the use of money in politics, a device believed by its champions to be a great step forward, should bring in its train new ways for spending money to get political results. Well grounded has been the complaint that long purses have had undue influence in advancing men. Now they are to have undue influence in advancing measures. Surely some method to prevent this ought to be devised.

How the People Vote

Under any form of the Referendum, whether combined with the Initiative or independent, there arises the question of whether the people vote more usefully than their representatives. Various factors affect the answer. Roughly they may be classified into those that concern motive and those that concern capacity.

Offhand the common impulse would be to say that the motives of the people are the better. There is a widespread impression that legislators are often impelled by improper ambition, by cowardice, greed, or other ignoble motives which are not found in the polling booth. This is not without some basis of fact, and yet my own conviction is that nine tenths of the lawmakers of the land are above the average of their constituents in point of honor, honesty, courage, unselfishness, and public spirit. Were it not so, they would not be elected. Instinctively an electorate chooses for its representative, as a rule, a man above its own average in these respects — not necessarily its best man, nor even a man from its best quarter or third, but a man above the average. If you doubt this, take a voting list and see where you will find the average.

Even if it were true that the representative is in character below the average of his constituency, yet would the balance of motive be commonly turned in his favor by a single factor — responsibility. He goes to the Legislature knowing that he has been entrusted with the duty of serving not his own interests but those of others. At times he may forget, but conscience is ever at hand to prick his memory. He may seem flippant, careless, indifferent to his trusteeship, and yet a hundred times a day he is reminded that he is a servant, for the address and salutation of every letter, the errand of every caller, the greeting on the street, the ceremonies of the assembly chamber, the little privileges and honors of office — all breathe to him of his relations with his constituents. Trusteeship involves responsibility. The trustee is held accountable. The reward or punishment of a representative may not always be tangible, but it is always real. He earns or forfeits respect, deference, honor, confidence, good-will.

How about the voter in the booth? Does he desire or fear what may be the result of his vote in any of these particulars? No, for it can have no such result. Is he accountable? Only to his own conscience, never to anybody else. Is he a trustee? If so, he does not know it. Unless he is that rare specimen, an altruist, he thinks only of himself and his personal relation to the question before him. Nothing of the dignity and solemnity of office affects him, for he is a non-official lawmaker. He knows his vote has very slight chance of influence, for he is but one of a hundred thousand or a million. Nobody will ever learn how he votes. No record of Yeas and Nays will inform his neighbors. If he evades by not voting at all, nothing will ever happen to him. What is the chance of his putting the common welfare above what he may think his own?

It has been argued that the situation will create a sense of responsibility, that unselfish, altruistic, patriotic impulse will be stirred to life, that a man will become conscious of his importance and will proudly answer the call of duty. So it may be with the few, but who knowing human nature can expect it of the many? Utopia has not yet arrived.

Rather is it probable that the secret ballot upon measures will enlarge the influence of prejudice and narrowness and ignorance.

The first use of the Initiative for amending the Constitution of Switzerland was directed against the Jewish method of slaughtering cattle, in 1893. The amendment commanded the support of less than a third of the members of either House, but was carried on popular vote by about three to two. Switzerland in 1882 rejected by the huge majority of 254,340 to 68,027 the law on epidemics, because vaccination was made compulsory and stringent regulations were laid down to secure isolation in case of illness. Ultimately compulsory vaccination was dropped and the law came into effect without a demand for the referendum. California in 1914 rejected an initiated statute for one day of rest in seven; Missouri in the same year a legislative amendment for pensions for the blind; Colorado an initiated statute for the probation of criminals; Washington an initiated statute for convict road work. Some of these may have been objectionable for collateral reasons, but probably not all of them, if any. Surely the record does not indicate altruism.

In point of capacity it is hard to understand how anybody can seriously maintain that an electorate will be superior to a Legislature. Official lawmakers are picked men, almost invariably above the mean in schooling, experience with affairs, and intelligence. Universal suffrage puts everybody on a level — trench digger and college professor, vagrant and bank president, degenerate and regenerate, sinner and saint. Huxley used a happy metaphor. Some experience of sea-life, he said, led him to think that he would be very sorry to find himself on board a ship in which the voices of the cook and the loblolly boys counted for as much as those of the officers, upon a question of steering, or reefing topsails; or where the "great heart" of the crew was called upon to settle the ship's course. "And there is no sea more dangerous than the ocean of practical politics — none in which there is more need of good pilotage and of a single, unfaltering purpose when the waves rise high." [1] Was not Huxley right in concluding that voting power, as a means of giving effect to opinion, is more likely to prove a curse than a blessing to the voters, unless that opinion is the result of sound judgment operating upon sound knowledge? And who can expect as to any but the most important measures either sound judgment or sound knowledge from a great part of the electorate?

It will be said that we assume the capacity of the electorate to

[1] T. H. Huxley, *On the Natural Inequality of Men, Method and Results*, 313.

choose its representatives, and if it may vote intelligently upon men, why not upon measures? The question can be turned upon the questioner, for a main argument in behalf of the new system is based on the allegation that the voters are incapable of electing honest and reasonably competent men to represent them. To this it will be rejoined that voting upon measures is a simpler thing than voting upon men, that a measure stands independently, presents a single issue, where the question of a man is complicated by party affiliations, views on various issues, and the many-sided personal factor.

Nevertheless, if capacity alone were to determine, the weight of conclusions drawn from experience would throw the scale in favor of chosen representatives.

Napoleon was not altogether wrong in his epigram: "The first duty of a prince is doubtless to do that which the people wants; but that which a people wants is hardly ever that which it says."[1] The record of mass voting upon measures throws grave doubt on the accuracy of such voting as an expression of the popular will. It is beside the mark to say that in the great majority of instances the people vote right (that is to say, as you would have voted, for it is the man with whom you disagree who votes wrong).

For example, it is well known that with only one or two questions on the ballot, "Yes" ordinarily has a better chance than "No." This may be in part due to the fact that many voters, like the people of Athens, always want some new thing, either because they find novelty attractive in itself or because their condition leads them to imagine any change is likely to be for the better. Doubtless also it is in part because of that trait of human nature which inclines more men to assent than to dissent.

Not a few, however, habitually dissent, on general principles. A striking illustration of this was given by the Massachusetts vote in 1919 on a rearrangement of the Constitution that had been made by a Constitutional Convention. The sole purpose was to make the Constitution more easy to consult, more intelligible. Not a voice had been raised against the committee report in the Convention. It would be impossible to imagine a valid reason for opposition by anybody other than a casuist.

---

[1] *Memorial de Sainte-Hélène*, ii, 110, Paris ed., 1824, cited by Francis Lieber, *Manual of Political Ethics*, 2nd ed., ii, 47 note.

Yet at the polls, with more than three fifths of the voters for Governor expressing their opinion in this matter, 64,978 out of 263,359 voted against the rearrangement. The inference is that nearly one fifth of the total electorate voted "No" without intelligent reason. In the case of 261 proposals scattered through twenty-seven States in 1914, only five had the opposition of less than one fifth of the voters. On four of these five the "No" vote was more than 19 per cent of the "Yes" and "No" combined; one was opposed by only about one seventh of those voting on it. In all probability some of these 261 measures were no more controversial than the Massachusetts rearrangement. The conclusion is irresistible that a material part of every mass vote is the result of instinctive hostility to change rather than of reasoned judgment.

On the other hand there are thoughtful men who are unwilling to approve any proposal on which they do not chance to feel adequately informed, and who argue that under such circumstances it is better to vote "No" than to refrain from voting.

To meet this situation the Missouri Convention of 1923 submitted to the people an amendment changing the form of a vote on a referendum to — "Shall the Act of the General Assembly be rejected?" The amendment failed, unfortunately, from the point of view of political science, for the effect of the change would have been instructive.

With many questions on the ballot, the tendency is to vote one way, either all "Yes" or all "No." The Massachusetts Convention of 1853 submitted eight propositions to the people and all were rejected. That of 1918 submitted nineteen and all were approved. In each case there was ground for thinking that the sentiment on a single proposition biassed the vote on the rest. Men seem sometimes to come to the polls in either an affirmative or a negative mood. In 1914 the Georgia electorate voted "Yes" on each of nine proposals, that of Missouri "No" on each of fifteen. The North Carolina electorate voted against each of ten proposals, and the people of South Carolina voted for each of ten. Wisconsin rejected each of ten. A little discrimination appeared in Oregon where four survived out of twenty-nine, South Dakota where one survived out of twelve, and Louisiana, where out of seventeen all but three were accepted.

At the very least this showing must be admitted to impeach the capacity of a material part of the electorate to exercise quite independent judgment on each of a numerous group of propositions.

Opinions differ as to the significance of the variations in the size of the vote on measures as compared with that on men, but if interest is a measure of capacity, here too the figures will raise doubts. Almost never has a larger vote been cast on measures than on candidates. In the thirty-one States that in 1914 voted on measures, on the average a trifle under seven tenths of the voters who expressed their choice of candidates, also expressed their judgment on measures. The percentage ran as low as 14.4 on one measure, in Georgia, but there were nine States where it rose above 90. Ten years later the average of the total was below six tenths, with a range from 12.5 per cent to 95.6 per cent.[1] Such variations are perplexing, but at any rate one fact stands out — that important questions have often been decided by a minor fraction of the electorate. For instance, Colorado in 1912 adopted a constitutional amendment for the recall of judicial decisions by a vote of 55,416 to 40,891 — total, 96,307 — at an election where 265,991 votes were cast for presidential electors. In the same year Denver adopted the commission form of government with the ratio about the same. Of the 90 proposals adopted throughout the country in 1924, the affirmative vote in the case of 79 was less than half the vote cast for officers; in the case of 59, less than 40 per cent; 16 received less than 25 per cent.

President Taft thinks a large vote for candidates and a small vote on legislative issues at the same election the best evidence that a majority of the electorate have neither interest nor information enough to lead them to vote on such issues, but do feel themselves competent to select representatives for the purpose.[2] Champions of the new system give a different turn to this by averring that the lack of an absolutely full vote is not a disadvantage, but the reverse. It means that only those who feel some interest in the subject, and are therefore prepared to act with a certain intelligence take the trouble to vote, and that the members of the unintelligent residuum voluntarily disfranchise themselves.[3] Furthermore the figures seem to indicate that with the use of the Initiative and Referendum there is at any rate

[1] *Political Science Quarterly*, vol. XL, no. 1.
[2] Wm. H. Taft, *Popular Government*, 21.
[3] S. E. Moffett, "The Constitutional Referendum in California," *Political Science Quarterly*, March, 1898.

less neglect or indifference. In 1924 when the average vote on measures was 57 per cent of that for officers, the average on constitutional amendments alone, far the greater part of which started in the old way, was 51.3 per cent. That on measures referred by the Legislature was 64.3 per cent; on measures referred by petition, 82.7 per cent; on initiated measures, 80.5 per cent.

Analysis is declared to show that the largest percentage of non-voters on proposed laws is to be found in city slum districts, where the greatest percentage of ignorance and illiteracy prevails. Indeed there are those who find here an effective and desirable educational test. Yet inquiry among intelligent men of serious purpose will disclose no small number of them who will avow that they refrained from voting on this or that question because they did not feel themselves well enough informed to pass judgment. The sword cuts both ways.

Many friends of the Referendum admit that the situation is serious enough to call for precaution; and approve taking it in the shape of requirement that a proposal shall be passed upon by a specified percentage of the electorate. The demand that it shall receive the support of an absolute majority of all voting appears to them unreasonable, and experience in the States where such a requirement exists, seems to justify them, from the practical point of view, but a requirement of approval by a third or so of the electorate is prudent and fair, and it has been imposed by a number of States. Nebraska, where an amendment must be approved by a majority of all persons voting at a general election, in order to carry, has adopted the plan of party endorsement, which is merely a mechanical device for counting the votes of those who really do not care to express themselves upon proposed measures. Idaho and some other States have adopted the separate ballot for constitutional proposals, and thus bring out a larger vote.

POWER OF MINORITIES AND MAJORITIES

There are those who fear that the Referendum, and also the Initiative when coupled with the Referendum, will work us harm through undue power given to minorities; and there are those who fear harm through undue power given to majorities. In spite of what seems a contradiction, neither fear is wholly groundless. Senator Lodge in his powerful arguments against any breaking down of the representative system emphasized repeatedly the fact that the decision of referenda is often made by the greater part of a minority, and this means that a small fraction of the electorate may dominate. Herbert Croly thinks that the Initiative and Referendum are instruments of minority rule and usually of the rule of a very small minority. None but an idolater, he declares, could believe for one moment that in the forms which they have ordinarily assumed they are instruments of majority rule. He points out that the ordinary mechanism of the Initiative operates so as to give to a small percentage of the voters the right to force the electorate either to accept or reject a specific legislative measure. "This is an extremely valuable privilege, because the right to force a vote on specific legislative projects, which cannot be discussed in detail or amended, but which must be approved or disapproved as a whole, places an enormous power in the hands of a skilful and persistent minority." [1] He recognizes that "it confides the leadership in legislation to small minorities, and allows to the majority only the negative function of submitting to the imposition or rejecting it." And he says (p. 307) "the friends of direct government do not pay enough attention to the fact that their proposed instruments of democracy entirely break down as agencies of majority rule."

If these contentions are right and if it is true that democracy cannot endure control by the lesser part, then danger follows.

On the other hand it can hardly be denied that the new device gives a readier instrument with which the majority can oppress the minority, than is at hand in the representative system. Government has long been recognized as existing largely for the purpose of preventing such oppression, and democracy itself has long been viewed with alarm by those who enlarge upon its possibilities of evil. Edmund Burke was certain that in a democracy the majority of the citizens is capable of exercising the most cruel oppressions upon the minority, and that oppression of the minority will extend to far greater numbers, and will be carried on with much greater fury than can almost ever be apprehended from the dominion of a single scepter. John C. Calhoun pointed out that the government of the uncontrolled numerical majority is but the absolute and despotic form of popular government, just as the uncontrolled will of one man is monarchy. In a decision holding a local option law invalid, Justice McKinstry voiced

[1] *Progressive Democracy*, 306.

the opinion of the California Supreme Court when saying: "Our government is a representative republic, not a simple democracy. Whenever it shall be transformed into the latter — as we are taught by the examples of history — the tyranny of a changeable majority will soon drive honest men to seek refuge beneath the despotism of a single ruler." [1]

How reconcile the two lines of thought? By recognizing that the majority must rule, but that the disparities of human intelligence will always enable minorities to impel majorities, and that danger comes not from giving power to either, but from excess of power, from power uncontrolled. Upon the champions of direct legislation rests the burden of proving that it gives too free a hand neither to majorities nor to minorities.

PROBABLE EFFECTS

What is likely to be the effect of the new system upon our old institutions is a question of vital importance even though that effect be remote. Attention must be paid to tendencies because tendencies will in time carry us past milestones. This alone can justify the warmth and vigor of the fight that has been waged by friends and foes of the innovation. Not remembering this, it would be hard, for example, to understand the earnestness of President Taft in declaring that the effect upon the legislative branch of the Government is necessarily to minimize its power, to take away its courage and independence of action, to destroy its sense of responsibility and to hold it up as unworthy of confidence. "Nothing would more certainly destroy the character of a lawmaking body. No one with just pride and proper self-respect would aspire to a position in which the sole standard of action must be the question what the majority of the electorate, or rather a minority likely to vote, will do with measures the details of which there is neither time nor proper means to make the public understand." [2]

Or observe the dictum of John S. Sheppard, Jr.: "Nothing is more natural than that the character and ability of our representatives should have deteriorated, under the tendency toward the 'direct' system. In the first place, we have not been sufficiently careful in our choice of representatives, because we have regarded the selection as of little consequence in view of the real

[1] Ex parte Wall, 48 Cal. 279 (1874).
[2] *Popular Government*, 63.

power being lodged in our own hands under the 'direct' plan. This thought has made us careless about whom we chose." [1]

Frankly, such opportunities for observation as have come to me have not presented any evidence whatever indicating such an effect. As a practical matter it is altogether improbable that unless the new system is carried much farther than has anywhere yet been attempted, the political ambition of capable men will be quenched or even discouraged. Only a comparatively small part of the work and the responsibility of legislators has yet been taken from them. Their office still brings with it plenty of chance for industry, and still is adorned with honors that may be petty and vain but are attractive.

Everywhere the Legislatures still see the beginning and the conclusion of a host of proposals, many of them far from trivial. Even of Oregon, where the new system has probably reached its greatest expansion, one may doubt the accuracy of the allegation that the Legislature, as far as really important constructive work is concerned, has ceased to exist. It is true that no personal knowledge lets me pass judgment on Oregon, and it must be admitted that those who have written of the workings of the system there seem to agree that it has made the Legislature inefficient, but a perusal of the matters that have been submitted to the people of that State in the course of fifteen years and have been approved, might well lead to the conclusion that if they exhausted the legislative capacity of Oregon, then Oregon must be wonderfully blessed with justice and contentment.

If argument that the personnel of Legislatures will be seriously affected is somewhat far-fetched, the counter-argument about the men likely to take the leadership in the use of the Initiative and Referendum is still more insubstantial and remote. It has been alleged that through direct legislation the State will offer an attractive field of usefulness for such of her citizens as do not care to give up their whole time to public life. Public-spirited citizens, it is said, without dislocation of business or profession, may and will devote a much larger share of their time than now to the consideration of public questions. If they conceive a desirable step in legislation, they will not have to contrive to get into office and to stay there long enough to accomplish their ends. They have a dignified and honorable method of presenting to the final authority, for adoption or rejection, the best fruits of

[1] "Representation in Popular Government," *Forum*, June, 1910.

their labors, free from the risk of mutilation or distortion by ill-formed, overworked, or corrupt Legislatures. This alone would be a powerful means of bringing spontaneously to the public service, and at no expense, a large amount of talent of the best possible sort for which there is now little encouragement in public life. This is the talent on which we should depend for the most serious lawmaking, and which we now have little chance to utilize. The Legislature will thus be facing a reasonable and wholesome competition, from which the public cannot fail to profit.[1]

If direct legislation in any considerable degree should become habitual and regular, something of such a desirable effect might be seen, but it is quite unlikely to take proportions of any consequence with that irregular and sporadic resort to the Initiative and Referendum which now seems probable.

Less visionary appear the predictions that the new system will have some influence in purifying certain of the Legislatures. It is said to have had this effect already in some of the Western Commonwealths, notably that of California. This would be reasonable to expect, and wherever a legislative body has sunk into the thraldom of selfish interests and has permitted its work to be vitiated by improper influences or by actual corruption, it may well be that a greater power of direct action by the electorate will result in a raising of legislative standards.

It does not follow that use of money in affecting legislation will be lessened. On the contrary more is likely to be spent, but the scene and the nature of the expenditure will be changed. To circulate petitions will cost money, much money. To shape opinion will cost more. Newspaper, billboard, and street-car advertising, booklets, pamphlets, circulars, speakers, automobiles, headquarters — these things for an effective State-wide campaign mount well up into the thousands. Selfish interests, invisible interests will find it just as advantageous to use this machinery as in the past they found it to use the lobby, just as advantageous and far more costly.

Much cry is heard because these interests work in the dark, noiselessly bending Legislatures to their will. Who is so simple as to imagine that they can be forced into the open if the appeal is to the electorate? We are told that the authors of four out of the five Oregon referenda of 1913 were not known with certainty

[1] L. S. Johnson, *The Initiative, Referendum and Recall*, W. B. Munro ed., 151.

if at all. The man who filed the petition against the Workman's Compensation Act of that year is said to have declared he himself did not know who was behind the movement. Misleading names of imaginary organizations were used to deceive the voters. The opponents of the appropriation for the University posed as "The Oregon Higher Institutions Betterment League." A scheme for saddling a toll-road on the State was fathered by "A Committee of Farmers." Chicanery like this can be perpetrated much more easily upon the electorate than upon a Legislature. The larger the multitude, the easier the deception. "You can fool all of the people part of the time."

You cannot, however, buy all the people at any time. Unfortunately bribery on a large scale is occasionally found in our elections, but with increasing rarity, and it has become altogether abnormal. Whether in recent years there have been more instances of buying Legislatures than of buying electors, would be no easy matter to determine. Anyhow to buy enough votes to affect materially the result of a State-wide poll would be much more costly than to buy the control of a Legislature, and would be usually out of the question. Therefore credit the Referendum with the likelihood of gain in this particular.

Also admit that a larger percentage of Representatives than of electors might be exposed to that milder form of venality which is bred by the prospect of direct pecuniary benefit, such as springs from measures to the advantage of corporations or involving the expenditure of public funds. Here, too, it is quite possible that temptation will have less of pernicious effect upon the electorates than it has had upon the Legislatures.

Furthermore it is manifestly impossible to bring pressure to bear upon the voters in any considerable numbers — the pressure familiar to every legislator. You cannot cajole, wheedle, or threaten the individual voter to any dangerous extent. He has no reëlection at stake. His vote will not endanger his business or professional income, nor cost him the good-will of any friend. In this respect the plebiscite has decidedly the advantage of the legislative roll-call.

On the other side of the account an entry of a less disagreeable nature may be made to the advantage of the Legislature. It concerns unwritten rules of action that involve no pains or penalties. A legislator, like a man of affairs, finds himself compelled to formulate for his own guidance certain tests by means of which he speedily reaches decision on various classes of questions. Perhaps unconsciously he will get into the way of opposing all increases of salary or favoring all proposals for home rule of cities. To the voter at the polls, decision has not become so habitual as to give occasion for any such mental standards. It is altogether improbable that he will be guided in the least by general principles. Expediency, the specific need, the impulse of the moment, will determine him. Surely this is no small matter. Our common use of language shows our intuitive sense of its importance, for we find few more opprobrious things to say of a man than that he is without principles, unprincipled. If principles are of such consequence in the daily relations of life, the individual relations, how much greater must be their need when the common welfare is at stake!

In point of mechanism both sides claim advantage. The quiet of the polling booth is contrasted with the turbulence of the assembly chamber, whereupon it is retorted that one is dead, the other alive. The merit of deliberation is advanced in behalf of each process, and each is accused of haste. The Legislature, blamed for enacting many bills on the closing day of a session, replies by ridiculing the voter asked to mark for or against thirty, forty, or fifty propositions in the few minutes that he may stay in the booth. The psychological conditions of a legislative assembly are said to militate against independent judgment; those at the polls are said to discourage caution. Perhaps the charges and counter-charges about offset each other.

There is no reason for expecting that in the long run campaigns for and against measures will differ essentially from campaigns for and against men who stand for measures, that is to say, party candidates in times when there are genuine party differences. If this prove to be the outcome, it is not easy to see why one should have upon the electorate an effect essentially different from the other. What matters it whether you choose between McKinley and Bryan, or between monometallism and bimetallism? To be sure the issues are seldom as clear cut as they were in that memorable campaign, but certainly we have had enough experience with political issues to warrant some inference as to their relations with the suffrage. Nevertheless many advocates of the Referendum seem to think that somehow it will differently affect the voters. It is expected to be more successful in meeting many of the suffrage difficulties already so familiar. We are told that the plebiscite in this new application will cure its own defects. It is urged that the imposing of responsibility will develop more responsibility, that the remedy for the ills of democracy is more democracy, that the use of the ballot will instruct in its use. As the French proverb says, "*En forgeant, on devient forgeron.*" Or as Emerson puts it, "Power educates the potentate." The essence of this may not be doubted by one who does not despair of democracy. He must admit that Dr. Freeman Snow was right in saying that the aim of popular government should be, not how best to govern the people, but how best to teach them to govern themselves.[1] To that end the people should, in fact, take as large a part as possible in the work of governing, but when Dr. Snow says this is equivalent to taking as large a part as possible in legislation, "for democracy means a government of law," the logic falters. Governing and legislation are two different things. They are allied but not synonymous.

Dr. Snow was writing in defense of congressional government and perhaps would not have carried his argument farther, but the champions of the Referendum use it and also err, as it seems to me, in confounding government and legislation. Thus an able writer in the "New Republic" (March 5, 1915) says that a measure of direct government is necessary in order to bring home to the people the extent and importance of their ultimate political responsibility. He thinks that the sense of popular political responsibility and the ability to use popular political power wisely is strengthened less by the delegation of authority than by its exercise. The electorate must learn how to govern chiefly by virtue of its participation in the work of government. The conclusive argument in favor of direct government is consequently educational. The conclusive objection to a representative or legalistic system which does not place occasional responsibility for important legislative decisions on the electorate is its dubious educational effect. If a political democracy is to learn its business it must participate directly in the transaction of its business. It must supplement its representative institutions and its constitutional forms with some method of direct political action, which will bring home to the people a sufficient sense of the stern reality of their ultimate political responsibility.

Here, it will be seen, is the constant assumption that gov-

[1] *Papers of the American Historical Association*, iv, 119.

ernment is legislation. How about the executive and judicial branches? If democracy is to learn its business by participating directly in the transaction thereof, should it occasionally try a murder case or a will case at the polls? Should it now and then by ballot issue the orders usually entrusted to the Chief of the Fire Department or the Insurance Commissioner or the Secretary of the Navy?

The educational contention is academic, not practical. Such use as bids fair to be made of the Referendum is not likely to have any material effect in making better citizens.

DEMOCRACY OR REPRESENTATIVE GOVERNMENT

Will the system hasten advance toward the millennium? With their destinies in their own hands, will the people move faster than would their representatives toward the goal of human progress?

Wholly conjectural though the answer must be, history suggests at any rate probabilities. Sir Henry Maine, the great authority on ancient law, a profound student of civilizations past and present, of peoples Oriental and Occidental, declares it to be indisputable that the greatest part of mankind have never shown a particle of desire to improve their civic conditions since the moment when external completeness was first given to those conditions by their embodiment in some permanent record. Maine further says: "The delusion that Democracy, when it has once had all things put under its feet, is a progressive form of government, lies deep in the convictions of a particular political school; but there can be no delusion grosser. It receives no countenance either from experience or from probability. Englishmen in the East come into contact with vast populations of high natural intelligence, to which the very notion of innovation is loathsome; and the very fact that such populations exist should suggest that the true difference between the East and the West lies merely in this, that in Western countries there is a larger minority of exceptional persons who, for good reasons or bad, have a real desire for change. All that has made England famous, and all that has made England wealthy, has been the work of minorities, sometimes very small ones." [1]

The result-producing minority is larger in a democracy, and therefore more powerful, but that it makes up a large enough

[1] *Popular Government*, 97 (1885).

percentage of the electorate under universal suffrage to sway the decision toward progress, merely by the number of votes, is altogether improbable. Rather is it likely that the minority will still now and then goad the oxen, the majority, to action. If it thinks it can more easily do this with the Initiative and Referendum than with a Legislature, it may have something to learn.

Surely the record thus far does not encourage such hope. It is admitted that in Switzerland the Initiative and the Referendum have proved more reactionary than progressive. This may not be said with confidence of the United States, but the figures are at any rate suggestive. Of 350 measures submitted to the people as a result of Initiative petitions in the course of a dozen years, three fifths were rejected. Of 286 measures submitted in all sorts of ways for State-wide vote in 1914, 58 per cent were rejected. No small part of those the people approved, would have been approved by their representatives; indeed many had been so approved — the constitutional amendments and ordinary laws submitted by the Legislatures themselves — as far as it may be assumed that submission implied approval. This leaves but a small number of measures actually enacted into law, of which we can assume that the Legislatures would not have approved.

Some inference can be drawn from the experience of Oklahoma, a State so young that there if anywhere we should find the new system revolutionary. After thirteen years of its operation, when forty-five measures had been voted on, John H. Bass said: "The prophecy that the Initiative and Referendum would lead to hasty and radical legislation has not been fulfilled." [1] After four years more of trial Blachly and Oatman declared: "Not a single amendment put into operation by the people, except the woman suffrage amendment, is in any degree progressive." [2] Here is no startling manifestation of popular unrest or swift seizure of the chance for change.

Broadening the inquiry, is it clear that an active share in the advancement of progress is a proper function of government? Undoubtedly government ought to protect every citizen in the pursuit of happiness, but ought it to pursue happiness for him? To try to answer these questions would plunge us into the interminable dispute between individualism and collectivism. Let

[1] *Southwestern Political Science Quarterly*, September, 1920.
[2] *The Government of Oklahoma*, 30.

us escape this by going no farther than to say that if direct legislation does no more than incorporate into law the will of the mass, nothing to-day indicates that it is going to advance collectivism among the great part of the peoples of the earth.

More to our present purpose is inquiry as to whether the new system is likely better to enact the public will than it is enacted by the representative system.

Lord Acton has said that America established a pure democracy, but it was democracy in its highest perfection, armed and vigilant, less against aristocracy and monarchy than against its own weakness and excess.[1]

Whether delegation of power to representatives is compatible with pure democracy might be questioned, but otherwise this characterization of what our fathers achieved is admirable.

They had studied the lessons of history. They knew what took place when the populace felt no restraint. They remembered how the Athenians, trying the unfortunate generals after the battle of Arginusae, met the reminder that the citizens were acting in direct contradiction to the law. The citizens exclaimed that they were the people; they made the laws; why should they not have the privilege of disregarding the laws? Euryptolemus and some others stood up for processes of law. "Some of the people approved of this," Xenophon records, "but the greater part cried out that it was strange if any one would not allow the people to do as it pleased."

The statesmen of Revolutionary times knew well the merits of popular assemblies, particularly in New England, where the town-meeting had been familiar for a century and a half; they also knew that although a pure democracy might be the best government for a small people that could meet in person, it was inapplicable to a great country; and they knew the faults of popular assemblies. Rarely have these faults been displayed more unhappily than they were in the local gatherings that wrangled over the Constitution that had been drawn by the Federal Convention of 1787. The long harangues, the specious arguments, the narrow views, the mean suspicions, the rabid charges that so nearly wrecked the beginnings of our nation, furnished the best of proof that its founders were right in their deliberate plan to give democracy a new form, and to arm it, in the phrase of Lord Acton, against its own weakness and excess.

[1] *History of Freedom*, 84.

Had the decision been taken in the town-meetings and at the county courts, it is altogether probable that the new Constitution would not have been adopted. Luckily the final word rested not with the people but with their representatives, gathered in State Conventions.

To one of these representative assemblies, that of Massachusetts, Fisher Ames gave the reason why democracy as it had been hitherto known would not meet the need. "A pure democracy," he said, "would be very burdensome, subject to faction and violence; decisions would often be made by surprise, in the precipitancy of passion, by men who either understand nothing, or care nothing about the subject, or by interested men, or by those who vote for their own indemnity. It would be government, not by laws, but by men. Such were the paltry democracies of Greece and Asia Minor, so much extolled and so often proposed as a model for our imitation. I desire to be thankful that our people are not under any temptation to adopt the advice. I think it will not be denied, that the people are gainers by the election of representatives. They may destroy, but they cannot exercise the powers of government, in person; but by their servants *they* govern. They do not renounce their power; they do not sacrifice their rights; they become the true sovereigns of the country, when they delegate that power, which they cannot use themselves, to their trustees." [1]

Observe here the definite declaration of intent to delegate power to trustees — the very doctrine in the very words nowadays roundly denounced and stoutly denied by many an advocate of direct legislation.

Thomas Jefferson was even more positive about the capacities of the people. In 1789 he wrote to a Paris correspondent: "We think in America that it is necessary to introduce the people into every department of government as far as they are capable of exercising it; and that this is the only way to ensure a long continued and honest administration of its powers. 1. They are not qualified to exercise themselves the Executive department; but they are qualified to name the person who shall exercise it. With us therefore they chuse this officer every four years. 2. They are not qualified to Legislate. With us therefore they only chuse the legislators." [2]

[1] *Debates of Mass. Convention of 1788*, 105.
[2] *Writings of Thomas Jefferson*, P. L. Ford ed., v, 103.

The Jeffersonian idea in our time found expression in the words of one who became a Jeffersonian President — Woodrow Wilson. "A government must have organs," he says; "it cannot act inorganically, by masses. It must have a lawmaking body; it can no more make law through its voters than it can make law through its newspapers." [1]

Yet the representative government that our fathers contemplated, a system based upon the complete delegation of power to trustees who should be held to account at regular intervals, in the course of time became unsatisfactory to many of the people. The doctrine of trusteeship was early attacked by those who wanted to substitute the doctrine of agency. With the fall of the Whigs and the rise of the Democrats came the demand that the representative should be considered as the servant of the people, subject to orders at all times.

Fault-finding grew as the representative system became less truly representative. With the gain of population, the flood of immigrants, and the diversification of pursuits, more and more was it matter of chance whether each group of ideas or interests secured representation in the ratio of its size. Some groups and some classes often failed to have any spokesmen at all in the assembly chamber. The two-party system made the situation worse by subordinating all other questions to the one issue chosen for the deciding test — the shibboleth. The views of a candidate on the other questions rarely affected the result of the poll, and so when those questions faced him as a Representative, he attached small weight to what might be the wishes of his constituents. Districts became so large that most of the voters had no personal acquaintance with candidates, and so could not of their own knowledge be confident in advance as to what would be the character of the representation. The voter found it hopeless to try to get his opinions voiced in legislative debate as a result of his markings upon the ballot. He could not express himself clearly, precisely, directly upon any public problem except that around which the campaign might be framed, and this was usually a national problem with no relation to State or local affairs. The matters nearest to the heart of the citizen were usually not involved at all in elections.

Also the representative system came to seem more dilatory than was necessary. It did not keep pace with the march of

[1] *Constitutional Government in the U.S.*, 191 (1908).

society. Evils in the train of the factory system, of new methods of transportation and locomotion, of growing disparities in wealth, of division into classes, of corporations, of all the other phenomena presented by modern society, met with correction delayed long after the occasion for remedy became apparent, or else met with no correction at all. Legislatures responded slowly, painfully, and imperfectly to the pressure of public opinion. Impatient sufferers reached the conclusion that the fathers had been needlessly drastic in their precautions against the whims, impulses, enthusiasms, and excitements of the populace, against the ill-advised and immature demands of transitory sentiment, against the hasty zeal of rash reformers. In the never-ending struggle between radicalism and conservatism, the radicals succeeded in advancing their lines.

Of course this has terrified the conservatives. They are full of forebodings. They predict the speedy collapse of the representative system. They dread Democracy unchained.

As usual they are unduly alarmed. Their fears are not being justified by what is developing. On the other hand the hopes of the radicals are not being realized to the degree expected.

It turns out that the new system, though at first used excessively and needlessly here and there, is for the most part accomplishing a desirable and defensible purpose. In the apt metaphor frequently heard, it for the most part proves to be the gun behind the door, the weapon ready at hand for emergency. Now for attack, again for defense, it compels or checks as the need may be. Its very presence without its use may bring benefits, if it serves constantly to remind the representatives of the people that whether trustees or agents, they are responsible, and that they must be honest, diligent, and amenable to reason.

Also experience already shows that the system of direct legislation, though it may usefully supplement, ought not to supplant and is not likely to supplant the representative system. For the great mass of legislation nothing better has ever been devised or is to-day suggested, than the representative assembly. The people have not the time, inclination, or capacity to handle more than a very small percentage of their problems. They will use the ballot for sporadic purposes, to supplement their Legislatures as the need may arise.

Of course your ultra-conservative denies that there is any need of supplementing the Legislature. He thinks that if Representatives do not do their duty, the remedy is to replace them with men who will. If the Legislature is controlled, subservient, venal, he says the recourse is to the bar of public opinion, which when informed and aroused, will meet the situation. He believes the public conscience has already been so stirred that the standards of legislative conduct have been raised greatly above the level of a generation ago. He avers that the Initiative and Referendum have secured the enactment of no measures of real value that could not have been secured in the old way. He alleges that a Legislature really representative would meet every need, and that such a Legislature is always within reach of the people.

Here comes the most serious argument that the champions of the new system have to meet. If the people cannot choose Representatives wisely, how can they wisely decide upon measures? It is not, however, a conclusive argument, even if weighty. Legislators are neither altogether good nor altogether bad. However admirable the system under which they work, it is not perfect. Theory may soundly advise against meeting its defects from the outside, but we are a practical people, standing in not too much awe of theory, and when we want results, we get them. So the academic beauties of the representative system will not deter the people from inroads upon its doctrines if they decide upon the practical need. With us the people are to govern and they are going to have their way. This does not in reality mean anything like a return to pure democracy. It does mean an adaptation of the representative system to new conditions.

That this adaptation is not in fact revolutionary, even in theory, is shown by the declarations of some at least of our courts. In Oregon a litigant contended that the Initiative and Referendum amendment abolished the republican form of government, substituting another form in its place. In reply to this the Supreme Court of that State answered: "The representative character of the government still remains. The people have simply reserved to themselves a larger share of representative power, but they have not overthrown the republican form of the government, or substituted another in its place. The government is still divided into the legislative, executive, and judicial departments, the duties of which are discharged by representatives selected by the people. Under this amendment, it is true, the people may exercise a legislative power, and may, in effect, veto or defeat bills passed and approved by the Legislature and the Governor, but the legislative and executive departments are not destroyed, nor are their powers or authority materially curtailed." [1]

When in another case [2] the question reached the Supreme Court of the United States, Chief Justice White, speaking for the Court, held that the question whether Oregon had a republican form of government was political and was for the judgment of Congress, and that until Congress acted upon any change in the government of Oregon, and declared it to be a violation of the Constitution, the Court would accept its status as determined by Congress when it admitted Oregon into the Union. Congress has virtually adjudicated the matter by admitting States with provisions for the Initiative and Referendum in their Constitutions.

There can be no question that the system has come to stay. It is not likely in our time to be anywhere formally repealed. Yet its friends assume too much in drawing any favorable conclusion from this. Everybody knows it is useless to try to recall any extension of power to the people, whether in the way of suffrage or in any other direction. The likelihood is that the people will presently learn how far they may profitably use this particular power, and will limit its use thereto almost unconsciously. Already they are learning that they cannot wisely legislate on complicated or technical matters, and are inclining to vote "No" on anything of the sort. Indeed reaction is carrying them in some States to the point of frowning on everything put on the ballot, whether complex or simple. In the course of the Great War interest in the subject notably declined, chiefly because the attention of the people was engrossed by other matters, but probably in part because the Progressive movement after reaching the crest of the wave in 1912, began a course rapidly downward. The War itself led to problems quite different from those of the structure and machinery of government, and was followed by no revival of interest in the Initiative and Referendum.

[1] Kadderly v. Portland, 44 Ore. 118 (1913).
[2] Pacific Tel. and Tel. Co. v. State of Oregon, 223 U.S. 118 (1912).

INDEX

INDEX

with Oregon in the matter of a fishery law, 592; attitude toward measures submitted in, 615

Watertown, raises a constitutional question in the Colony of Massachusetts Bay, 98

Webster, Daniel, thought general revision of the Massachusetts Constitution improbable, 145; and fractions in apportionment, 378; and the instructions of Michigan to Cass, 473; changes position on the tariff to correspond with that of his constituents, 501

Webster, Pelatiah, credited with the basic ideas of the Constitution, 544

Weed, Thurlow, criticizes single districts, 381

Wellington, the Duke of, praises the unreformed House of Commons, 270

Wells, Herbert George, characterizes elections in England, 207, 392

Wendell, Oliver, receives instructions, 449

West Virginia, the majority in, 237; instructions in, 455

Wethersfield. See Connecticut

Whigs, first known as Petitioners, 516

White, Edward Douglass, as to the majority of a quorum, 238; on the question of what is a republican form of government, 634

Whitelocke, Sir Bulstrode, as to difference between ordinance and statute, 28; says members of Parliament represent England, 435; on pledges, 483

Whitten, Robert Harvey, suggests method of amending Constitutions, 163

Wihtraed, and lawmaking, 65

Wilberforce, William, cost of electing, 408

Wilkes, John, and instructions, 441; and pledges, 483; shares in developing the power of the people, 535, 536

William the Conqueror, and the laws of England, 66, 70

William III, and the Bill of Rights, 39; and a more liberal policy as to colonial assemblies, 111; would not endure the religious franchise, 293; and the right of petition, 518

William and Mary College, receives the right to send a Burgess, 272

Williams, George, charged with corrupting voters, 414

Willoughby, Westel Woodbury, on custom in the development of law, 18; on sovereignty, 42, 44; as to the test of good government, 549

Wilmot proviso, and instructions, 473

Wilson, Henry, resignation of, raises a difficult constitutional question, 151; on the powers of a Convention, 154; and the majority requirement in Massachusetts, 229; favors population as the basis of apportionment, 363

Wilson, Woodrow, and the nature of law, 5, 17; theory of, as to the function of authorities, 19; and the sinking of the Lusitania, 50; view of, as to Parliaments, 67; and as to the function of Legislatures, 118; and the length of ballots, 218; the influence of writings of, 544; as to the need of a lawmaking body, 631

Winchester, Boyd, tells of the conservative effect of the Referendum in Switzerland, 605

Windsor. See Connecticut

Winthrop, John, and democracy, 33; and delegated authority, 36; records the first General Court in Massachusetts, 97; discusses the nature of the government, 98, 101; defeats Vane, 103; with his Council declines to solicit privileges from Parliament, 116; as to covenants and Constitutions, 125; and the fundamental laws in Massachusetts, 126, 127, 187; describes the method of election, 204; on petitions, 520

Winthrop, John, Jr., and an early use of the Referendum, 569

Winthrop, Robert Charles, and the vote in a Speakership election, 235; on the right of towns and cities to be represented, 346; on petitions, 528

Wisconsin, the majority in, 237; single districts in, 382; the gerrymander in, 400; voting one way in, 617

Witchcraft, and public opinion, 546

Witenagemot, the, and lawmaking, 13; described, 63; share of, in the creation of law, 563

Woman suffrage, 312, 313, 320, 438, 486

Wooddy, Carroll Hill, analyzes Senate votes from point of view of representation, 369

Woolsey, Theodore Dwight, as to minorities and majorities, 265; on